THROWN
upon the
WORLD

THROWN upon the WORLD
a true story

GEORGE KOLBER
CHARLES KOLBER

Copyright © 2018 George Kolber Charles Kolber.

All rights reserved. No part of this book may be used or reproduced by any means, graphic, electronic, or mechanical, including photocopying, recording, taping or by any information storage retrieval system without the written permission of the author except in the case of brief quotations embodied in critical articles and reviews.

Archway Publishing books may be ordered through booksellers or by contacting:

Archway Publishing
1663 Liberty Drive
Bloomington, IN 47403
www.archwaypublishing.com
1 (888) 242-5904

Because of the dynamic nature of the Internet, any web addresses or links contained in this book may have changed since publication and may no longer be valid. The views expressed in this work are solely those of the author and do not necessarily reflect the views of the publisher, and the publisher hereby disclaims any responsibility for them.

Any people depicted in stock imagery provided by Getty Images are models, and such images are being used for illustrative purposes only.
Certain stock imagery © Getty Images.

ISBN: 978-1-4808-6261-6 (sc)
ISBN: 978-1-4808-6262-3 (hc)
ISBN: 978-1-4808-6263-0 (e)

Library of Congress Control Number: 2018906715

Print information available on the last page.

Archway Publishing rev. date: 6/28/2018

Reared as we are, in quiet and in peace,
Now all at once we're thrown upon the world.

Johann Wolfgang von Goethe, *An Lottchen*

In memory of
Chao Chen Kolber

Contents

A Note to Our Readers xiii
Kolber and Chen Family Tree xv
Acknowledgments xvii
Prologue xix

CHAPTER 1	The Avalanche 1
CHAPTER 2	The Funeral 11
CHAPTER 3	The Piano Lesson 18
CHAPTER 4	Just Follow the Music 24
CHAPTER 5	Driven from Zhenru 32
CHAPTER 6	Salon on Julu Road 39
CHAPTER 7	Austria Is No More 46
CHAPTER 8	Broken Glass 61
CHAPTER 9	Separation 73
CHAPTER 10	The Red J 79
CHAPTER 11	The Shun Feng 93
CHAPTER 12	Finding a Partner 99
CHAPTER 13	A Riddle Wrapped in an Enigma 105
CHAPTER 14	Summer Heat 112
CHAPTER 15	The Lowendall Violin 118
CHAPTER 16	The Lucky Ones 127
CHAPTER 17	Gray Mourning Doves 138
CHAPTER 18	The Lesson 146
CHAPTER 19	Gondolas along the Grand Canal 151
CHAPTER 20	An Evening at Ciro's 157
CHAPTER 21	Three Ways Out 163
CHAPTER 22	A New Life 167
CHAPTER 23	Pearl Harbor 173

CHAPTER 24	Caught in the Act	182
CHAPTER 25	The Red Armbands	187
CHAPTER 26	To Repair the World	193
CHAPTER 27	The Solicitation	203
CHAPTER 28	Death at Sea	208
CHAPTER 29	The Typewriter Repair Shop	214
CHAPTER 30	Shabbat Dinner	218
CHAPTER 31	The Designated Area	227
CHAPTER 32	Spring in Wintertime	233
CHAPTER 33	Above the Factory	241
CHAPTER 34	The Red Dress	246
CHAPTER 35	The Recital	252
CHAPTER 36	One Drink Too Many	262
CHAPTER 37	Command Performance	272
CHAPTER 38	Closing Shop	279
CHAPTER 39	Anywhere but There	284
CHAPTER 40	We'll Make It	291
CHAPTER 41	The Nightingale's Song	298
CHAPTER 42	The Great Wall Crumbles	304
CHAPTER 43	Tables Turned	312
CHAPTER 44	Settling In	318
CHAPTER 45	The Doctor Will See You	328
CHAPTER 46	The Right Thing	333
CHAPTER 47	Wedding at the Promenaden Café	337
CHAPTER 48	The First Farewell	346
CHAPTER 49	The Lotus Flower	350
CHAPTER 50	Betrayals	357
CHAPTER 51	Disowned	363
CHAPTER 52	All at Sea	368
CHAPTER 53	Disembarkation	379
CHAPTER 54	Out of Tune	390
CHAPTER 55	Phantasmagoria	399
CHAPTER 56	Trapped	408
CHAPTER 57	The Red Shoes	415
CHAPTER 58	The Hotel Sacher	423
CHAPTER 59	Hotel Amadeus	429

CHAPTER 60	The Good Doctor	434
CHAPTER 61	America The Beautiful	438
CHAPTER 62	The Sale	446
CHAPTER 63	Summer Heat	451
CHAPTER 64	Overwhelmed	457
CHAPTER 65	The Breakdown	466
CHAPTER 66	The Promise	471
CHAPTER 67	The Arrival	482
CHAPTER 68	The Fourth Son	487
CHAPTER 69	Special Deliveries	494
CHAPTER 70	Journey's End	500
	Epilogue	503
	Afterword	507
	Family Photos	509
	Notes and References	511

A Note to Our Readers

To properly relate our families' complex stories, we found it necessary to fictionalize some characters and situations. Also, during our research we have identified a number of people who, to us, are unsung heroes. It was because of their passion and persistence, that we can tell this story at all.

We have taken certain liberties to make *Thrown Upon the World* friendlier to Western readers. Most notably, we have chosen to identify most Chinese characters by their given names first and family names second.

To assist our readers in understanding the relationship of our Kolber and Chen family members, we have provided three family trees, which highlight our main characters.

Kolber and Chen Family Tree

Josef Kolber Family

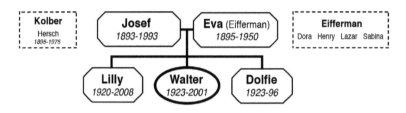

Gan Chen Family

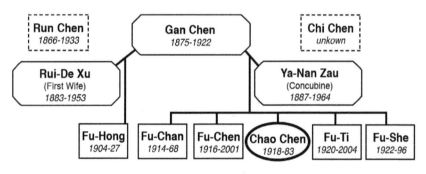

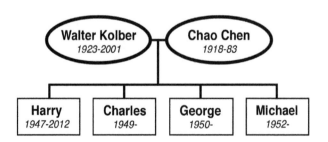

Acknowledgments

Enough cannot be said about the Hebrew Immigrant Aid Society (HIAS) and the Newark Jewish Family Services, which sponsored and found homes for the extraordinary number of refugees after World War II and arranged for us to be placed in the homes of caring foster families. Charles and Harry were placed with Rose and Harry Rothbloom, while George was placed with Joseph and Frieda Hirschfeld. We were immediately welcomed and loved by our respective families, and we remain a part of those families to this day. Were it not for their caring and guidance, we clearly would not have been able to tell this story.

Undoubtedly, Christa played a key role in the discovery of both families, which led to finding Uncle Fu-Ti Chen (Qian) in China and Aunt Lilly Kolber Ozer in Israel, both of whom were anxious to share the details of our families' histories.

We will be forever grateful to our collaborator, Loren Stephens, who not only helped with extensive research but provided tremendous insight and passion throughout.

We would like to thank Jerome M. Schottenstein, who was always encouraging and inspiring. He was a generous person who not only taught family values but led by example.

We would like to extend a special acknowledgment to the following people who helped provide critical research for our story:

Mary Au	Lea Bar-Ad	Elise Brancheau
Cindy Rothbloom Cohen	Paul G. Gaffney II	Lianne Goldsmith
Dr. Pan Guang	Robert Hirschfeld	Joseph Jedeikin
Tess Johnston	Perla Karney	Maria Kolber

Michael Kolber	Liang Pingan	Effy Pfefferman
Miri Ben Shalom	Rabbi Marvin Tokayer	Jenny Wang
Judith Ozer Zauberman	U.S. Representative Chris Smith	

Finally, we thank both Christa and Vita for putting up with years of unending history lessons and lively debates.

prologue
Promenaden Café, Shanghai

Sunday, December 15, 1946

Ya-Li walked quickly under the Shanghai sky filled with gray clouds blown westward by the wind off the Whangpoo River as it flowed into the East China Sea. She hurried up the stairs to the second floor of the squat building in an alleyway off Chusan Road and knocked on the door. Chao Chen let her in to the shabby one-room apartment. Other than an unmade bed, an upright piano with its bench, a hot plate and kettle, and a wardrobe with a cracked mirror, there was hardly a hint of its occupants: the elegant twenty-eight-year-old bride and her younger Austrian-Jewish lover, Walter Kolber.

Ya-Li inquired, "Why are you still in your nightgown, Chao Chen? The taxi will be here any minute."

"I needed to practice the piece Walter and I are supposed to perform after the ceremony. If I make any mistakes Walter will be furious with me. I guess the time just slipped away from me."

"Let me help you with your dress. I ironed it a few days ago. It should still be fresh."

Ya-Li took the red taffeta gown out of the wardrobe and instructed Chao Chen to step into it. The only time she had worn it was for the recital at the Shanghai Conservatory of Music was when she and Walter played the first movement of Beethoven's "Spring Sonata" for violin and piano. Of all the student performers, they were the only ones who received a standing ovation. And now, two years later, they were about to marry—and not a moment too soon.

Ya-Li struggled with the zipper. "Chao Chen, you're still tiny as a bird, but that baby inside you is taking up a lot of room around your waist. If you had waited much longer you would have had to buy another dress."

Chao Chen frowned. "And with what money? Walter and I are just scraping by. He's lost his job. The factory where he was working shut down, and the Jewish owners have gone to Canada." She sighed. "I just pray he finds another job soon or we'll be on the dole. The landlady is threatening to raise our rent now that so many Chinese are coming back from the countryside."

Tenderly patting Chao Chen's cheek, Ya-Li said, "Don't fret so. It's not healthy for you or your baby. Besides, it makes you look unattractive, and you're still so beautiful, especially in that dress. You look like a rose in full bloom. Now, put a smile on your face and let's meet your bridegroom at the Promenaden Café. I'm sure he's wondering where you are."

"Ya-Li, go downstairs and be on the lookout for the taxi. I need to feed my mourning doves. Who knows what time Walter and I will be back, and I don't want them to get hungry. Besides, they're afraid to be left alone for too long."

Ya-Li laughed. "How do you know that if you're not here?"

"I can't explain it. I just know." Chao Chen unconsciously rubbed her stomach. "They are like my babies."

After tending to her birds, Chao Chen inspected herself in the cracked mirror. Her eyes sparkled and her long, dark hair curled softly around her face. Her cheeks were flushed. She turned sideways. *I wonder if anyone will notice that I'm pregnant.* She answered herself out loud, which was becoming a habit of late. "No. You just look healthy, Chao Chen. Now lift your head up high and show everyone how happy you are."

She heard the taxi honking and grabbed her coat. Lifting the hem of her dress so she wouldn't trip, she ran down the stairs.

The day was cold, dictating that all the guests wear warm overcoats, hats, and gloves on their way to the marriage ceremony at the Promenaden Café on East Seward Road in Shanghai's poorest district. The officiant, Dr. Kurt Primo, seeing the darkening overcast skies, carried an umbrella. Better safe than sorry, he thought, especially since he had two more weddings to perform later in the day, although neither would be as unusual as this. If he wasn't being paid in American dollars he wouldn't have bothered. He could only guess what kind of trouble the groom had stepped into to be marrying a Chinese girl. The young man had a dubious reputation among the members of the Jewish B'nai B'rith Lodge. A shame, since his father, Josef Kolber, was such a fine and well-respected man. Dr. Primo sighed as he pushed his shoulder into the wind, wondering how many other young Jewish men had found themselves caught in the underbelly of war-torn Shanghai.

As Chao Chen and Ya-Li stepped out of the taxicab onto East Seward Road, the bride noticed the "In Bounds" sign posted in the window of the Promenaden Café, signaling that it was safe for U.S. military personnel to eat and drink there. It also guaranteed that the café would be crowded and overshadow the small wedding party, which had assembled in a dark corner, waiting for the bride's arrival.

Ya-Li grabbed Chao Chen's hand and guided her through the rowdy crowd. Some of the Seabees, sailors of the U.S. Navy's Construction Brigade sent to Shanghai to repair a deep-water pier severely damaged by Allied and Japanese bombing, whistled at her as she passed.

Sitting at the piano was Bobby Johnston, a well-known Negro jazz pianist from Philadelphia who played at the clubs and cafés around Shanghai, a city that could never get enough of American music, especially jazz. His raspy voice and nimble fingers earned him a silver tray full of tips whenever he performed.

Snapping their fingers and tapping their feet, the sailors added their off-key voices to his jazzy renditions of "Swinging on a Star" and "Twilight Time." A petite Chinese waitress worked her way through the crowd, balancing drink orders on a tray and shoving tips into her apron pocket, unable to protect herself from the sailors who pinched her cheek or patted her backside as if she were public property.

As Chao Chen and Ya-Li passed by, Bobby Johnston interrupted what he was playing, threw her an admiring glance, then broke into "The More I See You." The sailors sang out, "And there's nothing I wouldn't do for the rare delight of the sight of you."

Chao Chen wished she could just run away from this unwanted attention, but she willed her feet to keep moving toward her groom, who was laughing at something Professor Alfred Wittenberg was saying. As she neared, Walter caressed Chao Chen's neck and whispered in her ear, "I was beginning to worry about you. It's already past one o'clock."

"You didn't look too concerned, Walter. Weren't you just now laughing at one of Professor Wittenberg's jokes? I hoped you'd be waiting at the door to the café, looking out for me."

"You know how important it is that I appear to be hanging on his every word. I need his patronage. Without it I won't get anywhere."

Chao Chen sighed, resigned. "Sometimes I think you overdo it, Walter."

Walter signaled for the guests to gather around, and in a matter of only a few minutes the perfunctory civil ceremony concluded. Dr. Kurt Primo, the attorney Willi Schultz, and Fritz Weiss, who represented the Shanghai B'nai B'rith Lodge, signed the marriage certificate. The document was elaborately decorated with pink blossoms and birds and carried the seal of Shanghai's Jewish community, the *Jüdische Gemeinde* stamp.

Then, with everyone looking on, Walter embraced Chao Chen, bent her back at the waist, and kissed her on the lips with the false ardor of a movie star in a romantic scene. The guests applauded and then found their seats at the two tables reserved for the wedding party. Chao Chen, startled by her groom's sudden show of affection, wondered, *Did that kiss really mean anything to him?*

Weeks before the wedding, Chao Chen's brother Fu-Chan had offered to pay for the modest celebration at the Promenaden, one of the few Jewish cafés that accommodated weddings and known for its excellent European-style cuisine. He told Chao Chen, "I'm sorry, but that's the best I can do for you. I wish I had more money to spend on a more elaborate reception in one of those fancy hotels along the Bund, but I have the family to think about. I've only just started working again."

"Don't worry, Fu-Chan. I'm just glad that you and brother Fu-Ti will be there."

"It's the least we can do for you. But I'm sorry that you have chosen not to tell either Rui-De Xu or Ya-Nan that you are getting married."

"Why would I tell them? They made it clear they want nothing more to do with me when I told them I was moving out and would no longer give them money. Can you imagine how they would react if they knew I'm marrying a Jew? If they had their way they would have pawned me off to some wealthy widower with five children. In fact, they tried, but I refused."

Chao Chen whispered in her brother's ear, "The way Rui-De Xu carries on, you'd think she was the Empress of China instead of a pathetic widow. And as for our mother, Ya-Nan, since Father died... Well, you know, a concubine is a second-class citizen in the Chen family. If Father were alive he would be ashamed to see the way those two women behave, always squabbling over what's left of his estate."

Fu-Chan asked, "Will anyone be there from the Kolber family?"

"No. Walter kept our marriage a secret from his parents. Only his older sister, Lilly, knows about us, and she admitted to Walter that she didn't want to be disloyal to their parents and so she and her husband won't come either."

Fu-Chan ran his hands through his thick black hair, then adjusted his glasses as if to inspect his sister more closely. "You always were a rebel, Chao Chen. I've always liked that in you. But don't you think marrying a Jew is taking things too far?"

"So, you also disapprove of me marrying Walter?"

"I didn't say that. It's just... I worry what's going to happen to you. There aren't many mixed marriages in Shanghai, especially between Jews and Chinese. Neither side is particularly tolerant of the other, except when it comes to doing business together. But in matters of the heart, you and Walter will be alone, I'm afraid."

Chao Chen sighed. "We already are alone, Fu-Chan."

Chao Chen tried to push the memory of this painful conversation out of her head and concentrate on the guests seated at the tables. Out of respect to the bride, they conversed in English because Chao Chen knew only a few German words. Seated at the place of honor was Walter's violin teacher, Professor Alfred Wittenberg, who had been an illustrious member of Berlin's Schnabel Trio. He and his wife, like so many other Jews who found a safe haven in Shanghai, had narrowly escaped the Nazis. To his left, Chao Chen's piano teacher, Miss Liang, and her father, a well-known conductor and professor of music composition at the Conservatory, were deep in conversation with Deirdre Möller, the daughter of a Swedish Jew who owned a fleet of freighters and steamships. Deirdre had traveled all the way from Hong Kong to attend Chao Chen's wedding. They had met before the war when Chao Chen tutored her cousin in English. Sitting beside Ya-Li and Chao Chen's brothers were the Jewish officiant and witnesses, who expected a free meal in addition to their fee.

When Bobby Johnston took a break and after the dinner plates were cleared, Fu-Chan rose from his seat to deliver a toast to the bride and groom, his soft voice almost inaudible. The bride, lost in her memories, barely heard a word he was saying. She remembered when she and her brothers were young and carefree before the war, before their lives were turned upside down. Despite the crowded room and her new husband sitting beside her, she suddenly felt very lonely.

"Chao Chen, do you remember the beautiful lake at our estate and how you loved to row the boat past the pavilion?" Fu-Chan asked with a smile. Chao Chen was brought back to the present moment and returned her brother's smile. How could she ever forget gliding along on the lake in her little boat, free from all worry and completely at peace? She nodded, unable to speak, as Fu-Chan raised his glass. "May your marriage be as smooth as the surface of our lake, and may your journey together bring you as much joy as you had when riding in your little boat."

Everyone raised their glasses and then took a drink, and in the moment of quiet that followed, Professor Wittenberg seized the opportunity to deliver his own toast to the bride and groom. Miss Liang helped him to his feet because the cold December day meant his arthritis had flared up.

Professor Wittenberg, known for his ebullience, the very quality that endeared him to his students and that carried him through the gloomy days of the war, began his speech, which was characteristically lengthy. Chao Chen heard only about half of what he was saying; she felt as though she were in a daze. After expounding on Jewish numerology and the symbolism of their wedding date, Professor Wittenberg paused and lifted his glass, his eyes scanning the table to make sure everyone was hanging on his every word. Feeling as though she were a student in his class, Chao Chen straightened in her chair and focused on his words.

"It was Beethoven's 'Spring Sonata' for violin and piano that brought these two talented young people together," he said, beaming with pride. "As the seasons of their lives change from spring to summer, from summer to fall, and so on, may they always make beautiful music together." He raised his glass still higher and continued. "Let us make a toast to their health and happiness, and to the children they might someday be blessed to bring into a world that is finally at peace. May it always remain so."

Chao Chen blushed at the mention of children.

Then Professor Wittenberg reached under the table and handed Walter his violin case, nodding to the café's owner, Frau Reuben. "The Promenaden Café has graciously given Walter and Chao Chen permission to perform a short duet for us. Perhaps the other customers will temper their revelry for a few minutes." He turned around and scowled at the sailors, expecting that his expression would have the same effect on them it did on his music students, but they simply ignored him. It was only when Chao Chen was seated at the piano and Walter tuned his violin that a hush finally fell over the crowd.

Walter cleared his throat and announced, "My lovely bride, Chao Chen, and I would like to play a short duet for you." One sailor who'd had too much to drink booed and yelled, "Get off the stage! Bring Johnston back! We didn't pay to hear these two." Then he started stomping his feet. Someone grabbed him and pushed him back into his seat.

Trying to maintain his composure, Walter continued. "In all the commotion, I forgot to tell you the name of the piece we're going to play for you. It's 'Salut d'amour,' or 'Salute to Love' by Elgar. He wrote this little jewel for his fiancée, and in return she presented him with a poem, which he later set to music. Oh, they were perfectly suited for each other, just as Chao Chen and I are." Ignoring Chao Chen, he smiled out at the audience. Walter added, "One of my wife's suitors played this very piece two years ago at our first recital together. But he was a fool to have set his sights on her. I had already won her heart. Isn't that so, my dearest?"

Chao Chen was mortified that Walter had told such an intimate and untrue story. Forcing a smile, she nodded and then rested her hands on the piano keys, waiting for Walter to tune his violin so they could begin before the crowd lost patience.

Chao Chen played the first two measures, which she thought of as pulling back the curtain on the composition so that Walter's violin could take center stage. Except for a few measures toward the end of this romantic piece, the piano is there simply to accompany the violin. Walter took full advantage of his primacy, extending his bow, which he held in a French-Belgian grip, making sure that his wrist was relaxed and flexible, and showing off his mastery of the vibrato to infuse the piece with emotion and a sparkling brightness. Chao Chen complemented his style, adjusting her tempo to his, delicately pressing the pedal with the changing harmonies of the piece. It was a flawless performance, the happiness of the composer and his love for his fiancée finely communicated by Walter and Chao Chen.

As the final breath of music—played by Walter alone—hung suspended in the smoke-filled café, everyone stood up and cheered. Walter and Chao Chen took their bows and Bobby Johnston returned to the stage. "Your magnificent performance has brought tears to my eyes," Bobby said. "I'd like to give you a wedding gift, from one musician to another." Turning around, he handed Walter all the tip money that sat on his silver tray. The sailors broke out in applause and cheers.

Walter stuffed the money into his jacket pockets, thanked the pianist, and walked back to his guests. Chao Chen followed behind him, unable to hold back her tears. Anyone looking at her would have interpreted them as tears of joy.

chapter 1

The Avalanche

December 12, 1916

It was nearly midnight in a valley below Italy's majestic Mount Marmolada. The wind howled outside the army barracks, the moon hanging like a silver platter in the clear nighttime sky. Most of the soldiers were asleep, but twenty-three-year-old Josef Kolber hunched over the chess board lit only by a kerosene lantern as his opponent, Heinrich Eiferman, jammed his hands into the pockets of his heavy wool coat.

"It's a stalemate, Josef. That's the second time this week."

"Shows that we are pretty evenly matched."

"Either that or we've been playing together so long that we can anticipate each other's moves."

The two men, medics in the Austro-Hungarian Army, were stationed in South Tyrol at the foot of Mount Marmolada, part of the Isonzo Front campaign positioned to hold back Italian troops from advancing north. The snowy and treacherous terrain and the constant threat of avalanches made the region poorly suited to offensive operations. Like Josef and Heinrich's chess game, at least here, the war was at a stalemate.

The barracks' door flew open, letting in a blast of cold air. The telephone operator stamped his feet, took off his gloves, and blew on his fingers.

"What are you doing up?" Heinrich asked.

"I've just been with Field Marshall Lieutenant Goinger. He decided to keep our men up at the Gran Poz summit a few days ago. Now he's changed his mind. But it's too late. There's a sudden blizzard on top of the mountain and our guys are stranded up there."

"How many men?" Josef followed.

"Over three hundred, including Captain Rudolf Schmidt. We haven't been able to get food to them for a week."

Josef lamented, "Poor bastards. Let's hope the deepening snow does not give way and bury our comrades."

At five thirty the next morning the men were awakened by the echoes and concussions from Italian artillery fire calculated to set off an avalanche on the Austrians trapped below. After a single barrage, a thunderous sound reverberated through the mountain pass. Grabbing their coats and yanking on their heavy boots, Josef and Heinrich ran outside. Looking up toward Mount Marmolada, they could see snow and ice cascading down the mountainside, spitting enormous white clouds into the gray dawn's light. Most men in the encampment on the mountain were crushed to death. Only a few soldiers escaped, among them Captain Schmidt and his aide-de-camp.

That began three days of treacherous avalanches that would culminate on what became known as White Friday. Josef and Heinrich assisted the doctors in the makeshift operating room, lugging amputated limbs outside into the snow. The ground was too hard to bury the arms and legs, and so the gruesome pile of human limbs lay out in the open for all to see. Morphine was in short supply, and for many days the sound of patients crying out in pain as the surgeon's scalpel cut through flesh and bone drowned out the sound of the wind cracking through the valley.

Then Josef became a casualty. By mid-January, his chilblains had developed into a dire case of frostbite. The doctors feared that gangrene would set in before they could transport him to a civilian hospital, maybe to have his feet amputated, but he refused. "I'd rather die than lose my feet."

Heinrich was direct with his friend. "Are you sure, Josef?"

"Yes. I used to be the fastest Jewish kid in Nowy Sacz."

"From the look of things, I think your running career is finished, kaput."

"We'll see."

"Josef, I've always known you were an eternal optimist. We share the same Galician blood, but you didn't see what I saw. Perhaps, if you had, you would lose some of your optimism. I witnessed the worst atrocities perpetrated upon the Jews in Lemberg by the Russians two years ago. Our immediate family got out and is now living in Vienna, but some of my cousins, aunts, and uncles weren't so lucky."

"The doctors are sending me to Vienna for treatment. When the war is over, let's hope we shall meet again, dear Heinrich."

"God willing." Heinrich took out a piece of paper and wrote down his address. "Here, this is where you can find me, if I get out alive. And if you need a job, I might be able to arrange it. My family has set up a clothing business in Vienna."

Josef hugged Heinrich. "That's music to my ears, my friend. I don't have a trade, but I'm clever enough."

"Yes, I know that all too well. I thought you'd be an easy target, but you've managed to beat me at chess more times than I'll ever admit to."

"Don't worry. Your secret is safe with me."

Josef convinced the doctors at the Army Hospital in Vienna not to amputate his feet. Instead, he underwent a series of painful debridement sessions to remove the dead skin, and after six months, he recovered. The doctors insisted that he remain in the hospital under observation for sepsis, a fatal blood disease caused by gangrene, but it was Josef's good fortune that he was declared "sepsis-free," released from the hospital, and given an honorable medical discharge from the army in June 1917. The war was not yet over, but he was not sent back to the front despite the need for additional soldiers.

He rented a small room in a boardinghouse in the Leopoldstadt district of Vienna, an area known as Matzo Island because of the number of the Orthodox Jews from Galicia and other parts of Eastern Europe who had found their way to this cheap part of the city. Limping from store to store in search of work, he found a job as a clerk for a men's clothier. With the few Kronen left after paying his rent, he took his meals at a kosher restaurant and, on rare occasion, went to the Prater to ride the Ferris wheel or bought a ticket to a silent film or an operetta. Like everyone else in Vienna, he held his breath, waiting for news that the war was finally over.

Early in the morning on November 11, 1918, the battlefields of Europe fell silent; the Germans had signed an armistice and the Great War was finally over. It was unclear what price the Austro-Hungarians and Germans would be forced to pay as restitution for having lost the war. When the body count was issued, the world learned that more than ten million people had died during the four years of the war, six million of whom were civilians. This was a war that was played out not just on battlefields but on the streets of Europe's cities and towns.

Josef's army buddy Heinrich Eiferman survived unscathed and was soon put to work helping his father and sister, Eva, run the family's textile factory in Vienna, which had thrived as a supplier of uniforms, bandages, and underwear for the troops during the war. Now they returned to peacetime operations, using the same heavy sewing machines to manufacture men's and women's clothing bearing the label Eiferman and Company. Within a year's time the factory employed fifty Jewish laborers.

Eva Eiferman was raised to be a good Jewish wife and mother, but the war changed the course of her life, giving her the opportunity to work alongside her father rather than stay at home waiting for a man to appear at her door with a proposal in hand. At twenty-three she felt a sense of accomplishment that other young women of her generation could not imagine and did not desire. A handsome woman with chestnut-brown hair and hazel eyes, she did not hesitate to express her opinions; this boldness was encouraged by her doting father, while her mother worried that she was too headstrong to ever attract a man from a well-to-do Jewish family. And there were few available men from such families as it was. Thousands upon thousands of once-eligible Jewish bachelors lay six feet below the ground, casualties of the pogroms and the fiery battles of war.

A few months after the armistice, Josef Kolber had an epiphany: being a store clerk was not for him. He found the piece of paper that his army buddy Heinrich had given him with his address on it, and on a sunny Sunday in May, just as the blossoms were beginning to fall from the fruit trees, he walked from Leopoldstadt to the Eifermans' home. The house was modest in size but well maintained. The windows fronting the street were dressed in gauzy curtains, the heavy velvet draperies stored away until the following winter. Josef rang the doorbell, and a maid dressed in a black uniform with a starched white apron opened the door.

"Is Heinrich Eiferman here?"

"Who may I say is looking for him?"

"Josef Kolber. We were in the war together."

"Please wait here for a moment, sir."

The maid disappeared, and within seconds Heinrich stood in her place. He grabbed Josef in a hearty embrace and then led him into the well-appointed salon. "You're looking a lot better than the last time I saw you, Josef, and I am glad to see that your foot escaped the surgeon's scalpel. Come in right away. My sister, Eva, is at Lake Velden for the weekend with my mother, lucky for you, but my father is here. We'll have a chance to talk. When my mother and sister are around, we men can't get in a word. I've told my father about you, and he's aware that I mentioned the possibility of you coming to work for us. You see, I haven't forgotten. I hope you don't mind."

"Mind? Of course not. In fact, I'm elated. I wasn't sure if you were serious about offering me a job."

"My good man, we were Jewish comrades in arms. I can guess that things must have been difficult for you these past two years."

Abraham Eiferman, a portly gentleman in his late fifties, suddenly appeared and greeted Josef warmly. After a few minutes of polite conversation, Abraham got serious, "So, young man, Heinrich has told me all about you. And I like what I hear. He is a good judge of character, so let me cut right to the chase. Perhaps you are interested in working for our company?"

Josef could barely contain his excitement. "Well, sir, I would be honored, but I must tell you, outside of being a medic, I really haven't any professional training to speak of. However, I have been working as a store clerk for a men's clothier in Vienna for the past year. I have learned something about what men like to wear. So perhaps that would be of some value?"

"Indeed, it will. But you're going to have to learn the business from the ground up. We'll start you in the shipping and receiving department. You'll be expected to check all the deliveries to make sure that none of the *goniffs* out there are trying to cheat us, and when orders are ready for shipment, you'll count every piece to make sure the order is complete. And we'll just go from there. How does that sound to you?"

"Excellent, sir."

"Do you have any questions?"

"Not really, sir, other than the address of your factory."

Herr Eiferman laughed. "Aren't you interested in your salary?"

"Thank you for reminding me. I was so surprised by your offer that I forgot to ask. And frankly, the opportunity of working for you will give me the chance that I have been looking for. I don't see myself as a shop clerk forever."

"Good. I like a man with ambition. We'll start you at twenty Kronen a week. Now, I think our business is concluded. I'll leave you two boys to catch up. I'm off to the Café Mozart. Sundays are very crowded, although the maître d' usually reserves my regular table for me. Perhaps someday you'll join me, Josef."

"Indeed, sir. It would be my pleasure."

The factory was nearly empty at seven o'clock. Finished goods were piled high, ready for folding and packing. Only Eva and Josef were still in the office above the factory floor since it was Friday and everyone had gone home to prepare for Shabbat.

Eva looked quizzically at Josef. "What are you still doing here? Don't you have somewhere to go?"

Josef confessed, "Not really. I haven't a single relative in Vienna. Everyone in my family who survived the war is still living in Nowy Sacz. I'm here by myself. Shabbat dinner will be whatever is left over from what I bought at the delicatessen yesterday: dark bread, a slab of cheese, and a good dill pickle. Oh, and a glass of wine to say evening prayers."

"Sounds utterly miserable. Why don't you come to our home? After all, you already know my father and my brother. One more person at the Shabbat table won't be a big sacrifice, and you'll be able to meet my siblings, Lazar, Sabina, and Dora. Her fiancé, Herman, will be there too. I'll ask my mother, and perhaps next Friday evening you'll join us."

"I would be most honored, Fräulein Eva."

"Why don't you just call me Eva, Josef? We're hardly strangers. You've been working here two months already."

Josef could feel his face turning red. Eva laughed at his obvious discomfort. "Have I said something to embarrass you?"

"I didn't know that you even noticed me."

"Am I that hard to read? I noticed you from the first day you walked into the factory. And I have watched how hard you work. My father doesn't stop talking about the good job you are doing. I think that Heinrich is actually a little bit jealous, although he has no reason to be. After all, when all is said and done, the keys to the factory will be turned over to him."

Eva reached for her coat. Trying not to stammer, Josef warned, "It's getting dark. I would be most honored if you would allow me to walk you home."

After pulling on one glove and then the other and pinning a large, feathered hat atop her chestnut curls, Eva said, "I would like that very much, Josef. You never know who is lurking down a hidden alleyway."

Josef pushed on. "Is that the only reason you've agreed to allow me to walk you home, so that I can protect you?"

Eva leaned over and kissed Josef on the lips. "There is your answer. Now put your coat on and let's go. I don't want to be late for dinner."

Six months later, Josef, dressed in his only tailor-made suit and sporting a new pair of highly polished leather shoes, waited impatiently for Eva's father at the Café Mozart. He tapped nervously on the tabletop as a pianist played a Chopin melody in the background. Spotting Herr Abraham Eiferman, Josef jumped up from his chair to greet his employer, who unbuttoned his fur coat and signaled for the waiter to store it in the coat check room.

Josef waited politely for Herr Eiferman to settle himself, then sat down, signaling to a waiter. "I'll have a *Kaffee mit Schlag* and a *Sachertorte*, of course," Herr Eiferman ordered.

Josef smiled. "Make that two."

Looking around the room, Herr Eiferman raised his eyebrows. "I see that our competitor, Herr Weber, is seated in the corner. I'm in no mood to chat with him today, but if he comes our way, I'll introduce you."

"Let's hope that we won't be interrupted."

"And why is that, Josef?"

"Well, sir, I have something very important I want to ask of you."

"Are you going to ask me for a raise? If so, I can't possibly give you an answer. I'll need to confer with my daughter."

Josef laughed. "No, sir. You'll remember that, when you offered me a job, I neglected to ask about my salary. So it should come as no surprise that this is not the topic I wish to bring up with you today. It's something much more personal, but it does involve Eva."

"And what is that?"

"I wish to ask for your daughter's hand in marriage."

Eva had already told her father that she wanted to marry Josef Kolber and had secured his pledge that he would give his assent, and so Josef's question came as no surprise to Abraham Eiferman.

The older man thought it was an odd match to be sure. While both families were originally from Galicia, Josef Kolber was many rungs down the social ladder from the Eifermans. But Josef had proven himself to be industrious, intelligent, and loyal, and most importantly he was head-over-heels in love with Eva. Although they tried their best to hide their attraction for each other, it was obvious to everyone who saw the young couple working side by side.

"You are a very brave young man. My daughter Eva is a handful, although I must admit that I am partly to blame. Are you sure you can handle her?"

"Sir, I have no intention of 'handling' her. All I want to do is love her, make her happy, and if we are so blessed, bring children into this world with her."

"Well put, my boy. I see no reason, then, why I should withhold my permission."

Josef beamed. "You've made me the happiest man in all of Vienna, Herr Eiferman."

Herr Eiferman lifted his coffee cup and mouthed, "*L'chaim.*"

"Yes, to life."

A year after they were married, on July 20, 1920, Eva and Josef welcomed their daughter Lilly into the world. They brought her home from the hospital to a spacious apartment on Esteplatz, which was around the corner from the beautiful Stadtpark. The first year's rent had been paid by Herr Eiferman as a gift to the new parents. Three years later Eva gave birth to twin boys, Adolf and Walter.

At his wife's urging, and with her expertise and financial help, Josef struck out on his own in 1925. He started Kolber Textile Company, which made him a fairly well-to-do man.

Josef marveled at his good fortune. Just a few years earlier he had been one of the *Ostjuden* (Eastern Jews) barely eking out a living, and now here he was, living a good life among a highly assimilated upper-class Jewish community. He didn't deliberately turn his back on those who were less fortunate, but he needed to stay focused on building his business side by side with Eva, providing for his children, and making his family happy. He liked to joke that private schools, music lessons, summer vacations at Lake Velden, ski trips in the wintertime in Gstaad, and season tickets to the opera and theatre were all paid for one stitch at a time.

There were rumblings of discontent in the nascent First Republic. There was never a strong political majority to govern the country or a regal hand to guide its destiny. The Christian Socialist Party, closely allied with the Roman Catholic Church, dominated the countryside, while the Social Democrats held sway in Vienna. Occasionally, anti-Semitism reared its ugly head, especially in the poor quarters of Vienna, but Josef paid little attention to these incidents; neither did he take seriously the writings of novelists and Jewish journalists who tried to warn the Jews that something terrible was afoot.

One evening, as he sat in his library, he read a few pages of *Die Stadt ohne Juden* (*The City Without Jews*), which had been given to him by one of his business colleagues, Bernhard Altmann. He dropped the book on his desk, and the thumping sound caught Eva's attention. She had been concentrating on an intricate knitting pattern for the sweater she was making for three-year-old Walter.

Josef apologized. "Sorry to have disturbed you, *mein Liebling*. I can't decide if this book is simply the ramblings of a maniac or if we should all take heed."

"What's he saying?"

"It's pure fiction, mind you, but the author describes an Austria led by a fanatical anti-Semite who forces all Jews to leave Vienna."

"I've heard of this book. He is just an Expressionist with an all-too-vivid imagination. This city would be nothing without Jews, and everyone knows it."

"I hope you are right, but if the economy doesn't improve, there is no telling what might happen. Whenever there are problems, it is always the Jews who are first to be blamed."

Eva put her knitting down and came to him. Sitting on Josef's lap, she smoothed his hair and kissed his warm cheeks. "For once, I'm telling you not to worry."

Josef laughed. "You are usually seeing the dark clouds on the horizon, not I. It's very refreshing to see you like this. What's gotten into you?"

"Well, Papa has given us a trip to Venice for our seventh anniversary—just the two of us. My parents will stay here with the children for a few days, so we have nothing to worry about."

"Splendid."

Eva continued. "I have always dreamed about floating along the Grand Canal in a gondola and feeding the pigeons in the Piazza San Marco at dusk."

As twilight fell, Josef and Eva made a list of all the places in the world they might want to see. It was a happy distraction and *Die Stadt ohne Juden* remained on his desk until he threw it unceremoniously in the trash two weeks later.

chapter 2

The Funeral

Ya-Nan held her four-year-old daughter's hand tightly as they walked along the cobblestone streets of Zhenru. She wanted Chao Chen to see the hundreds of brightly lit lanterns floating over the canal drift into the night sky. She explained, "The Lantern Festival is to tell your father it's time for him to come home. Wherever he is, when he sees the lights, he'll know we are waiting for him."

Chao Chen craned her neck as the paper lanterns made a canopy over her head, temporarily blocking the stars.

Ya-Nan was unsure if her daughter remembered her father's face. It had been almost three months since Gan Chen had been home, and he stayed just long enough for her to conceive another child. He had brought with him a trunk full of gifts for his wife, Rui-De Xu, and a music box with a nightingale for his only daughter, Chao Chen. When he wound the key, the bird played a beautiful melody, opening and closing its beak and fanning its jeweled tail.

Ya-Nan shuddered when she saw Rui-De Xu's face as Chao Chen opened her present, but it was for her birthday—and why should Rui-De Xu be jealous? Gan Chen indulged his wife by giving her everything she coveted as recompense for taking Ya-Nan, his Shanghai mistress, into the red-chambered room, the same room in which Ya-Nan had birthed Gan Chen's four children. It was unfair of Rui-De Xu to deny Chao Chen this expression of a father's love, but Gan Chen's principal wife was a rapacious and vindictive woman. This past year she had pressured her husband into building an octagonal-roofed pavilion overlooking their willow-ringed lake. This always impressed the diplomats and government officials who often visited the estate to seek Gan Chen's advice and counsel. Every time Ya-Nan caught a glimpse of it, she thought of it as Rui-De Xu's consolation prize from Gan Chen, who favored his beautiful concubine over his now-barren wife.

As the full moon threw sharp shards of light across the black cobblestones, a crowd gathered around a group of male performers wearing red jackets and pajamas who were executing intricate movements on stilts while impersonating monks, clowns, and fishermen. A band of musicians clanging cymbals, ringing bells, and blowing on bamboo flutes accompanied the performers.

A vendor stood next to his cart nearby selling sticky-sweet rice balls. Chao Chen asked her mother if she could have one. "No, Chao Chen. I don't carry any money. Didn't you eat enough, or were you too excited to put anything in your stomach at dinner?"

The vendor, having overheard, quickly wrapped one of the sticky balls in a piece of brown paper and handed it to Ya-Nan. "There are rose petals and walnuts inside. Please take one for your little girl."

Ya-Nan hesitated. "I couldn't think of it, and we're not beggars, I assure you."

The vendor pushed the sticky rice ball into Ya-Nan's hand. "That I know very well. I have seen you in Zhenru with Magistrate Gan Chen. You live at the estate, no?"

"Yes."

"The magistrate reduced my father's tax burden so that we were able to hold on to our land after one of the worst floods in twenty years. Other magistrates would never have been so forgiving. My family is forever in his debt."

Ya-Nan's faced brightened. "Do you hear that, Chao Chen? Your father is a very important and generous man." She added, "Someday he will govern all of Jiangsu, but we must be patient for that day to arrive." She thought to herself, *When Rui-De Xu dies, I will stand at Gan Chen's side, reaping the rewards of his authority and beneficence.*

Ya-Nan gave the vendor her calling card. "Come to our gate and I will leave a few coins for you with the night watchman." The vendor bowed so low that his head nearly touched the ground. Chao Chen bit into the rice ball, its sweet taste filling her mouth.

In a nearby alleyway, a foreign-looking old man dressed in a shabby coat and torn pants set a tin cup next to his feet. Chao Chen watched as he took his fiddle out of its case and played a haunting and unfamiliar tune that echoed off the high stone wall. Tears slipped down his sunken cheeks as the last note seemed to hang in the air between him and the little girl.

Chao Chen asked, "Mama, why is he crying?"

"I don't know, Chao Chen. Maybe because the music is from his homeland, which is very far away."

"Will you give him your card so that he can come and play for us?"

"No, Chao Chen. Whatever gave you that idea?"

"Maybe he's hungry."

"Rui-De Xu would never allow him inside the compound." Wiping her daughter's face with a handkerchief, she said, "I think we've had enough of the Lantern Festival until next year." Ya-Nan took her daughter's hand. Chao Chen turned around to catch one last glimpse of the fiddle player, but he had disappeared.

Hearing Ya-Nan's voice, the night watchman opened the heavy wooden gates to the courtyard. Passing underneath the stone archway adorned with a silver plate signifying that this was the residence of a Hanlin scholar, the highest rank among China's bloated bureaucracy, Ya-Nan asked, "Has Magistrate Chen returned?"

"No, Madam."

The sound of splashing water in the courtyard fountain did nothing to soothe Ya-Nan's agitation. The red lanterns hanging underneath the carved eaves were still lit, but the living quarters were as dark as a tomb. At this late hour, her sons Fu-Chan, Fu-Chen, and Fu-Ti were already asleep, which was just as well because she didn't have the energy to listen to their imagined tales of adventure in the compound's bamboo forest or on the lake.

Ya-Nan tried to hide her disappointment from Chao Chen, but as she was tucking her daughter into bed, Chao Chen sympathetically threw her arms around her mother's neck. "The lanterns will find Papa, and he'll hurry home."

"Can you keep a secret, Chao Chen?" The child nodded earnestly. "I'm going to have another baby. Your father doesn't know yet, but he'll be happy when he hears the news. By the fall, you will have a fifth brother. I'm sure of it."

Chao Chen blurted, "I want a sister."

"One daughter is enough. Sons are what will make the Chen family strong." Ya-Nan knew that, with the birth of each son, her value to the family was further enhanced. Another daughter would add nothing to her personal currency.

After saying good night to Chao Chen, Ya-Nan tiptoed down the long hallway to her bedroom. Sitting at her dressing table, she unpinned her hair and rubbed face cream into her cheeks. Leaning toward the mirror, she examined the translucent skin underneath her kohl-lined eyes to make sure there were no telltale signs she might be losing her youthfulness and beauty. That is what attracted Gan Chen to her when he first saw her standing on the ladder in her father's shop in Shanghai's old quarter. Gan Chen, already a magistrate, and her father struck a bargain. He would pay off her father's debts in exchange for her, but Ya-Nan made her own demand of her lover: she would always be referred to as his second wife and not his concubine, even while Rui-De Xu was still alive. Gan Chen agreed, but then he told her, "A hand has five fingers, and of course each is important. But you must appreciate that Rui-De Xu will always be the thumb, and so you must be my cooperative wife number two."

Ya-Nan heard the creaking floorboards and smelled the lingering scent of incense and orange peel. Outside, the wind rustled the branches next to the shuttered windows. Turning down the kerosene lamp, she undressed in the dark and slipped beneath the covers, imagining that Gan Chen was pressing his strong body next to hers.

Ya-Nan woke up earlier than usual. She dreamed that it had snowed during the night, and she threw open the shutters to assure herself that it had been only her mind playing tricks on her. She shivered. Didn't dreams of snow portend a death?

Ya-Nan wrapped herself in a silk brocade robe and reached underneath her side of the bed for her slippers, placed there the night before by the maidservant, Ya-Li. Suddenly Chao Chen rushed into her chamber. "Mama, Mama, Father is home! But why is he sleeping on the ground?"

"I don't understand. Go back to your room. I'll come for you after I have properly greeted your father. I'm sure he's anxious to see me, and I'm bursting to tell him of the baby." For emphasis, she patted her stomach.

Ya-Nan rushed through the house and into the courtyard. Workmen stood under the portico as Rui-De Xu threw herself upon the body of Gan Chen. His cracked glasses were still resting on his nose, and his arms were folded across his mud-splattered coat. There was a gash on his right cheek, a vein of dried blood running from the wound to his neatly shaven chin. Rui-De Xu let out a piercing scream and shook her husband's body, willing him back to life, but it was too late.

Ya-Nan collapsed onto a stone bench underneath the portico. The carved lions adorning the red tile roof across the court yard taunted her. She imagined them telling her, "We are no longer going to protect you. Look what the gods have done to Gan Chen, dead at forty-six. All his virtuous deeds have not earned him another day."

Ya-Nan overheard the crew superintendent explaining to Gan Chen's older brother, Run Chen, "We waited several days for the rain to stop so the crew could start working again. It put us behind schedule. Magistrate Chen, trying to figure out how to make up for lost time for he promised the Hutai Coach Company that the East-West Road would be complete by summertime, had not slept for days. He was obviously suffering from exhaustion, and the weather didn't help: cold, windy, and soaking wet for days on end. Yesterday afternoon he was speaking with one of the crew's foremen, and before he could complete his thought, he fell over into the muddy embankment. He was screaming from the pain in his head. We lifted him into the bed of the truck and covered the fifty kilometers back to Zhenru as quickly as possible, but the old road was flooded in parts and we even had to push the truck through the water. I fear the delays cost Magistrate Chen his life. The very road that he was trying to complete would have saved him, I'm sure of it."

Run Chen observed, "My brother sacrificed his life serving China. There has never been a more devoted, more honest civil servant. He should receive a medal just as if he were a war hero who saved a battalion of soldiers. History will not forget all that he has accomplished."

Ya-Nan choked back her tears. *Yes, he is a hero, but he is also my husband and father to my four children. From this day forward, Rui-De Xu will declare herself my enemy. Until now she tried to hide her hatred of me and of my daughter, Chao Chen.* Ya-Nan realized that she would have to cement an alliance with Run Chen to secure her future. Now that Gan Chen was dead, she was a trapped woman.

Run Chen personally oversaw the preparation of his older brother's body for burial. Gan Chen was bathed and dressed in white linen pants and shirt, his gray hair combed away from his lined forehead, and his corpse was placed in an open casket made of dawn redwood and decorated with bronze curlicues and resting on two stools in the courtyard. An altar was assembled at the foot of the casket, and upon the altar was burning incense, a framed photograph of Magistrate Gan Chen taken during his speech before a gathering of the Provincial Senate, fresh fruit, bowls of rice, and white irises.

Carefully positioning a calligraphy set at the altar, Run Chen was solemn when he spoke. "Dearest brother, with this brush you inked important legislation. With it you created schools for the children of Zhenru and for the underemployed. Also, with the stroke of this brush, you shuttered vile opium dens that are destroying the people of our province. My brother, you have done so much for our country and family. Your memory shall be an inspiration to me and to all whom you have so valiantly served."

Rui-De Xu sat on a high-backed chair at Gan Chen's right shoulder, and his eldest son, eighteen-year-old Fu-Hong, sat to his left, both of them flanking Gan Chen's casket. During the vigil, hundreds of visitors passed daily through the archway, presenting envelopes of money and lighting joss sticks in tribute to Magistrate Gan Chen. Music was played as Buddhist priests chanted elegiac prayers, which could hardly be heard over the wailing and moaning of the visitors:

> *A cuckoo's song beckons me to return home;*
> *Hearing this, I tilt my head to see who*
> *has told me to run backwards.*
> *But do not ask me where I am head-*
> *ing, as I have this limitless world*
> *Where every step I take is my home.*

Outside the gate to the compound, men squatted on the pavement playing a game of dominoes through the night. They were there to guard the compound against evil spirits. The vigil continued for five days and nights.

Finally, on March 6, 1922, the lid of Gan Chen's casket was sealed, and the heavy cargo was lifted onto a palanquin. A marching band led the procession of three thousand mourners throughout the Chen estate. Behind the palanquin walked Run Chen, immediately followed by Rui-De Xu. She was carried in a sedan chair, her tiny bound feet peeking out from underneath her black mourning gown. Fu-Hong followed her, and then Ya-Nan and her children. Behind them, arranged in order of importance, were provincial officials, ministers from the central treasury, elite Jinsu and Hanlin scholars, wealthy landowners from throughout Baoshan County, tenant farmers who helped fill the Chen family coffers, the director of the vocational school established by Gan Chen, the principal of the girls' school, and the Christian missionaries.

The procession weaved about the estate, passing through its beautiful gardens, around the lake with its rowboats neatly tied up, and past the pavilion until the casket reached its resting place at the ancestral hall.

The tributes went on for hours as the mourners quietly passed the casket, paying their final respects to the deceased and his family, the reverent silence occasionally interrupted by wailing.

After the tributes, the casket was silently moved to the family tomb across the road and the Gan Chen was laid to rest next to his father, Erming Chen, who was beside his mother, Yang Shi, and all the other Chen family members who came before.

Chao Chen did not understand the meaning of all the wailing and moaning that filled the courtyard from morning until night, but she knew that Ya-Nan's red eyes and tear-stained face meant that something terrible had happened.

On the day of the funeral, Ya-Nan explained, "Chao Chen, remember the night we saw the lanterns floating up into the sky? That is where your father is now. He is never coming back, but he'll be watching you. So you'd better be a good girl, and that means you must obey me or he'll find a way to punish you. I can assure you of that. So, do you promise you'll listen to me and do exactly as I tell you?"

Chao Chen silently nodded and then ran to her room. Turning the key of her music box, she repeatedly listened to its song, hoping she would hear her father's voice telling her he was proud of her and always would be. An inexpressible sadness enveloped Chao Chen. She could not articulate her feelings, but she instinctively felt that the one person in the Chen family who truly cherished her was gone from the earth.

chapter 3

The Piano Lesson

Responsibility for Gan Chen's widow, his concubine and his six children, rested on the shoulders of his elder brother. Besides managing the estate, Run Chen worked part-time for the government as head of the local district's Bureau of Statistics. He made many shrewd investments in real estate and securities, giving him the wherewithal to cover the middle school tuition and boarding fees of the boys as they came of age.

When Chao Chen, Gan Chen's only daughter, was six years old, she entered first grade at the local Pengcheng Primary School for Girls. The school was funded by her father and uncle for the children of Zhenru Township and neighboring villages. Sitting at her desk next to the window that opened onto an orchard, she could hear the birds chirping in the trees. She was easily distracted because the lessons did not hold her attention. Her older brother, Fu-Chan, had already drilled her in basic arithmetic and taught her to read and write forty Chinese characters. Fu-Chan told Chao Chen, "A well-educated person must know four thousand characters, so you have a long way to go, but you are already one percent of the way there."

Chao Chen frowned. "How long will that take me? And what does one percent mean? All I know is that I want to read all the books in Papa's library."

"Don't ask so many questions, Chao Chen. Let's just say that you must still learn more than three thousand characters, but once you have memorized all of them, you can combine one character with another character, and in that way, you can write whatever is on your mind—even if you are a girl."

Chao Chen playfully punched her brother in the arm. "I'm going to be just as smart as you are, Fu-Chan. Maybe even smarter."

By the time Chao Chen reached the age of eleven, she was the brightest child in her class. She could hardly wait until she graduated to middle school and made no secret of her ambition to do so.

Her mother, Ya-Nan, cautioned her, "I wouldn't count on it. Your uncle is old fashioned in his thinking. Like so many men, he is afraid that an educated woman makes for an undesirable wife. He has promised me that he will put money away for your dowry, which he considers more important than giving you an education beyond primary school. Besides, he'll also need to pay for schooling for your two younger brothers when the time comes. I overheard him complaining to Rui-De Xu that all of this is a drain on the family's finances. I'll do what I can to plead your case, Chao Chen, but I have very little say in what goes on in this family now that your father is gone. And unfortunately, Gan Chen left me with very little money of my own. It's embarrassing, but I must ask your uncle for every yuan I wish to spend on myself. He usually gives me what I want, but it is only because I have borne four sons to carry on the Chen family name. If it were up to Rui-De Xu, I'd be walking around in rags." She smoothed the skirt of her elaborately embroidered cheongsam and turned her head ever so slightly so that the sunlight danced off her pearl-and-gold earrings.

Chao Chen argued, "All the more reason that I should get a good education. I never want to be a prisoner to my family, or to any man, as you are now, Mother."

Chao Chen could tell from the look on Ya-Nan's face that she had hurt her mother deeply, but she was too angry and disappointed to apologize. She realized that her mother was not her ally and she had only herself to rely upon.

Her uncle gave her the bad news. "You've had enough schooling, for a girl, that is. You are at an age when you should be practicing your domestic skills, not filling your head with learning." He lit his pipe, his eyes following the smoke into the air as if he were calling upon the gods to grant his wish. "What I expect of you is to marry a rich landowner whose assets will aggrandize the Chen family's wealth, as your father did when he married Rui-De

Xu. Marriages are for power and money, and the sooner you accept that fact, the easier your life will be, my dear niece."

Chao Chen bit her lip and tried to hold back her tears. Arguing with her uncle was pointless. From what her mother had told her, her brothers were the family's priority and she was at best an afterthought.

Chao Chen felt as if her life had stopped. Every day was like the one before it: embroidery lessons, watching Rui-De Xu and her mother play mahjong, caring for her canaries, memorizing ancient Chinese poems, and playing with her two younger brothers. If she was very lucky, she was invited by her mother to sit in the front seat of the Pierce-Arrow for an outing to Shanghai, where Ya-Nan shopped at the Sincere Department Store on Nanking Road.

On one occasion, mother and daughter stopped at the Astor House Hotel on Nanking Road for tea and finger sandwiches. The strains of a romantic Strauss waltz, which was played by a German pianist for the enjoyment of the hotel's guests, drifted into the dining room from the adjacent lobby.

As they were leaving, Chao Chen hesitated and smiled shyly at the handsome pianist. In fluent Mandarin he said, "Come back again, pretty girl."

Chao Chen asked, "What tune are you playing, sir?"

"Ah, 'The Blue Danube,' a waltz. It's a pleasant piece, is it not?"

Chao Chen answered, "The most beautiful music I have ever heard."

Ya-Nan yanked Chao Chen by the arm. "I don't want you speaking to strangers, especially foreigners. Now help me with my packages. The car will be along any minute." Chao Chen thought about the pianist and his music all the way back along the cobblestone streets of Zhenru. She knew immediately that she had to learn how to play.

Chao Chen could not stop thinking about the way she felt listening to the pianist at the Astor House Hotel long after she returned home. It was as if this strange and beautiful music had transported her to another world, a world free of the constraints placed on her by her family. She took out her nightingale music box and turned the key. When its song ended, her mind was made up. She would ask her uncle to find her a piano teacher.

Chao Chen confided in Ya-Li, her childhood *amah*. "I want more than anything in the world to learn to play the piano."

"That's a very fine idea, Chao Chen. I see how bored you are. But what makes you think your uncle will permit such a thing?"

Chao Chen twirled a lock of her thick black hair around her finger while she tried to come up with an answer. "I have an idea. Since my oldest brother's death, Rui-De Xu has never had a smile on her face."

"Who can blame her? She lost her only son, and under rather suspicious circumstances. Rumor has it that Fu-Hong died of a drug overdose. You must not breathe a word of this to anyone."

"If Father were still alive…"

Ya-Li nodded. "I know, I know. It would never have happened. But what does this tragedy have to do with piano lessons?"

"Well, if I learn how to play the piano, perhaps I can lift Rui-De Xu's spirits. Nothing seems to please her these days, and she is meaner than ever."

"You will be doing all of us a favor if you can do that." Ya-Li put her arms around Chao Chen. "Summon up your courage and ask your uncle. I believe he will say yes."

Miss Song Yuan Liang answered the advertisement for a piano teacher that Uncle Run Chen placed in *Shen Bao*, Shanghai's daily newspaper. She arrived by the Hutai coach on April 18, 1930 carrying an umbrella, an overnight bag in case the rain forced the road closed, and a leather satchel filled with piano music, which she had selected for her first pupil, twelve-year-old Chao Chen.

Miss Liang's father was a renowned faculty member of the Shanghai Conservatory of Music. He had studied at the famous conservatory in Leipzig, Germany and was reputed to be one of the finest teachers of the classical European repertoire. Among his star pupils was his twenty-three-year-old daughter, Song Yuan Liang.

After Miss Liang had been led to the music room, she looked at her young student and said, "Let's sit next to each other at the piano. I will demonstrate, and you will imitate me, Chao Chen."

"Can you show me how to play 'The Blue Danube' waltz, Miss Liang? I heard it once at the Astor House Hotel."

"So, you want to run before you can walk. You need to learn the basics. There is an order, a progression to learning the piano, and you can't skip the fundamentals. So, how many different notes are there on the piano?"

"I don't know."

"Well, there are eighty-eight keys on the piano but only twelve notes in a scale, just like there are twelve months of the year. These twelve notes are repeated over and over again, up and down the keyboard."

And so they began. The time flew by, and when the lesson finished they heard the rain pelting against the windows behind the lattice shutters.

"Chao Chen, I'm afraid I'm going to have to impose upon you. The coach is certainly not going to be returning to Shanghai in this weather."

"My brother Fu-Hong's room is empty. You are welcome to stay for the night and leave tomorrow morning. We are all going to see *The Butterfly Lovers* this evening. The troupe is presenting the opera in the temple courtyard right here in Zhenru. So let's hope the rain stops by nightfall or the performance will be cancelled." And then Chao Chen added, "It's my birthday today, so I hope I won't be disappointed."

Showing her positive nature, Miss Liang smiled. "We will just think good thoughts and all will be well in honor of your birthday."

The night air was damp after the heavy rainfall. The temple caretakers swept away the puddles on the stone pathway into the courtyard. There was not an empty seat; it seemed everyone in Zhenru was there. Chao Chen was familiar with the ancient tale of the two star-crossed lovers, Shanbo Liang and Yingtai Zhu. She identified with Yingtai, the ninth child and only daughter of the Zhu family. She remembered how her mother would tell her the story: Women were discouraged from taking up scholarly pursuits, but Yingtai convinced her father to allow her to attend classes disguised as a man. She fell in love with a classmate, Shanbo Liang, who did not realize that she was a woman; but many years later, she revealed her true identity to him and he returned her affection. Unfortunately, she was betrothed to another, and when her lover learned of this, he was heartbroken and died.

In the final, tragic scene of the opera, the heroine left the wedding procession and visited the grave of her lover, begging the gods to open the grave, and they did so. Chao Chen sat on the edge of her seat as the final scene unfolded. As the drums beat loudly to represent a clap of thunder, Yingtai Zhu threw herself into her lover's grave to be forever reunited with him in death. Then, with a trick of theatrical magic, the lovers turned into butterflies and disappeared into the bamboo forest.

The entire audience applauded, and most were in tears. The performers took their bows, and then the red lanterns were extinguished one by one as

Chao Chen and Miss Liang climbed into the back seat of the Pierce-Arrow and returned to the Chen compound.

Despite the lateness of the hour, Chao Chen struggled to fall asleep. She didn't want to let go of what had been the happiest day of her life.

chapter 4

Just Follow the Music

Miss Liang walked from the bus station to the Chen compound wearing her lightest summer dress and a wide-brimmed straw hat. She carried a parasol to shield herself from the burning August sun. In the fields around Zhenru, the farmers struggled to stay upright, their backs glistening with sweat. Anyone who had the luxury of staying indoors or sitting quietly on a shaded terrace did so, waiting for the combination of heat and humidity to loosen its grip.

Chao Chen greeted Miss Liang with a glass of iced tea, and after she had a moment to refresh herself, they began their weekly piano lesson. In just a year, Chao Chen had advanced from elementary one-handed pieces to complex two-handed compositions. On this day, Miss Liang put away the metronome. "Really, you don't need this meter counter any longer. I don't believe in it anyway; it is just a silly convention, but I'm forced to use it to the point my student is ready to play without it. You have reached that point. Music is an expression of the soul, and with all this ticking and clicking you will never really hear what the notes are meant to express: sadness, gaiety, longing, and the new word we in Shanghai are starting to use, love."

Chao Chen had a quizzical look on her lovely face. She was turning from an awkward youngster into a beautiful young girl. "What does 'love' mean, Miss Liang? It is a word I do not really understand."

"We Chinese are borrowing it from the Westerners among us, like the Christian missionaries who speak of it in religious terms. For example, their holy book says, 'Love thy neighbor as thy self.' But the novels of romance and passion illustrate other meanings, like the love between a man and woman as the connection of one heart to another, which can lead to a state of divine happiness. But there is also a dark side to love. Love can drive the beloved to do destructive and dangerous things. Remember what happened to the two young people in the opera *The Butterfly Lovers*? Death. Perhaps someday you will experience what romantic love is. I have not been so fortunate, but I have my music. Now, enough of this chatter. If your uncle hears us, he may decide that today's lesson is not worth what I'm charging."

Chao Chen hesitated for a moment, then placed her hands on the keyboard. She did not need to look at the score because she had memorized every note to "The Blue Danube." When she finished playing, Miss Liang asked, "How did that feel to you?"

"I'm not sure. I might have made a mistake or two."

"Stop being the humble Chinese maiden, Chao Chen. You played beautifully. I think we can move on to another piece. What do you think about trying Mozart's *"Eine kleine Nachtmusik"*? It is a lovely piece—the title means "A Little Night Music." It is intended for a chamber ensemble, but since there is just one of you, I have a piano version. Let me play it for you."

Miss Liang sat down at the piano and played. When she finished, Rui-De Xu, who had come in from the garden, said, "Ah, Miss Liang. That was exquisite. I knew the moment that you struck the first note that it couldn't have been Chao Chen playing. I really don't hold out much hope for her. In fact, whenever she makes a mistake during her practice time, I want to hide in my chambers. Her playing is really an affront to my ears."

"Forgive me for saying this, but Chao Chen needs some encouragement. No student will flourish in the face of incessant criticism. All my students make mistakes when they practice. It is to be expected. Let me assure you, Chao Chen is one of my most gifted students and, if she keeps up with her lessons, she might even have a career in music."

"Well, *if* that happens, all the money we have been paying you will not have been wasted. If you are not going to play anything further, I will go back to my game of mahjong. Good day, Miss Liang." Rui-De Xu walked through the drawing room doors and closed them behind her.

Chao Chen looked at her teacher. "Did you really mean what you said, or were you just trying to defend me?"

"Both. I don't like the way Rui-De Xu spoke to you."

Chao Chen admitted, "I'm used to it." She closed the lid over the piano keys while Miss Liang gathered her belongings. "If I understand the word correctly, she doesn't love me. In fact, I can say that she hates me, or at least she has little use for me. Whatever love she has is given to my brothers." Chao Chen sighed. Not wanting her teacher to leave, she made a bold suggestion. "I'd like to take our rowboat out on the lake. Would you accompany me?"

Miss Liang glanced at her watch. The coach would not be arriving for another hour at least. "That sounds very pleasant, and it will give us a chance to discuss something that has been on my mind for some time."

The green wooden rowboat was moored to a small dock at the edge of the lake. Chao Chen held it steady as her teacher settled herself on one of the seats, and then Chao Chen sat down facing her. She picked up the oars and placed them into the iron cleats, then steered the boat toward the middle of the lake. Miss Liang leaned forward and pushed the brow of Chao Chen's hat down so her face would be shaded from the glaring afternoon sun. The sound of the oars through the water, the intermittent croaking of the frogs, the chirping of the crickets, and the rustling of the weeping willow leaves were a pleasant backdrop to the conversation that followed.

Miss Liang took off her hat so Chao Chen could clearly see the determination in her eyes. "Chao Chen, I don't want to meddle in your family's affairs, but I think that you should be allowed to go to school. I have spoken with the headmistress of the Wuben School for Girls in Shanghai. I am sure that you could pass the test and earn a place. And if your family will not cover the tuition, there are a number of scholarships available for outstanding applicants."

"I am already too old for the first year of that school. All the entrants are ten years old. On my next birthday, I'll be thirteen."

"You look much younger. One day that will be to your advantage. Maybe even now."

Chao Chen forgot to keep rowing. The boat drifted toward the pavilion and got stuck in the lily pads lining the edge of the lake. She put her oar into the water, and after a few attempts, the boat was free again.

Chao Chen looked back across the lake. She could see Rui-De Xu still sitting at the table, playing her regular game of mahjong, which went on and on. And where was Ya-Nan? She suspected that she was lying on her bed in her red chamber with the shutters closed, taking an afternoon nap or reading the latest issue of a fashion magazine.

Chao Chen contemplated Miss Liang's suggestion. It was as if a door which had been forever closed to her suddenly opened a crack. "I won't mention this idea to Uncle Run Chen. If I pass the entrance examination, then I'll have to ask his permission, but I will not speak of this until then."

"That is the wisest strategy. The next examination is in late September. We will tell everyone that I have invited you to a concert at the Shanghai Conservatory of Music. In fact, my father will be performing there on the same day as the examination, and so we won't really be telling a lie. I've already gotten an application for you. It's tucked away in my satchel. I'll leave it with you, and you can give it to me at our next lesson. Then, with your uncle's permission, I'll present it to the school's headmistress. She and I are good friends, which will give you an advantage, I hope."

Chao Chen rowed the boat to the shore, and the two "accomplices" climbed out onto the dock and walked back along the gravel path toward the mansion, their steps in unison.

Chao Chen reminded herself to write in April 18, 1921 where the application required her birth date. She answered all the other questions truthfully, and she checked off the box labeled "scholarship requested," knowing that her uncle would object to paying for her tuition. In the brochure describing the features of the school, it stated that "Wuben School is connected with Utopia University, a liberal center of learning with an emphasis on Western pedagogy and a fine music department for those students interested in pursuing a career in music. All our students are required to board at the school during the week so that they can devote all their attention to their studies. Applicants who are accepted must obtain their family's permission in order to attend classes."

Chao Chen passed the entrance examination with flying colors, and with the intervention of Miss Liang, she was granted a full scholarship.

In response to the unexpected news that Chao Chen was a candidate for the Wuben School for Girls in Shanghai, Run Chen smiled. "You don't give up, do you, Chao Chen?"

"No, Uncle. When it is something that means the world to me, I will strive to move the heavens and earth."

"I admire that in you, Chao Chen, but I cannot pay the tuition at this time. The skirmishes to the north between the Japanese and our courageous soldiers are wreaking havoc on the economy, and we here in Zhenru are suffering. I'm afraid your little scheme to further your education was all for naught."

Run Chen thought that this would be the end of their discussion, but Chao Chen proudly told him she had been given a full scholarship. "So, Uncle, all you need do is sign this piece of paper and I am on my way."

Run Chen scanned the official-looking document and signed it, stamping the family seal on the paper. He looked at his niece. "Your father would be very proud of you."

Chao Chen choked back her tears, overcome by her uncle's generosity of spirit.

Chao Chen sat alone in the waiting room for the coach that would take her to Shanghai. She kept one hand on her valise to make sure that no one could take it, and tucked beneath her clothes was her piano music and a locked wooden box containing her most prized possession: the jeweled nightingale music box. She didn't dare leave it behind, afraid that Rui-De Xu might steal it.

As she climbed aboard the coach, her heart was pounding from a mixture of fear and excitement. She took a seat in the back of the coach and looked out the rear window as the town of Zhenru receded into the distance.

The Wuben School for Girls was located in the Nanshi District of Shanghai within the Old City. Despite its rigorous curriculum, which included classes in English and French, Chao Chen received top honors and was invited to skip two grades at the end of her first academic year. She was also able to continue her piano lessons with Miss Liang because the school had hired her to teach their most gifted students.

On Wednesdays Chao Chen took a trolley from the Old City into the French Concession, where the Liang family lived in a villa. Several of the public rooms were converted into practice studios, and one had been made into a small recital hall. The villa was home for some of the city's most famous Chinese conductors and musicians who concertized with Miss Liang's father. The professor often invited American musicians to play, like Negro trumpeter Buck Clayton and the Caucasian bandleader Whitey Smith, who played at the clover-leafed Majestic Hotel ballroom, one of the finest venues in all of Shanghai. Chao Chen could not get enough of what the Americans called jazz, its heady syncopated rhythms and catchy dance tunes. She imagined herself dressed in a beautiful evening gown, escorted to the Majestic by one of Shanghai's eligible bachelors. Here she would meet a man she didn't yet know, someone of spectacular charm and gallant in his bearing. She was convinced he would be waiting in the wings until the day he swept her off her feet and onto the dance floor. There was only one problem with this fantasy: she didn't know how to dance. *But*, she thought, *as with everything else in life, I can learn, can't I?*

Twilight slowly descended over Shanghai as Chao Chen left the Liang villa after one of her piano lessons. The Custom House clock rang on the hour from its distinctive tower overlooking the Bund and the Whangpoo River. Fashionably dressed pedestrians stopped for a minute to listen to its distinctive *bong*, checking their watches, and then proceeded along the boulevard en route to a private club, a reception at one of the many consulates in Shanghai, or perhaps a high-class house of prostitution, an opium den, or the seven o'clock showing of *Shanghai Express* at the Great World amusement center at the corner of Avenue Edward VII and Yu Ya Ching Road. Chao Chen wished she could just sit on a bench and catch snippets of conversation in French, English, and Mandarin, but she had a history test the next day and pages of reading awaited her.

The school's night watchman swung the dormitory door open. "Ten minutes more, Miss Chen, and you would have been locked out for the evening." He reached into his pocket and handed her a telegram. "This was delivered for you earlier today." He then bid her a good evening as she raced up the stairs to her room.

Her hands trembled as she opened the envelope, anticipating that it contained bad news, and she was right:

ZHENRU, NOVEMBER 12, 1933. UNCLE RUN CHEN DEAD. CAR WILL BE SENT FOR YOU AND YOUR BROTHER TOMORROW MORNING AT 8 A.M. MOTHER RUI-DE XU.

Chao Chen thought back to her many encounters with her sixty-seven-year-old uncle, and other than his agreement to pay for her piano lessons and giving her permission to attend middle school, she was ashamed to admit to herself that she felt indifferent to the news of his death. However, he had been running the family's estate since her father's death. Who would take care of such things now? She doubted that her nineteen-year-old brother Fu-Chan would be willing to give up his lucrative job at the Central Research Institute in Shanghai and return to provincial Zhenru, even for the sake of the family.

The next morning the Pierce-Arrow pulled up to the front steps of the Wuben School; Fu-Chan jumped from the back seat and embraced his sister. They had not seen each other in more than a year. "You look like a blossoming flower, Chao Chen."

"And you look very important in your business suit, Fu-Chan."

They loaded her few things into the car and took their seats, and before the Pierce-Arrow had even passed through the school gates, Chao Chen blurted, "Who besides you can run the estate now?"

Her brother answered, "At one time, it would have been up to me to run the estate, but I have no intention of leaving Shanghai to muck around in the fields collecting rents from the peasant farmers, who would just as soon kill us as reach into their pockets. But don't worry. I'll help Mother find someone to take over until our younger brother Fu-She is old enough to carry on, if he wants to. In my opinion, the entire family would be better off in Shanghai. We should just sell our properties now. If Emperor Hirohito gets his way, Baoshan County will, sooner or later, be under the thumb of those merciless dwarf Japs and all the landowners will be working for them. In fact, sooner or later, all of China will be controlled by the Japanese. The Republic does not have the wherewithal to resist them. It's really laughable. Think about it. The Chinese invented gun powder and we have millions upon millions of people who should be ready to fight, but we are not united behind one country and one cause."

Chao Chen could hardly believe what her brother was saying. He was predicting the death of a way of life that the Chen family had known for hundreds of years.

He continued, "Don't look so sad, Chao Chen. There is really nothing for us in Zhenru. The city is where young people like us belong. If not Shanghai, then Hong Kong. Just think of it. The entire world is opening up to us. We don't need to be stuck living out our lives next to the tombs of our ancestors, paying our daily respects to dead people."

"Even Father?"

"Even Father. Trust me. If he were still alive, he'd be encouraging you to make a life for yourself in the city where the possibilities for a smart girl like you are endless."

chapter 5

Driven from Zhenru

Contrary to Chao Chen's brother's thoughts on the matter, the Chen family held on to their land, but the family's fortunes suffered one blow after another over the next four years: punishing weather, an outbreak of cholera, a robbery, and the migration of tenant farmers into the cities to the north and south, leaving their land fallow and unproductive. To the north, Japanese troops had captured Manchuria, now renamed Manchukuo, and were planning a major mobilization southward and westward into China.

Chao Chen continued her education on a scholarship and graduated from a prestigious high school in Shanghai with near fluency in English. During her senior year she was given the opportunity to perform in a recital with some of Miss Liang's other students. She chose a piano transcription of Sergei Rachmaninoff's "Vocalise."

Before Chao Chen's name was announced, Miss Liang told her, "Just remember that it is *you* playing this piece. We want to hear *your* interpretation, *your* emotions, *your* soul, if you will let us. That is just as important as playing the notes correctly. You know the proper technique, but you have yet to fully express yourself through Rachmaninoff's music."

Chao Chen sat down in front of the piano as the other students stared at her. She wondered, *Are they waiting for me to make a mistake?* Out of the corner of her eye, she could see her tutor standing at the back of the studio. She took a deep breath and centered herself. And then, from the first note to the last, she felt as if she were in a trance, carried away by the sheer sadness and beauty of the composition. Lifting her head after the final chord, she looked out across the audience, which seemed to hold its breath with her.

Then they broke into applause. Miss Liang was smiling at her and clapping right along with the students.

Chao Chen curtsied and then walked back to her seat as the next student took his place. There was no one in her family to present her with flowers or to give her their congratulations. Not even her elder brother Fu-Chan bothered to come to her recital. Maybe one day they would buy a ticket to hear her perform in a real concert hall. That was her dream.

After receiving her high school diploma with honors, Chao Chen packed up all her things in the same valise she had brought with her four years earlier and reluctantly returned by coach to Zhenru. She was unsure of what her next step in life would be, but she prayed that the long summer days would bring her some clarity. Sitting on the bus, she tried to concentrate on the novel her English teacher had given her as a graduation present, but all she could think about was Rui-De Xu's angry face and petty demands.

Entering the courtyard of the Chen family mansion, Chao Chen was surprised by the silence. She wished she could turn right around and get back on the coach to Shanghai, but where would she live and how would she support herself? She opened her bedroom door, and to her relief, she found Ya-Li mopping the floor. She rushed into her arms, nearly tipping over the pail of soapy water.

Ya-Li confessed, "I'm so glad to see you, my dearest. Now I'll have someone to commiserate with and fuss over."

"Where are my brothers?"

"They'll be back soon, and then I'll have my hands full taking care of all of you."

"What about the other servants?"

"We had to let most of them go. Besides, one of them was a real troublemaker. Rui-De Xu caught him stealing from the pantry. When she confronted him, he told her, 'Well, what do you expect? You don't pay us enough and so we just have to help ourselves.' From what I hear, it's the same story everywhere in Zhenru." Ya-Li picked up her mop and pail.

Chao Chen looked at her. "Why do you stay, Ya-Li?"

"Where would I go? My parents are dead, and my three brothers have been recruited by the Communists to fight against Republican troops somewhere to the west. For better or worse, this is my home."

"I promise you, I'm going to figure out a way to get out of here, or else I'll die." Chao Chen was determined.

Ya-Li laughed. "Don't be so melodramatic, Chao Chen. Once all your brothers are home things will look much brighter, I promise you. And by the end of the summer, your Miss Liang will be back from Salzburg—isn't that where she is right now?—and you can resume your piano lessons. Now, if you want to be of some use around here, help me in the kitchen."

Chao Chen practiced her scales and chords so she would not lose her dexterity. In the middle of a run of C-sharp scales, her mother interrupted her. "Chao Chen, Rui-De Xu and I would like to speak with you. Come into the garden." Chao Chen took a handkerchief out of her skirt pocket and wiped the perspiration from her neck. She had not realized how still and hot the air was in the drawing room.

Rui-De Xu was drumming her long fingernails on the rosewood table. Ya-Li refilled her glass with iced tea and placed a fresh mint leaf in it. Rui-De Xu's eyes wandered across the lake to the pavilion, and then she rested her gaze on Chao Chen.

Ya-Nan snapped her fan open and closed. She motioned for Chao Chen to sit down in the east chair.

Rui-De Xu dabbed her lips with a lace napkin and then spoke to Chao Chen as if she were simply picking up a conversation interrupted midsentence. "Master Kao, a colleague of your father's, has contacted me with a proposal of marriage between you and his son. We did not need to go through the usual qualifying phase since both families have been eyeing one another for many years. Master Kao's son is thirty-five years old and a widower with four children, all boys, I believe. His wife died of cholera two years ago, and he has been looking for a wife ever since."

Ya-Nan picked up the conversation. "The Kaos have agreed to accept the amount of money in your dowry, so long as Rui-De Xu also presents them with her antique porcelain blue-and-white dragon vase. It is worth a fortune, but she has generously consented to sacrifice it for your future."

Rui-De Xu added, "A small price to pay to ensure your happiness, Chao Chen."

Both women turned to Chao Chen, awaiting her response. Without hesitating, Chao Chen asked, "How could you think that I would agree to marry a man sixteen years older than me—and with four children? Are you worried that at nineteen I am undesirable to a man my own age? And why do you think I would agree to a 'blind marriage,' saddling myself with someone I have not even met? I wouldn't say yes even if he was the heir to the British throne or the son of the last Emperor of China." She took a gulp of iced tea and continued before either woman could interrupt her. "I didn't win a scholarship and study hard at school so that I could be pawned off to some widower. I don't even know if I will ever marry, but if I do, it will be to someone I am in love with. Preferably someone who shares the same interests and passions I do."

"And what might those be?" Ya-Nan inquired.

"Do you know so little about your own daughter that you need to ask that question? Music, of course, and languages and literature, and everything that is beautiful and kind in this world." And then, just in case they did not fully comprehend the depth of her conviction, she stood up, and leaning with both hands on the table, said, "I would rather throw myself into the Yangtze than agree to this."

Before she could run off, Rui-De Xu grabbed her by the arm, digging her fingernails into her flesh. "If that is your decision, so be it. But we will expect you to help the family out financially, as if you were a man instead of an impudent girl."

Later that night, Chao Chen sat in front of her mirror, which reflected her red eyes. She brushed her bobbed hair until her scalp stung from the bristles. Through the open window she could hear Ya-Nan and Rui-De Xu arguing, but they were too far away for her to make out what they were saying. Her canaries flew around their cage, and when she filled their container with birdseed, they rewarded her by chirping and chattering. She lay down on her bed and imagined that the birds were telling her, "Don't worry, Chao Chen. Everything will be all right." If only she could believe them. Underneath her anger were feelings of panic and fear. Her stomach was in knots.

Still wearing his white linen business suit, Fu-Chan handed his jacket to Ya-Li and sat down for dinner at the head of the table. From her seat at the other end of the table, Chao Chen could still make out the plum trees in the fading evening light through the window. She remembered that it was the summer solstice, when the sun reached its highest point in the sky and the longest day of 1937. It made her wistful as she imagined young couples in love walking through the cobblestone streets of Zhenru after nightfall and watching the firecrackers rocketing into the star-filled sky.

After a dinner of watermelon, chicken, duck wrapped in shark fins, and rice cakes, Fu-Chan announced, "Chao Chen, I see that you're off somewhere else. Pay attention. What I am about to say involves everyone in the family, you included.

"As you all know, I have been in Shanghai for the past two days. Fu-She and I found a villa on Rue Tenant de la Tour in the heart of the French Concession. We are all moving there immediately. It's not safe for us to stay in Zhenru any longer. We have learned that Japanese warships are heading for the coast. There will be a confrontation and we could be caught in the middle.

"We will be better off in Shanghai, even if fighting breaks out in the city. The French Concession has its own protection, but it's highly doubtful that the Japanese will attack that area anyway. I don't think they want to risk bringing France into the war, or Great Britain for that matter, which, along with the Americans, is in charge of the International Concession."

Trying to paint a more positive picture, Fu-She added to his brother's comments. "The house has hot and cold running water, a working toilet, and electricity. Each of us will have our own bedroom. The house is really quite spacious, and there is a garden. The owners have agreed to leave their piano so you can practice, Chao Chen."

A scowl on her face, Rui-De Xu said curtly, "How long will we have to live in Shanghai? As far as I am concerned, it is a city of gangsters, prostitutes, vermin, and disease. And what's worse, there are places in the city where even the highest-ranking Chinese, people like us, are not allowed to go. I have heard that there are signs on some buildings and gardens that say 'No dogs or Chinese allowed.'"

Fu-Chan answered, "That is an exaggeration, Mother. But as for how long we will be there, I have no idea. The reports coming out of Nanking indicate this could be the beginning of another long and bloody war with Japan. They have taken Manchuria and Peking, and now they have their sights set on the rest of China.

"Fu-She and I have signed a three-year lease on the house as a precautionary measure, although we hope that we will not be stuck in Shanghai that long. I have already arranged for the members of the local militia to help us pack. Two trucks will be arriving in the morning. We will only be able to transport basic household items and furniture, and one of our remaining servants will stay behind to watch over the estate while we are gone. I don't wish to alarm you, but this really is a matter of life and death."

Rui-De Xu rapped her knuckles against the table. "So, we are being run out of Zhenru by those devils, are we? I have worked hard to turn our estate into a showplace. The gardens, the pavilion, and all our antiques are the envy of Baoshan County—even all of Jiangsu Province. I have no intention of leaving. You can go without me."

Fu-Chan argued, "Mother, please be reasonable. I promise we will be very comfortable in Shanghai. Just think of it. You will be welcomed with open arms by all of the most important Chinese families Father helped when he was in office."

Rui-De Xu raised her eyebrows. "Perhaps you are right. But you must promise me that the minute that, this inconvenient war is at an end, we are to return to Zhenru; and you must promise that I will be buried in the Chen Tombs, alongside Gan Chen, when the time comes."

"Of course, Mother."

Chao Chen could barely suppress a smile listening to this conversation. Her brother's news was the answer to Chao Chen's prayers. She felt confident that in Shanghai she would find more ways to pursue her academic studies and musical training, and she craved the hustle and bustle of the city.

"Can we bring Ya-Li with us?"

Rui-De Xu nodded. "As long as she can cook a meal as delicious as this one, I see no reason to let her go."

In cavalcade fashion, the old Pierce-Arrow led the way and trucks laden with clothing and household goods followed closely behind. The Chen family traveled southeast to Shanghai over the very roads that Gan Chen sacrificed his life to build. They were settled into their modest home on Rue Tenant de la Tour in the French Concession within a week of arriving. Their exodus was not a moment too soon. By mid-July, eager to show the world that China could defend itself, Chiang Kai-shek had declared a war of resistance against Japanese forces. He also wanted to gain the upper hand against the Communists, who were intent upon challenging his authority.

On August 13, 1937, Republic of China air force bombers staged an attack against the Japanese warship *Izumo* as it floated menacingly in the

Whangpoo River, its guns aimed at the Bund. Several of the Chinese firebombs missed their target and landed in the middle of the International Concession, damaging Sir Victor Sassoon's International Cathay Hotel, portions of the Wing On and Sincere department stores on Nanking Road, and the Great World entertainment center, where *Swing Time*, starring Fred Astaire and Ginger Rogers, played to sold-out audiences. Upwards of three thousand civilians were killed in the crossfire within a three-day period.

The Chen family hid in their new home, keeping their windows and doors shut, but ash and the smell of smoke seeped in through the cracks. Rue Tenant de la Tour was left unscathed, but some of their neighbors lost loved ones in the conflagration for this was a war that made no distinction between soldier and civilian. On August 23, for example, the Japanese dropped eight firebombs into a crowded waiting room at Shanghai's south train station.

A source of stability for the frightened Shanghai civilians during these attacks were the few English newspapers that survived destruction. Also, makeshift radio transmitters offered businesses and individuals the opportunity to communicate to family and friends. Messages were broadcast continuously, offering comfort and hope in a time of great fear and uncertainty.

The hospitals were overrun with the injured and the streets were littered with dead bodies, many of which could not be disposed of. Instead they piled up in the streets, causing health hazards, to say nothing of the smells and general dismay of all who passed by. The infestation of flies overwhelmed the authorities and carried many diseases.

The first telephone call to the Chen family after the phone lines were restored, which took several weeks, was from one of their servants left behind to guard the estate in Zhenru. Rui-De Xu heard the telephone ring but did not rush to pick it up; that was someone else's job, not hers. But the caller insisted on speaking with her.

She pressed the receiver against her ear.

"Madam Rui-De Xu, I have very bad news. Not more than three days after your departure, a posse of wild bandits broke into the house, ransacked it, and set it on fire. Only the shell of the original mansion remains. The town militia came too late to do anything."

Chao Chen watched as Rui-De Xu's face turned ashen. She hung up the telephone, and for the first time Chao Chen could ever remember, Rui-De Xu wept. Tears poured down the rivulets of her deeply-lined face.

chapter 6

Salon on Julu Road

In November 1937, three hundred kilometers northwest of Shanghai, Jiangsu's capital city, Nanking, was attacked by the Japanese Imperial Army. Over the next six months Japanese troops engaged in rape, murder, theft, and arson. Girls as young as twelve years old, screaming to be saved from their unspeakable fates, were taken from their homes by Japanese soldiers and driven away in trucks.

By the time the carnage was over, more than 300,000 civilians and soldiers had been slaughtered—half the population of Nanking. As many as 80,000 women had been raped, including infants and the elderly. "Rapes were often performed in public during the day, sometimes in front of spouses or family members. ... The women were then killed immediately after the rape, often by mutilation. There [were] even stories of Japanese troops forcing families to commit acts of incest. ... Monks who had declared a life of celibacy were forced to rape women for the amusement of the Japanese. Chinese men were forced to have sex with corpses. Any resistance would be met with summary executions.

The International Settlement and the French Concession remained islands of safety in Shanghai. How long that would last was anyone's guess, but for the time being, those with wealth and political power, which were mostly one and the same, carried on with the business of making money and socializing. So it came as a pleasant surprise when Rui-De Xu received an invitation from Madam Rose Jisheng to attend a ladies' luncheon in late January at the family's villa on Julu Road. Her husband, Liu Jisheng, was one of China's richest coal magnates and among its most influential citizens. The invitation could not have come at a better time.

Rui-De Xu was desperate to make contact with Madam Rose and the other ladies of whom, with sufficient patience and strategic diplomacy, she could take advantage. As her son Fu-Chan reminded her, she had been invited because Liu Jisheng, like so many other industrialists, had sought her husband's wise counsel during the years that Gan Chen served as a minister in the Republic of China's Ministry of Transport. Gan Chen had been a skillful negotiator and problem solver who could literally move mountains.

January of 1938 was bitterly cold. Rui-De Xu wore her finest fox fur-lined brocade coat over a jacket of white silk and a long wraparound dove-gray skirt that skimmed the floor, hiding her lotus slippers. She knew that the younger women attending Madam Rose Jisheng's luncheon would be wearing fashionable cheongsam dresses, but at her age, she wasn't about to change her style; and, admittedly, when she had tried on a cheongsam dress, the mirror told her that this style did her no favors. To complete her outfit, Rui-De Xu picked out an exquisite hairpiece of tourmaline, jade, seed pearls, and red coral that had belonged to her mother. She was ready to go into battle.

The Jisheng villa was one of the finest private residences on Julu Road in the French Concession. Designed by Hungarian architect László Hudec, the Italian Renaissance-style villa was built by Rose Jisheng's husband as a fortieth-birthday present. Rui-De Xu stepped out of the Pierce-Arrow in front of the columned entry and was led by a servant dressed in an English butler's uniform through the grand hallway with its spiral staircase, large crystal chandelier, and black-and-white marble floor.

Rui-De Xu took a deep breath as Madam Jisheng approached her.

"Ah, Madam Chen, welcome to my home. I have been looking forward to meeting you. My husband speaks so highly of your husband. How many years has it been since his premature death?"

"Fifteen years. It seems like yesterday that he met with your husband to conclude a business transaction. Of course, I was not privy to the details, but I understand that your husband profited greatly from Gan Chen's intercession."

"Yes. And of course, transporting coal from the mines in the north has been greatly facilitated by the North-South Hutai Road, which your husband was responsible for building."

Rui-De Xu sighed. "It was on one of his forays into the countryside while overseeing the construction that he was struck down. Oh, the workers spared me no detail. My poor husband landed face-first in the mud—it had been raining for weeks—and he was transported home by truck. But it was too late. I believe that Gan Chan dedicated his life to the Republic of China. Wouldn't you agree?"

Rui-De Xu had practiced this speech in front of a mirror, raising and lowering her eyebrows to punctuate its meaning, which was that this woman owed her wealth and position to Gan Chen. She wanted to be sure that there was no doubt of that since she had an important favor to ask of her and wanted to be sure that granting it would be a form of reciprocity. Yes, she could be conniving when it came to the well-being of her family.

The other women drifted into a circle around Madam Jisheng, curious about this woman with bound feet and slightly out-of-fashion attire. "Please let me introduce you," Madam Rose said. As each woman's name was announced, Rui-De Xu became even more certain that her mission would be accomplished: Madam Soong, the wife of T.V. Soong and sister-in-law of Chiang Kai-shek; the wives of the four richest industrialists in Shanghai, including Madam Rong; and Madam Liu.

"And this is today's guest of honor, Madam Chao Pei-Pa. She is the director of choral singing at the Shanghai Conservatory of Music. At the risk of embarrassing you, Madam Chao Pei-Pa, may I say how impressed we are with all that you are doing to use music as a means to unite our country."

Madam Chao Pei-Pa bowed. "A rather novel concept, this nation-building, but a necessity if we are to stop our enemies from taking advantage of our people and our land."

The ladies nodded in unison.

Madam Rose added, "And we owe a debt of gratitude to our guest, Madam Rui-De Xu. You've all heard of her husband, Magistrate Gan Chen, I presume?"

Once again they nodded, and Rui-De Xu practically smacked her lips thinking about the victory that was practically within reach.

The butler struck a gong, and the ladies filed into the dining room. Instead of sitting at the large banquet table, they were led to a small circular table set in the alcove to facilitate conversation. In the European fashion, sterling silverware had replaced chopsticks; the plates were Wedgwood china, the crystal goblets imported from Czechoslovakia, and in front of each place setting was a name card. Rui-De Xu could see the formal garden from her seat, its centerpiece a graceful marble fountain with a naked woman holding an urn over her head. Rui-De Xu averted her eyes and took in what was being said.

Rose Jisheng, as was her prerogative as hostess, tried to steer the conversation in another direction, but all anyone could speak about was the war. The women traded intelligence gleaned from conversations with their husbands.

Madam Rong reported, "My husband is planning to move some of his operations from Wuhan into Shanghai, where it is safer." She picked up her fork and took a bite of the cheese soufflé.

Madam Liu contradicted her. "Really? My husband has heard that the Republic is demanding many factories in the north be relocated. Imagine what this city will become if everyone moves their factories into Shanghai? The 'Pearl of the Orient' is going to become the cesspool of the Orient, and we certainly can't let that happen. Think of our beautiful rose gardens and our lovely parks. They will all be covered in a layer of soot and smog, to say nothing of the workers who will need to be housed here. They'll all end up living on the wharves and in the streets, which are crowded enough as it is."

Madam Song argued, "But look what happened in Nanking—mass murder and devastation everywhere! The Japanese dwarfs were merciless. We cannot expose our workers to the prospect of such cruelty. And now the Japanese military is marching south through Zhenru." She turned to Rui-De Xu. "That is where you are from, is it not, Madam Chen?"

Holding back her tears, Rui-De Xu nodded. "Yes. Our estate was overrun and set on fire. I don't know if I will ever be able to return. What's to be done? Our military is going to have to call upon other countries to help us defeat the Japanese."

Madam Song nodded. "You are correct. General Chiang Kai-shek is trying to bring the Soviets in, but my husband says he does not see that happening. We are alone, at least for the foreseeable future." She cut into the filet mignon surrounded by haricots verts and button mushrooms. "Rose, this is just delicious. You are fortunate to have such a well-trained chef."

Before their attention was focused elsewhere, Rui-De Xu confided, "I'm very worried that my four sons may be called to military service."

"How old are your children?" Madam Rose seemed genuinely interested.

"My sons are twenty-four, twenty-two, eighteen, and sixteen. The youngest may not be eligible yet, but the other three certainly are. Oh, I also have a daughter. She's just graduated high school." Straightening her back, she bragged, "She is studying to be a concert pianist at the Conservatory." Rui-De Xu would never admit to Chao Chen that she was in the least bit proud of her daughter, but she knew this fact would impress the ladies, most especially the guest of honor.

Dabbing her lips with her napkin, Rose Jisheng smiled, "My sons will be going into the family businesses once they finish their university studies. The Republic sees that as a form of service. That is not the case with your sons, since there is no family business for them to go into, and for the time being, your land is lying fallow since all the farmers have abandoned the fields to go into hiding or have joined the Communists. It is simply wretched what is happening." She cleared her throat. "Obviously bad news has a way of traveling throughout our little community." All the ladies nodded in unison. Rose Jisheng continued, "But given who their father is, I'm sure we can find a way to exempt your sons from military service, Madam Chen. I will speak to my husband immediately."

The guests knew that, whenever Rose asked something of Liu Jisheng, he gladly obliged. Wasn't this magnificent villa, and all the treasures in it, proof of her influence over her devoted husband? And whatever Liu Jisheng requested of government officials, they were only too eager to comply.

Rui-De Xu breathed a sigh of relief. She barely paid attention to the rest of the conversation. She was so excited she could hardly take a bite of the English trifle brimming with strawberries that had been placed in front of her. After the dessert plates were cleared, Madam Chao Pei-Pa gave a short talk about her upcoming concert at the Shanghai Conservatory of Music. The ladies applauded and assured her they would attend and bring their husbands, knowing full well that none of the men were interested in anything other than making money.

Rose Jisheng then announced, "To continue our luncheon salons, I have invited Xiao Hong in February. Some of you may have read her recent novel, *The Field of Life and Death*. Her feminist views have caused quite a stir. Not everyone will agree with her, but I found her argument quite compelling. And for March, the American Jewess Miss Emily Hahn has agreed to join us. I've told her she is welcome to bring her pet gibbon, Mr. Mills. Truthfully, although I hear that he is quite well behaved, for a gibbon, that is, I'm afraid he might climb up my silk curtains."

"Miss Hahn is a journalist, and she is the lover of the poet Sinmay Zau. Of course, she is fluent in Mandarin, so we will have no trouble conversing with her. I'm curious to meet her. Perhaps she'll give us some idea of what the United States' President Roosevelt intends to do about what is happening here and in Europe as well. I'm speaking of Adolf Hitler."

The ladies did not want to admit their ignorance of this Adolf Hitler, and so they simply nodded. After finishing their tea, all the guests stood up, thanked their hostess, and passed through the hallway to the chauffeur-driven cars parked in the circular driveway. Rui-De Xu was the last guest to leave, both by design and because she could not walk as quickly as the younger women.

Rose put her hand firmly on her shoulder. "Let me tell you this as delicately as possible." Her eyes narrowed. "In my experience, Madam Chen, you will need to offer a substantial amount of money for each one of your sons to keep them out of the military." She stipulated an amount. "Are you prepared for this?"

"Yes. We were able to secretly transfer gold into the Bank of Shanghai before we escaped from Zhenru." Until that moment she had never used the word "escaped," but now realized that is exactly what she and her family had done.

"Good. I will let you know in a few days if my husband has been successful." And then Rose's faced relaxed. "I do hope you will join us for the February luncheon."

"With pleasure. And may I say how grateful I am to you?"

"No need. I do what I can for my 'sisters.'"

The telephone rang a few days later. Rui-De Xu did not wait for Ya-Li to answer it. She picked up the receiver immediately, hoping that it was the call she had been waiting for. She recognized the voice on the other end. "Madam Rose, how lovely to hear from you. I hope you received my thank you note for your kind hospitality. I so enjoyed the luncheon."

"Let me get right to the point, Madam Chen. Everything has been taken care of. A representative from my husband's office here in Shanghai will be at your home tomorrow. He will present his documents so that you have no question as to his identity. Please have the transaction fees we discussed."

"I understand." There was a click and the telephone went dead. A smile passed across Rui-De Xu's lips. She knew exactly where she would find the money to save the boys. Chao Chen's dowry more than covered the agreed upon amount, and with the money left over, she would buy herself a pretty bejeweled hairpiece she had long admired at Sincere to reward herself. Perhaps moving to Shanghai wasn't such a terrible fate. After all, it had saved her sons from risking getting caught in the crosshairs of a Japanese rifle.

In March the Chinese military won their first major battle against the invading Japanese troops by massively outnumbering the enemy. But their euphoria over their success at the Battle of Tai'erzhuang was short-lived. The Japanese called up reinforcements and, with their superior technology, smashed Chinese resistance during the six-month battle for control of Wuhan on the Yangtze.

In a desperate measure to blockade Japanese advancement farther west, Chiang Kai-shek ordered the dikes of the Yellow River blown up, causing extensive flooding and displacing millions of Chinese. Some of the homeless now looked eastward toward Shanghai, and those who could found their way into the city, draining its already strained resources and increasing the homeless population.

In November 1938 Austrian and German Jews escaping the Nazis began arriving in Shanghai. Eight months earlier, no Jewish family could have imagined that they would find themselves seeking a safe haven in the city by the Whangpoo, the last tributary of the Yangtze River before it empties into the East China Sea.

chapter 7
Austria Is No More

On March 11, 1938, just before Shabbat, the concierge opened the heavy glass-and-brass door into the marble lobby of 10 Esteplatz in Vienna's fashionable Third District, where well-to-do Jewish families resided, just blocks from the Belvedere Palace and the Palais Albert Rothschild on the Ringstrasse. Normally, Josef Kolber would have taken the elevator to his second-floor apartment, but on this particular evening, he was too impatient to wait for the carriage to descend and instead climbed the stairs, two at a time, holding on to the wrought iron railing. Out of breath, he reached into his suit pocket for his handkerchief and wiped his brow.

Opening the door to his apartment, he recognized the final words of Mozart's *Don Giovanni: "Questo è il fin di chi fa mal; e de' perfidi la morte alla vita è sempre ugual!"* ("Such is the end of the evildoers; and in this life, scoundrels always receive their just deserts.") Josef and Eva had seen a performance of the opera during the 1937 Vienna opera season, and as a surprise gift to his wife, he had bought her this recording. That it was playing now on the gramophone was a hint that Eva and their daughter, Lilly, were already home from the family-owned Eva's House of Fashion, enjoying a brief musical interlude before dinner at six thirty.

How ironic that these lyrics should greet him tonight. Just the day before the German Wehrmacht had crossed into Austria, welcomed with fluttering Nazi flags. A national referendum was scheduled for the next day that would legitimize Hitler's rise to power and the reunification of Germany with Austria. Josef could not believe that his fellow countrymen would sanction Hitler's actions. Didn't they hear what he was saying about the Jews, that they were responsible for all of Austria's ills? And didn't they worry that he claimed he alone could bring the Reich back to its former glory?

As Josef unbuttoned his coat he admired the opulent salon's burgundy velvet curtains, already drawn, tapestry pillows accenting the large sofa upholstered in dark green brocade, and two Oriental rugs that grounded the room. A vitrine filled with Eva's favorite Meissen porcelain was lit by shiny brass sconces. The music stand next to the Bösendorfer piano still held the sonata his fifteen-year-old son Walter was practicing for his violin recital. On the walls were oil paintings depicting hunting scenes and lakeside villas that reminded Josef of family trips to Attersee and Salzburg. He knew his tastes were a bit conservative, but he simply purchased what he liked and resisted the urge to go after the works of the secessionists such as Gustav Klimt and Egon Schiele, which he thought too risqué—and too expensive for his pocketbook if truth be told.

He followed the sound of Mozart's music down the hallway and into the library. His daughter Lilly jumped up from her chair to greet her father with a big kiss. Every time Josef saw her, he was startled by how beautiful she had become, blooming from an awkward young girl into a sophisticated seventeen-year-old, one who was very sure of herself. His wife's beauty, at age forty-three, was dimming—to be expected after nineteen years of marriage and three children—but her sharp mind and inner strength earned her the appellation *gnädige Frau* (gracious Madam) from her customers and friends. Josef adored his wife, Eva Eiferman, and was grateful to her, and to her family, for launching their successful clothing business that made their comfortable lifestyle possible. He had married well.

Josef sighed, prompting Eva to ask, "What's the matter, Josef? You don't seem yourself." After so many years of marriage, the couple could read each other's moods with a simple glance.

"We'll speak of it later. Now, where are the twins?"

"In their bedroom. They need to study. Tomorrow is their geology test. Dolfie is, as usual, prepared, but Walter has been spending too much time on the soccer field and not enough time on his studies. I am worried about him."

"Dolfie" was a nickname for Adolf, and everyone preferred using it these days.

"Well, two heads are better than one, I always say. Dolfie will bring Walter up to speed, and I'm sure they'll both pass the examination with flying colors."

Eva smiled. "Always the optimist."

"Not always."

The needle on the gramophone slid into the center groove, making a hissing and clicking sound. Lilly got up and lifted the arm. "*Finito*, Papa."

"Just in time," said Eva.

Their housekeeper, Agneza, entered the library to announce that dinner was ready. "If you don't come now, everything will be cold." To a schooled ear she spoke German with a decidedly Slovak accent. Josef looked at his pocket watch: six thirty exactly. He laughed to himself. Why did he bother to check the time? Agneza was as punctual as the trains that ran in and out of Vienna's Westbahnhof station.

Eva instructed her daughter, "Call your brothers. They need to eat if they expect to do well on their examination."

"Yes, Mutti."

It was Shabbat, but the ritual lighting of the candles and the blessing over the challah and wine had long been abandoned by the family. Only the silver candlesticks at the center of the table were a reminder of the Orthodox Jewish community in Lemberg, Galicia (Austria-Hungary) that Josef and Eva had left behind, where their families had once devoutly followed the daily, weekly, and monthly Jewish rituals.

Tonight's menu included chicken paprika, spätzle, brussels sprouts, and for dessert, a jelly roll with homemade preserves covered in icing made with Belgian chocolate, a Kolber family favorite.

Over dessert Josef quizzed the boys. "So, who wants to tell me how thick the earth's crust is?" Neither said a word. "Well, Dolfie, why don't you answer the question?"

"Papa, I know the answer, but I was hoping Walter would tell you. We just went over this and I want to be sure that he's ready for the examination."

Lilly put down her dessert fork. "Show off."

Eva remarked, "Not at all. I think it's admirable that Dolfie wants to help his brother."

Walter kicked Lilly under the table. "I was just playing with you, Papa. I know the answer. The earth's crust ranges from thirty to fifty kilometers."

"Is he correct, Dolfie?"

"Yes, Papa,"

"Well done, boys. I'm glad to see that all the money Mutti and I are spending on your school tuition is not going to waste." The nearby Gymnasium was not only one of the most expensive private boys' schools in Vienna, but one of the oldest and most prestigious. It followed a traditional curriculum but included classes in English language proficiency and literature, preparing its elite graduates for entrance into a university at home or abroad. Eva and Josef expected both boys to enter the university and hoped that at least one of them would take over the family business someday.

Turning to Lilly, Josef asked, "And my little beauty, did Frau Klopstein come into the store today to pick up her evening gown?"

"Yes, and it fits her perfectly. While she was trying it on I showed her a black wool crepe day jacket we just made from one of our factory remnants, and she bought that as well."

Walter smirked. "Bragger."

Eva came to her daughter's defense. "Lilly is a great help to me. We have been busier than usual, with Pesach[1]* just around the corner. Josef, tell Lilly what we have in mind for her this summer."

"Instead of going with the family to Lake Attersee, how would you like to go to Paris for a month? One of my customers runs a fashionable store on Rue Saint-Guillaume on the Left Bank. He has offered to apprentice you, and you can stay with his family. They have a daughter about your age, so it would be perfect."

Lilly was dumbstruck. "You'd let me leave Vienna by myself?"

Eva observed, "It's time you saw more of the Continent. Consider it part of your education. Who knows? Maybe you'll even pick up a few customers for the factory. You should be sure to go to the Galeries Lafayette on Boulevard Haussmann. They carry ready-to-wear for men and women and it's one of Paris's chicest department stores."

"Could I invite Maria Alsfelder to go with me? Her French is even better than mine." Maria and Lilly were lifelong friends. The two girls had graduated together from the Eugenie Schwarzwald School and had competed for the school's top prizes, Lilly winning the first prize in English language proficiency and Maria winning in French.

Josef was thoughtful. "Well, I'll have to speak with her father first. He just made a small loan to me from his bank to buy two more sewing machines

---

[1] * Passover

for the factory. Let's see what he says. And if his answer is yes, what will you do?"

"I'll go, of course," Lilly answered. "And it will give me a chance to get away from these two matching bookends," she added, pointing to the twins.

Walter laughed. "Our good luck, for sure."

Josef sipped the last drops of coffee and then checked his watch again. Seven thirty. In less than fifteen minutes there was to be an announcement on the radio. He lit a cigar and then pushed his chair away from the table, signaling the end of dinner. Eva rang the silver bell for Agneza to clear the dessert plates.

Walter and Dolfie asked to be excused. Josef was emphatic in his answer. "No. I want the entire family together. Lilly, go into the kitchen and ask Agneza to join us. She needs to hear what is going on as well." Agneza, five years older than Eva, had worked for the Kolbers, first as a nanny, and now was their cook and maid. She was part of the family. Eva often brought her into her confidence, and Lilly and the twins treated her like a second mother.

With a look of grave concern on his face, Josef turned on the radio in the library. He was not sure what he would hear, but he knew that something momentous was about to happen. He didn't have long to wait. The radio announcer interrupted the music. "The planned March twelfth vote to unite Austria with Germany has been cancelled. In a few minutes we will hear from Austrian Chancellor Schuschnigg."

Eva mumbled, "Schuschnigg promised that our beautiful flag would never fall to the Nazis. I remember what he said: 'Red-White-Red until we're dead!'"

Josef nodded. He ground his cigar into the crystal ashtray on his desk. The music on the radio resumed for a few minutes, and then the familiar voice of Chancellor Schuschnigg addressed the Austrian people:

"Austrian men and women! This day has brought us face-to-face with a serious and decisive situation. The German Third Reich has presented a time-limited ultimatum to Federal President Wilhelm Miklas. He must appoint a candidate chosen by the Third Reich Government to the office of the Chancellor. Should the federal president not accept this ultimatum, then German troops would begin to cross our frontiers at this very hour. The federal president has instructed me to inform the nation that we are giving way to brute force. Because we refuse to shed German blood, even in this tragic hour, we have ordered our armed forces…to withdraw without serious resistance. So, in this hour, I bid farewell to the people of Austria and a wish from the bottom of my heart: 'God save Austria.'"

After some silence, Agneza was the first to speak. "What does this mean, Herr Kolber?"

"Austria will become part of Germany. This is what Hitler has been planning for months. No, for years. And the Nazi Party, which has up until now been declared illegal, will steal the reins of power from our legitimate government. We Jews will have to learn to navigate this new world order, and hopefully we will survive with our businesses and homes intact."

Eva demurred. "Josef, you're sorely mistaken. Like the Jews in Germany, we will be targets of Hitler and his thugs, and it will only be a matter of time before the heel of the Nazis will come down on our heads."

Everyone nervously sat close to the radio, and at midnight there was another announcement: "All schools and businesses will be closed on Monday, March 14, to make way for a celebration through the streets of Vienna. All citizens are asked to wear swastikas as a show of support for the Führer."

Walter said, "That's a stroke of good luck. With our examination postponed, I can study an extra day so I'll be sure to get one hundred percent. That should make you happy, Mutti."

Eva could not contain herself. "Do you not understand what is happening? Our government, which was voted in by the people of Austria, is to be swept aside; and that monster, Hitler, who blames the Jews for everything that is wrong with the Republic, is going to be put in charge."

Dolfie turned to his father. "What do you think, Papa? Are we in any danger?"

Unbuttoning his jacket and loosening his silk cravat, Josef answered, "Let's hope the good people of Austria will prevail."

The family, trying not to allow their imaginations to run wild, finally retired to their bedrooms at three o'clock in the morning. Eva spoke her mind. "Josef, we must leave Vienna as soon as possible."

"But Eva, we have obligations here. You have the store to run. I have fifty employees in the factory who are counting on me for their livelihood. Our customers count on us. The boys need to continue with their studies. There's no need to panic."

"It's common knowledge that the names of prominent Viennese Jews are kept on a list, and after the Nazis get their hands on it, we're done for."

"I can't make a decision right now. Let's try and get some sleep. Things will be clearer in the light of day. They always are." Josef put his arms around his wife. "Don't worry. So long as we are all together, we'll be all right." And then he added, as much to convince himself as her, "And don't forget, I served in the army during the Great War. No doubt the Nazis will respect that. I have a medal and a bum foot to prove it!"

German troops crossed the border into Austria on March 12 without resistance. It was announced that control of the Austrian government would be turned over to the Nazis and Arthur Seyss-Inquart would be at the helm during a brief transition. Nazi flags were hung from government buildings and thousands of people lined the streets to watch the parade of soldiers marching through the streets. All the cafés, normally filled with Jewish patrons reading the daily *Neue Freie Presse* or arguing political ideology, were empty. Josef stayed home throughout the day with the family, telephoning friends and colleagues and trying to learn what was happening. The news was all bad for the Jews.

By late afternoon German aircraft flew over Vienna, very effectively symbolizing that Austria was under the full control of the Nazis. The unification of Austria and Germany (*Anschluss*) was a fait accompli. Hitler spent the day in his hometown of Linz, Austria, where he was greeted by cheering crowds. This was the moment he had been waiting for. On Monday, March 14, with a huge entourage, Hitler made his grand entrance into Vienna. His motorcade headed for the Heldenplatz (Heroes' Square), where a crowd of over two hundred thousand supporters waving Nazi flags amassed to support their new leader. The *Anschluss* complete, Seyss-Inquart was removed, making way for Hitler as the leader of Austria, now part of the Third Reich.

Hitler stayed at the Hotel Imperial across the street from the Vienna State Opera. The symbolism of this was not lost on Hitler or his detractors. The Hotel Imperial was where Hitler had once worked as "a half-starved day laborer, shoveling snow off the sidewalk outside the entrance and respectfully removing his cap as wealthy guests came and went. He directed the motorcade to make a victory tour around the Ringstrasse, past the sumptuous palaces of the city's richest Jews: the Rothschilds (bankers), the Altmanns (textile merchants), and the Ephrussis (wheat merchants and food brokers). Behind the windows of their palaces were rare art collections, stately furniture, and safes filled with money and jewels, all of which would soon be plundered by the Nazis.

The Jewish community was stunned by the seamlessness of the takeover, which could not have been accomplished without planning by Nazi sympathizers who had waited patiently for just this triumphant moment. Thousands of Austrians, covertly or openly, ascribed to Hitler's plan for *Anschluss*. Within weeks, the Nuremberg Laws,[2]* which had been adopted in Germany in 1935, were enforced throughout the German Third Reich, which now included Austria. Jews could no longer hold government jobs or employ Christian women under forty-five as domestic workers, and intermarriage between Jews and Christians was declared illegal. The law even defined who was a Jew. A referendum was held on April 10 to reaffirm the population's support of *Anschluss*. Ninety-nine percent of the city voted in favor of it.

Two weeks later Reichsmarschall Hermann Göring addressed a gathering at the Northwest Railroad Terminal in Vienna. He said that three hundred thousand Jews were parasitically living in Vienna and promised his audience "their city would, within four years, be *judenrein* [purged of Jews]." He described Jews as vermin and lice and blamed the Jews for the ills of the Third Reich, including the loss of the Great War.

Eva turned off the radio. "I have heard enough. Josef, if you had any doubt about where the Nazis stand regarding Jews, this should clear your head. We need to leave, *mach schnell*!"

Josef tried to calm his wife. "I agree, but we need to come up with a viable plan for ourselves and the children. And that is going to take some time."

"You have already said this. So what is the plan?" Before he could answer, Eva laid out a strategy. "We have to find a country that will take us in, and sooner rather than later. I have heard rumblings that Argentina may be hospitable to the Jews, at least for now, and there may be other places as well. You need to start making inquiries, or perhaps you would prefer that I go to the various consulates here in the city. A woman sometimes has a better chance of getting the answer she seeks than a man does."

Josef was so overwhelmed that he left the entire matter in Eva's hands,

---

[2] * The Law for the Protection of German Blood and Honor and The Reich Citizenship Law

wishing that he could just close his eyes and have everything return to the way it once was. But the situation got worse. Thousands of prominent Jews, including their neighbor and friend Henrik Kahn, were imprisoned or sent to concentration camps. Nazi thugs randomly pushed Jews down in the dirt and prohibited them from sitting on park benches or using the sidewalks. On April 23, rabbis in the Leopoldstadt district were rounded up and forced to cut the grass in the Prater with their teeth, and middle-aged women were told to take off their coats and use them as rags to clean the cobblestone streets. Every manner of humiliation was conjured up, the average Viennese citizen watching without sympathy. The Nazis announced their intention to Aryanize all Jewish businesses and give Christians who had lost property and income during the Depression a second chance at wealth by redistributing whatever they grabbed from the Jews.

On April 26 the German government demanded that all Jews register their real estate and other assets exceeding five thousand marks with the authorities. The *Israelitische Kultusgemeinde* (IKG) was charged with pulling together records and being the intermediary between the Jewish community and the Nazi government as of May 1938. The headquarters of the organization was in Vienna's oldest synagogue, the Stadttempel, in the city's First District.

Jewish assets recorded by the IKG amounted to eight hundred million dollars. The Nazis planned to auction off these assets to the underemployed Austrian Christian populace to ensure their loyalty and to use the proceeds of plunder to fuel the war chest they were amassing. The apparel and textile industry was a plum sector of the economy. Almost seventy-five percent of all clothing factories were owned and operated by Jews, and the largest and most successful was the Bernhard Altmann Knitwear Company in the Eighteenth District. Bernhard Altmann employed over one thousand workers in 1938.

Josef Kolber's business was not serious competition for Bernhard Altmann's operation, but the two men knew each other and shared industry information. It was Altmann who recommended that Josef purchase only Pfaff sewing machines, even though they were more expensive, because they were the most reliable. Whatever confidence Josef had that "things couldn't get worse" was shaken to the core when he learned that Bernhard Altmann had moved his immediate family to London in April. Altmann was later forced to sign over his business to the Nazis in exchange for freeing his brother, who had been imprisoned in the Dachau concentration camp. Throughout the Third Reich, Jewish entrepreneurs were coerced into selling their businesses for next to nothing to their Christian employees, a tactic used by the Nazis to buy the loyalty of managers who could not otherwise have afforded to establish their own enterprises.

Jewish men and boys between the ages of sixteen and sixty were particularly at risk of being arrested, interrogated, and then sent back home if their families could pay extortion money; if not they were taken away to labor camps, some never to be seen again. Eva begged Josef to stay away from the factory in case the Gestapo paid them an unexpected visit.

Josef argued, "What's the point of hiding out? No place is safe. If they want to come and get me, they will."

Eva quickly replied, "No one will come looking for you at Herr Volker's house. He's one of the few Christians working for us we can trust. I'm sure you can stay at his house during the day and come home after dark when the street patrols have returned to headquarters. And of course, we will pay him for his troubles."

"How do you know he'll agree to this? We're putting him in danger."

"Leave it to me, Josef. I gave him money a few years ago so he could send his son to a good school."

"You never asked me."

"I thought it hardly mattered at the time, and now my decision may just save your life, my dearest."

Eva and Lilly tried to keep the dress shop open, but it was not unusual for them to arrive at the shop in the morning and see a Jewish star and *"Jude"* scrawled across the storefront window. Lilly would take a bucket and rag to scrub off the graffiti, knowing it would appear again only a few days later. Regular customers stayed away, and their shop girl was forced to quit, afraid of violating the Nuremberg Laws. Traveling to work became more difficult because Jews were forbidden to occupy trolley car seats, and so Eva and Lilly would have to cling to straphangers for the journey. They also closed the shop before sunset so as not to have to travel after dark. Park benches were off limits to the Jews of Vienna, and in some sections of the city they were forced off the sidewalks and had to walk in the streets, only to be covered in mud by the passing automobiles.

Dolfie and Walter continued at the Gymnasium *but* were now required to sit in the back of the classroom. Some of their classmates had proudly joined the Hitler Youth movement, and they shoved, cursed, and continuously bullied the twins, who avoided eye contact with anyone wearing a swastika. Their teacher, who also wore a Nazi armband and sported a swastika lapel pin, never called upon the twins.

In June one worker at the Kolber Textile Factory reported to the Gestapo that some of the sewing machines had disappeared. They suspected that the Kolbers were slowly disassembling the factory, intending to ship the equipment out of the country. Two Gestapo agents barged into the office to investigate. They were greeted by Eva, who was spending most days at the factory while Lilly did what she could to keep the dress shop open.

The Gestapo officer barked at Eva, "And where is Herr Kolber?"

"Ah, he had to make an unexpected trip to one of our suppliers in Prague, and so I'm in charge here. What can I do for you, gentlemen?" She felt as if she might faint, but she willed herself to remain calm.

"We want to review your business ledgers to make sure that the amount you have reported to the IKG is accurate and that you aren't hiding anything from us."

After what seemed like an eternity, the inspector who had walked through the factory and counted the machines demanded, "The ledger and the number of machines do not match up. Where are you hiding the equipment?"

Eva concocted a story: "Some of our Aryan employees quit, stealing equipment along with hundreds of bolts of fabric. And with my husband away, I was helpless to stop them."

"Even if you're telling the truth, Frau Kolber, they didn't *steal* the equipment or fabric. They took what is rightfully theirs."

Eva bit her lip. She wanted to scream, "Liar, pig!" But instead she added, "And now our customers are simply refusing to pay us for the merchandise we delivered. They think that, because we are Jews, they don't have to stand by their financial obligations. So, as you can see in the ledger, every month our income is less and less. We will soon be forced to shut our doors."

"This is why you should be selling your business to us. If you're smart, you'll sell now before we just take it."

"But what price will you give us?"

"You have your nerve asking such a question, you Jew whore." He picked up the letter opener lying on the desk, brandished it in the air, and then slammed the point into the desk. "You'll take whatever we offer. This is not a negotiation between equal parties. Now, before we leave, may I remind you that once you have paid the *Reichsfluchtsteuer* [the emigration tax] you owe the Third Reich, you will have one month to get out of Vienna. And you will need to show us proof that you have tickets and a place to go. Am I clear?"

"Yes."

"Yes, sir," he said sharply.

Eva closed the ledgers and repeated, "Yes, sir."

And then they were gone. Eva collapsed into the chair. Putting her head in her hands, she wept bitter tears for a few minutes. When she could compose herself, she took a handkerchief out of her leather purse and wiped the tears from her cheeks. The notice from the Argentinean Consulate was inside her purse, and upon reading it she cried again. Her request for a visa had been denied. The wave of anti-Semitism now spreading throughout the world had apparently reached as far as Argentina. In recent months, Jews who had emigrated there, promising to stay in rural areas, had ended up in the cities, taking jobs away from Argentinean professionals who were less educated and fomenting resentment among the Christian majority. So Argentina had closed its doors. Jews were no longer welcome, but even if the Kolbers had been given permission to emigrate to Argentina, there were no tickets to be had on any of the ocean liners. Every cabin was booked months in advance.

Eva's head was throbbing. She could barely manage to look at the bills on the desk. Forcing herself to do so, one jumped out at her. It was from a silk manufacturer in Shanghai. Not wanting to touch the letter opener, she opened the envelope with her finger and took out the bill. Staring at the address on Chusan Road, she was suddenly struck by an idea: *What if we were to go to Shanghai?* She had heard that a few Jews in Vienna were already planning their exodus to Shanghai since the city was one of the only places in the world where an entry visa was not required. She knew that it was an international port city with a small Sephardic Jewish community whose members, with names like Kadoorie and Sassoon, reputed to be as rich as the Rothschilds, had emigrated from Baghdad, New Delhi, and Bombay in the 1800s. Shanghai was also home to Russian Ashkenazi Jews who had escaped the pogroms. Eva thought, *Isn't it written in the Torah that one Jew must help another?* She didn't know if that was in fact true, but she prayed that it was.

That evening, after Lilly and the twins were asleep, Eva described her ordeal to Josef, who had managed to make it back to Esteplatz without being apprehended on the ten-block walk from Herr Volker's. "Thank God you weren't at the factory today, Josef. Who knows what those *Schweinehunde* might have done to you. They went through our books and asked me about some of our sewing machines. Where are they?"

"They are sitting in a warehouse in Trieste. You can't imagine how many officials I had to pay off to manage that. What a farce. Supposedly the money is to go to Vienna's poorest, but all it's doing is lining the pockets of 'expediters.' But at least we'll have something to take with us when we eventually get out of here."

Eva opened her purse and handed him the letter from the Argentinean Consulate. "This was waiting for me when I got to the factory this morning."

Josef read the official document denying them a visa. "Now what? Where are we to go? Perhaps we can go to Palestine?"

"Josef, you're dreaming. The British have imposed a quota on immigration there to appease the Arabs, who hate our guts. No, the only place remotely feasible is Shanghai."

"Really? Haven't you heard? There is a war going on between China and Japan. At least that is what I've read in the newspapers."

"That's true, but Shanghai is protected by the Americans, the French, and the British, and after all, it's a wealthy international port city. We don't need a visa to go there. And to get out of Austria, we only need to show that we have tickets to somewhere else and that we've paid whatever taxes those criminals are going to squeeze out of us. And once we're there, we'll figure out a way to set up a clothing factory."

Josef poured himself a glass of cognac from a crystal decanter and took a sip, mulling over his wife's idea. "You may be right. We can divert the new Pfaff sewing machines that are still on order to Trieste, and ship everything to Shanghai."

"What about my sister Dora and her husband Herman? They should come with us. Herman can help with the books and Dora will work the factory floor." Eva paced back and forth to relieve some of her nervous energy.

"The twins can help out until we find a school for them, and Lilly can design and sew clothes. We'll just start over again, Josef. Anyway, what choice do we have?"

The library clock struck midnight. Josef took the last sip of his cognac. It was strange to see that nothing had changed inside the apartment on Esteplatz while the outside world was falling apart. "Let's go to bed. Honestly, I haven't felt so hopeful in months."

"Maybe you'll sleep through the night without tossing and turning for a change."

Josef playfully patted Eva's derriere. "And maybe you won't snore for a change."

The Gestapo established the Central Office of Emigration in Vienna in the largest of the Rothschild family's palaces, placing it under the direction of Adolf Eichmann. Fleeing families were forced to abandon their treasures. Eichmann, assisted by the IKG, made sure that all the *Reichsfluchtsteuer* due the Third Reich were paid before any Jew could leave the country. Only those Jews with connections, money, and valuables to bribe the German authorities could get through Eichmann's bureaucracy and obtain the necessary documentation. And the requirements for emigration kept changing, adding to the confusion.

An international conference was held in Évian-les-Bains, France from July 6 until July 15 to address the looming "European" refugee crisis, but everyone there knew this meant a "Jewish" refugee crisis. Nothing positive came out of the nine-day conference, which was attended by thirty-two nations, including the United States, and numerous international relief organizations.

Hitler had assumed that no country would step up to help the Jews. In fact, he regarded the Évian conference a mandate to accelerate his plan to get rid of the Jews, to squeeze them out of the Third Reich. Indeed, like a noose slowly tightening around the Jews, Switzerland asked Germany to prominently mark all Jewish German passports with the red letter J so border officials could stop Jews from entering their country. Previously, German citizens, which now included Austrians, could cross from Austria into Switzerland without a visa, but now all Austrians were required to turn in their old passports and apply for German passports from the Third Reich—an Austrian passport was no longer considered valid because Austria was no longer an independent country—and the passports of all Jewish petitioners would be stamped with that red J.

Sitting in the library with the lights turned off and the curtains drawn to ensure that no one could see into the apartment, Josef listened to Mozart's unfinished Requiem. It was a hot summer evening, but Josef didn't dare open the window to let in the cool night air. As the first movement of the "Requiem aeternam" abruptly ended, tears filled his eyes. He kept turning this thought over in his mind: *Austria is no more.*

chapter 8

Broken Glass

A degenerate exhibition of art and photography named *Der ewige Jude* ("The Eternal Jew") opened in Munich in 1937, where it was seen by thousands. The cover of the exhibition catalogue featured a Semitic-looking man in a caftan holding gold coins in one hand and a map of Russia under his arm. The exhibition, which became the basis for a propaganda film produced by Joseph Goebbels, traveled to Vienna, where it opened to enthusiastic crowds on August 2, 1938.

Eva didn't dare go to the exhibition, and so she sent her maid Agneza, instructing her to buy the catalogue. She wanted to see the vitriolic messages that were drawing enthusiastic crowds of Nazi supporters with her own eyes.

"I'm almost afraid to give this to you, Frau Kolber," Agneza said when she returned, a look of anguish on her face.

Eva scanned the pages, gasping at the racist cartoons portraying the worst Jewish stereotypes. "I will take this with me to Shanghai as a bitter reminder of what this city has become. Whenever I feel a pang of nostalgia, I need only look at this." She handed it back to Agneza. "Put it at the bottom of my suitcase. I don't want the children seeing it."

"Frau Kolber, it took me almost two hours to get into the exhibition. People stood in the rain, undeterred by the heat and humidity, telling one another that the Jews of Vienna were getting what they deserved—and that they all should be deported. Some of the women were wearing crosses around their necks. I cannot believe these God-fearing Christians, like myself, would spew such hatred. I am ashamed to call myself a Christian." She began to weep. "Is there any way that I can go with you to Shanghai, Frau Kolber?"

"I'm afraid not. We've had a hard enough time finding a way for us to leave. And you should take some comfort in the fact that you have a home and a family to return to. Prague is beyond the reach of the Nazis. Be sure you never tell anyone you worked for a Jewish family, however. That could get you into trouble." Eva patted Agneza's hand. "You have been a wonderful help to me all these years. I couldn't have raised the children without you. You do know that, don't you?"

"Yes, Frau Kolber. I love all of you as if you were my true family. It breaks my heart to see what is happening to you," Agneza cried harder, her body now heaving with grief.

Eva waited a minute for Agneza to gather herself. "Enough of that. Now, help me fill these boxes. Before we know it, it will be dinnertime."

"Will Herr Kolber be joining you and the children for dinner?"

"No. We have decided it is too dangerous for him to be here any longer. He's going to be staying with trustworthy friends until it's time for him to leave for Shanghai with Dolfie and Walter. They will leave in a few weeks."

"You mean hiding out?"

"That's exactly what I mean. We've had too many close calls. Do you remember the Kahns who used to live across the hall from us?"

"I was here the night the Gestapo took Herr Kahn away, and then Frau Kahn went to live with her mother in Leopoldstadt."

"I can still hear her screams as they took him away. I hate to tell you this, Agneza, but I heard from Frau Klopstein that the Nazis sent Herr Kahn to Dachau, and shortly afterward his wife, dear Adele, committed suicide. Can you imagine? And she is not the only Jew in the city who has taken their life. But that is not going to happen to us, not while I have a single breath left in my body. Now let's get to work."

The two women labored side by side for the next few hours. Everything they might be able to use in their new life would be packed up. Eva debated whether she really needed her china and silverware, but she could not part with these treasures for sentimental reasons. She rationalized to herself, *If we need money we can always sell some of it. Please, God, don't let it come to that.*

Looking around the nearly barren salon, she thought back to her forty-second birthday a year ago when her friends and family gathered around the piano, Lilly at the keyboard and Dolfie and Walter playing their violins. Oh, they had practiced for weeks learning one of Sarasate's Spanish dances. Walter and his sister played beautifully, but unfortunately the piece was beyond Dolfie's capabilities. Nevertheless, everyone applauded politely when the trio finished.

Agneza interrupted Eva's daydreaming. "Frau Kolber, should we roll up the Oriental rugs and pack them as well?"

"We're going to have to leave them here." Eva allowed herself to reminisce, telling Agneza, "Josef and I bought these rugs in Venice as an anniversary gift to each other. The merchant wanted too much money, but I argued him down to a reasonable price. They're still beautiful after all these years, don't you think? Maybe you can find a way to take them after we're gone."

"You're sure you don't want them?"

"We don't have enough room in the shipping crates. If you don't take them, the Gestapo thugs will help themselves." Eva didn't tell Agneza that they were not only transporting their household goods but Josef had arranged to have eighteen sewing machines from the factory accompany them by train to Trieste. There they would be loaded onto the ocean liner together with the newly purchased Pfaff machines. The less she knew about their plans, the better, in case the Gestapo tried to get information out of her.

Miraculously, Josef had secured tickets for himself and the boys on the *Conte Verde,* which would leave the port of Trieste on November 1, 1938. Part of the Lloyd Triestino Far Eastern Line, the *Conte Verde* was one of the few ocean liners sailing to Shanghai. It would eventually become a lifeboat for Jews escaping the Third Reich. The Italian ship's route would take them through the Suez Canal and around the Arabian Peninsula, traversing the Indian Ocean with stops at various ports along the way. The ship was scheduled to arrive in Shanghai on November 24. It would be up to Josef and the boys to make sure that the crates were unloaded at the dock and transported to a safe location.

Josef and Eva agreed that there was no point in subjecting the entire family to a month-long sea voyage. "*Mein Schatzi,*" Josef warned, "remember the last time we were on a boat, sailing the Danube to Budapest? You got sick, and there was hardly a cloud in the sky or a ripple on the river. It's best that you and Lilly go overland by train. The trip is considerably shorter, and the trains across Siberia and through Manchuria have first-class accommodations. It will be quite a lovely adventure, and before you know it, we'll all be together again in Shanghai."

Josef secured train tickets for Eva, Lilly, Dora, and Herman; they would be leaving Vienna on November 11. First they'd stop in Berlin, where they would meet up with Josef's brother Hersch and his wife, Sara. From Berlin, their itinerary took them through Warsaw and on to Moscow, where they would board the Trans-Siberian Railway for a six-day journey to Chita, Siberia and then head south toward China, first on the Trans-Manchurian Railway to Harbin and then to Nanking, finally connecting to Shanghai. If all went well, they would arrive in Shanghai the last week of November, perhaps just a few days after Josef and the boys.

Handing Eva all the tickets, Josef said, "I would be very worried if you and Lilly were traveling alone. Two women are vulnerable to unwanted attention by men, but with Herman to protect you, I won't be as concerned."

Josef put his arms around his wife. "You and I have never been apart since the day we married, even for just a few weeks."

Eva tried to sound convincing. "This is the best plan. We'll make a good life for ourselves in Shanghai."

Josef nodded. "Then, after the Nazis are kicked out, we'll come back to Vienna, where we belong. After all, doesn't goodness always triumph over evil?"

"Now that's where you're wrong, Josef. Only a fool returns to an inn where he has been kicked out!"

On September 30, 1938, the major European powers, excluding the Soviet Union, signed the Munich Agreement giving Hitler the right to annex portions of Czechoslovakia along the country's border where mostly German-speaking people lived. The new territory was called Sudetenland, and the agreement was designed to appease Hitler, thereby avoiding an all-out war. On October 3, just three weeks before Josef and the twins were to begin their sea voyage to Shanghai, cheering crowds greeted Hitler upon his arrival in the spa town of Eger, Czechoslovakia.

Josef read the newspaper headlines in disbelief: HITLER LIBERATES THE SUDETENLAND. The article was accompanied by a photograph of Hitler and Heinrich Himmler being treated to glasses of curative spring water in Eger.

Eva muttered, "I wish someone would have poisoned their drinks."

There was not a single dissenting German voice in the crowd as Hitler delivered a victory speech in the Marketplatz as "the blood-red cloth with the black spider on a white field waved from even the out-of-the-way farmsteads" and from the windows overlooking the square.

The practicality of traveling by separate routes to Shanghai did nothing to lessen the sadness that enveloped the family. Josef tried to remain optimistic, telling the twins, "This is going to be a great adventure. And I'm counting on both of you to be *mensches* and help me get everything in order for Mutti and Lilly once we arrive in Shanghai."

Listening to her father's attempt at lightheartedness, Lilly complained, "You and Mutti promised I could go to Paris, but now I'm going to be stuck in Shanghai! What am I supposed to do there?"

Eva interjected, "Consider this, my darling. There is an area in Shanghai known as the French Concession. You'll be able to practice your French there, and we can open a dress shop for the wealthy Chinese and international ladies who live in Shanghai. I hear there are fancy nightclubs and racetracks for the British who live in what they call the International Settlement. Also, there are amusement parks where the latest movies are shown, and even a music conservatory. The guidebook says that lovely ferryboats go up and down the rivers that run through the Chinese countryside, including where the finest silks are made."

Lilly made a face. "Really? I thought Shanghai was overrun by filthy coolies and Japanese soldiers."

Josef lost his temper. "Where do you get these ideas, Lilly? How many times do I have to remind you that we are getting out of Vienna before it's too late? Had I not listened to your mother, God only knows what might have happened to me and to all of us. There is nothing here for us now. The factory is gone, the dress shop shuttered, and any day we'll hear the Gestapo knocking on our door."

Lilly apologized, "I'm sorry, Papa. You're right. I'm acting like a spoiled child."

Josef's hands were shaking as he struggled to open his briefcase. For the second time that day he checked to make sure that his passport, issued to Josef Israel Kolber and stamped with a red letter J for *Jude*, was secured along with his tickets. The twins each had their own passport, and he carried a document confirming that the Kolbers had paid all the exit taxes to the Third Reich.

Early on the morning of October 29, the ringing of the doorbell reverberated through the nearly empty apartment. Agneza looked through the keyhole to make sure that it was the taxicab driver here to take Josef and the twins to the train station. Josef and the boys gathered around Lilly and Eva to say their goodbyes. Lilly asked, "Why aren't we going to the train station to see you off, Papa?"

"We don't want to bring attention to ourselves. The station will be crawling with Gestapo. You are safer here, and from now until the time you leave, it's best that you go out on the street as infrequently as possible. All your papers are in order, but I don't trust these thugs. They might get it into their heads to detain you for no reason."

It was a heart-wrenching scene by any measure with much weeping and promises of imminent reunion, but if one could spy into the windows of other Jewish homes throughout the city, one might see a similar tableau unfolding.

Josef announced, "We'll be waiting for you at the Shanghai train station. We get there on November 24, and you should arrive just a few days later. Anyway, we will let the synagogue know where we are if you don't find us waiting for you."

"Which synagogue, Papa?" Lilly asked.

"The largest one, of course. I don't know the name, but I'm sure you can just ask anyone on the street and they'll be able to tell you." The naïveté of this remark was not lost on Eva, but she kept silent. Instead she embraced her husband one last time and kissed her boys, praying that she would see them again in just a few weeks' time, all safe and sound.

The three women listened behind the door as Josef and the twins' footsteps reverberated down the stairs. They rushed to the front window and pulled back the curtain a few inches. The women watched the taxicab pull away from the curb and head toward the Bahnhof. It was raining. A street vendor stood next to his horse and wagon, waiting for a customer to come by; a young couple sauntered down the street arm in arm; behind them, a well-dressed woman allowed her dachshund to gambol through the leaves that had fallen onto the pavement. In all, a deceptively pleasant scene in a play that could end only in tragedy.

"Shall I build a fire in the fireplace?" asked Agneza, needing something to occupy herself.

Looking around the barren salon, Eva observed, "There is really nowhere for us to sit. Let's go into the library. It's cozier there, and we can listen to the gramophone. A bit of music will cheer me up, I'm sure of it."

But, unfortunately, the music had the opposite effect, the way a sunny day at a funeral heightens the mourners' grief.

Eva and Lilly felt like prisoners in the apartment on Esteplatz, unable to go anywhere without fearing for their lives. For the Christians of Vienna, life was still gay. The opera season was in full swing. Mozart's *"Die Zauberflöte"* ("The Magic Flute") was scheduled to open on November 9; but, unless the tickets were resold at a discount to someone who might not have been able to afford a seat until now, the Kolbers' seats would be empty. At the Burgtheater, Friedrich Schiller's *Die Jungfrau von Orleans* ("The Maid of Orleans") was in rehearsal, although the Jewish actors had been kicked out of the company in compliance with the Nuremberg Laws.

Eva asked her daughter, "What is that famous line in the play, something about stupidity?"

Lilly knew the play by heart because she had performed the role of Johanna during her senior year of high school. She recited, "'Against stupidity, the heavenly gods contend in vain.'"

"That's it," Eva recalled.

Pretending to take the stage, Lilly swooned and, looking up at the ceiling, continued:

> "See you the rainbow yonder in the air?
> Its golden portals heaven doth wide unfold
> Amid the angel choir she radiant stands
> The eternal Son she claspeth to her breast, et cetera et cetera.
> Light clouds bear me up—
> My ponderous mail becomes a winged robe;
> I mount—I fly—back rolls the dwindling earth—
> Brief is the sorrow—endless is the joy."

And with that, Lilly climbed onto her father's desk, pretending to reach toward heaven itself. Then she jumped off the table and curtsied. Eva and Agneza applauded. For the first time in days, Eva smiled. "Who needs the Burgtheater when we have Lilly Kolber?"

"Oh, Mutti, I'm just an amateur, but it feels good to take my mind off worrying about Papa and the twins."

Agneza smiled. "Thank you for your lovely performance, Fräulein Lilly."

Looking at her watch, she added, "I'd better go now. The butcher shop closes early on Saturday, and all the good cuts of beef will have been sold."

After Agneza left, the ticking clock and the clicking of Eva's knitting needles were the only sounds that broke the stillness. Lilly picked her head up from the book she was reading. "Mutti, do you miss Papa and the twins as much as I do?"

"I can't get inside your head, Lilly, but I'm worried about them, terribly. They've only been gone a week, but it feels like an eternity, doesn't it?"

Lilly could only nod. The "ingénue" had lost her voice.

Both women turned as they heard Agneza's key in the lock. Agneza, her gray hair wet and her eyes filled with tears, said, "Frau Kolber, I paid the butcher for a kilo of fresh ground beef. As he was wrapping it, he spit on it, and then he handed it to me, screaming so that everyone in the shop could hear, 'I know you work for that dirty Jewess, Frau Kolber.' I couldn't take the package and so we won't have anything to eat tonight."

Eva embraced her. "Please don't cry. That won't help anything, will it?"

"How could he do such a disgusting thing? You have been his good customer for years."

"Apparently that no longer matters. Let's go into the kitchen and see if we can put something together for dinner, shall we?"

The last few nights before their scheduled departure for Shanghai, Eva and Lilly shared a bed, hoping to ward off terrible thoughts of Gestapo boots, barking police dogs, and the daily disappearance of Jewish men. It was rumored that they were being sent to labor camps and detention centers where their only chance of being released was to pay extortion money.

Lilly was worried. "What if someone comes to the door?"

"We will do what Frau Klopstein did. You'll get under the bed covers and I'll tell the authorities that you are running a high fever and you desperately need the attention of a doctor. Hopefully they'll not want to catch what you have and so they'll leave us alone."

"And what if they take you away, Mutti?"

"Agneza will still be here, and I'll manage to talk my way out of whatever they might try to do with me. You know that I can make a real nuisance of myself when necessary." Both women managed a laugh, but their worries did not go away.

On November 7, four days before their intended departure, Eva and Lilly listened to an announcement over the Nazi-controlled radio station that Ernst vom Rath, the Third Secretary of the German embassy in Paris, had been murdered by a seventeen-year-old Polish Jew, Herschel Grynszpan. Days earlier Grynszpan had received word that his parents, who were living in Germany, had been expelled from the Third Reich and deported back to Poland. As retribution against the German Third Reich, Grynszpan shot vom Rath.

This incident provided the perfect excuse to launch a bloodbath against the Jews. Goebbels, Reich Minister of Propaganda, issued a directive two days after the murder: "The Führer has decided that demonstrations should not be prepared or organized by the Party, but insofar as they erupt spontaneously, they are not to be hampered." In other words, the Nazis turned a blind eye toward any and all acts of retribution for vom Rath's murder, the match igniting a fire underneath the feet of the Jews throughout the Third Reich.

The concierge at Esteplatz warned Eva that she should be prepared for a visit from the Gestapo.

"And how do you know this?"

"My son saw the Kolber name on a list. That's all I know."

"Are you going to let them into the building?"

"What choice do I have, Frau Kolber? If I fail to cooperate with the Nazis, who knows what they'll do to me or to my son? I want to see my grandchildren born someday. I hope you understand."

Eva shrugged. "I understand. If I were standing in your shoes, I might very well do the same thing. Family always comes first, does it not?"

Looking relieved, the concierge replied, "I'm glad you won't judge me too harshly, Frau Kolber."

Eva stopped on the first step of the stairway and stared into his eyes. "What difference would it make if I did? None!"

Riots broke out throughout the Third Reich on November 9 in reaction to the Grynszpan assassination of vom Rath. Synagogues in Germany, Austria, and Nazi-occupied territories, 267 in total, were destroyed. Storm troopers shattered shop windows of about 7,500 Jewish-owned businesses and looted merchandise. Jewish cemeteries were desecrated, and almost thirty thousand Jewish men between the ages of sixteen and sixty were rounded up, thrown into prisons, and then sent off to Dachau; ninety-one Jewish men, women, and children were killed between November 9 and 10.

The roving bands of crazed Nazi sympathizers were instructed by the authorities to spare Viennese businesses owned by non-Jews, and to spare certain Jewish buildings that, if set on fire, might damage neighboring establishments. The main Jewish synagogue in the First District was spared because it was connected to other buildings. There was another reason that the Stadttempel was left standing: All the records of the IKG were housed there, with the names and addresses of all the Jews in Vienna and a comprehensive list of their assets, such as their real estate holdings, local bank accounts, businesses, and retail shops.

This pogrom became known as *Kristallnacht*, the Night of Broken Glass. Many years later, a Jew from Berlin said of *Kristallnacht*: "Is this the people of Goethe and Schiller? I couldn't digest it – not emotionally, not intellectually." Nothing had prepared the Jewish communities in the Third Reich for the utter chaos and devastation that took place.

Throughout the night, Eva and Lilly heard glass smashing and marauding gangs running through the streets. The smell of smoke seeped through the heavy curtains still covering their apartment windows overlooking Esteplatz. Throughout the city the screams of victims pushed into the burning buildings could be heard over the roaring wind caused by the fires.

The next morning the rioting continued unabated. Eva was frantic. What if they couldn't leave Vienna? Steeling her courage, she told Lilly that they would find a way out of the city. "Even if we have to walk."

Lilly couldn't stop her teeth from chattering. Eva poured her a shot of whiskey. "Here. Drink this. We still have packing to do."

Eva and Lilly sat on their bed with a sewing basket between them and a fur coat lying across their laps. Eva carefully snipped the stitches along the seam of the lining and tucked a pouch with several pieces of valuable jewelry into the lining. Threading a needle, Lilly re-sewed the seam.

Suddenly there was thundering bang, bang, bang on the front door. Eva grabbed the coat and hid it underneath the bed, while Lilly, still in her nightgown, slid under the covers. Eva rushed into the salon.

Agneza opened the door. Two Gestapo officers elbowed their way into the apartment, stamping their feet on the Oriental rug to get rid of the mud caking their leather boots. Their black wool coats reeked of smoke and were covered with a thin dusting of ashes.

Pointing at Eva, the older commanding officer yelled, "Jewess, where is your husband?"

Eva lied. "I don't know. You people hauled him away days ago. I've been frantic. Where did you take him? We're leaving Vienna tomorrow."

He ignored her plea. "Who else is in the apartment with you?"

"Other than our maid, Agneza Backorik, there is only my daughter. She's in her bedroom. I'm afraid that she has the flu, or worse. She's running a high fever, so it's best that you not disturb her."

"Do we look like a fever would deter us from doing our job, you bitch?" the officer spat. Just as they started to search the apartment, Lilly let out a hacking cough.

The younger-looking officer walked down the hallway, peered into Lilly's bedroom, and reported back to his superior, "Sir, the Jewess is telling the truth. There is only her daughter there and she sounds seriously ill." He pulled off his leather gloves and, gesturing to the barren salon, asked, "Where's all your furniture?"

Eva improvised. "We had to sell everything, including our furniture, just to survive. Our factory is gone and my store has been closed for several months. But you already know this. Everything has been recorded at the IKG and was presented to the authorities when the Reich granted my family permission to leave."

"Good news doesn't always travel fast. You Jews always try to play tricks on us, but we have a way of finding out who's lying." The younger officer snapped his riding crop against his leather boot and sneered at Eva.

Her heart pounding, Eva felt the bile rising in her throat. But she forced herself to remain calm and say nothing. Through the window she heard a loudspeaker blaring directions at pedestrians to clear the street to make way for a convoy of Nazi soldiers on their way to the Ringstrasse.

The commanding officer warned her, "We'll be back in two days. By the way, that's a beautiful Bösendorfer piano. My son Gregor is learning how to play." His meaty hands clasped behind his back, he marched over to one of the paintings still hanging on the wall. "I needn't remind you that it's against the law for you Jews to take artwork out of the country. Our commandant will appreciate your art. He has a particular fondness for hunting scenes like this one. Since you all will be gone by November 11, I wish you good riddance. I assume you only purchased one-way tickets. And where is it that you are headed?"

"We are going to Shanghai. But where did you take my husband? Please, we can't leave without him!"

Once again ignoring Eva's question, he laughed. "Those idiotic Chinese. They will soon realize they're making a big mistake allowing you Jews into their country. Once they see that you vermin will want to further contaminate their inferior blood, once they see that you will try to take over their businesses and destroy their economy as you have done here, they'll push you into the sea and the rest of the world will laugh right along with us."

Before leaving the apartment, he added, "We expect you to be gone when we come back—all three of you."

As soon as they left, Eva rushed into the bedroom. "Lilly, my little actress, our ruse worked."

"Did they try to take our train tickets, Mutti?"

"No. They didn't even ask to see them. I think they were here to see what they could take once we've left. I suspect they know our plans and just wanted to give us a warning. Oh, the older officer was salivating over your father's favorite paintings and the piano. They can have all of it as far as I'm concerned! Thank God we will be on our way tomorrow, and not a moment too soon."

That night Eva lay awake in bed replaying the confrontation with the Gestapo in her mind. Riots continued throughout the night. She felt a blanket of terror enveloping her as she wondered whether she and Lilly should have gone with the twins and Josef. What was a bout of seasickness compared to the nightmare they were living through? Perhaps the officers would be back first thing in the morning and take them away. Fearing the worst, Eva wrapped her arms around her daughter and listened to her even breathing, but sleep escaped her.

chapter 9

Separation

The *Conte Verde*'s first stop out of Trieste was Port Said. An Arab boarded the ship there, and while strolling along the deck as the ship passed through the Suez Canal, he saw a pretty, blond-haired young woman and immediately offered to buy her as his wife. The passengers tried to explain in halting English that this was not the custom in the German Reich. Dolfie and Walter overheard this exchange and had a good laugh. Walter joked, "I wonder how much our sister would go for."

Dolfie answered, "I don't know, but I'm sure that, after he bought her, he'd probably pay Papa three times as much to take her back. Lilly can be a real pain in the neck."

"That's true, and I can't believe I'm saying this, but I miss her, and Mutti too," Walter confessed. As the brothers stared at the horizon, Dolfie put his arm around Walter's shoulder, as much to comfort himself as his brother.

The dinner chime rang, and passengers uncurled themselves from deck chairs and lined up to wait for the salon doors to open. Walter whispered to Dolfie, "Another night of pasta and tomato sauce. I wish they'd serve some decent German food. I'm aching for a slice of pot roast with spaetzle."

"Aren't we all?"

Some of the tables in the dining room were suspiciously empty. It was rumored that a number of Jewish passengers had simply disappeared into the crowd at Port Said, intending to find their way to Palestine rather than continue on to Shanghai.

On November 11, 1938, the *Conte Verde* docked in the Bombay harbor. Josef led the twins down the gangplank. A group of British tourists stood at the dock, waiting to greet arriving passengers. An attractive young Indian woman stared at Walter and Dolfie, who were dressed in expertly tailored light wool jackets, white shirts, and fashionable silk bowties. When Walter returned her gaze, she blushed and turned away.

"Did you see that girl, Dolfie? I believe she was flirting with us."

"You think every girl is flirting with you, Walter. She's probably never seen twins before. That's all."

Their father quickened his pace, waving for the boys to hurry along. This was the day Eva and Lilly were to leave for Berlin, and he was eager to learn what was happening in Europe. Perhaps he'd find an international newspaper or be able to ask someone who had heard recent radio broadcasts from the West.

American, British, and Japanese flags fluttered in the breeze atop the Victorian-style buildings along Bombay's crescent harbor. Josef and the twins entered the lobby of the elegant Taj Mahal Palace Hotel, which overlooked the Arabian Sea. It was evident from the worried looks on the faces of many guests loitering in the lobby that something terrible had occurred. A uniformed representative of the British India Line was seated in one of the rattan chairs holding a newspaper. Josef instructed Walter to politely ask him what was going on.

Looking over the edge of his newspaper, the representative asked Walter, "Where are you from, young man?"

"Vienna. We're on our way to Shanghai."

"Passengers on the *Conte Verde*, eh?"

Walter nodded.

"Are you Jews by any chance?"

"Yes. Why do you ask?"

"My office has received word that the Nazis have gone on a rampage against the Jews. They are attacking Jewish establishments throughout the Third Reich, and there have been mass arrests and deportations. It's been going on for the past two days. Shops have been broken into, buildings burned down. Vienna has been hit very hard. Berlin too."

Walter gave his father the terrible news. Josef's face turned ashen and he grabbed the edge of the seat to steady himself. The man stood up, saying,

"Please sit down." Josef collapsed into the chair and buried his head in his hands.

Dolfie asked his father, "Do you think we can send Mutti a telegram?"

"Impossible. Where would we send it? Who knows if she and Lilly have even managed to get out of Vienna?"

Always looking for a way to outshine his brother, Walter spoke up, "And if Mutti did get a telegram, she couldn't very well answer it, could she? Once we get out of Bombay, we'll be at sea until we reach Hong Kong, which will take nine days."

Josef nodded in agreement. "Your mother is always resourceful. Let's hope that at this very minute she is with Aunt Dora and Uncle Herman and they are boarding the train for the Polish border."

Looking at his watch, the man advised, "You have a few hours before you need to reboard the *Conte Verde*. Perhaps you would like to go to the restaurant in the hotel and get something to eat. Your father looks like he could use a bit of sustenance, maybe a cold Pimm's Cup. We fancy that in Bombay. It's quite refreshing, really. Here is my business card. Just present it to the maître d' and your bill will be taken care of."

Walter said, "I'll tell my father of your generous offer. That's most kind of you."

"Well then, young man, I'll be off. I wish you a smooth journey to Shanghai." He doffed his panama hat and walked through the lobby and into the noonday sun. Walter looked at the name and title on the card: ROBERT ROTHSTEIN, REPRESENTATIVE OF THE BRITISH-INDIAN LINES, BOMBAY, INDIA.

"Rothstein. That's a Jewish name, isn't it, Papa?"

"Yes, which explains why he's showed us such courtesy. We might as well take advantage of his offer. I don't fancy getting back to the ship any sooner than we have to."

On November 11 the Westbahnhof Station was crowded with people desperate to leave Vienna. Long lines leading to the ticket booths snaked through the station and out onto the street. Most trains were already sold out to every destination in all directions. People hoping to buy a ticket were summarily sent away empty handed or told to try again in a few days.

Eva and Lilly, wearing their fur coats and each carrying two valises, made their way through the crowd toward the Vienna-to-Berlin platform. A porter, his blond hair peeking out from under his cap, pushed a rolling car laden with luggage. Unable to see in front of him, he bumped into Eva. Instead of apologizing, he barked at her, "*Mach schnell.*"

Eva whispered to Lilly, "Where are his manners?"

"Mutti, he has none," Lilly replied. Then she added, "I suspect that, when he's not working at the station, he's training with Hitler's Youth Corps. But he's right. We must move along quickly, before someone stops us."

Just then Lilly and Dora spotted each other on the platform. As Eva moved toward her sister, Dora waved her away—Gestapo officers were approaching her and Herman.

Just then the conductor shouted, "All aboard."

Eva and Lilly boarded the train quickly, wondering if Dora and Herman would even make it onboard. It seemed like an eternity, but after several heart-stopping minutes, Dora and Herman joined them in their first-class compartment, both smiling and crying.

They arrived in Berlin four hours later, and Eva, Lilly, Dora, and Herman were met at the station by Josef's brother Hersch, with whom the foursome was to spend two nights. An angry mob was marching near the Bahnhof carrying placards, temporarily blocking their taxicab. One placard read: ALL JUDAH WANTS IS WAR WITH THE GOOD PEOPLE OF THE THIRD REICH.

Hersch was frustrated. "If you were to ask how things are in Berlin, there's my answer. Mobs of hooligans roam the streets while the police just turn away and shrug their shoulders. The caretaker of the synagogue in the Prinzregentenstraße is reported to have been burnt to death together with his family. Two Jews were lynched in Berlin's East End in plain sight as mobs cheered. I heard that a mother even held up her child to get a better look. Thousands of Jewish-owned businesses in Berlin have been completely wrecked. Millinery shops and dress shops like Altaba and Rosner are nothing but a mass of torn materials, hats, and articles of clothing that have been trodden underfoot. Crowds have watched in frenzied delight."

After pausing for a moment, he continued, "Hundreds of Berlin's wealthier Jews have driven their cars into the countryside, fearing for their lives. My wife, Sara, tells me that Jews trying to withdraw money from the banks were informed that their accounts have been frozen, and at most they've gotten twenty or thirty marks. There is nothing more to say."[1]

Eva nodded in acknowledgment. "It's happening everywhere."

As dawn broke on the morning of November 13, Dora, Herman, Eva, and Lilly ate breakfast while listening to the radio. The broadcaster, without the slightest hint of irony in his voice, announced, "The Jews of Germany are to pay the government nine hundred ninety-six million Reichsmarks for the destruction of businesses and property in the preceding two days. Any insurance claims made by Jews will be immediately turned over to the German Reich."

Hersch turned the dial, but every station carried the same news. He pulled the cord out of the wall angrily. The outside buzzer sounded, announcing that the taxicab was waiting to take them to the train station. Grabbing a valise, Hersch urged everyone to hurry before the neighbors saw them leaving the building.

Eva hugged her brother-in-law. "Hersch, if your plans to go to Palestine fall through, I beg you to join us in Shanghai."

When the train reached the German-Polish border at the Frankfurt/Oder station, all passengers were ordered off the train by the Gestapo and herded into the waiting area. Anyone whose passport was stamped with a red J was told they would be detained until their belongings were inspected for any contraband.

Standing on a crate and speaking through a bullhorn, an officer demanded, "Get in line! Whoever is carrying any valuables, currencies, or jewelry on your person or in your luggage, turn it over now or you will be sent to a concentration camp." Following orders, a passenger opened his suitcase and reluctantly handed over a beautiful Jugendstil clock. He was teary-eyed as the officer examined it and stuffed it into a black canvas bag.

When it was Eva's turn, she unbuttoned her coat, then reluctantly tore the lining and found her pouch filled with jewelry. She handed it over. The officer quickly slipped the pouch containing her memories directly into his coat pocket. "Now go!" he barked. "You can wait outside in the rain for the next train to Warsaw."

Everyone crowded under a small overhang to stay out of the rain, but the wind had picked up and even those passengers with umbrellas gave up and snapped them shut. A young mother tried to comfort her baby, but the infant wailed, fraying the already strained nerves of everyone around them. After waiting for over an hour, the next train finally pulled into the Frankfurt station, and the bedraggled passengers, numbering in the hundreds, fought to get onboard. Not everyone made it.

Herman handed their tickets to the conductor and they were led to their reserved seats. Herman lifted their suitcases onto to the overhead racks while the three women unbuttoned their wet coats and hung them on hooks to dry. The veil on Eva's hat stuck to her face and she could barely peel her leather gloves from her fingers. Still shaking from their ordeal, the foursome sat facing one another in silence.

Eva blinked, trying to hold back her tears. "My wedding ring, the diamond pin Josef bought for me when Lilly was born, and my beautiful emerald ring, an anniversary gift, were all in that bag. I can't bear the thought of that Nazi cur giving them to his tight-lipped Aryan wife as a Christmas present or to some zaftig *Fräulein* he is running after."

Dora said, "Let's try to put all of this unpleasantness behind us. If things go well for us in Shanghai, Josef will buy you whatever you want. I hear there are hundreds of European-style shops in the city catering to clientele like us."

"You mean like we *were*. What if the business fails? Then what?"

Dora argued, "We mustn't think that way. Once we get things going in Shanghai, we're bound to succeed. We just need to work hard and stick together."

Exhausted from her ordeal, Eva leaned her head against the window and fell into a tortured sleep. When the train came to a halt at the station in Warsaw, she awoke with a start, not sure where she was or why she was there.

Lilly told her mother, "While you were sleeping, a conductor came by to tell us that we are going to have to stay in Warsaw for several days. Train service between Warsaw and Moscow has been interrupted. Something about the soldiers being transported to the border taking up all the seats. So we are just going to have to wait."

To their great relief, the group was met at the station by the members of local Jewish organizations who arranged for accommodations and meals. Four days later they continued to Moscow, arriving on November 19. For the first time since leaving the Third Reich, Eva no longer felt like a hunted animal.

chapter 10

The Red J

A Soviet official wearing an *ushanka* hat, a full-length wool coat lined with fur, and high boots to ward off the cold signaled for Eva, Lilly, Herman, and Dora to follow him out of the Moscow train station with the other passengers. Speaking in halting German, he announced, "My government knows that you will be staying in our city for three days, until you board a train on the great Trans-Siberian Railway. Marvelous, marvelous! You will be guests of the Union of Soviet Socialist Republics, and as such, we have reserved rooms for all of you at our most excellent Hotel Metropol. It has all the finest luxuries for the most discerning of travelers. You have heard of it?"

Herman spoke on behalf of the family, "Of course! The Metropol is world famous. Dignitaries always stay there."

"Yes, yes. Sergei Prokofiev, Bertolt Brecht, e. e. cummings—too many to name—have all stayed there. And now you people will stay there all together on the very same floor, the eighth, I believe. Just high enough to get a wonderful view of the Kremlin and our famous theatres."

Eva suspected that the government wanted to keep an eye on them, and what better way to do so than to put everyone in the same hotel? Her suspicion was confirmed when he added, "Tour guides just for your group will show you around our city and introduce you to Communist hospitality. Wandering around alone is forbidden." And with that he bowed and ushered them into a caravan of waiting limousines.

When the uniformed bellhop unlocked the door to their luxurious room, Lilly was overjoyed. As soon as he placed their suitcases on the luggage rack at the foot of their beds and shut the door behind him, Lilly ran into the marble bathroom and turned on the tub tap. "I feel as if I haven't had a bath in weeks." When the tub was filled, she dropped her clothes on the tile floor and sank into the hot water, her hair floating around her face.

Eva commented, "You look just like a Raphael painting. Don't dawdle for too long. We're expected in the dining room in an hour, and I want to take a bath too and change my clothes."

The opulent main dining room of the Hotel Metropol boasted a magnificent stained-glass ceiling, marble fountain, and wrought iron lanterns. An orchestra played discreetly in the background. Later that evening, couples would be invited to dance to the latest Western tunes. The restaurant staff looked as if they had worked there since the time of the Czar, and as any well-trained waiter would, they anticipated each guest's needs, filling crystal goblets with water and wine without being summoned. It was rumored that the entire staff, including chambermaids, were instructed to eavesdrop on the clientele and report any conversations of a suspicious nature to the *Narodnyi Komissariat Vnutrennikh Del* (NKVD), the Soviet's secret police, headquartered just a few blocks from the hotel.

Eva and Lilly walked among the tables to the far corner where their fellow travelers were seated. When they joined the others, the men at the table stood up and the women stared at their fashionable clothes. Everyone exchanged pleasantries, keeping their conversation light.

Lilly chirped happily, "We are directly across the street from the Bolshoi Theatre. I would love to see a ballet—I really don't care what's playing. I haven't been to the theatre or ballet in almost a year."

Their Soviet chaperone smiled. "I'm terribly sorry, but every performance of *Swan Lake* is sold out during your stay, even the matinees. The next time you visit our city, if you give me advance notice, I'll arrange for tickets for you and your lovely mother." He then handed Lilly his engraved card.

Lilly read it aloud: "Sergei Oblomov, Official Guide of the Soviet Socialist Republic. Am I pronouncing your name correctly, Herr Oblomov? If I recall, Oblomov is the title of a famous Russian novel about an indecisive nobleman. Right?"

"Touché, Fräulein Kolber. Are you a lover of Russian literature?"

"I haven't read enough to say whether I am or not." She then fluttered her eyelashes and asked, "Those tickets you promised, will they be free, Herr Oblomov?"

"For you? Of course, Fräulein Kolber."

Overhearing their conversation, another diner spoke up, "In the spirit of true equality, which I believe is the hallmark of communism, may I assume that all of us will receive the same courtesy?"

Squirming in his seat, Oblomov answered, "Why, of course."

"Well, then, would you pass your business card to the rest of us?"

"I'm afraid I've run out. I'll be sure to give each of you one tomorrow, since we will be spending the day together."

In the privacy of their hotel room, Eva warned her daughter, "Don't encourage Herr Oblomov. Behind that charming smile is a sinister man, I assure you."

"Oh Mutti, don't be so serious. I was only playing with him a little bit. He looks harmless enough."

Eva grabbed Lilly's arm. "Do you hear me, Lilly? I don't want you flirting with that young man."

"All right, Mutti. I promise I'll behave myself. But you can't blame me. He has the most beautiful blue eyes and long black eyelashes. And he's very tall. He looks like a Russian prince."

For the next two days Sergei Oblomov led his charges around Moscow, a city where the old world of bearded and dirty *izvoshiks* (drivers) clicking their tongues to urge their emaciated horses through the streets existed alongside the new world of shiny motorcars. As her mother instructed, Lilly kept her distance from Herr Oblomov, but she couldn't help imagining his arms around her waist as they danced to the lively orchestra at the Hotel Metropol.

Trudging past Saint Basil's Cathedral with its colorful onion-shaped domes, Oblomov announced, "Byzantine architecture. The domes represent fire reaching toward heaven. The building is now a state-run museum. Stalin is not sure if he will keep it. It blocks the progress of important demonstrations and military processions. Instead of the museum, we will go to Vladimir Lenin's tomb. You will find it very interesting."

Lilly suspected several people in the group would rather have waited outside, not wishing to see an embalmed corpse, but they feared the repercussions of not following orders and so they reluctantly went inside. They were escorted to the front of the line of tourists who were eager to catch a glimpse of the Bolshevik leader lying in an enormous canopied glass coffin on a raised platform.

Eva whispered to Herman, "Horrible. He's been dead since 1924. What must they pump him full of to keep him from disintegrating? Hot air?"

Herman restrained himself from laughing.

After doing a quick head count, Oblomov announced, "Now, if you'll follow me, ladies and gentlemen, we will descend into Moscow's magnificent subway station. Notice the marble throughout, a gift to the proletariat. The train will take us back to the hotel for our final dinner together this evening. I do hope that you will carry fond memories of your stay with us as you ride the Trans-Siberian Railway tomorrow."

The Yaroslavskaya railway station on Komsomolskaya Square was the busiest of Moscow's train stations, the terminus of the Trans-Siberian Railway, which, at over nine thousand kilometers, was the longest railroad in the world. Built between 1891 and 1916 during the reigns of Czar Alexander III and his son Czar Nicholas II, the railroad connected Moscow to Vladivostok. At Chita, about 6500 kilometers (4,000 miles) east of Moscow, passengers would have to change trains to travel southeast through Manchukuo to Harbin.

Eva, Lilly, Herman, and Dora boarded the aptly named "Czar's train" late in the afternoon of November 22, grateful to be on their way and anticipating a reunion with Josef and the twins in Shanghai.

At the same time, Josef, Walter, and Dolfie stood on the upper deck of the *Conte Verde*, looking out at the Hong Kong harbor. The gangplank was lowered so waiting passengers could board the ocean liner for the final leg of its journey to Shanghai.

Walter asked his father, "So where are Mutti and Lilly now, if everything has gone according to plan?"

Josef pulled their itinerary out of his pocket. "Let's see. They should be in China by now."

Dolfie added, "Why don't we ask one of the boarding passengers for news of what's going on? Maybe they'll have something to tell us. We haven't been able to learn anything from the ship's staff since we left Bombay."

An hour after the *Conte Verde* set sail, the lunch bell rang. Sitting in the dining room next to Josef were a well-dressed Englishman and his wife. Taking advantage of this seating arrangement, Josef asked the couple, "Do you speak German?"

"Why, of course. Let me introduce myself. I'm Henry Thompson, and this is my wife, Heidi. We've been living in Hong Kong for the past six years, and before that in Berlin, where I met my wife. I work for Lloyds of London."

"Are you by any chance Jewish?"

"Yes. And you?"

"Yes, and these are my sons, Walter and Dolfie. I don't mean to impose upon you, but in your position, might you have some information about what's happening to the Jews since the *Kristallnacht* pogrom? I've been worried about my wife and daughter. They should have left Vienna on the eleventh and be in China by now. They're traveling on the Trans-Siberian Railway. I didn't want them having to make the long sea journey because my wife has a delicate constitution." Trying to make light of his story, he added, "A trip up the Danube and she gets sick. She should have crossed into China by now."

As Henry Thompson expertly twirled his pasta around the tines of his fork, he said, "I don't have much to report. The British government continues to follow a policy of appeasing Hitler. The last thing they want is to drag England into another war. So, for the time being, we are tempering our outrage. More wine, Herr Kolber?"

"Please. Perhaps it will calm my nerves."

"Since the Évian Conference, it seems that no one cares about the Jews, not even the United States. I'm sorry I don't have more encouraging news to offer you. Now what is it that you do?"

"My wife and I owned a textile factory in Vienna. We are hoping to start a new business in Shanghai."

"You're going to the right place, Herr Kolber, I can assure you. Shanghai is the Paris of the East. As you'll see, it lives up to its reputation."

Mrs. Thompson spoke up for the first time. "The shops and department stores rival anything in Europe. In fact, this dress I'm wearing is from the Wing On department store on Nanking Road."

Josef smiled. "It's very lovely and suits you. The fabric is shantung, I believe."

"Yes. It comes from Shandong Province, the fabric, that is."

Josef tried to show some interest, but his mind was elsewhere. He had hardly touched his meal, but Walter and Dolfie, their appetites fueled by the sea air, finished their servings.

"Forgive me for being rude, but I feel the need to lie down. Will you excuse us?"

"Of course, Herr Kolber. I wish you a pleasant afternoon."

Josef found an empty deck chair, pulled a blanket over his legs, and closed his eyes, wishing for sleep to rescue him from the engulfing sadness. Walter and Dolfie amused themselves by playing a game of ping-pong and then took a refreshing dip in the ship's small saltwater pool.

As Josef napped and the *Conte Verde* sailed out into the open sea, the Czar's train pulled out of the Moscow station. Eva and Lilly's first-class tickets entitled them to a private cabin, which was roughly nine square meters (eighty-five square feet) and appointed with a sink and hot and cold running water. The cabin had two facing sofas that converted into beds. Toilets were at the end of the corridor. Dora and Herman's cabin was next door so they could all be together whenever they felt the need for one another's company.

Cabin attendants served first-class passengers tea and coffee from large samovars well into the evening. Passengers in first class were served their meals on fine china with silverware in the ornate central dining room. The less fortunate travelers who could only afford second or third-class tickets found themselves forced to sit upright on hard benches in crowded coaches for the entire journey eastward.

Sitting across from Lilly, Eva concluded, "The worst must surely be behind us now." She took out the train tickets and looked over the itinerary. "If everything goes smoothly, we will be arriving in Shanghai on December 8. We'll be ten days late, but what can we do? Hopefully, Papa will have found us someplace to live, and then we can focus our attention on getting the factory together and your brothers into a decent school."

Lilly giggled.

"What's so funny?" Eva asked. "Are you thinking about the way that Oblomov looked like a lovesick puppy when we said our goodbyes?"

"I've forgotten all about him. I was thinking about Walter and Dolfie leaning over the railing of the *Conte Verde* feeding the fish, sick as dogs, while we are sitting here in comfort with nothing to disturb us but the sound of the wheels hurtling along the tracks."

As night enveloped the land, it was impossible to see out of the train windows, and so it was not until the next morning that Eva and Lilly caught sight of the snow-covered countryside. Dense pine forests, gold and diamonds and coal reportedly just below the ground, marked the landscape. The railroad was built in part to carry these natural resources to the major cities of the West and East, and it was the only access route for the small villages and towns that planted themselves along the train tracks. Every such village looked the same: a cluster of wooden huts next to an onion-domed church.

Peasants riding in horse-drawn sleighs or skating across frozen ponds waved at the passing train. During the short daylight hours, it was so cold and windy that few passengers disembarked to stretch their legs when the train stopped at villages along the train route. For those passengers who ventured outside, there were vendors offering boiled eggs, cucumbers, and sausages. At night packs of howling Siberian wolves followed the train for short distances. The temperature outside dropped to ten below zero Celsius.

To break the monotony, Eva and Dora played card games, knitted, or worked on their needlepoint. Eva frequently lost her ability to concentrate, admitting to her sister how worried she was about Josef and the twins. "What if they aren't there when we arrive in Shanghai? What if something has happened to them?"

Speaking like an older sister, Dora said, "Calm down, Eva. I'm sure that Josef is managing quite well without you."

Eva was sarcastic. "He rarely does. Why should today be any different?"

Herman came to Josef's defense. "Given half a chance, I'm sure your husband will prove himself to be very resourceful. For most of your marriage, my dear Eva, you have been in charge. In fact, realistically, he's in effect been working for you."

"I've never heard him complain about his circumstances."

Herman stood up. "I think I'll take a walk along the corridor. Maybe I'll be lucky and pick up a card game."

Dora apologized for Herman's comment after he left. "We are all on edge. He didn't really mean anything by what he said."

Eva stared at her sister. "The only reason he would say such a thing is if you had repeated something I told you in confidence. In the future I trust that you'll keep what I tell you to yourself, or our time together will not go well for either of us. We need each other now more than ever, Dora. Do you promise me?"

"I promise." Dora added, "What was it that I used to call you when you were a little girl? *Moppelchen*. Little chubby one. And you used to call me *Grosse Ohren*. Big ears. And then we'd start fighting and Mutti would take a wooden spoon and chase us around the kitchen."

"It seems like such a long time ago, doesn't it? How silly we were."

The two sisters hugged each other and went back to their handiwork.

Lilly buried her head in her book. She estimated she'd have just enough time to read *Madame Bovary* from cover to cover before they arrived in Shanghai:

> You forget everything. The hours slip by. You travel in your chair through centuries you seem to see before you, your thoughts are caught up in the story, dallying with the details or following the course of the plot, you enter into characters, so that it seems as if it were your own heart beating beneath their costumes.

She reread this passage and wondered what life held in store for her.

The train reached Lake Baikal, the deepest freshwater lake in the world, five days after leaving Moscow. Ominous-looking shards of ice protruded from its surface; horse-drawn sleds hugged its shores. Men sat on wooden crates next to holes cut into the ice, fishing for omul. Their thick fur *ushankas* were pulled down over their ears to ward off the bitter cold. At one time passengers were ferried across Lake Baikal, but by the early twentieth century, train tracks and bridges were laid down, permitting uninterrupted travel around the lake.

As the Russian writer Maxim Gorky described it, Siberia was truly "the land of chains and ice," where only the hardiest souls survived and where political prisoners of the Czar were banished for what remained of their miserable lives.

The train arrived in Chita on December 2. Eva and Lilly disembarked with Dora and Herman and transferred to another train heading south on the Trans-Manchurian Railway. When they arrived at the border town of Manzhouli, situated between Russia and Japanese-occupied Manchukuo (formerly Manchuria), local border guards accompanied by Japanese soldiers boarded the train carrying rifles. Shouting in Mandarin and then again in Russian, they instructed the passengers to show their passports and visas. A fellow traveler volunteered to translate their commands into Yiddish: "All bags must be ready for inspection."

Eva whispered to Herman, "What are we going to do? We don't have visas."

Herman had the answer. "I'll just hand over all our passports together. Maybe it will be all right." He then turned to the Yiddish-speaking translator. "If they ask, will you inform them that we don't have visas because we are going to Shanghai? We are merely in transit. We don't plan on stopping anywhere. Show them our tickets and slip them this money."

"Sir, if I try to bribe them, that will only make matters worse, for you and for me. Keep your money."

The passport control official compared the passport pictures to their faces and then inspected each passport closely. "What does this red J mean? Where are your visas?"

Herman answered, "The German Reich requires that all people of the Jewish faith have passports stamped with the letter J."

Confused by the explanation, the Japanese officer demanded, "Get off this train—*now*. We cannot let you go across the border until we clear your documents with our superiors. You have no visa and we have never seen passports with a red J. We need to call our superiors." The other passengers watched in stunned silence as the foursome was forced off the train and onto the snow-covered platform. The guard repeated in broken English, "Come back tomorrow. I must ask superiors. Now you must wait. You look for beds."

Lilly was tearful. "Mutti, now what? Where do we go? Can they send us back home?"

A curious street vendor selling eggs approached. Herman pulled him aside and explained their unfortunate situation. After some discussion, Herman proudly announced, "Good news. Jacob here is Jewish and owns a chicken farm nearby. He said he and his wife Zipporah are happy to give us a place to stay."

Jacob bowed to the ladies and ushered them out of the station and into his horse-drawn sleigh. Everyone held on to their suitcases, hoping that the ride would be over quickly before their noses froze. Eva shivered. "I can't believe it. Even my teeth feel like they're starting to freeze."

Jacob and Zipporah's home was little more than a hut, but it was warm and welcoming. The hosts proved to be most gracious, and Zipporah prepared a hearty meal of chicken soup with rice.

Jacob explained, "We were newlyweds when we escaped the Kiev pogroms in 1919, and together we found safe haven here in isolated Manzhouli. I was trained as an engineer, but today we make a living as chicken farmers. Strange how life turns out."

"A year ago we were living the good life in Vienna, and today we don't know what is going to happen to us." Eva paused. "But tonight we are thankful to you for a warm place to sleep and food. I don't know how we'll be able to repay you."

Zipporah smiled. "Being able to help fellow Jews is compensation enough."

Later the four guests found themselves sharing a small room and, of course, the communal outhouse.

Early the next morning, with Jacob by his side, Herman approached the Manchu border guard. "Have you heard anything?"

"You must understand that it will take time. We just sent out the dispatch yesterday. You must be patient."

Meanwhile, Eva and Lilly volunteered to collect eggs while Dora and Herman fed the chickens. They were not used to this kind of work or to the bitter cold, but it was a small price for food, shelter, and friendship.

Another day and another trip to the guardhouse had the same result: "We've not heard anything yet. Maybe this afternoon."

Back at Jacob's house, Lilly was bored, frustrated, and scared. She cried out, "Is it possible that we will never get an answer? How long do we have to wait in this frozen wasteland? Then where do we go?"

Eva tried to adopt a calming voice. "Be patient. It will all work out. It just takes time." She almost believed it.

Lilly complained, "I simply cannot use their filthy, smelly outhouse, Mutti!"

Eva lost her patience. "Then you'll just have to go into the woods, but watch out for the wolves. And there's something else. I heard our host mention that there is a golem hiding under a rock a few meters from the house, just past the chicken coop." At the sight of Lilly's horrified face, Eva and Dora burst out laughing.

Again the next morning Herman and Jacob went to the border guards, and again they were turned away. Then, on December 7, a communiqué dispatched by Japanese officials from Tokyo informed the border guards:

> ALLOW TRAVELERS WITH RED J TO PROCEED. NO FURTHER DETAINMENT NECESSARY.

When the 4:15 train pulled into the station at Manzhouli, the official handed back their passports and directed them to board the train headed for Harbin.

One of the other passengers was a man named Israel Kaufman, a Russian Jewish businessman with a home in Harbin. Curious as to why people would climb aboard at the border crossing, he quickly befriended the group. Eva was all too willing to explain everything that had happened to them since they left Vienna over a month ago.

"Your travel story is unbelievable," Israel said. "My family escaped the Odessa pogrom in 1905. But your journey sounds even more difficult. So tell me, how will you continue on to Shanghai from Harbin?"

"It should not be so hard." Eva smiled. "At Harbin we change trains to Nanking, and from Nanking we take the train to Shanghai. So, as you can see, we are only a few days away. After what we've been through, this part should be easy."

"I hate to tell you this, but it won't be so easy. That route is very unsafe, and I don't see how you can get through. The Japanese are at war with both the Chinese Communists and Nationalists. There is constant fighting in that area, and they use the railroad to move troops and supplies. Many trains and tracks are wrecked. Anyway, you don't want to go near Nanking. Didn't you hear about the Rape of Nanking? The Japs horrifically tortured and murdered hundreds of thousands of civilians: men, women, and children. I am sorry to tell you that you must find another way, a way that is sure and safe."

The four looked at one another, speechless. Their silence was finally broken when Eva spoke up. "Do you know of another way?"

"Perhaps. If we can get you to the Port of Dalian on the East China Sea, you'll find a ship, probably a freighter, that goes to Shanghai. But that will take some planning. In the meantime, you can all stay with me when we arrive in Harbin. There we'll figure everything out. There is nothing we can do right now anyway."

Located 1,000 kilometers (650 miles) east of the Russian border and 1,000 kilometers north of Peking, Harbin was the administrative headquarters for building the Chinese Eastern Railroad at the turn of the twentieth century. Czar Nicholas II offered the persecuted and beleaguered Jews an opportunity to leave Russia if they agreed to settle in Manchuria, thus bringing their trading skills and ingenuity to the area for the benefit of Mother Russia. The Czar and his advisors reasoned that no one would be willing to go to this barren outpost beyond civilization besides the filthy Jews. Jewish settlers made their living as bankers, bakers, shopkeepers, and restaurant owners, turning Harbin into the "Saint Petersburg of the East." The Jewish population eventually reached twenty thousand by the 1920s. At one time there were more than twenty Jewish newspapers, and the language of commerce was Russian, not Mandarin.

The train arrived on the morning of Friday, December 9, and Israel Kaufman led the travelers to his comfortable home. He invited them to join his wife and five children and his brother Abraham's large family of seven for Shabbat dinner in his home. Israel asked Eva and Dora, as his "very esteemed guests," to join the other ladies in the lighting of the candles. Then everyone recited the blessings over the wine and freshly baked challah.

He intoned, "Let us not forget the true significance of Shabbat. It is a time of observance and remembrance." Everyone nodded, and he took this as a sign to continue. "Remember that you were a slave in the land of Egypt, and the Lord brought you forth from there with a mighty hand." And then, looking around the room, he said, "May it ever be so that God will deliver the Jews from harm. Amen." He then urged his guests, "Eat! Eat! You must all be yearning for some good Jewish cooking. My wife and sister-in-law are the best cooks. There is plenty here."

Herman thanked their host on behalf of his family. Then he waited a few minutes until the platters of stuffed cabbage, boiled potatoes, and steamed carrots had been passed around the table before asking the question that weighed on everyone's minds: "Can anyone tell us what is happening in Vienna and Berlin? We've been traveling for four weeks and it's been nearly impossible to get any information."

Abraham adjusted his glasses and took a deep breath. "We don't know how accurate the reports coming to us from Moscow are, but it seems that things have only gotten worse for the Jews. The Nazis have made it clear that harassment and, ultimately, deportation of all Jews is their primary goal."

Eva grabbed Lilly's hand and squeezed it, trying to give her daughter the courage to hear this terrible news.

And then Abraham added more bad news. "France and Germany just signed a no-war pact, and right on the heels of the Munich Agreement. It supposedly wiped out the traditional enmity between the two countries. Seeing that photo in the newspaper of those two negotiators toasting each other with glasses of champagne made my stomach turn." For emphasis, Abraham set his wineglass down on the lace tablecloth. "Hitler is now free to continue his advance into Eastern Europe, assured that the French will do nothing. Hitler is even intimidating Mussolini, who has eighty million Nazi sympathizers right across Italy's border."

"My dear husband, Josef, nearly lost his life fighting on the border of Italy and Austro-Hungary. And what good did it do us? His Iron Cross for heroism during the Great War counted for nothing."

Nodding sympathetically, Abraham continued, "I hope that our Shabbat dinner gives you some measure of comfort and that you will remember us fondly as you resume your journey. To conclude our meal, let us recite the Shemah reaffirming God's love for his chosen people, who have survived for thousands of years despite our enemies."

After the last word was sung, everyone stood up, wrapped themselves in warm overcoats, and walked briskly along the snow-covered street. The moonlight transformed the snow into a glistening white carpet, and the only sounds were the crunching of boots in the snow and a lone stray dog barking into the darkness.

On December 12, 1938, the family boarded the Harbin-to-Mukden train. Looking around the train car, Lilly whispered to her mother, "Did you notice that family of coolies getting on the train ahead of us? I hope they don't sit near us, now that we are no longer in first class."

"They are hardly coolies, my dear. Coolies are low-class Chinese. The women are wearing stylish fur coats and elegant velvet hats, and those feathers must have cost them a fortune. And the men are sporting ivory-handled canes. You'd better get used to being around Chinese people if you expect them to do business with us once we are settled in Shanghai."

"So you intend to sell to the Chinese?"

"Of course. Their money is as good as anyone else's, Lilly. And they will make up the biggest part of our clientele." Eva changed the topic. "How many hours will we be sitting on these uncomfortable benches?"

"At dinner Israel said the trip is about seven hours. Then, when we get to Mukden, we're to go straight to the next train for Dalian."

"It's going to be a long day, my dear, but with each hour that passes, at least we are an hour closer to Shanghai."

Lilly declared, "And I'll be pages closer to finishing *Madame Bovary*."

As the train slowed down at Mukden North, *Madame Bovary* moved Lilly to tears. Rereading one of her favorite passages, she felt Emma's longing at the very core of her being:

> Oh, if somewhere there were a being strong and handsome, a valiant heart, passionate and sensitive at once, a poet's spirit in an angel's form, a lyre with strings of steel, sounding sweet-sad epithalamiums to the heavens, then why should she not find that being?

Lilly wondered whether it was possible to find such a man, a man who was strong, sensitive, handsome, and also brave. At eighteen Lilly knew nothing about love except what she had read in novels, but she was determined to discover its magic, so long as she didn't have to give up her dream to become the next Coco Chanel.

chapter 11
The Shun Feng

The streets of Mukden, China were filled with Japanese soldiers and government officials. Since capturing the city in September 1931, the Japanese had taken over the railroad lines, deforested the wilderness, and plundered the area's other natural resources. In a symbolic gesture to the Chinese people, the Japanese appointed Puyi, the deposed emperor of the Qing dynasty, as the emperor of Manchukuo, and he took up residence in the Mukden Imperial Palace. The Japanese trotted Puyi out for ceremonial occasions, a puppet of the occupiers with no real authority.

Many Chinese families who had lived in Mukden for centuries fled the city; those who remained were placed under the boot of the Japanese and selectively relocated to the poorest quarters of the city to build factories, dig in the coal mines, and load lumber onto trains headed to port cities. Fewer than 250 Jewish families lived among the Chinese, Russians, and Japanese.

The train rumbled into the Mukden station as the four Caucasian travelers climbed onto the platform. They hoped it would be a short wait for the train to the Port of Dalian. But Eva, Lilly, Dora, and Herman soon realized they were lost. There were so many signs, and were they written in Japanese, or was it Chinese? It made no difference, as they could not read any sign and certainly couldn't speak to anyone. Their Western faces, and especially Lilly's auburn hair, drew stares from virtually everyone who passed, but no one offered of help.

Herman approached a uniformed Japanese guard to get information about the train to Dalian. He was pointing to Dalian on the map in his hand when the guard unexpectedly motioned with the barrel of his rifle, grunting and directing everyone into a small office. There they were met by a uniformed man who seemed to be of some importance. Speaking in broken English, the officer demanded, "Where you are going?"

Lilly answered in English. "Sir, we want to get on the next train to Dalian, and from there we're taking a boat to Shanghai." Choking with emotion, she continued, "That is where my father and brothers are waiting for us. Please help us."

"You have travel papers?"

Lilly handed over their passports. He pointed to the red J. "What this mean?"

"We are Jewish. We have left the Third Reich. Austria. You can see that our passports were stamped by the Japanese authorities at the Manzhouli border. There we were given permission to enter China and go to Shanghai."

"Ah. But where is your travel permit? Everyone must have travel permits."

"This is all that we have. Please, just let us go on to Shanghai."

"You must wait. I must get permission." He stopped and thought for a moment. "For now, go with that guard."

Lilly tried to control herself. "Mutti, how can this be happening again? This is too much! Now what is going to happen to us?"

They found themselves in a one-room schoolhouse without running water that was already occupied by ten Chinese men dressed in rags. They leaned against the walls smoking foul-smelling cigarettes. Lilly thought, *Definitely coolies.* Adjacent to the building was a filthy outhouse. The guard threw blankets down on the floor. A single window let in what little daylight there was. A Japanese soldier stood guard outside the building. Everyone was given a bowl of rice and water.

Lilly complained to Eva, "I'm going to starve to death if we have to spend even a day here. Who can eat this?"

Eva tried to change the subject. "Dora and I can afford to lose a few kilograms, but you're already too thin."

Pulling on the waistband of her skirt, Lilly remarked, "Look how loose it is. When we started this trip it fit me like a glove."

"That was a month ago. We should have taken the *Conte Verde* with your father and brothers. We would have been in Shanghai weeks ago. Instead we've been stuck in one hellhole after another. It was my decision, but now I regret it."

Dora chimed in. "It hasn't all been so bad, Eva. The Hotel Metropol was delightful, and we were treated with the utmost courtesy by our acquaintances in Harbin."

"Do me a favor, Dora, stop talking. I'm in no mood to be humored."

When Lilly put her head down at night, she could hear the scratching of rats in the walls, and outside, drunken Japanese soldiers wandered the streets, singing and yelling. She tried to keep one eye open as she clutched her valise in her arms, afraid that one of the coolies might try to steal it, but she was so tired that sleep finally overtook her.

Her mother lay next to her, most likely trying to suppress her fears. The uncertainty and the boredom were taking a toll on everyone.

Finally, on the morning of December 16, the same Japanese official from the train station appeared in the doorway. He pointed to the Westerners. "Get your belongings. Officials in Shanghai confirmed that you can go there without permits. Sorry, but we never heard this. Quick, quick! A train for Dalian will be leaving in a half hour."

Without the benefit of a mirror, Eva tried to tidy herself up, anchoring her hairpins into her bun. Turning to her sister, she asked, "How do I look, Dora?"

"About the same as I do, I'm sure. Like you have been on a train far too long and detained at every turn. Now let's get going before someone changes their mind."

On December 16, the *Shun Feng*, a Chinese freighter owned by the Chung Wei Steamship Company, docked in the Port of Dalian. The freighter had been commandeered by the Japanese during the Sino-Japanese War in 1937.

The ship's captain, a man named Zheng, stood shoulder to shoulder with a Japanese officer who oversaw his every move. The two men motioned to the family to proceed up the gangplank. Captain Zheng, speaking rudimentary English, instructed them to leave their valises on the deck. He explained, "One of our crew will bring suitcases. We have one cabin room only. It belongs to crew, but they will sleep elsewhere. You will be comfortable. You share toilet down hallway. It has washing tub too."

Lilly told the captain, "Thank you, but we'll handle our own luggage." She didn't want anyone touching her valise.

"As you wish. Dinner will be served at six o'clock exactly. You eat with me. Pleasant surprise: chicken with rice on menu."

"What is today's date, Captain?" Lilly knew all of her traveling companions had lost track of the date too.

"It's December twentieth, madam."

The four squeezed into their tiny shared quarters. Any hint of modesty had long since left them.

At dinner, Captain Zheng, enamored with the pretty young girl with auburn hair, insisted that Lilly sit next to him. Speaking in English, she became the translator for the group, "Captain, how long before we arrive in Shanghai?"

"Sometimes it takes us five days, sometimes seven days, and sometimes more depending upon the weather and the amount of freight we carry. I do my best to keep you comfortable, but we don't usually have passengers."

Eva asked the captain a question, and Lilly translated: "Are you expecting a storm, Captain?"

"Maybe yes, maybe no. Radio from headquarters say some ships ahead of us have run into problems. But no worries. This is strong ship."

Fortunately, the seas remained calm, and other than the miserable accommodations and the tasteless food, the journey was relatively comfortable and without incident. Seven days after boarding the *Shun Feng*, the freighter maneuvered into the port of Shanghai.

Eva and Lilly were unprepared for the grandeur of Shanghai's European-style Bund. Dozens of magnificent commercial buildings in the beaux arts style lined the streets along the Whangpoo River in the International Settlement just north of the walled Old City. But the wind blowing off the Whangpoo River brought with it all kinds of unfamiliar and vile smells from debris in the water: human waste, garbage thrown from the Chinese sampans, dead animals collected by street cleaners and dumped into the river, and bilge from the ocean liners anchored in the harbor.

They were dazed by all the commotion on the dock. Desperate for the sight of Josef and the boys, Herman suddenly spotted one of the twins. Not sure whether it was Walter or Dolfie, he shouted out both names. The boy seemed not to have heard him over the noise of the harbor and the yells of peddlers hawking their wares on the dock, and so Lilly stood on top of her suitcase and waved a handkerchief to catch her brother's attention.

Walter was surprised. Each day over the last month either he or his brother waited at the docks, hoping to catch sight of them. He waved back vigorously as he elbowed his way through the crowd. Everyone had tears in their eyes as Eva grabbed the boy—she saw it was Walter—and smothered him with kisses.

"And where are Dolfie and your father? What are you doing here by yourself? Is someone sick?"

"No, Mutti. We are all fine. When you didn't show up at the end of November, we were afraid that you might not even have made it out of Vienna. But we refused to give up hope. For a few weeks we went to the train station every day, but we were informed that service between Nanking and Shanghai has been cut off. So we decided to come down to the wharf to look for you instead. And now, here you are. Papa will be so relieved. Our stomachs have been sick with worry. Honestly, I thought Papa was going to have a heart attack. He's been going to the synagogue nearly every night to pray for you."

Teasing her brother, Lilly joked, "Is it my imagination or have you gotten bigger and uglier in the past month and a half?"

Walter replied, "I must have put on some muscle unloading our household goods. Papa rented a very pleasant house for us right in the middle of the French Concession on Rue de la Soeur. A German Jewish family who was living there is off to America, and so Papa took over the lease. We were very lucky! Decent housing is at a premium in Shanghai, especially in the French Concession." Turning to his aunt and uncle, he said, "We even have enough room for you in the apartment. Papa will help you find your own place, but that may take some time. It's wonderful that you have arrived just in time to celebrate the New Year. It seems the Westerners here go overboard with cocktail parties and elegant balls. It should be quite gay."

Lilly immediately shared her first thought. "I'm curious to see what the women wear here."

Walter answered, "I wouldn't know, but judging from the ladies I've seen walking along the Bund, Shanghai is a very fashionable place. Let's go and you can see for yourself." Walter waved his hand to catch the attention of some rickshaw drivers lined up along the wharf, all waiting for a good fare. As they climbed into the rickshaws, Walter was still excited, "I can't wait to tell you about our trip on the *Conte Verde*. What an adventure. By the way, what took you so long getting here?"

Eva was exhausted. "You have no idea, Walter. You just have no idea."

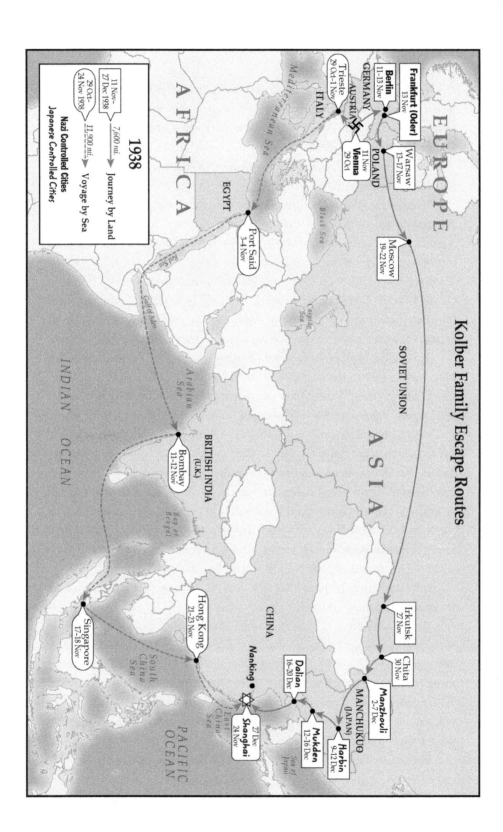

chapter 12

Finding a Partner

There was a light dusting of snow on Rue de la Soeur as Shanghai rang in the New Year. Peering out of the window of their first-floor apartment, Lilly spied well-heeled guests dressed in tuxedos and long dresses stepping out of chauffeur-driven limousines across the wide avenue. At midnight the clocks throughout the city chimed as one, announcing the arrival of 1939. Dance bands played until the wee hours of the morning. Wrapping a shawl around her shoulders, Lilly walked outside and listened to their lively tunes: "Begin the Beguine," the rollicking "Nice Work If You Can Get It," and finally "Goodnight, Ladies," tipping off the guests that the band was quitting.

Blessed with the resilience of youth, Lilly pushed the horrors of *Kristallnacht* and the detention by the Japanese soldiers out of her mind and breathed in the cool air as the last strains of "Auld Lang Syne" echoed through the streets. She imagined herself dancing the fox-trot, chattering away in French, German, and English, and meeting a handsome young man who would escort her to afternoon tea dances at the international hotels on the Bund that she had read about in the Shanghai travel guide. She wanted to discover for herself why Shanghai was called the Paris of the Orient. Isn't that what her mother promised her it would be like? She wasn't sure how she would find her way into Shanghai's Jewish elite, but if anyone could unlock that door, it would be her mother.

Eva, however, had more important things on her mind than worrying about her daughter's social life. That would have to wait until she and Josef figured out how they were going to support the family. She was disappointed to learn how little Josef had accomplished during their separation. He told her, "Eva, our sewing machines are still sitting in a warehouse near the wharf. But I do have some good news for you, *Schatzi*. I went to Shabbat at the Ohel Moishe Synagogue in Hongkew last Friday evening before you got here. I met a gentleman there by the name of Samuel Jedeikin. We chatted for a few minutes. He lived in Japan for years, working for his brother, who owns a successful watch business in Switzerland. Now both brothers are here in Shanghai. I think they are originally from Latvia, but he speaks fluent German and Japanese too."

"And what does this Samuel Jedeikin have to do with us, Josef?"

"I'm getting to that. The atmosphere was very congenial at the synagogue, and after we had a few glasses of wine, he asked me what I did in Vienna. I told him about our textile factory, and I told him that your family was in the business as well. He pumped me with questions. I think he was trying to see if I was a legitimate businessman. I mentioned my association with Bernhard Altmann and other well-connected people in Vienna. I have no idea if Samuel Jedeikin has ever heard of these prominent Jews, but what's the harm in a little name-dropping? I've discovered that there are a lot of foreigners in Shanghai who just try to pull the wool over your eyes, and I am sure a man like Samuel Jedeikin must be very cautious."

Eva was becoming impatient with all this back story. "And so…?"

"Anyway, I told him how successful we were until the Nazis shut us down. I even mentioned your dress shop. He was very impressed, I believe."

"Did you mention our sewing machines, especially the new ones? I'm sure no one in Shanghai has even seen what they can do."

Josef clapped his hands as if to cheer himself on. "I did. He said he may want to back us, maybe set up some kind of partnership. He'll find a location and provide the capital, and we'll put up our sewing machines and run the factory. I told him I'd let him know if we are interested after I'd spoken with you. What do you think?"

The sound of china breaking came to them from the kitchen. Startled, Eva left Josef standing in the parlor and rushed down the hallway to see what was happening. Mei-Li, a young Chinese girl whom Josef hired to do the housework, had broken a piece of Meissen china. She was on her hands and knees trying to pick up the pieces. In between gasps and sobs, she said in thick pidgin English, "So sorry, missy."

"Don't worry. You didn't mean to do it. Just be more careful." What had seemed so precious to Eva a few months ago was now just a possession that she could do without if she had to. Her priorities had totally shifted. She was just grateful that she, Josef, and the children were alive and safe. That was all that mattered—that and finding a way to make money. What little they had taken out of Vienna was not going to last them for long.

Eva rejoined Josef in the parlor. He looked up from the article he was reading in the *8-UhrAbenblatt* ("Eight O'clock in the Evening"), which reported that almost 1,500 European Jews had found their way into Shanghai. "Eva, what happened in there?"

"Nothing, really. Mei-Li broke one of my plates. She was crying so hard I thought her eyes would pop out of her head." She smoothed the folds of her dress and continued. "I think we should accept Jedeikin's offer, so long as we can negotiate a fair buyout agreement. Eventually we won't need him or his money. And the sooner we make this deal, the better."

"You're right. It says here in the paper that Jews are slowly trickling into Shanghai. Eventually that trickle will turn into a flood if Hitler gets his way, and then there will be a lot more competition. Perhaps Jedeikin will find someone else to back who has more to offer than just twenty sewing machines."

"Ah, Josef, that's the least of what we have to offer. We have the know-how and the fashion sense, and we're hardworking. He'll be thanking his lucky stars he went into business with the Kolbers, I can assure you."

Josef uncrossed his legs and sat ramrod-straight in his chair. "Right again. I should be so confident as you, Eva."

"Do you have his business card?"

Josef reached into his vest pocket. "It's right here, but I thought I'd wait until I see him next Friday night at synagogue. Let's make it seem like we're not so desperate for his money."

"A man like Jedeikin is either out on the town or counting his money. Since you are feeling so confident, I suggest you call him right now and make an appointment. What's the point of procrastinating? I'd rather know one way or the other if he's serious."

"But it's already eight o'clock."

Eva was adamant. "Are you going to call him or do I have to?"

Josef smiled, reluctant. "I'll do it."

Eva poured him a glass of cognac. "Here. This will put a little fire in your belly."

Samuel Jedeikin agreed to meet with Josef the following morning at the Kolbers' apartment on Rue de la Soeur. Samuel sat across the dining table from Eva and Josef. In the middle of the table was a rum raisin babka that Eva had just taken out of the oven. She cut Samuel a generous piece and then rang the bell for Mei-Li to pour their guest a cup of coffee, which was also the signal for Lilly to barge into the dining room as if on her way out the door.

"Oh, forgive me, Papa. I didn't know you and Mutti had a visitor."

Lilly had taken extra care with her hair and was wearing a chic hunter green velvet suit with black jet beads and a matching cloche hat, her appearance as orchestrated as her intrusion.

As Josef introduced their daughter, Samuel stood up. "Enchanté, Mademoiselle Lilly."

Lilly made a slight curtsy. "I'd better go or I'll miss the start of *You Can't Take It with You*. I've been dying to see the film, and it will only be at the Great Amusement Center for another week or so."

"You understand English?"

"Of course, and French too."

"Not only beautiful but also intelligent," said Samuel, blushing slightly underneath his well-manicured beard.

Lilly buttoned her wool coat and waved goodbye.

Josef served himself a piece of babka, took a sip of coffee, and turned to Samuel. "Shall we get down to business?"

"I have a number of conditions I need you to agree to before I'm willing to put up money for your business,"

Eva reached for Josef's hand underneath the table and squeezed it. Trying to remain calm, she asked, "What do you have in mind?"

"That you only hire Chinese labor in the factory. I've promised the Shanghai Municipal Council that we will put these people to work wherever I make an investment. Unemployment is a huge problem here. Their wages will be substantially lower than what foreigners will ask for, and their skills are excellent."

Josef and Eva looked at each other. Josef knew what was on Eva's mind. "We have no problem hiring Chinese labor, but we plan on bringing our family members into the operation. Eva's brother-in-law, Herman, is an accountant; he'll do the bookkeeping. And her sister Dora is an excellent seamstress. She will also help oversee the workers on the floor to make sure there are no mistakes, and nothing goes to waste."

Samuel replied, "If they are necessary to manage the business, then I have no objection, but I must insist that their employment is conditional on our profitability."

Josef spoke up. "I assure you, Samuel, you will not regret putting them on the payroll. What are your other conditions?"

"That you open a ladies' apparel store. As you explained, whatever piece goods we have left over after filling our customers' orders in the factory will be used to make clothes to sell in the store. With my brother Louis's contacts and my own, we can steer customers to both operations. I assume that Eva will be put in charge of that end of things?"

"Yes, but she'll need help finding a suitable location, preferably somewhere in the International Concession on Nanking Road that's close to Sincere and Wing On. And, of course, the store will have to have large windows opening onto the street to attract customers."

Samuel nodded. "Window shopping has become quite a sport among the well-heeled ladies here in Shanghai." He took another bite of babka and then looked toward the door as if waiting for inspiration to walk in. "And since you have mentioned that you'd like to put your family to work, what about your daughter? She'd make a very attractive salesgirl."

This was what Eva had envisioned, but it was much better that Samuel Jedeikin made the suggestion himself. "Lilly is not only an excellent salesgirl, but she's also a gifted dress designer. The outfit she was wearing today is one of her creations—and she knows what appeals to the modern woman."

Samuel was convinced. "Here is the deal. I will provide the location and you will provide the equipment. You will run the operation and we will share the profits fifty-fifty. I will provide some short-term cash that must get repaid quickly. Think about my offer and we'll iron out the details tomorrow."

As Samuel prepared to leave, Eva instructed Mei-Li to bring their guest his overcoat and walking stick, and then Eva and Josef watched Samuel walk to his shiny Bugatti waiting at the curb. The chauffeur opened the door and Samuel settled into the back seat. After the car drove off, Eva and Josef went back inside. Closing the door, Josef smiled at his wife. "Well, we got everything we wanted, didn't we?"

"No, but his offer will have to do for now." Then she added, "Once the factory is up and running, we'll need to get the boys into a good school. I imagine that Samuel Jedeikin can pull a few strings to make a place for them."

Josef nodded. "Dolfie will get in anywhere he applies. He has a good head on his shoulders and the grades to prove it. But as for Walter, he was already lagging in his studies in Vienna. If he has his way, he'd be on the soccer field or playing his violin for a pretty girl instead of studying."

Eva grimaced. "*Ach*, he's no different than most boys his age. He'll eventually take life more seriously. And as for our Lilly, she's going to be a real asset. Did you see the way she turned Jedeikin's head, just as I expected she would? And with her pretty face and figure, I'm sure that she'll find a good match for herself—even in this insect-infested city." For emphasis, Eva swatted a black fly that had landed on the half-eaten babka.

chapter 13

A Riddle Wrapped in an Enigma

After comparing high schools, Eva decided that the Shanghai Jewish School on Seymour Road in the International Settlement would be a suitable place for Walter and Dolfie to continue their studies. Located within the Ohel Rachel Synagogue, a Greco-Roman building with marble pillars and limestone-and-brick exterior, it looked more like a palace than a synagogue. Seven hundred worshippers could easily fit into the main sanctuary, and upstairs balconies allowed the men, who were seated downstairs, and the women to exchange appreciative glances during services. Built in 1920 by Sir Jacob Elias Sassoon in honor of his deceased wife, it was the first of seven synagogues in Shanghai.

Eva was amazed by its grandeur but more impressed that it was right out in the open, not hidden from view like most synagogues in Vienna.

Classes at the school were held in English and German, and the curriculum included Judaic studies, which was of no interest to the twins, who thought that once they had completed their bar mitzvahs they could put all that "religious nonsense" behind them.

When they complained, Josef insisted. "Will it kill you to take Hebrew lessons so that you can read Rashi and Maimonides and understand what these prophets have to teach us? Looking back on it, your mother and I are to be blamed for your indifference to Judaism. All we wanted was to be assimilated, to have the same rights and privileges as our Christian brethren in Austria. With all that is happening in Vienna now, I see how naïve we were. Our so-called Christian friends and neighbors were just waiting to put a noose around our necks and drag us across the Ringstrasse. There is no such person as an assimilated Jew. We are different, and you might as well figure out why and be proud of the fact. The Jewish people, without a homeland, have managed to survive in spite of everything for five thousand years, and with the Lord's help, we will continue to survive."

With a smirk on his face, Walter responded, "Are you finished, Papa? If we weren't Jewish, we wouldn't be stuck here in Shanghai. We'd be sipping *Kaffee mit Schlag* at the Hotel Sacher while the Nazis went about their horrible business."

Dolfie's mouth dropped wide open. For an instant Eva thought her husband would hit Walter squarely between the eyes, but Josef just let out a sigh of resignation and watched his son head to his bedroom.

Josef picked up his evening newspaper as Eva threaded a needle, continuing to work on a piece of embroidery. Dolfie opened his science book. From the back of the apartment, the notes of a violin subtly underscored this domestic scene. Eva listened as the music continued. "Felix Mendelssohn, I believe. Walter plays so beautifully, doesn't he, Josef?"

"Yes. I wonder if he knows that the composer he is so enamored with is from a prominent German Jewish family."

Eva ignored this remark. "I think it is time for us to get Walter a quality violin." Josef peered at his wife over the top of his newspaper. "After the way Walter spoke to me? I think he needs to apologize. And he'd better start showing more dedication to his studies or he'll be kicked out of school in no time."

As Josef and Samuel Jedeikin strolled along the Bund, Josef was amazed at how similar the waterfront buildings were to those in Europe. For a moment he was transported to the Thames, or perhaps the Seine, as he fondly remembered the elegant and imposing buildings that dotted the banks of rivers closer to home. If he closed his eyes, the sound of the water lapping the shores of the Whangpoo River could be the sound of the gentle waves of Lake Velden in Austria.

Interrupting his reverie, Samuel Jedeikin told Josef, "I made a few telephone calls to the right people and we're all set to open the factory for business. I need to introduce you to the heavyweights on the Shanghai Municipal Council. The chairman is Cornell Franklin, an American lawyer from Mississippi. He succeeded my good friend H. E. Arnhold, who is with Greyhound Association Limited. They operate the Canidrome, a dog-racing stadium here in Shanghai. Arnhold is a Jew and is in business with Sir Victor Sassoon. The rest of the Council is made up of other Americans, Brits, and of course Chinese businessmen. All fine gentlemen.

"Arnhold also helped me find a vacant store for us to lease at 450 Nanking Road. It is within walking distance of what's left of the Sincere and Wing On department stores. In no time foot traffic will be back to what it was before the unfortunate bombings in '37. Can you believe it? The Chinese intended to bomb the Japanese warship in the harbor, but their bombs hit the International Settlement. I'm afraid that the Chinese don't know what they are doing when it comes to fighting a modern war. They are no match for the Japanese pilots. That's why they have relied upon German know-how. Much of their artillery comes from the Germans. You knew that, didn't you?"

Josef's startled look was enough to communicate how shocked he was to hear this. What else did he not know about this strange city and this strange country? He was grateful that he had Samuel as a partner and relieved that Samuel shielded him from some of the clandestine deals that had to be struck in order to do business in Shanghai. It would not have surprised him if Samuel, in an effort to secure their business license, had made a "contribution" to the Green Gang, the city's most notorious gang that controlled the opium dens, houses of prostitution, and the black market.

"Nanking Road. I couldn't have asked for a better location."

Samuel nodded in agreement. "Just as you recommended. And it has large storefront windows. Have your daughter Lilly do some research on what is fashionable for European ladies. You can produce copies and sell them for a lot less than what it would cost our customers to buy them at the big, fancy department stores."

"And we'll advertise our clothing as custom-made. Eva and I thought of a name for the store: The Vienna House of Fashion."

Samuel put his hand in his pocket and rubbed a few coins together. "I like it. Anything with a European name appeals to the Shanghailanders and the wealthy Chinese, as well as our Japanese friends."

The clock in the Custom House chimed in the five o'clock hour. Josef took out his pocket watch to make sure it was keeping accurate time. Suddenly it rained. Both gentlemen snapped open their umbrellas. Samuel said, "Let's hail a cab before this turns into a deluge. I'll drop you off at Rue de la Soeur and then head home. My wife is having a dinner party tonight and I promised

I wouldn't be late. I apologize for not including you and Eva on our guest list, but we will another time. We have quite a lovely apartment not far from you at the Normandie on Rue Ferguson."

Josef understood. "It is we who should be inviting you for dinner and not the other way around. I look forward to meeting your wife, and your brother as well." Josef thought to himself, *Would Eva think that I'm being too much of a sycophant?* He let the thought pass as they stepped into the back seat of a taxicab just as an army truck carrying uniformed Japanese soldiers came barreling down the street from the opposite direction.

The JEKO Knitting Factory, named after Samuel *Je*deikin and Josef *Ko*lber, was in the International Settlement at 33 Chusan Road in the heart of the Hongkew District where many of Shanghai's Chinese working poor lived. This area had suffered bombings by the Japanese in 1937, but most of the buildings escaped destruction. Many Chinese families who had been displaced by the bombing in other parts of the city crowded into small houses left standing in the narrow lanes off Chusan Road. The alleys were populated by outdoor markets and shops selling everything from blocks of ice and hot water to hand-embroidered fabrics and exotic birds. Chinese peddlers worked in the lanes, attending to their braziers upon which they grilled meat and fish, or they walked through the lanes carrying buckets filled with water, or they pushed handcarts with household goods for sale. It was not uncommon to see a funeral procession winding its way through the lanes with a tiny coffin in front of the mourners, a casualty of dysentery, cholera, tuberculosis, or malnutrition, illnesses that plagued the city's poorest residents.

The JEKO Factory was housed in a two-story redbrick building leased to the partners by the Kadoorie family, fabulously wealthy Baghdadi Sephardic Jews who had settled in China and India in the mid-1800s and made fortunes in the legal opium trade, shipping, rubber plantations, and real estate. The Kadoories and other prominent Sephardic families, such as the Sassoons and the Hardoons, controlled much of the wealth of Shanghai. More than ninety percent of the seats on the Shanghai stock exchange were held by these few Sephardic Jews, and the skyline of Shanghai was a panorama of art deco buildings owned and operated by these families. Proud of their religious heritage and very philanthropic, they contributed to many important Jewish causes, including synagogues, schools, and charities that served the poorest of the Chinese.

By March 1939 the factory was up and running, and almost immediately Samuel Jedeikin stirred up enough orders from his business connections to keep the forty Chinese workers hired by Josef and Eva busy from seven in the morning to seven at night.

Josef and Eva rode the early morning trolley with Dora and Herman from the French Concession across Soochow Creek into Hongkew. At the Garden Bridge the trolley was forced to stop; all passengers had to take off their hats and bow to the Japanese sentry. Hongkew had been a Japanese-occupied zone since the '37 war, although foreigners could still move relatively freely from one section of the city to the other.

After a short ride from the bridge, the foursome walked along Chusan Road to the JEKO Knitting Factory. A line of Chinese workers stood outside the building waiting for the doors to open. All were skilled and grateful to have a job after months of unemployment. They had finally found a way to put food on the table for their families. Their faces were gaunt from malnourishment, but when Eva spoke with them through an interpreter, every one of them assured her they were capable of hard work and eager to be of service.

The factory was a scaled-down version of the Kolbers' cut, make, and trim operation in Vienna. If the cutters arranged and cut the patterns efficiently, there would be plenty of surplus fabric that could be used at the Vienna House of Fashion. There, the Jewish seamstresses would embellish the garments, which would be displayed in the windows on Nanking Road to entice upscale customers into the store. If everything went according to plan, the operation would be seamless and nothing would go to waste.

Eva was put in charge of purchasing textiles from the various local merchants, while Josef handled the orders for textiles from Japan and India. Eva could drive a hard bargain because Chinese businessmen, who routinely negotiated just for sport, felt it was beneath them to deal with a woman. So they gave in rather quickly. It was easier for them to say yes to her terms than try to squeeze a few extra yuan out of her. Chinese textile merchants were frequently seen exiting the JEKO Factory swearing they'd never do business with that foreign devil woman again or hitting an assistant for allowing them to make such a bad deal. But a month later every one of them would be back with an order pad in hand.

Herman did the bookkeeping. His most important job, other than making sure that customers paid their bills on time, was to prepare the monthly reports for their partner, Samuel Jedeikin.

Sitting in the office above the factory floor, Josef told his brother-in-law, "No red ink. I don't care what you have to do to show a profit, but do it!"

Herman poured two cups of steaming hot tea. Josef took a sip. "I can't get used to drinking this stuff. What I wouldn't give for a cup of strong Viennese coffee and a cruller."

Herman reminisced. "I used to go to a café on Maria-Theresien-Platz every morning before work. But that's all in the past. Maybe someday…" Without finishing his thought, he placed the March and April expense and revenue reports on Josef's desk. "Look these over. Things are going quite well without massaging the numbers. We're getting solid orders from Wing On, Sun Sun, and Dah Sun. I think they're very impressed with the quality of our Western-style garments."

"We can thank Samuel Jedeikin for making introductions to the buyers there. He's turned out to be worth his weight in gold."

"You've only been in Shanghai since November, and in just six months you've managed to learn how to do business here."

"I've hardly scratched the surface. Doing business in this strange land is still a puzzle. Do you think we'll ever get used to seeing all these Chinese faces or understand their culture?"

Herman laughed. "They're probably thinking, 'Will we ever get used to seeing all these German Jews?' We're as strange to them as they are to us."

Later that afternoon Josef locked his desk drawer and he and Herman walked through the factory. As they passed, with the Chinese workers hunched over their sewing machines, they heard the *tat-tat-tat* of the needles against the sewing machine plates comingling with the gentle hum of workers singing to themselves. Josef wondered, *How did I get here? At least I'm the owner of a factory in Shanghai.*

Dora stopped them at the front door to the factory. "Where are you two going? It's only four o'clock. The factory won't be closed for another three hours."

Josef answered, "One of the Jews who came from Berlin has taken a master lease on a lovely villa in the French Concession right on Rue des

Fleurs, a short walk from our apartment. They are turning the property into a rooming house. I understand there is a room available with access to a shared bathroom, which sounds as if it might be a decent place for you and Herman. After all, we really can't ask the children to continue sharing their bedrooms with you much longer."

Dora whispered to her husband, "Herman, I know this is my sister's idea, but please don't sign a lease until I have had a chance to see the rooming house."

"If we don't act right now, the room will no doubt be rented to someone else by tomorrow. Jews are now pouring into the city every day. Anyway, we can't keep living with your sister indefinitely. We can make it a nice place for us. Trust me. Everything will be fine."

Dora smiled. "You're beginning to sound just like Josef."

Walking to the trolley, Josef and Herman passed a street peddler selling roasted chestnuts from a coal-heated oven on wheels. Josef enjoyed the smell. "Shall we?"

Herman nodded. Josef held up two fingers, and the peddler scooped chestnuts into paper bags. Herman took out his wallet, but Josef pushed his hand aside. "Please, Herman, let me pay. It's the least I can do under the circumstances. Truthfully, I'm feeling very guilty about asking you and Dora to move out, but Eva has put her foot down."

Herman cracked open one of the chestnuts. "You don't have to apologize. I understand. If the business continues to do well, I'm sure you'll give us a raise and then we won't have any trouble finding more spacious quarters."

"That will depend entirely on how the business is doing. Honestly, having a partner has its drawbacks; but without him I'd be selling stitched goods from a pushcart."

The men continued walking, enjoying the heat of the chestnuts on their tongues and the warmth of the bags in their coat pockets.

chapter 14

Summer Heat

The wave of Jews fleeing the Nazis grew month by month, taxing Shanghai's infrastructure. To find housing for these refugees and provide basic services, several camps, known as *Heime*, were set up in Hongkew by the Committee for the Assistance of Jewish Refugees. Living quarters for men and women were set up dormitory-style, sheets hung between cots to provide some privacy. The barracks were overcrowded and unsanitary, and disease spread rapidly from one resident to the next.

Most refugees from the Third Reich arrived in Shanghai with only the clothes on their backs. A few smuggled out precious treasures that would eventually be pawned for next to nothing. Bartering had become commonplace. They would do whatever they could to earn money, even take menial jobs, but they were competing with Chinese labor. At least until now, only the poorest Chinese worked with their hands.

Besides the *Heime*, the Committee set up charity hospitals, a maternity ward, a dental clinic, and a medical dispensary for the refugees. Initially, charitable funds came from the Baghdadi Jews and from generous donors abroad through the American Joint Distribution Committee ("JDC"), which by December 1939 had sent $100,000. But as time went on, all prosperous Shanghai Jews were asked to do their part to support their brethren.

Josef warned Eva, "Any day now someone is going to show up at our door with a tzedakah box and asking us to make a donation."

"And what will you do, Josef?"

"Make a donation, of course."

"But we have school tuition and private violin lessons to pay for."

"That's all true, but how would it look to Samuel Jedeikin and his associates if we did nothing to help our people?"

"*Ach*, you're always worrying about what other people think. We need to put our needs first."

"Eva, you walk by the *Heime* every day. You see how these Jews are living. They are a shameful reminder of what Hitler has done to us. We can't just turn our backs on them."

"Don't promise anything without consulting with me, Josef. You're an easy mark. I know you too well. You'd give the shirt off your back if someone asked you."

"Yes, dear, but I have you to make sure that I don't."

The Vienna House of Fashion, which opened its doors in April 1939, succeeded in appealing to the elite and privileged of Shanghai society. The wooden mannequins in one window displayed afternoon tea dresses made of silk, rayon crepe, and cotton with fine detailing, such as decorative covered buttons, shirring and ruching, bows, faux flowers, and trim. Two-piece suits in nubby fabrics advertised as "the rougher the smarter" were also displayed in this window. The other window featured mannequins in evening dresses made of crepe de chine or printed chiffon. The showstopper was a metallic lamé dress with a front hem that brushed the floor. The back of the dress, which could be appreciated only when the ladies came into the shop to see the dress from behind, plunged dramatically and had a subtle train. The fashions that lured customers away from the big department stores and into the shop seemed straight out of Hollywood, and indeed Lilly spent hours going to the movie houses where the popular American films were playing, to copy dress styles for the store. And her instincts were on target: foreign women in Shanghai were more interested in what starlets Eleanor Powell and Jean Harlow were wearing than what was being turned out in the European fashion houses. Parisian couturier Madame Madeleine Vionnet was being eclipsed by Hollywood costume designers Adrian Greenberg and Bernard Newman.

Eva hired three highly skilled Jewish seamstresses to interpret Lilly's sketches. Lilly told her mother, "We should also have a display case inside the store for special accessories, things that don't need to be sized like evening purses with jeweled clasps and little pochettes."

Eva added, "And fake flowers for hair ornaments. They're all the rage right now. I'll leave it up to you to find some Chinese workers who can make these items for us. We'll put our label on the finished goods and mark them up."

By early summer Eva was shuttling back and forth from the store to the factory, and so on many days Lilly struggled to keep up with the steady stream of customers who came into the shop.

Eva placed an advertisement in the English-language *North China Daily News* for a sales assistant and model who could also speak Mandarin. Of the fifty girls who showed up for the job, Lilly and Eva chose Monique LeBoutin, the daughter of a French diplomat and his Eurasian wife.

Lilly and Monique were a study in contrasts. Monique was a petite blonde with sparkling blue eyes, and Lilly was an auburn-haired beauty with hauntingly brown eyes. While modeling dresses made by the Vienna House of Fashion and discussing choices with their customers, Lilly and Monique showed how the clothes might look on women of completely different colorings, complexions, and heights. The full cash register at the end of each day reflected how well this strategy was working.

Shoppers were drawn to the store not only because of its chic and reasonably priced merchandise but because of its two stunning salesgirls. By the middle of the summer engraved invitations from some of Shanghai's elite private clubs were hand-delivered to "Mademoiselles Lilly Kolber and Monique LeBoutin."

On a humid July evening Lilly and Monique attended a party at the luxurious Shanghai Jewish Club. The taxicab entered the circular gravel driveway and stopped at the front door. Through the high-arched windows the girls could see couples swaying to an eight-piece dance band. The tune the group was playing drifted through the windows and into the garden. Lilly recognized the song as Johnny Mercer's "Day In, Day Out."

The girls made quite a sensation as they hovered on the edges of the dance floor, waiting for an invitation to dance. They were both dressed in Lilly's designs, Monique in a pale rose chiffon dress and Lilly a hyacinth-blue silk dress with an apple-green taffeta sash and matching T-strap dance shoes.

Lilly did not have long to wait. Within minutes a man named David Ozer spotted Lilly and confidently asked her to dance. He was elegantly dressed in the uniform of the Jewish Volunteer Corps, one of seventy Russian Jews who served in this unit, which was part of the Shanghai Volunteer Corps established in the late 1800s to protect the International Concession. As they fox-trotted across the ballroom, Lilly couldn't help but admire David's trim physique, jet-black hair, and well-groomed mustache that fringed his ample upper lip. By the time the music stopped she was already imagining herself kissing him.

David asked Lilly, "When did you come to Shanghai? That's what we ask everyone these days."

"In late December 1938, via the Trans-Siberian Railway and then by boat from Dalian. It took seven weeks."

"You were one of the early arrivals from Vienna, yes?" Lilly nodded. David continued, "And your pretty friend in the rose-colored dress?"

"Monique has been here for quite a while. Her father was part of the French diplomatic corps. And what about you, Monsieur Ozer? You speak English with a bit of an accent, but I can't quite place it."

"My family got out of Russia during the Revolution. They lived in Harbin until 1930 and then moved to Shanghai with other Russian Jews. It became very difficult for my father to earn a living in Harbin once the Japanese infiltrated the city."

"And what do you do, if I might ask?"

"Are you trying to size me up?"

Lilly laughed. "Well, if you must know, I am."

"My family is in the textile brokerage business. We import and export fabric from all over the Far East. We also buy goods right here in Shanghai from the Chinese mills."

"How interesting! My father just started a sewing factory in Hongkew. Perhaps I should introduce you to him and the two of you could do some business together. He's always on the lookout for honest suppliers."

"I would be delighted to meet him. It's very impressive that he was able to establish himself so quickly in Shanghai. Money is tight, and only the most well connected Shanghailanders have access to capital."

"So I've been told."

David took out a gold case from his vest pocket and lit a cigarette. Then he waved his hand to attract the attention of the butler. "May I offer you a glass of champagne?"

"Absolutely. It's so hot in here."

"Would you like to go out on the veranda? It won't be much cooler, but at least we don't have to shout to be heard."

Lilly hesitated "I shouldn't disappear. Monique will wonder where I've gone, and I feel responsible for her."

David pressed on. "She's busy on the dance floor with one of my fellow captains. I don't think she'll miss you one bit."

David put his hand at the base of Lilly's back and gently steered her outside. She could feel her heart beating. The moon cast long shadows across the lawn and lit up David's handsome face. Leaning against the marble balustrade, he asked, "Where did you buy your dress, Mademoiselle Lilly?"

"At our store, the Vienna House of Fashion on Nanking Road. I'm working there as a salesgirl, and so is Monique. To be quite honest, I'm hoping that a few of the ladies here this evening, will take notice of our dresses and come to the store." Spontaneously she twirled around. "I designed it myself."

"So you're not only beautiful but talented as well." Before Lilly could react to his compliment, he added, "I believe my mother may have been in your shop quite recently."

"I don't remember meeting her. She must just have been browsing. We keep track of all our customers so we can send them news of sales and special designs."

"May I be honest with you?"

"Of course. A lie is the ruination of any relationship, at least that's what I was taught in high school."

"Your teachers were very wise to give you that piece of advice."

Lilly took a sip of champagne. "So what is this confession you are compelled to make, Captain Ozer?"

"After my mother saw you at your store, she instructed me to send you an invitation to this evening's soiree. You see, my mother is a bit of a matchmaker."

"Really? I'm very flattered."

"You do know that you are the most beautiful girl here, don't you?"

"I haven't given it much thought, but hearing you say so makes me think that perhaps it's true—at least in your eyes."

Without speaking, David clasped Lilly's hand. The band played another tune and the crooner's voice floated out into the garden:

"Falling in love with love is falling for make-believe.
Falling in love with love is playing the fool.
Caring too much is such a juvenile fancy.
Learning to trust is just for children in school."

Lilly shivered. "Is the singer trying to give us fair warning?"

"I don't know how to answer your question. I've never been in love. Now, why don't we take another spin around the dance floor so you can show off your dress and I can let my mates know that you're mine—at least for tonight?"

When the party ended, David asked Lilly if she would accompany him for an afternoon of sightseeing in the Yu Garden in the Old City, and she didn't hesitate for a moment to accept his invitation. She had never been there, and she had never been in love before either, but somehow, she intuitively felt that David Ozer was the man she would marry. She was already imagining her wedding dress, something in white satin, cut on the bias and skimming her hips, with dolman sleeves and a train. By her side was her groom in his elegant uniform, or perhaps wearing a tailored tuxedo that would show off his broad shoulders and trim waist. She knew she was getting ahead of herself, but she didn't care. She was certain she had found her Jewish prince, even though he was Russian rather than Austrian, as her mother would have wished.

chapter 15

The Lowendall Violin

On August 14, 1939, the Shanghai Municipal Council and the occupying Japanese military officials announced measures to restrict future immigration of Jews, except for those refugees who had sufficient capital to start their own businesses or demonstrable support from residents of the city, into the International Settlement. Shanghai's Jewish community reacted to this news with a mixture of horror and relief: horror that Shanghai could no longer provide a safe haven for persecuted Jews trying to escape the Nazis, and relief that the city's resources would no longer be taxed to the breaking point.

The timing could not have been worse for Jews stranded in Europe. Jews had been counting on the Soviets to stop Hitler, but on August 23, 1939, the Soviets and Germans signed a nonaggression pact that essentially gave both countries carte blanche to invade Poland.

By September the British Empire, except for Ireland, and France declared war on Germany in response to Germany's invasion of Poland, and World War II became a reality. Japan would not officially take Germany's side in the war for almost a year, but Japanese propaganda characterized Germany as a "good friend." At the very least they shared hatred of the Soviet Union and its Communist ideology.

Yom Kippur services were held in Shanghai on September 22, 1939 at Ashkenazi and Sephardic synagogues, and in temporary venues like the Broadway Theater. The Kolbers were invited by David Ozer and his parents to attend services at the Ohel Moishe Synagogue on Ward Road in Hongkew. Eva was not entirely pleased that Lilly was romantically involved with David, but she and Josef accepted the Ozers' invitation.

As they were getting dressed for the holiest day of the Jewish year, Eva told her husband, "I wish Lilly had found herself a nice cultured young man from Vienna or Berlin instead of a Russian Jew."

"Eva, don't be such a *yekke*. He makes a very good living. Did you see that he has his own private rickshaw and driver taking him around town? And he's an excellent businessman. He made sure to fill our fabric orders ahead of time."

"That's all well and good, but he's not our kind."

Josef seemed to lose his patience. "Eva, my dear, we aren't the Rothschilds. I predict that David will be a good husband to Lilly. What is most important is that he loves her very much, and his parents are over the moon about her. His family will make sure that the young couple are well taken care of financially, just as you and I were by your dear parents."

"Ah, you're such a romantic. When the war is over, he's going to want to stay in Shanghai. We'll not only be losing our daughter but in all likelihood our grandchildren as well to this disease-infested city. We don't belong here, and neither does our Lilly."

"Eva, again you are getting ahead of yourself. Don't worry. They will work it out."

Josef and Eva continued getting dressed and then waited in the hallway for Walter, Dolfie, and Lilly. Although it was Yom Kippur, they would not walk to the synagogue. A typhoon had blown through Shanghai a week before, leaving behind a steady rain and enormous puddles filled with garbage that emanated pungent smells and made the sidewalks and streets barely passable. In some parts of the city, floodwaters reached the tops of automobile tires because storm drains were clogged with debris.

A taxicab arrived and drove the family to the synagogue, which was packed upstairs and downstairs. Just as in Vienna, Yom Kippur was one holiday that even nonreligious Jews felt compelled to observe.

The service at Ohel Moishe was led by Rabbi Meir Ashkenazi, the chief rabbi of Shanghai. Josef sensed the anxiety of the congregation over the war, and that was all anyone could talk about during the breaks in the service. It was ironic that the *Parashat Bamidbar* reading for that week observed that "the Jewish people will be likened to the sand of the sea that cannot be measured or counted." And yet fifteen thousand Jewish refugees were counted by the authorities in Shanghai as the doors of the city were slowly closing to future Jews.

Josef felt the presence of his sons on either side of him, and lifting his gaze, he admired his daughter and wife sitting together with the other women in the balcony, their heads bowed in prayer. He felt overwhelmed by feelings of gratitude and grief in equal measure. As the shofar sounded, the Shemah was repeated by the congregation and then the wooden doors of the Ark were closed. Tears rolled down Josef's cheeks. Like so many others sitting in the synagogue, his thoughts and prayers were with his family members who had been left behind.

The telephone rang in the JEKO office. Josef picked up the receiver, anticipating another order from the Wing On department store or Sun Sun, but he was sorely mistaken. It was Professor Günter Gassenheimer, the headmaster of the Shanghai Jewish School.

"Herr Kolber, I am sorry to be the bearer of bad news. Your son Walter has been skipping class. When I confronted him, he told me that he's been selling soap to the refugees living in the *Heim* on Ward Road instead of attending class."

"Where did he come up with such an idea? This is outrageous," Josef exclaimed.

"Mr. Pan Lin, who runs a soap factory in Chapei near the North Station, approached him. He gave your son a bicycle, which, according to Walter, he has been hiding on the school premises. He uses it to pick up supplies from the factory. I warned him many times, but he won't listen to me. At this point there is no way that he can catch up with the rest of the class. He's already a year behind his grade level. I regret to inform you, Herr Kolber, that we're going to have to expel him. Of course, your son Dolfie is still welcome here. He's one of our star pupils and has even begun tutoring a few of our slower students in science and math. That boy has quite a bright future ahead of him."

"I wish you had spoken with me sooner," Josef said. Then he pleaded, "Can I do nothing to convince you to give Walter another chance?"

"We have a waiting list of students who are serious about their studies. I do have one suggestion for you, Herr Kolber. Walter brags that he is a wonderful violinist. Perhaps you can encourage him in that direction. Get him private lessons and maybe he'll apply himself to music."

"Professor Gassenheimer, I would appreciate it if you would not mention this to any of the other families. Can we keep this between ourselves? They'll find out soon enough; but if Walter does, in fact, apply himself to the violin while working part-time, it will seem this was a deliberate decision on our part and not a failure on his."

"Of course, Herr Kolber. Have a good day."

Josef felt his blood pressure rise when he confronted Walter. "What are you thinking? You know that education comes first! What are you going to do now, sell soap for the rest of your life? I didn't raise you to be a street peddler."

Walter tried to explain. "Papa, I'm not cut out for school. I thought you'd be proud of me for taking advantage of this opportunity. A lot of the boys my age are working in the streets, and their families are grateful for the money. I thought you would be too."

"Since when have you been concerned about the family's finances, Walter? I expect you to pay me back for the tuition I've already paid the school. Now we're going to have to find you a decent job."

With a false note of contrition, Walter agreed. "Whatever you think is best, Papa."

Despite the many refugees in dire need of work, Josef found an apprenticeship for Walter with the Star Garage on Nanking Road, which was owned by Abraham Cohen. He also owned Asia's largest fleet of rickshaws. Josef hoped that Walter would learn something about the value of an honest day's work and familiarize himself with different tools and machines, which would prepare him to work in the JEKO Factory.

Eva was not in the habit of harboring any regrets where Walter was concerned. She indulged him and seemed to find amusement in his rebellious and artistic spirit, an attitude that ran counter to her husband's. She didn't like that he was being made to work in a garage. Manual labor was not something she expected her son to be relegated to, but if Josef expected him to pay back whatever tuition had been forfeited by his antics, then so be it. She wouldn't argue with her husband—not on that point anyway.

With business going well at JEKO and at Vienna House of Fashion, Eva had enough money to put her latest plans for Walter into motion. She would find him a violin teacher, and she would buy him another violin, one that was perhaps beyond his skill level but would inspire him to take his music lessons seriously. If he showed he had real talent, he could give up his job at the garage and concentrate on his music career.

When Eva heard about Solly and Martha Leschnik at the synagogue, she was intrigued. Dora had informed her that the Leschniks, who had owned a hat store on the Kurfürstendamm, one of Berlin's fanciest streets, arrived from Berlin in February 1939. Somehow the Leschniks had managed to smuggle enough money out of Berlin to start their store, All For You, in Shanghai. The store carried a wide assortment of new merchandise. It was also a place where Jewish refugees could consign or pawn their treasures.

Like Eva, Martha Leschnik was in her mid-forties, and she was delighted that Eva had found her way into All For You. They chattered away in German about life in Shanghai. Martha complained, "The dirty water, the coolies spitting and urinating in the street—it's more than one should have to bear. But at least we're alive."

"So true. That's what my husband keeps saying,"

Martha got down to business. "Was there something special you were looking for, Eva? May I call you Eva?"

"I was wondering if you have any violins for sale."

Martha led Eva through a curtain to the back of the shop. Propped against the wall was an assortment of musical instruments: violins, violas, oboes, trumpets, and even a few cellos, as well as numerous bows made of Brazilian and cherry wood. Martha disclosed, "I must tell you, I have seen many a tear shed when the owners had to part with their instruments. Heartbreaking, really. Some of them begged me just to hold them for safekeeping, but what can I do? We need to eat too."

Eva knew little about violins, but relying on her keen eye and instinct, she picked up a beautiful instrument with a warm, sienna-brown patina. The original label and stamp were still inside the body of the violin: Louis Lowendall – Dresden. Ah, this maker she had heard about.

"That one is a real beauty with an important provenance. It comes from Dresden, from the hand of a master violin maker, Louis Lowendall. According to its owner, it was probably made in 1885 or thereabouts. It has a beautiful sweet sound. This is a serious investment, and so I could let you have it overnight on approval."

"What is the price?"

"One hundred seventy-five dollars, U.S."

"That can't possibly be your best price."

Martha knew the game of negotiation and played it as well. "Someone else is also interested in this violin, a professor at the Shanghai Conservatory of Music who wants it for one of his students. He said that he will let me know at the end of the week if he wants to buy it, although I warned him that it may be gone by the time he makes up his mind." She laughed. "And here you are. If you buy it now, I'll give you a ten percent discount."

Eva had no intention of taking the violin home "on approval." She knew that Josef would not allow her to buy such an expensive instrument for Walter. She feigned indecision, hoping that Martha would lower the price, but Frau Leschnik did not budge. After several minutes of haggling, Eva opened her pocketbook and counted out one hundred fifty American dollars. "Here, this should do it."

Martha accepted the money. "We also have several beautiful bows of the same period. Would you be interested in one of them as well?"

"No, my son has a perfectly fine bow. It is his violin that is not up to his potential."

"If you want to bring his violin in, I can see if we can sell it for you. Some of the young Chinese students come in here looking for a 'starter' violin. It is amazing to see how Western classical music is catching on in Shanghai." Martha prepared a receipt and handed Eva the violin in its case. "I am sure that your son will be very pleased with the Lowendall. Please let me know when he gives a recital."

Eva politely smiled and then, so as not to let an opportunity pass, said, "Martha, you must visit me at our fashion shop on Nanking Road." She took a flyer out of her pocketbook and slid it across the counter. "We sell both made-to-order and ready-made items, depending upon your preference, as well as beautiful accessories. Most of the custom clothing is designed by my daughter, Lilly. Please be sure to tell your friends about us as well. I'll make sure they get a discount." With her hand on the doorknob, Eva asked, "What was the name of that professor at the Conservatory? I am looking for someone to give violin lessons to my son Walter."

"Professor Alfred Wittenberg, a recent refugee from Nazi Germany. He is one of Hitler's gifts to Shanghai." Then Frau Leschnik added, "And be sure to tell him I referred you."

David Ozer instructed his rickshaw driver to take him to G. Stepanoff Jewelers at 800 Avenue Joffre in the French Concession. He knew the proprietor, whose mother was one of the store's better clients, and he trusted that the store carried only the highest-quality gemstones. It was common knowledge that many jewelers in Shanghai sold fake gems.

Mr. Stepanoff himself opened the glass door, but before David could enter, a beggar accosted him, pleading, "No rice. No yams. No coal. A few coins and into heaven." David reached into his pocket and gave the man some money. Mr. Stepanoff sighed and apologized, adding, "The same beggar will probably be waiting for you with his wife and three children when you leave."

"I can afford to be generous. It's the least I can do."

Mr. Stepanoff observed, "Frankly, if the rich Chinese families in Shanghai were more generous to their own, we wouldn't see so many beggars on the street. We have our hands full with our own brethren in the *Heime*. A representative of the Komor Committee was here just the other day asking for a donation. Of course, I was more than happy to oblige, but I am quite sure his visit is just the first of many."

"We will all need to do what we can. We cannot just rely upon the Baghdadi Jews and the Americans to shoulder the burden of our refugees."

"Absolutely, Monsieur Ozer. And now to the business at hand. After you telephoned me yesterday, I selected a few engagement rings for you to choose from." He took out a black velvet tray and placed five rings, one by one, under the light for David to examine.

David picked up a gold ring with a natural pearl and diamond clusters. "Lovely, but I think Lilly would like a gemstone better. This seems a bit subdued for her personality."

"What do you think of this one? The ring is in the art deco style. The center cabochon ruby is approximately two carats and is surrounded by pavé diamonds in a platinum setting. It takes a very sophisticated woman to wear this well. I myself adore rubies. It is said that Emperor Kublai Khan exchanged an entire city for a single perfect ruby."

"I think the color is too dark for my taste. It reminds me of blood. And

I'd prefer something larger." Pointing to another ring on the tray, he said, "Tell me about this one."

"Ah, you have exquisite taste. It is a natural Burmese sapphire set in a pavé diamond-and-platinum openwork mount. It's French from around 1910, and very unusual. The cornflower-blue color reminds me of the summer sky in Provence."

"And what is the significance of a sapphire, if I may ask?"

"It is considered a symbol of the heavens, the celestial sapphire, and the woman who wears it is said to be faithful and loyal. Good qualities for a wife, wouldn't you agree, Monsieur Ozer?"

"I think this is the one for my Lilly."

"An excellent choice. And the price—"

David interrupted him. "It's the one I want. I'm sure you will give me a fair price. Just put it on our charge account, if you don't mind. I'll pay it off in monthly installments."

"It's a bit unusual for me not to require payment in full, but for you I'll make an exception." Mr. Stepanoff placed the ring in a black velvet box and handed it to David along with a bill of sale. "Please do come back when you and your fiancée are ready to choose a wedding ring for her."

David laughed. "She hasn't said yes yet, but I like your optimism, Mr. Stepanoff—and your salesmanship."

"Well then, good luck, Monsieur Ozer, and good day."

David felt like the conquering hero as he left the jewelry shop, but his mood quickly sank at the sight of the beggar who, as Mr. Stepanoff had predicted, had returned. This time he was with his pregnant wife and three rag-clad urchins. Suddenly, the youngest child cried and threw his arms around David's leg. Horrified, his mother pulled him away and spanked him on the backside, which made him cry even harder.

David implored in Mandarin, "Please don't punish your son, madam. Here is one yuan. I hope that it does you some good." David wasn't sure if he was motivated by having just spent a small fortune on Lilly's ring or the painful sight of these sad souls. It didn't really matter. What was it his rabbi would always say about the purpose of life? *Tikkun olam.* "To repair the world." Wasn't that what he was doing with this small gesture? He shivered to think of the destiny of another baby coming into this world. Would the mother leave it on the steps of one of the Shanghai churches or dump it in a bed of straw in the streets? These discoveries were becoming more common as disease and starvation swelled to unmanageable proportions among the poorest of the Chinese population. He had seen these sad little bundles, abandoned in the lanes of Hongkew, with his own eyes.

David climbed into his rickshaw and kept his hand in his pocket to make sure that the bumping of the wheels along the rutted pavement would not dislodge Lilly's engagement ring. Despite the torrential rain, David instructed his rickshaw driver to take him to the JEKO factory. He didn't want to waste another minute. He would ask Lilly's father for her hand in marriage.

After listening to what David Ozer had to say, Herr Kolber cleared his throat. "If my daughter says 'yes' to your proposal, then I have no problem with the two of you getting married. But I'm not so sure my wife is of the same opinion. But leave it to me. I'll see if I can convince her that the decision should be Lilly's, not ours. After all, this is the twentieth century and we are in Shanghai."

"What does Frau Kolber have against me?"

"My wife is somewhat provincial in her thinking. It's not that she dislikes you, quite the contrary, but she has always imagined our daughter marrying a nice Jewish boy from Vienna. It's really quite ludicrous, in my opinion. But don't lose heart, my boy. I think you'll make Lilly a fine husband, and she's deeply in love with you, of that you can be sure."

"As I am with her, sir."

After telling Eva about David Ozer's marriage proposal, they argued well into the night; but Eva finally capitulated, having wrung an agreement out of Josef: if she let Lilly do what she wanted regarding "that Russian," then Josef must not make a fuss about the Lowendall violin she had bought for Walter or about his music lessons.

Josef was just glad it was all over. "*Ach*, Eva, you drive a hard bargain. But that is why I love you so much. What would I do without you?"

"You needn't worry about that, *mein Liebchen*." She took his hand and led him toward their bedroom. "Besides, who else would put up with me and where would I go?"

Josef turned off the lamp, and as the rain tapped lightly against the bedroom window, they found each other in the darkness.

chapter 16

The Lucky Ones

It was one of Shanghai's perfect June evenings: not a cloud in the sky and just a soft breeze coming from the west. David kissed Lilly's neck and breathed in the lovely scent of her perfume, a blend of the exotic and the sweet. He held her hand as the Ozers' driver steered the family's white Citroën along the tree-lined streets of the French Concession toward Nanking Road.

Lilly knew this was the night that David was going to propose marriage to her. Her father had alerted her and given her his blessing, but she feigned ignorance, not wanting to steal David's thunder. Better to have him think that it was a big surprise. She might even make him work a bit for her answer. Men loved the chase, especially someone like David. In truth, she was passionately in love with him. And why shouldn't she be? He was undeniably handsome, he was making quite a success of himself, and he was a hero of sorts in the Shanghai Volunteer Corps' Jewish Company. Over the past few months, as Japan's hold on the city tightened, the Corps had marched around the International Settlement and the French Concession in full kit, carrying bayonets to show residents that they were living in "protected areas." David had interfered in several skirmishes and shown considerable bravery.

The Citroën pulled up in front of the twenty-three-story Park Hotel. As he and Lilly stepped out of the car, David instructed the driver, "I'll have the maître d' call you when we're ready to leave. In the meantime, my mother expects you to pick her up. She and my father have an engagement at the Möller villa." The chauffeur bowed and slid back into the driver's seat as a red Bugatti pulled up behind them.

The hotel elevator stopped at the Sky Terrace on the fourteenth floor.

The upper vaults of the ballroom had "art deco motifs of bandleaders, musical notes and nude women running around a skylight that opened to the stars on a summer night. Pillars were decorated with gold scroll-like patterns." This gave the room a slightly Oriental appearance, a nod to the Chinese businessmen who owned the hotel.

Although it was just nine o'clock, the tables were already filling up with a diverse international crowd: young Chinese blue bloods (*xiao kai*), the scions of rich bankers and businessmen; expatriates; and diplomats and politicians. Everyone had adopted the Sky Terrace as a favorite spot among the many posh nightclubs of Shanghai.

Following the maître d' to their table by the window, David whispered the names of some faces in the crowd to Lilly. "That's our commander, Noel Jacobs, sitting next to his wife. the woman in the midnight blue dress. And there's Mr. Kwok with his retinue. He controls the Wing On department store chain. And do you see that gentleman sitting way over in the corner with the beautiful woman who is definitely not his wife? He's the general manager of the Bank of Shanghai, Zhang Gongquan. I must introduce your father to him."

The maître d' pulled Lilly's chair out for her. "I think this seat will give you the best view of the city, Mademoiselle." A bottle of champagne was already nested in an ice bucket next to the table. "May I open the bottle, Monsieur Ozer?"

"Yes. I want to make a toast." As the maître d' leaned over to fill his glass, David whispered something in his ear and slipped him a U.S. dollar bill.

Lilly looked out the window. Down below was the Canidrome, where men with money to burn bet on greyhounds, Mongolian ponies, and thoroughbreds. In the distance the phosphorescent sign over the Power and Electric building flashed its green-and-red neon message in capital letters: LIGHT, HEAT, POWER. Lilly overheard the gentleman sitting behind her say, "Shanghai is a city that consists of a narrow layer of heaven on top of a thick layer of hell."

His dinner companion commented, "If I'm not mistaken, you are quoting Christopher William Bradshaw Isherwood."

"Indeed I am. It's from his latest book, *Journey to a War*, which he penned with Auden. You must read it. They are a bit naïve about the Chinese Communists, but they got a lot of things awfully right."

Lilly thanked her lucky stars that she was dwelling in Shanghai's "heaven." She didn't know how long she would get to stay there, but she was determined to enjoy every minute of it with David by her side.

The band that evening was led by Don Jose Alindada, a Filipino expat; his fans followed him from one ballroom to the next. He was not only popular with the "men who walked with the Manila swagger," as the Filipinos were called, but with the Brits, Americans, Russians, French, and Chinese looking for a posh place to dance the night away. Some evenings the audience wouldn't let Alindada leave the podium, even after he had played "Goodnight, Ladies" at least three times.

Couples took to the dance floor with the opening bars of "All or Nothing at All," but David insisted that he and Lilly sit this one out. "Do you know this song, Lilly?"

"Not really. It sounds like a Cole Porter tune."

"I'm not sure, but I arranged for the band to play it just for us. The lyrics say everything that I want to tell you tonight."

"And what's that?" Lilly was trying not to reveal that she knew exactly what was on David's mind, but she was hardly able to hide her excitement.

"Forgive my accent. I'm not as fluent in English as you are. But they go something like this." He reached into his pocket. Lilly held her breath, thinking that David would present her with a ring, but instead he surprised her by taking out a piece of paper. As the band played in the background, he read a few lines of what he had written down to prepare for this moment: "'All or nothing at all. Half a love never appealed to me.'"

David put the paper back into his pocket. Lilly could see that his hands were shaking. And then he took out a velvet box and placed it between the two glasses of bubbling champagne on the table.

"So, what is your answer, Lilly? Is it 'all or nothing at all'?"

He opened the box and Lilly forgot all about giving David a hard time. The blue sapphire-and-diamond ring sparkled and winked at her like the stars that must have been shining down on Shanghai that evening.

"Are you asking me to marry you, David?"

"Yes, Lilly. I'm so in love with you that I can barely think of anything else."

She quickly admitted, "I feel the same about you. The minute I saw you at the Shanghai Jewish Club, I knew you were the man for me. Until that moment I never believed in love at first sight, but seeing you, so handsome in your captain's uniform, took my breath away. I've been wondering how long it would take you to ask me to be your bride."

David laughed. "You're an impatient princess. It's only been seven months, but it does seem as if we have known each other much longer. Maybe it has something to do with the terrible times we're living in."

Lilly wrinkled her nose. "Don't spoil this moment. I don't want to think about anything but us. Not now. Not ever."

David waited until the song ended. "So, Mademoiselle Lilly Kolber, will you make me the happiest man in all of Shanghai by becoming my wife?"

For the first time in her life, Lilly was speechless. All she could do was nod and smile.

Then David slipped the ring on Lilly's finger and led her to the dance floor. The band was playing another tune: "I've Got You Under My Skin." Lilly knew some of the lyrics and whispered them into David's ear: "'I've got you deep in the heart of me, so deep in my heart that you're really a part of me.'" The young couple floated across the dance floor as the neon sign on the rooftop of the Power and Electric building blinked on and off.

Eva shifted into high gear planning her daughter's wedding. There was no point in further expressing her objections. Lilly, headstrong and independent, was bound and determined to marry this handsome Russian. Eva would just have to learn to accept David Ozer as her son-in-law and the Ozers as *mishpucha*. She asked Madam Ozer to reserve the sanctuary of the Ohel Moishe Synagogue for Sunday, September 29, 1940 for the wedding, a week before Rosh Hashanah, with Rabbi Abraham Ashkenazi officiating. Madam Ozer offered to hold the reception at their spacious home in the French Concession, where they had a dining room large enough to seat thirty guests comfortably and a salon with a grand piano.

The German seamstresses at the Vienna House of Fashion worked overtime to make Lilly's wedding dress, which she had designed herself. Monique LeBoutin was dispatched to buy ivory silk and lace from Chinese merchants on Canton Road, where the highest-quality textiles were available. Lilly also designed her mother's floor-length lilac chiffon dress.

The Avenue Joffre Flower Shop was engaged to provide Lilly's bouquet, which was made of cymbidium white orchids laid onto a carved ivory fan.

Eva called her hairdresser, Margot Rosengart, reserving her for the entire day and into the evening so she could do touch-ups. The Shanghai weather did terrible things to a woman's coif, and it was important that she and Lilly both looked their very best because the Jewish newspaper intended to run photographs of the wedding on the society page. Eva spoke with the editor to make sure the captions underneath the photographs would read: "Dresses of the bride and mother of the bride from the Vienna House of Fashion on Nanking Road."

Eva went over the guest list with her husband. "Josef, which JEKO customers do you want to invite?"

"Certainly the buyers from Sincere and Wing On, but we'll have to be sure to seat them as far away from one another as possible."

"Who else?"

"I'd like to invite Milia Ionis and Leo Hanin and their wives."

"Fine, but make sure they don't start blathering on about Betar and why we Jews should all be going to Palestine. This is not a political meeting. It's our daughter's wedding."

"You are right, Eva, although I suspect that there are many Zionists who will be invited by the Ozers."

"We don't want to alienate anyone, do we?"

"Again, you are right, *Liebchen*."

The war on the European front went from bad to worse for the Allies. The German occupation of Paris was a fait accompli on June 14, 1940. A giant Nazi swastika flag was hung from the Arc de Triomphe as Hitler toured the city. Tanks rolled down the Champs-Élysées. The new Vichy government, sympathetic to the Germans, established itself in the south; the rest of the country was gobbled up by Germany and Italy. As word of Hitler's invasion of Paris spread through Shanghai's French Concession and the International Settlement, people wept in the streets.

Two months later the German Air Force launched bombing strikes on London. The newspapers reported that Prime Minister Churchill inveighed against President Franklin D. Roosevelt to enter into the war, but Roosevelt, convinced that Americans were not willing to fight another war in Europe, refused. Churchill was quoted as saying of Roosevelt, "An appeaser is one who feeds a crocodile, hoping it will eat him last." Roosevelt deflected Churchill's criticism by pointing out that he had ordered all American assets of German and Italian companies frozen.

On September 27, just two days before Lilly and David were to be married, Germany, Italy, and Japan signed the Tripartite Pact that cemented their alliance, leaving the Shanghai Jewish community wondering what the implications of this pact might be for their own safety and security. Would the Japanese, who were crawling all over the city, take orders from the Germans? And if that were the case, what might happen to the Jewish refugees who, until now, felt securely beyond Hitler's reach? Would the Japanese in Shanghai suddenly turn on them, ending the uneasy accommodation that existed between the Jewish and Japanese communities?

Eva hurried into Lilly's bedroom as Monique adjusted her veil for her. Tears were streaming down Lilly's cheeks.

"What is it, *Schatzi*? This should be the happiest day of your life. I have grown very fond of your David in spite of myself."

"How can I be happy when the world is falling apart around us? Maybe the Japanese will side with the Germans and do awful things to the Jews right here in Shanghai. I still have nightmares of *Kristallnacht*."

"Lilly, we can't live in fear. We are here today, the sun is shining, and everyone is waiting for you at the synagogue to witness this blessed event. Dry your tears and put a smile on your beautiful face. Just remember we are the lucky ones."

Monique picked up Lilly's bouquet, and the three women, together with Lilly's proud father and brothers, settled themselves into the passenger seats of the limousine for the short ride to Ohel Moishe Synagogue.

Monique LeBoutin sat next to the chauffeur in the front. Eva noticed Walter examining her profile, her perfectly turned-up nose, her lovely, creamy complexion. She frowned but supposed she couldn't blame her son; Monique was quite beautiful. A tress of shiny blond hair had fallen out of her floral headband. She tucked it back in and looked out the window. Both Eva and Walter followed her gaze to a convertible coupe carrying German uniformed officials driving on the opposite side of the road, a Nazi flag attached to the front bumper snapping back and forth as the car passed by, as if to warn the wedding party.

The rabbi's blessings and prayers for David and Lilly took on special meaning for the entire congregation. He read words of hope from the book of

Genesis: "Now look toward the heavens and count the stars, if you are able. So shall your descendants be." Then came the *Sheva Brachot* ("seven blessings"), asking God to "grant perfect joy to this loving couple," and then the breaking of the glass, which was not only the traditional symbol of the destruction of the temple but the shattering of what was and what could have been. Then everyone proclaimed, *"Mazel tov!"*

David and Lilly beamed as the newspaper's photographer took their picture outside the synagogue, and then the couple gathered with their family and guests at the Ozers' home. Eva was seated next to Eric Möller and Josef next to Eric's wife, Ingrid. The Möllers, Swedish Jews in the shipping business, lived on Seymour Road at the edge of the French Concession.

Speaking in German, Eva asked, "Do you have children, Herr Möller?"

"Six, and quite a menagerie of dogs and cats. My children love animals, and so I try to do what I can to please them."

"You sound very devoted to your family."

"To my family and to my horses. My Arabian stud, Blonic Hill, is quite a prize."

Eva raised her eyebrows. "I didn't know Jews were interested in horse racing."

"It is a favorite pastime, especially among the Sephardim, here in the Far East. Victor Kadoorie loves to say, 'There is only one race that is better than the Derby, and that is the Jewish race.' Or maybe it is the other way around."

"Really? I had never heard that. How amusing. And how are your children getting along here in Shanghai?"

"Very well. Most of them were born in China. Recently my nephew from Stockholm has joined us. He'll be working with me at Möller & Co. I just hired an English-speaking tutor to instruct him in Mandarin. The teacher, Chao Chen, is from a very prominent Chinese family from Zhenru just outside Shanghai. Her father was a scholar-bureaucrat of the highest order. In 1937 the family fled to Shanghai to escape the Japanese invasion, and now they live in the French Concession."

"So running from an enemy is not just the plight of the Jews, Herr Möller?"

"How right you are. Anyway, I met with Chao Chen's father, Gan Chen, on numerous occasions regarding the Möller Steamboat Line when he headed the Central Chinese Transportation Bureau. I owe a great deal to him, and so hiring his daughter to tutor my nephew is one way that I can do something for the family."

"I would think that Mr. Chen, being a government official, is somewhat inoculated from Shanghai's economic problems."

"Unfortunately, Gan Chen died almost seventeen years ago. He was just forty-seven, I believe. The family estate has temporarily been abandoned, until the war is over between the Japanese and Chinese. The Chens are living off whatever they managed to put aside during the good years, but theirs is not an unusual story. Many Chinese landowners have fallen on hard times."

Eva tried to stay focused on Herr Möller, but she was losing interest in his long-winded discourse on Miss Chao Chen and her family. But to her dismay, he continued. "Frau Kolber, if you or your children wish to learn Mandarin, I can tell you how to get in touch with her."

"Actually, I don't have time to learn the language. A few words of English is about all I can manage. I have my hands full running our store on Nanking Road and helping my husband at his factory. Most of our customers are Shanghailanders, and so I have little need of the Chinese language, actually." Then, so as not to miss an opportunity, she said. "I don't think I told you the name of our store. It's the Vienna House of Fashion. I do hope Frau Möller will visit us. We would be happy to make her something very special. My daughter's wedding dress was, of course, made there."

"And yours as well? You look very lovely in it. Lilac is my favorite color."

Eva blushed, which was very unlike her, but despite his talkativeness, she found Eric Möller quite charming. She laughed to herself. *I guess I'm not dead yet when it comes to attractive men.*

Herr Möller turned to the woman on his left and launched into another story, this time in French. Eva took a deep breath, realizing in that moment that the stress of the last few months, what with getting ready for her daughter's wedding and working two jobs, had taken a toll on her. She took a sip of champagne to revive herself.

Before Lilly and David cut their wedding cake, the pianist stood up and cleared his throat. "The bride's brother and I have prepared a little musical interlude for you. May I introduce Herr Walter Kolber."

Carrying his violin and bow, Walter joined the pianist. He looked very grown-up in his formal white dinner jacket, white bow tie, and black dress pants. His brown hair was wavy and thick, and he gave off an air of self-confidence, even bravado. Some of that was due to his teacher, Professor Alfred Wittenberg, who told his mother, "Your son Walter shows great promise. With dedication and hard work, he may one day be concertizing all over the world."

Standing at the piano, Walter addressed the wedding party. "We're going to play Tchaikovsky's *Valse-Scherzo*, which is not too short and not too long." Walter closed his eyes and began; he played with his whole body, as if he were making love to the violin. His performance was mesmerizing. When he finished, the audience exhaled as one and then erupted in wild applause.

He bowed and introduced the next piece. "For obvious reasons, we have chosen Saint-Saëns's *Wedding Cake Caprice-Valse*. It is normally played with piano and strings, but one violin will have to do this evening. Thank goodness it's a Lowendall."

Those guests who knew anything about the provenance of violins reacted with oohs and aahs.

Walter gave a lovely interpretation of the composition, and he and the pianist were rewarded with another enthusiastic round of applause.

Lilly, knowing that Walter had rehearsed one final piece, asked her brother, "Will you indulge us with an encore?"

"Anything for you, my dearest Lilly, but I must warn you that it is a romantic piece written to break one's heart, a melody from Gluck's *Orfeo ed Euridice* arranged for violin and piano by Kreisler. I hope you and David enjoy it."

After the wedding cake was served, some of the guests strolled into the garden. The pianist left the classical repertoire behind and played a selection of jazzy dance tunes.

Walter followed Monique LeBoutin into the garden, carrying two glasses of champagne. He offered her one. She hesitated for a moment, and then laughed. "Oh, *pourquoi non*? Do you think your mother will disapprove of my sipping a glass of champagne?"

"Why should she? You're off duty now."

"I don't want her thinking ill of me. One wrong step and there are fifty girls just waiting in line to take my place at the shop."

"But none of them are as pretty as you. I can't take my eyes off you."

"Aren't you being a little forward, Walter?"

"We have so little time. Who knows what tomorrow will bring?" He tried to put his arm around her waist, but she pulled away. "Can't fault a man for trying," he muttered.

"More like a boy. How old are you? Seventeen? Eighteen?"

"What difference does it make? Older men with younger women, older women with younger men, Chinese with Brits, and so on."

"It makes no difference according to whom?"

Walter laughed. "I just made that up, but it does seem that anything goes in Shanghai. Haven't you noticed?"

Monique looked at her watch and handed him her glass. "It's getting late. I have to work tomorrow. I need to go."

"Can I see you again?"

"I'm at the store every day. You can come in anytime."

"I mean for a date."

"I don't think your mother would like us to be going out."

"And why is that? Because you're Catholic?"

"Among other things."

"Well, that is exactly why I want to go out with you, among other reasons. Jewish women bore me to tears."

Monique looked over Walter's shoulder. "I see your mother coming this way. Do me a favor and go away."

"Only if you say yes to a date with me." He touched her.

"Please don't do that. I'll think about it." And then she was gone.

Waiting for his mother to gush over his performance, Walter took an unrestrained gulp of champagne. But she never made her way through the crowd of well-wishers. Instead, Dolfie popped out of the darkness. "Well, brother, you certainly outdid yourself tonight. That was quite a performance."

"I did it just for Lilly, but I think it had an effect on that little shop girl, Monique."

"I saw you flirting with her. She's very lovely, but she's much older than we are. She's probably twenty if she's a day. Why would she have any interest in you, Walter?"

Walter laughed. "Dolfie, if you paid more attention to the opposite sex and less attention to sucking up to Papa, you'd know the answer to that question."

His brother winced. "You know, you're an ass!"

"I was only kidding. Here's something for you to remember. This just slays me, but supposedly Paganini said, 'I am not handsome, but when women hear me play, they come crawling to my feet.' I'm not Paganini, not yet anyway, but I'm a lot more handsome. That's why Mademoiselle Monique is going to go out with me." And then he drained the last drop of champagne from his glass.

chapter 17

Gray Mourning Doves

Ya-Li pulled the curtains apart to let in the morning sunshine. "Time to get up, Chao Chen. Your brother Fu-Ti is waiting for you."

Chao Chen groaned. Her notebook was still open on the table next to the wooden birdcage. She had studied until two o'clock in the morning to make sure that she would do well on the advanced English examination. If she achieved an A, she was promised a position in the Möller household tutoring Mandarin Chinese to one of the family members. Herr Möller's secretary had spoken to her so quickly that she was unclear about who her pupil would be, but they settled on a fee and a date, April 10, 1940, on which to begin the lessons.

Chao Chen gently lifted the floral cover off the birdcage to wish her canaries *zao shang hao* ("good morning"), but they were both dead, lying on the floor of their wooden cage, their tiny legs sticking straight up in the air. She screamed. What could have happened? She had recently bought a bag of seeds from a street vendor in Hongkew when the last of the supply grown in Zhenru had run out. Could these seeds have been poisoned? That was the rational explanation, but she knew the real reason. Her canaries had died of homesickness. It had been three years since they last breathed the fresh air of their village or heard the singing of the nightingale in the forest beyond the Chen estate.

Chao Chen found a wooden box and put their tiny bodies inside, swaddling them in a lace handkerchief. When she returned in the afternoon she'd find a place to bury them in the garden. She would say a prayer so their spirits could fly free. Dressing hurriedly in a simple black skirt and cotton blouse, she brushed her long hair and stuck a barrette in it to keep her locks out of her eyes. Grabbing a heavy quilted jacket, she stuffed her notebook into her leather satchel so that she could study on the trolley car until the last possible moment.

The trolley rumbled through the French Concession to Xinzha Road, where Datong University had set up temporary quarters after its main campus was destroyed in the bombings of 1937.

Fu-Ti tried to engage his sister in idle chatter, but Chao Chen admonished him. "Can't you just be quiet? I need to look over my notes."

"You know you'll pass. You always do. I know you're the smartest student in your class."

"That may be, but I never like to take anything for granted. And passing is not enough. I need an A in order to qualify for a tutoring job with the Möllers."

Chao Chen and Fu-Ti separated at the front gates of the school. He headed for the engineering building and she walked quickly to the examination hall, trying to repeat some of the most difficult English words she had memorized: pathos, perfidy, quixotic, regurgitate, syllogism, tenacious, unctuous, vitriolic, wastrel, xenophobia, yearling, zealot… The specter of her dead canaries kept popping into her head no matter how hard she tried to concentrate, and her eyes filled with tears. She had done her best to be a good mother to them, but her best wasn't good enough.

The examination was easier than she had expected. Some of the other students squirmed in their seats, stared out the window as if seeking divine inspiration, and groaned; but when the proctor called "time," Chao Chen happily jumped out of her seat, handed in her test paper, and ran to catch the trolley car home.

Rui-De Xu and Ya-Nan were sitting in the salon listening to a Chinese opera on the gramophone. Chao Chen dropped her backpack. She recognized the music; it was from *The Legend of the White Snake*. As the cymbals clanged and the reed instruments wailed, the Abbott of Gold Mountain Temple sang, "Demon! My duty is to protect unsuspecting humans such as you."

Ya-Nan lifted the needle off the record and addressed Chao Chen. "Rui-De Xu and I were in your bedroom this morning to make sure that Ya-Li was doing a proper job of dusting the furniture and mopping the floor. We happened to see a wooden box next to the empty birdcage."

Chao Chen let out a sob. She explained, "I found Pélleas and Mélisande dead this morning. I'm going to bury them now underneath one of the rosebushes in the garden. In May, when the flowers bloom, my birds will have a beautiful place to rest."

Ya-Nan cleared her throat. "We already threw them out. They looked diseased. We don't want anything put in the garden that might contaminate the plants, and so we got rid of them. And I suggest that you not replace them. The same thing will happen again. You have your nightingale music box." She sneered at Chao Chen. "Let that be enough."

Chao Chen became teary. She knew this came at the urging of Rui-De Xu, who after all these years was still jealous of that small token of her father's love for her, but still she could not believe her own mother could be so cruel.

"Oh, stop your bawling," Ya-Nan, complained. "You are a twenty-two-year-old girl but you're acting like a self-involved ninny. You should count your blessings that you have a roof over your head, food on the table, and the prospect of a tutoring job with the Möllers. Most unmarried women your age are working at some menial job or renting out their bodies to satisfy the sailors who hang around the wharves."

Rui-De Xu kept nodding her head as Ya-Nan spoke, and then she informed Chao Chen that she was expected to contribute a portion of whatever the Möllers pay her to be used toward the upkeep of the Chen household.

"No. I am going to use my earnings to continue studying piano with Miss Liang,"

Ya-Nan argued, "That's what you think? Well, you're wrong. If you want to study with Miss Liang, you'll have to figure something else out. After all, you were clever enough to get yourself a scholarship for middle school and high school."

"What about the money that Father Gan Chen put aside for my dowry? I can use that for my piano lessons, can't I?"

The two older women paused and looked at each other. Ya-Nan stood up. "I have something to attend to. I'll let Rui-De Xu tell you what she has done with your money. I'm sure you'll agree that she made a wise decision."

Chao Chen felt her legs collapsing underneath her. She grabbed the arm of a chair and sat down.

Rui-De Xu slowly admitted, "Ya-Nan and I were afraid that your brothers might be called up to serve in the military. Imagine your brothers face-to-face with those heartless Jap dwarfs. I'm sure you wouldn't be able to live with yourself if one of your brothers were killed in battle just for the sake of your dowry. What I'm trying to tell you, Chao Chen, is that I used your dowry to bribe certain officials to exempt your brothers from military service. After all, they need to continue to support our family"

Stunned, Chao Chen remained silent. Rui-De Xu added, "And your brothers don't know anything about this. I was very lucky to have made the right connections here in Shanghai. I'm not at liberty to tell you who performed this miracle, but let's just say your father had something to do with it. His influence lives on to this day among the most important industrialists of Jiangsu." She sighed. "When we're able to go home again and visit the ancestral tomb, you and I will certainly have to say a special prayer of thanks to your dearly departed father."

"You did this without asking me?"

"Chao Chen, your opinion means nothing. I will spend whatever money we have for the betterment of the entire family. Haven't you heard the expression 'money is the best cure to problems?' Case closed."

Chao Chen looked around at the antique vases, carved furniture, and silkscreens transported from Zhenru. "I have no idea what you mean, but what I do know is that any one of these valuables is worth more than my dowry."

Rui-De Xu growled, "How dare you suggest that I sell any of our family's treasures? Now, what's done is done. If you marry someday, I am sure your brothers will be generous to you after they find out what you sacrificed for them. You wouldn't want them to think that you were not in favor of my decision, would you?"

Chao Chen felt herself pushed into a corner. "You're right. My brothers mean everything to me." She would have been devastated if her brothers had been wounded or killed in battle, but still she thought, *Why am I always expected to sacrifice for everyone? Don't I matter at all to this family?* After what Rui-De Xu had done, she knew the answer.

With a perfunctory wave of her hand, Rui-De Xu dismissed her. Despondent, Chao Chen threw herself on her bed and hid her face in the pillow so that no one would hear her crying. She slept through the evening and into the next morning. When she awoke, she was confronted with the sight of the empty birdcage and got teary once more. This time her tears were born of anger toward Ya-Nan and Rui-De Xu rather than sadness over the death of her beloved canaries. She turned the key of her music box and listened to its tune as the nightingale cocked its head and spread its sparkling tail, but it was not the same as hearing the sweet chirping of live songbirds.

A few days later, Chao Chen received notification from Datong University that she had received an A on her English language examination. There was a handwritten note beneath the grade:

> Congratulations, Miss Chen. You are the only student to have answered every question correctly, which has earned you the number one place in the class. We hope you will continue your studies with us. You show great promise in English language studies.
>
> Yours truly,
> Professor Edward Thompson

Chao Chen was overjoyed that she had done well enough on her examination to qualify for a tutoring position with the Möllers, but she was afraid that her wages would be confiscated by Rui-De Xu.

Chao Chen felt worthy of some small reward for her accomplishment, and so she bought another pair of birds despite her mother's warning. She passed a large brick tenement building on Ward Road in the Hongkew District of the International Settlement. Men dressed in business suits and women, most carrying babies and holding the hands of small children, in ill-fitting coats stood in long lines. They waited their turn for the soup to be ladled into tin cups by volunteer workers. She could see into the building. Laundry was hanging on clotheslines and cots were stacked one on top of the other, filling the dormitory-style rooms. Along the side of the building was an empty lot cleared of the debris from the bombings of 1937. Boys were kicking around a soccer ball while girls played hopscotch or jumped rope. Even in these difficult circumstances, children found ways to amuse themselves. Radios were tuned to local stations that carried live jazz and classical music. Chao Chen heard people yelling at one another in a strange language that one day she would recognize as Yiddish.

Chao Chen crossed Ward Road onto Chusan Road, the heart of what had become known as Little Vienna, a place where Jewish refugees struggled to earn a living. Delicatessens, restaurants, and clubs with names like Marlene Sweet abounded. There was the Sidas Restaurant, known for its Wiener schnitzel, and the Café Europa. An old movie theatre had been commandeered by a Jewish impresario for operettas and dramatic plays.

Chao Chen stopped for a moment to take in the smell of strange foods wafting from the restaurants and the sounds of foreign languages spoken by pedestrians rushing by. She turned on to Chusan Road. There was a small factory with a sign over the front door: JEKO KNITTING COMPANY. Chinese workers sat outside smoking cigarettes in the cold March air. Suddenly the door flew open and an imposing woman clapped her hands as if to tell them that their work break was over. They hurried back into the factory and the door slammed shut behind them.

Chao Chen found what she was looking for down a dark and narrow alley: stall after stall of bird sellers. She had never seen such an assortment of birds: canaries, finches, thrushes, parrots, all housed in wooden cages hanging over coal braziers to keep the birds and their vendors warm. A large colorful parrot stuck his beak through his cage and screamed, "Missy, missy, ten cents," trying to catch Chao Chen's attention. He was an extraordinary creature, but he didn't have a mate and Chao Chen wanted at least two birds.

A pair of gray mourning doves sat cooing on their perch. The street vendor, who looked as if he had just awakened from an opium-induced sleep, rested on his haunches and was slurping a bowl of noodles. He showed no interest in Chao Chen. She stood by the cage and waited for him to finish eating. "How much for your birds, sir?"

"For you, pretty lady, twenty yuan."

"That's too much. Will you take ten yuan?"

After a few minutes of haggling, the birds were hers. The vendor also sold her a bag of seeds, assuring her that they were clean. "No bugs. No poison."

Chao Chen found a second-class seat on the trolley car. Across the aisle was a well-dressed foreign woman in her early twenties with a little boy sitting on her lap. He was sucking a lollipop and the syrup dribbled down his chin. His mother pulled out a lace handkerchief from her coat pocket and wiped his face. "Ah, *Schatzi*, you are making such a mess."

The little boy squirmed out of his mother's arms and stood next to Chao Chen, holding on to her arm to steady himself as the trolley swerved along its tracks. He stared into the birdcage and then exclaimed, "*Die Vögel.*" Chao Chen guessed that his words meant "birds." She nodded and smiled. He was such a beautiful boy with his big brown eyes and curly hair. His mother grabbed the child's hand and blushed. "*Entschuldingen Sie, bitte.* Please excuse my son."

Chao Chen was pleased that she could speak to her in English, since she didn't know a word of German. "I don't mind at all. Your son is very beautiful."

"Thank you."

"May I ask where you are from?"

"Vienna. We are here *sechs Monats*, excuse me, six months."

"How do you find Shanghai?"

"It is like heaven after you have been living in hell."

The trolley stopped near Rue Tenant de la Tour. Chao Chen picked up her birdcage and waved goodbye. The little boy threw her a kiss. She was so startled that she nearly tripped getting off the trolley car.

Ya-Li opened the door when she rang the bell. "Where are Rui-De Xu and my mother?"

"You're lucky. They are taking their afternoon naps. Otherwise they would not let you bring those birds into the house."

"They can't tell me what I can and cannot do any longer. I'm going to be making my own money."

"Good for you, Chao Chen." Ya-Li smiled and then added, "Please don't tell them I said that. You'll get me into trouble."

"You have nothing to worry about."

"Do you know how much you will be paid by those people?"

"Yes." Chao Chen lowered her voice. "But it's a secret. I don't want Rui-De Xu knowing how much, because she expects me to give her half my wages."

"How will you hide the truth from her? She's bound to find out sooner or later."

Chao Chen had come up with a plan. "I'm going to ask the Möllers to pay a portion of my wages directly to Miss Liang for my piano lessons."

Ya-Li clapped her hands. "My sweet Chao Chen, you are your father's daughter!"

Chao Chen placed the birdcage on a table in her bedroom next to the window, filled a small cup with water, and poured the seeds into a feeding dish. The mourning doves hopped from their perch and pecked at the seeds. Chao Chen would have to wait until morning to make sure she had not been tricked and the birdseed was in fact safe for her babies to eat.

She took out her English notebook, and on a blank page she made a list of famous romantic couples from literature and music: Romeo and Juliet, Elizabeth Barrett and Robert Browning, Tristan and Isolde, Caesar and Cleopatra. None of these names appealed to her. She turned on the radio. Chopin's "C-sharp Minor Nocturne for Violin and Piano" was playing. It was just the inspiration she needed. She would call her mourning doves George and Frédéric after the unconventional couple who turned Paris upside down.

chapter 18

The Lesson

April coaxed the leaves of the plane trees that lined the boulevards of the French Concession into lacey profusion. It was a lovely time of year in Shanghai. The temperature was moderate, and rain fell only sporadically most days. Chao Chen debated whether to carry an umbrella. There was not a cloud in the sky, but she erred on the side of caution and carried one in her leather satchel. She had chosen her outfit carefully in order to make a good first impression on the Möllers: Her hair tied back in a ponytail, she wore a plain white blouse, black pleated skirt, matching black jacket, and what the English called "sensible shoes." She looked like a proper schoolmarm.

The Möller villa was located on Seymour Road at the northwest corner of the French Concession. Chao Chen had heard that Herr Möller, a rich Swedish Jew in the shipping business, had built the villa for his youngest daughter, Deirdre, after she told him of a dream she had of living in a castle. This was just a made-up story, the truth far less fanciful. The villa, with its Gothic and Tudor-inspired steeples, brown tiled roof, elegant porte-cochère and formal gardens, looked like something out of a Hans Christian Andersen fairytale, the reason this story was concocted by tour guides trying to entertain foreign visitors to Shanghai.

Along the property's frontage was a low brick wall with two stone Chinese lions guarding the villa. They reminded Chao Chen of the legendary gold lions that pedestrians rubbed for good luck in front of the Hongkong and Shanghai Bank. She passed her hand over one stone lion's head. She felt nervous at the prospect of tutoring a Möller child because they were such an important family and this was her first real job, but she was also excited that she could finally earn her own money and therefore no longer totally dependent upon Rui-De Xu. This was the beginning of a new chapter in her life. She felt as if she were finally a grown-up.

Standing at the front door, she checked her briefcase just to make sure she had remembered to pack the books that Professor Thompson had recommended. She read the titles out loud one more time, careful to pronounce each word clearly and correctly: *"Easy Lessons in Chinese* and *A Syllabic Dictionary of the Chinese Language."*

A Chinese butler answered the doorbell. Chao Chen handed him her umbrella, which he placed in a brass stand by the entryway. He then gestured for her to follow him. She had never seen a villa like this one. All the walls and ceilings were covered in dark wood paneling and the floors were made of inlaid parquet. In the grand salon were large upholstered sofas and chairs and a fireplace with a carved wooden mantel. Blue-and-white Chinese vases rested on the windowsills, and silver-framed family portraits were displayed on tables throughout the salon. As she passed through the hallway leading into the library, Chao Chen noticed several photographs of Herr Möller and his champion racehorses lining the walls.

The butler opened the door to the library and announced Chao Chen's arrival to Deirdre Möller, who smiled and greeted her in fluent Mandarin. "Ah, Miss Chen, you are right on time. May I introduce my cousin, Hans Möller. He's your pupil."

Chao Chen's gaze shifted to Hans Möller, whom she had not noticed before. As he stood she saw that he was over six feet tall with wavy blond hair and light blue eyes. When he smiled Chao Chen thought she might faint.

Switching to English, Deirdre explained, "Hans just completed his studies in maritime engineering at the KTH Royal Institute of Technology in Stockholm, and he'll be working with my father here in Shanghai. Papa thinks it's essential for Hans to learn Mandarin. He will eventually oversee our ship maintenance department. Most of our employees are, of course, Chinese. It is more effective to speak to them in their native tongue than in English—fewer mistakes that way."

Regaining her composure, Chao Chen opened her satchel and placed her books on the table. "I will do my best to prepare Herr Möller for his most important position."

"We have every confidence that you will do an excellent job. My father is particularly pleased that you will be in our employ. He speaks very fondly of your father, Magistrate Gan Chen. He credits him with single-handedly modernizing Jiangsu's transportation system and introducing many of China's business leaders to Western economic principles. And there are others who share my father's opinion of Magistrate Gan Chen."

"*Xièxie*. It means 'thank you' in Mandarin, Herr Möller."

Hans smiled. "I gathered as much, and may I say that I'm most impressed with your family background."

Deidre stood up. "Before I leave, would you two like coffee or tea and sweets? The cook has just baked some *drömmar and hallongrottor*."

Not understanding what she was being offered, Chao Chen politely refused.

"Now, Deirdre, make sure you don't eat them all. They're my favorite cookies," Hans warned.

Deirdre put on a mock frown. "Don't be so rude, Hans. You know I'm watching my weight. Otherwise, I won't fit into my dress for your wedding."

"I was only teasing. You're already thin as a reed. Besides, Elise and I are not getting married for another three months and so you have plenty of time to go on a diet. Honestly, I don't understand you women at all. Men admire women who have a little meat on their bones – more to have and to hold."

"All right, Hans. You've made your point." Deirdre turned to Chao Chen and placed an envelope on the table. "My father asked me to give this to you. I trust the amount is correct."

"I'm sure that it is, but I have a favor to ask of you. Would you take half of my pay and send it to my piano teacher, Miss Liang?" Chao Chen reached into her satchel and gave Deirdre a piece of paper. "This is her address. I know it is a bit unusual, but I want to be sure, since I don't yet have a checking account in my own name, that her fee doesn't get lost in our household account. My mother isn't quite as forward-thinking as my father was."

"Most certainly, Miss Chen."

After Deirdre left, Chao Chen kept her trembling hands hidden on her lap so Hans would not see just how nervous she was. She tried to keep her voice steady. "I notice that you have a notebook. Very good. I'd like you to take notes so that you can review today's lesson. Let me begin by explaining the use of Chinese intonations. Have you heard about them?"

"Isn't it like singing?"

"Not exactly. There are four tones and one neutral tone. Word pronunciation is constructed by pairing tones together. For example, *'nee hau,'* which means 'hello,' combines the highest, or first, tone with a neutral tone. Repeat after me."

Hans followed Chao Chen's example.

"Very good. Now listen to my intonation when I say *'woh hun hau,'* which means 'I'm very good.'"

"Yes, yes."

Chao Chen proceeded through several words over the next hour, giving examples of various tone combinations from highest to lowest. At the end of their session, when Hans yawned, Chao Chen thought he had lost interest.

"I hope I am not boring you."

"Not at all. It's just that Mandarin is quite complex," he said with a charming grin.

"Don't worry. Just study what we have covered today, and by the time I see you next week for your next lesson, it will be very easy. I promise you. Then we will go on to the concept of asking questions. I'll teach you how to use the word *'ma'* and where it goes in a question."

"Wait a minute. Next Wednesday is *Pesach* and so I won't be able to meet with you."

Chao Chen held back her disappointment. She needed the money to pay Miss Liang, but there was another reason: she had a crush on her pupil. Suppressing her feelings she asked, "Excuse me, but I don't know that word. It isn't English, is it?"

"No, Miss Chen. It's Hebrew. Pesach is an important Jewish holiday. We sit down at a big table, eat a special meal, repeat a lot of different prayers, sing songs, and tell stories about how the Jewish people escaped the pharaoh of Egypt and ended up in the land of Israel as free people. The Jews have been doing this for a long time."

"Escaping?"

"Celebrating Pesach, but come to think of it, we've been running away from enemies for thousands of years too. The pharaoh of Egypt, the Catholics during the Spanish Inquisition, and now the Nazis in the Third Reich, just to name the 'big three.' And there are plenty more."

"Just like how my family ran away from our home in Zhenru to Shanghai to escape the Japanese."

"Exactly. Anyway, we'll have to wait two weeks for my next lesson. Pesach goes on for an entire week. With us Jews, one day of observance and celebration is never enough!"

"So I'll see you again the first week of May? Is that correct?" she asked as she put her books and the envelope into her briefcase and snapped the latch.

"Yes. That will give me plenty of time to practice my intonations."

"So you *were* paying attention."

He nodded. "Let me escort you to the door."

"That won't be necessary. I can find my way out."

At the arched doorway to the library, she turned around. The lights had been turned off and Hans had disappeared.

Chao Chen was halfway home when the rain started, and she realized that she had forgotten her umbrella at the Möller villa. She thought, *You always leave something behind if you hope to return.*

chapter 19

Gondolas along the Grand Canal

Chao Chen opened the envelope that Deirdre Möller had given her. When she let out a gasp, her mourning doves, George and Frédéric, hopped off their perch and cocked their delicate heads as if signaling their curiosity. The Möllers had paid her double the fee that had been agreed upon. At first she thought there had been some mistake, but the next envelope she received two weeks later at the end of her tutoring session with Hans contained the same amount. Rui-De Xu counted out half of what was in the envelope, permitting Chao Chen to keep the rest, not knowing that one half of her actual wages had already been sent to Miss Liang. Chao Chen prayed that she'd be able to continue to hide the truth from Rui-De Xu.

At the end of May the weather turned hot and humid almost overnight. The city streets seemed to be bathed in sweat, and the stench from Soochow Creek and the Whangpoo River actually burned the eyes, forcing those who could afford them to wear dark glasses and wide-brimmed straw hats. People sought refuge from the heat in air-conditioned offices, hotels, and clubs, and they ordered glasses of cold lemonade in cafés where the ice was safe. The city was plagued by an infestation of disease-carrying insects. The municipal authorities called upon the city's residents to protect themselves by installing screens on windows and doors and hanging sticky paper, which turned black from fly carcasses within a matter of hours. Stinging caterpillars devoured the rose bushes and devastated the foliage in public gardens. Shanghailanders tried various petroleum-based insecticides out of desperation, but more often than not the plants could not withstand the spray and simply shriveled up and died. The cure was worse than the blight.

Chao Chen was eager to see her teacher again and arrived early at Miss Liang's studio. She had diligently practiced the same sonatas over and over, to maintain her technique, but she was eager to try a new composition. She had fallen in love with the works of the French composer Gabriel Fauré and hoped that Miss Liang might judge her ready to tackle one of his barcarolles.

A foreign-looking man held Miss Liang's studio door open for Chao Chen. He was carrying a toolbox, and his winter jacket and baggy pants seemed too large for his slight frame. Beads of perspiration glistened on his forehead. He thanked Miss Liang, tipped the brim of his hat with a finger, and wished both women, "Zao an" ("good morning").

Miss Liang hugged Chao Chen, clearly delighted to see her pupil. She looked her up and down. "You look quite chic. I like your hairstyle, very French, and you have gained a little weight. It's very becoming on you. And when did you start wearing lipstick and powdering your nose? I hope these are all signs that you have a boyfriend, or at least that you have your eye on someone. Am I right?"

"No. I just decided I needed to start looking my age. I have a job now. I'm teaching Mr. Eric Möller's nephew how to speak Mandarin. He's working for his uncle."

"And how old is this nephew of the rich Mr. Möller?"

"I'm not sure. I think Hans is twenty-six or twenty-seven, a few years older than me."

"Well, you must tell me more later."

Miss Liang motioned for Chao Chen to sit down at the bench. "The piano has just been tuned. In this humidity Herr Grünfelder has to come every three weeks, but I'm glad to give him the work. He doesn't even have enough money for a summer suit. He's still wearing what he had on when he arrived in Shanghai last winter with his wife and children. Herr Grünfelder is among our Jewish refugees living in Hongkew in one of the overcrowded *Heime*. It is terrible there, isn't it?"

"Yes. I've walked past one of the camps on Ward Road several times and seen many Jews lining up at the soup kitchen. You are very kind to employ him."

"That's the least I can do for him. In Vienna, he was not just a piano tuner but a well known teacher and performer. But here…" Her voice trailed off. "Now, why don't you play Rachmaninoff's 'Vocalise' for me?"

Chao Chen adjusted the bench and rested her hands over the keyboard. After taking a deep breath, she played the piece she had practiced, suddenly unaware of her teacher's presence, the sound of papers fluttering from the slight breeze coming through the window, and the ticking of the clock.

When she was finished, Miss Liang put her hand on Chao Chen's shoulder. "That was deeply emotional. Your playing has matured. You've made good use of our time apart. Brava, my dear. So, let's take a look at Gabriel Fauré. Which of his barcarolles do you have in mind?"

"I don't really know. I've heard several of his pieces on the radio, and they are all gorgeous."

"Let's start with his first." She placed a score on the piano desk stand. "Before I play this piece, you should know a bit about it and about our Monsieur Fauré. He wrote it when he was thirty-five, and although he was married, he dedicated it to one of his mistresses, who I believe was of Jewish descent and also married. Extremely attractive to women and with a passionate nature, Monsieur Fauré went on to have several more affairs. A typical European, *n'est-ce pas*? Like 'Vocalise,' this is very dreamy and romantic. 'Barcarolle' comes from the Italian word meaning 'boat'; barcarolles are the songs Venetian gondoliers sing, perhaps to entertain the honeymooners riding in their boats on their way to a petite hotel along the Grand Canal. The meter is very waltz-like. You will quickly recognize the theme, which he establishes at the beginning and returns to at the end. And so, here we go riding along the Grand Canal. Please note that there are many chords in the B section, but we do not attack them. We play them with the same delicacy as the arpeggios in the A section."

When Miss Liang finished playing the piece, she observed, "Lovely, isn't it? You have to play the piece with feeling, and it pays you back. Just listening to this piece brings up deeply felt emotions. I see the tears in your eyes, Chao Chen, and so Monsieur Fauré and I have, together, done our magic. Now, tell me what is going on? Do your tears have something to do with the Möller nephew?"

"His name is Hans. I can't stop thinking about him."

"And do you think he might have an interest in you?"

"Not at all. He teases me and sometimes flirts, but that's just part of his nature. He acts the same way with his cousin Deirdre. He's very handsome and smart."

"That can be a lethal combination."

"It is. And the worst part is that he's engaged to be married. The wedding is in just a few weeks."

"Oh my."

"What can I do? Every time I see him, I just want to embrace him. I can barely concentrate on our lessons. It's ludicrous."

"'The Heart wants what it wants—or else it does not care.' Emily Dickinson, an American poet, wrote that. You'll just have to get over him. Even if he were not engaged, the Jewish people are very insular. They rarely get involved with outsiders. They may seek a dalliance now and then, but when it comes time to pick a wife, that's a different story. For now, just concentrate on your piano studies, and someday a man will come along who is just right for you."

"Do you honestly believe that, Miss Liang? Now that I have met Hans, I cannot imagine anyone measuring up to him."

Miss Liang was about to answer when the telephone rang. She picked up the receiver. "Ah, Professor Wittenberg. How nice to hear from you." She pressed the receiver against her ear, straining to hear him. His thick German accent made it hard to understand his English, and he had a habit of speaking in a whisper. "Very well," Miss Liang said after a moment. "I have a few students in mind who might be good candidates. I'll ring you back shortly."

Chao Chen touched the piano keys lightly, picking out a few of the notes in the Fauré composition.

"Chao Chen, that was Professor Wittenberg at the Shanghai Conservatory of Music. He and my father concertize together, and he has observed me teaching here at the studio. He has several violin students who show great promise, and he'd like to pair them with my best piano students for duet practice. It won't be for another six months or so, but if you work very hard, I think you might be a good candidate. You'll have to audition for him when the time comes, and so I can't guarantee you a spot, but are you interested?"

"Yes, oh yes, absolutely."

"Good. This will be something to take your mind off Hans Möller and you can put your fascination with him where it belongs." She handed Chao Chen the music of Fauré's "Barcarolle No. 1." Touching her cheek, she said, "And to answer your question, you will find someone who is right for you, and when you least expect it."

"And what happened to the poetess Emily Dickinson? Did she ever find love?"

"That is a mystery. For years she never left her house. It is said that, by the age of thirty, she was suffering from a terrible depression. Late in life she struck up a relationship with a much older man, a judge, I believe. But Emily Dickinson scholars are not sure if this was a deep companionship or an affair of the heart. One of her poems begins: 'Hope is the thing with feathers / That perches in the soul / And sings the tune without the words / And never stops at all….'"

"What am I to take from these words, Miss Liang?"

"That you must always hold on to hope because, without it, the soul dies. But with hope, anything is possible."

It was past midnight and the house was as still as Emperor Qin Shi Huang's tomb. Chao Chen propped her back up with a pillow, her notebook lying open to a blank page on her lap. She made a list of things she needed to do:

1. *Practice, practice, practice the barcarolle.*
2. *Find a copy of Emily Dickinson's* Collected Works.
3. *Prepare next week's lesson for Hans Möller.*

She let out a sigh and absentmindedly began drawing tiny hearts and flowers in the margin of the page. And then she wrote Hans Möller's name five times (four was bad luck) with her name next to his.

She heard an automobile engine outside and then a door slamming shut. It was her brother Fu-Ti. Closing her notebook, she called his name as he passed by her bedroom door.

"I haven't seen you in days, Fu-Ti. Where were you tonight? Gallivanting around town, I suppose."

"Not at all. I had a date with Jin Hua Lee. We went to the Great World Amusement Center in the International Settlement to see *The Rains Came* with Tyrone Power and Myrna Loy. It's a real tearjerker. You should see it."

She grimaced. "I'm not in the mood for a tragedy."

"Well, then I have good news for you. I proposed to Jin Hua Lee tonight and she said yes. I'm so happy."

"So soon? You've only known each other a few months."

"Why wait? We are in love and we both want the same things in life."

"Well, then I'm very happy for you, and Rui-De Xu will be pleased. I know that she approves of the girl's family because they are well-off and, luckily, her dowry should be substantial."

"All of that is just icing on the cake. I would marry her even if her father was a rickshaw driver."

"But he's not, and Rui-De Xu would never allow it."

"Thanks for giving me a reality check, my dearest sister." He looked at his watch. "It's getting late. I still need to do some studying, and so I'll say goodnight. When you're in a better mood, maybe we can all celebrate. I have bragged so much about you to Jin Hua Lee that I think she's a bit intimidated. But I have assured her that you're the most generous and loving sister in the world."

"I hope she knows how lucky she is to have captured your heart."

Fu-Ti laughed. "I try to remind her of that fact every day so she doesn't change her mind."

After her brother's footsteps faded down the hallway, Chao Chen opened her notebook and blinked at what she had just written five times: *Hans Möller and Chao Chen*. She was furious with herself for doing something so stupid. Tearing the page out of her notebook, she ripped it into tiny pieces and slipped under her comforter, forcing herself not to think of Hans Möller for one more minute. But "the Heart wants what it wants," and his name was on her lips when she finally drifted off to sleep.

Chapter 20

An Evening at Ciro's

Josef savored the last few sips of his morning tea as he shuffled into the kitchen. He smiled to himself as he recalled the night before. Lilly and David had presented him and Eva with the joyous news of Lilly's pregnancy. While he could not quite imagine being a grandfather, he and Eva were both thrilled. They had celebrated long into the evening, and for those few precious hours, Josef had forgotten about the troubles of the world and the uncertainty they faced every day.

He picked up the pile of mail that had been pushed through the slot in the door and took it to his office. His smile immediately disappeared when he saw that he had received a letter from Samuel Jedeikin. It was unusual for Samuel Jedeikin to write Josef a letter. They usually met over coffee and a cruller at one of the German cafés on Chusan Road or spoke by telephone. Josef intuitively knew that something was wrong. The joy he had felt just moments ago was turning to dread as he sliced the envelope open, settled into his desk chair, and turned on the gooseneck lamp. Although there was no one else in the room, he read the letter[3*] aloud:

10 March 1941

Dear Josef,

I see from your monthly financial statements that JEKO is doing well despite the downturn in the economy. I predict

---

[3] * Letter recreated based upon interviews with Dolfie Kolber and Lilly Ozer.

that the tug-of-war between Chiang Kai-shek and Wang Jingwei for control over our country and its currency will eventually have a negative effect overall. You should know that a number of my other investments have not done as well as I had hoped, and therefore I am looking to diversify by opening another business here in Shanghai, which will require all my energy and a good bit of capital.

Therefore, I am afraid that I must decline your recent request for a short-term loan. However, I do not intend to sell my interest in JEKO because I have every confidence that you and Eva will maintain its profitability and that it will be worth a lot more in the long term. Please understand that I just can't extend myself further.

I trust that you will find another source of funding soon. If it becomes necessary, I can make a few introductions, but JEKO's balance sheet is strong enough so you should have no problem. Please keep me informed.

Yours truly,

Samuel Jedeikin

Josef pounded his fist on his desk and let out an audible sigh just as Eva walked into the office.

"What's the matter, Josef?"

Josef waved Jedeikin's letter in the air. "I can't believe it. Jedeikin is sending us up Soochow Creek without a paddle. Just when we have more orders than we can fill and the cost of fabric has gone through the roof, he says he won't give us a loan. What are we going to do?"

Eva grabbed the letter from her husband. "Well, he's certainly made himself clear, hasn't he? Obviously, we'll just have to go elsewhere." Eva sat down across from Josef. "*Ach*, my legs are swelling, and my feet are killing me. I'm going to need a larger pair of shoes by summertime. The doctor wants me to start taking pills for my arthritis."

Josef knew that all this talk about her health was Eva's way of sorting her thoughts and coming up with a solution. "Why don't you follow the doctor's orders? We're lucky to have so many fine German physicians here in Shanghai. I'm sure they know what they're doing. And they cost next to nothing. They're grateful for our business."

"At my age pills only make me blow up like a balloon. I have enough trouble keeping my weight down as it is." Eva leaned over and rubbed her left foot. Turning her attention back to Jedeikin's letter, she said, "Our son-in-law has excellent banking relationships here in Shanghai. Now that Lilly is about to make him a father, I'm sure David will do anything in his power to help us. He wouldn't want his child's grandparents to end up in a diseased-infested *Heim*, would he?"

"That's not going to happen any time soon, my dearest. Thanks to Herman we are in pretty good financial shape because he stays after those who are slow to pay. But, as usual, you've come up with an excellent idea. Who should ask David, you or me?"

"I'll mention it to Lilly and she can ask him."

The telephone rang. Eva leaned across Josef's desk and picked it up before he could reach it. "Hello, Walter." Then she paused, her brow furrowing as if she was straining to understand what he was saying. "Where are you? The noise around you is deafening."

Josef leaned in next to Eva and heard Walter's excited voice on the other end of the line.

"I'm at the dog track at the Canidrome. I just won a boatload of money, and so I thought you and Papa might like to meet me for dinner at Ciro's. My treat, of course."

Josef looked at Eva, who raised her eyebrows and tucked in a stray hair that had escaped one of her hairpins. "I'm hardly dressed appropriately for such a fancy restaurant," she spoke into the phone. "Let's meet at home so I can change my clothes and go from there together."

"See you at eight. Oh, I'm also bringing a date,"

Josef saw Eva make a face. "Who?"

"Someone I met at the Conservatory. You'll approve. She's from Berlin, Jewish, and very rich. She's studying the cello."

"That's a relief. I thought you might be bringing Monique from the store, and that would never do." Josef chuckled to himself.

"Why would you think that, Mutti? Just because she has a crush on me? Honestly, she's just a pretty little shop girl. I can do a lot better than her."

"My sentiments exactly. *À bientôt!*" Eva hung up the phone.

Eva was relieved that Monique was out of the picture. Now what was she going to wear this evening? Something that would catch every man's eye at Ciro's and not just her husband's. Even at forty-six she still considered herself an attractive advertisement for the Vienna House of Fashion.

Before they left the office, Eva got serious, "Josef, I know what Jedeikin said about not wanting to sell his interest in our company, but I recall that we can exercise our option to buy him out. So, when you meet with the banker, and I'm sure that David will set something up for us, I want you to bring this up. Kill two birds with one stone, as it were."

Josef knew this scenario was unlikely, but he'd do what he could just to make his wife happy. "Leave it to me."

"That's exactly what I intend to do."

Josef and Walter waited in the taxi for Eva, who couldn't decide on what to wear to one of Shanghai's finest nightclubs, which was owned by Sir Victor Sassoon. She finally settled on a long wine-colored gown with an attached cowl hood that drew attention to her still-youthful face and drew attention away from her thickening waistline. She slid into the back seat of the taxi next to her husband.

Walter asked, "What's that perfume you are wearing, Mutti?"

"Shalimar by Guerlain."

"It's lovely, almost as lovely as you are."

"Are you practicing compliments on me or do you really mean it?"

"Both."

Not to be outshone by his seventeen-year-old son, Josef quickly chimed in. "Your mother is just as beautiful as the day I married her." He then leaned over and gave her a peck on the cheek.

The taxi turned into the U-shaped driveway off Bubbling Well Road in the International Concession. The tall neon Ciro's sign sparkled against the soft rose-colored sky, beckoning the Kolbers to a glamorous evening of dining and dancing.

The threesome entered the lobby of the art deco building. Walter looked around and spotted his date, Annalise Berglas, standing at the foot of the staircase. She was wearing a belted copper-brown three-quarter-length taffeta dress and looked every bit the wealthy, well-bred young girl that he knew she was. He rushed over to her and waited for his parents to catch up. After exchanging introductions, Walter took Annalise's hand and guided her up the stairs.

Walter was sincere. "Annalise, you look simply stunning in that dress. I'm sure my mother will want to copy it for her dress shop."

"Mutti bought it for me for my eighteenth birthday. This is the first chance I've had to wear it. I'm glad you like it."

"It's not just that I like it. I like you in it. You look just like a Hollywood movie star."

Eva put her hand gently on Walter's shoulder as if to silently say, "That's enough."

Walter had reserved a table in the upstairs dining room along the metal railing overlooking the dance floor. As they were seated the band played a spirited version of "Puttin' On the Ritz."

Josef observed, "Makes you want to get up and dance, doesn't it?"

Eva retorted, "Not now. We'd like to get to know Annalise, wouldn't we?"

"Of course." Taking his wife's cue, Josef asked Annalise, "Are you any relation to the banker Jakob Berglas from Berlin?"

"He's my uncle, my father's brother. Thanks to him, my parents, my brother, and I got out in '38."

Walter lit a cigarette and blew a ring of smoke into the air. Annalise wrinkled her nose. "Walter, I told you I don't like it when you smoke."

He stubbed the cigarette out and laughed. "Anything else you don't like about me?"

Annalise blushed. "Nothing that I can think of—at the moment."

The band began playing "Let There Be Love" to begin the set. Walter was unfamiliar with the lyrics, but he hummed along as the singer crooned:

> "Let there be birds to sing in the trees,
> Someone to bless me whenever I sneeze.
> Let there be cuckoos, a lark, and a dove,
> But first of all, please let there be love."

Walter took Annalise's arm. "Would you give me the honor of this dance before the music ends?"

Turning to Eva and Josef, Annalise said politely, "Do you mind?"

Eva answered, "Not at all. You two should take advantage of this lovely dance floor. Go on, and I'll order us some food while you're enjoying yourselves."

Walter and Annalise danced for a few numbers and then returned to the table when their meals were served. After several decadent courses and a rich dessert, Eva signaled their waiter for the check.

Walter put his hand on his mother's arm as she reached for her pocketbook. "No, Mutti, this is my treat. Please tell the waiter just to leave the bill at my place."

"As you wish."

As Walter led Annalise back onto the dance floor, he thought, *Mutti is so clever. She wanted to make sure that Annalise knows who is paying for this expensive evening.*

Walter was grateful that the dance floor was crowded so that he had no choice but to hold Annalise close to him. They caught the rhythm of the band and moved together effortlessly. When the song ended, Walter suggested, "One more and then we'll go."

"But–"

"Don't worry about my parents. I'm sure they're already planning what to serve at our wedding."

"Walter, don't get too carried away. We hardly know each other, and I'm much too young to even think about getting married. So are you."

"I can dream, can't I?"

One of the tuxedoed guests on the dance floor made a request of the bandleader and the music started up again. It was *"Schön ist die Nacht"* ("Beautiful is the Night"). Walter couldn't have picked a more appropriate song to end the evening.

chapter 21
Three Ways Out

David arranged a meeting with K. P. Chen, the president of the Shanghai Commercial and Savings Bank. The bank did not need to occupy the city's priciest real estate to prove its importance as one of Shanghai's leading Chinese-owned financial institutions.

Walking south from the Bund, David told his father-in-law that he had already sent a memorandum to Mr. Chen and the banker was favorably inclined to structure a secured loan for JEKO. "Chen is one of China's modern bankers. He's from a family in Jiangsu Province, who excelled academically and somehow matriculated to the University of Pennsylvania's Wharton School. So he is very familiar with American business practices and enthusiastic about new entrepreneurs. Unfortunately, he doesn't speak German. So you'll have to rely on me to speak on your behalf. Are you comfortable with that?"

"Of course," said Josef. "But I do have a great favor to ask. Eva has gotten it into her head that we should buy out our partner, Jedeikin. Although he has made it clear he wants to hold on to his stake in JEKO, if we have the money, we may be able to force his hand."

"One step at a time. If Chen sees that you are a man of your word and that JEKO can meet the terms of the agreement he structures, we can bring this up at a later date. Remember, you don't have a track record with him yet."

Josef shifted his briefcase from one hand to the other. "This is not going to sit well with Eva. You know how obstinate she can be."

"Yes, but regardless, we're not in a strong negotiating position. There are a lot of other companies in dire need of cash, and if the war in the Pacific escalates, there is no telling what's going to happen. The Japanese may decide to commandeer all the foreign banks doing business here in Shanghai." Josef sighed. David continued, "Look at it this way. You and Eva will become grandparents in July. She's going to have things on her mind other than making you both the sole owners of JEKO."

Josef patted his son-in-law on the back. "You don't know Eva. Maybe you're right and having a little one to coo over will preoccupy her. But your mother-in-law is a force to be reckoned with, and while she will manage to be kvelling over her grandchild one minute, she will be poring over JEKO's finances the next." Josef thought to himself, *David's a real mensch. And to think that Eva was against his marrying our Lilly. How wrong she was.*

The two men waited only a few minutes before they were led into the bank president's office by his personal secretary. Mr. Chen stood up, and after the obligatory handshakes, he requested, "Please be seated." He then addressed his secretary: "Ask Miss Wang to join us, and please bring us some iced tea. It is unseasonably warm, even with the air-conditioning." He sat down and lit a cigarette. Taking just a single puff, he ground the cigarette into the bronze ashtray on his horseshoe-shaped desk. "Nasty habit. I'm trying to break myself of it."

David asked, "Who is Miss Wang?"

"One of the bank's rising stars. You'll be interested to know that her father is president of one of China's leading textile mills. Even though she's a woman, she is a real asset to us."

Without knocking, Miss Wang entered the room and quietly took a seat next to Josef. In her mid-twenties, she was the model of a modern Chinese aristocrat. Mr. Chen handed the typewritten memorandum to Miss Wang, which included JEKO's balance sheet and income statement and a three-year projection of income and expenses.

Speaking excellent German, Miss Wang looked at Josef, "How many Chinese employees do you have working for you at JEKO?"

"Since opening the factory in '39, we have consistently employed forty Chinese workers on two shifts."

"And who are your major customers?"

"Primarily the various Shanghai department stores. We aren't able to transport our garments by rail or ship presently due to the fighting, but there are plenty of customers right here in Shanghai, I can assure you."

"And I see that you have a retail operation."

"Yes, my wife is in charge of that end of our operation. She has four seamstresses working for her, German Jewish refugees. Until recently our clientele were primarily Shanghailanders, but lately we have been attracting well-to-do Chinese women."

Miss Wang smiled. "I've passed the Vienna House of Fashion on Nanking Road on several occasions. I'm quite impressed with the fashions in the window. I've been tempted to go inside."

"Please do. My wife Eva would be only too happy to assist you. My daughter Lilly, who is Monsieur Ozer's wife, designs many of our dresses, and we use a lot of the fabric overage from the factory to make our clothing. So, you can there's a lot of economy in our business."

Mr. Chen lit another cigarette, and speaking directly to David in Mandarin, he explained, "After extensively reviewing the JEKO customer list, we would consider factoring up to seventy percent of your receivables at an interest rate of eighteen percent plus administrative fees. I know it may seem high, but it's the best we can do."

David translated. Swallowing hard, his father-in-law was slow to respond. "Indeed, it is a very high rate, but given the current situation, I have no choice but to accept. Now we'll just have to make sure that everyone pays their bills on time. And as I am sure you are aware, that won't be a simple matter. We often find that some our customers would just as soon pay late penalties rather than pay their accounts in full. But be assured that we will do our best to collect our receivables in a timely manner, Mr. Chen."

Mr. Chen continued, "Since you'll be signing the agreement, we will look first to you and your wife personally. I understand your partner, Mr. Jedeikin, will not sign this agreement and so he will have no personal obligation."

"I understand," Josef said after David had translated.

"Experience has taught me that one must always have at least three types of security on a loan. One is, of course, your receivables. The second is your personal signature. And what might we look to as our third form of 'insurance?'"

Josef was dumbfounded, but his son-in-law came to his rescue. "You know me. What if I agree to co-sign the loan?" David offered. "I'm sure that my wife, Lilly, would be gravely disappointed if I did not make this offer."

"Then we have an agreement. Monsieur Ozer, please tell your business partners that I am most appreciative for this introduction. Shanghai Commercial and Savings Bank looks forward to being of service to you, Mr. Kolber."

Josef was relieved the meeting was over. "I look forward to a long and fruitful relationship with you and Miss Wang." He picked up his briefcase and wished Mr. Chen and Miss Wang *auf Wiedersehen*.

The two men walked out of the bank as the Custom House clock chimed in the half hour. Josef observed, "Mr. Chen is certainly a 'belt and suspenders' banker, isn't he?"

"Indeed. Some of our other lenders here in Shanghai could take a few pages from his book. It would help stop them from making so many bad loans."

"David, I can't thank you enough for your offer to co-sign the note. Do you think Lilly will be concerned?"

"She really doesn't have to know. All Lilly cares about is that there is enough money in her bank account to spend on whatever she wants. And so far, that's been the case. I have to keep a close watch on her. For every penny I make she'd like to spend ten. I wonder where she gets that from."

Josef laughed. "Unfortunately, Eva and I spoiled all our children. But I have a feeling you will be just as generous to your children when the time comes."

His son-in-law looked at his watch. "Is it too early to get a whiskey to celebrate our success?"

"In Manhattan we'd be right on time for a nightcap. Let's go."

chapter 22

A New Life

Lilly remained at the B'nai B'rith Polyclinic on Rue Pichon for eight days after giving birth to a healthy baby boy on July 10, 1941. The hospital's director, Dr. Max Steinman, made sure that all members of the immediate family had received their annual inoculation against cholera before the infant was brought home so as not to endanger the baby or the mother. Dr. Steinman had lost several patients among the Jewish refugees, many of whom had not paid attention to the precautions prescribed by the doctors as protection against Shanghai's rampant diseases and contaminated food and water. A single fly bite, a single cube of contaminated ice, or a single bite from a rat could end in disaster.

During Lilly's confinement, Eva organized the bris, conferring with her son-in-law's mother, Bacha Ozer, on the finer points of the ceremony. They met on the terrace of the Ozer home. As she looked out at the garden, Eva could hardly believe that it was just two and a half years ago that she and her daughter had reluctantly set foot on the banks of the Whangpoo River. Shanghai had been good to the Kolbers, and Eva no longer thought of Shanghai as the "sink of iniquity." In fact, she had begun to rather like Shanghailanders who, like the Ozers and the Möllers, she found to be very pleasant people. Now, if she could just meet some of the important Sephardic Jews, such as the Hardoons, Sassoons, and Kadoories, her social circle would be complete. But while those prominent families were involved financially and charitably in every aspect of the Jewish community, they tended to keep to themselves socially.

"And who is to be the *Sandek* at the bris?" asked Bacha Ozer.

"Lilly would like her father to have that honor."

"Fair enough." Wiping the perspiration from her neck with a handkerchief, Bacha reminded her, "We haven't yet heard what the child's name will be, although 'Mischa' has been mentioned. A good Russian name, don't you think, Eva?"

Eva bit her lip. "Yes. It's also a good Hebrew name, so if that's the name the children choose, they will be satisfying two masters. *Das ist nicht wahr?*"

"We'll have to wait until the bris to learn what it will be, won't we?"

"Yes. I've tried to pry my grandson's name out of Lilly, but she's very good at keeping secrets." Eva looked at her watch. "My goodness. Where has the time gone? I had better get back to the store. We are having a sale on ladies' summer trousers. They're very popular, thanks to Katharine Hepburn."

Bacha smoothed the front of her skirt. "I don't know. They might be suitable for young women like Lilly, but for women of a certain age, I think they're inappropriate—to say nothing of how uncomfortable they must be in this heat."

The sound of tires over gravel caught the women's attention. Bacha enthused, "What luck! Our driver is back from taking my brother to the Russian Jewish Club. Would you like a ride?"

"Thank you. I didn't fancy having to ride the trolley on such a hot day. And my legs are really bothering me." As Eva stepped into the car she thanked Bacha. "It's been lovely visiting with you. Till Sunday."

"Till Sunday."

Although it was a Sunday, the corner of Bubbling Well and Seymour Roads in the International Concession was bustling at two o'clock in the afternoon. Pedestrians, many of whom had attended church earlier in the day, strolled along the street, stopping in one of the many cafés, or headed a few blocks away to stand under the canopy of mulberry trees surrounding the palatial Hardoon estate. A Sikh dressed in a stark beige uniform and red turban cautioned the steady stream of cars to come to a complete halt, averting an accident as a limousine with Japanese officials inside sped through the intersection honking its horn.

Lilly and David Ozer's apartment was located at this busy corner on the sixth floor of the seven-story circumjacent redbrick building. On the first floor was the famous Uptown Theater, which showed second-run features that had long since left the screens of the Great World amusement center.

Walter stopped to read the theatre's poster announcing *The Great Ziegfeld*, a film with William Powell in the title role and Viennese actress Luise Rainer playing the first of his three wives. He addressed Dolfie out of earshot of his parents, who were already waiting for the elevator inside the apartment building. "Dolfie, you want to catch the movie later? I've got enough money to buy a ticket for both of us."

"I have a date later this afternoon, as it happens, with Mother's hairdresser, Margot Rosengart."

"I've heard a lot of things about her. Like meow, meow."

"Could you show a little more respect? Anyway, she and I are going to meet next door at the Federal Café, after the bris. You can join us if you want to."

"No offense, but I'd rather go to the movies. Maybe there will be someone at the bris who catches my fancy and I can invite her. I hear the film is a real tearjerker, just the kind of movie that women need a shoulder to cry on for."

"Walter, this isn't really a social occasion."

"Every occasion is a social occasion when I'm there."

"I thought you had your eye on Annalise Berglas."

"I do, but it's always good to hedge your bets. And when a girl thinks there's someone else waiting in the wings, that revs up their motor, although nothing would make Mutti happier than if I were to ask Annalise to marry me and she were to say yes."

"And what about Monique? She'll probably be here. She and Lilly have become good friends."

Walter made a face. "To tell you the truth, she dumped me. She didn't want to have sex. It's going to be a bit awkward seeing her again, but *c'est la vie*"

"You really are incorrigible, Walter."

"When I see an opportunity, I go after it."

Eva motioned for the boys to hurry. "The elevator is here."

There was plenty of room for all the family members and guests to sit in the high-ceilinged salon of Lilly and David's seven-room apartment overlooking Bubbling Well Road. The parents carried their infant son on a white pillow and placed him in his grandfather Josef's lap for the circumcision.

Before executing his duties, the *mohel* said in Hebrew, "Blessed is the one who has arrived." Lilly passed a drop of wine across her son's lips to dull the inevitable pain, but the baby let out a healthy cry when the circumcision was completed. David recited God's commandment to bring his son into the covenant of Abraham.

The *mohel* lifted a silver goblet, which had been in the Ozer family for generations, and announced the baby's Hebrew name, "Mischa," which he translated as "like unto God." Lilly and David relieved Grandfather Kolber of his precious burden. Josef was so overcome with emotion that he could not stand up. Dolfie rushed over to his father's side carrying a glass of water, and he held his father's arm to help him out of his seat.

Eva whispered to Bacha, "You were indeed right about our grandson's name."

Bacha, the eternal optimist, smiled and said, "I'm sure that, with such wonderful parents and grandparents, he will live up to his name. And may there be more children to follow, at least a daughter—one as beautiful as our Lilly."

"She is indeed beautiful. And what is that necklace she is wearing? I haven't seen it before."

"My son just bought it for her to commemorate the baby's birth."

"David certainly has good taste. And that necklace must have cost him a small fortune."

"We all love our daughter-in-law," said Bacha, implying that she had had something to do with the purchase. "Nothing is too good for our Lilly."

The baby was soon whisked away by a nursemaid, and the guests jockeyed for position around the dining room table for light refreshments. Eva had ordered special continental cakes and fresh strawberries from Eisfelder's Café Louis as part of their contribution to the occasion.

A Chinese houseboy served white and red wine as well as locally brewed weak beer mixed with raspberry syrup, a drink known as a *Berliner Weiße*, a specialty of the café. It was too hot outside to serve coffee, and besides, beans were in short supply, as were many other items that could not be locally grown or manufactured.

While the women gathered around Lilly in her bedroom to offer baby-rearing advice (Let your baby cry it out and don't pick him up…; Keep

Mischa on a strict feeding and sleep schedule, or otherwise he'll turn out to be a spoiled child…; Wake him up during the night to change his diaper…), the men stayed in the salon, trading facts and rumors about the war on both fronts while smoking Lauzon cigars, which David had passed out in honor of his son's birth.

Bernard Rosenberg, one of the leaders of the German-speaking Zionist organization, reported to the gentlemen guests what he knew about Germany's "Operation Barbarossa," the Nazi invasion of the Soviet Union. "Back in June, German forces stormed through the Baltic states without much resistance. They launched a major strike with their Axis allies across the Soviet border. The Soviets were caught unprepared, and at first Hitler had the upper hand, but later his troops got bogged down because of heavy rainstorms. Now the Soviet troops have a chance to mobilize and beat the German forces back before they get to Moscow. If those bastards get stuck in the Russian countryside with winter bearing down on them, they're going to freeze to death."

David asked, "And what about the United States? Where is Roosevelt in all of this?"

Mr. Klebanoff, the owner of the Siberian Fur Store on Nanking Road, piped up. "Soviet radio is reporting that he's funneling weapons into the Soviet Union and China under the terms of the Lend-Lease Act, but the American people don't want to go to war. He's gambling that the Brits, the Soviets, and the Allies can stop Hitler without American troops and fighter planes."

David Ozer signaled to the houseboy to refill his guests' glasses and then opened the window wider to let out the smoke that had filled the salon as he addressed Eric Möller: "My friend, where does China stand against the Japanese?"

"The Chinese have strengthened their resolve to resist the Japs, and by virtue of their sheer numbers and the size of the country, they are slowing Japan's advance into the interior. The Communist forces and Nationalist forces are cooperating with each other for a change, and since the Battle of South Shanxi in May, things seem to be at a virtual stalemate. The Republic has adopted the tactic of 'land for time,' and the people in the rural areas are abandoning their farms and factories and moving west, trying to drag the Japs into difficult terrain. On the other hand, Chinese armaments and fighter planes are inferior to the Japanese war machine. We at Möller and Company are seeing firsthand a dramatic buildup of Japanese warships in the East China Sea, and because of the oil embargo, Japan will soon be running out of fuel for domestic use. All their reserves will be diverted to the military, choking the Japanese domestic economy, and so they will have to invade oil-rich areas to fuel their economy and their war planes and ships."

Dr. Steinman observed, "Our hospital will soon run out of medicine. We may have to turn to the Japanese to supply us with drugs to take care of our patients and ensure that disease doesn't spread throughout the city. We're not only taking care of the Jews. We're being called upon to help the Chinese locals. Their hospitals are woefully inadequate, but I'm quite impressed with some of their doctors who've received training abroad."

With a skeptical look on his face, Mr. Klebanoff warned, "I still wouldn't trust them to take care of me or my children."

The other men nodded in agreement.

At that moment Eva led the ladies back into the salon, ending the men's conversation.

Walter noticed that Monique was not among the group of women who had just entered the salon. She had obviously slipped out before he had had a chance to speak to her. Walter thought, *Just as well. Monique is no more than a dalliance. Annalise is the real thing. Now I just have to win her over.*

The sound of Mischa's cries and the chiming of the Custom House clock in the distance reminded everyone it was time to leave. Lilly needed to attend to her infant, but before she retired, her father lifted the silver cup once again and, with tears in his eyes, addressed the gathering:

"Eva and I, together with Lilly and David and our family, want to thank you all for joining us today. We are so blessed to be receiving a new Jewish life into the covenant of Abraham in the midst of so much pain and suffering in the world. Let us hope that soon we will enjoy the blessings of peace so that we may turn over a better world to our grandson Mischa and the generations to follow."

Chapter 23

Pearl Harbor

It was early in the morning on Monday, December 8, 1941[4*]. Walter tiptoed down the hallway in the dark so as not to awaken his parents. Dolfie was fast asleep, curled up underneath a heavy wool blanket to ward off the cold winter air. The twins still shared a bedroom, but other than their physical proximity and similar looks, they had nothing in common.

Walter dropped his clothes, which reeked of cheap perfume and cigarettes, in a pile on the floor and crawled into bed. He'd had too much to drink. The room kept spinning around and he had to close his eyes to keep from getting dizzy. Spring Peony, one of his favorite girls in Shanghai's red-light district, had given him a run for his money. When he arrived at the brothel the night before, he was delighted to see that her name was up on the red lantern and he asked for her by name. The madam told Walter, "Spring Peony always looks forward to you, young Mr. K. Just wait here. She'll be right down."

He would not tell Dolfie where he'd been, although his brother could probably have guessed his whereabouts. Walter could never talk his brother into going with him to a brothel. As far as he could tell, Dolfie was still a virgin. What a shame. He didn't know what he was missing. Walter wondered what Annalise Berglas would think if she knew what he was up to on the evenings they were not together. With a little luck she wouldn't find out, and when the time was right, he'd share with her everything he had learned from Spring Peony.

---

[4] * December 7, 1941 Hawaiian time

With Annalise's name on his lips, he fell into a deep sleep.

He woke to the sounds of trucks and tanks rumbling in the distance. Dolfie's bed was empty. Walter assumed that he had already left for JEKO because it was a work day and he was managing the first shift. He wrapped a wool robe around himself, slid into his slippers, and ambled down the hallway.

His parents were sitting in the dining room still in their nightclothes. "What's going on?" Walter asked.

His father answered, "I don't know. The Japs are taking over the whole city." He pulled back the curtains. "It seems the Jap troops are everywhere!"

Eva blurted, "Are they going to come after us? Why are they driving through a residential district at this hour of the morning?"

Josef said, "Let's stay calm, but we shouldn't go outside. We'll just have to listen to the radio for now."

Eva panicked. "Where is Dolfie? Has he already left for the factory? It was his morning to open up."

Walter reported, "He wasn't in his bed when I got up just now. He must have gone out earlier."

Eva said quietly, "God in heaven, I hope he's all right."

Josef turned the radio on and found a station that was broadcasting from somewhere outside Shanghai. While the transmission was full of static, they could still make out the announcer in midsentence: "...Japanese battleships also turned their guns on American and British gunboats in the Shanghai harbor near the International Settlement. It's been reported that Brits sank their own ship before the Japanese could commandeer it. To repeat, a United States naval base in Pearl Harbor, Hawaii was bombed by the Japanese in a surprise attack against the Americans. We don't have all the details yet but..."

Josef turned the dial to a local Shanghai station controlled by the Japanese propaganda network. The announcer stated in a soothing voice, "Everyone needs to remain calm. The Japanese soldiers patrolling the streets are *your* friends, there only to ensure everyone's safety and to maintain law and order. If you obey the soldiers patrolling the streets, no one will get hurt."

Dolfie appeared at the front door out of breath. He explained that all the trolley cars had stopped running and he had been unable to get to the factory. The radio announcer continued: "Japanese troops armed with bayonets are marching through the streets. A Japanese flag has been unfurled on the facade of the American Club in the International Settlement. The French Concession has been left untouched for the time being."

Eva spoke over the radio announcer. "We should have known that something bad was about to happen when the U.S. Marines left Shanghai a few weeks ago. Martha Leschnik told me that she stood on the sidewalk of Bubbling Well Road as the Marines marched down the street toward the Customs' jetty. She mentioned something about a big American ship, the *President Madison*, leaving the harbor with hundreds of U.S. Marines on board. The bystanders were waving American flags, and a group of people broke out singing the 'Marseillaise.' A lot of people were crying."

There was a pensive silence while Walter filled a cup with hot water from the urn sitting on the sideboard and squeezed a slice of lemon into it for some flavor. "Well, I for one am not going to sit around here all day. My lesson with Professor Wittenberg is at two o'clock at the Conservatory, and tonight I have a date with Annalise Berglas. We're going to see the play *Fremde Erde*, if it's still on in the midst of all this."

Eva asked, "What is this play about, Walter?"

"It's rather morose. Believe me I wouldn't have picked it myself, but Annalise wants to see it. It's about a German woman's love affair with a Chinese man." He lifted his cup. "It's not really my cup of tea, so to speak, but I'm all about pleasing Annalise. I quite like her."

"And what's not to like?"

"Exactly."

"Have you met her parents yet?"

"She says it's too soon, but I'm going to ask her again tonight. We've been seeing each other since August. Let's just hope the play isn't cancelled; if it is, I'm going to have to wait even longer."

Josef tried to make a point as he pried, "And when her father asks what you do for a living, what are you going to tell him?"

Walter laughed. "Shall I tell him that I'm a member of the Green Gang and make my money on the Shanghai lottery and at the racetrack?"

"Not if you intend to make a good impression on them. Be serious for once, Walter."

"Annalise knows that I have my heart set on becoming a concert violinist. I'm sure they will be impressed. After all, she is studying cello full-time at the Conservatory."

Josef interjected, "So you'll be two starving musicians. Wonderful! If you plan on marrying her, you'd better start saving money. And I wouldn't count on the Berglas family to be your patrons. They aren't the de Medicis."

Walter tied the belt of his bathrobe more tightly. "Papa, maybe you can get me a job with the Möllers. They seem to be very chummy with the Ozers. I saw you chatting with Herr Möller at Mischa's bris, and if I remember correctly, you sat next to him at Lilly's wedding, Mutti. He seemed rather enchanted by you."

Josef answered, "Neither your mother nor I know Herr Möller well enough. You're just going to have to find a part-time job on your own. I can't go calling in any more favors for you after your short stint at Cohen's garage. He told me that you hardly ever showed up on time, and when you did you were trying to engage the workers in a game of cards."

Ignoring this, Walter informed them, "I hear there may be a part-time job at a typewriter repair shop on Avenue Joffre. The owner is a widow from Düsseldorf. She needs help picking up and delivering typewriters, so she can run the shop."

Josef perked up. "Maybe you could even bring in some business from the Conservatory, eh?"

"Aren't we getting ahead of ourselves? I don't even have the job yet."

Eva insisted, "There's no harm in planning ahead, is there? Just try and stick with it for a change. I don't want you leaving another employer in the lurch. You'll soon get a bad reputation in the Jewish community."

Walter kissed his mother on the cheek. "It's probably already too late to worry about that. I suspect that Mr. Cohen has spread lies about me to his friends, saying that I'm unreliable. And quite honestly, I'm not cut out for a laborer's job. I have to protect my hands for the violin. Now, if you'll excuse me, I need to practice before my lesson with Professor Wittenberg."

"But aren't you going to eat something first?"

"No, my stomach is on the fritz. I think I might have had too much to drink last night."

After he left the room, Eva looked at Josef. "If he weren't so handsome and so talented, I'd give him a good swift kick in the tuchus."

Josef added, "And if you didn't spoil him rotten, maybe he'd be more responsible. When I was his age—"

Eva cut him off. "I know all about 'when I was his age.' He's still going through a period of adjustment. We all are." She turned away from Josef, took a sticky sweet *Schnecken* from the sideboard, and closed the curtains.

A light drizzle started in the early morning hours and continued into the afternoon. Walter stepped onto Rue de la Soeur, pulled his hat down over his ears, and opened his umbrella. A cold wind rustled the bare branches of the plane trees and his teeth started to chatter. The street seemed eerily empty for a Monday afternoon, as if people in the French Concession were in hiding, waiting for the all clear signal.

The severity of the morning's news suddenly hit Walter when he saw his fellow students standing in a line in front of the Conservatory entrance as Japanese officials handed out a stack of proclamations:

> As of December 8, 1941, Japan is at war with the United States and Britain. It is promised that law and order will be maintained. Everyone is to carry on as before the Occupation. It should be noted that all clocks will now be set to Tokyo time. In the next few days, armbands will be handed out to all residents of Shanghai. Ethnic Asians, including Filipinos, will be exempt from wearing armbands.[2]

After entering the Conservatory, Walter closed his umbrella and unbuttoned his coat. He was late, but Professor Wittenberg was still with someone in the practice room. Walter could hear the music coming through the partially open door. He recognized the piece, a Fauré barcarolle for piano, though he didn't know which one. The pianist was exceptional. When the music stopped, Walter absentmindedly dropped the piece of paper he held in his hand. Professor Wittenberg applauded the pianist, which was very unlike him, and opened the door all the way.

"Come in, Walter. Let me introduce you to Miss Liang and her student, Miss Chao Chen. Speak English because Miss Chen doesn't understand German."

Walter exaggerated a deep bow. "You play very beautifully, Miss Chen."

Professor Wittenberg explained, "Miss Chen is auditioning for one of my chamber music groups. Or, come to think of it, she might be a good duet partner for you, Walter." Then turning to Miss Liang, he said, "I'm quite impressed with your student. I think I may have a place for her. Please give me a call in January. Let's hope that things will have quieted down by then."

Chao Chen was obviously appreciative of the opportunity. "Thank you for allowing me to play for you today. It was such an honor. I do hope that I have not disappointed you too much."

"To the contrary. I thank you for coming."

Walter bowed again. "*Zaijian,* ladies," and wished them a good day as they left the practice room.

"So, Walter," Professor Wittenberg said as they closed the door behind them, "remind me what piece we are working on. I have had a hard time keeping my concentration today. In fact, I almost cancelled our lesson, but that would have given those Jap bastards the upper hand."

"I'm glad you didn't, Professor Wittenberg. I appreciate that you made such an effort for me."

"Don't flatter yourself, my boy. I have four other students today, and I also wanted to hear Miss Chen play. She's quite good, isn't she?"

"And quite beautiful, if you have a taste for Oriental women, which I do."

Professor Wittenberg tied a knitted wool scarf around his neck. "I feel as if I'm coming down with a cold. This weather is killing me." He rubbed his hands together, trying to force the circulation into his fingers. "All right. What are you working on?"

"The first movement of Johann Sebastian Bach's *Partita in D Minor.*"

"The allemande. Do you need to look at the music?"

"No, I've already memorized it. You always tell me that you cannot master a piece if you are constantly looking at the music."

"Correct. Now, remember that Bach primarily wrote for the organ. You have only four strings at your disposal to communicate the majesty of this piece. Don't forget the vibrato. Without it your playing will sound one-dimensional. *Verstehen?*"

"Yes, Professor." Walter removed his Lowendall violin and bow from the case. Professor Wittenberg played middle C on the piano. When both were satisfied that the violin was properly tuned, Professor Wittenberg signaled for Walter to begin.

The lesson did not go well. Professor Wittenberg found fault at almost every measure, and when the hour was up Walter had barely gotten through half the movement. He was seething inside, but his anger was mostly directly at himself because he knew he had not practiced enough. Too much drinking and too many dalliances had taken their toll.

Professor Wittenberg warned him, "Walter, you are very talented, but you aren't properly applying yourself. And what's more, you look disheveled. I suggest that you spend less time with the ladies and more time with Maestro Lowendall's instrument. You are lucky to have such a beautiful violin. You should show it the respect it deserves."

"My apologies, Professor Wittenberg. Did I do nothing correctly?"

"Well, you have managed to memorize a very difficult piece, but that's as far as it goes. I expect you to practice at least three hours every day until I see you next week. You heard me say that I have you in mind to play with Miss Chen, but if you don't show marked improvement, I'm going to have to find someone else, someone who is up to her ability."

Walter felt stung by his remarks. Since when could he not hold his own with a woman musician, and a Chinese one at that? "I promise I'll work very hard, although I must tell you that my father is pushing me to get a job, which will cut into my practice time."

"I don't need your excuses. I need results. There is nothing wrong with getting a part-time job. When I was your age I worked at a tailor shop in Berlin to help my parents. That's what responsible children do."

Walter nodded.

"Now, go. I have another student who will be here any minute and I need to relax for a few moments. My nerves are rattled by the news of Pearl Harbor. It's really too much to comprehend. And, Walter, be careful out on the streets. I assume you are walking home?"

"Yes."

"By the way, please tell your mother that my wife very much appreciated the special discount she extended for the dress she bought at her store. My wife said that there were so many lovely styles to choose from she had a hard time making up her mind. The dress she bought looks splendid on her. She's planning to wear it to the Conservatory's New Year's Eve party. That is, if there is one."

"I'll let Mutti know. At least one of the Kolbers has done something right, Professor."

"Listen, Walter. I'm being hard on you because you have potential. If you didn't, I wouldn't give you the time of day. I have a long list of students who wish to study with me, but few of them have your talent. Don't throw it away. I expect you to be in top form the next time I see you. Do you understand?"

"Yes, Professor Wittenberg. I won't disappoint you. And then maybe you'll consider me a worthy duet partner for the pretty Miss Chen."

"We'll see. Now don't forget your umbrella. And remember, I expect you to practice at least three hours a day."

Walter sang, "Come rain or come shine."

"Yes. And stop listening to all that American music. Now go."

Walter left the building feeling very dejected. The rain had finally let up, and a ray of sunlight sliced through the branches of the trees. He heard someone call his name. Looking up, he saw Annalise Berglas walking toward him carrying her cello case. She was dressed in a fitted navy-blue cashmere coat, her dark curls tucked under a matching felt hat. She looked the picture of a fashionable Berliner.

Walter's mood immediately lifted. "You are looking ravishing, as always."

"Thank you, but I don't feel so ravishing today. I heard that the Japanese are starting to round up some of the Brits and Americans in the International Settlement. My papa says that they are being dragged off to a detention camp on the outskirts of the city and will be held for God knows how long. There is also talk that they are going to go after the Baghdadi Jews who hold British passports. I have heard that some of the Sassoons have already left Shanghai."

"This city can't run without foreign know-how. The Japanese will soon come to their senses." Walter put his hand on Annalise's shoulder. "So, should we take a gamble that the play has not been cancelled this evening? I have the tickets right here over my heart."

Annalise blushed. "Since you went to so much trouble, we should make the effort. I hear the play is sold out for the entire run."

"Why don't I order a taxi and pick you up at your house? That way I can meet your parents."

"I'm having dinner with them at a German restaurant not far from the Broadway Theater, so just give me my ticket in case I am running late. I'll find you at our seats."

"Very well." He dug into his breast pocket. "You'll at least let me take you home after the theatre?"

"All right. I shouldn't be traveling around the city at night alone now anyway."

Walter leaned over to give Annalise a kiss on the cheek, but she gently pushed him away.

"Not in public, Walter! Someone might see us."

"And so?"

"And so it is not proper." She smiled shyly and then added, "Till tonight."

chapter 24

Caught in the Act

Annalise Berglas still had not arrived at the Broadway Theater. It was 8:45 p.m. and the lights flashed on and off in the lobby, signaling that the audience should take their seats. The usherette handed Walter a program, and he flipped through it in a desultory fashion. On the back cover was an advertisement for a show starring the popular comedian Gerhard Gottschalk. Walter would much rather have seen that than *Fremde Erde*. He kept checking his watch, and at nine o'clock the curtain went up. The seat next to him was still empty at intermission, and so he left the theatre. He wanted an explanation for Annalise's absence. He thought, *She'd better have a very good excuse. I paid a lot of money for the tickets to a play I didn't even want to see.*

A taxicab was waiting curbside near the theatre on Wayside Road. He instructed the driver to take him to one of the brothels near the Bund. He had enough money in his pocket from a winning lottery ticket to pay for one of the fancy Russian girls working there. At least the evening would not be a total loss, but this was certainly not the way he expected it would turn out.

The Indian driver spoke German well enough for Walter to understand him. "Mister, you are pretty young for Madam Colette's."

Walter snapped at him, "Why don't you mind your own business and just take me there?"

Walter paid the fare without leaving a tip and slammed the door. The driver rolled down the window and shouted at Walter, "Next time I see you, I won't bother to pick you up, you cheapskate."

The next morning at breakfast, Eva drilled Walter about his date with Annalise. When he told her that she never showed up, Eva was angry. As his mother, it was her prerogative to point out Walter's shortcomings to him, but when it came to the rest of the world, she expected them to appreciate his background and talent. "Doesn't she know that you're going to be a famous violinist someday and that you come from a fine Viennese family?"

Josef rolled his eyes. "Eva, you aren't doing your son any favors by giving him a swelled head."

Dolfie, dressed in a heavy winter coat, rushed into the dining room. He grabbed a cruller and waved goodbye.

Walter followed his brother out the door with his eyes. "There goes your perfect son, Mutti. You should save your compliments for him, now that he's your full-time schlepper at the factory; and from what I hear, he's doing a very good job. Isn't that right, Papa?"

Josef folded the newspaper and took his reading glasses off. "Walter, what's gotten into you? You really have a vicious tongue. Just because you were stood up by that Berglas girl doesn't mean you have the right to be disrespectful toward your brother."

"You're right. I'm just peeved. I spent a lot of money on those tickets. If not for her I would have been at a comedy club or at home practicing the violin. Professor Wittenberg expects me to put in at least three hours a day. Otherwise he's going to cut me loose, and I can't let that happen."

Eva put her knitting down. "He actually said that? Now that would be a real *schanda*. The only reason I've stopped complaining about living in this godforsaken city is that you have been given the opportunity to study with a world-class violin teacher, and the only thing that keeps me going is to imagine you on the stage of a great concert hall—and I don't mean one in Shanghai. No, I expect to see you at…at…," Eva stuttered. "At Carnegie Hall in New York City."

"Do you hear that, Walter?" Josef dreamed along. "That should be ample motivation for you to buckle down. You don't want to disappoint your mother, do you?"

"Of course not!"

Walter peeked through the window of the rehearsal room to see Annalise with her cello along with four other students. At exactly three o'clock the students gathered their musical scores, packed up their instruments, and walked into the hallway. Annalise was laughing at something one of the boys said to her, but when she caught sight of Walter, and the scowl on his face, her expression turned serious.

"*Entschuldingen Sie*, Ralphie," she said to the boy. "I'll see you tomorrow."

"You sure you don't want to join us at the café for a little sweet?" Ralphie asked.

"No, there's someone waiting for me. I need to speak with him right away."

"As you wish, Annalise."

Trying to keep his temper in check, Walter declared, "I don't like being stood up, Annalise. Where were you last night? Out with another boyfriend? You were supposed to meet me at the Broadway Theater. My God, I had to sit through that insufferable play alone. The only reason I got the tickets was to spend time with you. Believe me, I would much rather have been at a light comedy than being subjected to that lugubrious drivel!"

Annalise whispered, "Please don't make a scene. Let's go outside so I can explain what happened. I don't want anyone hearing what I have to say."

It was a mild and clear winter day, the sun's rays needling their way through the spaces between barren tree branches. Walter put his hat on and buttoned his overcoat. He did not offer to carry Annalise's cello case for her. Pointing to a bench just outside the gates of the Conservatory, she asked, "Why don't we sit there, Walter?"

He retrieved a cigarette, cupped his hand around the match, and took a puff just to annoy Annalise. "Well, what have you got to say for yourself?"

"I don't want to lie to you. I was having dinner with my parents and my brother Joshua at the Colibri Restaurant. There would have been plenty of time for me to get to the theatre before the curtain went up. I was truly excited not only about seeing the play but spending the evening with you. Of course, I didn't tell my parents that I was meeting you. I just said that I was going with a group of friends from the Conservatory, but my brother knew of our rendezvous. Even though I had sworn him to secrecy, Joshua broke his promise, and with good reason."

"So, you still haven't told your parents about me? Why not?"

"Because there are things I know about you that my father would disapprove of. He's very conventional in his ways."

"Such as?"

"That you haven't been able to hold down a job for more than a few weeks."

"Are you referring to that job I had at the garage? I don't see the point of working at some menial job and risking injuring my hands. I must be able to practice."

She ignored his defense and went on. "It wasn't just that you quit. I heard that you were fired for not showing up and for doing a mediocre job. And this happened not once, not twice, but three times. It didn't matter to me, but I knew my father wouldn't have approved. I believed that you'd eventually find steady employment somewhere and then I could introduce you to my parents."

"So you can't stand up for your boyfriend just because he doesn't want to get his hands dirty? Well, guess what. I'm about to accept a job at a typewriter repair shop. The lady who owns it knows I'll be a real asset to her. And I plan on sticking with it. She has a good clientele, and I won't have to get dirt under my nails." Walter made a smoke ring and watched it float into the air. "There must be more to the story than my employment history to explain why you stood me up last night."

"Walter, we live in a small community. There are no secrets. A few of my brother's friends told him you are a serious gambler and, what's more, you've been visiting numerous brothels in the worst part of town." Tears rolling down her cheeks, she said, "It's true, Walter, isn't it?"

Walter was quick to reply. "Your brother is a liar. It wasn't his so-called friends who saw me. It was your brother because he was there too. Once I even saw him coming out of an opium den. Did he tell your father that?"

She was stunned and teary. "No—that can't be true about Joshua."

"Well, take my word for it. And anyway, I was certainly not getting anything from you."

Annalise gasped.

Walter realized he had gone too far, and so he quickly backpedaled. "Annalise, I respect you too much to expect us to have sex just yet. But I can't believe that you would bend to your parents' wishes. I thought you were in love with me."

"I never said I was in love with you, did I?"

"No, but the way you look at me, the way you take my hand and let me kiss you on the lips… What would you call that?" He tried to turn the tables. "I guess you were leading me on. If you weren't serious you should have stopped seeing me and spared me a broken heart, and that is what I have right now. All those girls at the brothels are just playthings. They mean nothing to me. If you said you'd continue seeing me if I stopped going there, I would give them up before you could say '*Shabbat shalom*.' Won't you give me a chance to redeem myself and show you that I can be a faithful boyfriend, someone worthy of your attention?"

"I'm afraid the damage has already been done. I'd appreciate it if you would stay away from me. We can be cordial to each other. In fact, we may even find ourselves sitting in the same orchestra or chamber music group at the Conservatory, but that's as far as our interaction can go."

Walter could feel himself getting angrier and angrier with each word out of her mouth. Suddenly he grabbed her arm. Annalise let out an involuntary scream, and some students coming out of the building looked in their direction.

Walter let go of her arm. "So, your family thinks I'm not good enough for you? Well, the truth is, you're not good enough for me. There are much prettier girls than you in Shanghai who think I'm a catch!"

Tearfully, Annalise turned, picked up her cello case, and ran off.

Walter wanted to chase after Annalise and slap some sense into her. He had never experienced such rage against another person before, but then again, no one had ever exposed his misdeeds so irrefutably. He had been caught with his pants down around his knees, as it were. How could he have let the beautiful Annalise slip through his fingers? In utter denial, Walter told himself, *If it weren't for her snitch of a brother, pretty Annalise could have been mine. I am sure of that.*

But Walter had no genuine feelings of shame or guilt. Struggling to calm his angry heart, he headed toward Avenue Joffre to pay a surprise visit to Frau Weinstein, the owner of RIPO, a typewriter repair shop. He'd talk his way into a job, and this time he'd stick with it just to show everyone how dependable he really was when he put his mind to it. He hummed a few bars from Mozart's *Don Giovanni* and breathed in the refreshing afternoon air, undeterred by what had just happened with Annalise.

chapter 25

The Red Armbands

Chao Chen carried her satchel with her prepared notes for that day's Mandarin lesson with Hans Möller. Hans was a quick learner and challenged her to turn him into a native speaker so that he would live up to the expectations of his uncle, who was grooming him for a top position with Möller & Co. Just thinking about Hans, with his movie star good looks and endearing sense of humor, made her blush. She was infatuated with him. She whispered his name as she lay in bed and dreamed about him at night, imagining that they were seated in a gondola as they floated along the Grand Canal in Venice, traveling together to see the world. She knew that she was suffering from more than a schoolgirl crush. Hans was now a married man, and his wife, Ingrid, was about to have their first child; and still she couldn't stop fantasizing about him.

Passing a newsstand on her way to the Möller villa, Chao Chen bought a copy of the *Chinese Daily*, which reported that Hong Kong had been attacked by the Japanese six hours after Pearl Harbor was bombed. The British crown colony was in danger of falling to the enemy, which meant that every major city on the eastern coast of China would be under the control of the Japanese.

Just as startling to Chao Chen was the news that Hitler had declared war on the United States. The editor opined:

> [F]rom the invasion of Poland through the Battle of Britain, the fall of France, the U-boat war in the Atlantic, and Hitler's invasion of the Soviet Union, America was the most reluctant of warriors. Hitler solved Roosevelt's problem [to

stay out of a war with Germany] by unilaterally declaring war on the United States on December 11, 1941.

The editorial went on to say that Hitler decided "that Japan's bold stroke in the Pacific gave him the opening he needed to control the Atlantic." With the United States embroiled in the Far East, the United States wouldn't, the writer believed, have the resources to pay attention to what was happening in Eastern Europe—it would be Hitler's for the taking all the way to Moscow.

A limousine with the flags of occupied Shanghai was parked in the driveway of the Möller villa. Chao Chen was instructed by the butler to wait outside. The villa's heavy wooden door swung open and a delegation of Chinese officials from the mayor's office stepped outside and into the waiting limousine.

The butler signaled for Chao Chen to come inside. Hans was standing alone in the entryway. She heard a door slam shut at the far end of the hallway. She suspected it was Herr Eric Möller and that whatever had happened between the mayor's entourage and the Möllers had been unpleasant.

Hans greeted her. "Sorry to keep you waiting. My uncle and I had an unexpected visit from Gongbo Chen. Have you ever heard of him?"

"No."

"He is the mayor of Shanghai appointed by President Wang Jingwei, the head of the Nanking Nationalist government. They are both in cahoots with the Japanese. Gongbo Chen is not a bad chap. He went to Columbia University in New York City, and for a time he was allied with Chiang Kai-shek. But things have changed and now he is under the thumb of the Japanese occupiers."

"Why was he here?"

"It's top secret but suffice it to say, he is working with us to make sure our freighters stay out of harm's way going up and down the coast and out to sea."

Chao Chen breathed a sigh of relief. "That's very good news."

"Whether it is or it isn't will depend upon how many pounds of flesh these Jap devils extract from us."

"What does that mean, pounds of flesh?"

"It's a turn of phrase coined by Shakespeare, a metaphor. He used it in a speech delivered by the Jewish moneylender, Shylock, in *The Merchant of Venice*." Then he recited:

> "The pound of flesh, which I demand of him,
> Is dearly bought; 'tis mine and I will have it.
> If you deny me, fie upon your law!
> There is no force in the decrees of Venice.
> I stand for judgment: answer; shall I have it?"

Hans continued, "Shakespeare didn't do the Jews any favors when he wrote *The Merchant of Venice*. Read the play and you'll see why. Before you leave today, I'll see if I can find a copy for you in our library. So, let's get started with our lesson, shall we?"

Chao Chen followed Hans down the paneled hallway, past the now-familiar victory photographs of Eric Möller and his racehorses. Her head was spinning. There was so much she didn't know about the world. Would she ever have the time to continue her education, to learn about Shakespeare and about these mysterious people, the Jews? She knew nothing about world religions, since neither Rui-De Xu nor Ya-Nan were the least bit observant. Their only gods seemed to be money and status.

Hans seemed very preoccupied. At first Chao Chen assumed he had been disturbed by the meeting with the mayor, but she later learned that something far more personal was on his mind.

Chao Chen opened her notebook and indicated for Hans to do the same. "Today we will speak about time and location. Unlike many other languages, such as German and English, the Chinese don't conjugate verbs. There are no plurals or singulars, no past or present tenses, but the context is everything. So, our language is really quite simple in many respects."

"I'm glad you feel that way."

"And as you know, our word order is the same as English. Chinese is not like Latin, where the object of the sentence and the subject of the sentence have their special places. For example, *'woh see-ahng chih fahn,'* which means 'I would like to eat rice.' Can you try saying that?"

Hans repeated it a few times.

"Perfect. Now, if you just get the tones right, you'll be one hundred percent correct. I have my dictionary, which will be helpful going forward when we learn new words and phrases. You're really doing quite well already."

Hans smiled. "Thanks to you."

Chao Chen felt very proud of herself for having earned a compliment from Hans. She turned the page of her notebook. "I thought you might like to cover the ways in which we ask questions."

"Really?" And then Hans laughed because he had just asked a question.

"Yes. We have a miracle word. The word is '*ma*.' Say it using a neutral tone."

"*Ma. Ma. Ma.* I sound like a baby, don't I?"

"Not really. Anyway, you just put the word '*ma*' at the end of a phrase and it becomes a question. Here's an example: '*Ni shi Hans ma?*' which means 'Are you Hans?' but is constructed like a statement: 'You are Hans?'"

He nodded and said, "*Ni shi Chao Chen ma?*"

Chao Chen smiled. "Exactly."

"How do I say, 'Can you speak English?'"

"*Ni hui shuo Yingwen ma?*"

"And so, 'Can you speak Chinese?' must be *Ni hui shuo Zhongwen ma?*"

"You must remember one other thing, however."

"Why is it that women always say, 'There is just one more thing'?"

"I don't know. Maybe it is because we are complicated beings and we don't see things as black-and-white. Our minds see all the nuances of life. The yin and the yang—the light and the dark, the masculine and feminine aspects of the world, the active and the passive—but also the many shades in between."

"Well put, Chao Chen. Do you mind if I tell my wife, Ingrid, what you just said?"

"With pleasure." Chao Chen wished that Hans would not mention his wife's name. For just an hour she wanted to pretend that he was hers forever and ever and that these lessons were a prelude to a romance.

She continued, "The only thing I was going to add is that you cannot use the word '*ma*' when you expect an answer other than 'yes' or 'no.' So when you need to know who, what, when, where, why, and how, the structure of the sentence dictates the question. And the sentence ends with the thing that needs answering. So, for example, you don't say, 'What is this?' You say, 'This is what?' You don't say, 'Who are you?' Instead you say, 'You are who?'"

Chao Chen continued guiding Hans through the process of interrogation, leaving out the one example that would have ripped off the mask hiding her true feelings: *Ni ai wo ma?* Do you love me?

The library clock struck three fifteen. They had gone over their usual time together.

"Ingrid will be wondering where I am. I promised her that I'd see her exactly at three. She's not feeling well."

"Oh, I'm sorry. I hope it isn't anything serious."

"The doctors have put her on complete bed rest for the remainder of her pregnancy. I don't think that Shanghai agrees with her. The weather, the food, and being so far away from her family… It's a lot for her to deal with. But she's being very brave. I'm so proud of her, and before you know it, we'll be parents. It's just a matter of weeks now."

"How wonderful." Chao Chen put her notebook back into her satchel. She hesitated for a moment, then said, "Hans, might I impose upon you for that copy of *The Merchant of Venice?* You have piqued my curiosity about this Shylock and his demand for a pound of flesh. I really know very little about Shakespeare and still less about the Jewish people."

"I really don't have time to look for it now, but I'll have it for you when you come back for our next lesson. I do have something for you right now. In the state I'm in, I almost forgot."

He reached into his pocket and took out an envelope. "Here's your pay for today, but there's something else. I bought two tickets to a recital of European classical music at the Doumer Theatre next month. It's on January 25. In Ingrid's condition, I don't think I should count on going. Would you like the tickets? The concert promises to be quite extraordinary. Many of the finest Jewish refugee artists will be performing. It's a fundraiser for the American Jewish Joint Distribution Committee, which is helping many of the Jewish refugees. We now have more than 2,500 people currently living in five camps, and many more throughout Hongkew and elsewhere who are dependent upon the soup kitchens for at least one meal a day." He handed her the envelope. "I'm sure you'll enjoy the concert. Do you have a nice young man to invite as your escort?"

Chao Chen blushed. "No. I have neither the time nor the interest in striking up a relationship with anyone just now."

"I apologize. I shouldn't have asked such a personal question. Forgive me."

"Of course. I just don't like being put on the spot like that. If you want to know the truth, I've never even had a boyfriend, and now most of the men my age are in the military. So what chance do I have of meeting someone?"

"That is a bit of a dilemma, isn't it? Let's hope, now that the United States is finally engaged in the war on both fronts, we'll see a quick end to the fighting."

Hans led Chao Chen to the front door and held out her coat. She slipped into it and picked up her satchel. There was a pile of red armbands on the antique Chinese altar table in the hallway. Hans held one up. "Have you seen these? A parting gift this morning from the mayor. Orders of the Japanese. It's unbelievable. All residents of Shanghai who are considered enemies of the Japanese are expected to wear these. The Möllers are British citizens, and therefore…" He picked up one with a letter B printed on it. "My uncle is livid, but we have no choice."

Before Chao Chen could react, a woman's voice called out Hans's name from upstairs. "My wife. I'd better go. *Zaijian*, Chao Chen."

"Thank you for the tickets. That was most generous of you," Chao Chen said while walking out the door. Hans stood at the door and waved. Trying not to blush, Chao Chen looked back, "Until we meet again."

chapter 26
To Repair the World

Chao Chen threw the bedcovers off and ran barefoot across the cold wooden floor. It was already seven thirty. The calendar hanging on the wall confirmed what she already knew: today was the benefit concert at the Doumer Theatre. She had been counting the days since Hans Möller gave her the two tickets. Fortunately, Miss Liang, her piano teacher, had agreed to accompany her. She couldn't imagine going to a concert by herself, especially one where most of the audience was Jewish.

She took the blanket off the birdcage and filled the birds' food cup with seeds. Six months earlier two chicks had been born, and now all the mourning doves huddled together on their perch trying to stay warm. Chao Chen added a few spare coals to the brazier underneath the cage to give off some much-needed warmth. It was a marvel to Chao Chen that her birds had procreated in this inhospitable city. Shivering, she wished them all a good morning and then wrapped herself in a wool robe.

Ya-Li was in the kitchen preparing breakfast. "So, what would you like, Chao Chen?"

"I'll just have some tea. I'm too excited to eat anything. I need to be at the theatre by eleven thirty."

"You have plenty of time."

"Not really. I need to practice first. Miss Liang has me on a very strict schedule. She thinks I might one day be good enough to perform before a paying audience."

"Is that what you want for yourself, Chao Chen?"

"Yes, but you're the only person I can admit this to. Rui-De Xu and

193

Ya-Nan only care that I marry a rich man who will take me off their hands. I've told them I have no intention of doing so."

Ya-Li nodded. "Follow your dreams. And if you meet a man whom you truly love, only then should you marry."

"And how is it that you are so modern in your thinking, Ya-Li?"

"It's something your wise father, Magistrate Gan Chen, would have said."

The kettle let out a shrill whistle. Ya-Li poured the boiling water through a sieve filled with tea leaves and handed a cup to Chao Chen. "Now go practice. But don't play too loudly. You don't want to wake the ladies, do you? They need their beauty sleep." Ya-Li tried not to smile, but when Chao Chen burst out laughing, her maidservant joined in.

For the next three hours, Chao Chen was unaware of time passing. She couldn't remember how many times she repeated Franz Schubert's *Impromptu in G-flat Major*, softly caressing the notes to bring out the deep sadness of the music. By the end of her practice session, Chao Chen wept. She felt as if she had achieved a higher level in her playing and that she and the music were one. She thought of the poet Yeats' famous lines:

> O body swayed to music, O brightening glance,
> How can we know the dancer from the dance?

She was still in a trance when Ya-Li announced with some alarm, "Chao Chen, it's already ten thirty!"

"What?"

Ya-Li repeated herself, then warned, "If you want to be at the concert on time, you'd better get dressed. You can't go in your nightclothes, can you?"

Standing among a crowd of Europeans in the lobby of the Doumer Theatre, Chao Chen felt out of place. A movie poster advertising the showing of *Adam Had Four Sons*, starring Ingrid Bergman and Susan Hayward, hung just inside the entrance. The theatre had been rented by the American Jewish Joint Distribution Committee just for the benefit concert this morning, and then it would return to its use as a movie house. Because of the lineup of talent and the urgent need to raise money for the Jewish refugees, the recital was sold out.

Well-dressed Jews, many wearing armbands, enthusiastically greeted one another, the women double-kissing one another on their powdered cheeks and the men doffing their hats. Some of the concertgoers milled about, waiting for the doors to open so they could take their seats, furtively glancing in Chao Chen's direction. She tried to meet their eyes with a shy smile, but it was easier to follow the pattern in the carpet, to examine the garishly painted ceiling or read the slogan on the movie poster: Love Conquers Betrayal. She breathed a sigh of relief when Miss Liang tapped her on the shoulder.

Chao Chen said, "Now there are at least two of us."

"What are you talking about, Chao Chen?"

"I think we are the only two Chinese women here. I feel as if my slip is showing or I have a piece of spinach caught between my two front teeth."

"Nonsense. Let's take our seats."

Chao Chen continued, "I wish I were half as confident as you."

"And I wish I were half as pretty as you. If anyone is staring at you, it is because they admire the way you look in that gray suit. It fits you perfectly. Honestly, with a little more makeup and your hair styled by a professional hairdresser, you could be a calendar girl."

Chao Chen blushed. She was convinced that she was a plain and tidy girl with an unremarkable face and figure, and she definitely was not used to compliments.

Chao Chen picked up the program on her seat. It was written in German and she could not decipher its meaning. Miss Liang came to her rescue. "We are to be treated to eight extraordinary operatic voices—Max Warschauer, Ferdinand Adler, Sabine Rapp, Fritz Melchior, and Rosl Albach Gerstell—singing the works of Gounod, Verdi, Dvořák, Schumann, Schubert, and Strauss."

"I practiced Schubert's *Impromptu* all morning. What else of his is being offered?"

"'*Die Allmacht.*' That means 'The Omnipotent One.' Most of the selections on today's program are religiously inspired. For example, the Dvořák piece 'Gott ist mein Hirte' comes from a psalm that starts with the words 'The Lord is my shepherd.' It's very beautiful. One of the other lines is: 'Yea, though I walk through the valley of the shadow of death, I will fear no evil, for thou art with me.'"

"Is that what the Jewish people believe?"

"I don't know. Perhaps you can ask Hans Möller when you see him again. And please be sure to thank him for these seats. I'm sure he paid a lot of money for them."

Chao Chen was puzzled. "Aren't all the seats the same price?"

"Oh no. These are the premier seats. I wouldn't be surprised if the Möllers are recognized for a special donation by the speakers. And here they come."

The audience quieted as a woman in her late thirties stood at the podium in front of the grand piano. Wearing a simple black dress with a white lace collar and what might be generously referred to as "practical shoes," her short black hair was parted down the middle and curled under her ears. She had a handsome face with intelligent brown eyes that looked out over the audience with a determination that Chao Chen had never seen before in a woman.

With a German translator to her right, the woman spoke in English without notes. "Good day, ladies and gentlemen. I'm Laura Margolis, and on behalf of the American Jewish Joint Distribution Committee and my colleague Manny Siegel, I'd like to thank you all for your presence here today. I'd also like to thank the marvelous artists who have generously given of their time and talent on such short notice to help raise funds for the thousands of Jewish refugees living in squalid conditions in Hongkew's *Heime,* all in desperate need of your help. As all of you are aware, support from the United States has been cut off since the attack on Pearl Harbor. For all intents and purposes, Shanghai's Jewish community is stranded. Funds from the JDC are technically frozen. Hopefully we will be able to prevail on Captain Koreshige Inuzuka to get some help from the Japanese. He was my upstairs neighbor while I was staying at the Cathay Hotel, and we were on good speaking terms. Of course, I have since been removed from the hotel, but I think he remembers me with some fondness. At least until this." She waved the newspaper in her hand, as much a prop as a piece of evidence. "I'm sure that many of you have read the January fifteenth issue of the *Shanghai Times* with the headline STARVING REFUGEES IN HONGKEW, and perhaps you have heard the subsequent radio broadcast before the airwaves were jammed. I don't think Captain Koreshige Inuzuka, who is the head of the Imperial Navy's Advisory Board on Jewish Affairs here in Shanghai, is very happy about this bad publicity and the threat of Jews rioting in the streets; but when a reporter calls me, what am I supposed to do?" She laughed, and with a gleam in her eye, continued. "I responded frankly, saying that the flow of funds into our aid agencies is currently at a standstill. I am hopeful that this matter will be resolved shortly and we will come to some agreement to access frozen funds and receive permission to borrow money either locally or abroad, which will be funneled through the Committee for the Rescue of Eastern European Refugees, headed by your very own Michael Speelman." She raised her eyebrows for emphasis. "Unfortunately, he could not be with us today."

She cleared her throat and continued. "We are also working with the American Red Cross. At present, their hands are also tied, and they have been prohibited from distributing supplies of cracked wheat for our food pantries. We are down to serving just one paltry meal a day to those in need, and there is no guarantee we can continue doing so for very much longer if our negotiations with the Japanese are unsuccessful. I have looked over the number of aid workers on our staff, and we currently have almost five hundred people on our payroll. That is going to have to change. I know that giving our Jewish refugees jobs is important, but filling more empty stomachs, albeit with fewer hands, is more important. And lastly, I have taken a tour of the kitchen facilities. The ovens are in a deplorable condition. We will need to buy updated equipment in order to improve the efficiency of our operation."

Laura Margolis paused again to let her message sink in. For the first time Chao Chen understood the enormity of the Jewish refugee problem in Shanghai. She saw people shifting uncomfortably in their seats, and some audience members coughed into their handkerchiefs.

"I'd like to officially thank some of our most generous donors, including the Möller family, the Toeg family, the Berglas family, and the Ozers. I'd also like to say a special thank-you to those in our community who have opened their homes to many of the refugee children whose parents turned them over to your care to spare them the difficult living conditions in the *Heime*: cockroaches, rats, rampant disease, freezing cold weather, no hot running water or private toilets, and a single meal served off a tin plate washed in cold water. I say to the rest of you, please consider taking in a child if you have a spare room or a spare bed to share. I am sure that your children will learn an important lesson in compassion if they are asked to give up a little space of their own to save another life.

"In the next several weeks, my colleague Manny Siegel and I will be meeting with many of you individually to solicit your support, whether an outright gift, a temporary loan, or shelter. Buying a ticket to today's recital is but the beginning of what will be asked of you. I make no apologies for this. With your help, we will go from strength to strength, and without it, we shall all perish in the end.

"In closing, let me remind you of the wisdom of the sages who taught the value of *Tikkun olam*, which has come to mean 'to repair the world.' That is our duty as Jews. We alone are responsible for improving the world by doing acts of loving kindness.

"And now I will turn the podium over to Maestro Ervin Marcus. May the music you are about to hear touch your hearts and remind you of your humanity."

The audience sat in stunned silence. Then someone clapped, and suddenly there was a tidal wave of applause as Miss Margolis left the stage.

For the next hour, the music of Schubert and Dvořák filled the theatre, triggering memories of family and friends. Frau Klein in seat B10 thought of her mother, Gerda, last seen being dragged by the Nazis out of their spacious apartment in the Ringstrasse; Herr Silberman in seat F20 remembered the faces of his daughters, Perla and Clara, as they waved goodbye aboard one of the *Kindertransport* trains pulling out of the station; Frau Orenstein in seat Q30 repeated to herself the last letter to reach her from her brother, Heime, assuring her that he had made the right decision to go to Palestine "before it's too late."

The recital concluded with a few light pieces, and the lyrics of the songs sung in French, German, and Yiddish filled the theatre with much-needed laughter.

As the crowd pushed its way into the lobby, Chao Chen spotted two young men who looked familiar to her. What was so strange was that they resembled each other: Both had dark, wavy hair and what was commonly referred to as "patrician noses," and they had the same physique: medium height with broad shoulders. But one was casually dressed in a wool turtleneck sweater and sporty pants with a white silk scarf wrapped around his neck, while the other wore a finely tailored suit and an expensive-looking silk tie. Chao Chen pointed them out to Miss Liang.

"Isn't the one wearing the scarf Professor Wittenberg's violin student?" her teacher observed.

"You're right. And that must be his twin. Have you ever seen two brothers look so alike?"

"One looks a bit cocky, and the other looks a bit stiff, I'd say."

Chao Chen nodded. "Maybe I'll see the violinist again, if Professor Wittenberg finally chooses me for one of his chamber music groups."

"With your talent and dedication, I'm hopeful that you'll have the chance very soon."

Outside the theatre, a newspaper boy was hawking the January 25, 1942 edition of the *Shanghai News*. The headlines read: THAILAND DECLARES WAR ON THE UNITED STATES AND THE UNITED KINGDOM. Another article described the Japanese invasion of the Solomon Islands, a British protectorate. A reader looking for news of the war in Europe would have been frustrated that no mention was made of what was happening in the Western Front. What went unreported was the outcome of the Wannsee Conference held in Berlin days earlier, during which the Germans hammered out the final solution to the "Jewish question," leading to the relocation and extermination of the Jews. In the days that followed, news of the conference spread like an iron wind throughout the Jewish community via Moscow radio, which reached all the way to Shanghai.

Prior to the benefit concert at the Doumer Theatre, Laura Margolis called an emergency meeting of the *Jüdische Gemeinde* to inform the leadership that there was only enough money to feed eight thousand starving Jews for four more days or four thousand Jews for eight days. On January 11, 1942, the board elected to feed four thousand refugees and issued a proclamation. Some of the provisions included:

> 1. Each family that cooks its own meal shall also provide a meal for one needy person.
> 2. Families that do not cook their own meal shall pay U.S. $1.25 per month for food.
> 3. Cafés shall collect from each guest a ten percent emergency surcharge, and grocery stores shall collect a five percent surcharge.[3]

These measures were not sufficient to make up for the temporary loss of financial support from the Joint Distribution Committee, however. After weeks of negotiating, Captain Inuzuka agreed to allow the Committee to borrow money locally, with the proviso that only those individuals who were not considered enemy aliens should be allowed to lend money and the names of the lenders would be made known to the Japanese authorities. This second provision was of grave concern; why would one choose to be on a "list" that could be used for nefarious purposes in the future? Who could guarantee that Captain Inuzuka and his minions might not seek revenge against those Jews who had answered the call of their brethren? Despite this major stumbling block, Laura Margolis and Manny Siegel managed to pull together a loan of U.S. $180,000 in April 1942, led by a U.S. $10,000 commitment from Fritz Kauffmann, a longtime German Jewish resident of Shanghai.

Sipping a cup of twice-brewed coffee at breakfast, Josef told Eva, "Fritz Kauffman, who owns his own import-export firm, recently sold some essential goods to the Japanese military and came into a lot of money."

"And where did the rest of the loan money come from?"

"Joseph Bitker and David Rabinovich, the editor of *Unser Leben*, went door-to-door, so to speak, with their *pushke* container in hand and came up with what was needed for the moment. But this is only the beginning, I assure you. I've hesitated to tell you, but that American woman, Laura Margolis, called me the other day and asked for a meeting to discuss how we're going to help."

"And what did you tell her? Did you point out that the Russian Jews have recently built a new club for their members and that they should be solicited for funds? If they have enough money for a new building, they should have enough money to help the poorest among us. This isn't just a problem for the German Jews of Shanghai."

Josef nodded. "I totally agree. The Ozers have already made an outright gift, and I know they are prepared to do more if they are called upon. What I suggest is that we all meet at the factory. We're certainly not rich, but neither are we poor. We do have an obligation to help out, don't you agree?"

"Did you tell Miss Margolis that we're against the Jewish community catering to the Mir Yeshiva students from Poland who've been dumped on us, demanding separate living quarters and kosher meals outside Hongkew?"

"No, I didn't. At the meeting of the Betar Zionist movement we all reluctantly agreed that the rabbi and his students should be given special treatment so that they can observe their strict religious traditions. Besides, a number of the Sephardim are supporting them, and so, for right now, only a small amount of money raised by the JDC is being distributed to them."

Eva pulled the embroidered shawl she was wearing tightly across her ample chest. She squeezed her eyes shut, trying to hold back her tears, but it was no use. Sobbing, her shoulders bobbed up and down as if she were drowning in a sea of her own despair. After several minutes, she regained her composure. Josef sat paralyzed, not knowing what to do or say to comfort her.

Eva confessed to her husband, "Every day I worry that something terrible might happen to you or our children. I worry that the business is going to go to ruin and that we will end up in Hongkew, living in one of the camps." She wiped her eyes and went on. "You know, Josef, when I was listening to the music at the Doumer Theatre, all I could think about was our life in Vienna before the trouble started: our beautiful apartment, our summer vacations at the lake, boat rides up the Danube, and picnics in the Prater. I took it all for granted. I could never have imagined what's happened to us." She sobbed even louder. "I miss our old life, and that's all there is to it."

Josef stood and tenderly caressed Eva's neck. "I'm glad that you're able to express your true feelings to me. You always appear so strong, so in control, but what is the point of lying to each other? But I honestly believe that we will all get through this in one piece."

"And then what?"

"Once the war is over, the best place for us will be Palestine. We'll have many opportunities there, and at least we Jews will be together."

Eva looked horrified. "Josef, I'm not going to that desert called Palestine—and that's that. I'm not made for feeding chickens or digging trenches in the middle of a sun-drenched desert where my skin will turn into shoe leather in a matter of weeks and, instead of the Japanese and Chinese, I'll have to deal with hostile Arabs who would just as soon cut our throats as share a meal with us."

A wind suddenly lifted the dining room curtains and a bolt of lightning, followed by a clap of thunder, announced the arrival of a storm. Eva stood up to close the window just in time to keep the rain from drenching the dining room. A bug skittered across the floor and dove between the floor planks, narrowly avoiding Eva's heel.

Leaving their argument hanging in the humid air, Eva knocked on Walter's bedroom door. "Come in, Mutti," she heard him call.

"Sorry to intrude," she said as she poked her head into his room. "I know you need to practice, but I wanted to make sure your window is closed. I know how engrossed you become. There could have been a flood in here and you wouldn't have noticed."

Walter laughed. "You're right. I am right in the middle of a piece I'm preparing for Professor Wittenberg. He is, at long last, pleased with my progress, and I've been chosen to play a duet with one of the Chinese piano students under his friend's wing. I heard her play a Fauré barcarolle at his studio some time ago, and she is quite talented. Professor Wittenberg assures me that she is up to my standards, but we'll have to wait and see, won't we? Honestly, I'd rather play with one of the German students, but Professor Wittenberg wants to give this Miss Chen a chance."

"What is it that you're going to be playing with her?"

"Beethoven's *Spring Sonata* for violin and piano. Would you like to hear a few measures of the violin part?"

"Of course. I've had a difficult morning with your father. These days, listening to you play is my greatest and only pleasure, to be sure."

"Well then, sit down and I'll give it a go. But just a bit because I need the freedom to make mistakes, and with you here, I want everything to be perfect—and it won't be. I've just started learning the piece."

Walter turned his back to his mother and posed in front of a full-length mirror hanging on the bedroom wall. He brushed his hair back from his eyes and tucked his violin under his chin. Taking a few breaths to put himself in the proper frame of mind, he picked up his bow, glanced down at the music, and began.

Eva sat entranced for every moment, and when he stopped playing, she begged, "Oh, please go on, Walter."

"No, Mutti. It's best that you leave me alone now. I have another two hours of practice ahead of me."

She quietly closed his bedroom door and wandered down the dark hallway to her bedroom. The maid had already straightened up and her bed was neat and tidy, but she felt so tired that she lay down on top of the comforter and closed her eyes, imagining herself applauding as her famous son took yet another bow to shouts of "Encore, encore!"

chapter 27

The Solicitation

Laura Margolis arranged a meeting with Josef and Eva Kolber at the JEKO Factory shortly after Pesach, on April 12, 1942, since fundraising was considered unacceptable during the holiday. Josef had his son-in-law join them, thinking that his advice would be helpful in negotiating with this formidable representative of the JDC.

Eva met Laura Margolis at the front door of the factory. "I do hope you didn't have too much difficulty finding us,"

Laura Margolis replied, "It took me almost two hours to get here. I am staying with a Russian family not far from Hongkew, but with public transportation almost nonexistent now, it took me longer than I expected. But not to worry. A small inconvenience for what I expect will be a very worthwhile meeting."

Eva led Miss Margolis through the factory. The Chinese laborers sat hunched over their sewing machines, not even bothering to look up as the two women passed. Many stations were unoccupied due to the dramatic decline in business.

Eva pointed this out to Miss Margolis. "We have had to let some of our employees go in the last month or so. Our most important clients, the major department stores, cut their orders significantly. And what's worse, we have had a tough time getting the piece goods. The Japanese now control all transportation and most of the supply of raw cotton, and they are strangling the Chinese-owned mills here in Shanghai, normally our best suppliers."

"Hmm, so I've heard."

Eva continued, "And what material is available to us is costing us a fortune. Runaway inflation is going to strangle us."

"I understand your dilemma, Frau Kolber. But I cannot concern myself with macroeconomics. I must deal with what's right under my nose, and that is putting food into the mouths of starving Jewish refugees and clothes on their backs. I'm sure you understand that, don't you?"

Eva felt her face turning red from anger and then embarrassment, and she sputtered, "Yes, yes, of course. Now, if you'll follow me upstairs, we'll be more comfortable." Eva grabbed the handrail and took one slow step after another. At forty-seven, her arthritis was getting worse in the humidity of Shanghai. Some days she felt as if she were becoming a cripple, but sheer stubbornness carried her onward.

Opening the door to the office, Eva said, "I'd like to introduce you to my husband, Josef. You have already met our son-in-law, David Ozer. He is married to our daughter Lilly, who is at home taking care of our grandson, Mischa."

Laura Margolis seized the opportunity. "How lucky you are to have a grandson. *L'dor vador* – 'from generation to generation.' So many in Hongkew are not so fortunate. Why, in just the past few weeks, we have had several infant deaths. But I'm sure you already know that the conditions in the *Heime* are becoming grimmer by the day."

Josef pointed to a chair in front of his desk. "Please sit down, Miss Margolis. May I offer you some coffee?"

Laura Margolis shook her head. "No, thank you, Herr Kolber. You know, I never understood how you all insist on drinking hot coffee even in this heat and humidity. I saw the same phenomenon when I was working for the JDC in Havana. But I would appreciate a glass of water, if you don't mind."

Josef spoke into the intercom. "Dolfie, can you bring a glass of water to the office for our guest?" He looked back to Miss Margolis. "My son will be up in just a minute."

Miss Margolis took a report out of her briefcase and ran her finger down a list. "K-O-L – Kolb…Kolber. Ah, I see that you have two sons. Twins, I believe. Is that correct?"

Eva jumped in. "Yes, Dolfie and Walter, who's working part-time for Frau Weinstein at the RIPO typewriter repair shop while at he same time he's taking violin lessons with Professor Wittenberg at the Shanghai Conservatory."

"That job must be quite recent. I don't see his employment information noted here. We are trying to keep accurate records of all the Jewish refugees for planning purposes. Unfortunately, the Japanese have requested copies as well."

Josef observed, "No good will come of that." Remembering he was on the Nazi's list in 1938, he pulled at the collar of his shirt as if it was suddenly too tight.

Dolfie brought a glass of water on a tray and placed it on his father's desk in front of Miss Margolis. "It's still a little warm, I am afraid. I boiled it just to make sure it would be safe to drink. We've run out of bottled water. I'm very sorry."

Miss Margolis waved her hand in the air. "That's the least of my problems." She took a healthy gulp to quench her thirst. Without bothering to introduce him, Josef instructed Dolfie to get back to work. "And close the door behind you."

Miss Margolis cleared her throat. "I'm sure you know why I'm here. Now, what are you prepared to do to help us?"

There was dead silence. Josef touched a pile of papers on his desk. "These are our unpaid bills." He then pointed to a much smaller pile. "And these are our pending orders. In a nutshell, we are barely managing to keep the business afloat. And to add to our problems, we have a loan outstanding with one of the Chinese-owned banks. They expect to be paid every month, come rain or shine."

"I've already spoken with Mr. Chen at the bank. He is willing to restructure your loan and reduce your monthly payments for the foreseeable future in consideration for keeping your existing Chinese workers on the payroll, even at a reduced salary."

Josef raised his eyebrows. "That comes as wonderful news. I had no idea the JDC had so much influence with the bank."

"The bank has seen many of their borrowers forced out of business by the Japanese, and so they have no chance of being repaid for those loans. At least you are still in business. And the Japanese have not come knocking at your door…like the Nazis did in Vienna." Miss Margolis took a sip of water and then continued. "One of the biggest problems we are facing among our refugees, besides food shortages and disease, is a lack of clothing. Many of the Jews are wearing the same heavy suits and dresses they wore when they stepped off the boat. Recently, some of the refugees have taken the Red Cross burlap bags used for wheat, and turned them into lightweight pants and shirts. They hate being helpless. They have even put in some vegetable gardens in the *Heime* and are turning over the produce to the soup kitchens as a way of making some contribution."

Eva observed, "How admirable. But what is it you need from us?"

"We'd like JEKO to manufacture basic clothing: white shirts and black pants for the men and housedresses for the women. Given your excess capacity, do you think this will be possible?"

"But who will pay for what we manufacture?"

"We can't possibly pay you much, but we can certainly see to it that your machines are not idle."

Josef replied, "Maybe so, but there's another problem. Where do we get the fabric to fill these orders?"

Josef's son-in-law, who had been listening attentively, knew this was the moment for him to step in. "I've recently spoken with my good friends at Guojun Liu's textile group, and they expect to be back in business by May. The group's gotten the go-ahead from Japanese officials by promising their support of Wei Wang's collaborationist government. They've been given assurance that there will be enough electricity to keep at least seven thousand spindles running at their factory in the International Settlement. Also, Liu has successfully speculated in various currencies and commodities on the side, and so I'm sure he'll be willing to sell us his fabric on good terms."

"So it seems that all the pieces are falling into place," Miss Margolis confirmed, "but we still need to settle on a price that the JDC can pay you." Referring to a second list in her briefcase, she asked, "How much would you charge?"

Josef answered, "Our price will depend upon how much we will have to pay for labor and materials."

Not missing a beat, Miss Margolis responded, "All right. Why don't we just settle on a percentage over your cost? Let's say three percent?"

Josef coughed and took a gulp of coffee. Before he could clear his throat, Eva countered. "I was going to offer five percent over our cost, but why don't we split it down the middle?" She stared at Miss Margolis, waiting for her to blink.

Finally, Miss Margolis made a proposal. "Shall we say five percent on the first thousand units, four percent on the second, and three percent for all orders over and above that? Hopefully by the time we hit five thousand units, the war will be over."

Eva agreed. "I think we can live with that."

Then Miss Margolis informed them, "Oh, and by the way, for this you must hire Jewish labor and also provide them with lunch every day."

And just when Eva and Josef thought negotiations were over, Miss Margolis added, "Not that we question your integrity in any way, but we will need our accountants to look over your books on a monthly basis just to make sure everything is kosher, and you are living up to this agreement. Really, this provision is only because we have so many Jewish accountants looking for something to do."

Josef, who didn't appreciate his integrity being questioned, was ready to kick Miss Margolis out of his office, but he held his temper in check. "That won't be a problem. We're already providing monthly reports to the bank and to our partner, Herr Jedeikin."

Miss Margolis asked, "Samuel or Louis?"

"Samuel. We've been partners in JEKO from day one. He secured the lease on this building from the Kadoories and contributed most of the capital. We contributed our sewing machines and sweat equity. It's been an amicable arrangement."

"Others have not been so fortunate, which is why I knew you would bend over backward to help us out," Miss Margolis said with a smile.

Eva stood up. "Well, I guess our business is done here. Miss Margolis, thank you for everything you are doing, under what is surely a daunting and unpredictable set of circumstances. Every day there is a new edict and a new set of problems."

"Frau Kolber, our dire circumstances in Shanghai are nothing compared to what is happening to the Jews in Europe. Now, may I thank you all for your generosity and wish you a good day. No need for you to show me out. I can find my way."

chapter 28

Death at Sea

Chao Chen dispatched Ya-Li to the St. John's University campus on Jessfield Road to borrow a copy of Shakespeare's *The Merchant of Venice* from their library. Chao Chen read the play three times, trying to understand the English text. But without a background in European and Jewish history, she had many questions she hoped that Hans Möller could answer: Why were the Jewish people so maligned? Was there really a ghetto in Venice, and why could the Jews not walk freely about the city? Were Jewish people allowed to marry outside their faith?

This was the first time she would see Hans since he had become a father and since he had been promoted to general manager of his uncle's shipping company. Walking briskly toward the Möller villa despite the sweltering August heat, Chao Chen recited one of her favorite passages from *The Merchant of Venice*, Lorenzo's speech to his bride, Jessica:

> "The man that hath no music in himself,
> Nor is not moved with concord of sweet sounds,
> Is fit for treasons, stratagems, and spoils.
> The motions of his spirit are dull as night,
> And his affections dark as Erebus.
> Let no such man be trusted. Mark the music."

She thought, *Jessica is fortunate to have found a man with such exquisite sensibilities.* Could there be such a man, or did he exist only in Shakespeare's play? Mulling over this puzzle, she nearly walked right past the stone lions at the entrance to the villa.

Before ringing the doorbell, Chao Chen wiped the perspiration from her neck and quickly reapplied her lipstick. Tucking her damp hair behind her ears, she waited patiently for one of the servants to open the door. After waiting a few minutes, she thought it odd a servant had not answered the door, so she rang the bell a second time. When the door finally opened, she was surprised to see Hans's cousin Deirdre standing there dressed in black, her eyes red and swollen from crying.

"What are you doing here, Chao Chen?"

"Hans and I made an appointment several weeks ago to resume our lessons today. I didn't want to disappoint him, and so here I am. Did I make a mistake?"

"Someone from my father's office should have called you, but clearly, they were not made aware of my cousin's appointment with you." She gestured for Chao Chen to come inside.

The two women stood in the dark hallway. Chao Chen heard a baby crying upstairs, and then the soothing voice of a woman singing a familiar Chinese lullaby to calm the baby: "Oh little lotus flower, gone, gone too soon." Porcelain vases filled with flowers decorated the side table in the hallway, emitting a lovely perfume.

Deirdre said, "Please, sit down. What I'm about to say is very difficult for me. I know that you were extremely fond of Hans. I could see it in your eyes and the way you spoke to him. I know he was fond of you as well." Chao Chen blushed. *Was I so transparent?*

Deidre continued. "Don't be embarrassed. My cousin was a charmer. Everyone loved and admired him." She stopped for a moment, took a deep breath, and then continued. "Hans was sent out on one of Daddy's freighters a week ago into the South China Sea. All our ships fly the British flag, but we were assured by the maritime officials reporting to the Japanese that the ship would be guaranteed safe passage. But the telegram from Shanghai's mayor never made it to the proper authorities, and a Japanese warship attacked the freighter. Eight people on board were killed, including my cousin."

Chao Chen gasped. "This can't be!"

"Sadly, it's true. Hans's body was transported back to Shanghai and the funeral was held yesterday. He is buried in our family's cemetery plot here in Shanghai, but when the war is over, he will be reinterred in Stockholm, close to his parents. As you can hear, his baby son is with us for now, and his widow as well. We're all doing what we can to help her, but she's inconsolable. There are days when I feel the same way, but we must go on, mustn't we?"

Chao Chen was stunned, and as she wept, she said, "I don't know what to say."

Pointing to the vases, Deirdre took in a deep breath. "The flowers keep coming. I've already had to throw out those that are more than a day or two old. The climate here in Shanghai is inhospitable to living things—except mosquitoes and flies."

Chao Chen wistfully observed, "It seems as if some of the most beautiful things have but a short life, like flowers and fireflies and music. A note disappears into the ether as soon as it is struck."

"You're right." Deidre stood up. "Since you went to all the trouble of coming here today, it's only fair that I pay you for Hans's lesson." She opened a drawer in the sideboard, took out several American dollars, and handed them to Chao Chen.

"Please, I can't let you do that."

"I insist. Hans told me you're studying to become a concert pianist. Consider this a contribution from the Möller family to your career, Chao Chen. Hans would have insisted too. Now, if you'll excuse me, I must look after Ingrid. Perhaps we shall see each other again under happier circumstances."

The street seemed to swim in front of Chao Chen's eyes, blurred by her tears. She looked away as a caravan of trucks raced down Seymour Road, the Japanese flag displayed on the front hoods. She wanted to scream, "Murderers!" But instead she bowed her head, praying that they would not stop and arrest her. After all, she was their enemy, and they were hers.

Chao Chen had forgotten her house key. Ya-Li opened the door, and Chao Chen collapsed crying into her arms. "He's dead. He's dead."

"Who, my little lamb?"

"Hans Möller." She explained the circumstances of his death and then confessed, "I loved him. I thought I'd go insane all these months waiting to see him. And now he's gone from my life forever."

Ya-Li stroked her hair and held her tightly. "Shh, my dearest. We don't want Rui-De Xu hearing you cry, do we?"

"I'd rather die than have her suspect that I even cared about Herr Möller. Ya-Li, you must tell her what happened. I don't have the strength to give her the terrible news."

"If you wish, but she'll berate me once she finds out that you came home empty handed. She's been counting on her share of your wages."

Chao Chen's grief suddenly turned to rage. "You can tell Rui-De Xu that I have her money. The Möllers are the most generous people. Despite all that they have suffered, they wanted to pay me. Can you believe it?"

Ya-Li observed, "I'm glad you took the money. I overheard Rui-De Xu telling Ya-Nan that she wanted the driver to go to Sun Sun to buy her a pot of French rouge before the store runs out."

Chao Chen couldn't help saying the words that flew out of her mouth: "She is pathetic. People are starving to death in Shanghai and she's trying to look like a twenty-five-year-old. And where's the driver going to get the petrol? The boulevards are empty except for German and Japanese vehicles. Soon we'll need a horse to pull our car."

Ya-Li knew should could be honest with Chao Chen. "Rui-De Xu is living in a dream world. She's going to be fifty-nine this year. I think she's beginning to take leave of her senses."

Chao Chen screamed, "I wish she were dead instead of Hans," and then ran to her bedroom, leaving Ya-Li to deal with Rui-De Xu.

Chao Chen lost her appetite, refusing to eat dinner that night or the next day. Her eyes burned from crying, her stomach was in knots, and she had a splitting headache. She couldn't chase the images of Hans from her head, and besides occasionally feeding her mourning doves, she could barely rouse herself from her bed. She kept the curtains closed despite the oppressive heat. Eventually hunger pains drove her into the kitchen, and Ya-Li prepared a light meal for her.

Chao Chen handed her *The Merchant of Venice*. "Ya-Li, can you take this back to the library? It's long overdue, and I can't bear to look at it another minute. It reminds me of Herr Möller and I am trying my best to stop grieving, but I can't seem to pull myself out of the darkness. Honestly, there are moments when I think about suicide."

Ya-Li gasped. "Chao Chen, you have your whole life ahead of you."

"I'm twenty-four years old and I have accomplished so little. Who would really care if I disappeared? My mother wants only one thing from me, money. And where am I going to get another job? The city is overrun with refugees who are far more talented than I am, and they are standing in long lines at soup kitchens in Hongkew, just hoping for one hot meal a day."

"Don't speak this way. You and I will figure something out." Ya-Li stirred the soup she was making, and then, as if its vapors had given her an idea, she said, "I heard that there is a glove business operating out of the villa across the street. Perhaps you could apply for a job there. Their Chinese maid said that a Frau Götz from Berlin runs the place."

"Why would she hire me?"

"Well, they might need someone who is fluent in Mandarin and English." And then she lowered her voice. "And there are several members of the Green Gang living not far from here. They have all the money in the world, collecting bribes and running the best nightclubs that are still in business. Their wives and mistresses only want the finest of everything, and I've been told that the gloves being made across the street are very fashionable. So maybe you could sell to them."

Chao Chen wrapped her arms around Ya-Li. "At least there might be a chance that they would hire me."

"And then you won't have to give up your piano lessons."

Just then the telephone interrupted their conversation. Chao Chen picked up the receiver quickly, before her mother would think to listen in on the call.

It was Miss Liang. "Chao Chen, I just heard from Professor Alfred Wittenberg at the Conservatory. He has asked that you audition for him next week, on September 14, just after the Jewish New Year. He says that he has a violin student who might make a good duet partner with you. I think he said that it's that young German man we met some months ago, Herr Walter Kolber. I need you to come into my studio tomorrow so that we can get you ready."

"I'll be there, Miss Liang." Chao Chen put the receiver back in its cradle.

Ya-Li said, "Judging by the smile on your face, you must have had good news."

"Finally some good news. Professor Wittenberg is at last ready to audition me."

"So life isn't so grim after all, is it, Chao Chen?"

"Now I have a reason for being."

"And someday I'll be sitting in a concert hall listening to you play, then standing up with the rest of the audience to show our appreciation for your artistry. It is only a matter of time."

"One step at a time, Ya-Li. First I have to impress Professor Wittenberg."

chapter 29

The Typewriter Repair Shop

RIPO, the typewriter repair shop on Avenue Joffre, the main artery of the French Concession, was not far from the Cathay Theatre. Walter stopped to look at the movie poster advertising *The Shanghai Gesture* directed by Josef von Sternberg and starring Gene Tierney, Walter Huston, Victor Mature, and Ona Munson, who played a Chinese madam. Reading the advertisement on the poster, he laughed to himself. Yes, Shanghai was a city "where almost anything can happen…and does!" Walter was only twenty, but he indulged in every vice the city offered—usually without getting caught. He had recently hatched a new scheme to amuse himself, and he was about to put it in motion.

The bell over the RIPO door gave a happy tinkle as he entered the shop. Frau Weinstein was on the telephone and signaled for Walter to put on a jacket with the initials RIPO embroidered on the label. As Walter's eyes adjusted to the dimly lit space, he saw an array of Corona, L. C. Smith, Underwood and Royal typewriters sitting on the shelves. Some of models made at the turn of the century had been discontinued, and so customers came to Frau Weinstein's shop to have old parts replaced. The chirpy tone in her voice meant she was speaking to a customer.

"Ah yes, Herr Orenstein. My repairman, Mr. Deng, will be on his way momentarily. What is the model of your typewriters at the Shanghai Conservatory? Very good. We also have exactly the ribbons you need." She paused. "Thank you for your business, and have a good day."

After hanging up she addressed Walter. "Your visit to the accounting office at the Conservatory paid off. We have just gotten our first order to service their typewriters. I must say, Walter, you landed a big one."

"I promised you when you hired me that I'd do my best to bring in business, and I hope I can continue to prove myself a worthy employee."

"So far, so good. Of course, you will keep it up, won't you?"

Mr. Chun Hsien Deng appeared from his workshop located just on the other side of the shelves. Bent over from an injury he had suffered at the hands of a Japanese sentry some weeks earlier, he carried his worn and heavy black leather bag with difficulty. Inside the bag were typewriter spare parts, screwdrivers and pliers, and new ribbons and cleaning solutions.

Frau Weinstein instructed him to go directly to Herr Orenstein's office at the Conservatory. "Unfortunately, it's probably going to take you the rest of the afternoon to get there and back."

"No worries, missy. I walk."

"Take Herr Kolber's bicycle. He has a basket on the handlebars. You don't mind, do you, Walter?"

"Just so long as you get back by six, Mr. Deng." He hated to admit that he was still living at home because it made him sound like a child, but he explained, "Mutti expects me to join them for Shabbat dinner this evening. My father's business partner, Herr Jedeikin, and his wife are invited, and she'd like me to play the violin for them." He pretended to hold up his violin, fingering the imaginary strings and moving his bow. "Mutti likes to show off my talents."

"I would do the same if I had a son with such a gift. Unfortunately, Herr Weinstein and I could never have children. We were married for only five years when he died in an auto accident. He hit his brakes on a patch of ice in the Austrian Alps and ended up at the bottom of a cliff. He always did drive too fast. But what's the point of dredging all that up?" She adjusted the collar of her blue-green cotton dress that had buttons from the neckline to the hem. "Life goes on, doesn't it?" Then, touching the nape of her neck, she added seductively, "Although it can be awfully lonely sometimes."

Mr. Deng left the shop, which was now empty except for Frau Weinstein and Walter. Walter couldn't help staring at her ample bosom.

"I just had my hair bleached to make it look blonder. I didn't want those German guttersnipes to mistake me for a Jew now that I've converted to Christianity."

Walter raised his eyebrow. "Really?"

"Yes. There are Christian missionaries in Shanghai eager to sell conversions. I thought that it would be best to do so if I expect to ride out this war. I was never very religious anyway, and so it makes no difference to me whether I walk around as a Christian or a Jew. You aren't shocked, are you, Walter?"

Walter answered diplomatically, "Who am I to judge you, Frau Weinstein? The war makes us do strange things just to stay alive. I've heard that a few young Jewish girls in Hongkew are keeping company with Japanese officers to make money and earn favors. Their mothers are just as ashamed as their daughters, but what else can they do?"

"I've seen the way those little yellow arrogant bastards look at me on the street. I've attracted their attention from time to time."

Now was the moment Walter had been waiting for. "Well, you've certainly attracted mine, Frau Weinstein." He slipped behind the counter and put his arm around her slim waist, and then, without hesitating, kissed her on the lips.

He expected that she might slap him on the face, but she leaned into him. "There is a cot in the back where Mr. Deng sleeps when he is here late. If we hurry, we can enjoy ourselves for a few moments." She picked up a sign that read: Out to Lunch. Be back at 2 p.m. and hung it on the door.

Laughing, she led Walter into the dark back room. He noticed the smell of ink and grease underneath the scent of her intoxicating perfume. Hanging his jacket on a hook, he turned away to take his damp shirt and pants off. When he turned around, Frau Weinstein was naked except for the tiny gold cross and chain she wore around her neck. At nearly thirty she still had a shapely figure, and she didn't hesitate to show herself off.

Walter was at ease in bed, and he matched Frau Weinstein's ardor. He proved himself to be a skillful lover, willingly accommodating whatever she wanted from his body. When they finished, Walter tried to engage Frau Weinstein in playful banter, but she quickly changed the mood. Throwing off the covers, she shoved Walter onto the floor.

In a petulant voice, Walter asked, "Why did you do that? I thought we might go another round. You certainly seemed to be enjoying yourself."

Frau Weinstein buttoned her dress. "I'm expecting a delivery any time now." Standing in front of a mirror, she vigorously brushed her blond hair and reapplied her lipstick. As Walter finished putting his trousers back on, she warned, "If you intend to end up on this cot again, and I assume you do, you must promise you'll tell no one. Is that understood?"

"Of course, Frau Weinstein. A woman needs to protect her reputation, especially if she hopes to marry again. What would a potential suitor think about a thirty-year-old woman sleeping with a twenty-year-old?"

"Ouch. But I suppose I deserved that. Now, finish getting dressed and straighten up the cot. We don't want to shock Mr. Deng, do we?"

Walter shrugged his shoulders. "I really don't care what that little Chinaman thinks. He'd just better bring my bicycle back on time. If I wasn't trying to please you, I never would have let him take it. Who knows? What if he tries to sell it?. Those people can't be trusted."

"You're wrong about Mr. Deng. He's a perfectly honorable man, and he desperately needs this job. If you expect me to keep you on here, Walter, you'd better adjust your thinking."

"That's the second request you've made of me in less than five minutes." He bowed and then broke out laughing. "Is there anything else my lady wishes me to do?"

"Go out and take that sign off the front door. We don't want to lose a customer, do we?"

chapter 30

Shabbat Dinner

Eva stood back to admire the Shabbat table. She had made sure the maid, Mei-Li, had polished the silverware, the candlesticks, and the Kiddush cup and that the Meissen chinaware and the Czech crystal wine goblets were placed correctly. Perhaps the table would distract her guests from the meal; she knew that the brisket was tough, and she had had to substitute yams for boiled white potatoes. Normal staples were becoming harder to come by, but she was able to find uncontaminated flour, fine chocolate, and apricot jam to bake a *Sachertorte*. She could have bought a cake at one of the many bakeries in Little Vienna, but she wanted to show off her culinary skills so that the Jedeikins would realize that she was not only a clever business woman but a fine hostess from a fine Jewish family.

Eva looked at herself in the mirror hanging over the sideboard. Her hairdresser, Margot Rosengart, had given her a modern style, which hid some of the gray streaks that had seemingly appeared overnight. Eva had to admit that, at forty-seven, she was beginning to show signs of aging; but fortunately, she had an instinctive sense of style and knew how to enhance her best features: her creamy complexion and her deep, chocolate-brown eyes. Lilly had designed a new dress for her, and she thought that this evening would be the perfect occasion to debut it. The seamstresses at the Vienna House of Fashion had cut and fit the dress to perfection. No matter what Frau Jedeikin wore, Eva felt confident that her simple dark green matte dress with its embellished waistband was nonpareil. So as not to look overdone, she chose an understated necklace of jet beads and matching earrings. She always told her customers that "simplicity is often elegant," and this was true for her as well.

Eva heard the front door open. It was her husband and Dolfie.

"Sorry we're late, my dearest." Josef was obviously annoyed. "I hope you weren't worried. Dolfie and I had to wait almost an hour for a trolley car, and when one finally arrived, we were packed in like sardines into a can. We had to stand for the entire trip. There are fewer automobiles out and about, and public transportation is becoming unreliable." After putting down his briefcase, Josef kissed his wife on the cheek.

Eva was impatient. "Our guests are due in half an hour! You'd both better hurry, change your shirts and freshen up. I hope that there is enough hot water."

"We'll make do. And where is Walter? I don't hear him practicing."

"He telephoned from the typewriter repair shop. Something about having to wait for the repairman to return his bicycle."

And on that note, Walter appeared. He smiled and explained, rather sheepishly, "I had quite a workout getting home. I blew a tire on my bicycle and had to run with it the entire way. And to top it off, it's beginning to rain and I forgot my coat." He started unbuttoning his shirt, which clung to his toned body.

"Do that in your room. I don't want the maid seeing you half-naked."

"She might enjoy the view."

Eva drew the curtains across the dining room windows. She didn't want anyone who passed by to see the family lighting Shabbat candles. She remembered how, earlier in the week, as they were leaving shul after Yom Kippur services on September 21, 1942, she overheard Robert Bitker, the leader of the Zionist movement in Shanghai, telling Josef that the presence of Nazi officials in Shanghai had risen dramatically since the summer.

"We estimate that there may be as many as four hundred high-ranking Nazis in the city. And naturally, they have their eyes on all of us."

Josef pondered, "I wonder why the interest in Shanghai?"

"It's simple. Hitler is hell-bent on eradicating the Jews wherever they are and whatever the cost. If he thinks he can pressure the Japanese to do his dirty work by sending a few hundred of his henchmen to Shanghai, he will. What's not clear is whether the Japanese will ultimately cooperate with the Nazis."

Eva flinched as she was brought back to the present moment when Josef called out, "Our guests have arrived. I'll answer the door."

There was a flurry of activity as Mei-Li took coats and umbrellas while Josef and Eva greeted the Jedeikins with "*Shana Tovah*" and introduced the couple to Walter.

Samuel pumped Walter's hand. "Ah, the violinist. Your father promised me you would play something for us after dinner. Am I right?"

"Yes, sir, with pleasure."

Samuel then turned to Dolfie and slapped him on the back, exclaiming, "Good to see you, my boy. Your father tells me he's put you in charge of our refugee seamstresses and cutters at JEKO. And I understand that you are helping your uncle Herman with the bookkeeping. Keep it up and you might have your own operation someday. I speak from experience. Hard work always pays off—especially in difficult times."

Sonia Jedeikin interrupted her husband. "Let's not talk about work tonight. This is a social occasion."

Eva turned to Josef. "Why don't we all proceed into the dining room and welcome the Shabbat?"

After the women lit the Shabbat candles and everyone recited the blessings over the wine and bread, Walter pulled out Frau Jedeikin's chair and Dolfie did the same for his mother. Eva was pleased that Walter seemed to be on his best behavior. Eva waited for Mei-Li to serve dinner before telling Sonia how much she admired her silver-gray pearl necklace.

Sonia smiled and looked adoringly at her husband. "I know I said we shouldn't discuss business, but perhaps this is an exception. Samuel gave these to me. He is in partnership with an Italian here in Shanghai. They are importing South Sea Island pearls like mine. When the war is over, they plan to export them throughout Europe. Jewelry stores there are anxious to get their hands on them."

Josef looked surprised. "Samuel, things must have turned around for you since you informed me by letter that you couldn't put any more money into JEKO."

"Fortunately, they have. Right now my brother Louis and I are buying up real estate here in Shanghai."

"I recall that you were looking into another business in order to diversify your investment portfolio."

"Yes. I'm the sole investor and operator of the Duncan Metals and Fastener Company over on Great Western Road in the International Settlement. It's not far from the Sung Sung Dairy where most of the café owners buy their milk."

Eva joined in. "And your brother, what business is he involved in?"

"He currently owns a paint manufacturing company, a good business to be in during wartime, what with ships, buildings, and all that. Both he and I have had to reinvent ourselves, so to speak. As you know, before Louis came to Shanghai, he lived in Switzerland where he ran the family watch business. I was in Kobe, Japan handling our interests there. By '37 the family business was practically kaput. Louis was afraid that Hitler might invade Switzerland, and so he started making plans to leave."

Josef chimed in. "So far Switzerland has maintained its status of armed neutrality, but who knows how long that will last."

"My brother's sentiments exactly. In 1940, he and his wife, Vera, left with their children for Shanghai. We had already moved here, and our son Leon was born right here in Shanghai. Thank God we are all together. Family means everything to me. Walter and Dolfie, you both must know how special it is to have a brother. Louis and I are best friends, and our wives get along beautifully as well. I hope that someday you will be as fortunate when you marry. Do either of you have a special girl? I know a few lovely Jewish women about your ages who are looking to get married and raise a family."

Seizing the opportunity to speak, Walter disclosed, "Dolfie already has a serious girlfriend. I like her. As for myself, I don't have time for a real romance. I'm working part-time at the RIPO typewriter repair shop and practicing the violin three hours every day. Plus, I have my weekly lessons with Professor Wittenberg at the Conservatory. It's about all I can manage. But maybe someday I'll find the right girl who loves music and who loves me."

Eva intended to put a stop to this chatter. Walter was revealing too much about himself when the two families barely knew one another. She rang the dinner bell, signaling Mei-Li to clear the dinner plates and serve dessert and coffee. She felt fairly certain that her *Sachertorte* would be more than satisfactory, but she wasn't so sure about the coffee; it had taken Mei-Li several trips to market to find roasted beans. But at least there would *be* coffee. They had gone without it for several weeks.

Eva was pleased to see that there was not a morsel of *Sachertorte* left on anyone's plate when dessert ended. She suggested, "Why doesn't everyone bring their coffee into the living room. Tonight, instead of singing one of the traditional Shabbat songs to end our evening together, Walter will play a few short selections on his violin."

Samuel suddenly announced, "I have some rather unpleasant news, which I thought you should be aware of. It's probably best to tell you now so that Walter's music can bring us some solace, as music always does."

Eva felt a sudden chill. The rain beat against the windowpane behind the drawn curtains.

"My brother is privy to a lot of intelligence about Nazi activity in Shanghai."

Josef commented, "I went by the German Club the other day, and would you believe it, there were youngsters in Nazi uniforms marching on the grounds and singing fight songs as if they were parading through the streets of the Third Reich."

Samuel nodded. "Nazi SS Colonel Josef Meisinger arrived in Shanghai from Tokyo in July. He's supposed to be overseeing all Nazi activities regarding the Jews in the Far East. Meisinger has been holding secret meetings with numerous Japanese military and diplomatic personnel."

"If they are secret, how do you know about them?"

"There are some Japanese in the Naval Intelligence Bureau and the consulate who are leaking information to us. I can't say who. Anyway, Meisinger has one chilling message for the Japanese: 'You should follow our policy.' And he has laid out a plan for the total eradication of all the Jews, including those in Shanghai. They are universally referring to this plan as the 'Final Solution.' All Jews in Shanghai, whether from the Third Reich or anywhere else for that matter, were to have been rounded up and arrested in a 'surprise attack' during Rosh Hashanah. Obviously, that didn't happen. And what do you think he planned to do with all of us Jews?"

Everyone around the table sat frozen in their chairs, waiting for the answer.

Samuel continued. "Get rid of them, of course. And how, you might ask. Meisinger presented a number of, how shall I say it, *creative* solutions. Put all Jews on ships and set them adrift in the East China Sea, where they would all starve to death or just sink the ships. Or send them up the Whangpoo River to work in abandoned salt mines, where they'd die of exhaustion. Or send them to concentration camps on Chongming Island, where they'd be subjected to hideous medical experiments and chemical weapons."

Josef observed, "We've heard that many of our Sephardic brethren carrying British passports have been hauled off to detention camps and their properties confiscated by the Japanese. Sir Elly Kadoorie was taken to a prisoner of war camp, and Ellis Hayim, whose family is originally from Bombay, is sitting in the Bridge House jail in Hongkew at this very minute. Who would have believed that the former chairman of the Shanghai Stock Exchange would be treated so inhumanely? The Japanese have also detained numerous Americans they accuse of being spies."

Samuel was quick to reply. "Josef, you aren't telling me anything I don't already know. The Japanese have taken their own unilateral action against anyone they consider enemy aliens, regardless of their religious affiliation, but this is totally different. What the Nazis are demanding of the Japanese is the wholesale murder of all Jews, regardless of their nationality. So far the Japanese have stood their ground and said no to Meisinger. They've bought themselves some time, but we expect that the Japanese may do something to appease the Germans by next February at the latest. That gives us a few months to figure out what our options are."

Josef asked, "What are we to do now?"

"For the moment there is nothing you can do."

The Shabbat candles sputtered and crackled as if in protest of all that Samuel had divulged. Eva, already tired, now felt terribly sad. "I feel as if one evening, maybe very soon, I will wake up and it will be *Kristallnacht* all over again."

Josef said, "Let us all take comfort in the blessings of the Sabbath." Together they all bowed their heads and recited the closing prayer:

> "Be pleased, O Lord our God, to fortify us by thy commandments, and especially by the commandment of the seventh day, this great and holy Sabbath, since this day is great and holy before thee, that we may rest and repose thereon in love in accordance with the precept of thy will. In thy favor, O Lord our God, grant us such repose that there be no trouble, grief or lamenting on the day of our rest. Let us, O Lord our God, behold the consolation of Zion thy city, and the rebuilding of Jerusalem thy holy city, for thou art the Lord of salvation and of consolation."

Eve broke the spell that had descended over the room. She looked at her watch and exclaimed, "Goodness, it's already past eight o'clock. Shall we retire to the living room?" Eva turned on the wall sconces and motioned for the Jedeikins to settle themselves on the cushioned sofa. Suddenly a moth flew into the light, its wings beating against the bulb. Eva waved her handkerchief to chase the insect away. "I don't know how those beastly creatures get into the apartment, but they do."

As the moth flew behind the drawn curtains, Walter positioned himself in front of the guests and adjusted his music stand. Then Eva asked Walter to give a brief introduction to the piece he would play. "His selection will be a surprise for me," she explained. "I've been so busy at the shop that I haven't heard Walter practice in weeks."

Walter pointed to the music with his bow. "I'm going to play the short intermezzo from Jules Massenet's opera, *Thaïs*. At the end of the first scene in the second act, the Christian monk Athanaël tries to convince the beautiful courtesan Thaïs to renounce her sinful ways. She laughs at him, but by the end of the first scene, she repents and breaks down in tears. In the next scene, she follows him into the desert. By the opera's end, the monk realizes that his obsession for Thaïs is driven by lust, not faith, and she in turn dies with a pure heart. This 'Méditation' builds to a passionate crescendo. In working on this piece, I have tried to capture the emotions of the monk and the courtesan."

Walter scarcely looked at the score, and as he reached the end of the piece, he held his audience in the palm of his hand. Sonia Jedeikin was the first to applaud, and then the others enthusiastically joined in. Walter was pleased with himself. "Do you have time for one more piece?"

Sonia responded, "By all means. What have you planned for us as an encore?"

"I thought you might enjoy 'Liebesfreud' by Fritz Kreisler. As I am sure you know, he was from a Viennese Jewish family but at the age of thirteen he converted to Christianity. He fell in love with an American divorcée and they had a wonderful marriage. They eventually settled in the United States after the Great War, but they toured the world. Both greatly admired the Orient. During a performance of his own work, he said, 'Music is the tongue that speaks to all civilized humanity.' This little piece, which Kreisler used often as an encore, is normally played with piano accompaniment. But I'll do my best so that you won't miss the piano voice too much."

The tune was reminiscent of old Vienna, and Walter played with gusto, changing the tempo in subtle ways—speeding up and slowing down to suit his taste—and ended with a flourish of his bow high above his head.

His parents beamed with pride as Samuel and Sonia stood up. "Bravo!" said Samuel. "You have given us a very special gift this evening. I am reminded of what Martin Luther wrote: 'Beautiful music is one of the most magnificent and delightful presents God has given us.'"

Walter responded, "I don't believe in God, Herr Jedeikin, but I do believe in Fritz Kreisler. If anyone is to be thanked, it is him, for giving us such a lively and joyous piece of music to forget our troubles."

Samuel laughed. "Well, you certainly know how to speak your mind, Walter, although I don't agree with you. But you know what they say about the Jews: 'Two Jews, three synagogues.' We always enjoy a good argument, even for argument's sake."

Josef was appalled. "I hope you aren't offended by Walter's remarks."

Samuel assured him he was not. Then he turned to his wife. "Sonia, my dearest, I think we've overstayed our welcome."

"Not at all. May I offer you a glass of sherry?"

"Another time. It's been a most memorable evening. And by the way, Eva, your *Sachertorte* was just delicious."

As the Jedeikins put on their overcoats, Samuel pulled Josef aside. "At the risk of breaking my wife's request not to discuss business on Shabbat, I wanted to give you some good news. I've spoken to one of my Japanese contacts, and he's assured me that delivery of electricity into the factory will continue without interruption, even when some of your neighbors on Chusan Road and elsewhere are suffering from power outages."

"It certainly pays to have friends in high places, doesn't it?"

"Yes, and it also helps to speak Japanese."

"Thank you for letting me know."

"Keep up the good work, Josef. You and Eva are doing a splendid job!"

Josef opened the front door and watched the Jedeikins as they climbed into the back seat of their chauffeur-driven Rolls-Royce Wraith. A car passing in the opposite direction threw up a plume of water from one of the many puddles that had formed during the storm. Humming the melody of *"Liebesfreud,"* Josef shut the door and turned the lock. He saw that the Shabbat candles were almost extinguished; what little light was left threw long shadows against the dining room walls.

Alone in the living room, Eva poured herself a glass of sherry and drank it in a few short gulps. "Something to calm my nerves, Josef."

Taking her hand, he led Eva down the hallway to their bedroom. Josef still took delight in watching his wife slowly undress without modesty or shame, and then the long-married couple slipped beneath the bedcovers, finding temporary comfort in their lovemaking.

chapter 31
The Designated Area

The Lederers, Hungarian Jews who lived in Vienna before the war, occupied the floor above Lilly and David in their apartment building on Bubbling Well Road. Veola Lederer had given birth to a baby boy within days of Mischa's birth, so on sunny days the two toddlers and their mothers were in the habit of taking a morning stroll up to the Hardoon villa and back. February 18, 1943 wasn't supposed to be an exception. Sunlight streamed through the tall windows of the Ozers' apartment, and Mischa played with a set of wooden blocks while Lilly finished a cup of breakfast tea. Still dressed in her nightgown and peignoir, she was planning what she would wear for their daily outing. She asked her maid about the outside temperature.

"Ah, missy, it's zero degrees today. Very cold and very windy."

Lilly smiled at the opportunity. "Well, then I'll just have to wear my fur coat." She paused for a moment, then instructed the maid to lay out her favorite pink sweater and black wool skirt. The skirt was still one of the bestsellers at the Vienna House of Fashion. Wealthy Chinese clients liked the simplicity of the cut and its versatility. It could be worn with a jacket or, as Lilly planned, with a sweater underneath a coat.

"And would you mind polishing my black leather heels, the ones with the gold buckles? It was raining the last time I wore them, and I forgot to give them to you when I took them off. They're in my closet."

Mischa, carrying one of his blocks, climbed up on the sofa next to his mother. At a year and a half, he was a handsome little boy with jet-black hair and dark brown eyes. Lilly thought he looked just like his father, but

Eva insisted he was the spitting image of the twins when they were his age. Mischa tugged at his mother's sleeve.

"What is it, my little angel?"

Mischa held a wooden block in his hand. Letters of the alphabet were carved on all four sides. He pointed to the K and asked, "B, Mama?"

"No, my pet. That is a K, like *Katze*. And what sound does a *Katze* make?"

"Meow, meow."

Lilly clapped her hands and then gave him a kiss on the forehead. "Just so."

Mischa turned the block over and was about to try and name the letter B for *Bahn* ("choo choo train") when David rushed in interrupting their happy play. He was waving the English-language *North China Daily News*. Lilly had never seen her husband so agitated.

"What's the matter, David?"

"My English is not as good as yours, but I get the gist of what the newspaper is reporting. The Japanese have announced the establishment of what they are referring to as a 'designated area for stateless refugees,' which is nothing more than a code word for us Jews. Here. Read this out loud." David picked up his son and put him down on the carpet so he could look over his wife's shoulder as she read:

> "In a joint proclamation issued today, the Imperial Japanese Army and Navy authorities announced the restriction of residences and places of business of stateless refugees in Shanghai to a designated area comprising sections of the Wayside and Yangtzepoo districts as of May 18, 1943. Stateless refugees are European refugees who have arrived in Shanghai since 1937."

Lilly gasped.

"Go on. What does the rest say?" David urged. She continued:

> "The designated area is bordered on the west by the line connecting Chaoufoong, Muirhead, and Dent Roads; on the east by Yangtze Creek; on the south by the line connecting

East Seward, Muirhead, and Wayside Roads; and on the north by the boundary of the International Settlement."

It took a few moments for David to absorb this. "In other words they are talking about a two-and-a-half square kilometer [one square mile] area of Hongkew. There are already 100,000 Chinese living there as well as Jewish refugees who are being housed in the *Heime* or renting rooms in the lanes. And where exactly do the Japanese expect to accommodate all these people who are currently living throughout the International Settlement and the French Concession?"

Lilly read portions of the proclamation:

> "Permission must be obtained from the Japanese authorities for the transfer, sale, purchase, or lease of rooms, houses, shops, or any other establishments situated outside the designated area and now occupied by the stateless refugees."

Lilly scanned the rest of the article. "The Japanese authorities justified this action by saying, 'This measure is motivated by military necessity, and is therefore not an arbitrary action intended to oppress their legitimate occupation.'"

David laughed. "What hogwash. What they mean by 'stateless refugees' are the Jews who have come to Shanghai since '37 from the Third Reich, Poland, and elsewhere. This is a deliberate attempt on the part of the Japanese to create a ghetto, so they can keep an eye on the refugees and confiscate their businesses and other property."

"What's behind this?"

"Lilly, the question is not *what* but *who*. The Nazis, of course. The city is crawling with vermin: Baron Jesco von Puttkamer, Lothar Eisentrager, and of course, Josef Meisinger."

Lilly interrupted her husband. "Our neighbor, Veola Lederer, saw Meisinger on the street less than a week ago. She said he is one of the ugliest men she ever laid eyes on. Tall, with a large face that only the devil could bear to look at. The Jews are calling him the 'Butcher of Warsaw.' I shudder to imagine what earned him such a name."

"As I was about to say, the Japanese military has had to come up with a scheme to placate these thugs. And think about it. If the Jews must move into Hongkew, vacating their comfortable homes and well-equipped businesses, the Japanese can step right through the door and lie down in their beds. So the terms of the proclamation are advantageous to them. That's why they agreed to it. That and the fact that the Japanese are suffering strategic losses in the war in the Pacific and need the Germans."

"What's to happen to us, David?"

"We Ozers came here from Harbin in 1930, so we are exempt. I can't say the same for your family, however. Unless the Jedeikins can come up with some reason to convince their Jap contacts that they should keep their hands off your family, I'm afraid your parents and the twins, as well as Dora and Herman, will be forced to squeeze into the ghetto—that is what this is. I don't care what they are calling it."

"And what about the shop? The building is prime real estate and right in the middle of the International Settlement."

"According to the proclamation the shop will have to be relocated, sold, or closed down. But there again, Samuel Jedeikin might have a trick or two up his sleeve to protect his interests. After all, the shop is still doing relatively well."

Lilly nodded. "Mother tells me that, just the other day, a wife of a Japanese military officer came into the shop and placed an order for five cocktail dresses, made from the finest Chinese embroidered silk robes. The customer told Mother, 'I got the robes for next to nothing. The woman who sold them to me used to be the wife of some wealthy landowner in Jiangsu Province.' I have no idea where that is, but I can't wait to see what our seamstresses come up with for her."

David rubbed Lilly's neck. "My darling, it just amazes me that after four years, you still know almost nothing about Shanghai. It is as if you have blinders on."

"We're going to leave as soon as this miserable war is over, aren't we?"

"Shanghai is my home, and I hoped that it would become yours as well, now that we are married and have a son to raise. I can't imagine living anywhere else, really."

Lilly replied, "My father has been babbling on about going to Palestine. Every time he brings it up my mother wants to cut his head off. Poor Papa. He's the long-suffering husband, but I can understand why my mother is so against Palestine. It sounds utterly wretched. Nothing but desert, heat, and hostile Arabs."

Bored with his blocks, Mischa pulled on his father's pant leg, interrupting their conversation. David picked his son up. "Do you want to play horsey? You've been such a good little boy, not making a sound while your mama and I have been having a serious talk."

"Yes, Papa." David got down on his hands and knees so that Mischa could climb up onto his back. After circling the living room once, David stopped in front of Lilly.

"That's enough playing with your papa. We need to get ready to go to the park." And then she hesitated. "David, do you think it's safe for us to go outside today?"

"I'll instruct my driver to follow a few feet behind you and Veola with his rickshaw in case there's trouble on the street."

Remembering her mother's confrontation with the Nazis, Lilli suggested, "And I suppose I shouldn't wear my new fur coat, although I had my heart set on it."

"An excellent idea, Lilly. You'll have plenty of occasions to show it off when things calm down."

"And when will that be, David?"

David didn't answer.

By early March, their neighbors, Veola and Ludwig Lederer and their son, moved out of their spacious apartment. Veola explained to Lilly, "We're afraid, if we wait until May to find accommodations in Hongkew, we might be forced to live in absolute squalor."

"Don't you know anyone you can pay off, Veola? This city survives on bribes. And how do the Japs even know that you are here?"

"Someone plastered a notice on our door the other day instructing us to leave our premises. An emigrant Russian Jew, a Mr. Rogovin, is now the head of CentroJew. The Japanese expect him to coordinate the relocation program and to oversee the fees the Japanese and Chinese are charging the refugees for apartments and rooms in Hongkew. I am afraid that, once apartments and rooms become scarce, we will all be held hostage to their demands and they can ask whatever they want, regardless of Mr. Rogovin and his staff. So Ludwig thought it best that we move now."

Lilly was shaken. "So where are you going to live, my dear friend?"

"Ludwig got in touch with a very nice Chinese pediatrician who has an apartment and clinic on Wayside Road in Hongkew. It is a short walk from your parents' factory on Chusan Road. We will move there and he will take over our apartment here. So, you are in luck Lilly. If Mischa gets sick, God forbid, you'll have a doctor living upstairs. He has excellent training. Ludwig tells me he went to medical school in Vienna."

Lilly was horrified. "You don't expect me to take Mischa to a Chinese doctor, do you?"

"From the expression on your face, I guess not."

"Is there anything I can do to help you?"

"Just don't forget us, Lilly. And when all of this is over, hopefully we will be neighbors just as before."

Chapter 32

Spring in Wintertime

Chao Chen hurried up the steps of the Shanghai Conservatory of Music as the chimes in the bell tower on the Bund marked the two o'clock hour. She breathed a sigh of relief that she was on time for her appointment with Miss Liang, Professor Wittenberg, and his violin student.

On this day of all days, her employer, Frau Götz, had asked her to stay late to finish stitching six pairs of leather gloves for a rush order from the Wing On department store. Several of the Jewish women who lived in Hongkew had come down with a case of cholera, leaving their employer shorthanded. Out of desperation Frau Götz had turned to Chao Chen to help out with the stitching, reassuring her that this was just for a few days, just until the women returned or until she could find other workers to take their place.

"There are plenty of Jewish refugees looking for work," Frau Götz had said, annoyed. "You are much too valuable to me as a salesgirl to do stitching, and if we don't get this order out on time, Wing On will go somewhere else—and we need their business." She handed Chao Chen a pair of scissors and a thimble. "Use this so you don't prick your finger. And be sure to cut your thread on an angle."

"Yes, madam. When I was a girl, our servant Ya-Li, taught me the basics of embroidery. I'll do my best."

Chao Chen put her head down and tried to concentrate. The smell of cabbage simmering in a pot on the stove had made her nose itch. She much preferred the loamy scent of the tanned leather hides being cut on the large dining room table. Chao Chen kept checking her wristwatch. It was already noon and she still had two pairs of gloves to sew. Rushing to finish her work, the thimble slipped off her finger and she pricked her thumb. She cried out in pain as a drop of blood stained the piece of leather she was working on.

Chao Chen wrapped a handkerchief around her thumb to staunch the blood. Mortified, she showed Frau Götz what she had done.

"I knew I shouldn't have asked you to do this!" Frau Götz exclaimed. "You are not cut out for this kind of work. And don't waste your tears. It's not going to make things any better."

Changing her tone, Frau Götz then opened a bottle of Mercurochrome and lightly painted it onto Chao Chen's thumb. "There. That will keep it from getting infected. We can't be too careful." She wrinkled her nose. "This city is infested with germs we Germans don't even have a name for."

"Thank you for being so understanding, madam." Chao Chen noticed the other women staring at her. She couldn't understand what they were saying, but she saw from the looks on their faces that they resented the way Frau Götz treated her, as if she were meant for something better than what they were paid to do day in and day out. She knew that many of these German ladies once had servants to do their bidding and now they were forced to stitch for a free meal and for money to support their families.

Frau Götz suggested to Chao Chen, "Why don't you get your things together? Don't you have an important engagement with Professor Wittenberg today? I'll finish these myself." She closed her eyes and sighed. "Some years ago, my father, may he rest in peace, took me to a performance of the Schnabel Trio in Berlin. I don't remember the selections, but Professor Wittenberg played beautifully. As I remember, he is also a piano virtuoso. You're indeed a very lucky young lady." She stroked Chao Chen's hair as if she were petting a prized Pekingese.

As she put on her winter coat and tied a scarf around her neck, Chao Chen had apologized. "Madam, please deduct the glove I ruined from my salary this week."

"Nonsense. It was an accident. Don't think twice about it. I'll pull the stitches out and we can use the side of the leather that is still perfectly good. Now go, or you'll be late."

Chao Chen made up her mind to ignore the throbbing in her thumb as she made her way through the streets. Would she remember this day as the day that a door to her career as a performer would open a crack or be slammed shut in her face?

She kept shifting her satchel from one hand to the other so as not to put undue strain on either; in the satchel was the music to Beethoven's *Spring Sonata*, the piece that Professor Wittenberg and Miss Liang had selected for her to play with the violin student. Miss Liang had told Chao Chen, "This is a very common audition piece. What Professor Wittenberg will be looking for is that you and his violin student complement each other. The two instruments converse with each other, the melody alternating back and forth. In the opening of the piece, the violin has the melody and the pianist's right hand plays the harmony while the left hand provides the bass. Later on, the violin takes the harmony while the piano plays the melody, some harmony, and the bass."

"I'm so nervous. Do you think I'm ready, Miss Liang?'

"Of course, or I wouldn't have agreed to this. Do you think I want to embarrass myself? This is my chance to show my skill as a master teacher. Professor Wittenberg knows this very well. He wants to help advance my career, not just yours or that of his student violinist, Walter Kolber. You remember him, don't you? He was the professor's next pupil the day you auditioned for the maestro a year ago. He is quite a charming young man—handsome too."

Chao Chen felt her cheeks turning red. She vividly remembered him. Hadn't she seen him at the benefit concert walking up the aisle, a white scarf wrapped around his neck? He had made a lasting impression on her, but she wouldn't dare admit this to Miss Liang.

"Do you know anything else about him, Miss Liang? How long has he been playing?"

"I don't know. He is not a full-time student at the Conservatory. He studies with Professor Wittenberg privately. I believe they have mutual friends in the German Jewish community. I recall that his parents are from Vienna originally and now own a clothing factory on Chusan Road, as well as a fashionable ladies' shop in the International Settlement. I have often thought of going there myself, but I hear the prices are quite high. Certainly not within the reach of a piano teacher."

"Well, if Herr Kolber and I get along, perhaps he can arrange a discount for us."

"I wouldn't count on it. The Jewish people are out to make as much money as they can, just like the rest of us, so that they won't be a burden on their community. The few wealthy Jews have their hands full taking care of the thousands of refugees who have no jobs and nothing to barter. It's really a pity."

Chao Chen thought of her own sacrifices, like knocking on doors to sell Frau Götz's handmade gloves instead of practicing and dealing with her mother's selfishness. These indignities paled in comparison to what so many others were forced to endure, not only in Shanghai but in the countryside, where thousands of Chinese soldiers and civilians had died by bullets, starvation, or torture.

All thoughts of war and personal struggle melted away as Chao Chen entered the Shanghai Conservatory of Music. The corridor was crowded with German-speaking students on their way to and from class. The best of the local Chinese students who had also set their sights on a classical music career were also there. She couldn't figure out where Professor Wittenberg's practice studio was located. She felt a wave of panic wash over her. She didn't know which way to turn and stood paralyzed as students rushed past her.

She dug into her pocket and pulled out a piece of paper on which she had written Professor Wittenberg's name and the room number. A handsome young man carrying a violin case approached Chao Chen. He asked in English, "Can I help you? You look lost."

Chao Chen recognized the young man as Walter Kolber. She handed him her note and replied in English: "I am looking for Professor Wittenberg's studio, number one hundred ten."

"Follow me. You are Fräulein Chao Chen, I believe?"

"Yes."

"We have met before." He bowed. "You are even prettier than I remember. My lucky day!"

Chao Chen was not used to receiving compliments from a young man, especially one as handsome as Walter Kolber. She felt oddly attracted as she looked into his mischievous brown eyes. "If you're as good a violinist as you are a flirt, it will be my lucky day too."

Professor Wittenberg was in his early sixties but exuded the energy of a much younger man. Waving his arms as if conducting a symphony, he ushered Walter and Chao Chen into the practice studio. Miss Liang greeted Chao Chen with a sweet smile, giving no hint of how important this moment was to their mutual careers.

Professor Wittenberg gestured for Chao Chen to take a seat at the piano. She placed her music, which had notations made by Miss Liang, on the stand. Walter took out his violin and bow. Walter bragged, "I don't need the music. I've already memorized the first movement, as Professor Wittenberg recommended."

Chao Chen tried to remain calm, but his comment unnerved her.

Turning to Chao Chen, Professor Wittenberg asked in English, "And what is the tempo, please?"

"Allegro."

"What does that mean to you?"

"Quick."

"Yes, but quick means different things to different performers, and so you and Walter will have to interpret this together. For example, a young man might think a relationship is proceeding too slowly while the young woman wants to slow it down so she can uncover his true nature. They must come to an understanding or their budding romance will be doomed to failure. Yes?"

Miss Liang addressed Chao Chen in Mandarin: "Professor Wittenberg has a playful sense of humor. He enjoys teasing his pupils every now and then. Don't be uncomfortable, my dear. And don't pay any attention to Walter's bragging. He is just trying to diminish you. But I know you. You are a fighter."

Professor Wittenberg had an impish grin on his face, but he quickly turned back to the task at hand. "Let us assume for a moment that you both are technically up to this piece. You understand the fingering, the tempo, and so forth. But technique is just one aspect of artistry. Bringing out the emotion and imagery of a piece of music is what creates the magic. There are two competing themes in the *Spring Sonata*, which are presented right away in the first movement. What are they?"

Walter spoke up. "The first is pastoral and light, like a beautiful spring day."

"And the second, Chao Chen?"

"Threatening, like a storm building on the horizon that is about to burst forth at any minute."

"Bravo. Well put. So, as you play, keep these two competing themes in mind. We know that this piece is written in F major, but in order for Walter to tune his instrument properly, we will need Miss Chen to please play an A-major chord."

As Chao Chen sustained the chord on the piano, Walter adjusted the pegs of his violin several times, nodding when he was satisfied that the two instruments were in tune with each other.

Professor Wittenberg continued, "Both of you need to start together in the opening measure. The piano's eighth note sets the tempo of the piece. So, Walter, you must follow Miss Chen. I suggest that you face Miss Chen for your first attempt. Later on, when you are more comfortable with each other, you can assume the traditional position of the violinist, your body turned away from the piano and toward the audience. So, shall we give it a try?"

Walter gave an emphatic "yes" while Chao Chen simply nodded.

Miss Liang turned the pages of the score for Chao Chen while Professor Wittenberg sat with his eyes closed, listening to the students as they stumbled through the piece. He suddenly leaped out of his chair and clapped his hands. "That's enough."

Chao Chen was visibly upset. "Was I that awful?"

To her amazement, Professor Wittenberg smiled. "Not bad. Not bad at all for your first attempt. What do you think, Miss Liang?"

"I think they show great promise as duet partners."

Professor Wittenberg placed his hands on Walter's shoulders. "You have played this sonata with me enough times to know that you need to know your collaborator's part so that your playing will fit together seamlessly, like a pair of gloves. You cannot simply concentrate on your part to the detriment of Miss Chen. And there is something else—I want you to give yourself over to the music. You know all the notes, but you must show us that you also connect with the music on a visceral level. You need to show us more emotion."

"Yes, Professor."

"And you, Miss Chen, your playing is too tentative." To make a point, he caressed the piano. "Take command of your instrument. Show more courage and trust your talent because it is there for you to rely upon. Be bold.

"And both of you need to play the runs more brightly. Some of the passages sound as muddy as the Whangpoo River. They must be as crystal clear as a mountain spring when the winter snows melt."

Professor Wittenberg picked up his violin and brilliantly played a few measures of the sonata, and then he abruptly put the instrument down. "I think you both will do well with this piece. It is not so difficult that you will drown, but it is challenging enough that you will have a chance to develop your talent. I'm planning a public recital for strings and piano this June at the Lyceum Theatre. If you both apply yourselves, the first movement will fit nicely into the program. Six months may seem like a long time to prepare yourselves, but with your other commitments, you will have just enough time to get ready."

Chao Chen could not believe her ears. Judging by the look on Walter's face, he seemed rather indifferent to this news. She thought perhaps that he didn't want to appear with her, but she tried to push this notion aside.

"For the next four weeks you both will practice with Miss Liang. Walter, we will also continue our private lessons here as usual. Miss Liang, please stay for a few more minutes; the two of you are dismissed."

Walter held the door open for Chao Chen and they walked into the cold winter air. "What happened to your thumb? You're wearing a tiny bandage, aren't you?"

Chao Chen was surprised that he noticed. "Did my playing suffer?"

"No, not really. I was just curious about what happened."

She told him of pricking her finger earlier in the day. "I work for Frau Götz so that I can afford lessons with Miss Liang."

"I'm working as well, at a typewriter repair shop. Maybe someday I'll have a patron like Beethoven did, and then I can just concentrate on my violin; but for the time being, I'm in the same boat as you."

Chao Chen smiled shyly. "I hope you will have such a patron, Herr Kolber. You are very talented. I am very lucky to have been chosen to play with you. I'm sure that there are many other pianists who would serve you better than me."

"You're being much too modest, Chao Chen. But that is the Chinese way, isn't it? You're probably thinking, 'This German boy can't hold a candle to me.' Am I right?"

"Not at all, Walter. Why on earth would you say such a thing?"

"Oh, I'm just playing with you a little bit."

Chao Chen suddenly felt annoyed. "Please don't. I've sacrificed a lot to get this far, and I don't like you or any man playing with my feelings."

"I'm not sure I understand what you are saying, but from the look on your pretty face, I must have said something wrong. I apologize."

"Apology accepted. I must go now. I'll see you at Miss Liang's next week."

Walter grinned. "I'll count the days." He turned and walked away.

Chao Chen stood at the gate to the Conservatory for a moment, then headed in the opposite direction. She smiled at the thought of what might come to be.

As Walter walked away from the Conservatory, he wondered how this sensitive and emotional Miss Chao Chen might be in bed. She looked like a fine porcelain doll that might easily break if accidently dropped.

chapter 33
Above the Factory

Eva was despondent. The prospect of moving from their comfortable apartment on Rue de la Soeur to the overcrowded squalor of Hongkew, now called the "Designated Area," was abhorrent. Unable to control her frustration or her tears, she berated Josef, "Can't you do anything to avoid this insult? I understand that some of the refugees have found ways to get around this proclamation. Look at Frau Götz. The Japanese have allowed her to stay in her house and her glove business is thriving. She came into the shop the other day just to look around, and when I mentioned the proclamation, she said that, for the time being, she was 'staying put.' She gave me no explanation, nor did she offer us a way out of this mess."

Josef reasoned, "That's because she's making gloves for the Japanese troops, and probably at no cost to them. Do you want JEKO to start sewing their military uniforms? It's bad enough that we have to make clothes at little or no profit for the residents in the *Heime*, but at least that's helping to keep our operation going and we're doing something good for the Jews. We haven't been forced to sell our soul—at least not yet."

"Have you spoken to Samuel Jedeikin?"

"Yes. He's worked something out so the store can stay open right where it is, and we have been assured that electricity in the factory won't be cut off. But that's all the help he can give us. So we're going to have to move before May 18. There's no getting around that."

"And where do you suggest we go? It's already March."

Josef was quick to answer. "I've thought of that already. We can move into the office above the factory floor and take over the storage area. We won't have to pay rent, and there's just enough room for the four of us to live comfortably, at least compared to some families who are trying to find living quarters next to the Chinese families in the lanes. We can partition some space by hanging sheets, and we have boxes to store your china and stemware."

"Have you lost your mind? There isn't even a proper bathroom or a kitchen, and there are no walls! We'll be sleeping right on top of Walter and Dolfie!"

"But think of all the money we'll be able to save. I've heard that key money has skyrocketed and families are paying a fortune to find some space to share with people they don't even know."

"And how are we expected to bring all our belongings?"

"Most of our furniture will have to stay right here. The Japanese captain who intends to move in here *says* he will take care of everything that we don't schlep into Hongkew."

"So, you've rented out our apartment already?" Eva stared at Josef.

"Eva." Josef paused. "We had no choice."

Eva was angry. "Do you really think we can trust him to take care of our belongings?" Then she wept. "First it was the Lemberg pogrom, then the Nazis run us out of Austria and now the Japanese are forcing us into a ghetto. Will this ever end?"

"Eva, no one is happy. What is it that my mother used to say when I was a little boy? *'Nit mit sheltn un nit mit lakhn ken men di velt ibermakhn.'* 'Neither cursing nor laughing can change the world.'"

"Josef, you know how I hate it when you speak Yiddish. You sound like a peasant, not a cultured Viennese."

Then, although not sure if it would cheer Eva up, Josef said, "When I told the captain we wanted to observe Pesach right here, he agreed to give us until April 30 to move out."

"Did you invite him to join us?" she said sarcastically.

Josef bit his tongue. "Of course not, my dear."

"And where do you expect my sister Dora and Herman to live? We are responsible for them too. They're going to be forced to leave the rooming house in the French Concession."

Josef replied, "Lilly tells me her neighbors on Bubbling Well Road, the Lederers, I believe, have moved into a small house on Wayside Road. Their landlord is subdividing the building into separate tiny living quarters and there is still one bedroom available. They will have to move real fast, and indeed, it already may be too late. There is a common toilet and running water, and so by Hongkew standards, luxurious. One of the Jewish tenants is a musician who works at the Café Atlantic. When he comes home he plays some jazz tunes in the dark, since electricity is almost nonexistent at this point and they don't want to waste the few candles they have in reserve for an emergency."

"You make it all sound so *gemütlich*, but I know better, Josef."

On May 18, 1943, the rain held off for several hours, just enough time for the Kolbers to move their belongings into their makeshift living quarters above the factory. Dolfie instructed the men at the cutting tables to stop what they were doing and help carry the trunks, wooden crates, folding cots, a large clay pot with an iron grill on top that would serve as a stove, a trough for a bath, a honey pot to be used for toileting, and other various household essentials up the stairs. And there were the Meissen chinaware and the silver candlesticks Eva insisted on bringing. Some of the workers were so emaciated it was a miracle they didn't fall under the weight of their cargo as they carried it up to the second floor.

Walter put off telling his parents that Frau Weinstein had fired him from his job at the typewriter repair shop. She had accused him of stealing from the cash register. At first he denied everything and pointed the finger at Mr. Deng. In truth he had borrowed money from time to time to bet on the greyhounds, and usually he was able to cover his tracks; but recently he had made several bad bets and lost quite a bit of money. Just as Mr. Deng was about to be fired, Walter, knowing that the Chinaman had a wife and child to support, felt a tinge of remorse, so he confessed. He was certain that Frau Weinstein would do nothing because he had something far more incriminating to hold over her head than petty theft. He was wrong about her resolve.

Regardless, he had no regrets about losing his job. Frau Weinstein could never be satisfied sexually, and he was bored with her begging and whining. He'd much rather satisfy his healthy urges at one of the bordellos in the red-light district, where the girls expected nothing from him once he zipped up his pants, paid his bill, and promised to return. And if the lottery ticket he had just bought turned out to be a winner, he could pay Frau Weinstein back. He was only concerned about his parents' reaction, but with any luck, he'd find another part-time job soon enough. At least that's what he told himself.

One small window on the second floor of the JEKO Factory overlooked Chusan Road. It was the family's only source of ventilation and daylight, and when the window was open, the stench and the noise from the street below went on day and night: vendors hawking their wares, the honey pot collectors announcing their arrival in the early morning hours, the clanking of the factory door, and the strains of music and chatter from nearby cafés that carried on well after midnight.

Eva barked out instructions: "Walter, hang three cords from one side of the office to the other, and attach these sheets with clothespins. Dolfie, help your father push his desk into the far corner of the room so we have more space, and then go downstairs to see where the pipes are located. We're going to have to put in a water closet up here somehow or I swear I'm going to die. I just can't continue to climb onto the roof and use that clay pot. Now, Josef, help me find a place for my china. God knows when I'm ever going to use it in this hellhole, but I couldn't leave it behind, could I?"

"No, my dearest. I know how much it means to you." Josef paused as the hum of the sewing machines carried up from the floor below. "Well, there is one advantage to living here."

"And what could that possibly be?"

"We have a much shorter commute than when we were living on Rue de la Soeur, and we don't have to worry about the trolleys not running or someone stealing from us."

Walter looked around the room. "Papa, do you remember reading us Sholem Aleichem when we were little? I recall something he observed about the Jews, and today proves that it's true: 'You can take a Jew out of the *shtetl* but you cannot take the *shtetl* out of a Jew.'"

Eva grabbed Walter by the collar and smacked him across the face. "Sometimes I think you don't have the sense you were born with. How dare you say such a thing?"

"Oh Mutti, I was only making light of a grim situation. I really didn't mean to upset you so."

Her hand still stung. "Why is it that I think you're lying, Walter?"

Dolfie chimed in, "Because he is."

Samuel Jedeikin paid a visit to the JEKO factory. While examining some finished goods sewn by the refugees, he told Josef, "I just learned that more than eight thousand Jewish refugees have had to give up over a thousand residences in other parts of the city to move into Hongkew."

Josef was worried. "And what about their businesses?"

Samuel reported, "About three hundred businesses have had to shut down, and the owners are scrambling to relocate if they have the money to do so. Most of them have gone to the JDC trying to get loans, but we are having a tough time getting money through Switzerland from the United States."

Josef inquired, "What's happened to Laura Margolis? She strikes me as a woman who won't take 'no' for an answer. Look at the deal she negotiated with us."

Samuel sighed. "She's been taken to a Japanese prisoner of war camp in Chapei. I hear that she is in 'good company.' Some of the American executives from Chase Bank and Standard Oil are there as well, and they've organized themselves into various task forces to feed the prisoners and get news in and out of the camp without being detected."

As the date on which all "stateless people" were expected to move into Hongkew drew near, some of the Jewish refugees gambled that the Japanese authorities would simply overlook them and refused to move. By August 1943 they realized that they had made an egregious mistake; the Japanese officials hunted down the heads of households and threw them into a lice-infested jail on Wayside Road. When they were released, their families still had to scramble to find a place to live, which by that time was nearly impossible. Many prisoners ended up in the Wayside Hospital, afflicted with all manner of diseases—from which many never recovered. By hesitating they had written their own death sentence.

Chapter 34

The Red Dress

Frau Götz was one of the fortunate Jewish refugees living in the French Concession given permission by the Japanese authorities to remain in her house and continue to run her business. Her house on Rue Tenant de la Tour was across the street from the Chen family residence, making it a simple matter for Chao Chen to show up for work every morning. Chao Chen became Frau Götz's right hand, keeping track of the books, selling to the Chinese-owned department stores, and checking the deliveries of leather and other supplies. Unfortunately, all of Frau Götz's skilled Jewish seamstresses lived in Hongkew and now needed to obtain a pass to leave the Designated Area. The official letter with Frau Götz's name engraved on it was sufficient to earn each a three-month pass, which meant she was guaranteed a stable workforce at least through the summer. But there was no telling when the Japanese would enforce tighter restrictions on the movement of the Jewish refugees to and from Hongkew. The rules governing the special passes were devised by the quixotic and sadistic Japanese official Kano Ghoya, who took delight in taunting the Jews on a whim.

Speaking in English and in a whisper to shield Chao Chen from the jealousy palpable among the refugee workers, Frau Götz asked, "Chao Chen, what do you intend to wear to the Shanghai Conservatory recital?"

"I don't know. I have only two dresses, and at this point they are so threadbare that I'm embarrassed to think of myself on stage wearing either. I'll look like a peasant, but my mother refuses to buy me a new dress. She doesn't even plan to attend the recital."

"And why is that? Isn't she thrilled that you will have your first public performance? Everyone is talking about it. Herr Götz and I already have our tickets."

Chao Chen had never before spoken of her complicated family situation. She confessed, "Rui-De Xu doesn't leave the house now except to go to Madam Soong's salons, and my mother, Ya-Nan is not well. She stays in bed all day and wanders around the house late at night. She's at the mercy of Rui-De Xu, who despises her because my father favored her. Ya-Nan was his concubine, but he always treated her as the love of his life. It is not an unusual situation among families such as the Chens. I'm sure it must seem very strange to you."

"I shouldn't have pried. It's really none of my business." Frau Götz took a sip of water to cool herself. Even with the windows open and the fan rotating overhead, it was stifling in the house. Shanghai was imprisoned in an insufferable heat wave, and even the nights brought no relief from the heat.

"This is a special event, so I'd like to buy you something new to wear," Frau Götz continued. "I've discussed it with Herr Götz and he's in total agreement. We both appreciate the excellent job you're doing. I hear that the Vienna House of Fashion is having a sale. We might be able to find something for you there."

Chao Chen blushed. "My recital partner, Herr Walter Kolber, is the owner's son."

Frau Götz smiled. "What a happy coincidence. Have you met Eva Kolber? I've seen her once in a while in synagogue."

"No, but Walter tells me his parents will most assuredly be at the recital."

"Well, this will be a perfect opportunity for you to meet Frau Kolber, and we can also bring a few samples of my gloves when we shop for a dress for you. They have very up-to-the-minute fashions. I've been to the store a number of times to look over what they carry; and they have feathered hats, pochettes, and pretty barrettes in the accessory cases, but no gloves."

Chao Chen's lower lip quivered. She felt unprepared to meet Walter's mother. He described his mother as somewhat domineering, a woman who disliked anyone who disagreed with her.

A Chinese salesgirl greeted Frau Götz and Chao Chen. Despite the big SALE sign in the window, they were the only customers in the store. Speaking in fluent English, the salesgirl asked, "Ladies, are you looking for something special?"

Frau Götz responded, "Yes. My assistant, Chao Chen, needs a new dress for her recital at the Lyceum Theatre next week. She is a pianist, and so we'd like a full-length dress with a pretty neckline, something that will look elegant on stage."

The salesgirl nodded. She disappeared behind a curtain, and within seconds she returned with two dresses, both dresses cut from the same pattern. One was made from a Chinese brocade remnant with pink peonies, the other out of a dazzling red taffeta that shimmered in the light. "Do either of these appeal to you? They are the same price."

Frau Götz suggested, "Why don't you try both of them on?"

Chao Chen hesitated. "If it's all the same to you, Frau Götz, I prefer the red dress. In China we believe red is the color of good luck."

The salesgirl smiled in agreement and pointed to the dressing room. Chao Chen hung her skirt and blouse over a chair and stepped into the dress, but only after she had wiped the perspiration off her neck and back. She stared at herself in the full-length mirror. The dress was too large but it was beautiful, and the color enhanced the luminosity of her skin and dark hair.

Frau Götz clapped in amazement when she stepped out of the dressing room. "You're so petite that the dress needs to be taken in and shortened, but it suits you, Chao Chen."

"It's the most beautiful dress I've ever seen. I would be thrilled to wear it." Losing her inhibitions, she twirled across the parquet floor.

The bell over the door tinkled. The salesgirl tilted her head and announced, "Ah, Frau Kolber has arrived. I am sure she would like to see you in this dress."

Chao Chen froze.

Frau Kolber addressed Frau Götz in German. "Who is this girl to you?"

"She works for me, and she is a student at the Conservatory."

Eva nodded and continued. "Tell her to take one more turn. She looks charming in that dress. Most young ladies look cheap in red, but she looks quite *raffinée*. Ah, the gifts of youth."

Chao Chen did as she was instructed as Frau Götz added, "She's the pianist performing a Beethoven sonata with your son next week. My husband and I are so excited to hear Chao Chen perform."

Frau Kolber raised her eyebrows and put her glasses on to get a better look at Chao Chen. "How interesting. Walter didn't mention who is to accompany him."

"I believe the violin and piano share equal billing."

Continuing in German, Frau Kolber leaned in and whispered to Frau Götz, "Not when Walter is on stage. He's always the star and anyone who plays with him must surely know that."

Frau Götz laughed. "Spoken like a true mother."

Frau Kolber turned to Chao Chen and asked in German, "So are you satisfied with this dress? It is of the moment, and so no one could possibly think that it's been hanging in your wardrobe for years. Or would you like to see something else? For example, the dress made of Chinese silk. That might be more appropriate for you."

Frau Götz translated for Chao Chen and then explained to Frau Kolber that this was the dress that Chao Chen preferred.

Frau Kolber bore down on Chao Chen. "Is there anything else you might need? We have some very smart suits designed by my own daughter, Lilly. She used to work with me in the store, but now that she has a son, she has her hands full. Such a devoted and loving mother. It makes my heart sing."

Frau Götz admired them. "How lovely, but I don't think we'll be needing anything else, although she will need a pair of gloves. I see you don't have any for sale. Do you mind if I show you some samples that we've made at my workshop?"

Chao Chen understood that she was no longer part of this conversation, and so she stepped back into the dressing room to allow the two women to begin their negotiations. Her hands shook as she unzipped the dress. She took several deep breaths and then put her skirt and blouse on again. She felt embarrassed at how plain she looked.

Frau Götz was in the middle of showing Frau Kolber a selection of her dress gloves. "And this is one of our finest models. The cording is, of course, hand-stitched onto the leather. This one we call the 'half 'n half' because of the length. It is perfect with a cocktail dress or a suit."

"I can see your gloves are very well made. I would consider carrying them in the store and seeing how we do with them."

"What if I give these to you in exchange for a reduction in the price of the dress?"

Frau Kolber hesitated for a moment. "The dress is already on sale. How much are we talking about here?"

"Would you be willing to reduce the price by another twenty percent?"

"Frau Götz, you must be joking. I'll give you a discount of ten percent, and that's as far as I can go."

"That's much less than I was hoping for, but we have a deal so long as you have your seamstress fit the dress properly at no extra cost."

"Fair enough. We do that as a courtesy for our customers anyway. It's one way that we can compete with the department stores down the street. Tell Miss Chen to put the dress back on so the seamstress can fit it. We'll have it ready for her in time for the recital."

Chao Chen stood on the fitting box while the seamstress pinned it, all the while wishing she could simply disappear. She looked down at the seamstress, trying to avoid her own reflection in the mirror. She noticed the woman's thinning hair and bony shoulders, signs of malnutrition.

"Where do you want the hemline, Frau Götz?"

"Let's just make it full-length. It must look very ladylike when she's at the keyboard."

When the seamstress finished making all the adjustments, Frau Götz pronounced the dress perfect.

Frau Kolber was delighted. "Tell Miss Chen I look forward to seeing her on stage in our dress. Will she be coming back to pick it up?"

"No. Here's my card. Just telephone me when it's ready and I'll have my husband come by and pick it up."

The salesgirl held the door open as Frau Kolber wished Chao Chen and Frau Götz a pleasant afternoon. It had begun to rain. The two women huddled under one umbrella and walked briskly, synchronizing their pace and being careful not to step in the puddles beginning to gather on the pavement.

Frau Götz complained, "That woman is an insufferable, self-important snob. But I'm willing to tolerate her for the sake of the business. Something in my insides tells me that you would be well-advised to stay out of her way. Does her son take after her?"

"Which one? Walter has a twin brother, Dolfie."

"Don't be evasive with me, Chao Chen. I am speaking of Walter, of course."

"He has always treated me with the utmost kindness and civility. He didn't object when Professor Wittenberg and my teacher suggested that we perform together."

"Chao Chen, I have friends on the faculty of the Conservatory who told me that of the two of you, you're the finer musician. Does that surprise you?"

"I had no idea."

"Well, it's true. And I can assure you that, when you step onto the stage in your red dress, you'll be the talk of Shanghai."

chapter 35

The Recital

Walter and Chao Chen stood off by themselves in a dark corner backstage at the Lyceum Theatre, which the Shanghai Conservatory had rented for the recital. Walter watched as Chao Chen paced nervously back and forth. "I'm so terrified," she whispered. "I'm afraid I might throw up or pass out at any minute." Then she confessed, "Walter, I'm afraid I may be unable to go on."

"Don't be ridiculous, Chao Chen. What's there to be nervous about? We've rehearsed this damn piece until my fingers are numb. To be honest I'm annoyed we're not being allowed to play all four movements since we've managed to work on all of them. Look, I expect you to do your best; otherwise my performance will suffer, and that can't happen. My parents are sitting in the audience, and who knows who else is out there. We must show everyone that we are as good as, if not better than, the full-time Conservatory students. I've heard some of them rehearsing, and honestly, some sound like a cat scratching on a tattered rug compared to me."

"I wish I were as confident as you, Walter." Then she whispered in his ear, "That's why I admire you."

Walter squeezed her hand. "And that's why I adore you. You believe in me."

After having practiced together for months, Walter and Chao Chen had become close, and not just as rehearsal partners. Walter was drawn to her exotic beauty and found her susceptible to his charms. Knowing how Chao Chen responded to compliments, he went one step further. "You are by far the most enchanting girl here tonight. You look utterly stunning in that red dress. My mother should be very pleased. You're a walking advertisement for the Vienna House of Fashion. I'll put money on it that someone is going to ask you where you bought it. That will please her to no end. Anything to get a customer, that's my mother."

"I'm not sure she'd be pleased with anything I might do. In all the time that we have been practicing and going out together, you've never once invited me to meet your parents."

Walter quickly changed the subject. "See that girl with the cello? That's Annalise Berglas. She and I went out together once, but that was long before I met you, of course."

"She's very beautiful."

"Perhaps, but she can't hold a candle to you. Besides, she's very unpleasant and so I ended it with her. *Kaput.*"

"Really?"

Walter lied with ease. "Yes. She's very stuck-up. She's only out for someone with money, and that's not me. Not yet, anyway."

Chao Chen observed, "I believe Annalise Berglas is also performing a Beethoven piece, *Sonata Number Three* for cello and piano."

Walter feigned indifference. Chao Chen handed him the printed program. "Take a look." Walter read:

Shanghai Conservatory of Music
Recital
Lyceum Theatre
June 10, 1943

1. Violin Sonata no. 26 in B-flat Major, K. 378, Allegro
Moderato (Wolfgang Amadeus Mozart)
Xue Guowei, violin; Annette Birnbaum, piano

2. Cello Sonata no. 3 with piano, Adagio cantabile –
Allegro vivace (Ludwig van Beethoven)
Annalise Berglas, cello; Bruno Rogovin, piano

3. Impromptu, op. 90, no. 3 in G-flat Major for piano (Franz Schubert)
Edvard Eisenstein, piano

> 4. Violin Sonata no. 5 in F Major, op. 24 with
> piano, Allegro (Ludwig van Beethoven)
> Walter Kolber, violin; Chao Chen, piano
>
> 5. "Salut d'amour," op. 12 (Edward Elgar)
> He Tang, violin; Dimitri Tsarskey, piano
>
> 6. Nocturne in E-flat Major, op. 9, no. 2 (Frédéric Chopin)
> Albert Offenbach, piano

Walter observed, "A nicely balanced program, although maybe just a bit schmaltzy for my taste." He laughed. "Did you notice that the piece following ours is *'Salut d'amour'*? 'Salute to Love.' I'd like to believe that Tang and his duet partner are performing it just for us, Chao Chen."

"I know He Tang. He has a girlfriend, and if he is playing for anyone, it's for her."

"I thought you were going to say you went out with him."

"He doesn't interest me in the least. He's just too provincial for my taste. I need someone who has seen more of the world than Jiangsu Province and the Yangtze River. And you know I've never had a boyfriend before. You are my first, my one and only."

"Either I'm the luckiest guy in the world or other men are just plain stupid or blind to not notice how beautiful and sensual you are. I can never get enough of you."

Chao Chen blushed. "I'd better look at the score once more so that I don't disappoint you or Miss Liang."

Walter pulled out his pocket watch. "I wonder what's taking so long. It's already ten past six. The recital was supposed to start exactly at six o'clock."

As if on cue Professor Wittenberg clapped his hands to gain the attention of the musicians backstage. "All right, everyone. We will begin in just a few minutes. We have a sold-out crowd this evening. There are more than six hundred people in the audience, which shows that music transcends all barriers. Many in the audience have had a difficult time getting here, and a few were denied passes to leave the Designated Area until I personally called Commandant Kano Ghoya's office and prevailed upon his staff. I've had to hold the curtain for a few minutes to wait until he arrived with his entourage, but they are finally all seated now in the front row and so we can begin."

Edvard Eisenstein looked visibly shaken. "Professor Wittenberg, I've had several run-ins with that little Japanese monster. I hope Ghoya isn't going to cause trouble for us this evening."

Professor Wittenberg assured him, "He will be on his best behavior. Ghoya loves classical music. He plays the violin, badly but he plays. He fancies himself a violinist in spite of barely being able to keep time, in fact, but you can be sure I haven't pointed this out to him. When I've been forced to play with him, he saws away and I try to follow his lead as best I can. It's insufferable. Nevertheless, we should be grateful that he has allowed this recital to proceed tonight. He could force us to cancel if he wanted to, and so I put up with his nonsense."

The musicians breathed a collective sigh of relief.

"And now, my musicians, are you ready?" Professor Wittenberg asked enthusiastically.

"Yes, maestro," they answered together.

"Wonderful. When you go on stage, remember that you are instruments of the Divine. Yes?"

In unison they responded again, "Yes, maestro."

The audience waited impatiently, fanning themselves with their programs; the concert hall was sweltering without air-conditioning, but due to rationing, there was only enough electricity to run the lights.

Professor Wittenberg parted the curtains and stepped out on stage to greet the audience. "Welcome, ladies and gentlemen. I'm thrilled and delighted to see so many of you with us this evening to enjoy this program of romantic music. My apologies for starting a few minutes late. I know how anxious you are to hear the wonderful students who will be playing their hearts out for you tonight, but I felt it only right that we wait until our esteemed guest, Commandant Ghoya, and his entourage were here. Now that they have arrived, please give this special patron of music the round of applause he deserves."

Ghoya stood and a smattering of applause echoed through the theatre, and then the lights dimmed as the first violinist and pianist took center stage for the first of the six selections. The brightly played opening notes of the

Mozart piece pitched the audience onto the edge of their seats, and whatever fatigue they had brought in with them was quickly erased by the sheer beauty and vivacity of the music.

As each selection was played, the separate emotions of the men and women there, whether Chinese, German, Japanese, or Scandinavian, melted into one collective beating heart.

When Walter and Chao Chen took their places on stage, there was an audible murmur of admiration for the stunning couple. It soon became apparent that their physical attractiveness was more than matched by the beauty of their performance.

It was the first time that Chao Chen had ever received a standing ovation. She was overwhelmed. Walter, on the other hand, seemed to take it in stride; Chao Chen suspected that in his mind *he* had earned it for both of them.

When student pianist Albert Offenbach bowed his head as he struck the last chord of the Chopin Nocturne, the audience would not let him off the stage. Their applause was meant for the collective group of performers, but it was left to him to extend the recital for a few more minutes with a planned encore, Chopin's *Mazurka in F Minor, op. 68, no. 4*, a brief and heartbreaking final tribute to the composer's Polish heritage.

After the musicians, standing shoulder to shoulder, took their bows to thunderous applause, Commandant Ghoya smiled, and reaching up to the stage, he shook Professor Wittenberg's hand. Then leading his entourage, he marched down the aisle holding himself erect to compensate for his short stature, looking left and right to make sure the audience paid attention to him. Everyone waited quietly in their seats until he left the theatre, wanting to avoid any contact with the man who so arrogantly called himself the "King of the Jews." As the audience filtered into the lobby, the ushers opened the doors onto Moulmein Road to cool down the room. The sound of Ghoya's speeding motorcade could be heard over the shouts of congratulations as the musicians joined their families and friends.

Walter pressed his hand against Chao Chen's back, pushing her into the crowd. "Ah, I see my family over there. I want you to meet them."

"You know I've already met your mother. I'm not so sure she'll be pleased to see me."

"Oh, don't be such a timid mouse, Chao Chen. You look ravishing in her dress, and I can just hear Mutti bragging about the perfect fit, et cetera and so forth. And by the way, you played extremely well tonight."

"I thought I might have made a few mistakes in tempo."

"Not really. You managed to keep up with me, and because of you, I outdid myself. I can't wait to hear what Professor Wittenberg has to say. I might even get a mention in the newspaper tomorrow."

Chao Chen wondered, *What about me? Could I possibly be worthy of a mention as well?* Miss Liang appeared carrying a bouquet of flowers. "There you are. You both played magnificently. I'm very proud of you." She handed Chao Chen the bouquet. Hardly able to contain her excitement, Miss Liang disclosed, "A reporter asked me if you were my protégée, Chao Chen. You know what that means? That means, if he writes something nice in the newspaper, I'll soon have more private students than I can handle."

Walter was curt. "Wasn't that the main reason I was paired with Chao Chen, to showcase you, Miss Liang?"

Miss Liang forced a smile. "In part." With impatience in her voice she said, "Now, if you'll excuse me, I must find my father. He's here somewhere. He wanted to be sure to hear Chao Chen this evening. He's already quite a fan of hers!"

Walter bowed and then pushed his way into the center of the lobby. Chao Chen trailed behind him. His parents, surrounded by Walter's twin brother Dolfie, his older sister Lilly, and her husband, waved.

Lilly embraced her brother. "Walter, you did the Kolber family proud this evening. Papa must be pleased that he hasn't wasted his money on all those violin lessons for you. He can stop his grumbling."

Herr Kolber retorted, "Did I have a choice? Your mother would have put me out onto Chusan Road with nothing but the clothes on my back, just like the poor Jewish refugees, if I had stopped paying for your lessons."

Lilly laughed. "You're right." Turning to Chao Chen, she spoke in English. "It's a pleasure to meet you, Miss Chen. Walter, why don't you introduce Miss Chen to Mutti and Papa?"

Frau Kolber spoke up. "Walter, tell Miss Chen that she looks quite nice in my dress."

Chao Chen smiled graciously despite feeling as if everyone was being condescending toward her.

Walter's father scanned the lobby, and then he waved at another man across the room. "Oh, there's Samuel Jedeikin," he said aloud to no one in particular. "We must say hello. *Gute Nacht*, Fräulein Chen." And with that they all turned their backs and quickly left.

Standing by herself amid the celebratory crowd, tears filled Chao Chen's eyes. Turning around to look back at her, Walter shrugged his shoulders and mouthed, "Sorry."

Frau Götz and her husband came to Chao Chen's rescue. Seeing them push their way through the crowd, Chao Chen practically fell into Frau Götz's arms as the woman smiled at her like a proud mother. "You were marvelous, *Liebchen*."

Herr Götz leaned in to give Chao Chen a kiss on both cheeks. "Why don't you ride with us? We have a rickshaw waiting outside the theatre. That is, unless you'll be taking a coffee and some sweets with Walter and his family."

"No. I wasn't invited. Thank you. I'd be most grateful for the ride."

Frau Götz wrinkled her nose. "So that little *mamzer* doesn't have the manners he was born with."

"What does that word mean?" Chao Chen only knew that it wasn't a nice word.

"I should bite my tongue but I can't help it. We have an expression: 'God will strike me dead for saying a mean word, but he'll bring me back to life for speaking the truth.'"

Herr Götz laughed at his wife's quick wit, but Chao Chen waited for an explanation. Frau Götz continued. "*Mamzer* is a Yiddish word that has a few meanings. In this case I mean 'rascal,' but it can also mean a child born out of wedlock or from a marriage forbidden by Judaism."

Chao Chen looked visibly shaken. Herr Götz jumped in. "Come, ladies. We can all use some fresh air."

As the threesome was leaving the theatre, the violinist Xue Guowei approached Chao Chen. "Congratulations on a beautiful rendition of the first movement of the *Spring Sonata*. If you are ever looking for another violinist to play with, I'm your man."

"Thank you. That is very kind of you to offer, as you played the Mozart with extraordinary brio; but for the moment, Walter Kolber and I are committed to playing together."

Xue Gouwei added, "If you change your mind, let Professor Wittenberg know and perhaps he can arrange something for us."

"Indeed."

Once they were outside the theatre, Frau Götz asked Chao Chen what she and that "very handsome young man" had discussed. After Chao Chen explained, she added, "When word gets out about your performance, you'll have your pick of partners, my dear."

Neither Rui-De Xu nor Ya-Nan cared to wait up to hear anything about the recital. Chao Chen placed her flowers in a vase, making sure that she chose one of little importance to avoid being roundly criticized. As she carried it down the dark hallway and into her bedroom, Ya-Li appeared out of the shadows. "Chao Chen, how did you do? I want to hear every last detail."

"I thought I would faint from nervousness, but the minute I sat down at the piano, I forgot all about the butterflies in my stomach—and miraculously I didn't make a single mistake."

"And what about Walter?"

"Oh, Ya-Li, he was magnificent! I wouldn't be surprised if he is offered a position in one of Shanghai's orchestras by next year. I'll be lucky if I find a job playing with a chamber music group in a hotel lobby at best."

"You're too modest, Chao Chen. I'm sure you did brilliantly. I hope he thanked you for all your hard work. Did he give you those lovely flowers?"

Chao Chen smiled. "No. They're from Frau Götz and her husband, but Walter's taking me to see the American movie, *The Constant Nymph*, tomorrow night. It's playing at the Eastern Theatre on Wayside Road. I just finished the novel and I'm dying to see the film. The casting is strange. It's hard to believe, but Joan Fontaine, who is twenty-six according to the movie magazine I read, is playing a fourteen-year-old girl named Tessa. Her romantic rival, Alexis Smith, is actually two years younger than she is. Both are in love with Charles Boyer. He plays the role of a composer and pianist who's down on his luck. He's a bit of a cad, married to one woman and enamored of another."

"And how does this love triangle end?"

"Badly. Tessa dies of heart failure and the composer's wife renounces him when she realizes his heart is elsewhere. He regrets the choices he's made, of course. He never achieves the fame he craves, and he ruins the lives of the two women who love him."

Chao Chen jumped off her bed, startling her mourning doves, which fluttered about in their cage. "I want to read you something. Let's see if I can translate it for you." Opening the English novel on her night table, she flipped through the pages. "Ah, here's what I'm looking for. It's a description of Lewis Dodd, the composer in the novel." She read aloud:

> "'His young face was deeply furrowed, nor was there any reassurance to be found in his thin, rather cruel mouth, nor in light, observant eyes, so intent that they rarely betrayed him. His companion, distrusting his countenance, found, nevertheless, a wonderful beauty in his hands, which gave a look of extreme intelligence to everything he did, as though an extra brain was lodged in each finger. Their strength and delicacy contradicted the harsh lines of his face....'

"Isn't that extraordinary? 'An extra brain was lodged in each finger?' If I were clever enough, I would describe Walter's genius with the violin the same way." She gently closed the book and sighed.

"What are you going to wear tomorrow night for your date with this genius of yours?" Ya-Li asked.

"I have so little to choose from." Chao Chen opened her wardrobe and held up a light cotton shirtwaist dress in pale pink. "This will have to do. Can you iron it for me? Although it's so humid that I'm sure it will be wrinkled in no time. Nothing stays crisp in this weather. Sometimes I wish that it were winter all year round. But then I'd be yearning for summer, wouldn't I?"

"I can't deal with your philosophizing, Chao Chen. You'll have to have this conversation with your genius violinist."

"Stop calling him that. I know you're just teasing me."

"In a way I am, but I'm also trying to warn you to keep your eyes open." Then Ya-Li was emphatic, "And your legs closed. The worst thing that could happen is for you to become pregnant. Just be careful. Herr Kolber may say he loves you—at least that's what you've told me—but I'm sure his parents would never accept his marrying outside his own kind. The Jewish people may like us as customers, they may want us as business partners, and they may hire us as cheap labor, but that's as far as it goes. When the war is over, they'll leave Shanghai, and then what will become of you, Chao Chen?"

With each word that Ya-Li uttered, Chao Chen became more agitated. She felt like one of her little birds fluttering around in its cage. "Miss Liang told me the same thing, but I'm afraid it's too late. But she also said, 'The Heart wants what it wants,' and for better or worse, I want Walter Kolber. When he touches me, I just can't resist him. And the fact that he is Jewish intrigues me. After all, wasn't Hans Jewish? I had a hopeless crush on him. I still think about him every now and then."

"Oh, Chao Chen, you are sounding like a silly schoolgirl instead of a grown woman. What am I going to do with you?"

"Trust that everything will turn out as it should. After all, didn't I pick out a piece of cake on my first birthday? At least that is what I was told. And that means that I'll know how to enjoy all the pleasures that life holds for me."

Ya-Li continued, "I can see that I can't talk any sense into your head, but I can still worry about you."

Chao Chen yawned. "I should go to bed. I need to be at Frau Götz's tomorrow and then…" Her voice trailed off.

"And then you have a date with your Prince Charming. Is that better?"

"Yes. And let's hope he proves to be just that."

Chapter 36

One Drink Too Many

The next morning, Eva sent Dolfie to buy the early edition of the *Shanghai Jewish Chronicle* while Walter slept behind the sheet that divided his area from the rest of their living quarters. Although it was only eight o'clock, Chusan Road was already buzzing with activity. A band of emaciated and dirty Chinese street urchins followed a cart laden with muslin bags. One of the boys slit a bag open with a pocketknife and rice poured onto the street. The boys rushed to gather up as much as they could, stuffing it into small bags, which they would then sell to the poorest residents of Hongkew living in the dark streets. Dolfie watched in amazement at the speed with which they carried out the robbery. A little Chinese girl, her brown eyes running with an infection, approached him and asked for money. She was virtually naked except for the cotton stopper, referred to as a "cotton tail," intended to keep diarrhea from running down her legs.

Dolfie reached into his pocket and gave her a coin. She thanked him in pidgin English and then disappeared down an alleyway, no doubt to give the handout to her parents. Despite the heat, Dolfie's hands were cold and clammy. He sat down on a bench for a moment to catch his breath, and then he headed to a newsstand that was already open for business. "May I have a copy of the *Shanghai Jewish Chronicle*?"

"You're in luck. They're back in business." The vendor's hands were black with ink. "The paper was suspended for a few days because they printed an article that suggested a Chinese Nationalist victory was imminent in Chungking. The Japanese, of course, denied this. As punishment they shut the paper down. You never know what's going to infuriate them. And who knows if the news is even accurate? Probably not, since most of the true accounts won't get past their censors. The Japs are only interested in having us print their lies." He handed Dolfie a newspaper. "That will be twenty fen. And watch out for the ink. It hasn't dried yet."

Glad that he wouldn't disappoint his mother, Dolfie practically ran back to the factory. The Chinese and Jewish refugees were already busy at their machines. Frau Klein lifted her head and shouted over the *rat-tat-tat* of her sewing machine, "Dolfie, if you decide to break up with that Margot, let me know. I have a very pretty daughter, and I know she'd be pleased to go out with you. Do you want to see her picture?"

"That's very kind of you, Frau Klein. I have no intention of breaking up with my girlfriend, but perhaps you'd like me to ask my brother Walter if he'd be interested?"

Frau Klein made a face. "From what I've heard about your brother, I don't think he would be a good match for my Rosalie. But thanks anyway."

Walter had just washed his face in the sink when Dolfie ran upstairs. Looking in the mirror, Walter hollered, "I don't know how much longer I can tolerate shaving in ice-cold water. I should have one of the women downstairs heat some water for me."

Josef yelled, "Your mother wants to take a bath tonight. We'll have some hot water by five this evening. I'm sure she'll save some for you and Dolfie." Turning to Dolfie, he asked, "Do you have plans this evening?"

Dolfie nodded. "Margot and I are going to play cards."

Josef looked at Walter. "And what about you?"

"If I can get past the guards, we're going to catch an American movie."

"Walter, I don't know how you always manage to sneak out of the Designated Area and back." Josef paused, "And tell me, who is this 'we'?"

"A nice girl from the Conservatory," Walter lied. "You didn't get a chance to meet her. She couldn't make the recital. Too bad. She so wanted to hear me play."

Eva was impatient. "Enough of this chatter. Dolfie, give me that newspaper. I want to see what the reviewer has to say about Walter's performance with that China girl."

Eva put on her reading glasses and pulled up her chair next to the window, so the sunlight would illuminate the print better than the single light bulb hanging from the ceiling.

Finding what she was looking for, she scanned the review until she spotted Walter's name.

Walter grabbed the newspaper from his mother. "Let me see that." His eyes scanned the article quickly, his anger growing apparent on his face.

> One highlight of this glorious international recital—bringing together our Chinese hosts with the rest of the musical community—was Beethoven's Spring Sonata. Violinist Walter Kolber played with considerable flair, his notes clear and lively. But it was Miss Chao Chen who, like a flower blossoming in the springtime, gave the performance a rare beauty and passion. There was little eye contact between the two musicians, but it was as if their fingers knew intuitively just when to play the notes. We will look forward to hearing more from these two performers.

"This idiot gives more credit to Chao Chen than to me,"

Eva agreed. "Just remember that the *Jewish Chronicle* always has one eye on the Japanese. They probably told the reporter what to write."

"That makes no sense, Mutti. The Japanese are at war with the Chinese. If politics was the issue, they would have bent over backwards to praise me, not Miss Chen, who is Chinese."

Eva sputtered, "Well, maybe it's because the reviewer is ignorant." She was on a tear. "I suggest that you refuse to play with Miss Chen in the future."

Walter thought his mother had gone too far. "I can't do that. I have to follow Professor Wittenberg's orders, and for now, at least, he wants me to continue to perform with her."

"We'll see. And if you won't tell him, I will."

Josef intervened. "Eva, my dearest, you are overreacting. The review was very, very complimentary to Walter. I'm guessing that some of the other performers were not even mentioned. Am I right?"

Eva looked at the review a second time. "You're right. Annalise Berglas was totally ignored by the critic."

Josef kissed his wife on the top of her head. "My goodness, it's almost eight o'clock. The store will be open soon. Isn't it time for you to go?"

"Yes, it is, darling."

He handed her the brass button that indicated that she had a three-month pass out of Hongkew. "Don't forget this."

After pinning it on her collar, Eva looked at herself in the full-length mirror that hung on the back of the office door to make sure that her slip was not peeking out from underneath her hem. "I'm off."

The Constant Nymph did not disappoint. The French matinee idol, Charles Boyer, was convincing as the charming and notorious Lewis Dodd. After the film, Walter asked Chao Chen, "Can you imagine an old man like that falling in love with a young girl?"

"Does age really matter when you're in love?" Chao Chen had a reason for asking this question. She had hidden the fact that she was five years older than Walter. He had no idea that she was twenty-five because of her youthful appearance and childlike innocence.

"I agree with you. I've been with older women and younger women, and until now it was all the same to me. I got what I wanted and then let them go. But it wasn't love, which is what I feel for you."

For better or for worse, Walter had never hidden from her that he had had more than one sexual experience, even though she had told him she didn't like being reminded of that fact. When she thought about the possibility that he had frequented pleasure houses in the red-light district, it made her shudder but it was also strangely thrilling.

He kissed her hand. "When I'm around you, all I want to do is protect you. You seem so young and so vulnerable, like a delicate flower that will surely die in the winter's snow."

"Not quite. I've had to learn to be very independent and self-sufficient." She hesitated, "Even though I may seem like a 'delicate flower' to you, you'll find out that I'm more like a stalk of bamboo, bending in the wind so I won't break."

"It sounds like something Confucius would say."

"No. It's from an ancient Chinese poem. Bamboo is important in my culture because its deep roots denote resoluteness, its straight stem represents honorability, its interior modesty, and its clean exterior chastity. Bamboo also gives people strength when facing tough situations."

Walter joked, "I am in favor of all of that, well, except the chastity part."

Chao Chen, trying to avoid Walter's eyes, turned her head.

Walter sounded apologetic. "I didn't mean to upset you. Cheer up. I have something special planned for us this evening. I've reserved a table at ten o'clock at the roof garden at Wing On. Henry Rossetty and his quartet are playing there. What do you say?"

"I'm not properly dressed for such a fancy place. And I don't know how to dance."

"All you have to do is follow my steps. You'll pick it up in no time."

The cover over the roof garden on the seventh floor of Wing On was rolled back to reveal the starlit sky over Shanghai. The dance floor was crowded with patrons eager to forget their troubles and indulge in the alchemy of music, liquor, and laughter.

As Walter and Chao Chen sat down at a table near the dance floor, bulbs flashed near the entrance. Photographers followed a glamorous party that was quickly ushered to one of the gazebos at the far corner of the roof garden.

Chao Chen gasped as Walter asked, "Who are those people making all that commotion?"

"That's the movie star Yanyan Chen with the chairman of Wing On, Leon Kwok. The movie magazines call her 'The Swallow Next Door.' She's still making pictures here in Shanghai. Her latest is *Wedding Night*. It's playing all over town."

"You know I don't speak a word of Mandarin, and I'm not much interested in the local entertainment."

"Have you ever heard the expression 'when in Rome, do as the Romans?' You really are very parochial, Walter."

"And I intend to stay that way, except when it comes to romance. There is something about Oriental women. They are so mysterious, so alluring, so…"

"So unlike your mother."

Walter burst out laughing. "Yes, that's true. And what is it about me that attracts you?" His question sprang from an insatiable and deep-seated need to be admired, a trait that would turn into an incurable obsession that no woman could satisfy.

She leaned across the table and gently caressed his cheek. "I told you at the recital. It's your self-confidence. And you're extremely attractive. At least to me you are. When we are playing duets together, I have a hard time concentrating on the music."

Tapping his foot in time with the music, Walter ordered two gin fizzes, and after downing the first glass and ordering another, he stood up and glanced toward the dance floor. "Are you ready to take a whirl around the dance floor?"

"I don't know. I'll probably step all over your feet or trip over my own."

"Just relax. I'll put my hand on your back and steer you around. I don't recognize the music, but I think it's a fox-trot." Before Chao Chen could object, Walter had her in his arms, swaying to the music.

They stayed on the dance floor for a few numbers, and then Walter declared, "I'm dying of thirst. Let's sit the next one out." He picked up his drink. "Bottoms up."

Chao Chen imitated him. Within minutes she felt lightheaded. "I'm not feeling very well."

Walter paid the bill, but when she stood up she could barely keep her balance. Stepping into the empty elevator, Walter put his arm tightly around Chao Chen's waist; and as the elevator doors closed, he leaned in and kissed her passionately. "I've been wanting to do that all evening."

She slurred her words, "And I've been dying for you to do that." And then she fell into his arms.

When the elevator door opened, Walter helped Chao Chen through the lobby and out onto the street. He hoped that the breeze off the bay would sober her. She finally opened her eyes. "You'd better take me home, Walter. I think I'm going to be sick."

"You can't go home like that. My sister Lilly's apartment is not too far from here. I have an extra key. Why don't we spend the night there? In the morning you can go straight to Frau Götz's."

Chao Chen could have come up with a hundred reasons to say no, but none seemed to matter in her impaired state.

Walter hailed a pedicab. Chao Chen leaned against him, the fog enshrouding them. He took off his jacket and put it around her shoulders. After lighting a cigarette, he took a flask out of his jacket pocket and gulped a few swigs of whiskey.

When the pedicab stopped, Chao Chen asked, "Where are we?"

"Don't you remember anything, Chao Chen? We're spending the night at my sister's. You wouldn't want your mother to see you like this, would you? But don't worry. I'll be the perfect gentleman—unless you don't want me to be."

Chao Chen didn't answer. What would he think of her if she confessed that she wanted to lie naked in his arms, feel the beat of his heart next to hers, and hear him tell her that he loved her?

As Walter fumbled with the key the couple heard a baby screaming from the apartment. When he finally opened the door, Lilly stood before them. She was holding little Mischa in her arms, trying to calm him down. The toddler kept tugging at his ear, crying out in pain.

Lilly addressed her brother in German. "Mischa has a fever and an ear infection. I don't know what to do, and David is out with friends."

"Isn't your upstairs neighbor a doctor?"

"Yes, Dr. Lee, but he's Chinese. I wouldn't think of asking for his help."

"I don't think you have a choice. I'll have Chao Chen ring his doorbell and ask if he will see the boy."

Walter quickly explained the situation to Chao Chen. Lilly grabbed Chao Chen's arm. In English she asked urgently, "Will you do that, Miss Chen? I'd be so grateful."

"Of course, Miss Lilly."

Despite the lateness of the hour, light was visible underneath Dr. Lee's door, which told Chao Chen that the doctor had not retired for the evening. After a few rings of the bell he answered the door. Chao Chen introduced herself and apologized for disturbing him. "Dr. Lee, can you come downstairs? The little boy, Mischa Ozer, is sick."

"Why don't you ask his mother to bring him up here? My treatment room is right here in the apartment, and I'll have a better chance of diagnosing the problem. I probably even have some medicine in my cabinet that might help. Hopefully it's nothing serious."

"I'll be back in just a minute."

Chao Chen ran down the stairs, the urgency temporarily clearing her head, which moments ago had been spinning. She helped Lilly bundle Mischa up. The two women hurried back to Dr. Lee's apartment, the toddler cradled in his mother's arms.

Now wearing a white coat instead of his street clothes, Dr. Lee ushered them into his examination room. "Miss Chen, will you tell Madam Ozer that

I'm going to look inside Mischa's ear with this instrument to see what's going on? She can hold him on her lap if she wishes."

Lilly looked to Chao Chen for guidance with pleading eyes.

Dr. Lee performed his examination swiftly and with gentleness so as not to frighten the little boy or his mother. "Your child has an infection of the middle ear. Nothing to worry about, but he will need antibiotics right away." He went to his medicine cabinet. "Ah, luckily I have the right dosage." As if he thought someone were spying on him, he lowered his voice. "Some of the doctors, even in the hospital clinics, can't get their hands on the medicines they need unless they know who to bribe. It's really a disgrace." He handed Lilly the pills and addressed Chao Chen. "Miss Chen, tell Madam Ozer that she must give her child two pills a day. They are to be mashed up and mixed with his food. And she is not to skip a dose. I'm also going to give her some ear drops to alleviate the pain. Please ask her if I have her permission to administer the drops now."

After Chao Chen translated, Lilly nodded and held Mischa's head still to make it easier for the doctor. Within minutes Mischa stopped crying and his eyelids drooped from exhaustion.

Dr. Lee observed, "Well, I guess our little patient is feeling more comfortable. He should sleep through the rest of the night."

Through Chao Chen acting as an interpreter, Lilly asked, "Dr. Lee, how much do I owe you?"

"Just pay me for the medicine. This evening's visit is free. And please bring Mischa back in five days. I want to be sure that the infection is clearing up." He reached into his coat pocket. "Here's my card. Please schedule a daytime appointment with my secretary." He then added, "My door is always open to you, Madam Ozer."

"I'm so grateful to you. And if there's ever anything I can do for you, Dr. Lee, please do not hesitate to ask. My husband will stop by in the morning with your money on his way to work. And again, please forgive us for barging in on you at this hour."

Chao Chen looked down at the sleeping boy in Lilly's arms. His dark curls were matted against his forehead and his long eyelashes brushed against his damp cheeks. She wondered if she might ever have the desire to be a mother. It seemed like an overwhelming responsibility, one she was not prepared to take on, at least not now.

Chao Chen helped put Mischa to bed. As the two women stood over his crib, Lilly turned to Chao Chen. "I'm sorry if I ruined your evening with my brother. I'm sure you didn't expect things to turn out this way."

"Please, think nothing of it. I'm glad I could be of help to you. Perhaps in time we'll get to know each other better."

Lilly whispered, "May I give you a bit of advice?"

Chao Chen wasn't sure she wanted to hear what was on Lilly's mind, but she thought it would be rude if she said no. She nodded.

Lilly continued in a whisper. "You're a lovely young woman, and a very talented one as well. Don't throw away your gifts on Walter. I adore him. That's why I gave him the key to our apartment. He has no privacy living with our brother and my parents, obviously. But I'm not sure he's capable of a meaningful relationship. Walter thinks about only one person—himself. And he can be very irresponsible."

"Forgive me, Madam Lilly, but I ask you to let me be the judge of that. I'm not a child."

"Fair enough. I'll keep your relationship with Walter a secret, but I must warn you that, if my parents find out you two are a couple, I'm not sure what the repercussions might be. They could stop paying for his violin lessons and more."

"From what Walter tells me, your mother encourages him in his career."

"You're right. But if you have any hopes of keeping Walter interested in you, I suggest you play hard to get. Do you understand what I mean?"

"Not really, Miss Lilly. Love is not a game to me."

"That's where you're wrong, my dear. The English have an expression: 'Why buy the cow when you can get the milk for free?' A man like Walter needs a challenge. If you climb into bed with him before he's made a real commitment to you, I predict that you'll be sorry. You understand?"

Chao Chen blushed.

Lilly continued, "I'll tell Walter to sleep on the sofa in the living room and you can take the bed in our guest room. The two of you can figure all this out when you're both thinking clearly. Knowing my brother as I do, he's probably had a few too many drinks by now." Then she added, "Let me fetch you a nightgown. You don't want to sleep in your street clothes, do you?"

Chao Chen shook her head. "No. It would be unbecoming to show up to work tomorrow morning in a wrinkled outfit, wouldn't it?"

"I'll be just a minute." Lilly slipped into her bedroom for a moment. When she returned she handed Chao Chen a nightgown. "Pleasant dreams and thank you again for coming to Mischa's rescue."

After Lilly closed the door to the guest room, Chao Chen lay awake wishing that Walter might find his way to her bed, but as the hours ticked by, she lost hope and finally fell into a deep sleep.

chapter 37

Command Performance

When Gan Chen was alive, his wife Rui-De Xu was always on everyone's guest list in Zhenru, and her own lavish parties were seen as an opportunity for others to spend a few moments with Magistrate Chen. Now, twenty years since his death, Rui-De Xu was no longer the envied hostess or desirable guest. So, it came as a surprise to her when she received an engraved invitation from Madam Zonghing Rong, whom she barely knew, to attend a tea on December 15, 1943 honoring Shanghailander Clarise Moise at the family villa on North Seymour Road in the International Settlement. At the bottom of the invitation was a handwritten note:

> Please be sure to bring your daughter, Chao Chen. I hope she will perform a short piano recital for our guests.

Rui-De Xu was livid that this invitation was not solely for her. Wasn't Madam Rong the wife of the "King of Flour and Textile," yet another Chinese businessman who had benefited from her husband's connections? She had a good mind to turn the invitation down, but it was so rare that she was invited anywhere these days, and the thought of an elaborate English tea gave her ample reason to change her mind and accept, despite her displeasure at the thought of introducing Chao Chen to anyone of importance.

She rang the bell at her elbow. "Ya-Li, tell Chao Chen to come here at once."

Chao Chen stood at her bedroom window as a light snow fell outside, dusting the branches of the yew trees.

Ya-Li opened the bedroom door. "Didn't you hear me knocking, Chao Chen?"

"No. I must have been daydreaming."

"About what? Or should I say, about *whom*?"

Chao Chen hesitated, then blurted out Walter's name. "No matter how I try to resist thinking of him, I'm hopelessly in love. He told me he feels the same about me. We've been seeing each other every week at Miss Liang's studio. And there's more."

"Such as…"

"His sister Lilly has a beautiful apartment with a spare bedroom. She gave Walter a key so that we can be together whenever we like."

Ya-Li gasped. "And have you?"

Chao Chen nodded. "I feel my entire body quiver when Walter touches me. I want to yell out to the world, like Madame Bovary, 'I have a lover!' I never thought I'd know the meaning of sexual passion, but now I do because of Walter. He may be younger than I am, but he has much more experience than I do and is teaching me everything he knows about love, or should I say, lovemaking."

"Chao Chen, I'm afraid you've gone quite mad."

Feeling a mixture of defiance and confusion, she answered, "Yes, I have."

"Pull yourself together this minute. Rui-De Xu wants to see you. I hope you don't owe her money. You know how furious she becomes if you are late in paying her."

"Don't worry, Ya-Li. I'm being her 'good and obedient slave.' It galls me that she keeps taking money from me. I hate that she holds the purse strings and controls my mother. Have you seen the way my mother looks lately? Sometimes I think she's barely alive. I don't know whether it's because she's worried about my brothers or because she has no rights in this house. If my father were alive, everything would be different, wouldn't it?"

Ya-Li whispered, "I don't have an answer, but you'd better go to Rui-De Xu before she throws something because I'll have to pick up the pieces."

Chao Chen bowed to Rui-De Xu and then waited for her to speak first.

"I haven't seen you in quite a while, Chao Chen. You're looking rather pretty today. I'm reminded of a blushing rose in full bloom."

Chao Chen eyed Rui-De Xu suspiciously; until this moment, the woman had given her only harsh criticism, and she would often slap her face, or worse, at the slightest provocation.

Rui-De Xu continued. "I've been invited to a tea at the home of Madam Rong." She waved the invitation in the air. "She asked that you perform for the guests. Madam Rong will even send a chauffeur for us."

"Will she pay me for performing?"

Rui-De Xu snorted. "Don't be ridiculous, Chao Chen. It is an honor just to have been asked."

"I'm not a monkey sitting on an organ-grinder's shoulder. I'm a serious pianist. I have sacrificed everything to get where I am, and without anyone's help. If you had been at the Conservatory recital or even read the reviews, you might have some appreciation for my musical ability. I imagine that Madam Rong was in the audience or she heard about my performance." Chao Chen had begun to accept that she had genuine talent.

Rui-De Xu growled, "I have no interest in your so-called musical career. It's not earning you any money, and it won't give you the opportunity to meet a suitable husband. Now, you're going to go to the tea with me and that's final!"

"Yes, but it's only because I want to perform, not because you're ordering me to." Chao Chen waited for a slap on the face, but instead, she handed Chao Chen a purse with money inside.

"Take this. Go with Ya-Li to the Sincere Department Store and buy yourself a new dress. I don't want you looking like a charwoman. The Gan Chen family has its reputation to uphold, and for better or worse, and as much as I hate to admit it, you're a part of this family."

As often as Rui-De Xu had insulted her, nothing she had said to Chao Chen in the past stung her deeper than this. Despite everything, she was still her father's daughter, and nothing would change that.

The entryway of the Rongs' villa was decorated with garlands and gilded wooden cherubs. A huge Christmas tree stood underneath the skylight, and hundreds of wrapped presents sat at the foot of the tree. On the carved reception table were rare fifteenth-century blue-and-white porcelain flasks. An English Christmas carol played on the Victrola.

Madam Rong was chatting with the guest of honor as Chao Chen and Rui-De Xu were escorted into the salon. "Rui-De Xu, I think you may have met most of the ladies here some time ago, and of course I recognize your beautiful daughter, Chao Chen, from the recital at the Lyceum Theatre. Let me introduce you to Madam Clarise Moise. She and her husband, Arthur de Carter Sowerby, founded the *China Journal* some years ago. We owe both of them a debt of gratitude for sharing their extensive knowledge of China with the United States and England. Her husband is the honorary chairman of the Shanghai Museum."

Turning toward Chao Chen and Rui-De Xu, Clarise asked in fluent Mandarin, "Have you been to the museum? It has quite an extensive collection of Chinese art and artifacts."

Rui-De Xu answered, "Unfortunately not. We've only lived in Shanghai for six years. My family was forced to abandon our estate in Zhenru Township in 1937. We narrowly escaped the Japanese invaders." She straightened her back and boasted, "Perhaps you know that my late husband, Gan Chen, was the minister of commerce at Nanking and head magistrate of Baoshan County during the early years of the Republic."

Clarise responded, "I'm very familiar with your husband's reputation because he approved many projects that my husband coordinated in Baoshan County and in northern China."

"And why was your husband in China, may I ask?"

"Arthur was on a mission financed by the American steel magnate Robert Sterling Clark. He served as a consultant for some important national projects. He told me that your husband worked tirelessly to help the people of China. As I recall, Gan Chen was a Hanlin scholar, was he not?"

Rui-De Xu, whose lips were usually frozen into a perpetual scowl, smiled. "I'm flattered that you know so much about my husband. He was indeed a Hanlin scholar, as was his father before him. Did you know my husband achieved fifth place in the imperial examination? He had to beat out thousands from around the country to get there. Oh, he was rather disappointed that he did not come in first. He was always mightily ambitious, though not for himself but for his family name. Then, nothing we did was for us." She glanced toward Chao Chen. "It's not like today. Young people have only one thing on their minds, to succeed and benefit only themselves."

Clarise ignored Rui-De Xu's remark so clearly aimed at Chao Chen. "I hope you will visit the museum. My husband has just mounted a show for David Ludwig Bloch, an émigré artist from Bavaria and quite a fascinating man. I believe he's a Jew who was released from the Dachau concentration camp and emigrated to Shanghai. His exhibition includes more than two hundred wood-block prints of everyday street life, like *Rickshaw*, *Beggars*, and *Beware of the Hat Snatcher*. He has been to our house for dinner with his girlfriend, Lilly Cheng. Both she and David are deaf, and so we sometimes struggle to communicate with one another. They're planning to marry."

Chao Chen listened intently. Unable to hide her curiosity, she blurted, "A Jewish man and a Chinese woman marrying? I didn't know that such a thing was possible."

Clarise replied, "It's very rare here in Shanghai, but it has happened."

Madam Rong stared at Rui-De Xu. "What do you think about interracial marriage?"

"I have no opinion about this Herr Bloch person, but I would never allow it for my children." Looking toward Chao Chen, she continued, "Why, this very minute I'm desperate to find a proper match for this old maid. She'll be twenty-five next April."

Mortified at her mother's remarks, Chao Chen could only look away.

Clarise insisted, "She's hardly an old maid, Madam Rui. She looks barely twenty. If you will let me play matchmaker, I might have someone in mind for her. He is from a wealthy Chinese family right here in Shanghai. Do give me your card and I promise to be in touch."

Rui-De Xu smiled even more broadly. "How very kind of you, Madam Clarise. I'm sure that Chao Chen will be only too happy to meet anyone you have in mind, and it will lift a great burden off my shoulders."

Clarise addressed Chao Chen. "You should know that we Americans don't stand on ceremony and can come off as a bit pushy. I'll try to make this introduction as comfortable as possible for you, my dear. I can see that the topic of marriage makes you very uneasy, and I don't blame you." She laughed. "If I hadn't met Arthur, I'd probably be unmarried to this day, but I found him irresistible and so here we are."

Chao Chen found Clarise Moise's forthrightness refreshing. "Oh, I've come across one American woman some might call 'pushy,' but to me she was so impressive. Miss Laura Margolis. Do you know her?"

"The Jew with the JDC? Of course I do. And you are so right. She is quite amazing, but unfortunately, she has been sent to a Japanese detention camp. My husband, who is British, and I have so far been exempted. But that could change any day now if and when the Japanese open more camps."

Madam Rong interrupted their conversation. "Let us take our conversation into the dining room where you can also enjoy tea and sandwiches."

Once tea had been served, Madam Rong stood up and announced, "I have had the pleasure of hearing the brilliant pianist Chao Chen, who was featured at a recital at the Shanghai Conservatory of Music some months ago, and I'm so glad that she is graciously willing to entertain us this afternoon."

The ladies applauded politely, and then Chao Chen confidently announced her program: "I will be playing Franz Schubert's *Impromptu in G-flat Majo*, followed by Frédéric Chopin's *Barcarolle in F-sharp Major*. And as a short finale, I have prepared Erik Satie's '*Je te veux*,' which means 'I want you.' The composer called this little waltz 'furniture music,' but I hope you'll agree with me that it is a very beautiful composition and much more impressive than simply a piece of furniture, even an antique one."

The ladies laughed at her witty observation.

Out of the corner of her eye Chao Chen saw that Rui-De Xu was staring at her with a look of amazement on her face, as if she were seeing her for the first time. When the performance ended, Madam Rong handed Chao Chen a bouquet of white orchids as the ladies clapped politely. Clarise Moise shouted, "Brava," and to Chao Chen's amazement, everyone joined her.

Chao Chen and Rui-De Xu settled into the back seat of Madam Rong's limousine on their way home after the tea. Passing by the Ohel Rachel Synagogue, Rui-De Xu picked up the thread of their conversation with Clarise Moise and Madam Rong. "I wonder if that American woman is serious about finding you a husband."

"Please don't speak to her about me. I don't want or need her help."

"Do you have something to tell me? Have you found someone who wants to marry you? Or are you afraid that I might disapprove of him and you're keeping it a secret?"

"It's not that. There are many men at the Conservatory who have shown an interest in me. I'm just weighing my options."

Rui-De Xu responded pointedly, "Well, aren't you the lucky girl? After they discover your true age they'll immediately lose interest in you."

"I doubt that."

"While you're weighing your options, be sure to count his money and carefully examine his background. You're a stupid fool if you believe that you can be happy marrying someone of a different race. It will only end badly. That story Clarise Moise told us is all well and good for two deaf people, but you're the daughter of the honorable Gan Chen. Don't ever forget it!"

"What would you do to me if I did marry a foreigner?"

"You'd be disinherited and permanently erased from the family records. And any hope of being buried in the family tombs… Well, you can just forget that."

Chao Chen laughed. "You can't be serious. You've already spent the dowry my father put aside for me, and without that, what Chinese man would ever want to marry me now? Now I have nothing to bring into the marriage, or at least that's what you have led me to believe."

Rui-De Xu interrupted, "Maybe one who is rich enough not to care what you are worth would be willing to marry you." Rui-De Xu examined her long fingernails, which had just been polished for this special occasion. Her eyes landed on the bouquet Chao Chen was holding. "Now give me those flowers."

"But I earned them."

Rui-De Xu snatched them out of her hands with a strength that defied her sixty years. "You're such an ungrateful girl. I have a good mind to throw you out on the street."

Chao Chen snapped at her, "If I had anywhere else to live, I'd be gone by tomorrow."

chapter 38
Closing Shop

Josef crawled out of bed at first light. Eva was still asleep. He sighed and looked at his watch: five thirty. The early morning sunlight pierced through the burlap window covering, the stench of human waste being collected on the street below seeping in through a crack in the glass windowpane. He closed his eyes for a moment, imagining himself once again lounging on the shore of Lake Wörthersee, sipping a glass of iced tea with Eva while his children sunned themselves on a raft, their healthy bodies glistening in the summer sunshine as a string quartet played a lovely Strauss waltz on the terrace of the Hotel Schloss Velden where they spent their summers so many years ago.

Josef put on his glasses. He knew the war was taking a heavy toll on everyone's business, and so he was not surprised when he went over JEKO's expense and revenue report for May, 1944. Herman's numbers merely confirmed what he already knew, huge losses from the Vienna House of Fashion. He was not looking forward to his meeting with his partner later that day at the Café Europa.

Josef anticipated that the store would have to be shuttered because there was no business to be had. Eva had done her best, but without Lilly's presence as its chic salesgirl, she could not keep things going. Besides, he needed his wife in the factory, at least until Dolfie was released from the hospital. He had contracted diphtheria six weeks earlier and was making a slow recovery, and so there was no telling how much longer he would be in the hospital. *However, not all the news is bleak,* Josef thought. Lilly was pregnant with her second child. The baby was due in September. *Is it still called a miracle if a child is born in the midst of all this misery?*

It was disappointing to Dolfie that Lilly never visited him in the hospital, but perhaps it was for the best. What if she contracted some terrible disease and passed it on to Mischa or her unborn child? Dolfie would just have to get over his resentment toward his sister.

As for Walter, while he didn't admit as much, Josef knew that he had a girlfriend living somewhere outside the Designated Area because he didn't come home most nights. Josef could only hope that this son would have the good sense to stay out of trouble. The thought that Walter might become a husband and father at twenty was worrisome. He lacked his twin brother's common sense and calm disposition that had won the heart of Margot Rosengart, Eva's hairdresser. The two had just announced that they were engaged.

Yes, there would be a wedding in the Kolber family when the war ended, which pleased Josef and Eva. Eva was very fond of Margot. In a former life in Königsberg, Germany, Margot's parents ran a successful business selling baby carriages. Now Margot was the family's major breadwinner. Although Margot's prices were higher than those of the clever Chinese hairdressers who worked in the beauty parlors in Hongkew from seven in the morning until nine at night for scant wages and a mattress to sleep on, Eva remained loyal to Margot as a way of helping the young couple out. Certainly, Dolfie deserved as much.

If Josef was being honest with himself, he had to admit that Walter was a "golden boy" who had musical talent and was just lucky in life. It seemed that the Pao Chia mandatory civilian patrol listed only Dolfie for service and somehow skipped over Walter altogether. Maybe being a Kolber with the same birthdate confused whoever did the scheduling. And then there was the upcoming concert in September; Walter had finally been chosen to play in a professional orchestra. Eva was *verklempt*.[5*]

On balance, looking at the ledger of his life, Josef told himself that he was "in the black."

Josef was startled by a hand on his shoulder. It was Walter, already dressed in a cream-colored linen suit. "Good morning, Papa."

"So, you decided to sleep here for a change. Honestly, I don't know

---

[5] * Yiddish, *Overcome with joy*

how you manage to avoid the curfews. One of these days you're going to get caught."

Walter shrugged his shoulders. "I have an appointment at the Deaman Gregg School of Business on Kwenming Road. I think it's high time I started making some money instead of being on the dole. I'm going to enroll in their secretarial program."

Josef was speechless for more than an instant. Finally, he said, "Am I hearing clearly? What explains this change of heart?"

"It's always good to have something to fall back on. I remember you telling me this a few years ago, and I really didn't believe you. But I see how unpredictable the life of a violinist can be and I want to prepare myself for whatever life hands me."

"Is it possible that you are finally growing up, Walter? I'm going to circle this day on the calendar. Here it is: June 6, 1944."

"While you are at it, circle September first as well. That's the day of my solo performance with the orchestra."

"Indeed, I will, although I'm sure your mother will remind me a hundred times until the day arrives. By the way, your brother has been asking that you visit him in the hospital. He's miserable there. I'm sure you could cheer him up."

"Tell him I'm sorry. I've been too busy. Tell him I'll try to make the time to see him."

The Café Europa was nearly empty. Frau Borenstein, the owner, greeted Josef. "And where is Eva?"

"She's feeling a bit under the weather. The heat and humidity aggravate her arthritis and her legs still bother her."

"Please give her my best and tell her I plan to come into the shop in the next few days. We have a bar mitzvah in the family in July."

Josef wished her *mazel tov* and then scanned the restaurant for Samuel Jedeikin, who was sitting in the corner making pencil marks on a piece of paper.

Josef found his way through the many tables. Samuel stood up when he saw him approaching and gave him a big bear hug.

"Sit down. What can I get you? You know the menu, of course." Samuel waved the waiter over. "This is one of the few places in the city where the kitchen can still manage to get chocolate. Who would have ever believed that a German would have to learn to live without chocolate and whipped cream, eh? That's why I love coming here."

Joseph already knew what he wanted. "I'll have a *Sachertorte* and a coffee."

"Have you heard what's going on in France as we are sitting here?"

"No. The Japs confiscated our radio and I haven't had a chance to read the morning papers. Not that you can fully trust anything printed here. Anyway, Eva couldn't join us. She's supervising our cutters. We're introducing a new jacket pattern and she wants to be sure that no mistakes are made. We can't afford to waste any fabric. Materials are getting more expensive every day. And one of the heavy-duty sewing machines is on the fritz. My mechanics work wonders, but parts are hard to come by and there are no new machines."

Samuel put his hand up. "Catch your breath, Josef, and just listen for a minute. American, British, and Canadian forces have staged an amphibious landing on the beaches of Normandy, France. While German troops have positioned themselves on top of the cliffs with long-range artillery, it appears—at least this is what Peter Adams is reporting—that the Allies are advancing under the protection of heavy aerial bombardments and will soon be heading inland. If this invasion succeeds, the war in Europe could soon be at an end. I know we've heard this kind of news before, but this time the report could be real!"

"And what about what's happening in the Pacific and right here in China?"

"According to shortwave broadcasts coming out of Australia, the Americans are 'hopscotching' from one Pacific island to another. The Japs have no idea which island will be the next target, and they're losing men, ships, and aircraft at a devastating rate. What's more, Chiang Kai-shek's strategy to draw Japanese troops deep into the countryside and away from the coastal cities seems to be working, although there are reports that the Japanese are using chemical weapons, killing innocent civilians by the thousands. In my opinion, when this war is over, it will be the Chinese who will have sustained the greatest losses—in the millions."

Josef glanced at his watch. It was almost four o'clock when his coffee appeared and they still had not gotten down to business. "I see that you've been looking over our most recent financial statement. I'm anxious to get your reaction."

Samuel Jedeikin adjusted his wire-rimmed glasses. "I've finally secured a buyer who is willing to pay for the Vienna House of Fashion. He'll pick up whatever merchandise is still hanging on the racks and pay overdue rent. I see that we are in arrears three months."

Joseph was suspicious, "How did you come up with a buyer when so many of the small shops are closing their doors?"

"Let's just say that it's going to be a bauble for the mistress of a rich Chinese merchant friend of mine right here in Shanghai who has connections and leave it at that. What he decides to do with the store is anybody's guess, but it will make his mistress very happy." Samuel folded the report and put it in his breast pocket.

"Samuel, this will be a sad moment for Eva. She and Lilly put their hearts and souls into the shop."

"I know this is a sad moment, but we must all move on. Please give my sincerest regards to your wife."

"And the same to Sonia."

Chapter 39

Anywhere but There

The leaves of the plane trees rustled in the morning breeze as the birds flitted from one tree branch to another. Chao Chen crossed the street to Frau Götz's house. She was feeling lighthearted and optimistic. She couldn't stop thinking about the look of pure joy on Lilly's face as she nursed her baby girl, Judith, who had been born just a week ago on September 7. The baby's bassinet was right next to Lilly's bed and would stay there for several months until Judith was old enough to sleep in the crib already waiting for her in the nursery. Then her brother Mischa would be moved into the guest bedroom where Chao Chen and Walter had spent their nights together.

Chao Chen asked Lilly, "May I hold the baby for just a moment?"

Lilly hesitated. "I don't think that's a good idea. Babies shouldn't be handled by anyone other than their parents just yet. But in a few weeks I'll happily let you take her off my hands. I promise."

Walter looked at the baby girl over Chao Chen's shoulder. "I swear she looks just like me when I was an infant."

Lilly made a face. "Hardly. I remember you as an ugly little runt. And now look at you. I have to admit that you've turned into a rather handsome man, although sadly you sometimes remind me of Dorian Gray—beautiful on the outside and corrupt on the inside."

"I don't know the reference, but I don't like what you're insinuating."

"Never mind, Walter. I'm only teasing you."

Chao Chen discounted Lilly's criticism of Walter. She viewed it simply as light banter between siblings, and she was even a bit jealous.

And there was another reason for Chao Chen's smile. Walter had passed his examination at the Deaman Gregg Business School, which meant that he would qualify for a bookkeeping position and then she and Walter could live together and stop hiding the secret of their love affair from the rest of the world. It crossed her mind to ask Deirdre Möller if there might be something for Walter in her father's company.

Chao Chen had a key to Frau Götz's front door and, expecting to see the ladies concentrating on their hand-stitching and carefully cutting a bolt of leather, let herself in. Instead, everyone was gathered around the dining room table as Frau Götz read aloud in German from a weatherworn book. Chao Chen could not understand what she was saying, but between phrases the ladies shrieked and wailed as if they were hearing their own death sentence leaping from the pages of the book.

When Frau Götz came to the end, she bowed her head and wept.

Chao Chen hardly knew what to do or say, but she didn't have to understand German to realize that something horrific had happened. She had never seen such communal grief before. Nor had she ever felt more like an outsider.

Slowly everyone resumed their work. Whatever catastrophe had struck the Jewish community, these ladies could not afford to lose a day's pay and Frau Götz could not afford to miss a delivery deadline, whatever the reason.

Chao Chen looked at Frau Götz, "What's happened?"

"Oh, my dearest, it is worse than we could ever have imagined." She picked up the book she had been reading from. "Until this moment we have all been kept in the dark about what the barbaric Nazis have been doing to the Jews." She choked back a sob. "Everyone in this room left someone behind to suffer at the hands of these madmen. Hitler wants to annihilate every Jew on the planet. The man who wrote this book is a firsthand witness to the atrocities that have been perpetrated on our innocent people."

Chao Chen looked at the cover and read the name of its author and title: "Jankiel Wiernik. *Ein Jahr in Treblinka*. What does this mean?"

"A year in Treblinka." Frau Götz sat down. Her hands were shaking. She tried to explain, but she herself was incredulous. "This book was snuck out of Poland and translated from Yiddish into German. Treblinka is a Nazi concentration camp where this man, a Jewish carpenter, was held prisoner for a year. He escaped in 1943 and wrote down what he saw. Let me see if I can translate some of it for you into English:

'Time and again I wake up in the middle of the night moaning pitifully. Ghastly nightmares break up the sleep I so badly need. I see thousands of skeletons extending their bony arms toward me, as if begging for mercy and life. I, drenched with sweat, feel incapable of giving any help. And then I jump up, rub my eyes and actually rejoice over it all being but a dream. My life is embittered. Phantoms of death haunt me, specters of children, little children, nothing but children.'"

Frau Götz turned a few pages. "When corpses of pregnant women were cremated, their bellies would burst open. The fetus would be exposed and could be seen burning up inside the mother's womb."

"Who could do such a thing?"

"The Nazis, of course. This man tells of loading corpses into wagons and sliding them into ovens with his own hands. He was forced to do this. Otherwise he would have been murdered right along with the rest of the prisoners."

"How can he live with himself?"

"He asks himself the same question. He has no answer, but he says he must write what happened to him with complete honesty so that the rest of the world will know what is happening. He believes that this is the only reason he escaped—to bear witness. He says, 'Perhaps I shall someday know how to laugh again.'"

"Do you think the Walter's parents know about this?"

"How could they not? This book has been passed from hand to hand throughout Hongkew. After reading this I cannot imagine ever going back to Austria or Germany when the war is over. The earth will be covered in the ashes of my people, the rivers filled with their blood."

"Where will you and your husband go, Frau Götz?"

"Anywhere but there."

Chao Chen thought about her future with Walter. Once the war was over, where would the Kolbers go—and would she be asked to follow Walter as his wife? She didn't have the answers, but she trusted that Walter would have ambitious plans for both of them. They would make their way together in the world as fellow musicians and helpmates. She had to believe this or everything that had happened between her and Walter would be a farce.

Frau Götz wiped her eyes. "I have been meaning to tell you that Frau Kolber stopped by just yesterday with a package. Inside was the last delivery of our gloves we made for her shop. She said they closed and she needed to return them. Normally I would not have taken them back or refunded her money, but because of your relationship with Walter, I made an exception."

Chao Chen could barely speak. "Frau Götz, you didn't say anything about Walter and me, did you? We have kept our relationship a secret from his parents. Only his sister Lilly knows that we are romantically involved."

"Of course not. I know with whom I'm dealing. I can only guess what she might say if she knew anything about the two of you."

Chao Chen relaxed. "Walter didn't mention that his mother's shop is closing."

"From what I know about Walter, I don't think he's very interested in the family business. Forgive me for saying this, Chao Chen, but I think that your young man has a selfish streak in him, and so the only reason he would be interested in what is happening to the family business is if it affects him in any way. And again, from what I know about Frau Kolber, she'll do whatever she can to keep her son living in the style to which he has become accustomed. Just look at the beautiful clothes he wears."

Chao Chen felt an ache in the pit of her stomach. This was the second time in a matter of days that someone had spoken ill of Walter, first his own sister and now Frau Götz. Was she so infatuated with him that she was blind to his faults?

Chao Chen buried herself in her work, checking the invoice dates on the completed orders, but after hearing what Frau Götz said about Walter, she felt very uneasy and had a tough time concentrating. She kept looking at the clock on the mantel. There was only one hour left before she'd be free to leave for her practice session with Walter at Miss Liang's studio. Until then, she'd have to live with her gnawing doubts about him.

Walter leaned against a tree in front of the Liang family residence and studio smoking a cigarette. The windows onto the street were wide open to let in fresh air. The curtains billowed like the skirts of beautiful young girls walking through the Stadtpark. Shielding his eyes from the sun, he watched

Chao Chen approach him. She rushed into his arms. He smelled the scent of lavender on her skin, and as he held her, he could feel her delicate backbone, which he loved to trace with his fingertips until she moaned with pleasure. And then he would... Well, there was always something new to explore with Chao Chen's body.

He threw his cigarette on the ground and picked up his violin case. "Let's go. Today we'll finish going through the second movement together: *Adagio molto espressivo*. It is much easier playing Beethoven with you than with Professor Wittenberg at the piano. Just looking at you puts me in the right mood."

"Walter, before we go in, I must tell you what happened this morning at Frau Götz's."

"You didn't lose your job, did you?"

"What would ever make you think such a thing? No. She told me that your mother has closed her shop. Why didn't you mention it to me?"

"I didn't think it was any concern of yours."

"How can you say that? Perhaps what you really mean is that it's of no concern to you!"

"Since when have you become Dr. Sigmund Freud?"

"You're right. I have overstepped. I apologize."

He kissed her on the lips. "You're forgiven."

"And there is something else, something unimaginably frightening that Frau Götz told me this morning."

"And what is that?" He pulled at the collar of his shirt and wiped a bead of perspiration from his forehead.

"What was just thought to be a rumor is now a proven fact. Hitler is not just waging a war against the Allies but a war against the Jews wherever they might be found. They are being rounded up and taken in cattle cars to be imprisoned in concentration camps, and there they are eventually gassed, and their bodies cremated." Chao Chen was teary.

"Stop crying, Chao Chen. Finish your story."

"Don't call it a story. It is a nightmare, and a real one. Frau Götz has a book to prove that what I'm telling you is true. All the ladies were crying, worrying about their relatives left behind in Europe. You still have family in Austria and Poland, don't you?"

"Yes, and perhaps that is why we haven't heard a word from anyone since we've been in Shanghai." He added, "My mother knew what she was doing when she forced us to leave Vienna in '38. If it had been up to my father, we'd all probably be on our way to one of those concentration camps. Come to think of it, we were pretty lucky, weren't we?"

Still weepy, Chao Chen nodded. "And we never would have met, would we?"

Walter handed her a clean handkerchief. "Here, dry your tears. Now, tell me what's really on your mind."

"Frau Götz said that she and her husband will leave Shanghai when the war is over. She said this city will never be their true home but they cannot return to Germany either, not after what has happened there. So, they will have to find somewhere else to live, but they don't know where."

"And you're concerned about my family and about the two of us? Is that what all this *Sturm und Drang* is about?"

"I don't know what you are saying, Walter. But from the tone of your voice, I can only guess. Please don't be so dismissive."

"You aren't to worry. Who knows how much longer we'll be here? And where is it written that, if my parents leave, I must follow them?" Walter continued, "I could very well stay in Shanghai with you if I achieve the success that I envision for myself. For that matter, I can live anywhere. All I'll have to do is pick up the telephone and say yes or no to an invitation to perform in any one of the concert halls in the world. That is the life of a musician anyway, isn't it? Traveling about? And of course you'll go with me. Besides, I don't share Frau Götz's abhorrence of Austria. Perhaps I'll go back there. We have beautiful concert halls in Vienna, and the city is built on the shoulders of the greatest composers that man has ever heard."

Chao Chen interrupted, "But Walter, I don't even speak the language. I know no one. And how many people in Austria look like me? I'd be completely out of place. I never told you, but when I went to the concert at the Doumer Theatre and Miss Margolis spoke there, I made sure to bring Miss Liang with me so that I wouldn't be the only Chinese face in the crowd and the only person who was not Jewish. Do you know what it feels like to be different? At least, here in Shanghai, I look like almost everyone else, don't I?"

Walter put his arms around Chao Chen once more. "Oh, my little sparrow, you are much more beautiful than any Jewish *Fräulein* I have ever laid eyes on. You'll be like an exotic bird that everyone will be drawn to."

Chao Chen wanted to believe Walter with all her heart but wishing something to be true did not make it so, she reminded herself.

"Has the storm lifted and the sun come out again, my Chao Chen? I certainly hope so because we're going to be late. We can continue this conversation at another time. For now let's show Miss Liang what a perfect pair we make, shall we?"

Their session went well enough for Miss Liang to recommend that Walter and Chao Chen move along to the third movement, the Scherzo: allegro molto, the shortest of the four movements. "This is Beethoven's little 'joke.' That's what *scherzo* means in Italian." Miss Liang motioned with her hands. "It's played with humor and brightness, and quick, quick, quick. But don't be fooled. You must commit to every note with the utmost seriousness. Do you understand?"

Walter and Chao Chen nodded and thanked Miss Liang for allowing them to advance toward the end of the piece.

"Don't thank me. You're doing the challenging work. I'm just here as your coach." She added, "You'll still have to please Professor Wittenberg. He'll be the final judge of your collaboration, not me."

chapter 40

We'll Make It

The winter of 1944 descended upon Shanghai, bringing with it the bitter cold once again. The Jewish refugees still living in the seven *Heime* wore every stitch of clothing in their meager wardrobes, and their Chinese neighbors living in the dark alleyways of Hongkew suffered right along with them. The atrocious living conditions were exacerbated by fears of air raids and fire bombings.

A witness recorded in his journal how the city had been drastically transformed in the three years since the Japanese bombing of Pearl Harbor in December 1941:

> The streets, never clean, had become filthier. Popular British double-decker buses had disappeared and single-decker bus service was irregular. Moreover, due to the lack of gasoline, a new contraption with a pipe spewing black smoke, which the French called "gazogene," was fitted on the front of most buses. The limousines of high-ranking Japanese officers had been likewise converted. One newspaper headline was vividly descriptive: "[Chinese] Man Gives Child to Hawker for One Sack of Rice." Nerves were frayed by the constantly increasing number of air-raid alarms, as U.S. bomber planes punctured the clouds over the city.[4]

Despite Japanese efforts to block radio communications, news of Allied victories in the Pacific made its way through the community. In January 1945 it was reported that the Japanese blockade of China was broken and that a major supply route from Burma to China, was finally completed. It was named the Stilwell Road by Chiang Kai-shek in honor of U.S. Army General Joseph Stilwell for providing much-needed men and munitions. With the aid of the United States and its allies, Chiang Kai-shek's strategy of drawing the Japanese away from the coast into the countryside was paying off.

In Western Europe, following the successful invasion of France at Normandy on June 6, 1944, Allied troops closed in on Germany and its occupied territories in the west while Soviet troops were advancing toward Germany from the east. In a desperate effort to gain the upper hand, Germany launched a major offensive on December 16, 1944 that was intended to drive a wedge between the American and British armies in France and the Low Countries and recapture the port of Antwerp in the Netherlands to deny the Allies use of the port facilities. The Battle of the Bulge, which lasted a month, turned out to be the largest battle fought on the Western Front, involving over a million soldiers, many of whom were underequipped and poorly clothed. More than ten percent lost their lives on both sides. But Hitler held on, and in the months following their defeat on the battlefield, the Nazis intensified their attacks against the Jews, turning Eastern Europe into a killing field. In February 1945, with victory in sight, President Franklin D. Roosevelt, Prime Minister Winston Churchill, and General Secretary Joseph Stalin met in Crimea for the Yalta Conference, where they hammered out an agreement that stated that the Allies would accept nothing less than the unconditional surrender from Germany. Among the other provisions was the agreement that the Soviet Union would finally enter the war in the Pacific, siding with the Allies against Japan—no more standing on the sidelines.

On May 7, 1945, the German High Command signed a document of unconditional surrender at General Dwight D. Eisenhower's headquarters in Reims, France. Another surrender agreement was signed two days later in Soviet-occupied Berlin at the insistence of Stalin. Days earlier the Soviets attested that Hitler and his mistress had committed suicide and that their remains had been discovered in a bunker beneath the Berlin Reichstag.

Josef heard the news of the Allied victory. Echoing what must surely have been on the minds of so many other Jews, Josef looked at Eva, "Now we can only hope that the Allies will concentrate all their military power on defeating the Japanese. I don't know how much longer we're going to be able to hold on before we're bankrupt. We're selling to customers who have no credit, and in some cases below our cost. And every time the telephone rings I expect that it's the bank reminding us that we're late. I wouldn't be surprised if they decided to call our loan. And if all this wasn't bad enough, I'm worried about our Lilly and her children. Since her father-in-law's death in January, David has been struggling to make ends meet. And now, on top of everything else, he has his mother to worry about in that fancy villa of hers."

Eva kept her voice down so as not to waken Dolfie. "Lilly tells me she's thinking about making children's clothes and selling them from their apartment. She says her neighbor, that Chinese doctor, has patients with children coming in and out of their apartment building at all hours of the day and night. And she's even willing to sell to the Nazis still in Shanghai. Some spend time at the café next door to their apartment building. Their children are growing just like anyone else's, and she knows how to make lederhosen and dirndls, which are all they're interested in buying for their *Kinder*."

Not expecting that she would have an answer, Josef asked Eva, "How much longer are we going to have to put up with the Nazis here in Shanghai? What are they still doing here?"

"I heard that some of these Nazis are helping Chiang Kai-shek. The Nazis and the Chinese Nationalists still have a common enemy, the Communists."

Rubbing his temples, Josef finally confessed, "I don't know how much longer I can keep going."

Eva put her arms around her husband. "We don't have any choice but to keep going, Josef."

They heard footsteps coming up the stairs. It was Walter. He had been out all night and looked like he had gotten into some kind of scuffle. Josef remarked, "Look what the cat dragged in. Where have you been?"

"I spent the night in jail. I think my luck is running out. When I left the French Concession late to get back into the Designated Area, I got caught at one of the checkpoints. I tried to talk my way out it, but the Jap guard didn't understand a word I was telling him. I even invoked Professor Wittenberg's name and told him that he was my teacher and a good friend to that Jap in charge, Kano Ghoya, but that didn't do the trick."

Then Walter doubled over in laughter and slapped his knees. "Oh, what an adventure! I was petrified that they would confiscate my violin. Then I had a brilliant idea. In the middle of the night, while other prisoners were trying to bargain their way out with a pack of cigarettes or scratching their bug bites and moaning, I took out my Lowendall and began playing. Naturally, the acoustics were not the best, but a calm descended over the prisoners and the guards tapped their boots in time to the music. I played a short Paganini caprice, my own private joke, because his 'Caprice No. 9' is called 'The Hunt' or 'La Chasse.' Of course, the Japanese missed the point, but by morning my cell door was unlocked, and *voilà*, here I am, free as a bird."

"And why were you out past curfew in the first place? You know how dangerous the city is!"

"It's better that you not know, Papa." He changed the subject. "It's a good thing I got out when I did because I finally got an interview for a bookkeeping job at one of the factories on Great Western Road. It's quite a distance, but with luck I can make the trip in under an hour and be back in time for my practice session with Professor Wittenberg."

Eva, visibly upset at the thought of what could have happened to her son, knew to move on. "If you intend to interview for a job, you'd better clean up. Josef, go downstairs and get a few of the workers to buy enough hot water for Walter to take a sitz bath. He smells awful. And make sure they don't overpay for the water!"

Dolfie, roused from a deep sleep by all the commotion, emerged from his room. He stood in his bare feet and his sweaty, crumpled nightshirt. He had only been out of the hospital for a few days and was still feeling the lingering effects of his illness.

Eva asked, "How are you feeling today?"

"Better, Mutti." He yawned, stretched his arms over his head, and then poured himself a cup of tea. "I couldn't help overhearing your tale of last night's adventure. Honestly, Walter, how is it that you step into a pile of horse manure and still come up smelling like a rose."

"You sound jealous. And what for? At least you have a secure job with Papa. I, on the other hand, am forced to go out and find work on my own."

Dolfie kept his temper in check, his response measured. "If I recall correctly, you showed very little aptitude or interest in the family business. And then you got yourself fired from your job at the garage, the typewriter shop, and everywhere else."

"Shut your mouth, Dolfie. You don't know what you're talking about."

Eva interrupted. "Stop your bickering. You're acting like you're still fifteen instead of twenty-two."

After soaking in the makeshift tub, Walter shaved in front of the mirror that hung by his bed and then patted a few drops of aftershave cologne on his face. Dispensing with a tie, he put on a freshly ironed shirt, light cotton jacket, and a pair of khaki summer pants cut to order by the seamstresses at JEKO. Stepping back to admire his reflection from head to toe, he was surprised to see how thin he had gotten. He pulled his belt to the tightest notch and then folded a handkerchief into his breast pocket.

The trolley took Walter within a few blocks of his destination on Great Western Road. He walked past the Country Hospital and the German Evangelical Church, where mourners tarried in the front courtyard as a casket was loaded onto a flatbed truck. Beyond the church was the Ash Civilian Assembly Center, one of six internment camps where British and American foreign nationals were kept under twenty-four-hour surveillance by Japanese guards.

Despite the distance and the unreliability of public transportation, Walter was on time for his interview with the owner of Schmidt Engineering Works. The sign outside the factory read: You need it; we'll make it. Many workers were highly trained Jewish engineers from Vienna and Berlin who accepted the most menial jobs, cobbling together all kinds of machinery on demand using whatever substitute materials they could get their hands on, including used tin cans, which they turned into stovepipes.

He knocked on the door to the factory office and was admitted by Herr Schmidt, who shook his hand briskly and ushered him to a seat.

Herr Schmidt looked Walter up and down. "Herr Deaman recommended you. We need someone to work part-time in the accounting department. I understand you received good grades in your class. Your name was mentioned by my neighbor here on Great Western Road, Samuel Jedeikin. He says he knows your father and vouched for you. Your father is Josef Kolber from Vienna, correct?"

"Yes, sir. We came here in '38."

"Small world, isn't it? Samuel speaks very highly of your family, and so I'm willing to give you a chance, but you'll be on probation for three months. That should be enough time to prove yourself."

"I promise I'll do my very best."

"Let's hope that's good enough. The salary for an entry-level bookkeeper is sixty fen an hour, and you'll be expected to work Monday to Friday from seven in the morning until noon."

Walter hesitated. That meant he'd have to get up at the crack of dawn, but he needed the money if he would ever be able to afford a room for Chao Chen and himself. "That shouldn't be a problem, sir."

"Very good. Now follow me. I want you to meet Clara Cohen, my niece and my eyes and ears in this factory. By the way, why aren't you working for your father at JEKO? According to Sam they are doing all right, even in these tough times."

"My father already employs my aunt and uncle and my twin brother, Dolfie. So here I am. I want to be on my own."

Herr Schmidt reacted in just the way Walter hoped he would. "Well, good for you! It doesn't hurt to make your own luck, does it, my boy?"

Herr Schmidt and Walter walked into the factory office. He addressed his niece, "Clara, this is Herr Walter Kolber. He's going to be your assistant starting tomorrow."

Clara lifted her head from her paperwork when she heard her uncle's voice. She had beautiful bright blue eyes, a slightly upturned nose, and a mane of thick, wavy blond hair that cascaded down her shoulders. Walter guessed that she was probably twenty-five or twenty-six.

"A pleasure to meet you, Frau Cohen," he said.

"It's Fräulein."

"My mistake. I couldn't imagine a woman as beautiful as you being single."

Clara was dismissive. "Herr Kolber, use your charms on someone else, if you don't mind. I'm interested in just one thing, that you help take some of this paperwork off my desk."

Walter bowed. "Please forgive me, Fräulein Cohen. I'm at your service."

Herr Schmidt escorted Walter to the door. "You'll find my niece to be a very independent-minded and ambitious young woman. Since I have no sons and my two daughters have no interest in the family business, I expect that Clara may one day be the future president of Schmidt Engineering Works—after she earns her engineering degree."

"A woman president. That's a novelty."

"Do you disapprove?"

"Of course not. Women should have as much opportunity as men these days. If the war has taught us Jews anything, it is that women are equal to men and, in many ways, more resourceful. How many women in Hongkew are now their family's primary breadwinner while their husbands sit by the window and stare out at the birds in a state of perpetual mourning?"

"You're right, Walter. It's a very sad state of affairs. Fortunately, I have managed to survive. There are always those people who land on their feet in good times and bad."

"Thank you for this tremendous opportunity, Herr Schmidt. I'd better hurry or I'll miss the trolley. I have an appointment at the Shanghai Conservatory."

"Not so fast, Walter. Don't forget that you're on probation. I want to be sure that you can satisfy Clara's expectations and that you're a hard worker. We don't tolerate slackers here."

"Of course. I promise to prove myself."

Herr Schmidt shook Walter's hand. "See you promptly at seven tomorrow morning."

Walter boarded the east-bound trolley. He held on to the strap as the trolley rocked back and forth. He felt as if he might lose his balance, but it was not the result of the trolley's movement but rather the effect that Clara Cohen had had on him. He was instantly attracted to her vitality and self-confidence. Walter stared out the window. A makeshift hearse, which Walter remembered had stood in the German Evangelical Church's courtyard on his trip here, followed alongside the trolley. It had obviously delivered its cargo to the nearby cemetery.

Walter smiled to himself. Yes, he would do his best to satisfy Clara Cohen's expectations, and any need she might have in mind. The thought of burying his face in her beautiful breasts made him dizzy.

chapter 41

The Nightingale's Song

Walter felt as if he were living a double life: in love with Chao Chen, promising that at any minute he'd have enough money to rent a room so they could be together; and at the same time infatuated with Clara Cohen, watching for the slightest hint that she might be open to the possibility of romance. He didn't know how he had gotten himself into this predicament, but he needed to figure it out.

He was irritable around Chao Chen, and during one of their practice sessions he snapped and threw the musical score across the room. "Why don't you pay attention, Chao Chen? We're never going to get through the last movement. It says '*allegro non troppo.*' I should find myself another partner. I really don't know why I put up with your ineptitude."

Chao Chen became teary-eyed. Miss Liang tapped her fan on Walter's shoulder. "You will not speak to Chao Chen in that manner! The *next* time you lose your temper is the *last* time I'll allow you in my studio. And may I point out that it is *you* who made the mistake, not Chao Chen."

Walter placed his violin and bow in his case, picked up his musical score, and stormed out of the studio.

As soon as he had slammed the door behind him, Chao Chen tried to make excuses for him. "Walter's under a lot of pressure. If he makes one mistake or shows up for work a minute late, he's afraid Herr Schmidt will fire him. There are five other junior bookkeepers standing in line for his job, and we need him to make his own money."

"Really?" Miss Liang cleared her throat. "Chao Chen, his behavior is inexcusable. You must surely know that, don't you?"

Chao Chen nodded.

"I think you need to take a very hard look at Walter Kolber. He has a dark side. Do you understand what I am saying?"

"Yes, Miss Liang, I do. But I keep hoping that his moodiness is just temporary and he'll revert back to the person I fell in love with."

Miss Liang asked, "Would you allow me to introduce you to someone? His name is Li Shutong, a vocalist studying at the Conservatory. He needs an accompanist to play a Schubert piece. At a minimum you'll be well paid, and who knows where it might lead? He is from a wealthy Shanghai family. His father and mine have known each other since boyhood."

Chao Chen hesitated to say what she suspected, and then in a torrent of words, admitted, "Walter has been very distant toward me, as if there is another woman in his life. I have no proof, of course. No smell of strange perfume, no lipstick on his collar, no love notes in his pocket."

"Chao Chen, you have been reading too many love stories in *Jindai Funuii*.[6]* If Walter is cheating on you, he's clever enough to hide the evidence, but that would surely explain his sudden bad behavior. I encourage you to trust your instinct. We women have a sixth sense when it comes to matters of the heart."

Chao Chen sighed. "Why is being in love so painful?"

"Don't be so melodramatic, my dear. You're not a prisoner to Walter Kolber's whims. I'm going to give you Mr. Li Shutong's telephone number, and the two of you can schedule a practice session at your home. Won't Rui-De Xu be surprised to see you with an upstanding Chinese gentleman?"

"At least it'll give her something to gossip about with Madam Rong if she ever sees her again."

"You haven't told Rui-De Xu or Ya-Nan of your involvement with Walter Kolber, have you?"

"Of course not."

"You are wise not to say anything. It is up to you to figure out what you want from life and with whom you want to spend it. You owe Walter nothing! Just because you were intimate with him does not mean that you are tied to him for all eternity. And you don't need to get married at all if you don't want to. Look at me. My career comes first, before any man. If I had to make a choice between music and a man, I'd always choose music."

---

[6] * *"Modern Woman"* (Chinese women's magazine)

Chao Chen watched through the window of the Chen family residence as the gray-and-maroon Italian coupe pulled up to the curb and the driver stepped out. Carrying a leather briefcase in one hand, he patted his straight dark hair with the other. Li Shutong was over six feet tall and walked up the path leading to the front door with long, self-assured strides.

Chao Chen, not wanting to appear overly impatient or anxious, waited for him to ring the bell before she opened the door. When he saw her, he smiled broadly. "Am I at the right address? Are you Miss Chao Chen?"

"Please come in." Chao Chen led him into the salon. "I apologize. The piano has not been tuned for months, but if we get past our first session together, I'll spend the money to have it tuned properly."

"No worries. I'm happy to send over a piano tuner."

"Would you like some water before we begin? It's unseasonably warm even for June."

"No, thank you, but I would like to take my jacket off, if you don't mind."

Chao Chen looked down at her shoes as he removed his jacket, trying not to stare.

"Ah, that's better." He took a sheet of music out of his briefcase. "As we agreed, I'd like to practice Schubert's '*Ständchen*' from the *Schwanengesang* cycle."

"Shall I translate it into Mandarin for you before we begin?" Chao Chen offered. "Understanding the words will lead us to a better interpretation of the music."

Li Shutong nodded as Chao Chen read:

> "My songs beckon softly
> Through the night to you;
> Below in the quiet grove,
> Come to me, beloved!
>
> The rustle of slender leaf tips whispers
> In the moonlight;
> Do not fear the evil spying
> Of the betrayer, my dear.

Do you hear the nightingale's call?
Ah, they beckon to you,
With the sweet sound of their singing
They beckon to you for me."

Chao Chen asked, "What do you think of the words?"

"It is very romantic, obviously, and tells of the man's longing for his lady love. He calls upon the nightingale to do his bidding. When I was still a young boy, my father gave me a nightingale music box, and I used to listen to its sweet tune for hours."

"What a strange coincidence. My father gave me a jeweled nightingale for my second birthday. It is my most prized possession because it is the only thing I have to remember him by."

"So, this song has a special meaning for both of us, yes?"

"Most certainly. Shall we try it all the way through? Don't worry about making a mistake. We can mark the sections that give you trouble and you can work on them alone."

Their hour together flew by. Li Shutong had a pleasant voice. Putting his music back into his briefcase, he asked, "Is my voice worth your time, Miss Chen? I do this solely for my own pleasure, so don't be afraid to say what's on your mind. You won't hurt my feelings, I assure you."

"You sing with feeling, which, as Professor Wittenberg says, counts for as much as technique— even more in some instances. So, I would be delighted to help you indulge in the pleasurable pursuit of Schubert's *Lieder*. May I ask what you do when you are not singing of nightingales and lovers?"

"Banking and investments. It's all rather boring. When this blasted war is over, and hopefully it will be over soon, I want to travel the world. I feel like a caged animal stuck here in Shanghai, but it's too dangerous to travel right now." Li Shutong reached into his pocket and pulled out a leather billfold as they walked toward the front door. "I almost forgot. What do I owe you for this delightful hour, Miss Chen?"

"I think we agreed upon one hundred yuan."

"And so it is. And here's a little extra for the conversation. I believe we've already set a date next week for our second session."

Chao Chen nodded, thinking to herself that a week seemed like an eternity.

Li Shutong smiled. "I shall look forward to it." He stepped out into the bright sunshine, opened the door of his coupe, revved the motor, and waved as he sped off.

Rui-De Xu crept up behind Chao Chen. "And who was that?"

"Don't spy on me. That was Li Shutong. He's paying me to accompany him on the piano."

"Shutong, you say. I have heard that name somewhere. I'm going to call Madam Rong and find out if he is who I think he is."

"Do what you want, but please don't embarrass me."

"How can you say that? I am only looking out for your well-being. I think the Shutongs are one of the wealthiest families in Shanghai."

Chao Chen did not want to give Rui-De Xu the satisfaction of being right. "I wouldn't know."

Realizing she had forgotten to fill her mourning doves' bird feeder, Chao Chen retreated to her bedroom. She poured the seeds into the cup, picking out the maggots that had burrowed themselves into the muslin bag. The little family of six mourning doves cocked their tiny heads toward her. "I'm sorry I ignored you. Will you forgive me?"

As if they understood what she was asking, the mother bird chirped happily and fluffed up her feathers. Chao Chen opened the cage door and coaxed one of the birds to sit on her finger. As she stroked his little body, he stared into her eyes, and then he flew back into the cage, nestling against his mother once again.

She heard a tapping on her bedroom door, and then it opened a crack. Ya-Li peeked inside. "May I come in, Chao Chen? I've made some fresh lemonade for you."

"Why do I suspect that the lemonade is just an excuse to find out about my visitor?"

"Well, if you must know, it is. I saw him leave a few minutes ago. I swear he looks just like a movie star. And that car of his must have cost him an emperor's treasury."

"I don't know anything about cars, but he is rather handsome, isn't he?"

"Does he have a chance with you? Or have you decided that Walter Kolber is the man for you?"

"How could I possibly know? I've only just met him. Besides, why would he have any interest in me?"

Ya-Li grabbed a hand mirror and thrust it in front of Chao Chen's face. "Just look at yourself. There's your answer. You are a beautiful young woman. And you are talented and smart and kind. I could go on and on." Then she stamped her foot on the floor. "You deserve better than that Walter Kolber. Face the facts. He's just a starving violinist with an insufferable sense of self-importance."

Chao Chen put her hands over her ears. "Ya-Li, you've said enough. Thank you. Now please take your tray and leave me alone."

In that moment, there was so little Chao Chen could be sure of.

chapter 42

The Great Wall Crumbles

Walter peered over Clara Cohen's shoulder as she worked at her desk. She waved her hand in the air as if swatting a fly.

"Do you mind, Walter? This is none of your business. You have plenty of things to occupy your time besides spying on me. I need you to go through the invoices so that I can prepare a monthly report for Uncle."

"That was very rude of me, but the intense look on your beautiful face aroused my curiosity."

"I suspect that I've aroused more than your curiosity."

"Guilty as charged." Noticing that the door to Herr Schmidt's office was closed, he decided that now was as good a time as any to turn their relationship into something more than strictly business. "I've been meaning to ask if you might consider going to the Mascot Roof Garden. My brother Dolfie and his fiancée are making an evening of it. Henry Rossetty and his band are playing there through the summer." He hummed a few bars of *"Bésame Mucho."*

"Give up, Walter. Take one of your Chinese girlfriends."

Walter narrowed his eyes. *How did she know about Chao Chen?* "What do you mean? I don't go out with Chinese girls. Let's just forget that I asked you out on a date, shall we?"

"And I'll pretend that you haven't been seen around town with a Chinese girl from the Conservatory."

Walter felt his face turning red. "Oh, you must be referring to Chao Chen. She is my duet partner, but I haven't the slightest interest in her beyond her musical talent. No, I'm looking for a pretty Jewish girl to take home to Mutti."

Clara smiled. "Good luck with that, Walter."

Walter tried to ignore her retort. "So, aren't you going to tell me what's on your desk? Is it something I can help you with? After all, that's what I'm here for, to make your life easier."

"If you must know, it's an application to the University of California. They are offering scholarships to foreign students, and I want to be first in line when they consider applicants. This war can't last forever. Once we are free to leave Shanghai, I'm going to get my engineering degree. Then I will come back to Shanghai to work for my uncle in a more senior position. That is, unless the Communists have their way. In which case I'll stay in the United States and find a job there."

Walter felt deflated. Why hadn't he taken Herr Schmidt's warning about Clara more seriously? He had been the model employee—showing up right on time, doing everything that was asked of him, however menial—just on the slim chance that he might crack Clara's seemingly impenetrable facade. What a waste of effort and energy. If he wasn't going to be rewarded with something more than money, what was the point of working so hard?

At noon Walter straightened up his desk. He thought about handing in his resignation, but he realized that his impulsive decision could be a mistake. He'd have to think about this frustrating turn of events. Perhaps a bird in the hand was worth two in the bush. He should start looking for a room for Chao Chen now that the door to romance with Clara had been slammed shut in his face.

But Walter missed all the signs she was pulling away from him. They had not spent a night together in over a month, and when they met at Miss Liang's studio, it was all business. They wrestled with the Rondo of the *Spring Sonata*, arguably the most challenging movement of the piece, which had similarities to a *bourrée*, a lively courtly French dance with quick steps. The relationship between piano and violin in this movement is one of a "call and response." It was this aspect of the final movement that gave Walter and Chao Chen difficulty, since they were barely speaking to each other by the end of the session.

Miss Liang addressed both. "I'm not interested in what is going on between the two of you. What I care about is your performance. If you expect to participate in Professor Wittenberg's next recital, I suggest you put your differences aside and concentrate on Beethoven. Can you do that?"

Walter was annoyed. "I don't know what you're talking about, Miss Liang. Chao Chen and I are getting along just fine. It's just that we have both been saddled with demanding jobs, which have unfortunately taken their toll on us. I assure you we'll be in perfect form the next time we meet. Isn't that right, Chao Chen?"

"Of course." Chao Chen looked at her watch. "Oh, I'd better hurry. I'm going to the opera this evening. I need to be ready by seven."

Walter felt as if he had been slapped in the face. "You didn't say anything about this to me."

"Since when do I need to account for my every minute? If you must know, the opera is called *The Great Wall* and it's based on one of China's well-known fables. I've been looking forward to it all month. I believe the libretto is in Mandarin, and so I assumed you would be bored to tears, which is why I didn't ask you to join us. This will be the opera's world premiere for the Russian composer, Aaron Avshalomov. He's created a work that melds classical Russian music with Chinese tonalities and instruments like clappers and gongs. Have you heard of the instruments? You seem to have no interest in my culture."

Walter shook his head. "It sounds a bit too experimental for my taste. I'll stick to Beethoven and Chopin." He snapped his violin case shut. "Enjoy your evening, Chao Chen. I'm off to the Canidrome. I'm suddenly feeling very lucky."

After Walter left, Miss Liang smiled. "Can I guess who invited you? Is it Li Shutong? Madam Rong telephoned to tell me that he's quite taken with you. And would you believe that he's the very same young man whom Clarise Moise had in mind to introduce you to some time ago?"

"Really? He never mentioned this to me."

"I don't think he wanted you to feel as if you were being trapped by all those ladies scheming to put the two of you together."

"Meeting Li Shutong through you, Miss Liang, seems much more natural, and he's paying me very generously for my time. Someday I'll be free to move out of the house and live on my own like a 'modern woman.' Only you know it, but I'll be twenty-eight on my next birthday."

"It's true that his family is looking for a young wife for him, but so far no one has satisfied him. The women in his social circle are just after his money and are dazzled by his good looks. You're a refreshing change for him."

Chao Chen confessed, "I'm sure that, if he finds out how old I am, he'll lose interest in me."

"Well, then you just won't tell him, will you?"

"The fact is, Walter Kolber has no idea how old I am either. But luckily I don't have to make a choice between either man right now, do I?"

Miss Liang rested her hands on Chao Chen's shoulders. "I see only heartache between you and Walter Kolber. You and he really have very little in common. How many couples intermarry? It is very rare, and for good reason. Neither family is happy. And then, when the children come along, who are they? What will you do when your children are called names and find they have no friends to play with?"

Chao Chen was dumbstruck. "Could that really happen?"

"Chao Chen, you have a much more optimistic view of the Jews and the Chinese than I do. We all have our prejudices, and it is hard to overcome them, even when love is involved. Believe me when I tell you that you'd have a much easier life with Li Shutong. I hope you'll give him a chance to win you over."

"I am giving him a chance. Why else would I have accepted his invitation to the opera this evening?"

Chao Chen examined her reflection in the mirror, looking for any telltale wrinkles on her forehead or lines running like rivers from her nose to her mouth. The makeup advertisements called them "laugh lines," but she found them anything but amusing. She was trying to pass for a younger woman. She twisted her hair into a fashionable chignon, then took a powder puff and lightly dusted her nose and applied a pink lipstick. After pinching her cheeks to bring some color to her face, she judged herself presentable. She wished her mourning doves a peaceful sleep and then covered the birdcage with a light blanket.

She stepped into her high-heeled shoes, then tiptoed down the corridor, hoping not to disturb Rui-De Xu. She didn't want to see her before she left, anticipating that she would throw a barb at her and disturb her happy mood—but there was no escaping her. Rui-De Xu hobbled out of her bedroom with a box in her hand.

Chao Chen held her breath.

Looking her up and down, Rui-De Xu said, "So you don't look like a servant girl, I'm giving you a strand of black pearls to wear just for this evening. I expect them back. You never know when I'll need them again. Let me help you put them on."

Chao Chen felt her cold hands touching her neck. "Let's hope they bring you good luck. Gan Chen gave them to me when we became engaged."

"Thank you, Rui-De Xu."

"What for? I consider it an investment in our future. If you are lucky enough to trap Li Shutong into marrying you, we'll all benefit from it."

Before Chao Chen could respond, Rui-De Xu disappeared. Chao Chen listened for the sound of Li Shutong's automobile. She wondered how he was able to find petrol when most of the city had come to a standstill.

Li Shutong opened the passenger door of his coupe. She breathed in the scent of real leather and looked at the dashboard with its tiny clock that lit up when Li Shutong turned on the headlights. He drove with an easy confidence. Glancing at her while keeping one eye on the road, he spoke first. "Chao Chen, you look particularly lovely this evening. I can't tell you how much I've been looking forward to taking you to the opera."

"I feel like Cinderella."

"Are you going to disappear at the stroke of midnight and turn back into a servant girl?"

"I certainly hope not."

"Well, if you do, I'll just have to bring you a glass slipper, won't I?"

"That won't be necessary. I have no intention of running away from you, at least not on our first date."

"And on our second?"

"We'll just have to wait and see, won't we?"

Li Shutong smiled, and then he concentrated on the road for the rest of the way to the theatre.

Once there, Li Shutong lightly touched Chao Chen's elbow to steer her up the stairs into the theatre. Chao Chen felt a palpable excitement in the air as they took their seats in the third row of the orchestra section.

The audience was curious to see the groundbreaking *The Great Wall*, an ambitious production requiring a sixty-piece orchestra, an elaborately costumed principal cast and chorus, and even flying sets painted to resemble the gardens and temples of the Qing dynasty. It was rumored that the Manchukuo Film Company, which was under the control of the Japanese, had financed the production, lending costumes from Chinese film projects made a few years earlier.

Chao Chen had just enough time to read the program before the lights went down and the curtain went up.

> Synopsis: Lady Meng Jiang is brokenhearted when her husband is pressed into service to build the Great Wall. Receiving no news from him for months and then years, she departs from her village with a package of clothes. When she reaches the Great Wall, she frantically tries to find her husband and learns that he has died. In her grief, she weeps so bitterly that a part of the Great Wall collapses.

Chao Chen tried to focus her attention on the opera, but all she could think about was Li Shutong sitting next to her. She kept her hands folded in her lap, wishing that he might reach over and entwine his fingers in hers. Did he have "intelligent fingers" like the composer Lewis Dodd? If he did, the slightest touch would have told him that she was falling in love with him.

She blinked when the lights went up at the end of the opera, and the audience expressed their approval of this odd synthesis of Western and Chinese music. Li Shutong followed Chao Chen up the aisle, and only when they had reached the lobby did he express his opinion. "That was very brave of Avshalomov to co-opt one of our jewels for his own purposes, but I think he did an admirable job."

Chao Chen admitted, "I had almost forgotten how sad a tale *The Great Wall* is. Imagine not knowing the fate of your loved one for so many years only to find out they are dead. I suspect that is how some of the Jewish refugees feel right now, waiting to hear who has survived the war in Europe. And the Great Wall collapsing—I wonder if the composer was thinking of Vienna, Berlin, or Krakow when he came to that part of the story."

"I never thought of that. How clever of you to come up with this interpretation."

"Other than music, literature was my best subject in school; but of course, there is so much that I don't know." She tried to be modest, but she was very flattered that Li Shutong appreciated her insight into the composer's inspiration.

As they passed through the throng of operagoers, Chao Chen spotted Walter standing at the bottom of the stairs outside the theatre. Her head throbbed and her throat went dry. She forced herself not to gasp.

Pushing through the crowd, Walter made his way toward the couple. "Good evening, Chao Chen. Did you enjoy *The Great Wall*?"

"Very much, Walter." Not knowing what to do, she stumbled on. "Let me introduce you to Li Shutong. He was kind enough to buy me a ticket to tonight's performance. He and I are practicing Schubert's *Lieder* together. He's studying at the Conservatory, and Miss Liang suggested that I'd make a suitable accompanist for him."

Walter smirked. "Well, you're a lucky fellow. My Chao Chen is quite a talented pianist, as I'm sure you've found out." He then addressed Chao Chen. "Funny that you haven't mentioned this to me. And may I presume that you have been keeping me a secret from him? Did you tell him that we're planning on moving in together?"

"No, Walter."

Li Shutong addressed Walter in perfect English. "Sir, I see that my automobile is being brought to the curb. Please let us pass."

Li Shutong slid into the driver's seat as the attendant opened the passenger door for Chao Chen. As they pulled away from the curb, Walter tipped his hat and then disappeared into the crowd.

Chao Chen was mortified.

Li Shutong was the first to speak. "It's very disheartening to me that you would keep Walter Kolber a secret. You and he obviously have something together, and I'm not in the habit of competing for anyone's affection—no matter how much I care for them. I hope he appreciates what he has in you. May I wish you all the happiness in the world, Chao Chen."

Cornered, Chao Chen tried to explain herself. "I didn't know that our relationship was anything other than professional until this evening. I didn't allow myself to think that you might actually be interested in me romantically." She unconsciously touched Rui-De Xu's pearl necklace and went on. "Do you not wish to continue our musical partnership? You were making a lot of progress."

"No, Chao Chen. Schubert was just a ruse to get to know you. There are many other pianists in the city, although none as enchanting as you."

Li Shutong stopped the car in front Chao Chen's house. He opened the door but did not offer her his hand to help her, making it clear that he didn't intend to walk her to the door. She looked up at him. He shook his head. "I'd best be going. Thanks for explaining *The Great Wall* to me."

Chao Chen stood in the doorway watching Li Shutong drive away. No sooner had she closed the door than she heard Rui-De Xu's shuffling footsteps coming toward her.

"So, Chao Chen. Give me back my necklace. Did it bring you luck as I hoped it would?"

"Yes, but not the way you would have wished, Rui-De Xu."

"And what do you mean by that?"

Chao Chen quickly lied. "Li Shutong admitted to me that he has someone else in his life and that it's best we not see each other again. I'm glad that he was so honest with me. Otherwise, I might have had my heart broken."

Rui-De Xu let out a piercing scream. "What a demon! To have gotten my hopes up only to have them crumble right before my eyes."

"Just like China's Great Wall, Rui-De Xu."

chapter 43

Tables Turned

Dolfie slipped on his Pao Chia armband and wrapped his hand through the strap of his billy club. He would be joining the other Jewish recruits for the civilian patrol on the morning of July 18, 1945. Service was mandatory, and he was assigned to patrol Ward Road near the prison. He felt an inexplicable sense of foreboding. He ran through a checklist in his head of the whereabouts of his loved ones: his fiancée, Margot, was at home with her parents; Walter was at the Schmidt Engineering factory on Great Western Road; and his parents, with his aunt and uncle, were at JEKO. He couldn't say for sure, but he assumed that Lilly and David were at home with their children, Mischa and Judith.

The air raids over Shanghai were a daily occurrence as the Allies intensified their attack against the Japanese. So far the Allied bombings had been precise, limiting their strafing to strategic industrial targets and avoiding civilian areas. If a direct attack occurred, the residents of Hongkew were instructed to run outside because there were no proper bomb shelters in the Designated Area. The water table was just beneath the surface of the streets, which made it impossible to create effective underground protection. Some people, speculating that the concrete Ward Road prison was the safest place to seek shelter, developed their own defensive strategy. It was common knowledge that the Japanese military was storing munitions throughout Hongkew, essentially using the Jews as human shields, and they thought it best to seek shelter in the most hardened buildings in the area.

Dolfie looked up at the overcast sky just as alarm sirens sounded. He checked his watch—it was almost one o'clock—when he heard an enormous explosion. American B-24 bombers dropped payloads directly onto Hongkew. Panic erupted as buildings collapsed and bodies were hurled into the streets. Anyone who remained unharmed was mobilized into action to help the injured and dying. They created makeshift stretchers to carry people to the nearest hospital.

Dolfie saw a former schoolmate lying in a pool of blood. He screamed out, "Help me! Help me!" but just as Dolfie tried to lift him, he became lifeless. At day's end, the bombing in Hongkew ceased; but the next morning, the bombing continued in other parts of the city.

After making sure that Margot and her parents were unharmed, Dolfie ran home. The factory was still standing, and his parents were safe. Walter couldn't come home from work because all public transportation had been suspended. It was not until midday that they heard from Lilly and David. They and the children were unharmed.

Thirty-One Jewish refugees were killed in the attack on the radio towers located in the Designated Area. Among the dead was Dr. Kardegg, the head of the Pao Chia. Many more refugees were injured. Several thousand Chinese lost their lives. The exact number was undetermined since most of the Chinese casualties went undocumented.

The *Shanghai Jewish Chronicle* carried news of the initial air raid in Hongkew, explaining that the target of the bombing was a Japanese-occupied building on Seward Road that had large rooftop radio antennae to signal incoming Japanese aircraft. More attacks followed, targeting the Shanghai Power Company, the Shanghai Waterworks Company, and the Shanghai Gas Company.[5]

Air raids over Shanghai finally ceased on July 23, but it would take days before the gears of the city began to turn again. It seemed that only the chiming of the clock in the Custom House reassured all of Shanghai that civilization had not come to an end. But neither had the war. The Japanese continued to hold out, refusing to surrender to the Allied forces.

Then, on August 6, 1945, the United States exploded an atomic bomb on Hiroshima and nature reacted. For days afterward, severe wind, rain, and flooding hit Shanghai. While flooding occurred frequently during the rainy season, this time the waves in the Whangpoo River were violent. Then a second atomic bomb was dropped on Nagasaki on August 10. In the days that followed the bombing, it was determined the number of civilian casualties would exceed two hundred thousand, and it was reported that the effects of the radiation would be felt for years. Both cities were decimated; it was impossible to recognize streets and buildings close to the epicenter of the bombings.

The residents of Shanghai learned within days that the Japanese had surrendered and the Soviets had finally taken up the cause of the Allies by invading Manchuria. The war was over, but it would take weeks for Japan to make their "unconditional surrender" a matter of record, and it would be months before Shanghai was entirely purged of Japanese administrators and officers.

Only when American military personnel arrived did the refugees accept that they were free to move about the city and the war was indeed over. In the weeks that followed the International Red Cross published the names of the confirmed fatalities in Europe. Jews stood in solemn lines anxiously awaiting a chance to read the list, hoping that the names of their loved ones would not be there. However, everyone knew that, even if a name did not appear on a list, it was no assurance that the person had survived the war. But as the lists grew, many in the Designated Area learned that some or all of their relatives had been killed at the hands of the Nazis.

Rosh Hashanah fell on Saturday, September 8, 1945. Josef, Eva, Walter, and Dolfie, together with Lilly and David Ozer and David's mother, attended the synagogue on Rue Tenant de la Tour to mark the head of the Jewish New Year, the day when God was believed to determine who will live and who will die in the year to come. The congregants gave thanks for having survived the war. During the Mourner's Kaddish, Josef and Eva whispered the names of their relatives still missing: Eva's siblings, Heinrich, Lazar, and Sabina; and Josef's mother, Schendel; and his brother Hersch. The anguish and grief of the congregants could hardly be contained within the walls of the synagogue. Anyone passing by could hear the wailing and heartbreaking sobs piercing the stained-glass windows.

And yet, in the midst of all this sadness and sorrow, there were celebrations in the streets now that the weight of Japanese domination had finally been lifted and the Jews were free to walk about the city. The boundaries of the Designated Area were removed. One of the Jewish worshippers recalled that, "as a sign of victory, the streets were adorned with tall sugarcane stalks artfully bundled together. In some places the graceful plants were put on both sides of the street, making a beautiful arch. Chinese music erupted from everywhere, and masses of people strolled on the streets. It was a mild evening and the whole scene was bathed in light. For the first time in years there was no blackout. It was magical."[6]

Standing in the hallway of their apartment for the first time in more than two years, Eva was overcome by the spaciousness of the rooms and the sight of her furniture and belongings, which she had left behind. She thought back to the day she had first walked into the apartment when she and Lilly arrived in the city. She remembered complaining to Josef that the apartment was much too small for the family. Now it seemed like a palace compared to their makeshift quarters above the factory floor in Hongkew. She examined each piece of furniture to make sure there were no scratches or cigar burns left by the Japanese captain. Opening the cupboards in the kitchen, she was relieved that none of Tanaka's provisions had been left behind other than a half-opened can of sardines, which had attracted a swarm of black flies. Eva wrapped the can in an old newspaper and threw it in the garbage. She sat down at the kitchen table, grateful that she was "home" at last.

Resting her head on her hand, she was reminded of an old Jewish folktale about a farmer, Yankele, whose wife complains that their hut is too small. To teach her a lesson, he brings in all the farm animals one by one, and the family is crowded into a small corner of the hut. He then returns the animals to the stables and the yard, and the wife tells her husband, "Yankele, our hut is so big." *Do they live happily ever after?* Eva laughed to herself. What Jewish couple ever lives happily ever after? There is always something to complain about, but at that moment, all she could think about was gathering her family around the dining room table once again to enjoy a delicious Shabbat dinner—that is if she could find all the ingredients.

With the arrival of American troops into Shanghai came newsreels depicting the Nazi concentration and death camps. For the first time the Jews could actually see what tragically happened to their brethren.

Jobs were now becoming available. The American military placed help wanted ads in the local and Jewish press for stenographers, truck drivers, laborers, cooks and clerks. But the pullout of the Japanese had also left a political and administrative vacuum. Chiang Kai-shek's brother-in-law T.V. Soong, was installed to institute monetary policies meant to stimulate the domestic economy and reduce inflation.

Soong met with Manuel Siegel, the principal representative of the JDC, to discuss the twelve thousand Jewish refugees who were still receiving housing and food. One third were over the age of fifty and unemployable, while seven thousand were still stuck in the *Heime*, suffering from illness, malnutrition and severe depression. It was an enormous burden that neither the JDC nor the city officials wanted to shoulder.

Soong and Siegel recognized that the only answer to the Jewish refugee problem was to evacuate the destitute Jews to other countries, as quickly as possible. But who would have them? According to U.S. Army Chaplain Rabbi Alvin Fine, the one bright light in this otherwise bleak picture was that "many of the youngsters [were] now studying in JDC-supported classrooms, learning English and Hebrew as well as other academic subjects."

Much to the consternation of American officials aid relief became a big business that was largely benefitting Chinese officials. Chiang Kai-shek created the Chinese National Relief and Rehabilitation Administration which was established solely to control the distribution of foreign aid. Soong was put in charge leveraging it politically while using it to increase his personal wealth. Many complaints were voiced that supplies were inequitably distributed, mainly reaching Nationalist supporters. Only a portion of rations ever reached the intended refugees in Hongkew.

Eva was elated to see a small truck parked on Chusan Road in front of the factory. Miraculously, Josef had found one to transport their belongings back to the apartment. She entered the factory, and without speaking to the workers hunched over their sewing machines, slowly climbed the stairs. Her legs and feet were swollen, and she felt enervated from the trek to the apartment and back.

Walter was standing on a chair, taking down the sheet that had served as a partition. "What do you want me to do with this, Mutti? It's rather filthy."

"We can donate all the sheets to the *Heime*. And our towels, as well."

"And what about the stove, the tub, and the leftover wood pellets?"

"Give them to our Chinese workers downstairs. I'm sure they can use them."

Josef held up a catalogue he had discovered underneath papers in his desk drawer. He looked at Eva. "What is this piece of garbage?"

Eva gasped. "That's the catalogue for *The Wandering Jew*. I asked Agneza to buy it for me so I would have no regrets about leaving Vienna. Let me see it." Josef handed her the program, and Eva's hands shook as she turned the pages. "Do you remember how the good people of Vienna lined up to see this exhibition?"

Josef could only nod.

"It still breaks my heart to think that we will never return to Vienna, but after everything that has happened, how our fellow Austrians welcomed Hitler with open arms, how they turned a blind eye when the Nazis pushed Jews into the Danube or sent them off to concentration camps to die… Nothing could make me want to go back."

Walter and Dolfie stared at their mother as she tore the catalogue to shreds.

chapter 44

Settling In

Living under the same roof as Rui-De Xu was a fate worse than death; Chao Chen had to move out. Ya-Li admitted to Chao Chen that she had been instructed to "accidentally" break her phonograph records and to do away with the mourning doves by whatever means. She warned Chao Chen, "Rui-De Xu will stop at nothing to make your life a living hell now that money is getting tight and you have no prospects. Sooner or later I'm going to have to do as she tells me or I'll be punished right along with you."

"Don't fret, Ya-Li. I'll think of something. I'm going to look for a room to rent, but I need to figure out how I'm going to pay for it. I've already asked my brother Fu-Chan for money, now that he's back from Chungking; but he tells me that, if Rui-De Xu finds out, she'll make things miserable for him and he needs her help until he's found employment here in Shanghai."

Ya-Li heard a bell ring. "That's Ya-Nan. She wants me to clear her breakfast tray. I wish I could convince her to leave her bedroom, but she refuses. I don't think she's had a ray of sunshine on her face in two years. It's a pity. She used to be such a beautiful woman. You know, Chao Chen, I see her beauty in you every day."

Chao Chen shuddered, but then her face brightened. "I need to practice for a few hours. Today Walter and I present the entire Beethoven *Spring Sonata* for Professor Wittenberg. He's going to decide if we'll be selected to perform all four movements at the next Conservatory recital in April. I'm not feeling very confident. Walter and I have been fighting and it's showing up in our collaboration. It's not easy for us to set aside our differences. He's been extremely vindictive toward me since he saw me with Li Shutong."

"Chao Chen, most men are somewhat possessive when they are in love, but Walter has taken it to an extreme, following you to the opera the way he did."

"Do you think so, Ya-Li? I'm afraid I'm terribly naïve, aren't I?"

"Yes. But it's not your fault. After all, neither Rui-De Xu nor Ya-Nan has taken you under their wing. Although, come to think of it, how much do *they* really know anyway?"

Chao Chen and Ya-Li burst out laughing. Chao Chen hugged Ya-Li. "Oh, it feels so good to laugh every once in a while. Now, I'd better get to work or I'm going to be an abysmal failure this afternoon."

Walter and Chao Chen left the studio at the Conservatory after their audition. Chao Chen was shocked when Professor Wittenberg told them, "After listening to the way you performed today, I'm going to do both of you a favor. You should not be performing together at the upcoming recital. You are fighting each other with this duet. Instead, Walter, we should discuss a solo piece for you that you'll have enough time to prepare. And as for you, Chao Chen, I suggest that you and Miss Liang find another opportunity to perform in public. Perhaps Miss Liang's father is going to hold a recital at their home. As painful as this is for all of us, I'm sure you understand my decision. In the long run, I think both of your careers will benefit from this separation. In fact, I'm sure of it."

Chao Chen thought she had glimpsed a shadow of a smile cross Walter's lips, but she convinced herself that she must have been mistaken. The two students nodded and left the studio. Once outside Chao Chen stumbled to the nearest bench. Walter sat down next to her, saying, "I can't believe that he would do that to us after all the time we have spent practicing together."

Chao Chen rationalized, "Perhaps it's for the best. Now we're each free to pursue our studies independently. We can still play together for our own enjoyment. Frankly, I'm almost relieved because this way I won't hold you back."

Walter gazed into the distance as if he were looking out at his audience rather than listening to Chao Chen. "What do you think about my playing Johann Sebastian Bach's *Sarabande in D Minor* for the recital? And if Professor Wittenberg organizes the recital chronologically by composer, I'll probably be first, which is almost as good as going last. The first performer sets the tone for the entire recital."

Chao Chen smiled. "Unless someone else plays Vivaldi."

"How right you are. You are a much better student of the classical music repertoire than I am. If I were as diligent as you, I'd be a lot further along in my career. What do you think?"

"I'm sure that you'll play the Bach brilliantly. Didn't the conductor of the Shanghai Symphony Orchestra say that you played the Dvořák beautifully at their performance last year?" Chao Chen hoped she bolstered his ego.

"What's so great about that? He didn't call me back again. And I wasn't sitting in first chair, was I? But someday I will be, and then I'll be on my way to a solo performance." Walter put his arm around Chao Chen's shoulder somewhat tentatively. She leaned against him, feeling her resentment and anger toward him fading away despite herself.

Walter whispered in her ear, "I've missed lying next to you, Chao Chen. Please don't keep me at a distance any longer. You know it's been agony for me to see you at Miss Liang's all this time and not be able to take you in my arms and feel your heart beating next to mine. Don't you love me still?"

Chao Chen confessed, "Walter, I was very confused by what happened that night at the opera. I felt as if you were following me, and not because you truly cared about me but because you suspected you might be losing me to someone else."

"You're right. That was an act of pure jealousy on my part. I couldn't believe that there could be another man in your life. For all I know you are still interested in Li Shutong. From what I've learned about him, he's quite a catch. Rich, handsome, and single. Am I right?"

Chao Chen debated whether to let Walter believe he still had a romantic adversary, but she wanted something from him so desperately that she admitted, "After what you did and said that night, Li Shutong is no longer interested in seeing me. And it's just as well because all he was doing was making me confused about my feelings for you. Now that he's no longer in the picture, I realize that you and I are meant to be together." Then, trying to lighten the moment, she added, "Even if Professor Wittenberg doesn't agree. But then again, I'm not speaking of making music together. I'm speaking of making a life together."

Walter breathed a sigh of relief and tried to kiss Chao Chen on the lips.

"Not here, Walter. One of the Chinese students might see us and tell Rui-De Xu or someone in her ladies' circle. Gossip is one of their favorite pastimes." And then she confessed, "I cannot go on living in that house. I must find a way out. What am I to do?" She held her breath, praying that Walter would offer her a way out.

"Chao Chen, I'm lucky enough to still have my job at Schmidt's Engineering, and now that the owner's niece has left for the United States, he gave me a small raise and has me working more hours. With my salary and what you're making at Frau Götz's... You're still working there, aren't you?"

"Yes, she tells me that I've become indispensable to her."

"Well, then, we'll be able to get a room together in Hongkew. All the Jewish refugees who still have money are moving back into the former International Settlement or the French Concession, and suddenly there are quite a few rooms for rent. It won't be paradise, but it's cheap and will do for a start. I'll continue to live with my parents because they would be suspicious if I didn't make an appearance every now and again, but for all intents and purposes, we'll be just like a happily married couple."

"Is that what you want? To marry me?"

"Of course that's what I want, but I can't marry you until my future is more secure. The life of a concert violinist is unpredictable at best. One day you are the darling of the critics, and the next day they will kick you by the side of the road for one false note."

"Then why do you want it so badly?"

"It's my obsession, just as you are, Chao Chen. Now let's find us a room to rent, shall we?"

The landlady, Madam Han, didn't ask the young couple too many questions. So long as they paid the key money and agreed to the rent, the room on the second floor of the building on a lane off Kungpin Road was theirs.

Ya-Li helped Chao Chen get settled. Stealing rags, a mop, soap, and a pail from the house, she cleaned the floor, polished the mirror, and scraped the dirt and grime off the brazier left behind by the former occupants. Only a few days earlier the room had been home to a family of six. The tiles in the bathroom were covered in mold, and it took her hours of work before they finally sparkled. Then she unpacked Chao Chen's suitcase and hung her clothes in the lone wardrobe closet. "I'm going to find you an iron and a board."

Chao Chen made a face. "You know I've never learned how to iron anything. I've always had you to help me."

"It's really very easy. You wash a blouse, hang it up, and when it is still a little damp, you iron it. Back and front panels first, then the sleeves, and finally the collar. And if the material starts to get too dry, you just sprinkle a little water on it—like this." Ya-Li turned on the tap, wet her fingers, and flicked a few drops playfully in Chao Chen's face.

Chao Chen laughed as she wiped her face dry with a towel. "I'll try to remember your instructions, Ya-Li. And what am I supposed to do about cooking a meal?"

"That might take you a little longer to learn, but I'm sure you'll manage, although your repertoire is going to be limited to what you can prepare on that hotplate and in a kettle. Let's hope that you and Walter move into something a bit more comfortable soon."

With a worried expression on her face, Chao Chen placed her birdcage next to the window. "I'm sorry that you don't have much of a view, my little darlings, but I promise we'll be happy here so long as I can hear you sing to me."

Ya-Li looked around. "This isn't much, but I hope you'll be comfortable here." She pretended to look under the bed. "I just wanted to make sure that Rui-De Xu hasn't sneaked in here while our backs were turned."

They both laughed again, and then Chao Chen hugged her and tried to give her a mother-of-pearl hair comb as a gift.

Ya-Li refused to take it. "You have always been so kind to me. Helping you move here is the least I can do for you. I'll miss you." Before Chao Chen could say anything in response, Ya-Li rushed out the door and down the stairs.

Chao Chen spent the afternoon reading a cookbook and looking at her watch. Walter had promised he would be there by seven o'clock. He finally arrived two hours later with a big apology and a gift-wrapped box. "It's Shabbat. Mutti insisted I have dinner with the family. And Dolfie and Margot had some news for all of us. They are getting married in August and moving into her parents' apartment. Honestly, I think Mutti was relieved. One less mouth to feed, or to put it another way, more money for her to spend on herself."

"Is your mother really like that? She's beginning to sound a lot like Rui-De Xu."

"Perhaps I'm being a bit hard on her, but it galls me to see the way she is fussing over Dolfie and Margot. You'd think theirs was the first wedding in the family. Lilly and David were married five years ago and I played violin for the happy couple. Oh, it was marvelous. Or should I say, *I* was marvelous."

"I'm sure you were, Walter. And do you intend to invite me to Dolfie's wedding?"

"We have almost two months to figure out a way for me to tell my parents about us. Don't pressure me, Chao Chen." He then handed her the beautifully wrapped box.

"Is this for me? What's the occasion?"

Walter kissed her hard on the lips and patted her backside "It's a housewarming present. And I went to a lot of trouble to find it, so you'd better like it."

Chao Chen carefully unwrapped the gift so as not to tear the paper, and then she slowly opened the box. Inside was a silver hand mirror embossed with birds, hearts, and flowers in an ornate Viennese style. Chao Chen held the mirror up to her face and looked at her reflection.

Walter was excited. "What do you think of it?"

"It's very beautiful. Do I deserve such a gift? You must have paid a lot of money for it."

"Don't worry about the cost. I bought it at the same shop where my mother bought my Lowendall. The owner, Frau Leschnik, is a friend of the family and so she gave me a good price as a favor. Of course, I didn't tell her why I was buying it. But she'll know soon enough when we announce our engagement."

Before Chao Chen could ask when that might be, Walter took her hand and led her toward the bed that was pushed into one corner of the small room. As she undressed, Walter placed a record onto the Victrola: Dvořák's *Romance in F Minor* for violin and piano, the perfect accompaniment to their lovemaking. He turned around and saw that Chao Chen was already naked underneath the thin sheet. He quickly undressed and climbed into the narrow bed with her.

Resting his head on her breast, he said, "Is it safe, Chao Chen? I have no interest in becoming a father, and I'm sure that motherhood is the furthest thing from your mind. We have our whole lives ahead of us to be parents.

Just think of it, a little Walter and a little Chao Chen sitting at our feet by the fire while we listen to beautiful music."

"You make it all sound like a wonderful dream,"

Walter put his hand over her mouth. "Stop talking, my little nightingale, and use your mouth for more pleasurable purposes."

The early morning light filtered through the curtains as Chao Chen listened to Walter grumble, "If I don't get going right now I'll be late for work. Honestly, I hate that job. One of these days I'm going to quit. Herr Schmidt has found a new head of the accounting department, and he and I don't get along. Things were much better when Fräulein Clara Cohen was in charge. At least she was pretty to look at."

Chao Chen made a face. "Are you trying to make me jealous, Walter? It's a good thing she's far away or I'd be worried."

Walter rolled out of bed and put his pants on, then stood in front of the sink. Holding up Chao Chen's hand mirror, Walter brushed his thick, wavy dark hair and then examined his face to make sure that he had removed all traces of shaving cream. He spun around. "How do I look?"

"Like an international violin virtuoso."

"Good." He picked up his violin case and opened the door.

"Will I see you this evening, Walter?"

"I don't know. Probably."

Chao Chen stayed in bed until she could no longer hear Walter's footsteps on the stairs. She closed the window, took the blanket off the birdcage and opened it to let the mourning doves fly around the room. Then she put birdseed in their food dish and the doves, hungry for their breakfast, flitted back into the cage. "There you are, my little angels. Don't ever fly away from me."

She sighed and put a kettle on the hotplate, made herself a cup of tea, and took a bath to ready herself for work. She looked forward to seeing Frau Götz's friendly face and hearing her kind words, grateful that she still had a job to go to.

The trolley rocked back and forth on its way into the French Concession. She recognized one of Frau Götz's workers boarding the trolley on the last stop out of Hongkew. Chao Chen waved at her and gestured to sit in the seat next to her, but the woman shook her head and found a seat toward the front of the trolley car. When they disembarked, Chao Chen tried to catch up to her, but the woman quickened her footsteps. Even after all this time working for Frau Götz, not one of the other women made any effort to befriend her. Chao Chen thought, *Is it because we don't speak the same language or do they have something against the Chinese or is it that they just don't like me?*

She wished she could ask Frau Götz, but she was too embarrassed to bring up the subject. Instead, she took her seat at her desk and carefully reviewed the bills. She noticed that the price of supplies had dramatically increased, by thirty-three percent over the past several months. Frau Götz would be forced to increase the prices of her gloves to keep up with inflation, which could jeopardize her sales if other glove makers did not follow suit.

As if reading her mind, Frau Götz declared, "We are really in a pickle. If the Chinese government doesn't do something soon to stabilize the yuan, we won't be able to keep our doors open. Our biggest customers, Wing On and Sun Sun, will continue to lose sales and that will affect us immediately."

Chao Chen's mind was racing. "Do you think Walter's parents are in the same predicament?"

"Of course. We all are. Most Jews are already making plans to leave Shanghai. But it won't happen overnight. It's almost impossible to get a visa right now, unless you have someone to sponsor you. And for now, at least we have the U.S. military pumping money into the economy. In fact, I just received a very nice order from American headquarters for work gloves for the Seabees repairing the piers. So, for now, we are 'keeping the wolf from the door,' as their generals like to say." Sniffing the air, Frau Götz announced, "Lunch is almost ready. I hope you will join us at the kitchen table, Chao Chen."

"No, thank you. I want to finish what I am doing before I leave for my piano lesson."

"I'm glad to hear that you're continuing with your studies. I was afraid that you wouldn't have a piano when you moved out of your mother's house."

"I don't. I just study the music and try to imagine a keyboard. So far I've been managing." She forced a smile. "I'm sure my neighbors are grateful they aren't bothered by scales and arpeggios for hours on end. It's noisy enough in the lane."

"Nonsense. They should consider themselves lucky to have a pianist as talented as you in their midst."

Frau Götz abruptly disappeared into her office, and Chao Chen overheard a heated argument between her and her husband. And then Frau Götz practically skipped back into the room, which looked slightly comical for a woman of forty with a thick waistline and generous bosom. "Herr Götz agrees with me that we no longer have any use for our little upright piano. It has been doing nothing but gathering dust since I gave up playing several years ago. You didn't know that I played, did you?" She hurried on. "That's why I do so appreciate your talent, Chao Chen. I know a gifted pianist when I hear one. So, Herr Götz and I have decided to give you our upright. We'll arrange to have it delivered to your room tomorrow."

"I have never known such boundless kindness from anyone before. How can I ever thank you?"

"Just invite us to your next recital, whenever it is."

"I will, I promise. Miss Liang's father, a professor at the Conservatory, may be organizing something in the near future. And hopefully he'll allow me to play then."

"What about Professor Wittenberg? Are you no longer working with him? When I lived in Berlin, I used to hear him in concert. What a genius. He is equally amazing on the piano and the violin."

"Yes, but now I'm just studying with Miss Liang. He felt that it was better for Walter's career, and of course Walter's career comes first, doesn't it?"

Frau Götz shook Chao Chen by the shoulder. "No, my dearest, your career is equally important. You shouldn't have to sacrifice anything for that young man. But fortunately for you, Miss Liang is a gifted teacher as well and so you shouldn't suffer from this decision."

"You're right, Frau Götz. I must stop sounding like an obedient Chinese girl and more like an independent woman who knows her own mind."

"Exactly. And let our gift be a reminder of that, or our so-called generosity will be for naught."

A few days after the piano arrived at her apartment, there was a knock on Chao Chen's door. She expected the worst, but instead of being asked to stop practicing, a woman holding a young boy's hand stood there.

"Forgive me, madam, but I live in the room just below you, and I have been listening to you practice. I can't pay very much, but might you consider giving my little boy, Jian, piano lessons? He's nine years old and very much wants to be a musician someday. I don't know where he gets these ideas, but it's all he talks about, and his school doesn't have a teacher for him."

Chao Chen looked at the little boy. Before she could answer, Jian ran around her and sat down at the piano and struck the keys with a look of amazement on his face. Chao Chen was fascinated by his reaction. "I would be happy to teach him. I'm sure we can come to some arrangement, especially if you bring me more students from the neighborhood. By the way, my name is Chao Chen."

Jian ran back to his mother and pulled at her skirt.

"And my name is Shu-Au. I'd better be going. My little one is getting hungry. Again, thank you so much for agreeing to teach him the piano. It will bring both him, and me, the greatest joy."

chapter 45

The Doctor Will See You

On a rare occasion Walter was in a generous mood, he and Chao Chen went to see the Rex Harrison film *The Rake's Progress* playing at the Eastern Theatre, and then to the Chocolate Shop, a popular spot for American soldiers and sailors stationed in Shanghai.

Seated at a center table in the Chocolate Shop was an American journalist for the *North China Daily News*, his wife, and their two children. Walter commented to Chao Chen, "Too bad Lilly isn't here to give that family her business card. My sister's making quite a go of her children's clothing business from her home. At Dolfie and Margot's wedding reception, she bragged that the Hardoon ladies were customers of hers. They even invited her to have tea with them at their estate." Then to avoid the inevitable question, Walter raced on: "Lilly tells me that the Hardoon estate looks like a gymnasium with so many children running around, a palatial gymnasium, of course."

Chao Chen put down her spoon. "Your brother and his fiancée got married?"

"I already mentioned to you that they were planning on it. They were married on August 22. My mother cried her eyes out. What drama! And I played the violin at the reception. One of the guests gave me his business card and asked that I play at his daughter's wedding. I wanted to tell him I'm not a fiddler for hire, but then I thought about us and said, 'I'd be honored, Herr Bernstein.' Ugh!"

Walter took a long gulp of his ice cream soda, then looked at Chao Chen, whose face had fallen. "What's the matter with you? I treat you to a movie and dessert and you are pouting like a spoiled child."

"I'm hurt that you didn't invite me to the wedding. How long are you going to hide me from your family? Are you ashamed of me?"

"It's just that Mutti and Papa would disapprove. You know that already. Your Rui-De Xu would feel the same way about me. Can you imagine what she would do if you introduced me as your Jewish fiancé? She'd probably try to rip my eyes out."

"I don't care what she thinks. I'm a grown woman and I can do as I please. She doesn't own me. And you should stand up to your parents, but it's obvious that you can't—or won't."

He signaled for the bill. "I'll tell them in due time. I didn't think I should say anything while they were in the throes of Dolfie's wedding. That's all my mother has been thinking about. She's really quite fond of Margot, even if she's only a hairdresser." He leaned across the table and caressed Chao Chen's hand. "I have a plan. I'm going to enlist Lilly's help with my parents. She's on our side. She hasn't forgotten how you helped her when her son Mischa was so sick. Yes, she is very fond of you. Now let's get out of here before one of those GIs tries to steal you away from me."

While giving a piano lesson to Jian, Chao Chen felt dizzy. A wave of nausea gripped her, and she bolted into the bathroom to throw up. She splashed cold water on her face, which was already dripping with perspiration, and brushed her teeth.

She returned to her student and his mother, embarrassed. "I'm so sorry, Madam Au. I must have eaten something spoiled. We still can't be too careful. Why, just the other day, my neighbor complained about a bad can of beans. Now, where were we?"

Jian pointed to the music, Brahms's Lullaby. "Here. The second measure."

Chao Chen tried to concentrate, but she was afraid she might get sick all over again. She was relieved when the hour was up.

As Jian gathered his music, he asked, "How did I do today, Madam Chen?"

"Very well. But I expect you to memorize this piece. Do you think you can do that by our next lesson?"

"I'll try my best, but it's hard when you can only practice on an imaginary piano."

Opening the door, she smiled weakly. "That's true, but I know you can do it." She watched him as he ran down the stairs to his family's apartment on the first floor, his mother close behind him.

Chao Chen didn't want to tell Walter what she suspected until she saw Dr. Lee. She ran to the telephone booth outside the rooming house and dialed his number. The doctor could hear the desperation in her voice. "Come over tomorrow at ten o'clock."

"I'm so sorry, but I work until noon and can't afford to miss a day's pay."

"Well, then come as soon as you can and I'll make time for you."

Dr. Lee's waiting room was filled with children and their anxious parents. Chao Chen expected that she'd wait a long time to see him, but when she gave her name to the nurse, she was told to come right in to an examination room. "The doctor will be along momentarily," the nurse informed her.

Dressed in his formal white coat with a stethoscope around his neck, Dr. Lee smiled broadly when he saw Chao Chen. "We haven't seen each other in a very long time, Miss Chen. Other than the fact that you are much thinner and look a bit tired, I'm relieved that the war has not taken too great a toll on you. Now, tell me. What's bothering you?"

"I'm afraid I'm pregnant."

"From the tone of your voice, I must assume that you aren't married; or if you are then this is happening at a most inauspicious time. Which is it?"

"My fiancé is Walter Kolber, your neighbor's brother. He and I plan on getting married, but we haven't set a date and we certainly didn't plan on becoming parents for at least a year or two."

"How old are you, Miss Chen?"

"It's a secret, but I can trust you not to say anything. I'm twenty-eight, five years older than Walter. He thinks I'm much younger. He's only twenty-three, which is not really an issue for me, but if he knew my real age he might be less keen on marrying me. Especially if he wants to have a large family, and I believe he does. Oh, the way he goes on about his nephew and niece…" She knew she was telling an untruth, but somehow saying these things gave her a cover of dignity to wrap herself in.

"And you? Do you intend to have many children?"

"Well, I come from a family of six children, but I haven't really thought about it very much. I have been totally focused on my musical career and just making ends meet." She sighed and then asked, "You won't say anything about my age if you run into Walter?"

"Your secret is safe with me. Now, let me listen to your heart and lungs." He leaned over and pressed his stethoscope against her heart, and then, placing the instrument on her back, asked her to cough. "All clear. In my experience, women usually know when they're pregnant. When was your last menstruation?"

"It's been nearly two months."

"Are your breasts tender to the touch?"

Chao Chen blushed. "I haven't noticed."

"All right. I'll need a urine sample. I should have the results back in a few days. Make an appointment for next week. In the meantime, try to keep your stomach full. That will stave off the nausea. As I said, you don't look as if you've been eating enough."

"Thank you, Doctor Lee." Then she asked, "If I'm pregnant, will you take care of me and arrange to have the baby delivered?"

"So, you plan on bringing this baby to term? I suggest you discuss this with Herr Kolber."

Chao Chen lied. "I'm sure he'll be thrilled."

Dr. Lee raised his eyebrows. "I hope you're correct, Miss Chen, but be prepared if he isn't."

When Chao Chen returned for a follow-up visit, Dr. Lee confirmed that Chao Chen was indeed pregnant. He smiled kindly. "I need to examine you so that I can determine generally when your baby is due. Here's a gown to put on. I'll be back in just a minute with my nurse."

Lying on the table, Chao Chen tried to remain calm, but she kept gasping for air and her teeth started to chatter. The nurse came in and held her hand. "Oh my dear, don't be afraid. This won't hurt a bit."

"Thank you. I'm not very brave, am I? I'm not used to being examined by a doctor."

"Well, all that's about to change. We'll expect to see you every four weeks right until the time that you deliver to make sure you and your baby stay healthy. Now just relax."

Dr. Lee entered the room and snapped on his rubber gloves. "I'll be as gentle as possible."

Chao Chen shut her eyes again. She could feel herself being poked and prodded.

"I'd say you're about eight or nine weeks pregnant, Miss Chen, and so your baby will be born sometime in June of next year."

The nurse smiled. "The sign of the Pig. Children of that sign are usually considerate, responsible, independent, and optimistic."

"Are there any negative qualities associated with this sign?" Chao Chen was still haunted by old Chinese superstitions.

"Mothers don't usually ask such questions at a time like this. Let me think. Sometimes they can be lazy, and their pure hearts will let them be cheated in everyday life."

Chao Chen thought for a moment. "So, it's best that I watch out so that no one takes advantage of my child."

Dr. Lee laughed. "You don't really believe all that, do you? Children's personalities are a balance between nature and nurture. They come into this world with certain inherited traits, and then life's events combine with their upbringing to form the person they turn out to be. If you and Herr Kolber are attentive parents, and if you guide and discipline your child, chances are you will be amply rewarded."

"If what you say is true, Dr. Lee, I can look forward to having an angelic child because I plan to shower my baby with love."

"That's only part of the equation. You must also set boundaries for your child or they will grow up to be selfish and self-centered."

"Yes… Well, I've taken up enough of your time, Dr. Lee. Thank you for seeing me today."

"Don't forget to make another appointment in a few weeks. I want to be sure that you are eating properly and taking good care of yourself and your baby. Everything you do and everything you feel affects your unborn child. So, keep a smile on your face and your stomach full."

Chao Chen, her worst suspicion proved true, had only one thought. How would she tell Walter?

chapter 46

The Right Thing

Lilly and David's maid, Liu Yang, answered the doorbell and instructed Walter to wait in the living room. "Madam Ozer is paying the seamstresses. She'll be with you in just a moment."

"Where are Mischa and Judith?" Walter asked. "I ought to say hello to them. I haven't seen them in quite a while."

"They're visiting Monsieur Ozer's mother. They are not expected back for at least another hour."

Walter was not in fact in any mood to see his nephew and niece, and so the news came as a relief. He wasn't fond of either of them, and at five and two years of age, they bored him to tears.

Walter lit a cigarette and sat down on the sofa. Now that the dining room had been turned into a sewing room, a small table was set for dinner; but other than that minor adjustment to accommodate Lilly's business, the apartment had not changed. Since they never had to move to the ghetto, Lilly and David had survived the war without making too many sacrifices. *Just like Lilly to have all the luck while the rest of us suffer.*

Lilly glided into the living room. She was a beautiful woman of twenty-six. Wearing a fashionable linen dress of her own design, she flopped down on the sofa next to her brother. "What's so urgent, Walter, that you had to rush over here?"

"Chao Chen is pregnant."

"What? Are you certain she's not just trying to trap you into marrying her?"

"She went to see your upstairs neighbor, Dr. Lee, and he gave her the news."

"Give me one of those foul cigarettes. I need to calm my nerves." She took a long draw on the cigarette and followed the smoke with her eyes as it floated toward the ceiling.

Walter laughed. "You look as if you're praying to God Almighty."

"No, but that's what you should be doing. When Mutti and Papa get wind of this, there'll be hell to pay. Is it too late to do something about this?"

"Chao Chen is about two months pregnant. I suppose she could terminate the pregnancy, but honestly, as much of an inconvenience as this is going to be, I can't imagine murdering my own child. And, although if I put my foot down she'd probably do what I tell her, she's against an abortion as well."

"So, your minds are made up to have this half-breed?"

Walter hesitated and then admitted, "Ouch. That's a harsh thing to say to me, Lilly."

"Well, you'd better get used to it because that's what people are going to say when they see your child."

Walter admitted, "I'd rather it not have happened at all. I honestly don't know who is to blame, her or myself, but I guess I should take some responsibility for this."

Lilly looked surprised. "Well, that's refreshing. For once you're not looking to point the finger at someone else. Maybe, at twenty-three, you're finally becoming a mensch." She stood up and paced back and forth. "All of us are trying to figure out where we're going to go now. It's becoming clearer by the day that Chiang Kai-shek is losing his power base. If the Commies take over, we're done for. The state will do away with private enterprise. We'll be forced to give up our business. Anyway, we've put our names on various lists to emigrate—to the United States, Palestine, even South America."

"What has this got to do with Chao Chen and me?"

"Walter, sometimes I don't think you have the brains you were born with. Make a plan to get out of Shanghai, the sooner the better. That way you won't have to sneak around with a Chinese wife and baby for very long. And in the meantime, *you* can keep it from Mutti and Papa. I certainly won't tell them. You've heard the expression 'don't kill the messenger?' Well, Mutti might not know that one and she'll murder me just for speaking the words. I'll do what I can to help you. I've always favored you to Dolfie. He's really a dullard, I'm afraid. As much as I hate to say it, you can be very amusing and charming when you want to be. And you have musical talent, something that poor Dolfie is totally lacking. When do you plan on getting married? Soon, I expect. You owe Chao Chen that much."

"Chao Chen spoke to her brothers. They've offered to pay for our wedding reception, such as it will be. I'm not sure how I'm going to arrange for all our official marriage documents with the *Jüdische Gemeinde* without Mutti and Papa hearing of it. If I could get married under a different name, I would. But I don't think that's possible."

"Have you set a date?"

"We're looking at Sunday, December 15. It will be a rather low-key affair, to say the least, at the Promenaden Café in Hongkew. That's where a lot of the secular weddings among Jewish couples are being held these days, what with so many couples tying the knot—or should I say the noose."

"Is that how you really feel, Walter? Because if it is, you shouldn't go through with this."

"Look, I have to do the right thing by Chao Chen. And there is something that you don't know about her. The Chen family is very rich, at least that's the rumor. Her father was a provincial governor and they owned a lot of land outside Shanghai. They had to leave all that behind when the Japs invaded, but they managed to sock away a lot of money. I've heard that their house in the French Concession is filled with priceless antiques. Chao Chen may even have a dowry, but I haven't had the nerve to ask her. Then she'd think I'm just marrying her for her money. There's some truth to that, but between us, I would never admit to it."

"You really think that her family would give her a dowry for marrying a Jew? Don't be ridiculous, Walter. They're just as against intermarriage as the Jews are. Honestly, I can't wait to see the look on Mutti's face when you tell her."

Walter cleared his throat. "I was thinking that, when and if the time came that our parents find out about all this, you could be the one to tell them."

"Oh really, Walter? You want me to do your dirty work for you? I don't think so. But we can talk about it later."

"I just have one favor to ask of you right now."

"What is it?"

"Will you and David act as our witnesses at the wedding ceremony?"

Pausing as if to delay having to give him an answer, she said, "When did you say it was?"

"Two days before the start of Chanukah. By then Chao Chen will be three months pregnant."

"Hmm, hopefully she won't be showing." Lilly put her hand on her own stomach. "I remember when I was three months pregnant with Mischa. You'd never have suspected a thing. But it was a different story with Judith. By then I was as big as a watermelon and could barely fit into my clothes."

"Fascinating. Now will you come to our wedding or not?"

"Walter, you are putting me in a very difficult position. As much as I'd like to be there to show my support for you and Chao Chen, I really think it's for the best that David and I not go."

"And why is that? Are you ashamed that someone might put two and two together and realize that you have a Chinese sister-in-law?"

"If you must know, yes. And if someone we know spotted us there, someone who was once a customer in the shop or who is friends with Mutti and Papa, I'd have a lot of explaining to do."

"That's just like you, Lilly, to do what's in your best interest—and the rest is just hogwash. You don't want our parents to think that you are in any way involved with Chao Chen and me, do you?"

"My first loyalty is to our parents, but I'll do what I can to help you. You can trust me not to tell anyone."

chapter 47

Wedding at the Promenaden Café

The alarm woke Walter out of a sound sleep. With his eyes still partially shut, he groped around for the clock and held it at just the right angle so he could confirm that it was ten o'clock.

He buried his head in his pillow and groaned, fighting the urge to go back to sleep and just forget about everything, but his stomach was growling. The smell of freshly baked cinnamon buns and strong coffee wafting from the kitchen was too enticing. He threw off the covers and stood naked on the cold bedroom floor. Ambling over to the full-length mirror, he examined his body. Despite hard living, his body was still toned, and at twenty-three, his face as of yet unlined. He smiled at his reflection and began to sing Schumann's *"Ich will meine Seele tauchen"*:

> "I want to plunge my soul
> Into the chalice of the lily;
> The lily shall resoundingly exhale
> A song of my beloved.
>
> The song shall quiver and tremble
> Like the kiss from her mouth
> That she once gave me
> In a wonderfully sweet hour!"

What a song, and so full of sexual symbolism. What a clever man Schumann was! If only Walter had a better voice, he'd sing it to Chao

Chen, his budding bride. She was clever enough to understand its full intent if he translated it for her. Too bad she didn't understand a word of German. Well, all of that would have to change once he put his plan into motion.

But first things first: he had a wedding to go to, his own at the Promenaden Café, later that morning. He wrapped a wool robe around himself and sneaked into the bathroom. Turning on the shower, he let the room fill up with steam and then stepped into the stream of hot water to release the tension in his neck and back. He squeezed the bar of soap and it popped out of his hand, landing on the tile floor. Pushing aside the shower curtain, he stepped cautiously on the wet floor to retrieve it just as his mother banged on the door. "What's taking you so long in there, Walter?"

"I'm almost finished, Mutti. Just give me five more minutes." He jumped back in the shower and rinsed himself off, then grabbed a towel and quickly dried himself. So much for a last leisurely shower as a single man. Putting his robe back on, he opened the door. His mother was still in her robe.

"I'm surprised you're still here, Mutti."

"I wasn't feeling well this morning, so your father went to the factory without me. Now get out of my way. I need to use the bathroom badly. My stomach has been on the fritz."

Opening his closet, Walter laid out a dark blue suit and then took out a crisp white shirt that had been sent to the laundry. Oh, it was delightful to finally have things properly attended to. It was one of the few luxuries that his mother spent money on these days. "Fresh sheets make for a good night's sleep, and an ironed shirt makes for a gentleman," she liked to say, and he agreed. He wished that Chao Chen could do more than just wash their bed linens. Why didn't she bother to iron them? It never occurred to him to ask her. In her condition, she was becoming emotional over just about anything. She'd probably take his remark as a criticism, and with so much on his mind, he didn't have the patience for it.

While buttoning his shirt he muttered to himself, "*Ach*, what have I gotten myself into? You really are an idiot, Walter." But then he thought about that first blush of passion with Chao Chen. Maybe, once the baby was born, she'd get over all these mood swings and revert to the sensuous, beautiful young woman he had first laid eyes on at the Shanghai Conservatory of Music three years ago. Had it really been that long? The war had distorted time.

Not knowing from one day to the next whether they would survive brought an immediacy to everything. Other Jewish refugees weren't so lucky, but that was really no concern of his.

Walter looked at himself once again in the full-length mirror. He adjusted his silk tie and checked his pocket to make sure he had the gold band he had bought for Chao Chen from a pawn shop in the Old City—far from prying eyes. He put a few coins in his pocket for the trolley that would take him from the French Concession into Hongkew. Now that he knew his father would be at the factory today, he would be extra vigilant when he and Chao Chen were out on the street. *Oh, this game of cat and mouse is tiresome. Lilly is right. The sooner we can leave Shanghai, the better.*

No one was in the dining room when he took one of his mother's Meissen plates, even though she kept the dinnerware for special occasions only, from the cupboard and helped himself to two buns. Then he poured a cup of coffee from the silver urn. It was very pleasant sitting here with no one bothering him.

No sooner had he stirred a heaping spoonful of sugar into his cup than his mother appeared in the doorway. "Where are you off to all dressed up like that? It's Sunday."

Walter had a ready answer. "Some of us from the Conservatory are getting together for a tea dance at the Blue Bird on Boulevard de Montigny. It's a Chinese-owned club and so we'll be slumming it. But it'll be fun."

"Just don't let one of those Chinese taxi dancers get into your pocket, Walter."

"Don't worry, Mutti. I have my eye on a pretty young thing from the Conservatory. And she's Jewish, so you needn't worry."

Eva seemed satisfied with Walter's explanation. She poured herself a cup of coffee and sat at the head of the table to read the morning newspaper. "Can you imagine?" she said as her eyes skimmed the front page. "France has reelected Léon Blum prime minister of France. Perhaps there is hope for Europe."

"Fascinating, Mutti. So the Frogs have decided that the Jews aren't so bad after all."

Walter took a last gulp of coffee. He stood up, brushed off a few crumbs of pastry that stuck to his jacket, and took his heavy wool coat from the coat rack in the hallway. He hesitated for a moment, and then he realized that he had forgotten his violin. He retrieved it from his bedroom and put it into a large brown paper bag.

Kissing his mother on the forehead, he looked in her eyes. "Take care of yourself, Mutti. You don't look so well."

"Will you be home tonight?"

"I don't know. It all depends..." He rushed out the door to avoid more questions stepping into the cold December air. He thought again, *Am I taking an enormous gamble marrying Chao Chen? No point in dwelling on all this right now. Der Würfel ist gefallen – the die is cast.*

He hopped onto the trolley that rode into Hongkew, and not wanting to sit down and crease his pants, he remained standing and held on to a strap. He smiled at the young woman dressed in a full-length fur coat who was staring at him. She took out a compact and reapplied her red lipstick. What an invitation. Under different circumstances he would have started a conversation with her, but he suppressed the urge to try to pick her up.

He tipped his hat at the attractive woman as he stepped off the trolley in front of the Promenaden Café. For once he was right on time. Prominently displayed in the window was the "In Bounds" sign, advertising that the café passed muster with the American liberators and so the troops and sailors could go into the café for a safe meal and entertainment. A poster with Bobby Johnston's picture, a popular Negro jazz pianist who made the rounds of the local cafés throughout Shanghai, was also displayed. His appearance would guarantee a lively scene. Walter opened the café door to a roar of U.S. soldiers in uniform drinking, smoking, and singing along to the syncopated rhythms of Bobby Johnston's piano-playing. The silver tip tray at the edge of the baby grand was already full even though it was only one o'clock. But this was Shanghai, and it didn't matter what time of day it was. Someone was always dancing, singing, drinking, and having a good time, especially now that the war was over.

Walter spotted Professor Wittenberg and Miss Liang standing at one of the three corner tables at the back of the room reserved for the wedding reception. Making his way through the room—but not before giving a friendly wave to Bobby Johnston as one musician to another—he greeted Professor Wittenberg and Miss Liang.

Miss Liang turned to the two men in conservative business suits who stood nearby and said in English, "Misters Chen, may I introduce you to your sister's groom, Walter Kolber. Walter, this is Fu-Chan and Fu-Ti Chen."

Fu-Chan and Fu-Ti bowed slightly. In the politest of voices, they each congratulated Walter. Fu-Chan confided, "You know, Herr Kolber, we love our sister very much. We expect that you will treat her like a rare and delicate flower. She has not had an easy life, as I am sure you know. We are counting on you to make her future bright and full of joy. Isn't that so, Fu-Ti?"

Fu-Ti nodded. "Chao Chen has always had a reputation for being headstrong. We hope that her independent nature will not get her into trouble." And then he reached out and squeezed Walter's hand as if warning him that both brothers would be watching him.

Ignoring this hostile gesture, Walter said, "It was very generous of you to cover the cost of our wedding reception. To be honest, I would have liked something more elegant for my rare and delicate flower, but the Promenaden is one of the few places in Hongkew that accommodates civil weddings, especially one such as ours, if you understand my meaning."

Fu-Ti and Fu-Chan looked at Walter with suspicion but were too polite to say anything.

Walter continued, "It's a pleasure to meet both of you. I'm sorry to say that none of my family will be here today. Now, if you'll excuse me for a moment, I must to speak with Professor Wittenberg. Chao Chen and I have prepared a surprise for our guests, and he's in on it."

He turned his back on Chao Chen's brothers. "Professor Wittenberg, would you take care of my violin until Chao Chen and I are ready to play? And have you cleared it with Frau Reuben? We will need to commandeer the piano for a few minutes. I don't want there to be any complications."

"She has already given her permission, and so you have nothing to worry about. In fact, she is quite excited to hear you and Chao Chen play once again, although I'm not sure this crowd of rowdy American GIs is going to appreciate what you have in store."

"Too bad." He laughed dismissively.

Looking toward the entrance, Professor Wittenberg announced, "Walter, I see your bride is here, and she looks quite stunning. You are indeed a very lucky young man. I hope you know that."

Walter turned around to see Chao Chen in her red dress. She was walking tentatively through the crowd, keeping her eyes down as soldiers and sailors hooted and hollered. She was led by Ya-Li, who cleared a path for her. When she at last looked up and saw Walter, Chao Chen rushed to his side. The couple was quickly surrounded by Chao Chen's brothers and the other guests.

Kurt Primo, the officiant for the ceremony, asked, "Are you ready? I am afraid that I have two other weddings to perform today and I can't be late for either of them, but I do want to have time to enjoy a luncheon banquet with you. The Promenaden has an excellent kitchen. In fact, they prepare the best Wiener schnitzel in all of Shanghai." After guiding the bride and groom to a table, he continued. "Here are the official marriage certificates for both of you to sign." The two witnesses, attorney Willi Schultz and Fritz Weiss from the Shanghai B'nai B'rith Lodge, watched expectantly.

Walter picked up the pen. Those standing near him could see that his hand was shaking. He leaned over, took a deep breath, and signed his name. Turning to Chao Chen, he said, "Don't use Chinese characters. The officials in Austria won't be able to read your name when we get there. Write your name in English. You know how to do that, don't you?" Why he chose to belittle her at this moment was beyond even his own understanding.

Chao Chen, aware that her groom was investigating the possibility of emigrating to Austria, did as Walter instructed. The couple stood in front of Kurt Primo, who read from a prepared script and elicited a perfunctory "I do" from the bride and groom. "Walter Kolber and Chao Chen, I now pronounce you man and wife by the power vested in me by the *Jüdische Gemeinde* and the city officials of Shanghai."

Keenly aware of all the expectant eyes upon them, Walter kissed his new bride while dipping her at the waist to the enthusiastic applause of his audience.

Walter and Chao Chen took their seats first, and then their guests found their places around the three tables. Walter signaled to the proprietress, Frau Reuben, to serve the first course and pour each guest a glass of champagne in anticipation of the toasts to come.

Despite the rowdiness and noise in the café, Chao Chen's older brother Fu-Chan stood up and, in a barely audible voice, wished the newlyweds good luck. "Today's date is the fifteenth. When its digits are added together, it makes the number six. We pronounce this as 'liu' in Mandarin, which means 'smooth' and 'well-off.' In Chinese people's eyes, this means that everything will go smoothly. So, Walter and Chao Chen, you both have nothing to worry about. Your marriage will go as smoothly as a fine piece of ivory or the surface of a lake on a still summer's day." And then he smiled. "Chao Chen, do you remember the beautiful lake at our estate and how you loved to row the boat past the pavilion?"

Chao Chen returned his smile as Walter thought to himself, *So it must be true what I've heard about how wealthy the Chens are.*

Then it was Professor Wittenberg's turn to toast the newlyweds. He acknowledged Fu-Chan's prediction. "I'm sure we all breathed a sigh of relief upon hearing that our bride and groom were to be married on a trouble-free day." Professor Wittenberg then launched into a lecture on the significance of the number fifteen in the Jewish tradition: "Fifteen is an allusion to the Divine Name. It is also a very auspicious number because our Passover holiday begins on the fifteenth day of the Hebrew month of Nisan, Sukkot on the fifteenth day of Tishrei, and Tu B'Shevat on the fifteenth day of Shevat—all important holidays in our Jewish calendar that dates back three thousand years, just a little further back than the Chinese civilization." He stopped for a moment as if coming up with a new insight. "Perhaps that is why our two newlyweds get along so well together. They are about the same age, historically speaking." He looked around the table expectantly as people politely chuckled and nodded. He continued: "It was Beethoven's *Spring Sonata* for violin and piano that brought these two talented young people together. As the seasons of their lives change from spring to summer, from summer to fall, and so on, may they always make beautiful music together." Then, making sure that everyone was paying close attention, he said enthusiastically, "Let us make a toast to their health and happiness and to their future children that they might someday be blessed to bring into a world that is finally at peace. May it always remain so."

Walter winced when he heard Professor Wittenberg mention children; he hoped no one noticed his reaction.

Once everyone had drained their glasses, Professor Wittenberg handed Walter his violin, which had been hiding under the table. Taking on the role of master of ceremonies, he announced, "The Promenaden Café has graciously given Walter and Chao Chen permission to perform a short duet for us. Perhaps the other customers will temper their revelry for a few minutes." He glared at the rowdy sailors at the other end of the restaurant, who ignored him.

Walter buttoned his jacket and straightened his tie. Taking Chao Chen's hand, he led her to the stage. She sat down on the piano bench, moving it closer to the keyboard. Passing her fingers lightly over the keys, she rested her feet against the pedals. Excited to be performing, Walter could feel the adrenaline pumping through his veins. He held his violin to his chin as he tuned it, and the room quieted expectantly. Then, as if teasing his audience, he put the violin down and addressed the crowd. "My lovely bride, Chao Chen, and I would like to play a short duet for you."

The rowdy crowd of sailors and soldiers voiced their displeasure, calling for Bobby Johnston to come back. One of the GIs yelled, "Get off the stage, you Kraut." And someone else yelled back, "Why don't you shut up for a minute and let them play? And did you take a gander at his wife? She's a real China doll." A few men whistled.

Speaking loudly and trying to maintain his composure, Walter continued. "In all the commotion I forgot to tell you the name of the piece we are going to play for you: '*Salut d'amour,*' or 'Salute to Love,' by Elgar. He wrote this little jewel for his fiancée, and in return she presented him with a poem, which he later set to music. Oh, they were perfectly suited for each other, just as Chao Chen and I are." Then, smirking, he couldn't resist adding, "One of my wife's suitors played this very piece two years ago at our first recital together. But he was a fool to have set his sights on her. I had already won her heart. Isn't that so, my dearest?" He looked at Chao Chen, who was blushing furiously. He got a perverse thrill from embarrassing her; after all, it was so easy to do.

After the crowd quieted again, they began to play. The music filled the room, and what minutes before had been a rowdy crowd turned into a collection of admirers. When the piece ended the couple was greeted by thunderous applause and stamping feet. Walter grabbed Chao Chen's hand and the couple took their bows.

As they left the stage, an appreciative Bobby Johnston handed Walter all the tip money on his silver plate, saying, "Your magnificent performance has brought tears to my eyes. I'd like to give you a wedding gift, from one musician to another."

Walter eagerly accepted the money, stuffing it into his coat pockets, and thanked Bobby. Holding his violin and bow, he left the stage with Chao Chen following closely behind him. She leaned into him and whispered, "Did I do all right, Walter? You weren't disappointed, were you?"

"You did fine. My performance was flawless. I'm just surprised they didn't ask for an encore, but it's just as well. We can get out of here and make love as husband and wife. That will be quite a novelty, won't it?"

Chao Chen didn't answer him, but Walter saw tears in her eyes. Most certainly they were tears of joy.

chapter 48

The First Farewell

Shanghai was a bloated city with a population soaring toward seven million people by 1947. Its harbors and waterways were clogged with freighters carrying every manner of cargo that had not reached the port throughout the war, such as drums of gasoline, bulk medical supplies, and construction materials. Peasants were migrating into the city from the countryside looking for work, and city dwellers were leaving the city in droves, looking for housing elsewhere. The main train station was glutted with passengers waiting for hours, sometimes even days, for trains that did not adhere to any particular schedule. It was not uncommon to see entire families bedded down in the street until they could finally board a train.

Letter-writers set up tables catering to the illiterate Chinese who were desperate to find family members. Upward of twenty million Chinese soldiers and civilians had died in battle or from famine or disease.

Inflation was out of control fostering a healthy black market where shoppers could buy nylon stockings, perfumes, canned goods, and other items still in scarce supply or overpriced in the department stores and legitimate Shanghai markets. Many of the foreign corporations doing business in Shanghai pulled up stakes and moved their headquarters south to Hong Kong, a British protectorate. An area of that city became known as "Little Shanghai."

Few Jewish refugees envisioned a future for themselves in Shanghai, especially as Communist forces expanded their control over parts of China and Manchuria and set their sights on the Pearl of the Orient.

By 1947 fewer than five thousand stateless Jews were still receiving some form of assistance from the JDC, a dramatic reduction from almost fifteen thousand the prior year. Jews hastened to put their name on waiting lists, seeking passage out of Shanghai to other countries willing to take them in. Those Jews who had overseas sponsors or money in their pockets and a skill had a better chance of quickly finding a new homeland.

News of departures was quickly spread throughout the refugee community, among the many: Eric Reisman, who worked for the American Air Transport Command as a mechanic, left with his family for Bolivia; Doris Gray, head nurse at the Emigrants Hospital in the Ward Road *Heim*, left Shanghai on the *Marine Lynx* for the United States; Herman and Ulse Krips took the first transport headed back to Berlin in August of 1947; and the Meyerowitz family left for Panama. Ralph Hirsch, whose family owned a candy store in Hongkew, left for the United States; Eric Culman, an apprentice in camera repair, secured passage to San Francisco; Ruth Summer married an American GI against her parents' wishes, and a month after arriving in the United States gave birth to a baby boy. Fred Gusberger joined his brother in Sydney; Rachel Koffman abandoned her couturier business in Shanghai and emigrated to Australia.

Dolfie and his wife were the first in the Kolber family to leave Shanghai. Margot had placed her name on a list to emigrate to the United States, but when she learned that only she and her parents would be allowed to go, she removed her name. Instead, the couple made plans to sail to Bolivia with her parents in January of 1947. Dolfie carried a letter on JEKO stationery and signed by his father that indicated to the authorities that "Adolf Kolber is a hardworking, reliable and responsible employee."

Josef and Eva huddled against each other on the wharf as a fierce January wind blew off the Whangpoo River. Dolfie looked around. "Where are Lilly and David? Aren't they coming to say goodbye to us? And what about Walter? Is he too busy playing his fiddle to see his own brother off?"

Eva responded, "The children both have colds, and Lilly doesn't want to take them out in this weather. As for Walter, I have no idea where he is. He'll probably be along just before you board. Besides, these boats never leave on time. Look at the crowd. It's going to take at least an hour before all the passengers are aboard."

Margot patted her husband's hand. "Don't fret. At least your Aunt Dora and Uncle Herman are here to see us off. If Walter doesn't show up, he'll surely come to regret it."

Dolfie smiled. "Margot, you always think the best of everyone. You really don't know my brother at all. I've told you that Walter was born without a heart. He only thinks of himself."

Eva interrupted. "Dolfie, is this how you want to spend our last few moments together, complaining about Walter?"

She winced in pain. Josef looked concerned. "Eva, you must go to the doctor. You can't keep ignoring the pains in your chest."

"It's nothing. I think I'm just overwrought. I can't believe that the family is scattering to the winds. I thought that somehow we'd all stay together. Nine years in Shanghai and now we are saying goodbye to one another. Who knows when we will all be together again?"

The ship's captain waved at the passengers standing on the dock as the Custom House clock chimed in the noon hour. Josef pulled out his pocket watch. "Right on time. Will miracles never cease?"

Eva lamented, tears in her eyes, "We've lost so much, haven't we, Josef?"

"And gained so much. We can be thankful for our grandchildren and for our sweet daughter-in-law, Margot. And there is some consolation knowing that Margot's parents are going with them. They won't be all alone."

"God only knows what's in store for them in La Paz."

Dolfie hugged his mother. "There you go again, Mutti. Try to see the bright side of things for once."

"At my age, why should I change my ways? I'll be fifty-three on my next birthday. I feel like I already have one foot in the grave."

A queue had formed. Josef slapped Dolfie on the back. "No point in dawdling. I am proud of you, Dolfie. Make a good life for yourself and Margot."

Dolfie grabbed his father and kissed him on both cheeks. "Papa, I'll look forward to a letter as soon as we're settled telling me that Mutti is feeling better."

Josef whispered to Dolfie, "And I'll look forward to news that you and Margot are going to be parents. And be sure and teach your children German so that, when we are all together, I can amuse them with stories about you and Walter when you were little boys."

Eva and Josef held hands as they watched the foursome make their way up the gangplank. Standing on the deck of the boat, Dolfie doffed his hat and Margot waved her gloved hand to her in-laws and Dora and Herman.

Eva refused to budge until Dolfie and Margot turned around and went below deck.

chapter 49

The Lotus Flower

As they stood in the long queue outside the office of the United Nations Rescue and Relief Administration, Walter warned Chao Chen, "Let me do the talking. You won't know what to say." For days, Walter had rehearsed the speech he would give the clerk: *Well, sir, I recently lost my day job at Schmidt Engineering. They've shut their doors like so many other Jewish businesses. So, as of right now, I'm not making any money at all. My wife has been giving piano lessons to make some extra money, but as you can easily see, she's about to give birth any day now and so we'll be virtually penniless soon. You ask what I'll do after we emigrate? Well, I'm a concert violinist. You may have already heard of me—Walter Kolber. I have a letter of reference from my professor, Alfred Wittenberg. He's a world-famous violinist and teaches at the Shanghai Conservatory of Music. Yes, yes, that's him. Anyway, I expect that this letter will open many doors for me. Thank you for helping us.*

After two hours of standing, while one Jewish refugee after another was processed, Walter and Chao Chen finally reached the front of the queue. Chao Chen could barely stand, but no one offered her a chair or a glass of water while they waited. She stood behind Walter, and as he started to deliver his rehearsed speech, the clerk quickly interrupted him. "Where do you and your wife wish to go, Herr Kolber?"

Walter had already handed over the forms he filled out. "As I have written, I wish to return to my home country, Austria. And from there, hopefully one day to the United States. Although I have no connections there yet, I expect that I will be invited to play at Carnegie Hall in New York or with the Philadelphia Orchestra. There are many possibilities for me, I can assure you."

Uninterested, the clerk asked, "When did you arrive in Shanghai?"

"1938."

"So, you've been here nine years?"

Walter nodded. "Yes. I came here with my family from Vienna. My wife and I were recently married here in Shanghai, on December 15, 1946."

The clerk stopped him again. "Your name sounds familiar. Now let me think. Oh yes, there was an Adolf Kolber here with his wife a short while ago. Are you any relation to him?"

Walter tried to remain calm but his hands were shaking. "Yes. He's my twin. He and his wife recently left for Bolivia, and from there they hope to go to the United States. With luck, we'll find one another there. Oh, I do miss Dolfie—that's what I call him—already."

The clerk observed, "You look nervous, Herr Kolber. Are you hiding something from me? Whatever it is, it will be easy enough for me to find out. We have very good records of the Jews here in Shanghai."

Walter leaned over the desk and whispered, "Please, sir. My parents don't know anything about my situation. I'm sure I needn't go into any detail, do I?"

The clerk, staring at Chao Chen's belly, raised his eyebrow. "So, young man, you're in a bit of a fix. But it's really none of my business. I'm here to expedite your departure, not to make trouble. We have been instructed to get as many Jewish refugees out of Shanghai as quickly as possible, to shift the burden, you might say."

Looking over Walter's application a second time, he said, "It seems as if everything is in order." He stamped the paper. "You and your Chinese wife and baby will have to wait your turn, as transportation is extremely limited. We won't allow your wife to travel until after she has the baby anyway. They don't have birthing facilities on the troop transport ship. So check back after the baby is born and then we'll get you out of here. When is she due?"

"In June. Will that give you enough time to book passage for us?"

"Who knows? We'll just have to wait and see. Now, please move on." He waved his hand and yelled, "Next!"

Walter led Chao Chen out to the street. "What did he say, Walter?"

"Once the baby is born we'll be on our way." He clapped his hands and then picked Chao Chen up and did a little waltz with her in his arms. Even with a distended belly she was as light as a feather.

"Walter, put me down before I have the baby right here."

Emboldened by the success of their visit to the immigration office, Walter asked, "Chao Chen, there's something I've been meaning to ask you for quite some time. It's rather awkward for me, but since we are in such dire financial straits, I thought it might be time for me to broach the subject."

"What is it, Walter? You should be able to discuss anything with me. I'm your wife, aren't I?"

"Yes, and I'm your husband, which means that it's my role to take care of you. But unfortunately, given our current circumstances, I can't afford to. Fortunately, the Hebrew Immigrant Aid Society is giving us a bit of a handout, but other than that, what can I really count on? So let me come right out and ask you. Do you think there's any chance that we might ask your family for some money? I mean, wasn't there any money put aside for you if you were to marry or have a child? I've heard that wealthy Chinese families do such things."

Chao Chen laughed. "Are you serious, Walter? Do you think that we would be living the way we are if there was any money for me? Do you think I like living in a tiny room down a dark lane in the poorest part of Shanghai instead of in a small home in the French Concession, which is where my mother spends her days and nights? Whatever money might have been mine was spent by Rui-De Xu years ago, a bribe so that my brothers wouldn't have to go into the military. I'm of no consequence to the family, and so if you married me hoping that I might bring a dowry with me, you are sorely mistaken." She took off her gloves and held out her hands. "All I have are these two hands and a heart full of love for you and our unborn baby. If that isn't enough for you, tell me now."

"More than enough. Please forget that I even brought this up." Caressing her cheek, he asked, "Can you do that?" He smiled his most ingratiating smile, which Chao Chen seemed to find irresistible on most occasions.

Chao Chen stared at Walter, and then, rubbing her belly, said, "Dr. Lee told me that I was not to become agitated over anything or it might affect our baby. A baby can sense when their mother is unhappy, and so I'm going to pretend this conversation never took place."

Although he had a key to their room in Hongkew, Walter rapped on the door to give Chao Chen fair warning that he had arrived right on time for once. They had plans to see a movie at the air-conditioned theatre on Bubbling Well Road, and then they would have a coffee with Lilly and David at the café downstairs from their apartment. Walter had orchestrated this rendezvous in order to ask his sister for money. He felt fairly certain that, when Lilly saw Chao Chen with her protruding belly, his sister would agree to give them a helping hand.

Walter kissed Chao Chen on her moist forehead. "You look just like a ripe peach ready to be plucked from the tree."

Chao Chen forced a laugh. "I feel more like an old prune than a ripe peach. Give me your hand. My feet are so swollen from this heat that I can barely take a step."

"Luckily I've got a taxicab waiting downstairs. I did fairly well at the racetrack today. It's going to be a bad day for me and those greyhounds if the Communists close the Canidrome."

"Walter, I wish you'd stay away from the track."

"You're beginning to sound just like my mother. I know what I'm doing. On balance, I've made more than I've lost. What's that the Americans like to say: 'You've got to spend money to make money.' That's capitalism for you."

Chao Chen knew better than to start an argument with Walter. "I've had a bad day. Our landlady knocked on our door shortly after you left, and I pretended I wasn't here because I didn't have the rent money." Chao Chen sighed. "And when one of my students came for his lesson this afternoon, I could barely concentrate. I kept listening for a knock on the door rather than paying attention to my student. Poor boy. He had practiced so diligently to please me. I feel guilty taking his mother's money, but what would we do without it?"

"Once we get to Austria, everything will take a turn for the better. I promise."

The seven-p.m. showing of *Till the End of Time* was almost sold out. Walter suspected that the popularity of the Hollywood film had as much to do with the theatre's air-conditioning as it did with the drama, which starred Robert Mitchum and Guy Madison, about U.S. Marine Corps buddies returning from World War II.

Just as the film's heroes were about to get into a fight with some former soldiers trying to enlist them into a veterans' group that "excludes Catholics, Jews, and Negroes," Chao Chen let out a shriek and grabbed Walter's arm.

"What's the matter? It's only a movie,"

"Walter, I think the baby's coming right now."

The couple rushed up the aisle. Pointing to a bench in the lobby, Walter said, "Wait here. I'll go next door to Lilly's apartment and notify Dr. Lee."

"Hurry, Walter. I don't know how long I can stand the pain."

Walter took the stairs two at a time to Lilly's apartment and kept his finger on the bell until Lilly opened the door.

"Walter, we weren't planning to see you for another hour. What's the matter?"

"Chao Chen is having the baby. Please get Dr. Lee. We need to go to the hospital right away."

Carrying his medical bag, Dr. Lee rushed downstairs and, together with Lilly, found the theatre and waited with Walter and Chao Chen for an ambulance to arrive. A small crowd had gathered around, and when someone offered Chao Chen a glass of water, Dr. Lee warned, "Don't drink that. It's better for you to have nothing in your stomach in case we have to give you anesthesia. Just breathe."

Within minutes two medics rushed into the lobby and put Chao Chen on a stretcher. Dr. Lee gave the driver instructions to take them to the Concord Women's Hospital on Rue Molière.

Lilly whispered to Walter, "It's a good thing we're not going to the hospital in Hongkew. Someone there might recognize you."

"You still haven't told Mutti or Papa, have you?"

"No... Not yet."

Walter could barely pay attention to Chao Chen. He was furious with his sister. "I get the distinct impression that you intend to say something to them. Am I right?"

"Now isn't the time to discuss this, Walter. We'll talk about it later."

"Don't you dare complicate things for me. I almost got caught by UNRRA. Just my luck the same clerk had taken care of Dolfie's application. He thought he recognized me. I was afraid he might contact Papa, but he dropped the matter and our papers have been processed. Now we just have to wait for one of the agencies to pay for our passage out of here." Walter took out his handkerchief and wiped the perspiration from Chao Chen's brow. He tried to appear interested in what was happening to her, but all he could think of was trying to figure out how he could pry some money out of Lilly and stop her from saying anything to his parents—at least until he had a chance to put his situation in the best possible light.

Walter and Lilly sat in the crowded hospital waiting room. They didn't have long to wait. At ten o'clock, Dr. Lee came out and told them that Chao Chen had given birth to a healthy baby boy. "You can see your wife now. She is still a little groggy from the anesthesia, but she keeps calling for you. Does she have any other family who should be informed?"

Walter shrugged his shoulders. "No. To be quite honest, her family has no interest in my wife, or me for that matter."

"That's a pity. The birth of a firstborn son is a very joyous occasion for Chinese families."

"Not in this case, I'm afraid."

Walter tiptoed into Chao Chen's hospital room. He was unprepared for the sight of his wife holding a baby in her arms. Until this moment, being a father and responsible for a child was just a story he repeated to engender sympathy from various aid workers. And now here was his baby in the flesh. "Well, I don't see much of myself in the boy."

Chao Chen was annoyed. "All babies look alike, Walter, wrinkled and red-faced. Just be patient. In a few weeks he'll probably be a spitting image of you—or perhaps a combination of both of us." She was visibly exhausted as she stroked the baby's tiny head. "What's today's date?"

"It's June 18, 1947."

"The number eighteen means that our baby will be rich someday, at least according to Chinese numerology."

"And eighteen in the Jewish tradition is double *Chai*, which is a very lucky number as well, and so this child has nothing to worry about. *Chai* means life, and so double *Chai* means that he will have a long life, and hopefully a prosperous one too." He then leaned over and kissed his wife on the head. "I'd better let you get some sleep. I'll be back tomorrow. In the meantime, I'm going to the offices of UNRRA to let them know that you've had the baby and they can make arrangements for our passage out of here. At least we can put our names on a list."

"Before you go, we need to settle on a name for our little one. What about Gan, after my father?"

"Are you serious, Chao Chen? That might make sense if we were staying in Shanghai, but he should have a popular Western name. What about

Robert, after the movie star Robert Mitchum? Or better yet, Harry, like President Harry S. Truman?"

Before Chao Chen could react, Walter slapped his knees. "Yes, that's it. Harry. It doesn't sound much like a baby's name, but he's sure to grow into it."

Chao Chen rested her head against the pillow. Her baby started to cry. She encouraged him to take her breast, but he resisted. What to do? She thought back to her own childhood, when one of the nursemaids rocked her brother in her arms and sang a lullaby, the same one that she had heard coming from the Möller's nursery years ago:

> Oh little lotus flower in the shadow of the great wall.
> Oh little lotus flower, far, far away.
> Oh little lotus flower, shining like the moon.
> Oh little lotus flower, gone, gone too soon.

After she repeated the sad lullaby three times, Harry finally quieted down, his eyelids fluttering closed. Chao Chen did the same, lulled into a deep sleep that carried her away momentarily from the turmoil that her beautiful baby was born into.

chapter 50

Betrayals

Josef sipped his morning coffee as the curtains fluttered in the breeze. A bird struck the window and then flew back to its perch among the thick leaves of the plane trees on Rue de la Soeur. Eva, bringing with her the morning newspaper, sat opposite him after helping herself to a large slice of pumpernickel bread and a plate of summer fruits. As soon as Josef glanced at the front page of the paper, he put down his coffee cup and pounded on the table. "*Mein Gott!* I can't believe this."

Eva stared at him. "What are you talking about?"

"Listen to this." He pushed his glasses back to the bridge of his nose and read:

> "The ship, which has been renamed *Exodus*, arrived back in French waters today. On board are 4,530 Jews. They are people without a country. The Jews—most of them refugees from Germany—left the French port of **Sète** on July 11 bound for Palestine. They changed the name of their ship from the SS *President Warfield* in the apparent hope that their crossing of the Mediterranean would be as fruitful as Moses' crossing of the Red Sea. It was not. The Jews were denied access to what they view as their Promised Land as the British refused to let them disembark at the port of Haifa. Officially, the British said, the Jews are displaced persons [DPs] and illegal immigrants to the Holy Land."[7]

Eva was appalled. "And what's to happen to those poor wretched souls? Aren't the immigration agencies going to step in and help them out?"

"The article goes on to say that, as of right now, they are sitting on the ship in the harbor of Marseilles and will in all likelihood be forced to go back to Germany. They'll probably end up in a displaced persons camp."

Eva was angry. "This just proves that your pipe dream of going to 'Eretz Yisrael,' as you call it, is ludicrous. We don't belong there any more than we belong in Austria. Eventually our names will come up on a list for the United States, Australia, or Canada. At least in those countries Jews are welcome."

"I'm not so sure about that either, Eva." Josef folded the newspaper and finished his cup of coffee. Trying not to arouse his wife's suspicion, he said in a rather offhanded manner, "I have an appointment this morning with our son-in-law." He continued fibbing. "He wants to introduce me to a prospective customer."

"And why don't they just come to the factory? We can show him around."

Josef stood. "I'm not quite sure why. I think the gentleman is in Shanghai for just a few days, and he's staying at the Cathay Hotel. I don't think he wants to schlep all the way to Hongkew just to see Chinese workers hunched over our sewing machines." Patting his stomach, he changed the subject, "That bread was just delicious. You haven't lost your touch, Eva."

"Don't be ridiculous. I bought it at Café Delikat. Who has time to bake these days?"

Without responding, Josef took his straw hat from the rack in the hallway and waved goodbye to his wife. After shutting the door, he breathed a sigh of relief that Eva did not cross-examine him.

He walked down the street and hailed a taxicab. Looking out the window of the cab, he was startled to see a group of Chinese university students marching with banners that read LOWER TUITION FEES, FIGHT HUNGER, and BETTER FOOD SO OUR MINDS WILL WORK TOWARD THE GREATER GOOD OF CHINA. Under his breath he muttered, "Those damn Commies. Next it will be the factory workers."

Overhearing his comment, the cab driver was obviously excited to speak. "Mister, surprise coming. Mao is strong leader. Chiang Kai-shek bad. You will see soon." Josef tried to ignore his comment, but the driver persisted. "What you think? Sir?"

"I really have no opinion. This is not my country." Josef waved for him to stop. "Let me off here. I think I'll walk a few blocks. I need the air." He handed the driver some coins and stepped out into the oppressive humidity.

Josef thought to himself, *Arrogant bastard. A few years ago he wouldn't have dared speak to me at all other than to say, "Thank you, sir."* Frowning, he walked the few blocks to Lilly and David's building.

Lilly opened the door before he had a chance to press the buzzer. "Where are my grandchildren, Lilly? I haven't seen them in weeks." Josef peeked around her to see if the two young ones were there.

"I told the maid to take them out for a while. I wanted us to have a chance to speak privately and without Mutti."

"Am I missing something? The children won't be able to understand whatever we have to say to each other anyway."

"Yes, but I'm afraid of your reaction. They are extremely sensitive these days, and I think they already sense some tension between their father and me."

"What's wrong?"

"My husband extended credit to customers during the war. Many of them just up and left, and who knows where they went? He's holding a stack of worthless IOUs. David's having a difficult time financially, and frankly, I'm not making it any easier on him. I told him the other day that he should give me a hand with the clothing business, and he didn't take very kindly to that."

"So, you're wearing the pants in the family these days?"

Lilly nodded.

"Well, just don't say something to him you'll later regret."

"I'm afraid I already have, but I'll think of a way to make amends. Anyhow, that's not why I asked you to come here. I almost forgot. May I offer you a drink?"

"Should I ask for a stiff scotch?"

"In this heat? A gin and tonic might be more appropriate."

Lilly went to the silver bar cart, measured a jigger of gin, opened a bottle of Schweppes, and poured it into a crystal glass she had filled with ice cubes. She handed him the drink. "Here, Papa."

He took a long gulp and then patted the sofa cushion next to him, gesturing for his daughter to sit down. "Now, what was it you wanted to discuss with me?"

"It's about Walter. He's gotten himself into a lot of trouble."

"There's nothing new about that. Your mother has spoiled him rotten."

"Let's not go into that. It's water under the bridge, as they say. I don't know quite how to tell you this... Walter got married in December. He's been living with his wife in Hongkew, practically right under your nose. It's a miracle that you haven't run into them."

Josef demanded, "And who is the foolish woman who has put her fate in his hands? Is it someone I know?"

"Yes and no. Do you remember the pretty young Chinese woman in the red dress who played a duet with Walter at the Shanghai Conservatory recital? Beethoven's *Spring Sonata*, if I'm not mistaken."

"That Chinagirl? Who—"

Lilly interrupted, "Papa, stop talking. I need to tell you she's Walter's wife. She was the pianist. And her name is Chao Chen." She swallowed. "And what's worse, a couple of weeks ago they had a son."

Josef raised his voice. "What are you saying? That Walter has married that Chinese woman and they had a baby together? A half-breed?"

"If you must put it that way, yes."

For the second time that day Josef invoked God's name. "*Gott im Himmel*, is the boy out of his mind?"

"I don't know. For some time he thought she was from a wealthy Chinese family and that she'd come into money, but he has recently learned otherwise. Naturally, that came as quite a blow to him. She speaks English fluently, which he sees as an advantage, and she's a gifted musician and so they have that much in common. Walter has convinced himself that Chao Chen will help him get ahead in his career. Of course, he certainly didn't plan on becoming a father so soon."

Josef was now shaking with anger. "So where do these two lovebirds expect to live?"

"Walter's waiting to hear from the UNRRA. He's planning on going back to Austria with Chao Chen and their son. He thinks he can land a permanent job with an orchestra or a chamber music group. Professor Wittenberg has given Walter a letter of introduction. What good that will do, I don't know, but Walter seems to think that a letter from the maestro will open doors for him."

"He's more of an idiot than I thought." Josef paused. "Is the kid slanty-eyed? This is going to kill your mother." Suddenly overcome with emotion, tears stinging his eyes, he smashed his fist on the table. "As far as I'm concerned, he's dead to me."

Lilly felt compelled to come to her brother's defense. "Papa, if we hadn't left Vienna this would never have happened. You'd probably be congratulating Walter on becoming engaged to some lovely Jewish girl this very minute. Blame Hitler if you need to blame someone, but please be careful how you tell Mutti. She's been through a lot. In fact, I'm a bit worried about her health. Haven't you noticed? She doesn't look well these days."

"I have. It's been weighing on my mind. I've even thought about asking your mother to stop working, but frankly, I need her at the factory now that Dolfie is gone. But getting back to Walter. What's to be done about him? I know that he doesn't have a pot to piss in."

"You're right. He's been living off international aid. Until a few weeks ago his wife was making some money teaching piano, but that ended. Except for two of her brothers, I don't think her family even knows she's married. I believe that Walter and Chao Chen will leave Shanghai without so much as a goodbye from her family. They are against this marriage just as much as you are."

Josef questioned, "You seem to know a great deal about their circumstances, Lilly. Did you know about the pregnancy? Did you go to the wedding?"

Lilly instantly lied. "Of course not, Papa. Walter has just now confided in me. He asked me for money but given our present circumstances, I'm in no position to help out."

Josef took another gulp of his drink. As the ice clinked against the inside of the glass, he reasoned, "I should consult with Willi Schultz. He's a good lawyer. Maybe their marriage isn't legal."

"I'm sorry to tell you, Papa, but I just found out that Willi and your friend Dr. Kurt Primo were the witness and the officiant at their wedding."

"So there are people in my community who know about this scandal? I can't believe no one has said anything to me! How I could have been so duped? Your mother will have to confront him because I'm washing my hands of that boy. If he wants to let you know of his whereabouts when he leaves Shanghai, so be it, but as far as I'm concerned, I now have only one son—and that's Dolfie." Josef slammed his empty glass down on the cocktail table in front of him and stood up by pushing down on the arm of the sofa.

"Nothing about Walter should surprise me, but I must say I never could have imagined he would make such a mess of his life."

Lilly reasoned, "Well, at least he was man enough to marry Chao Chen after he got her pregnant."

"She probably trapped him into it. A handsome young man from a fine Viennese family… She must have thought she'd caught herself a real prize and that he'd be her ticket to get out of this hellhole."

"Papa, I think that's where you're wrong. Shanghai is her home, with or without her family's blessings. She's going to have a very hard time living in Austria. She speaks no German, and then there is the matter of her race…" Lilly's voice trailed off.

"She should have thought of all that before she got herself into trouble with Walter."

Lilly opened the door for her father. She handed him his hat and kissed him on his warm cheek. "Maybe someday you'll find it in your heart to accept what's happened?"

"Never."

chapter 51

Disowned

Chao Chen tried not to worry because Dr. Lee told her that anxiety blocks the flow of breast milk, but she couldn't stop thinking about what Walter's parents would say to him when he finally told them of his marriage and the birth of their infant son, Harry. She prayed they would find it in their hearts to help them out, but from what little she knew of the Kolbers, she was doubtful. Trying to distract herself by preparing for their imminent departure, Chao Chen folded the leather lederhosen and the knitted blue wool sweater that Lilly had made and put them in a small suitcase. Thankfully, Harry slept peacefully in his basket so she could pack what was left of her belongings.

Chao Chen missed the chirping of her mourning doves. Knowing that she couldn't take them with her, she gave them, along with her piano, to her downstairs neighbor. When Shu-Au offered to pay her something, she refused. "No, the piano is a gift from me. Just promise me that you'll find another teacher to give Jian lessons. Your son has come very far in a short amount of time. Someday, if the Communists don't shut it down, I hope he'll apply to the Shanghai Conservatory of Music."

Shu-Au thanked Chao Chen profusely. Then she confessed, "We will both miss you greatly. There were many days when we barely had anything to eat, but hearing you play the piano so beautifully took our minds off our empty stomachs." Then she added, "I so admire your talent, and you're very brave, Madam Kolber. I can't imagine living anywhere else in the world but Shanghai."

Chao Chen reluctantly admitted, "It's going to be a big adjustment for me. But looking back on my life, I've always taken chances when others predicted that I would fail. So I must believe in myself. Isn't that the secret to succeeding in life, Madam Au?"

"I tell Jian every day: 'Believe in yourself and you'll be a concert pianist someday, just like Madam Kolber.'"

Chao Chen laughed. "Well, I'm not there quite yet. But perhaps someday, when Harry doesn't need all my attention, I can go back to practicing and then Walter and I can perform together. Just imagine the headlines: 'Chao Chen and Walter Kolber take Europe by storm!'"

Chao Chen's enthusiasm was infectious. Shu-Au said, "How exciting! Maybe you and your husband will come back to Shanghai and Jian and I can buy tickets to one of your concerts, then go backstage for your autographs!" Looking around the room at the suitcases, she asked, "Is there anything I can do for you?"

"Nothing really, except please take good care of my little birds. They are going to be heartbroken when I'm gone."

"I'll do my best, Madam Kolber, although I'm sure they'll be looking for you every day."

"Tell them that their mother misses them very much. And be sure to examine the birdseed very closely."

"Oh, I will. I promise."

After Madam Au left, Chao Chen resumed her packing. She picked up her mechanical nightingale and turned the key to listen to its now-familiar tune, *"Für Elise."* When the music stopped, she placed the nightingale in its brocade box, tied the satin ribbon, and tucked it underneath her clothes in her suitcase. Suddenly she imagined herself sitting at a window in a lovely house in Vienna, listening to its sweet tune as Harry played with a red wagon on the floor, a light snow dusting the trees in the garden below. And of course there would be music coming from upstairs where a famous pianist was practicing his arpeggios, perhaps a friend of Walter's he met while playing in one of the city's chamber music groups. Chao Chen told herself, *Life will be so grand.* And in the summertime they would all go to the Salzburg Music Festival, where Walter would be performing. She had seen photographs of quaint Tyrolean villages, and Miss Liang had told her about the many famous artists who had conducted there before the war, like Herbert van Karajan and Wilhelm Furtwängler. Maybe they'd all be returning to resume their careers.

Harry's wail startled Chao Chen out of her reverie. She picked him up and put him to her breast, but he continued to cry. "Have you soiled yourself, my little cherub?" She checked his diaper and was relieved it was still dry because those hanging on the line that was strung across the room were still damp. She told Harry, "Nothing dries in this heat and humidity." As if he understood, Harry stopped crying and looked at his mother, and then a little smile crossed his face. Hugging him, she exclaimed, "That's your first real smile! I can't wait to tell your papa. I'm sure he'll be so impressed! Maybe you'll do it again, in case he needs a bit of cheering up after visiting with his parents. Oh, I do hope his parents are kind to him."

Chao Chen settled him back in his basket and continued packing. One after another she gathered the various pieces of music she had played over the years and placed the scores in her suitcase: Fauré, Elgar, Satie, Mozart, Chopin, and of course, Beethoven. Flipping through the pages, she read the notations of her beloved teacher, Miss Liang: "Practice the fingering here. Don't be so tentative in your approach to this passage. Show more courage." She suspected that she would need a deep reservoir of that to carry her through the days and months ahead.

She picked up the boat tickets and itinerary that Walter had tossed on the wooden crate next to the door. The *Marine Lynx* would be departing Shanghai at ten o'clock a.m. on August 17, 1947 and was scheduled to arrive in Marseilles on September 17, 1947. Walter had explained, "Then we'll take a train to Vienna, and from there it's just another train ride to Linz."

"Can we stop in Paris? I'd love to see the Eiffel Tower and walk along the Seine, and then maybe spend a few days in Vienna. You could show me where you lived, and we could take Harry for a stroll in that park you told me about where you used to play as a little boy. What was the name of it?"

Ignoring her question, Walter snickered. "And maybe we could spend an afternoon sipping hot chocolate and eating a delicious torte at the Hotel Sacher, which was my father's favorite café before the war."

"That sounds wonderful, Walter. Do you mean it?"

"Chao Chen, how can I put this delicately? We are not on a tour of the Continent like some rich Americans. We are refugees and the only place we'll be seeing for a while is a DP camp."

"Forgive me, Walter. I don't mean to upset you. It's just that I've never been outside of China. I want to see the world." And then she added, "With you by my side, of course, and with our little Harry."

Replaying this scene in her head, Chao Chen felt a knot in her stomach and her head began to throb. She poured herself a glass of water and wiped the beads of sweat from her brow.

She felt a rush of air as Walter opened the door. Turning around, she waited for him to say something. She knew from the look on his face that the news he was bringing was not what they had hoped for.

Then unexpectedly, Walter burst out, "When I told my parents about us, my father yelled out the most hateful words. He used expressions that I haven't heard out of his mouth since the Nazis confiscated our factory in '38. He told me I'm a disgrace to the Kolber name, that I should be ashamed of myself, and on and on. He wouldn't allow Mutti to get in a single word, which is a feat in itself. That was probably the only moment worth remembering in the whole ugly scene. He stormed out of the room screaming that I was dead to him."

Walter's voice kept getting louder and louder as he recounted this confrontation. Chao Chen turned on the radio to drown out his shouting. Although most of the neighbors didn't speak a word of English, she didn't want anyone in the rooming house or across the alley to hear what he was saying.

"He was so angry that he forgot Mutti altogether. After he left the room, Mutti grabbed my hand and said, 'Your papa's right, but I still want you to be happy.' Then she slipped me three hundred American dollars and walked away. A lot of good that will do us, but I guess it's better than nothing."

"That must have been very hurtful, Walter."

"I really could have cared less about Papa, but Mutti is a different story. She has always been on my side. And to have her turn on me like that came as a shock."

Chao Chen started shaking. "Did they ask to see Harry and me before we leave?"

"No, they want nothing to do with you or me or their grandson. Think about it. They're no different than your pathetic mothers. Have they once ever inquired about me?"

"No. I'm a stranger to them now. I might as well be dead as far as they are concerned. Only my brothers have shown me some compassion, but their hands are tied. If they so much as hint that they have seen us, Rui-De Xu and Ya-Nan will cut them off."

Walter loosened his tie and unbuttoned his shirt. He went to the open window and covered his ears to block out the shouts of Chinese peddlers hawking their wares in the alley. "The sooner we leave Shanghai, the better. No matter how long I live here, I'll never get used to those coolies and their ching-chong singing. Now get me something to eat. I'm famished." And then a slow smile came over his face and he grabbed Chao Chen by the waist. "I've changed my mind. Let's get into bed before Harry starts whining. I'd rather have you than a meal of canned beans."

chapter 52

All at Sea

Walter kept a firm hand on his violin case as they boarded the USNS *Marine Lynx*, bound for Marseilles. After handing over their tickets at the gangway, a crew member carried their three suitcases down to the cramped cabin that would be their home for the next thirty-six days at sea. The corridors were packed with German and Yiddish-speaking refugees who were eager to find their accommodations aboard this converted five-hundred-foot troop transport ship operated by the American President Line. Many couples were separated and sent to men's and women's barracks, but Walter and Chao Chen were given their own quarters because they had an infant to care for.

As the ship left the harbor, Chao Chen strained to catch a final glimpse of Shanghai through the cabin's porthole. Walter leaned against her and kissed her on the neck. "Can you believe it? We're finally on our way. It was quite a pleasant surprise that Professor Wittenberg and Miss Liang came down to the dock to see us off."

"And what about Ya-Li? When we embraced there were tears in her eyes. I wish I could have taken her with us, Walter. She would be a great help to me."

"You know she's not a refugee, and what's more, she doesn't really like me. What did you tell her? She had a most unpleasant scowl on her face."

"Nothing, Walter. It's just that she's worried about how I'll manage to get along. Other than taking a ferry up the river, I've never been anywhere."

"She's overly protective of you. You'll do fine, and you have me standing right by your side to coach you. And once we are situated somewhere in Linz, I'm sure that the ladies in the camp will lend you a hand with Harry every now and again. I've heard that children are a treasure in the camps. They'll be calling him their little *Liebchen* in no time at all and fussing over the two of you."

"What does that mean?"

Walter pulled an English-German phrase book out of his suitcase and threw it onto the lower bunk. "I've bought this for you. If you know what's good for you, you'll start studying it now. Why don't you look it up? L-I-E-B-C-H-E-N."

Chao Chen sat down on the bed and turned the pages slowly until she found the word. "Oh, here it is. 'Dearest one.' Is that what they'll call him?"

"Yes, and you'll be his *Mutter* and my *Frau*."

"That's enough for today, Walter. I'm feeling a bit seasick."

"Chao Chen, it's all in your head. The weather is perfect and the sea is as smooth as glass right now. Why don't you lie down while I practice for a bit—if it won't disturb you or Harry?"

"Not at all, but what about our neighbors?"

"Too bad about them. If they knock on the door I'll just invite them into our cabin. I should charge them for the privilege of listening to me."

A bell rang at six o'clock signaling that dinner was to be served in the dining room. "Why don't you stay here with Harry, Chao Chen? I'll go up and have dinner by myself. I'll bring something back for you."

"Don't you want people thinking we are together? Are you embarrassed by me? I saw the way some of the passengers were staring at Harry and me as if they'd never seen a Chinese woman with her baby before. Maybe they're wondering why we're here at all."

"One of us has to stay here with the baby. We certainly can't bring him into the dining room. If you'd rather eat by yourself in the dining room, I'll watch Harry until you return."

"No. I won't feel comfortable eating all by myself. What would I say to these people? I'd just be staring into my soup bowl and wishing I could crawl under the table. Perhaps you're right. You go upstairs. Enjoy yourself."

A mirror hung over the sink in their cabin. Walter picked up his brush and ran it through his thick hair, straightened his tie, and splashed cologne on his face. Chao Chen watched as he smiled at his reflection as if immensely pleased with what he saw: a handsome twenty-four-year-old with high cheekbones and wavy hair. Without looking at Chao Chen or Harry, Walter slipped into his well-tailored summer jacket, opened the door, and bounded up the stairs as if he were a bird released from a cage.

Chao Chen unpacked her nightingale music box and turned the key. As the familiar melody filled the cabin, tears rolled down her cheeks. She tried to stop crying, but the more she resisted, the louder her sobs became. Harry woke up and started to cry too. Someone in the next cabin pounded on the wall and shouted in German, *"Halt die Klappe!"* She picked Harry up and walked in circles, trying to settle him down. His face became bright red and he continued wailing. In desperation, Chao Chen carried Harry up to the outside deck. The sun was low in the sky and there was a hint of a full moon ascending overhead. Taking a deep breath of the salty air, she could feel her nerves untangling as Harry relaxed and settled down in her arms.

She sat on a deck chair and watched the sun descend toward the horizon, casting a shimmering path of light over the water. She threw a blanket over herself and nursed Harry until he fell back to sleep. Sensing that someone had sat down in the deck chair next to hers, she turned her head. It was a young woman. She looked vaguely familiar. Summoning her courage, Chao Chen smiled and said, "Good evening, Fräulein."

"So you speak English, do you?"

"Yes, I studied it in school."

"And do you speak German also?"

"Not a word, unfortunately."

"And why is that a problem for you?"

"My husband and I are returning to Austria. He was born there."

"Your husband…is Jewish?"

"Yes. His family came to Shanghai in 1938. His parents are still there, but they plan to go to Palestine, I believe."

"So, the two of you and your baby are running away, so to speak?"

Chao Chen could feel her cheeks turning red. "Not at all. My husband is a violinist and I'm a pianist. We're going to Europe to establish our careers there."

"Good luck to that. By the way, I'm Annalise Berglas Schönfeld." She held out her hand. "And you are?"

"Chao Chen Kolber, and this is my son, Harry. He'll be three months in September."

Annalise peered at his face and then observed, "He looks just like you." Then she stood up and put her pocketbook on her arm. "We're bound to run into each other again. Do tell your husband we met. If he is who I think he is, Walter and I are acquainted. I studied cello at the Shanghai Conservatory. That is, until I got married. You too look somewhat familiar to me, Frau Kolber. Didn't you accompany your husband on the piano at the Shanghai Conservatory some years ago?"

"Yes. We played the first movement of the *Spring Sonata*. And you?"

"I played Beethoven's *Third Sonata*. It was quite a lovely evening, except for that Commandant Ghoya. He almost ruined it for everyone."

"Yes. But all of that is in the past, is it not?" Curious to know more about Annalise Schönfeld, Chao Chen asked, "And where are you going, if I might ask?"

"My husband and I are off to Paris for a brief stay and then on to the United States. We have family in New York who have agreed to sponsor us. I couldn't imagine returning to Vienna after what Austria did to the Jews. But to each his own, Frau Kolber. Perhaps your husband is more forgiving than I." She wrinkled her nose as if a foul odor had passed by.

Something about the tone of her voice and her expression suggested to Chao Chen that this woman did not think highly of Walter. "I'll be sure to let my husband know I met you. It was lovely speaking with you, Frau Schönfeld. Perhaps you and your husband will join us for dinner one of these evenings?"

"I don't think that would be advisable. Good luck, Frau Kolber. I hope that you find what you are looking for in Austria."

Chao Chen felt dejected. At first blush she thought she might make a friend in Annalise, but her parting words felt as if she were slamming the door in her face. She had a dim recollection that Frau Schönfeld and Walter had once had a disagreement, but she wasn't sure.

Opening his eyes, Harry's thick eyelashes grazed his cheeks. He looked up at his mother.

"Ah, Harry, you're my little angel. No matter where we are, I'll always take care of you. You don't have to worry about anything."

Harry blinked and then smiled at his mother as if to reassure her that he understood her promise.

Walter returned from dinner with a bowl of chicken soup, a piece of bread, and chocolate pudding for Chao Chen. He crowed, "You aren't going to believe this, but some of the passengers at my table were at a recital in Shanghai where I played the Bach partita. Can you imagine? They remembered me and asked me to give a little impromptu concert to pass the time. And who knows? Maybe one of them might have connections in music circles in Austria that I can take advantage of. I didn't want to be so bold as to ask them straightaway, but we're going to be stuck on this boat for a month and so I'm sure there'll be an opportune time to make inquiries." Walter started humming "The Blue Danube" waltz and took a quick turn around the cabin.

"I'm glad to see you so happy, Walter. I hope I won't dampen your spirits, but something strange occurred while you were enjoying your meal. Our next-door neighbors were yelling at me to quiet Harry. I couldn't understand what they were saying, but it didn't sound very kind. So I took Harry onto the deck to try to calm him down." Chao Chen dipped the bread into her soup and took a few bites before continuing.

"So…what happened? Did someone say something rude to you on the deck?"

"Not exactly. A well-dressed woman sat down next to me. She had shiny auburn hair and deep-set dark eyes. She looked to be our age, I think. She wore a diamond ring on her finger and diamond earrings to match. She's German, but her English is very good. We had a chance to converse for a few minutes, until she got up and left, and rather abruptly, I might add."

Chao Chen sensed Walter was beginning to lose his patience as he remarked, "You'll soon learn that many of the Germans and Austrians on this boat are a bit standoffish, even to me. That's their nature and so they can't help themselves. Even after everything we have been through, you'd think they'd be more tolerant. Anyway, go on."

"When I introduced myself as Chao Chen Kolber and mentioned to her that I'm a pianist and you're a violinist, she looked as if she had bitten into a rotten apple."

Walter pulled at his collar. "What's this woman's name? You know I do have a past. I've never hidden that fact from you, but I've always been faithful to you from the day we met, Chao Chen." He reverted to his habit of lavishing her with compliments whenever he thought he was about to stand on the razor's edge. "You are more than any man in his right mind could ask for: beautiful, intelligent, and talented."

Chao Chen put up her hand to halt his nattering. "Annalise Berglas Schönfeld. She said that she knew you at the Conservatory, and then we remembered that we both performed at the same recital."

"She's on this boat?"

"Where else? I didn't jump onto a life raft in the middle of the ocean. Yes, on this boat, Walter."

Walter paused as if trying to collect his thoughts. "Ah yes, Annalise Berglas. Remember her? She played the cello."

"I also recall that you said something about her to me, but I just can't remember what it was. Did you and she ever go out together?"

Walter ran his hand through his hair, which was messy from the wind that had suddenly intensified as darkness fell over the ocean. "Annalise and I dated for a short time, but she was very hurt when I dumped her. In fact, when I ended our relationship she spread nasty rumors about me to some of the Jewish girls in our circle of friends and tried to ruin my prospects. To be quite blunt, I have no use for her. That's why she reacted the way she did. Don't take it personally. You didn't do anything wrong. A woman scorned et cetera, et cetera."

"Well that explains it, Walter. But we're bound to run into her and her husband."

"If we do I'll be civil to her, and I'm sure she'll be the same toward me. She wouldn't want to provoke me." He paused and then added, "If she's unpleasant toward me, I might then be forced to tell her husband that I'd slept with his wife. I'm sure he thinks he married a virgin." He put his arms around Chao Chen. "She may be pretty, but inside she is rotten to the core."

Chao Chen suddenly realized that the ship had begun to rock and that there were ominous sounds of water sloshing against the porthole.

Walter warned, "I think we're heading into a storm. Let's hope that it clears out by morning." No sooner were these words out of his mouth than the ship listed dangerously to the port side. Chao Chen's nightingale music box, which had been sitting on the small table next to the lower bunk, slid onto the floor. She gasped, afraid that its wings might have been bent in the fall, but surprisingly, when she picked it up, it was undamaged.

Chao Chen climbed into bed and held on to the post with one hand and Harry's basket with the other. He seemed unperturbed by the motion of the ship. The sound of the straining engines carried up to their cabin all the way from the bowels of the ship. Through the wall Chao Chen heard people on both sides of their cabin praying. As the ship pitched up and down, their prayers grew louder until Walter shouted over the wind, "They probably have no use for God except when they're worried they're about to die." And with that he turned off the light and climbed into the upper bunk. Within minutes he was sound asleep, unaware that Chao Chen was terrified, fearing for her life and the life of her baby boy.

By morning the storm had passed and the seas were calm again. Chao Chen suggested to Walter, "Why don't we take a stroll together on deck? It will be pleasant to feel the sun on our faces. And it will do Harry some good to breathe in the fresh sea air. The cabin is so stuffy."

"Why don't you go without me? I need to practice. I'm going to play for the passengers this evening. Strike while the iron is hot, as they say. I'll play something schmaltzy, like Strauss's *Aschenbrödel*[7]* waltz. That will really get the tears flowing. And then a bit of Debussy, just for variety's sake." He opened his suitcase and pulled out his tuxedo and white shirt. "I thought I should wear these, but they're all creased. Fortunately, I packed a travel iron. You can use this table as an ironing board. You do know how to iron, don't you?"

Chao Chen had been given a brief lesson on the art of ironing from Ya-Li and had only managed to get the wrinkles out of one or two skirts. She wasn't confident and tried to hide it. "Of course I know how to iron. You'll look just like you stepped out of an advertisement in the *Tatler*."

Walter unfolded the Singer Durabilt travel iron and set the thermostat to the appropriate temperature for the jacket and pants. "There you go!" Then he turned and took out his violin from its case. After hitting the tuning fork, he played a few notes. "I can tell you that the sea air isn't doing my violin any favors."

Chao Chen plugged the small iron into the wall socket. Taking a deep breath, she ran the iron over the back of the tuxedo jacket, turned it over to press the front, and then worked her way up one arm and down the other. Placing it on a hangar, she felt emboldened and worked quickly to get the creases out of the pants. Then she laid out Walter's white shirt on the table.

---

[7] * *"Cinderella"*

But when she placed the hot iron on the back of the shirt, she saw a huge burn in the shape of the iron appear on the white fabric and a terrible smell of burning cotton filled the cabin.

"What in God's name have you done?" Walter cried.

"I don't know, Walter."

He grabbed the iron out of her hand. "You didn't lower the temperature. That's what the thermostat's for. Anyone but a bumbling idiot would know to do that!" He picked up his shirt. "It's ruined. What am I supposed to wear tonight? My undershirt?" He spit the words out of his mouth, waking Harry up from a sound sleep. Walter growled, "Give me the iron. I'll press the front myself. Maybe with my tuxedo jacket on no one will notice. I should have known better than to trust you to do this. Sometimes I wonder if you have the sense you were born with. Didn't Ya-Li teach you anything about being a good wife?"

Chao Chen tied her long hair back into a ponytail, washed her tear-stained face, and picked Harry up in her arms without uttering a word. She left the cramped cabin and climbed the stairs to the outside deck. Staring out toward the horizon without a sign of land anywhere, she felt as if she had lost her bearings.

She wrapped a shawl around her shoulders and sang softly to her baby, "Oh little lotus flower, gone, gone too soon." Looking into Harry's eyes, she murmured, "Don't you fret. Your papa will forgive me, I'm sure, and then everything will be as calm as the sea is today." Harry pulled hard on a strand of Chao Chen's hair. "Ouch! Are you angry with me too?" The tone of Chao Chen's voice seemed to scare Harry and he started to cry. She sat down on a deck chair, covered her breasts with her shawl, and nursed Harry until he quieted.

She felt a wave of hunger sweep over her. In all the commotion she had forgotten to eat. It was past one o'clock and the bell for lunch had long since rung.

One of the American crewmen saw Chao Chen hovering at the entrance to the dining room. A few passengers still lingered at their tables. "What can I do for you, madam?"

"Might I be able to get something to eat, or is it too late for lunch?"

"Sorry, but all the serving dishes have already been removed. If you don't mind following me into the kitchen, I might be able to find some leftovers, although these passengers act as if they haven't eaten in years and every meal we prepare seems like their first."

"I'd be most grateful."

The crewman, who was physically fit with dark hair and sparkling blue eyes, asked in a friendly tone, "I haven't seen you in the dining room. Where have you been hiding?"

"In our cabin. It's difficult to manage things with my baby."

"If you want, I could bring food to your cabin. Which one is it?"

"Number three hundred fifty-seven, but my husband wouldn't appreciate it."

"The jealous type, eh?"

"Not really. He usually brings me my meals, but today he's very preoccupied." With a hint of pride in her voice, she said, "Some of the passengers recognized my husband. He's a concert violinist and they asked him to give a recital later today. He'll be performing at four thirty today. I left our cabin so that he'd have a chance to practice without worrying that our baby might interrupt his concentration."

"So, we have a celebrity on board?"

"You might say that."

Taking long strides, the crewman escorted Chao Chen through the dining room. The few diners who were lingering over their meals picked their heads up and stared at her as she passed by their tables.

After pushing the swinging door open into the kitchen, he saw a large bowl of food on one of the steel tables that had not yet been refrigerated. "How about some chicken fricassee? It's a fancy way of saying 'chicken, mushrooms, and onions swimming in cream.' It's a popular American dish, especially in the Midwest, where I'm from. We serve it at almost every meal, except for breakfast, of course. Maybe you've already tried it?"

"No, but it sounds delicious."

This brief encounter lifted Chao Chen's spirits. After she had eaten her fill of the chicken fricassee, she thanked the crewman and returned to her cabin with Harry. She had almost forgotten the altercation that had occurred between her and Walter, but the minute she opened the cabin door, the entire episode flooded over her. She was relieved to see that Walter had already left their cabin.

She felt so tired. She stretched out on the bed and closed her eyes for what seemed like a few minutes, but when she awoke, it was already four o'clock. She looked at Harry, who was cooing happily in his basket, amusing himself by reaching for his chubby little feet.

She said, "Harry, once we are off this boat, I'm going to buy you some toys to play with." She then lifted him out of his basket. After nursing him and changing his diaper, she put on a blue cheongsam embroidered with gold butterflies. After just three months she had lost all the weight she had gained during her pregnancy, and so it fit her almost perfectly. It was still a little tight across her breasts. She slipped her feet into a pair of blue sandals and then picked up her silver mirror so she could carefully apply a light coat of pink lipstick and powder her nose. Examining her reflection, she wondered if Walter would be proud of the way she looked.

She was just in time for Walter's performance. He had instructed her to stand outside the salon if Harry started fussing, saying, "I don't want him ruining my performance."

Chao Chen noticed there was a piano off to one side of the salon. She thought, *Perhaps we can play one of our duets*, but she suspected that Walter would find a reason to reject this notion.

Speaking in German and then English, one of the ship's officers became a self-appointed master of ceremonies and introduced Walter: "It gives me great pleasure to introduce one of our fellow passengers, Herr Walter Kolber, a violinist and protégé of the renowned Alfred Wittenberg, whom you all know of. Herr Kolber is returning to Austria after a nine-year absence. He is very excited to play for you, and we should be excited to listen to him as he will be performing in Salzburg this fall and next year in Vienna. Please give a warm welcome to Walter Kolber."

In the midst of a difficult passage in the Debussy piece, Harry let out an enormous wail, causing Walter to make a mistake. He feigned indifference, but even from the back of the salon Chao Chen sensed his anger. There was no use trying to calm Harry down, and so she rushed back to the cabin and anxiously waited for Walter's return.

She tried to force herself to stay awake by studying the English-German phrase book, but after a few minutes, the words swam in front of her eyes and she could barely concentrate. At eleven o'clock, she lay down on her cot and turned off the light. The gentle rocking of the ship and the sound of the waves washing against the porthole should have lulled her to sleep, but she kept tossing and turning. She could hear the passengers in the cabins on either side arguing with one another, and then there was complete silence along the corridor. When the door to the cabin finally opened, it was after two in the morning. Chao Chen pretended to be asleep. She could hear Walter tiptoeing around the cabin in the dark. Then she heard a *thump* as Walter stubbed his toe. Letting out a yelp, Chao Chen sat up and yawned. "Oh goodness, Walter, are you all right?"

"Of course I'm all right. Go back to sleep."

"Now that I'm awake, tell me how your recital went?"

"It went nearly perfectly, no thanks to you and Harry. They asked for four encores after the three pieces I presented. Honestly, if I hadn't put my violin away they would have made me play all evening. I had to promise I'd give another performance before the trip is over."

"What were you doing up so late? Did you run into Annalise Schönfeld and her husband?"

"Fortunately for her, no. Three of the men wanted to play cards. They needed a fourth, and so I obliged them. I'm sure they are very sorry they asked me because I cleaned out their pockets. I should have let them get away with a few hands so that I wouldn't entirely scare off the competition, but once I started winning, there was no stopping me. I'll have to figure out another way to make some money while we're stuck on this floating bathtub. It's hardly the *Conte Verde*, but I guess beggars can't be choosers, eh?"

Chao Chen propped herself up by her elbow. Looking squarely into Walter's eyes, she asked, "Where did the master of ceremonies get the idea that you have received invitations from Salzburg and Vienna? Why would you keep such extraordinary news from me?"

"I made it up. But who cares? If the audience thinks you're on your way to Salzburg, they appreciate you more. Credentials are everything in my business. And before we know it, it'll be true anyway. So, what's the harm?"

"You're misrepresenting yourself, Walter. That's the harm."

"It isn't the first time and it certainly won't be the last."

chapter 53

Disembarkation

To Walter's great delight, he had become quite the celebrity aboard the *Marine Lynx*; and by the time the ship anchored in the port of Marseilles, he was convinced that he had a bright future ahead of him. Disembarking, Chao Chen carried Harry in her arms as Walter pushed his way through the crowd, doffing his hat at well-wishers and then queuing up in front of the UNRRA officials who sat behind long tables at the dock to process the refugees. The transfer from the dock to the St. Charles train station, where they would board a train to Vienna, went smoothly. All of Walter's and Chao Chen's papers were in order, thanks to the efficiency of the immigration officials in Shanghai. Chao Chen spotted Annalise and her husband walking toward them in the waiting room. She realized there was no way that they could avoid running into one another. She judged Annalise's husband, with his salt-and-pepper gray hair and vaguely lined face, to be quite a few years older than his wife. Dressed in a well-fitting suit, he gave off an air of self-satisfaction, both with himself and his wife, whom he touched as if she were a gem of the finest quality.

Chao Chen warned Walter of the likelihood they would have to acknowledge one another. Grabbing his arm, she pleaded, "Please be cordial to them. What's the point of starting a row?"

"Just our luck. They're heading right this way." Walter straightened his tie and acted surprised to see Annalise and her husband. "Well, well, if it isn't Annalise Berglas. How long has it been? Four years? And this must be your husband."

"Yes. May I introduce you to Ludwig Schönfeld. I've already met your charming wife, Chao Chen, and your sweet baby. Didn't she tell you that we met early on in our voyage? It's a small world, isn't it?"

"No, she didn't. She's been quite preoccupied taking care of our little *Liebchen*, Harry, and as you might have heard from some of our fellow passengers, I've given several impromptu violin recitals to break the monotony of the trip."

"I wouldn't have heard. My husband and I spent most of our time on the upper deck. It was just by chance that Frau Kolber and I happened to meet."

Walter replied, "Pity that we didn't have a chance to visit with one another." Then, during this awkward exchange, it was announced that the train for Paris was leaving the station in twenty minutes.

Ludwig Schönfeld extended his hand to Walter and bowed to Chao Chen. "I'm sorry, but we'd better hurry or we'll miss our train for Paris. And where are you headed?"

Walter answered, "To Vienna and then on to Linz."

Ludwig remarked, "Hitler's hometown? He was planning to build a museum there and fill it with all the artwork he plundered during the war. Pretty city right on the Danube, or at least it was before the war. I assume you are headed for the American zone?"

Annalise interrupted her husband. "Darling, we'd better be going." She avoided Walter's eyes and smiled at Chao Chen. "Good luck and goodbye, Frau Kolber."

Walter and Chao Chen found their seats on the train. After putting their luggage onto the overhead rack, Walter tucked his violin case underneath the seat. Chao Chen lifted Harry out of his basket and settled him on her lap. As the train lurched out of the station, she turned to Walter. "I'm quite proud of you. You were very cordial to Annalise."

Walter sneered. "Don't patronize me, Chao Chen. Seeing Annalise literally makes my blood boil. She's quite the self-satisfied bitch, isn't she?"

Chao Chen bit her lip. "I thought she was very gracious. Had it been me you scorned, I'm not sure I would have been so polite. It would have broken my heart to see you married to another woman."

"She's a good actress, but she was no happier about seeing me than I was seeing her. And that husband of hers, the old goat, seems a self-satisfied bourgeois."

Chao Chen opened her purse and took out a hard candy. "Would you like one, Walter?"

"No. What I really want is a stiff drink, but I don't think there's a bar on this train."

The Pöstlingberg Pilgrimage Church of Linz, which is dedicated to the Seven Sorrows of the Virgin Mary, sat on a verdant hilltop. Through the window of the bus that carried refugees from the main train station in Vienna to Linz, Walter caught sight of the church's double spire and imposing eighteenth-century stone façade. The sparkling water of the Danube River, which divided Linz into the American and Soviet zones, was below. After crossing the rebuilt Nibelungen Bridge, the bus headed toward one of the twelve camps in Austria that housed concentration camp survivors and displaced persons, some of whom were in transit.

An alphabet soup of humanitarian organizations and the American military police oversaw the welfare of almost one million displaced persons who had arrived in wave after wave since the liberation of the concentration camps in 1945. Many early residents of the camps in Germany and Austria were near starvation, carrying diseases, and close to suicide. The resources of the DP camps, which were intended only as short-term housing, were strained as famine and persecution of the Jews continued in Ukraine, Romania, and Hungary. By the end of 1947, there were more than twenty thousand Jews in DP camps in Austria's American zone alone.

Within the camps and assembly centers authorities had set up thirty elementary schools and kindergartens with instruction in Hebrew, catering to those Jews who intended to emigrate to Palestine, and thirteen vocational schools run by the Jewish Organization for Rehabilitation and Training (ORT). Jewish displaced persons were employed in JDC's sewing shops, carpentries, and bakeries, and there were courses in automobile mechanics, bookkeeping, and nursing to prepare the refugees for life after the camps.

There was also a thriving black market outside the confines of the camps. Jews traded in all manner of goods in direct competition with the legitimate businesses of the Austrian and German townspeople, which caused resentment and often led to fistfights that had to be stopped by the military personnel tasked with the job of keeping peace within the camps and in the nearby towns. When food was scarce due to ongoing famine in the winter of 1947, some of the camp residents foraged in the fields, angering the farmers trying to squeeze every last Reichsmark out of the hardened soil.

By 1947 the Austrian economy, including those businesses appropriated by the Soviets, reached a little more than half its prewar level. However, the country survived 1946 with rations remaining below two thousand calories per person per day, until the end of 1947. A harsh winter the prior year contributed to food scarcity, which was followed by a disastrous heat that kept the potato harvest to less than one third of pre-World War II levels. Food riots ensued, and in August 1947, just before Chao Chen and Walter set foot on Austrian soil, a food riot in Bad Ischl turned into a pogrom against local Jews. UNRRA stopped its food shipments in June of 1947, requiring the United States to ship $300 million in food rations. By the end of 1947 the United States had finalized the details of the Marshall Plan—and Austria was part of this aid rescue package.

Most refugees on the bus heading to Linz could not comprehend the chaotic situation they were about to face, least of all Chao Chen, whose only source of information was Walter. He did his best to present a rosy picture of the camps, but he knew hardly more than she did. The only difference between the two of them was that Walter spoke German and was cunning enough to take advantage of any and every opportunity, legal or otherwise, that came his way.

Looking out the bus window, Walter was elated to see the quaint Tyrolean streets and the majestic Alps, their snow-capped peaks gleaming in the distance, instead of the dirty Whangpoo River and the alleyways of Hongkew. All that seemed like a bad dream from which he was just awakening—until he looked over at his Chinese wife and infant son.

Whether they were trying to quell their apprehension for what lay ahead or were feeling a false sense of nostalgia for the way things used to be, the passengers on the bus started to sing *"Im wunderschönen Monat Mai."* Walter joined in.

Chao Chen was proud of herself for recognizing the music as one of Schumann's *Lieder*, but she couldn't understand the lyrics. "What are you singing? It sounds so very beautiful and so sad, as if someone's heart is breaking."

"The song describes the singer's unrequited love for a maiden. Let's see if I can translate it for you:

> In the lovely month of May
> When all the buds were bursting
> Then within my heart
> Love broke forth.
> In the lovely month of May
> When the birds all sang
> Then I confessed to her
> My longing and desire."

Chao Chen repeated the last line of the stanza to herself: "My longing and desire." How often had she been afflicted with these twin emotions? In truth, only twice: once for the handsome Hans Möller and then for Li Shutong. She dared not verbalize her feelings for her husband. Why had he so enthralled her in the early stages of their romance? She could certainly name his charms, but they were all just a cover-up for his devious and narcissistic nature. *There*, she thought, *I said it, at least within my own mind*. But did falling for his charms make her? She stared out the window at the unfamiliar countryside, fear and self-loathing gripping her heart as she traveled toward Linz, Austria on September 28, 1947.

The International Rescue Committee (IRC) officials and representatives of the American Joint Distribution Committee (AJDC) directed the refugees off the bus with their suitcases and packages and to line up outside the school building, which was used for processing. Harry began crying and Chao Chen was unable to calm him. Walter barked, "Can't you just shut him up? You're annoying everyone and calling attention to yourself."

"I'm sorry, Walter. I'd nurse our baby if I could, but there is no place for me to hide. So, if you don't mind, just apologize for me."

"I'll do no such thing. You tell them *'Bitte verzeihen Sie mir.'* It means 'Please forgive me.' Can you manage that?"

Chao Chen turned to the couple standing behind her and did her best to pronounce the German words. She must have made herself understood because the man shrugged his shoulders, smiled, and said, "*Babys sind so.*" But his wife refused to look at Chao Chen. She opened her pocketbook to take out a handkerchief, which she held to her mouth as if she were suppressing a cough.

When they reached the front of the line, Walter handed over their travel documents. The clerk, an American woman who spoke fluent German, looked down at her list and announced, "We've assigned you to the Asten Displaced Persons Camp outside Linz. It's fairly decent, with barracks as well as small private apartments. Unfortunately, all the apartments are occupied at this time, but residents are always in the process of relocating as soon as they can. If you are lucky you'll be moved into your own apartment soon."

The name on her official badge read LILLIAN COHEN. Addressing her by her name, Walter asked in German, "Is there anything you can do to speed that along? You see that I have a baby, and it's going to be difficult to manage living in a barracks. And then there's my Chinese wife...." His voice trailed off.

Lillian replied, "I understand what you're implying, Herr Kolber, but I assure you that everyone on staff will do their best to assist you and your wife in whatever way they can. Does your wife speak English?"

"Very well."

"The residents at Asten are from all over. The majority are Hungarian, but there are also Poles and Ukrainians as well as Germans from the former Third Reich like yourself. They are primarily Jewish, although of course there are Catholics and those from other religious groups who have also suffered dislocation during the war. Many of the aid workers assigned to Asten speak English very well, and there are American military personnel at the camps to ensure a safe and secure environment." Lillian Cohen turned to Chao Chen and said in English, "Welcome, Mrs. Kolber. You have a very beautiful baby boy. How old is he?"

"He'll be four months old this October," Chao Chen replied.

"I have three sons." Lillian held up three fingers just to make sure she was understood.

Chao Chen smiled. "You must be very proud."

Lillian nodded. "I see that you don't have a baby carriage for him. Let's see what I can do to remedy that. You'll be wanting to take him out—it's important that infants get sunshine on their faces. Yours too. You shouldn't be cooped up inside all day long. And if you walk around the camp, you'll get a chance to meet the other mothers. We've had a baby boom, what with so many young couples getting married. It's a miracle, really. When some of these women arrived from the concentration camps you would have thought that their poor bodies would never be able to carry a child. You'll see. Hopefully some of the ladies will speak English so you can trade baby-rearing secrets. Maybe you know a few things from your culture that will be helpful to them?"

"Not really, Mrs. Cohen. Harry is my first, and when my brothers were infants we had servants to take care of them. I'm from Zhenru, outside Shanghai."

"Yes, I see that on your paperwork. Well, your life is very different now, isn't it? But don't worry. All of us have had to adjust to many changes because of the war. Let me assure you, Mrs. Kolber, that we'll do whatever we can to help you."

Chao Chen adjusted Harry in her arms, and Walter said, "Thank you. We're both going to need it."

Lillian nodded and then instructed them to board another bus that would take them to Asten.

The UNRRA official gave Walter and Chao Chen a brief tour of the Asten Displaced Persons Camp located in the American zone. "Here are the men's bathrooms and showers, and on the opposite side of the corridor are the women's. Unfortunately, we don't have sinks in the individual rooms, but we are lucky that there is adequate hot water, at least for the present. I suggest that you bring your own towel and soap with you when you use the showers, and keep them in your room or they will be stolen."

Walter translated these instructions for Chao Chen as she held on to Harry.

On the left-hand side of the far end of the barracks, their escort opened a door that looked just like all the others and gestured for Walter and Chao Chen to enter. "Well, here's where you'll be staying. Lucky for you this is a corner room so you have not one but two windows. That will let in more light and air. And I see that Lillian Cohen has worked her magic. The baby carriage is for your exclusive use. Sorry about the bed situation, but you can push the two cots together and *voilà*, a marriage bed!"

Walter put down their luggage but held on to his violin case. He tried to avoid looking at Chao Chen, not wanting to see the disappointment on her face. "At least it's bigger than our room in the Hongkew ghetto."

Chao Chen shook her head. "Not really, but it is brighter."

The camp guide continued. "Here is the schedule for meals. We have a central dining hall. Food has been a problem of late, but the Austrian government has taken over providing food rations for the camp since August. You're allowed to use the hot plate when you wish to prepare meals for yourself, and there are some residents who have opened their own makeshift kitchens in their quarters as a way of making some money. In fact, Frau Hay, who lives a few doors down from you, is a pretty good cook—if you like goulash and chicken *paprikash*. I hope, as we are totally unprepared to accommodate Oriental people, your wife will acclimate herself to the food here. In fact, I have never seen an Oriental before."

Walter scowled. "My wife is Chinese. I'd prefer you refer to her that way." Then he edited the guide's remarks in his translation for Chao Chen.

She nodded and hesitantly said, "*Danke*."

The camp guide smiled. "Please tell your wife I admire her for trying to speak our language. I'm sure that it's not so easy for her."

"My wife will manage, I'm sure." Gesturing to his violin case, Walter changed the subject. "How do I get to Salzburg from here? I intend to meet with a number of chamber music groups and orchestra directors as soon as possible."

"There is train and bus service, but you'll have to buy your own ticket, I believe. Perhaps you should meet with the representatives of ORT here at the camp to see what sort of work might be available to you."

Walter raised his eyebrows. "Such as...?"

"Well, there are numerous crafts shops right here in the camps, and there's always janitorial work. And if you know how to drive, some of our residents drive the camp bus into Linz and back to go shopping and to the movies. A few of our drivers have made pretty good money because our residents like to see American movies whenever they can, especially if they have German subtitles. Why, just recently I saw *The Postman Always Rings Twice* with Lana Turner. She's quite the looker."

"If you say so. Now, if you'll excuse us, my wife and I would like to unpack our belongings and settle our baby. And if you don't mind, could you help move our beds together—unless it's too much of an imposition?"

The guide laughed. "It's not in my job description, but I'm happy to do so. Perhaps that will cheer your wife up a bit. She looks very unhappy."

Walter's tone betrayed his impatience. "It's just that she's very tired from our long journey. I'm sure she'll be herself again once she's rested. And she will be very happy about the baby carriage. After all, we weren't able to take very much with us on the ship."

The camp guide put his clipboard in front of his mouth as if he didn't trust that Chao Chen could not understand a word he was about to say. "Herr Kolber, may I give you a piece of advice? As you may have noticed, some of the residents here were staring at your wife as we walked down the corridor. They've probably never seen a Chinese woman before, and they might have some very strong feelings about the two of you being married." Hesitating for a moment, he then barreled on. "And might I also point out that there may be some resentment about a Chinese woman taking food out of the mouth of a starving Jew? It may sound cruel, but that's the reality of the situation. I even have to fight these feelings myself. After all, what did the Chinese go through during the war compared to what we've suffered?" He then tapped his clipboard for emphasis. "So, if I were you, I wouldn't leave your wife alone for very long. Some of the people here have been through hell and back, and they're not always on their best behavior. And who can blame them?"

"Thank you for your concern about my wife. Let's hope that their better natures prevail over their baser instincts. Isn't it written in Exodus, 'You shall not wrong a stranger or oppress him, for you were strangers in the land of Egypt'?"

"So, you are a religious person, Herr Kolber?"

Walter laughed. "Hardly, but I like to quote Scripture when I think it will elicit a positive response. I'm right, am I not?"

"I don't know, Herr Kolber. There are some residents here in the camp, as you will find out, who believe that God has forsaken them. And then there are other Jews who celebrate the Jewish holidays with an enthusiasm that is quite extraordinary. Perhaps it is because they are trying to create a sense of community. But what do I know? We are making up the rules as we go along to help all of you get back on your feet."

Walter replied, "My father used to remind me that the Jews were the chosen people. He told me to be proud of my heritage. When I ask myself what exactly we were chosen for, the only answer I come up with is that we are chosen to be persecuted." He looked around at his surroundings. "But I guess I shouldn't complain. We are still better off than most."

"Yes, Herr Kolber. At least you are alive, and your wife and child are as well. Many cannot say the same. Now let's push these two beds together, and then I need to get back to the office. We are expecting another busload of refugees later this afternoon. It is as if the spigot has been turned on and all the refugees of the war are flowing into Asten."

After the guide left, Walter and Chao Chen silently settled themselves into their room. Walter opened the window. They could hear boys shouting from a nearby play area. They were racing back and forth, pushing tires with wooden planks. Groups of women with baby carriages passed by the window chatting to one another.

Chao Chen observed, "How nice to see other ladies with their babies. As Lillian Cohen suggested, perhaps I can make some friends."

Walter's skepticism showed. "And how do you expect to do that?"

"Perhaps you can look after Harry once in a while and I can take German lessons a few times a week. My phrase book will only take me so far. Right now all I know is 'good day' and 'thank you.' And what is that you taught me earlier today? 'Please excuse me?'"

Stuffing a shirt into the only bureau in the room, Walter vented, "As if that's all I have to do, watch Harry while you go about socializing. You're just going to have to fend for yourself, Chao Chen. As soon as I can find a way to get to Salzburg, I'll be leaving. You don't want me to end up a janitor here, do you? That's what that prick was suggesting, that I should look for work here at the camp. He had the nerve to suggest that maybe I'd like to scrub toilets or drive a bus into Linz so some of these *mamzers* can go to the movies."

"You'd abandon me here?"

"You can't look at it that way. I'm trying to secure a future for us, and I certainly can't do that by hanging around here."

Holding Harry, Chao Chen sat down on one of the cots and cried. Seeing the tears rolling down Chao Chen's cheeks, Walter changed his tune. "I didn't mean to upset you. I know this is all strange and unfamiliar to you. I feel the same, but I need to summon my courage—for both of us—and get myself a real job with a chamber music group and eventually an orchestra. You do want that, don't you?"

"Of course. Isn't that why we're here?"

"Well, then you'll just have to be brave. You'll see. Everything's going to work out."

Chao Chen tucked Harry into his basket and took out her music box. Placing it on top of the dresser, she wound the key and she and Walter listened to its familiar tune. Chao Chen felt comforted. "I feel better already just hearing '*Für Elise*.'"

Walter observed, "Perhaps you should keep it hidden. The camp guide mentioned that things get stolen around here."

"Is that what he was telling you? I wish we could lock the door to our room." Chao Chen wrapped her arms around herself and shuddered involuntarily. "I feel so vulnerable."

Walter suggested, "If that will make you feel better, I'll see if I can get a lock and key." Then he kissed the tip of Chao Chen's nose. "My princess, your wish is my command. I'll do it first thing tomorrow. But right now I need to take a shower, and when I come back, you might want to do the same. And then, who knows? If Harry can keep his little mouth shut, we can take advantage of our fancy marriage bed. What do you say?"

Chao Chen paused, weighing her words carefully. "You must promise me that you won't stay away for more than a day or two at the most until I've become accustomed to this place. Can you do that?"

"Of course. Now hand me that bar of soap." And he was off.

chapter 54

Out of Tune

Walter's request for a lock and key went nowhere because the camp administrators insisted on periodically inspecting the barracks to make sure the rooms were kept clean. They were also on the lookout for stolen goods. A black market just outside the camp was thriving because the refugees were given only small allowances and so they needed to find a way to make money or trade stolen goods for simple luxuries.

Walter soon figured out a way to collect, barter, and even steal rations—packets of sugar, soap, coffee, butter, even American cigarettes and military shirts—which he traded or sold on the black market. He quickly became known around the barracks as the go-to man to fence various items, and every time something changed hands, he took a commission. This wasn't how he wanted to be known, but desperate times called for desperate measures; and as he saw his financial resources grow, he moved one step closer to buying a bus ticket to Salzburg.

Chao Chen made another request of Walter. "I don't feel comfortable taking a shower with the other ladies because they're constantly staring at me. I know it isn't my imagination. Do they think I have a tail or that horns are growing out of my head?" Before Walter could answer, she continued, "Can you ask someone for a washtub? There is a pump right outside the barracks. The water will be cold, but I can heat it a bit at a time on the hot plate. And then I can use the tub to wash Harry's dirty diapers. I don't like using the communal sink. I always make a mess."

Walter grimaced. "Wonderful. Our room will look like a public laundry."

"As a matter of fact, I've thought of taking in laundry for some of the ladies to make extra money. You seem to be able to get your hands on soap. If you can spare a few bars for me, I'll offer my services. You'll just have to tell me how to say 'laundry' in German and help me figure out how much I should charge."

Walter paused, seeming to contemplate Chao Chen's proposal. "Why not? Right now you're doing nothing to improve our situation here. I'll see if I can get you a washboard from the central laundry room. You do know what it's used for, right?"

Chao Chen felt as if Walter had slapped her in the face, but she just accepted it. "I saw my maid, Ya-Li, using one to remove stains from my clothes. I'm sure I can figure out what needs to be done, Walter."

"All right. I'll write out a few German phrases for you to memorize." Taking a pencil and a scrap of paper, he wrote down three phrases and spoke them so that Chao Chen could hear how they were pronounced: "*Haben Sie etwas Wäsche?* Do you have laundry? *Wie viel?* How much? *Es wird morgan fertig sein.* It will be ready by tomorrow."

Pointing to the phrases, Walter grinned. "If your little scheme works, who knows how much we could make? And this way I don't need to spend the three hundred dollars Mutti gave me. I've kept it hidden in my violin case. God forbid someone should find it. It's for a real emergency, and we haven't reached that point, at least not yet. You know, I'm still furious that those sneaky bastards wouldn't put a lock on our door. Do they think we're peasants, like some of the other people here, who can't keep their rooms clean?"

Chao Chen ignored his derogatory comments and intently studied the piece of paper. She then repeated the phrases over and over again. "How do I sound, Walter?"

"*Nicht schlecht.* Not bad. Keep practicing. Maybe you'll get lucky."

The next day Chao Chen hurriedly dressed Harry and tucked him into his baby carriage. She had observed the other mothers taking their babies out for a stroll in the morning hours. At ten thirty, two young women headed in Chao Chen's direction. They were pushing baby carriages and chattering to each other. Their coats were ill-fitting. Chao Chen guessed that the coats had probably been donated to them by the aid workers or traded by one resident to another.

Lisbeth Weisz observed to her two Hungarian companions, Frieda Koranji and Hannah Vogel, "Do you see who is standing at the corner? That Chinese woman, Frau Kolber, and her half-breed baby. She can see us coming. I'd like to cross to the other side of the street, but that would be much too obvious. So let's just ignore her. She wouldn't dare speak to us, would she?"

Frieda argued, "Honestly, you're such a snob. We just observed Sukkot, when we are supposed to rejoice in community. I feel sorry for her."

"And why is that?" Lisbeth snapped. "In addition to not being one of us, she is married to that *hondler*, Walter Kolber, who arrived here a couple of weeks ago. He's quite the braggart, telling everyone who'll listen that he's a concert violinist. In a pig's eye."

Hannah added, "Well, if she says something to us, I leave it up to you to speak to her since you seem to be in a rather charitable mood today. Although I can't understand why. You've just been complaining to me that we aren't getting enough to eat here."

Chao Chen waved hello to the three ladies. Smiling, she took out the piece of paper and handed it to Lisbeth. Lisbeth glanced at it and then gave the paper back to Chao Chen, replying briskly, "*Nein, danke.*" Since Chao Chen seemed confused, Lisbeth shook her head to indicate that none of the women were interested in having her do their laundry, and then they proceeded along the sidewalk without bothering to introduce themselves.

When they were out of earshot, Frieda remarked, "That poor woman. I'll bet her husband put her up to that. But honestly, I wouldn't let her touch anything of mine. Anyway, I'd rather do my own laundry. That way I know it will be done properly. She looks as helpless as a schoolgirl. Do you think there is anything we can do for her?"

Lisbeth was snarky. "Yes. Put her right back on a slow boat to China where she belongs."

"Show a little compassion, Lisbeth," said Hannah as her baby started to fuss. "Oh my, he probably needs to be changed. We should turn around. Is she still standing at the corner?"

Lisbeth looked over her shoulder. "No, she's had the good sense to go back inside."

Frieda admitted, "I have to admit that I'm curious about her. There is something about her eyes—and I don't mean the fact that they are slanted—that looks so terribly sad. Don't you agree?"

Chao Chen opened the door to their room at the end of the hallway. An envelope rested on one of the unmade cots. Her hands were shaking from the ordeal she had just endured, and she wanted to tell Walter of her defeat and hear a few words of encouragement from him. Instead, she read the letter he had left for her:

Chao Chen,

Off to Linz on the camp bus. Will be back tomorrow afternoon. I'm planning to meet with someone there who might have a job for me. I have my letter from Professor Wittenberg. Hopefully that will do the trick. Take care of yourself and Harry in the meantime, and good luck with your new business!

Your devoted husband,
Walter

How could Walter have left without so much as a goodbye or a simple mention of his plans? Surely he had known of his appointment for a few days, or did he intend to just knock on doors? And what if he got rejected? He would certainly throw a temper tantrum and take it out on her.

Chao Chen felt a pain in her stomach. She realized that it was from hunger. Once she had nursed Harry, she made her way to the dining hall in one of the other buildings. It was late enough that there were very few people still eating, and so she was able to have lunch without feeling scrutinized. She saw Frau Weisz and her friend sitting together at one of the tables. She wished that they might invite her over to join them, but when she smiled in their direction, they just looked down at their plates.

Chao Chen sighed. *So this is how it's going to be. Well, someday, when these ladies are sitting in a concert hall in Vienna and my Walter is up on stage as the guest violinist, they'll think twice about the way they treated me. I'm sure of it.* Then she turned toward Harry, who was sleeping in his baby carriage. She smoothed his blanket, stood up, and kissed him on the forehead. He woke up and smiled at his mother. She struggled to remain cheerful despite the morning's painful setbacks. "Ah, my little angel. I really don't need anything but your adorable face smiling at me to set me right again."

Walking slowly back to her room, she wondered why those three ladies had treated her with such disdain. She recalled the way Frau Götz had fussed over her and the generosity of the Möllers. Many of the Jews she knew in Shanghai were very kind to her. And why was that? She turned this question over in her mind, and the answer suddenly came to her: it was because they knew her to be a gifted pianist and an excellent English language teacher. Perhaps she might put one of these skills to good use here. And once they realized that she had some talent, some worth, perhaps these ladies might extend a friendly hand to her and allow her to wash their clothes so she could help support Walter in his quest.

The next day, instead of wearing a tired-looking blouse and skirt, she put on her prettiest cheongsam and matching silk slippers. Being careful not to step into a puddle from last night's rain, she found her way to the camp office. A U.S. military clerk shuffling through a pile of papers looked up from his work.

"What can I do for you, Miss…?"

"Mrs. Kolber. I'm staying at the end of the hall in building number two with my husband and my baby. It's nice to be able to speak English with someone."

"I remember when you arrived several weeks ago. What is it that you need, Mrs. Kolber? I hope it's not more food because we are just scraping by at the moment."

"No, sir. I was wondering if there is a piano somewhere on the camp grounds." She held up her music score. "I'm a pianist, and I so miss playing. I would love to practice, and perhaps some of the guests here…" She thought that sounded better than "refugees." "Perhaps the guests would enjoy an impromptu recital of sorts."

"Do you know any Jewish music?"

Chao Chen blushed. "I'm afraid not. But I do know the compositions of a number of Jewish composers. Will that do?"

"We have a makeshift theatre where the refugees sometimes stage plays and operettas from time to time. They're always in German or Yiddish, and I can't say I understand anything, but the audience usually laughs a lot and claps and so I guess they appreciate it."

"Where I'm from, Shanghai, there used to be a part of the city called Little Vienna. There were lots of theatres and clubs for the Jews there. But, like you, I don't understand their language. I'm trying to learn a few words, but it's pretty difficult. They say, if you haven't learned a language by the time you're twelve, it's a problem."

The clerk smiled. "I learn something new here every day. And by the way, you look very young to me. May I ask how old you are, Mrs. Kolber?"

"Don't they say you should never ask a woman her age? How old are you?"

"I'm twenty-two. I enlisted on my eighteenth birthday."

"I'm a few years older than you. So, about the piano?"

"Right. I don't think anything is planned for this evening, and so no one will be rehearsing. But I have to warn you, the piano is sorely out of tune. Although a lot of these people are pretty handy, I haven't been able to find anyone at the camp who knows how to tune it."

Chao Chen could barely contain her excitement as the clerk led her to the theatre. He unlocked the door and turned on the lights. Folding chairs were stacked up against the walls, and a blackboard with Hebrew letters scrawled across it was stuck over in a corner.

"I'll leave the door open. It's musty in here," he said.

"Thank you, sir."

"I'll be back in an hour to lock up. In the future I'll need to get permission for you to be allowed in here."

Thinking quickly, Chao Chen asked, "Do you know Mrs. Lillian Cohen in Linz? She has been ever so kind to my husband and me. I'm sure she'd approve."

"It's just a phone call. Shouldn't be a problem. I'll write her name down and we'll clear it with her. What do you say?"

"I'd say you've turned what started as a very bad day into a glorious one, sir."

After the clerk left, Chao Chen placed the music on the piano stand and adjusted the bench so that her feet reached the pedals. She positioned Harry's carriage so she could keep an eye on him, but he seemed quite content.

She ran through a few arpeggios and chords to test the piano's action and pedal depression and to hear its voice. It was an instrument severely needing attention, but Chao Chen was euphoric just to be sitting in front of the keyboard. Barely referring to the printed notes, she played Schubert's *Impromptu in G-flat Major*; each passage took her farther away from Asten, back to a time when her future was spread out before her with all its possibilities and none of its disappointments.

To Chao Chen, this Schubert piece held the saddest and quietest of moments but within which were encased the composer's desperate rage and anger. When she came to the end of the piece, she let her fingers rest on the keyboard, feeling the instrument's subtle vibration and heat. She sighed as Harry stirred in his carriage, but he didn't cry. He just smiled again and seemed content, as if the music was pleasing him.

"So, my little bird, what do you think of your mama's playing?" Chao Chen smiled back.

Walter barged into this tranquil scene carrying a washboard and large aluminum tub. "I stopped at the camp office on my way back to the barracks to get you these." He dropped what he was carrying on the floor but held on to his violin case. Chao Chen could see that his knuckles were white from the way he gripped the case's handle. "That smart-ass sitting behind the desk told me that you were in here. And so you are."

"Yes. He was very kind to me."

"He told me, 'You have a beautiful wife, Herr Kolber.' And I see what prompted him to say this. What were you thinking, putting on that dress?"

"I was trying to make a good impression, Walter."

"And so you did. Where did you get with the ladies yesterday? Did any of those *yekke* make you an offer, or are they too stuck-up to turn over their nighties to you?"

"I offered to do their laundry, but they said '*Nein, danke.*'"

Spying the blackboard, Walter dragged it next to the piano. He rubbed off the Hebrew letters with the eraser and grabbed a piece of chalk. "So, I'm going to write again what you are to say and you will repeat it ten times." He scrawled the words and then, brushing the chalk dust off his suit, rapped the board with his hand. "Begin."

"Must I? I brought the piece of paper with me and showed it to the ladies."

Walter leaned over and shook Chao Chen hard by her shoulders. "What did I say? Begin. And stand up while you're at it."

Realizing that Walter was beyond reason, Chao Chen did as she was told and repeated the phrases.

"Excellent. Now, I expect you to find some customers. I can't be solely responsible for you and Harry, and I forbid you to play the piano while we're here. If anyone is to play an instrument, it will be me!"

Walter and Chao Chen walked quickly back to their room without speaking to each other. Chao Chen suspected that he didn't want anyone overhearing what he had to say.

Walter slammed the door shut. "Today was a near disaster, made more so by your shenanigans." Then he lowered his voice. "I met with the concertmaster of the main cathedral of Linz, Professor Franz Xavier Müller. A pompous fop if there ever was one. Anyway, he asked me to play for him. I chose a Bach partita, and he had very nice things to say about my performance; but after I sweated through barely a quarter of the piece, he said that there was really nothing he could offer me at the present time. I don't know why he bothered to waste my time, although I didn't have an appointment with him and so I can't totally blame him. He knows Professor Wittenberg, of course. So I thought he might give me a chance, but no such luck. Bastard!"

Walter threw his suit jacket on the floor. Chao Chen picked it up and hung it on the back of a chair recently donated to them. Walter paced back and forth. "He pointed out that most of the important opportunities are in Salzburg and Vienna."

"Does that mean you're going to have to go there?"

"Of course. What do you think? He offered to make an appointment for me with Kurt Wöss, the principal conductor of the Tonkünstler Orchestra of Lower Austria. They perform in Vienna during the regular season and somewhere else during the summer months as part of a music festival. It's not the Vienna Philharmonic, but he knows they are looking for a violinist. He promised to get in touch with me as soon as he reached Herr Wöss."

Chao Chen forced a smile. "That's wonderful, Walter. Does that mean we'll be moving to Vienna?"

"Eventually, if things work out. For the time being, we're better off here. Everything is free and we'll have a chance to save enough money so that we can live in the best part of Vienna, not in some hovel. I've heard that apartments are scarce there, thanks to the Americans and the Brits bombing the hell out of the city. I wonder if my family's apartment building on Esteplatz is still standing."

Harry started to cry. Chao Chen picked him up and held him close to her breast. He quieted down. Walter lit a cigarette and poured himself a scotch, explaining, "I need to calm my nerves after the ordeal I've been through today."

Chao Chen sat down on her cot. "I should probably nurse Harry now."

"Good. And then we can make love. That's all I thought about riding back in the bus. Honestly, Chao Chen, you do look beautiful, even if that Chinese dress of yours is out of place."

Once Harry was sated and back in his basket, he closed his eyes and was soon fast asleep. Walter wasted no time unzipping Chao Chen's dress, and then he pushed her against the pillow. She turned her head away from him and stared out the window, praying that he'd be done with her quickly. What used to be a pleasure for her had become a tedious obligation.

Walter leaned his head against his elbow and ran his fingers down Chao Chen's body, tracing her spine. "This was well worth waiting for." His voice then softened. "Perhaps I was being a bit hasty when I said you were not to play the piano. What harm would there be in it? I think I was just so disappointed that Professor Müller didn't hire me on the spot that I took it out on you. I need to be more patient, don't I?"

"Oh, Walter, thank you. I've nearly been going out of my mind here with nothing to do except look after Harry, whom I love dearly, but I feel as if my mind is turning to mud. And you have no idea how those women look at me. I thought if I could present myself as having some musical talent they might be kinder to me and give me their laundry to wash. I'll be sure to pick music by Jewish composers, and maybe I can even learn a few Jewish songs. That might please them."

"I hadn't thought of that, Chao Chen. You are a clever girl, aren't you?" He pushed up against her and caressed her back. "Now, why don't you show me how grateful you are? Then I'll fetch you some water so you can try out that tub I bought you." This time Chao Chen tried to respond with more enthusiasm to her husband's ardor.

chapter 55

Phantasmagoria

Chao Chen recognized the irony in the bargain she had struck with Walter: the music she cherished for someone else's dirty laundry. It was worth the price. By December 1947, three months after their arrival to Asten, she had secured a few steady customers in Barracks Number Two. Sometimes they paid her in currency, and other times she was handed a box of matches, a bar of chocolate, a pack of cigarettes, or a slightly worn pair of shoes, which Walter promptly sold. Their financial resources were improving enough for Walter to travel back and forth to Vienna several times in search of work. Although nothing had yet materialized, he said he had a solid lead for a place in an orchestra slated to play at the 1948 Salzburg Music Festival the following summer.

Chao Chen adjusted to being without Walter for several days at a time. She told herself that she should mourn his absences, but in truth, she was relieved he was not around to criticize and badger her, to complain about the wet laundry hanging on the line across their meager surroundings, to accuse her of flirting with American officials who were still working in the office, or to yell at Harry, who at six months old was crawling on the floor and hoisting himself up on a chair leg like any other healthy baby. Walter seemed to take no pleasure in watching his son change as the months went by, but Chao Chen had enough love for Harry that the child showed no sign of being rejected or abandoned by his father.

Dressing him in the blue knitted sweater that Lilly had made for him, Chao Chen bundled Harry up in extra blankets. The weather had turned bitterly cold, but he needed to get some fresh air on a blustery December morning. Wearing a pair of oversized leather boots and a faded wool coat, Chao Chen pulled her hat over her ears and slipped her hands into a pair of exquisitely made gloves, a going-away present from Frau Götz. Every time she wore them she thought of all the kindness that Frau Götz and her husband had shown her.

She brushed away a strand of black hair that had escaped her hat and walked resolutely along the sidewalk, pushing Harry in his carriage. Chao Chen had not walked far when she saw the same women she asked to do their laundry. They were talking animatedly with another woman Chao Chen did not recognize. Feeling her cheeks flush with embarrassment at the memory of that day, she held her breath as they were about to pass by. She expected them to turn away, but instead she was greeted in English by the unfamiliar woman.

"Good morning, Madam Kolber. And that must be your little boy, Harry. What a sweet, round face he has."

Chao Chen was nearly dumbstruck and hesitated for a moment before thanking this stranger. "May I ask how you know our names?"

"I live in Barracks Number One, which is close to the room where I hear you practice every day. I inquired as to who was playing, and that friendly American military clerk told me all about you. He says that you are intending to give a recital for us. Is this true? If it is I would be delighted to spread the word. Do you have a date in mind?"

Chao Chen felt as if her heart would burst right out of her chest. "To tell you the truth, madam, I haven't decided on a program yet. I've been practicing a number of pieces, mostly classical pieces from the Romantic period." She surprised herself by continuing. "I'm not a fan of contemporary music, although I do understand its appeal."

"How rude of me not to introduce myself. I'm Hilda Marton. You might infer from my accent that I'm from Budapest. Anyway, I'm thrilled that what I heard was not just a rumor. Many of us play an instrument. I myself play the cello, although I'm very rusty. Do you have a date in mind?"

"No. What do you suggest?"

"Well, Hanukkah begins on December seventh this year. The camp turns itself inside out for the holiday and the occupants can think of nothing but dreidels, menorahs, and latkes. Do you know what they are?"

"No, I'm afraid not. My husband is not very religious, and I was brought up in a very different world than the one you come from—although there were many Jewish people in Shanghai during the war. That's where I met my husband, Walter. We were music students at the Conservatory. He's originally from Vienna. The family name is Kolber. I don't suppose you've heard of them?"

"No, but your story is very interesting. My friends and I were wondering how the two of you had found each other. War does make strange bedfellows, does it not? Anyway, my advice is that you present your recital in January after we've gotten through Hanukkah, which goes on for eight nights. Oh, it's so wonderful. You'll see. Maybe you could learn the dreidel song and play it on the piano for us. Everyone will smile. Ask your husband about it."

"I doubt that he'll be able to tell me very much. Is there a library at the camp where I might read about it?"

"Oh, you haven't discovered our lending library? Most of the books are in German, of course, but there are a few in English. Those of us who were able to save our books pass them among one another. Let me know if you'd like to visit it and I'd be more than happy to escort you. We can see if we can find something about the Jewish holidays. If you are here for any length of time, you should try to understand what we Jews are up to."

"Thank you, but my husband is hoping that we'll be leaving here very soon. He's in Vienna this very minute interviewing for a position with an orchestra."

"I wish him luck, Madam Kolber. Unfortunately, there are more gifted musicians around than there are seats to fill. But hope springs eternal, yes?"

"Yes, or what would be the point of going on?" Chao Chen could feel a weight in the pit of her stomach.

"The weather here is usually brutal in January. The wind comes down from the mountains, and sometimes we are forced to either stay inside for days on end or risk getting frostbite. So, having your recital to look forward to will lift our spirits. You'll be doing a *mitzvah*, I can assure you. Just about everyone in the camp is a music lover."

Hilda then turned to the other ladies and explained the nature of their exchange. For the first time since arriving at Asten, Chao Chen didn't feel like a pariah. No, now these ladies were looking her straight in the eye and there was just the hint of a smile on their faces.

Snowflakes started falling and the wind picked up, cutting their conversation short. Chao Chen said, "I'd best be going."

Hilda was polite. "So January it is. Just let me know what I can do to help."

Chao Chen practically flew back to her room. It was bitterly cold inside, the heat from the small radiator barely reaching the four corners of the small space. She kept her coat on. Harry lifted his arms to let his mother know that he wanted to crawl. She threw a blanket on the floor and handed him a set of wooden blocks that a child who had moved out of the camp had left behind. Hoping that Harry might amuse himself for a few minutes, she flipped through the pages of her music books. She talked to herself. "No, that piece won't do. This one is a possibility. Ah, this one will be perfect."

Harry let out a piercing cry. She looked up and saw that he had crawled over to the radiator and had touched one of the pipes. Even from a few feet away she could see that a big, red welt was forming on his little hand. Tears streamed down his face. She scooped him up in her arms, grabbed the blanket, wrapped him in it, and rushed down the hallway to the infirmary in the next building.

The waiting room was crowded with sneezing and wheezing patients; a little boy sitting on his mother's lap threw up and had to be rushed to the toilet. Chao Chen was frantic. She grabbed the arm of one of the nurses, showing her Harry's hand. Pointing to a chair, the nurse told her to wait, and in a matter of minutes Chao Chen and Harry were led into the doctor's examination room ahead of the other patients.

Communicating with each other in hand gestures, the doctor, Dr. Blum, put a thin coat of ointment on Harry's hand and then bandaged it to keep the medicine in place. He handed Chao Chen a tube and a small roll of gauze and tape, and then he held up two fingers, indicating that she should change the bandage twice daily. He then asked his nurse to make a follow-up appointment with Chao Chen in one week's time. The nurse wrote the date and time on a piece of paper and handed it, together with a lollipop for Harry, back to Chao Chen.

Chao Chen held on to the stick while Harry sucked on the candy. As she left the waiting room she felt as if everyone were staring at her, wondering why she had been given preferential treatment and judging her to be a neglectful mother.

Walter returned to Asten well after dark. Chao Chen threw her arms around him to distract him from discovering what had happened to Harry, but he immediately spied the bandage. He peeled Chao Chen's arms off his neck. "What happened here?"

"I took my eyes off Harry for just a split second and he burned himself on the radiator. I rushed him to the infirmary and the nice doctor took care of him right away. Oh, I've been just beside myself with worry, Walter."

Chao Chen was shocked when Walter slapped her across the face. She bit her lip to keep herself from crying out.

"You have almost nothing to do all day but look after Harry, and yet you are incompetent even in that regard!" Walter yelled.

Chao Chen accepted the blame. "You're right, Walter. It was all my fault. I promise it will never happen again."

"Don't apologize to me. You should be apologizing to your son. He's the one you injured. Can I even trust you with him?"

Chao Chen felt a sudden urge to hit back at Walter. She lifted her arm, but he caught it in midair and bent it behind her back. "Don't you ever lift a finger against me, Chao Chen. You don't know what I'm capable of when I'm angry."

"You're right. I'll never take my eyes off Harry again. I didn't realize that he was becoming so independent."

Walter released her arm roughly, then brushed the snow off his coat and hung it up on a peg by the door. After shaking out his hat, he brushed his damp hair back from his face with his hands. "I need to write a letter to Lilly," he said, putting the mirror down. "As far as I know, she and David are still in Shanghai. I'm sure she's wondering where we are and how we are managing. Can you keep Harry quiet so that I can concentrate, or is that too much to ask of you?"

"No, Walter. It's past his bedtime anyway. I was keeping him up so that you could say good night to him."

"Do you think it really matters to him at his age? Right now all he wants is his mother's breast. When he gets older, he and I will have plenty to do together; but right now all he does is eat, sleep, and dirty his diapers." Walter wrinkled his nose. "But if you insist, I'll give him a kiss on the head, and then I really must get something off in tomorrow's mail. I'm curious to hear from my sister. Perhaps she has some good news for me."

"Such as…?"

"Perhaps Papa regrets the way he treated me and now wants to help us out. When we left Shanghai, JEKO was still operating and making money."

"You mean your father may want to do a *mitzvah*?"

Walter looked surprised. "Yes, do a *mitzvah*. I cannot fathom how he could have disinherited me, especially now that I have a son. I know what it means to be a father and to want to take care of and protect your child." He got dramatic. "What is it that the Bible says? 'Bone of my bones and flesh of my flesh…'"

"I believe that was Adam speaking of Eve, Walter."

"No matter. It still applies. Now where did you learn about *mitzvah*?

"I met a lady from Budapest, Madam Marton. She speaks very good English. She used the word in a sentence and I figured out the meaning. Am I right? Does it mean 'a good deed'?"

"Yes. Maybe there is hope for you after all."

She thought, *Why does he find it necessary to denigrate me at every turn? Is this how it will be?*

Chao Chen had decided on which pieces of music she would play for her recital: one piece each from Mendelssohn's *Lieder ohne Worte* ("*Songs Without Words*"), Chopin's *Ballade No. 1 in G Minor*, and two selections by the Russian composer Alexander Glazunov, which she had never played before. There was something breathtakingly daring about including works unfamiliar to her in her recital, but she had three weeks to practice.

Jim, the helpful clerk who had shown her the piano, unlocked the door to the assembly room for her. He grinned. "Everyone is talking about your recital. Madam Marton asked me to run some announcements on the mimeograph machine so that she could hand them out in the dining hall a few days in advance. She's a big talker, and so you're sure to get a crowd in here."

"I hope you'll be in the audience, Jim. If it weren't for you, none of this would be happening."

He smiled. "And let's not forget Lillian Cohen. Maybe she'll come too. I'll let her know the date."

"She's my guardian angel. And so are you."

Once Jim had left her to practice, Chao Chen placed the music to the Mendelssohn piece on the piano and scanned the score. She had made her own notes and underlined certain passages she anticipated might trip her up with their difficult fingering. She looked at Harry. "Forgive me for keeping you penned up in that carriage of yours, but I have no choice. Try not to fuss so that Mama can practice, won't you?"

Harry waved his bandaged hand in the air and smiled lovingly at his mother.

"And so, we begin." Chao Chen played the first measures with little difficulty, and then her fingers froze. She rubbed her fingers together and tried again, and then again, but her fingers refused to move. Walter's face floated in front of her when she looked up at the music. His mouth was open as if he was screaming at her, and in the next instant she heard Rui-De Xu's voice berating her, and then Ya-Nan's face appeared over the notes. Chao Chen spoke directly to her mother's image: "Get out of my way." But her mother just laughed. Chao Chen put her hands over her ears, trying to block the noise, but it was no use. She realized that all this confusion was coming from inside her head. Something terrible was happening to her, something she couldn't name.

Chao Chen slammed the lid of the piano down over the keys. She felt suffocated. She could not force air into her lungs. Staggering to her feet, she pushed Harry's carriage through the door and back to her room. She lay down on the cot. Her head ached and her fingers felt as if she had submerged them in a bath of ice water. She looked out the window at the ground, which was covered in a thick blanket of snow.

There was a knock on the door. Chao Chen stood up and pushed the laundry hanging on the line to one side so her visitor would not see the room in such a state of disarray.

Jim was standing in the corridor. "You forgot these, Mrs. Kolber." He handed Chao Chen her music.

"Thank you."

"You don't look so well. Would you like me to bring you a cup of tea?"

"No, that won't be necessary. I can just use the hotplate to make myself a cup."

Jim shifted his weight from one foot to the other. He seemed to not know what to say in response to seeing Chao Chen in such an agitated state. He mumbled, "Well, I'm sure looking forward to your recital."

"There isn't going to be one. I've decided that I won't have enough time to get ready. I need to give my little Harry all of my attention right now."

"Really? You've been working so hard, and you play so beautifully. I can hear you through the wall in the office. Everyone is going to be so disappointed, especially Mrs. Marton. It's all she's talking about. Shall I tell her for you?"

"I'd appreciate it. To tell you the truth, I'm relieved now that I've made up my mind. It was putting too much pressure on me. I don't seem to have the stamina to practice the way I should in order to give a proper performance. I'd be humiliated if I couldn't do my best. You may not believe this, but music used to be all that I could think about, all that I wanted. Now I have other responsibilities." She looked down at Harry sitting up in his carriage. "Like my little Harry and my Walter. I was just fooling myself, thinking that I'd be ready for a recital. No, no, no. Just rip up the announcements and let's forget all about it. It was foolish of me to think that I could do this."

"Maybe in the spring you'll feel differently. The winters here make everyone very sad."

Trying to change the subject, she asked, "How long have you been here, Jim?"

"I've been stuck here in Austria for the past year. I just hope I get out of here before another war breaks out and I won't be able to go home. I swear, not seeing my family is just killing me."

Chao Chen sighed.

"I don't mean to worry you. Forget what I said about another war. It's just that the Commies are giving us all kinds of trouble. They've clamped down on Hungary and Czechoslovakia, and we don't know who is going to be next. Anyway, when you want to go back to the piano, just come and see me. I love… I mean, I like hearing you play. Seeing your pretty face brightens my day."

"Jim, please don't ever say that to me again. If my husband hears you, there's no telling what he'd do. He's the jealous type."

"Sorry if I was out of line. Well, good afternoon, and please take care of yourself." He then lowered his voice. "Just one more thing. If you were my wife, I'd be jealous too. I don't blame your husband for not wanting to see you talking with American soldiers around here."

Chao Chen stood in the doorway until Jim was at the far end of the building before she turned around and put her music away. She lifted Harry out of his baby carriage and held him so tightly that he tried to squirm out of her grip. "Sorry, my little one. It's just that Mama is feeling so sad today, and you are such a comfort to me. What would I do without you?"

chapter 56

Trapped

The hills beyond the Asten DP Camp were resplendent with blooming trees, springtime in full display, and a plot set aside for a vegetable garden had started showing little green shoots. Several children were given the task of watering the garden as part of their school day, and they happily tipped their watering cans to nurture the plants.

Chao Chen watched them from the window as they laughed and went about their gardening. Turning to Harry, who was continually standing and falling, she said, "See those children? Soon you'll be big like them and you can join in the fun."

Harry opened his mouth and said, "Mama."

Chao Chen clapped her hands with delight. "What a smart boy you are, my Harry! Your first word, and you're not even a year old! And can you say 'Papa'?"

Harry made a face and shook his head from side to side.

"Try. Your papa will be so pleased."

He pursed his lips and stared at her, the smile disappearing from his cherubic face.

"All right. Maybe another day. Now let's go to the office and see if there's a letter from your Aunt Lilly. Your father has been waiting for word from her." Imagining that he asked her, she answered, "Your papa will be home any day now. He's still in Salzburg. It looks as if he's going to be there all summer if he gets a proper job. Maybe we can go with him. Wouldn't that be wonderful? A change of scenery would do us good, and I hear that the music festival is very exciting. People from all over come to hear the concerts and watch the plays."

Jim was standing behind the office counter on the telephone. Chao Chen waited patiently but couldn't help overhearing what he was saying. "Thank you for letting me know." He raised a finger to Chao Chen, signaling that he'd just be another minute. "Nice of you to say, sir. I appreciate it. Goodbye, sir."

Jim jumped into the air while he hung up the receiver. "That was my commanding officer. I'm leaving here on June 15. I might even be home in time for the Fourth of July celebration. My home town goes all out."

Chao Chen didn't know whether to laugh at his boyish antics or to cry.

He explained, "July Fourth is a big holiday in the good ol' U.S. of A. Fireworks, parades, the whole nine yards. I'll put on my army uniform and march right at the front of the parade along with the other vets. Wow!"

"I'm happy for you. I really am."

"Then why do you look so sad, Mrs. Kolber?"

"I'll miss you. There is almost no one here I can talk to."

Jim leaned across the counter and touched her shoulder. Chao Chen pulled away. "I came in here today to see if my husband had received a letter from Shanghai."

"As a matter of fact, he has."

Jim went into a back office and returned with an envelope.

Chao Chen immediately noticed the Bubbling Well return address. "It's from my husband's sister. It's been nine months since they've exchanged letters. I'm almost as anxious as my husband to know what's happening there."

"And what about your family, Mrs. Kolber? I don't remember seeing any mail for you since you arrived."

Chao Chen's eyes narrowed. "They aren't interested in me. They never have been and they never will be."

Later that afternoon Chao Chen sat in the medical clinic's waiting room. A nurse who spoke passable English called out Chao Chen's name and escorted her into Dr. Aldrich's examination room. She handed her a white gown. "Please take your clothes off and put this on, Mrs. Kolber. The doctor will be with you in a few minutes. I'll come back. We have our rules, and doctors are not allowed to examine female patients without a nurse being present at all times."

Chao Chen folded her skirt and blouse and placed them on a chair, and then she put on the clean cotton gown.

Dr. Aldrich, the American gynecologist who rotated through the clinic on alternate Wednesdays asked, "*Sprechen Sie Deutsch?* Or do you speak English, Mrs. Kolber?"

"English, sir."

"That's a relief. My German is very rudimentary. I'd have to rely on my nurse to translate. It's always better if I can speak directly to my patient. What's bothering you, Mrs. Kolber?"

"I think I'm pregnant."

"Well, if you don't mind hopping up on the table, I'll take a look." Obviously trying to distract her to put her at ease, he commented, "Honestly, it must be something in the water. We're going to have a bumper crop of babies next winter if everyone carries to term. Let's hope the food situation improves."

Chao Chen stared up at the ceiling, trying to concentrate on what the doctor was saying.

"Well, Mrs. Kolber, since you've missed menstruating for two months, my guess is you're about nine or ten weeks pregnant. We'll have to wait for the results of the test, but you're showing all the signs. Since you've already had one child, I'm sure you know how your body feels when you are with child."

Chao Chen nodded and then handed Harry a stuffed animal from her pocketbook to keep him busy for the remaining few minutes of her visit.

The nurse instructed her to get dressed. After Dr. Aldrich left the room, she said to Chao Chen, "I don't want to get your hopes up, but I feel quite confident that congratulations are in order."

Unable to control herself, Chao Chen burst into tears. The nurse was surprised. "Oh my. That's not what I expected. I thought you'd be very happy. All the other ladies were ecstatic when they got the news."

Chao Chen covered her face with her hands and took deep breaths.

The nurse handed her a glass of water and provided some wisdom. "Having two children close in age is a good thing, really. They get to play with each other, and they're out of diapers within a year or so of each other. So, before you know it, you won't have two little ones hanging onto your skirt. Think of it that way, Frau Kolber."

Chao Chen blew her nose and wiped her face. "You're right. I don't know why I started to cry. Maybe it's because I so rarely see my husband. He's trying to get a job outside the camp."

The nurse laughed. "You know, there are many wives who would be delighted to see their husbands gone for a while. Then, when they are home, it's very romantic and the rest of the time you can do what you want without having them bothering you. But maybe what I'm saying is just how we German women feel. I hear that Chinese women are much more subservient. Is that true, Frau Kolber?"

Running her fingers through her long hair, Chao Chen shrugged her shoulders. "I can only speak for myself, and I really don't know what to think at the moment."

The nurse handed her a cup. "Please leave us a urine sample. Dr. Aldrich will let you know the results in a week or so. And cheer up, Frau Kolber. You're too pretty to have that sour expression on your face."

"I suppose I should thank you for the compliment. You do mean it as a compliment, don't you?"

Walter returned that evening with what, to him, was great news. "I've been asked to join a chamber music group that will be playing at the Salzburg Music Festival from July 28 to August 31. And then who knows what will be next? Maybe a chair with the Vienna Philharmonic. You'll be happy to know my perseverance has paid off, Chao Chen. I've arranged to stay in a boardinghouse. I'll have to share a room with another musician, which is not ideal but cheap." He feigned disappointment that he couldn't bring Chao Chen and Harry with him. The truth was that he'd be sharing a room with one of the actresses performing in the morality play *Jedermann*, whom he'd met taking a coffee and a Linzer torte at the Café Neimitz.

Chao Chen was enraged. "You'd leave me here for so long, and in my condition?"

"What are you talking about?"

"I went to see the doctor today. Dr. Aldrich says it looks like I'm pregnant. You're going to be a father again in January. What do you think of that?"

Walter sat down on the cot. "Is this your way of trapping me? Isn't one child enough in this hellhole of a place?"

"Why are you blaming me, Walter?"

"Wasn't one accident enough?"

Chao Chen blushed. "Is that what you think of Harry? That he was an accident?"

"Well, wasn't he? Neither of us was ready to be a parent. We did the right thing by getting married, but who needs another child right now? Why don't you think about getting an abortion?"

"Never. I couldn't live with myself. I'd sooner die than kill my unborn child."

From out of the corner of his eye, Walter saw Harry take his first step.

Chao Chen gushed, "Can you believe it? Harry is barely a year old and he's starting to walk." She picked him up in her arms. "And today he said his first word."

"And what was that?"

"What do you think? 'Mama,' of course."

Walter took Harry from Chao Chen and bounced him on his knee. "So, how about saying 'Papa'?"

Harry shook his head just as he had done earlier in the day with Chao Chen. Walter kept repeating "papa," and when Harry refused to perform, Walter accused him of being a slow learner. "He certainly doesn't take after me. I was speaking in full sentences by the time I was a year old. At least that's what Mutti said. Dolfie, on the other hand, didn't speak until he was almost two. He relied on me to speak for him. But what's to explain this one's doltishness? Does he take after one of the Chens?"

"What do you mean, Walter? My father was one of the highest-ranking scholars in all of China, just as his father before him." Enraged, she almost tripped over her words. "And for your information, I won a scholarship to middle school when my uncle refused to pay for my education. And I got the highest grades in my high school class and received an A in English at Datong University. As I recall, you never even finished high school, or was that your twin brother I'm thinking of?"

Chao Chen was pacing back and forth. Harry had climbed off Walter's lap and now cowered in the corner, startled by his mother's sudden outburst. Then she collapsed in a chair.

"Well, go on. What more do you have to say to me?" Walter sneered.

"Nothing." And then, as if none of this had occurred, she picked up the letter from your sister and handed it to Walter. "Is this what you've been waiting for, a special delivery letter from Shanghai?"

"Are you trying to make a feeble joke? It's not special delivery, and yes, that's what I've been waiting for. Give it to me." Walter scanned Lilly's letter and then translated it from German into English for Chao Chen—without censoring Lilly's unkind remarks:

1 June, 1948
Shanghai

Dear Walter,

I am writing back to you without our parents' knowledge. You have broken Mutti's and Papa's hearts, and they still mourn you as if you were dead. Papa is still lighting a *yahrzeit* candle in your name.

Since the establishment of the State of Israel on May 14, our parents have been planning to go there, even though fighting continues between Israel and its Arab neighbors.

We also have decided to go with them. David and I have made this decision in order to not break up the family. I can hardly see myself or Mutti and Papa living in a tent in the desert. Let's hope we can find an apartment soon. As you can imagine, many Jews are going to Israel now.

My husband is not happy about leaving Shanghai, but at this point he has no choice. His business is all but ruined. If the Chinese Communists have their way, all private enterprises will be shut down.

Wishing you good luck, Walter. Regards to Chao Chen.

The next time you hear from me, it will probably be from Eretz Yisrael.

Your sister,
Lilly

P.S. Mutti's health continues to deteriorate. Papa, on the other hand, is doing fine.

Walter lifted the letter and raised his voice, "If Lilly thinks that her letter is going to make me feel guilty, she's sorely mistaken. What kind of a Jew is my father anyway? He's a hypocrite, lighting a candle in my name. I should send him a picture of all of us as proof that I'm alive and that we doing just fine. And it will give me no end of pleasure to send him a program with my name on it. Oh, I can see Mutti crying and beating her breast." He raised his tone a few octaves, to imitate his mother: "'Oh, look at this, Josef. Our son, our son! He's a big shot now.' Yes, you and I are much better off here in Austria, as far away from my parents as we can get." Walter laughed. "Don't you think it's funny?"

Chao Chen could only shake her head.

"You know, Chao Chen, your sad face is becoming very tiresome. I've almost forgotten what attracted me to you in the first place."

"I feel as if some unseen force is draining the life blood out of me. I haven't felt like myself since I cancelled my recital. It's as if I just gave up. Perhaps after this baby is born I'll feel more like myself again. In the meantime, I ask for your patience, if you can find it in your heart."

Walter put his arms around Chao Chen. She breathed in his scent. She wondered if it was her imagination, but she thought she could detect the smell of a woman's perfume on his skin.

chapter 57

The Red Shoes

Walter paid no attention to the events dominating the world's headlines. The Berlin Blockade and the hostilities of the Cold War meant something to him only insofar as they might affect travel from one part of Austria to another. On January 26, 1949 he was right where he wanted to be, in a warm bed in Salzburg with twenty-year-old actress and singer Lotte Gruber. As he was waking up with Lotte in his arms, Chao Chen was going into labor and being transported by ambulance to the hospital in Linz with Dr. Aldrich in attendance.

Days earlier, Walter had informed Chao Chen, "I'm sorry to be leaving you at this precarious time, but Bernhard Paumgartner, who teaches at the Mozarteum in Salzburg and a renowned conductor, has agreed to consider me for a position there for their upcoming season. I cannot tell him that I'm unable to go because my wife is pregnant, can I?"

"I won't beg you to stay, Walter." She was emotionless.

The birth was quick, and as Walter fondled Lotte's milky-white breasts, Chao Chen was handed her infant son. Dr. Aldrich assured Chao Chen that her baby was perfect. He then asked, "Would you like us to contact your husband?"

Her voice quivered. "He's in Salzburg. I expect he will be back any day now, but I have no way to reach him. He didn't tell me where he is staying." And then she broke down sobbing, her tears falling on her new infant's innocent face.

The nurses found it impossible to calm her. Dr. Aldrich recommended a sedative, but Chao Chen refused. "Doctor, I am afraid it will contaminate my baby's milk."

Chao Chen begged the hospital to release her earlier than the time recommended for a mother recovering from childbirth. She did not want to be separated from Harry, who was being cared for in the nursery at the Displaced Persons Camp. She fretted that he might catch a cold or worse, and she was worried that he would be confused by her absence.

Carrying her newborn, Chao Chen boarded the bus from the hospital back to the camp, and when she arrived she immediately went to the nursery. Harry sat by himself in a corner, refusing to engage with the other children. When he saw his mother, he ran to her, but then stopped, seeing that she was carrying a bundle in her arms.

"My darling, this is your brother, Charles. We're going to take care of him together, yes?"

Harry stamped his foot and his lower lip quivered. "*Nein*, Mama, *nein*."

"What are you saying? When did you start speaking German?"

A young German woman in charge of ten children said, "It's amazing. In the few days that you have been away, Frau Kolber, little Harry has picked up quite a few words of German. But don't be worried. At his age, children do not confuse one language with another. And if you intend to stay here in Austria much longer, it is probably wise that he starts to learn our language."

Chao Chen nodded. Turning to Harry, she addressed him in English. "Come, my little angel. Let's go back to our room and get your brother settled."

The caregiver informed Chao Chen that the camp had found a crib for Harry, and several sweaters, a coat, and some pants that had been donated by other mothers. Chao Chen was embarrassed that her child would be wearing hand-me-downs, but she was grateful for the clothes since she had no money to buy anything for the children—or for herself for that matter. Any money that she and Walter had managed to make went toward Walter's auditions.

Walking down the corridor to her room, she noticed that many of the doors were open and that the personal effects of the residents had been packed up in preparation for their departure. Everything was in flux. Many residents had been given permission to emigrate to Israel and to the United States. Several camps in Austria and Germany had already closed, and others were slowly phasing out their operations. She heard that those displaced persons who still had nowhere else to go, like herself, were being relocated to vacated apartments in Linz. The prospect of having their own apartment after living in the barracks for a year and a half gave Chao Chen a glimmer of hope.

As Chao Chen put her hand on the doorknob to their room, she imagined Walter sitting on the cot reading the morning newspaper he had picked up in Salzburg; but when she looked inside, he wasn't there. She sighed and tucked Charles into the basket. Harry fetched a stuffed toy rabbit, put it next to Charles's face, and made little meowing sounds.

"Darling, that's the sound a cat makes, not a rabbit." Then Chao Chen thought for a moment. "You know, I don't know what a rabbit sounds like, but when we have our own house, we'll get a little pen for the yard and you can have as many rabbits as you like. Cats too, and maybe a few ducks. When I was a little girl, I lived right next to a lake and we had ducks and swans. Can you imagine? And I used to go out in a green rowboat and dangle my hand in the water. I wish I had a photograph to show you. It was so beautiful. But that was so long ago."

Harry didn't understand what his mother was saying, but he smiled in response to the sweet tone of her voice.

Chao Chen heard the door open behind her, and Walter stood there, covered in snow from head to foot.

"Damn it, the bus broke down and I had to walk all the way from the station back to camp." He stamped his feet to loosen the snow, and without bothering to wipe up the puddle that had begun to form on the floor, he looked at his newborn son without so much as giving Chao Chen a kiss. "So, we have another son, do we? I was hoping for a daughter, but I suppose it will be easier on us knowing what to expect the second time around."

"What do you think of him, Walter? Isn't he beautiful? He reminds me of my brothers when they were babies."

"Spoken like a mother. Hopefully in time he'll start favoring the Kolber side of the family. Harry is already beginning to look more like me, don't you think?"

Chao Chen bristled. "What took you so long getting back from Salzburg?"

"I had to make the rounds. Bernhard Paumgartner wasn't interested in me, but I got an audition with the director of the Vienna State Opera House.

He is in Salzburg scouting talent. They're mounting a traveling production of *Die Zauberflöte*. The pay is decent, but if I'm hired, I'll be on the road for at least three months this summer."

"Then what am I supposed to do while you are gallivanting from one Tyrolean village to another?"

"It's obvious. You'll have your hands full with these two little urchins." Walter sat down on the only chair in the room and pulled an envelope from his breast pocket. "The office handed this to me. I've already read it. You'll be very pleased. We're going to be moving to our own apartment in Vienna. The American woman who signed this letter, Lillian Cohen, arranged the whole thing. We leave next week, and so you'd better start packing." Walter pulled their three suitcases from under the cots into the middle of the room. Harry tried to climb into one. Pulling him by the arm, Walter shouted, "Get out of there, Harry! That's not a playpen. Go sit in the corner." He rolled a rubber ball in his direction. "Now leave me alone. I'm exhausted."

It didn't take Chao Chen long for her to gather all their possessions. She placed her music box lovingly in the bottom of one of the three suitcases. Hearing Walter snoring, she didn't bother to share her thoughts with him. Instead she addressed Gan Chen. "Ah, Father, what do you think of your daughter? I hope that you aren't ashamed of me. I hardly recognize myself." She put her hands over her mouth to squelch a sob.

Harry lifted his head and ran over to her. Patting her arm, he whispered, "Mama… Mama."

Lillian Cohen had done the Kolbers a great favor by assigning them to a clean and tidy apartment with a private bathroom in Währing, in the Eighteenth District in the center of Vienna. Primarily a residential area, Währing boasted the largest Jewish cemetery in the city; a church, the Währinger; and the Volksoper, one of Vienna's three opera houses that was situated right on the Währinger Straße.

Chao Chen suspected that their neighbors were less than thrilled to have this family in their midst: two noisy children, a pompous Viennese Jew who bragged to anyone who would listen that he was a concert violinist, and his strange Oriental wife who rarely smiled and didn't speak a word of German other than "*Entschuldigen Sie, bitte*"[8]* as she passed them on the stairs on her

---

8 * "Excuse me, please"

way to or from one of the neighborhood shops or the street market near their apartment on Bastiengasse. Occasionally she took the children to a park, but it was awkward for her to sit there while the other mothers chattered and laughed among themselves. She imagined that they were gossiping about her, especially when they glanced in her direction or refused to let their children dig in the sandbox with Harry, who wanted nothing more than to have a friend to play with.

In late July Walter packed his bags and joined the traveling company of *Die Zauberflöte*. He was elated because Lotte was appearing in the production as an attendant to the Queen of the Night. He spent most of the money he earned on presents for Lotte and late-night dinners and fancy bottles of wine at the local restaurants.

When he returned, he explained to Chao Chen, "I ended up having to pay for my own accommodations. It's unfortunate, but what could I do? If a musician complains, they're out on their ear. So I just kept my mouth shut, but next time, I'll know better. I'll make sure that all my living expenses are covered in my contract. One of these days I'll have an agent to look out for me."

Chao Chen counted the money Walter had put on the table. "That's half of what I was expecting, Walter."

"I know, Chao Chen. But look at it this way. We're still getting money from UNRRA. Between that and what I've brought home, I'm sure you'll find a way to make ends meet."

"What choice do I have, Walter?"

"None, but remember, this is only temporary. One of these days I'm going to get my big break." He fiddled with the radio dial, and when he found the station he was looking for, he sat down and listened to the strains of Beethoven's *Eroica* while Chao Chen nursed Charles and Harry spoke in gentle tones to his stuffed rabbit.

Passing a newsstand on her way to a nearby market, Chao Chen bought a copy of the English-language *International Herald Tribune*. She'd have to forego buying something on her list, but it had been so long since she had read a newspaper that she couldn't resist the urge.

That evening, after both children were sound asleep, she opened the newspaper, which was dated October 10, 1949. She heard a radio, which was playing a popular American tune, and feet shuffling across the bare floor in time to the music coming from the apartment above. Sipping a cup of tea to ward off the chill night air, she read that, on October 1, China was officially under the control of Mao Tse-Tung and that supporters of the Nationalist Party, fearing for their lives, were fleeing the country. She worried about her brothers, who were ardent supporters of Chiang Kai-shek. Would they be shot in the streets or sent to a labor camp? Thirty years ago her father had pushed her country toward modernization, and now the Communists wanted to turn back the clock.

Chao Chen heard the chiming of the church bells ringing in the ten o'clock hour through her window. She wrapped a wool shawl around her shoulders and turned to the advertisements in the newspaper for films playing at the local cinemas. The advertisement for *The Red Shoes* caught her attention: "Thrill to matchless music as Moira Shearer dances dangerously between two loves." Chao Chen didn't know when or how, but she wanted to see this film. If Walter wouldn't agree to take her, she'd have to find a way to go without him. She began plotting her foray: She'd steal a few Schillings from Walter's pockets, buy a map of Vienna and chart her route, mend her coat so she'd look halfway presentable when she bought her ticket, and then sit down next to other patrons in the theatre.

The music was still playing in the upstairs apartment when she got into bed, but the music had changed from a catchy American dance tune to a sultry ballad. She could make out the words: "All of me, why not take all of me? Can't you see, I'm no good without you?" After the song ended, someone turned off the radio. Exhausted, Chao Chen fell into a deep sleep, unaware when Walter slipped under the covers beside her.

A few nights later, Chao Chen left the bowl with the remains of Harry's dinner in the sink. She settled him in his crib and rubbed his back until he closed his eyes and drifted off. Nine-month-old Charles was already asleep. He was clutching Harry's little stuffed rabbit, which was passed back and forth between the boys.

Chao Chen buttoned her coat and tucked her hair under a knitted cap. Locking the door behind her, she hurried down the stairs and out into the street, which glistened from the rain that fell steadily. It was only a ten-minute walk to the movie theatre where *The Red Shoes* was playing. She had just enough money in her pocket to buy a ticket. She told herself not to worry about Harry and Charles; they were sound asleep, she'd be gone for only two hours, and what could possibly happen in that time? She had checked the stove to make sure that all the burners were turned off, locked the windows, and turned on the radio to give the impression that she was at home if someone passed by the door.

Chao Chen lost herself in the movie, sitting on the edge of her seat throughout the tragic final scene as the beautiful red-haired ballerina Victoria, under the spell of the Mephistophelian choreographer Lermontov, kills herself by jumping off a balcony at the train station, dying at the feet of her husband, the composer Julian Craster, whom she fears she has lost forever. When the lights went on after the credits rolled, Chao Chen sat there in a trance. As several patrons slid past her, she stood up and walked slowly through the theatre lobby and into the night.

Putting her key in the door of her apartment, she was puzzled to find that the door was unlocked. She was sure she had locked it when she left. Only Frau Waldheim, the building custodian, had a key to the door. And then she put two and two together: Walter had come home. She could feel her heart beating hard in her chest. When she opened the door, Walter was reading the *International Herald Tribune*. He had obviously rifled through her drawer and found it hidden underneath her things.

He threw the newspaper on the floor, grabbed her by the arm, and slapped her hard across the face. "Where have you been and with whom? Did you have a date with an admirer? I could hear Harry and Charles screaming as I came up the stairs. How could you leave them alone? Don't tell me that you were gone for just a few minutes to pick up something at a shop. I've been sitting here for over an hour. I was just about to ask Frau Waldheim to telephone the police and tell them that a Chinese woman had gone missing." Then he shook her by the shoulders.

She yelled, "Stop that! You're going to make me lose the baby."

"What in God's name are you talking about?"

"I'm pregnant again, Walter. And to answer your question, I went to the movies—alone." She waved her map in front of his eyes. "See? I marked the route to the movie theatre. There, you have your proof."

"The only conclusion I can draw is that you're out of your mind. Leaving two defenseless children alone? Who would do such a thing? And what do you think the neighbors will think of us?"

"Frankly, I don't care. They despise me as it is. This will just be something more they can hold against me. What do they know of my life, of what I have sacrificed to be with you?"

"Sacrificed? I should have left you back in Shanghai, but I took pity on you and did the right thing by marrying you. You cost me the love of my parents and whatever money I might have had coming to me when my parents die."

Chao Chen collapsed in the chair. She unbuttoned her coat, which smelled of damp wool, and took her cap off. "Please, let's not fight, Walter. I was wrong to leave the children. They are my life. I would cut off my arm to protect them. I'd die for them; I truly would. But I thought I would go crazy if I didn't get out of here for just a few hours. *The Red Shoes*—that's what I went to see—took my mind away from everything that is making me so terribly sad."

Walter suddenly turned into a needy child. "Chao Chen, don't you love me? Isn't my adoration enough for you?"

He caressed her cheek, still red from where he had slapped her. Then he fondled her breasts, which would soon be swollen from her pregnancy. He whispered in her ear, "My darling Chao Chen, you are my everything."

Why did his words remind her more of the evil Lermontov than Julian, Victoria's adoring husband?

chapter 58

The Hotel Sacher

Since his job with *Die Zauberflöte*, Walter was not having any luck finding work. He followed up on numerous leads, but no matter how often he auditioned for various conductors who praised his technique, he wasn't hired. Word was getting out that Walter Kolber was difficult to work with and had an inflated sense of his own importance.

While his star seemed in decline, his girlfriend, Lotte Gruber, had graduated from the chorus at the Volksoper into featured roles. It irked him that she was doing so well, but he had to admit that she had a beautiful soprano voice to complement her desirable body and angelic face. Whenever he was in bed with Chao Chen, he'd close his eyes and imagine Lotte. Although Chao Chen said nothing, he wondered if he sometimes mumbled Lotte's name in his sleep. If that happened, he had a ready answer for her prying question: "Oh, Lotte was my nursemaid when I was a little boy. She was just like a mother to me. I miss her to this day. She died at Auschwitz. What a pity." It was a good story.

Burdened by the prospect that he'd soon have a third child on his hands and a helpless wife to support, Walter answered an advertisement in the *Wiener Zeitung* for a violinist to play for the guests in the lobby of the Hotel Sacher.

Wearing his best wool suit that had been tailor-made for him in Shanghai, he took a trolley to the Hotel Sacher on Philharmonikerstrasse. Entering the hotel lobby was a bittersweet moment for him. If the war hadn't happened, if Hitler hadn't driven the Jews out of Austria, he might be sitting at a table sipping a coffee and eating a *Sachertorte* with a lovely young Jewish woman, perhaps his wife, who would be looking at him adoringly as he regaled her with stories of his latest success on stage while, at home, a Czech nanny cared for their *Kinder*.

With his Lowendall in its case, Walter stepped up to the concierge and asked for Herr Stade, the hotel manager.

Looking over his glasses, the guest register opened in front of him on the counter and large, gold room keys hanging in boxes behind him, the concierge asked, "Do you have an appointment?"

"No, but I thought I'd take a chance and check if he might be available to see me. I've come about the violinist position advertised in the newspaper." He handed the concierge a card with his name engraved on it.

The concierge picked up the telephone, dialed a number, and turned his back to Walter while he spoke. After he hung up, he faced Walter once again. "You're in luck. Herr Stade will see you. He just had a cancellation. Take the elevator to the second floor. The hotel offices are located there."

Walter bowed and walked with purpose and resolve to the elevator. When the doors opened, several American women, chattering away, stepped out. One was more beautiful than the next. Walter stared at each of them, and he could see the color rising in their cheeks. He couldn't resist and blurted out, "Good day, ladies."

They did not return his overture, but as the elevator door slowly closed, he heard one of them say to another, "Isn't he attractive? Let's hope we run into him again."

The other added, "Yes, and rather brazen, I might add." And then whatever else they said was lost as Walter stepped behind the closing elevator door.

Walter smiled and felt his spirits lift as the elevator ascended to the second floor.

He walked down the heavily carpeted hallway and found the office. He knocked on the door, and a woman's voice instructed him to come in. Then pointing to a leather chair next to a stack of newspapers and magazines, the receptionist, Fräulein Wyler, according to the name plate on her desk, said, "Have a seat. Herr Stade will be with you shortly." Fräulein Wyler appeared to be in her sixties; her hair was efficiently pulled into a tight bun at the base of her neck, and a pair of reading glasses dangled down the front of her prim black dress. From the dour expression on her face, Walter surmised that she had swallowed one of life's bitter pills.

He was all too familiar with that, but he knew the value of putting on a pleasant face when he wanted something.

Walter looked around the office at the many photographs of movie stars and Austrian nobility who had stayed in the Hotel Sacher. There was even a photograph of the president of Austria, Karl Renner, with his pointed mustache and pince-nez glasses, standing in front of the hotel.

Through the intercom he heard a barking command: "Send him in."

Walter stood in front of Herr Stade, who was puffing on a cigar and did not try to hide the fact that he was sipping brandy even though it was only eleven in the morning. His belly protruded over his belt and his tie was loosened. Walter imagined that his neck size had expanded from eating too much goose liver. This was not a man who had suffered during the war.

"Sit down, young man. Let me see your résumé."

Walter folded his hands on his lap and waited. Herr Stade let out a few grunts of recognition. "So, you are a student of Alfred Wittenberg, I see, and you studied with him in Shanghai. Jewish, are you?"

"Yes, sir. Does that make any difference?"

He took a puff of his cigar and blew the smoke toward the window, which opened out onto Philharmonikerstrasse, giving Walter a distant view of the Vienna State Opera House, just a three-minute stroll from the stately hotel.

"It would have a few years ago, but now we're over all of that. I was just curious, that's all. I see that you were born here in Vienna. The city's changed quite a bit, but fortunately for us, the Hotel Sacher is thriving thanks to the American military and tourists who are finally returning to our city. Slowly we are rebuilding what was destroyed, and before long, things will be as beautiful as they once were." He took a sip of his brandy.

Walter nodded. "Would you like me to play something for you? That's why I am here, isn't it?"

"How about 'The Blue Danube' waltz? That's always a crowd-pleaser in the lobby."

Walter took his violin out and turned the pegs and plucked the strings to make sure that it was properly tuned, then played the opening measures of a tune that made him want to scream out of frustration. He thought, *What kitsch. Is this what I have come to?* But he pretended to be enjoying himself as he watched Herr Stade's bloated face beam with satisfaction. He hummed along with Walter.

"Well, I think we've found the right violinist for the job. Do you have a tuxedo?"

"Yes, sir. Of course."

"Good. Can you start tomorrow night? We are expecting a tour group from San Francisco, California, and we don't want an unfriendly lobby greeting them upon their arrival."

"Of course, sir, but what's my salary?"

"Oh, you'll be playing for tips in the beginning, but if you do well, and if Herr Gürtler, the new owner of the Sacher, likes what he hears, we'll give you a regular salary in a month. Let's just say that you'll be auditioning for us."

Walter wanted to pick up the letter opener lying on Herr Stade's desk and stab it right into his neck, but he controlled his anger and simply smiled. "Herr Stade, I'm not in a position to simply work for tips alone. I have a family to support, a wife and two children and a third on the way. Things are a bit tight at the moment." He had learned from his mother never to accept the first offer, and he was not about to do so now—no matter how much he needed the job.

Herr Stade rolled his cigar around and drew in another puff of smoke, looking as if he was making a few calculations in his head. "All right. I'll pay you fifty Schillings a night, but I expect you to work from seven to midnight. Except on Mondays. We're usually slow at the beginning of the week."

"That's satisfactory, Herr Stade. I very much appreciate the opportunity to work here. Many years ago this was my father's favorite spot in all of Vienna."

Leaning forward on his desk, Herr Stade said, "Yes, you Jews always knew the best places in the city." He stood up and offered Walter a snifter of brandy. "Let's drink to our arrangement, shall we?"

Walter suspected that the offer was merely a test. "Ah, Herr Stade, I don't drink when I'm working, but thank you anyway."

"As you wish, my man."

Walter was pleased that he had gotten the job, but Herr Stade's comment about the Jews stuck in his craw. He thought about stopping at the Volksoper and inviting Lotte out for a quick coffee on his way home, but he remembered that she had a long day of rehearsal as a chorister in Richard Strauss's Der

Rosenkavalier. The opera was opening on Saturday, October 29, 1949, and at the last minute, she had been handpicked to understudy the role of Sophie von Faninal, the young daughter of a rich bourgeois gentleman, so Lotte had not one but two parts to rehearse.

He recalled with pleasure how she had lain in his arms, a worried frown knitting her beautiful brow. "Ach, the trio in the third act is going to kill me."

"Don't worry. The critics won't be able to take their eyes off you. Just be sure that your costume has enough of a décolletage to drive them wild."

She mused, "What if they are homosexual? Then what good will that do me?"

"Do you want me to play the melody for you so you can practice now? Or can you stop thinking about Sophie for another half hour?"

Lotte rolled over on top of Walter. "Here's your answer."

Walter wondered how long he could hide his affair with Lotte from Chao Chen. At least, as far as he knew, she did not know of his infidelity, but even if she did, what good would it do her anyway? She was helpless without him. That was both a curse and a blessing. And one day maybe he'd get up the nerve to leave his wife and run off with Lotte. Life was too short, if he was being honest with himself, to be saddled with a morose wife and children that he didn't want.

Emboldened by his successful interview at the Hotel Sacher, Walter made an appointment for an interview the next day with the manager of the Erste Österreichische Bank. The salary he had negotiated with Herr Stade was not adequate to indulge in his carnal pursuits, namely Lotte Gruber. And he had another reason for seeking a second job. It would give him an excuse to get out of the apartment when he wasn't going out for auditions. He was not meant to be a babysitter for his two sons, and he needed an escape from Chao Chen's harping.

Walter took off his hat and entered the air-conditioned marble lobby of the bank. He was a few minutes early for his appointment. At exactly ten o'clock, an attractive woman approached him and introduced herself. "Good morning, Herr Kolber. I'm Liesl Grün, Herr Richter's assistant. He's anxious to speak with you right away. He'll explain. Follow me."

Walter smiled. "With pleasure."

Liesl showed him to Herr Richter's office and then shut the door behind her as she left. Herr Richter pointed to a leather chair across from his desk. Dispensing with any pleasantries, he informed Walter, "We've been approached by several Jewish aid organizations to handle their checking accounts. We think that it's good public relations to have a Jew working here at the bank. You'll be the first. Is that a problem?"

"Not at all, sir."

"Good. As you know, this is a part-time bookkeeping position. Nine o'clock to two thirty Monday through Friday. Depending upon how things go, we might want to extend your hours."

"To be honest, sir, I have another job. I'm a violinist at the Hotel Sacher."

"Really? One of my favorite spots in all of Vienna. Many of our overseas clients stay there when they are in town for business. About your pay… Erste pays a Reichsmark an hour. No exceptions."

Walter feigned ignorance. "I had no idea. That's more than I expected. When I was working as a bookkeeper for Schmidt Engineering—you'll see that in my résumé, sir—I wasn't making nearly as much. So I'm just delighted."

Herr Richter stood up, and without shaking Walter's hand, simply said, "I think our business is concluded then. We'll have a plaque made with your name on it that you can prominently display on your desk. No one coming into the bank will miss it."

Walter smiled. "Good advertising, eh, Herr Richter?"

"You'll go far here, Herr Kolber. We'll see you tomorrow."

chapter 59

Hotel Amadeus

Walter was bereft. Lotte Gruber had left Vienna in early May for Salzburg to begin rehearsals for the Salzburg Music Festival scheduled to begin on July 27, 1950. She had been cast in the chorus of Mozart's *Don Giovanni* directed by Wilhelm Furtwängler, and she promised Walter that she would inquire about a position for him with one of the chamber music ensembles playing in the Großes Festspielhaus so they could spend the summer together.

After two weeks he could no longer stand their separation, which was made more painful by the chaos at home. He planned to visit her for two days, and Lotte assured him that she would secure an audition for him. She spoke to him in excited tones, thrilled that she would be standing on stage with Tito Gobbi, Elisabeth Schwarzkopf, Anton Dermota, and Ljuba Welitsch, who were among the greatest international operatic voices of the day. "Walter, this is where you must be this summer."

Walter needed no convincing.

Chao Chen could barely open her eyes each morning, exhausted from sleepless nights and arduous days as she coped with her two young sons and a difficult pregnancy. Harry was in constant need of attention. At three years old he wanted to be taken to the park to play with the other children, who eventually accepted him. He was a gentle little boy who was only too happy to share his shovel and bucket. When it rained, he stood at the window beating on the panes and trying to wipe the drops away from the glass so he could see down to the street below. Charles, still in diapers, had not begun to walk, although he was already a year old. He'd grab hold of a table leg as he tried to pull himself up to a standing position, but every time he took a step he fell, letting out a piercing scream that jangled Walter's nerves and made Chao Chen grimace in sympathy for him. Both children were clothed in hand-me-downs from the JDC. It embarrassed Walter to see them dressed so shabbily. He recalled his own wardrobe as a child. From as early as he could remember, he had been attired in the latest fashion. He and Dolfie even had dress-up "costumes" resembling the princes of the Ottoman Empire. His two half-breed sons looked a few notches above street urchins, and his wife's eyes were red from crying and her body no longer appealing to him.

Chao Chen was unable to prepare a decent meal, and so Walter usually snuck into the Hotel Sacher staff kitchen before returning home, stealing a bite to eat after long hours of taking requests from the guests seated in plush chairs in the hotel lobby, buckets of champagne at their elbows and ash trays that were constantly being emptied by attentive uniformed busboys.

The icebox in the apartment was always nearly empty. Occasionally, Walter volunteered to go to the nearest grocery store with a list of provisions that Chao Chen requested: a bottle of milk or two for the children, a box of detergent to wash their diapers and clothes, a few fresh apples and peaches that had come into season, cereal, and cans of beans and vegetables. But more often than not, he just sat in a chair, read the newspaper, and listened to the radio, content to let Chao Chen fend for herself. What was the saying? *Kinder, Küche, Kirche* – children, kitchen, and church.

When Walter told Chao Chen of his intention to go to Salzburg for a job interview, she flew into a rage. "How convenient for you that you are leaving." She rubbed her protruding belly. "This baby will be born in just a few weeks. What am I supposed to do if you're not here for this one too?"

"Frau Waldheim is well aware of your condition, Chao Chen." He snorted. "Who could miss it, really?" Ripping off his bow tie and dropping it on the floor, he continued, "If I'm still away when the time comes, she has offered to call you a taxicab to take you to the hospital—and I'll pay her in advance to stay with the boys until I return from Salzburg. Hopefully that won't be necessary, but if it is, you have nothing to worry about."

"I will need some money to tide me over while you're gone."

Walter took out his wallet and put one hundred Schillings on the table. "That should be more than enough for you and the boys. I'll only be gone for a night or two. I have several appointments lined up in Salzburg, thanks to my connections with some of the musicians who have already settled in. The season looks to be very exciting. They are presenting new productions of Britten's *The Rape of Lucretia* and Strauss's *Capriccio*. And of course there is always *Jedermann*. I can't for the life of me understand its popularity, but crowds seem to love seeing that old chestnut performed every summer."

Chao Chen complained, "I remember when you promised that you'd take me to Salzburg. Whatever happened to *all* the promises you made to me?"

"I thought things would be different here. I imagined that I'd be sitting on top of the world, that all my talent and training would have turned me into a celebrity. And look where I am. Playing violin in a hotel lobby and entering numbers in a ledger at the bank, where I'm their pet Jew. It's disgusting, really, but what else can I do? It's all for you and the boys. I can't count on more money from the Joint, since they've had to make up for what the UNRRA is no longer contributing." He took a breath. "I need your encouragement, Chao Chen, not your complaints. Perhaps this trip to Salzburg will be the break that we are both hoping for, and if not, we must start thinking about another course of action. I have been mulling over the possibility of going to the United States now that the Displaced Persons Act has been passed. Two hundred thousand refugees will be admitted into the country. It's about time. Maybe I'll have more luck there. You know what they say: 'A man is never a prophet in his own town.' I am violinist from Vienna, and a Jewish one at that, and all those rich Jews in New York are probably feeling guilty about what's gone on here in Europe and they'll bend over backwards to do something for me."

"Walter, you sat out the war in Shanghai while others suffered immeasurably in the concentration camps. I don't know that you can count on their sympathy."

"Well, we'll see."

Walter entered the train compartment and hoisted his valise onto the overhead rack. Across from him sat an elderly couple. As soon as the train left the station, the woman leaned her head against her husband's shoulder and was soon fast asleep. The husband tried reading the morning's newspaper, but it was hopeless. He grunted and slipped the newspaper into his leather briefcase, tucked his wire-rimmed glasses into his breast pocket, and after a few minutes of glancing at the passing landscape, he nodded off.

Walter was grateful that he wouldn't have to make idle chatter. The man's light snoring matched his wife's. Was that what it was like to be married for what he guessed was about fifty years? What an utter bore! He let his mind wander to Lotte's lovely unlined face, her rosy cheeks, and glistening blond hair. She was the picture of a well-endowed Austrian maiden, ripe for the plucking. And then there were her luscious red lips, which drove Walter to distraction. Only one small blemish marred the otherwise perfect picture of her he had painted in his mind.

After a romantic evening when he saw her last, Lotte had pressured him to divorce Chao Chen. "You've been complaining about her, Walter. You've told me that she's a stone around your neck. Cruel words, but if you really mean it, why don't you just leave her? Let the government take care of her, and those boys too, for that matter!"

Walter wouldn't dare tell Lotte that his wife was pregnant yet again. "Let me think about it. But I'm curious. Why do you want to be with me at all? I'm just a poor violinist."

"I can't argue with you about that."

"Then why? I know you like the finer things in life, and right now there is no way that I can give you what you should have. Look at you. You are breathtaking, and you have a beautiful voice and a body to match."

"Don't you know that women crave bad boys? And you, my darling, are one of the worst."

The train came to a screeching halt, jolting Walter out of his reverie. He reached for his valise and stepped down onto the platform. Lotte, dressed in a lovely spring frock, ran into Walter's arms. He breathed in the scent of freesia. "Ah, you're wearing Joy."

"Yes, a gift from an admirer. He came to the theatre the other night and gave it to me, along with a beautiful bouquet of flowers."

"Are you trying to make me jealous?"

"You have nothing to be jealous of. You are my one and only lover—at least for the moment. Speaking of that, I've rented a lovely room for us at the Hotel Amadeus not far from Mozart's childhood home. The proprietor, Frau Weisdorfer, is very discreet."

"And why can't we stay at your boardinghouse? I could barely afford the train ticket."

"Every room there is occupied by a gossipmonger. I don't want word to get out that you are my lover. It could ruin your chances of earning a place in the musical group I've arranged for you to audition with today."

"You are indeed a miracle worker, dearest Lotte."

"Let's hope they are impressed by you. Your audition is at three o'clock this afternoon with the music director, and then we are free to spend the rest of the day and evening at our leisure."

Walter climbed the red carpeted stairs to their guest room on the third floor of the Hotel Amadeus. Dressed in a silky, light blue peignoir that matched her eyes, Lotte lifted her head from the musical score she was studying. "And how did your audition go this afternoon? Was Musical Director Hans Steiner duly impressed with you?"

"Unfortunately, there were four other violinists auditioning—and one of them just happened to be his nephew. I found this out from speaking with Steiner's assistant. He had no intention of hiring me in the first place. I think that he was just doing you a favor by seeing me."

Lotte let her peignoir slip open and pressed herself against his body. "Oh, I'm so sorry, Walter. That wasn't very honest of him, was it? You just wasted your time traveling all this distance, and for what?"

"You know perfectly well for what. To see you, of course. Yes, I am disappointed, but I'm sure you'll make it up to me, won't you?"

Lotte led Walter to the pillow-laden bed. As he crossed the room, he stripped his clothes off and the lovers dove under the covers. Through the open window Walter heard a church bell marking the six o'clock hour ringing in the distance, but he was hungrier for the taste of Lotte's body than a good meal. That could wait.

chapter 60

The Good Doctor

The ambulance turned its siren on to clear the streets. The emergency medical personnel could tell instantly that Chao Chen Kolber was minutes from delivering her baby. Pulling up to the side entrance of the Spitalgasse Hospital, Chao Chen was lifted onto a stretcher and rolled into the delivery room, where an obstetrician and his team of nurses were already prepared to welcome Chao Chen's third son, George, into the world on May 25, 1950.

The hospital staff did their best to communicate with Frau Kolber, but the moment she came out from under the effects of anesthesia, she was unable to utter a single word in any language. Desperate to find a way to get through to her, the hospital contacted one of their medical staff, Dr. Fritz Jensen, because his wife, Wu-An, was Chinese.

Chao Chen's face was turned to the wall, but when she heard her name pronounced with just the right intonation by a calming voice, she turned around to see a Chinese woman who also appeared to be in her late twenties. The woman took her hand and introduced herself in Mandarin, "I'm Wu-An Wong from Peking, and this is my husband, Dr. Fritz Jensen. We're here to help you."

The touch of this woman's hand on hers proved to Chao Chen that she was not hallucinating. She never imagined that someone would speak to her in her native language here in Vienna. The woman's kindness opened a floodgate of sorrows in her, and she cried, "I'm here all by myself. I don't know when my husband will return from Salzburg. My two boys are being looked after by the custodian of our apartment building. Harry is just three years old and my little Charles is only a year and four months. I must get home immediately. There is hardly anything for them to eat. Please tell the doctors that I want to leave right away. I don't trust anyone else to take care of my babies." Then she fell against her pillow, exhausted.

Looking at her medical chart that hung at the foot of her bed, Dr. Jensen asked in fluent Mandarin, "Frau Kolber, may I call you Chao Chen?"

Chao Chen nodded at this tall, distinguished-looking gentleman who was perhaps in his late forties or early fifties. Dr. Jensen continued. "Thank you. You've had an episiotomy, and we'd like you to stay in the hospital for a few more days until the incision has healed. We don't want you to develop an infection. If your husband doesn't show up today, we'll try to get in touch with him somehow. My wife will go by your apartment to make sure that your children are doing well, and if need be, she'll go to the grocery store to pick up some things for them to eat. That will put your mind at ease, won't it?"

"Thank you so much, Dr. Jensen. Have you seen my baby? I want to make sure that he's all right. I haven't been feeling well these last few months, and I didn't see a doctor during my pregnancy. Perhaps that was foolish of me, but I had no one to watch the children. And I couldn't take them with me to the doctor's office, could I?" Chao Chen sensed that she was rambling.

"What do you mean when you say you weren't feeling well these last few months?"

Chao Chen straightened the sheet to cover herself and paused, unsure whether she should reveal more to this stranger, but his gentle demeanor prompted her to continue to unburden herself. "My husband, Walter, and I have been arguing. He has a bad temper, and there are times when I am afraid of him. He has slapped me more than once in front of the children."

Wu-An gasped but otherwise remained silent. Chao Chen went on: "He's a violinist, a very brilliant violinist, but he has been unable to find proper work and that has been very frustrating for him, and for me as well. He had to take a job at the Hotel Sacher, but right now he's in Salzburg for a day or so, speaking to someone about playing at the Festival this summer. That is why he is not by my side." She tucked a strand of hair, wet with perspiration, behind her ear. "At least, that is what he tells me."

Just as those words were out of Chao Chen's mouth, Walter appeared in the doorway and rushed to her bedside, "Oh my darling, please forgive me.

I arrived less than an hour ago, went directly to the apartment, and was told that you were here. Is it a girl?"

"No, Walter. We have another son. Perhaps Dr. Jensen will take you to the nursery so you can see him?"

Dr. Jensen smiled, more for Chao Chen's benefit than Walter's. "I'd be delighted to, but first I'd like to introduce you to my wife, Wu-An."

Walter couldn't hide his surprise at this turn of events. "So, another Austrian married to a Chinese woman? What a coincidence. I know of no other Austrian men married to Chinese women, although I heard of a few while I was living in Shanghai. That's where I met my lovely wife. Are you Jewish too, Dr. Jensen?"

Dr. Jensen politely replied, "Yes, I'm Jewish. My wife and I met in China during the war as well. I was working with the Communist troops, providing medical care, and my wife worked right alongside me."

Walter put on an ingratiating smile. "How interesting. My wife and I were brought together by my music teacher at the Shanghai Conservatory, Professor Alfred Wittenberg. I'm sure you've heard of him. I'm a concert violinist and my wife plays the piano, or at least she did. She hasn't played in quite some time, unfortunately. Hopefully, one day she will get back to it. She's quite a gifted artist. Isn't that true, darling?"

"Which part, that I'm gifted or that I'll get back to playing someday? I'm not sure I agree with either of those statements."

A nurse wheeled a cart into the hospital room and handed Chao Chen a glass of water and two pills. Turning to Dr. Jensen, she said, "Please tell our patient that these are to protect her from infection and stop her milk flow. I believe she doesn't want to nurse her baby. Every time I tried to put him to her breast, she pushes him away." Wu-An brushed a lock of hair out of Chao Chen's eyes and translated the nurse's comments. Chao Chen obediently swallowed the pills and sank into the pillow.

Walter kissed Chao Chen lightly on the forehead. "I'm going to look in on our new little angel and then go back to the apartment. I've asked Frau Waldheim to stay with Harry and Charles until I get back from the hotel tonight, and she'll continue in our employ until you're released from the hospital. And when will that be, Dr. Jensen?"

"I've explained to your wife that she will need to stay here for at least a few more days. We're concerned about her developing an infection."

"So, she's going to have a little vacation on Austria's money, eh? That's very nice for her, but it's going to cost us. I'll need to get Frau Waldheim to work more hours."

As they left Chao Chen's hospital room, Walter addressed Dr. Jensen in German. "I hope you'll get her discharged sooner. I don't want to keep paying someone else to take care of our boys. I'm working to support my family, not some charwoman who despises me and my wife."

Dr. Jensen snapped at Walter, "Sir, I will do what is in the best interest of your wife. If necessary, my wife would be more than happy to give you a hand. We can see the stress your wife is under."

Walter's eyes narrowed. "Has she said something to you, Dr. Jensen?"

"Just that having three children so close in age is going to be an enormous challenge. In my professional opinion, that is too much for any mother to handle. And with a husband traveling for work, as you are, her burden is compounded."

"Ah, so I see she has complained to you. Well, let me set the record straight. I have my own challenges. You can be sure of that. One of them is Chao Chen. If she'd learn to speak German, life would be much easier for both of us. But she refuses, and so here we are." Walter hastened his step. "Now, show me my boy! And then I need to go to work or Herr Stade will find reason to fire me."

Dr. Jensen continued, "Your wife tells us that you were in Salzburg for an audition. How did that go, Herr Kolber?"

"So, she was bragging about me? Let me tell you, the classical music community here in Austria is made up of an incestuous bunch of pricks. They would rather hire their cousin or their brother than someone like myself. It's been an uphill battle here. But we couldn't stay in Shanghai. I'm sure you understand." Walter shook his head and went on. "In my opinion, people here in Austria have no interest in China, and as for the refugees… Well, it's an unmanageable situation. Thank God for the Marshall Plan. Without it we'd all be starving to death. We can thank the great United States of America. That's where I hope to go sooner rather than later."

chapter 61

America The Beautiful

Walter burrowed down into the dark green velvet cushion of one of the lobby chairs, hiding his violin with the afternoon newspaper. He had been instructed by Herr Stade not to sit among the guests during his breaks, but the staff quarters smelled of garlic and paprika, the scents of which clung to his tuxedo. He was trying to limit the number of times each month he needed to have his jacket cleaned and pressed. Inspecting the fabric on the elbow of his jacket, he realized that he'd have to buy another one soon.

Aside from the concierge, who raised an eyebrow when he saw Walter settle himself, he felt sufficiently invisible and free to eavesdrop on the American guests loitering about. He caught snippets of their conversation:

"How long are you here, Joe?"

"Three days, and then we're off to Salzburg for the start of the music festival. My wife is dragging me there. Frankly, I'd much rather stay here in Vienna or go to Paris. I've never been to the Moulin Rouge. I hear it's quite a show, all those bare-breasted women dancing on stage. We don't have anything like that in Minneapolis."

Walter shifted his focus to eavesdropping on the two men sitting behind him. They were arguing. "This makes no sense at all. The Allied High Commission is allowing West Germany to regain control of their chemical industry. I don't trust those Krauts for a minute. They'll never stick to the restriction that they can only manufacture chemicals for peaceful purposes."

"Listen, we need a strong West Germany if we expect to keep the Soviets from running roughshod across Eastern Europe. Look at what's going on in Hungary."

"I don't know who is worse, the ex-Nazis hiding in plain sight or Stalin."

"Get the waiter. We need a drink. What'll you have?"

"Let's see. It's ten o'clock. Do you want to join me for a nice apricot liqueur? And then I think I'll go upstairs. My wife went to sleep hours ago." He laughed. "She's tuckered out from all the shopping."

Walter, realizing that he needed to get back to work, jumped up, folded his newspaper, and picked up his violin. Walking through the lobby to his post in the lounge, he saw a group of young American women. He sensed that they were following him with their eyes, and for a moment he turned around. They all smiled in his direction and then went back to their conversation.

Walter thought, *American women look so free and easy. I'm sure that I'd have a lot of success with one of them, given half the chance. And if she's a Rockefeller, that wouldn't hurt either.*

Walter finished his last set at midnight with the obligatory "The Blue Danube" and then returned his violin to its case. One of the women who had caught his eye earlier in the evening approached him. "Sir, you play so beautifully. My girlfriends and I enjoyed your performance. It's a shame that you aren't putting your talents to better use."

"Thank you, miss. Are you a lover of classical music?"

"My father is on the boards of several orchestras in the United States. He played the violin when he was a boy, and he always regretted not having followed his passion and so he does what he can to support classical music. All the arts, actually." She smiled and then handed Walter an engraved card.

He looked at it, then at her. "Miss Cornelia Annenberg. And I presume this is your telephone number?"

"Yes, for our main residence in Manhattan, although we don't live there all the time. If you ever come to the States, please call me and I'll introduce you to my father. He might be of some assistance to you."

Walter bowed so low that he felt slightly lightheaded when he stood up to his full height.

Cornelia added, "I'm sorry that my friends and I won't be here much longer. We are on the Grand Tour, a gift from our parents. Honestly, Daddy had a bet with one of his friends that I'd drop out of college and be married before my senior year. But I surprised him, and so here I am."

"Indeed. This must be my lucky day, Miss Annenberg. May I wish you a wonderful summer, and if you ever come back to Vienna, here's my card as well."

"Walter Kolber. You're Jewish, aren't you?"

Walter hesitated for a moment. "Yes. My parents and my sister and her husband are living in Israel, but I came back to Vienna to advance my career as a violinist." He laughed, knowing that modesty was an attractive trait to some women, or at least he suspected that true of this one. "But I'm not yet doing as well as I had expected."

"There's always tomorrow, Mr. Kolber."

"Yes. That's what's great about Americans. You are eternally optimistic. It's very refreshing. We Austrian Jews don't have a similar outlook."

She lightly touched him on the elbow. "Well, it's understandable after all that you have been through." Waving her hand, she said, "And now I'd best be heading off to bed. My roommate will be starting to worry about me. She loves playing the chaperone. You'd think I was sixteen instead of twenty-three."

"And a beautiful twenty-three at that."

Cornelia blushed. "Thank you. Good night."

As Walter stood in the middle of the lobby, he felt as if time had stopped. Stepping into the street, he felt the warm summer breeze off the Danube caress his cheek. He replayed this conversation over and over in his head and took it as a sign that it was time for him to act.

Chao Chen was still awake when he put the key in the door. She was pacing back and forth with George in her arms. "I can't settle him down. He just won't go to sleep, and if he keeps on crying he's going to wake Harry and Charles and then it will be pure bedlam in here."

"Why don't you just put him into the carriage and take him outside for a few minutes?" Walter's irritation showed. "I've had enough. Here, give him to me. You are so agitated, and I'm sure that's what's keeping him up."

"Since when did you become an expert in childrearing? You're never around."

Walter banged his fist on the table. "As if I can help that. I'm working two jobs now. What do you want me to do? Which should I quit? They both pay about the same, but one salary alone is not going to keep our heads above water." He unbuttoned his tuxedo jacket, unzipped his fly, and stepped out of his trousers. Chao Chen looked away. "What's the matter? It's not like you haven't seen me naked before. I can remember there was a time when you couldn't get enough of my body. Have you grown tired of me?"

"I'm tired of everything. This apartment, this city, and most of all, myself. Do you remember the story I told you about my first birthday?"

"Vaguely."

"Well, on my first birthday in Zhenru, my mother predicted that I'd know how to enjoy life when I chose a sticky-sweet rice ball. Silly, now that I think of it. What child wouldn't do that? Although my older brother picked out a stamp, which meant that he would be a public official or maybe an accountant. Instead, he died under mysterious circumstances. But I certainly did not live up to my mother's prediction. Nothing other than my babies brings me any joy. Not even you, Walter. I'm sorry. I wish I felt differently, but you wouldn't want me to lie to you, would you?"

"You've certainly said a mouthful, Chao Chen."

Chao Chen opened the window further and breathed deeply as the night air wafted into the apartment. She looked over at Walter and George, who was no longer crying. "Well, I see that you have worked your charms on George. He seems to have settled down. Thank you, Walter. I really mean it."

Walter pushed a dirty stuffed toy to one side of the crib and placed George onto his back. "I don't think he needs a blanket. I'll just let him sleep as he is."

Chao Chen leaned over the crib and swept George's matted hair from his forehead, then kissed Walter on the back of his neck.

Walter turned around and pulled Chao Chen's nightgown over her head. "If it's not asking too much..."

Chao Chen put her hand on his mouth and led him to their bed. Slipping his hand between her legs, he closed his eyes and imagined making love to Miss Cornelia Annenberg.

The next morning Walter felt in better spirits than he had in weeks. He had a plan of action and he was about to execute it. Aware that the American Embassy opened its doors at eight a.m., he got up earlier than usual and rushed out the door just as Chao Chen was preparing breakfast for the children.

"Where are you off to at this hour? You don't need to be at the bank until nine o'clock. Have they changed your hours?"

"I'm covering today for someone. His mother is in the hospital and it doesn't look good, and so he's taking the day off." Walter shut the door behind him without kissing Chao Chen or the boys goodbye.

A line snaked around the palatial American Embassy building on Boltzmanngasse in the Alsergrund, one of Vienna's most elegant districts. Walter put on his sunglasses and kept checking his watch. He opened his briefcase to make sure that he had his sons' birth certificates, all the papers documenting his stateless status, and Chao Chen's official visa from Shanghai. Everything seemed to be in order.

There was a special line for displaced persons, and before long he found himself standing in front of a young woman with short-cropped curly brown hair and an American flag pinned to her lapel. She quickly skimmed through his papers. Walter noted her name tag, which read ANITA JENKINS. She spoke to him in fluent German. "So, Herr Kolber, you know that it may take a while for you and your family to be cleared for immigration."

"Yes, I understand, but I'm very anxious to go to the United States while my children are young and can more easily adapt to another country. It will be a lot harder for all of us in a few years."

"I see that your wife is from Shanghai. However, because you are entering as a family, the fact she is Chinese should not be an obstacle. Otherwise she'd have a much harder time of it. The United States and China are no longer friends now that the Communists are in power, and naturally the quota for Chinese citizens is down to nil." She took a breath. "We'll be coordinating matters with the Hebrew Immigrant Aid Society. We'll need HIAS approval as well, and they'll have responsibility for some of the expenses associated with your immigration. Do you have any connections in the United States, Herr Kolber? And do you or your wife know of anyone who could assist you in finding a job in the United States once you are there? That could help speed things along."

"Not presently, although I have met a few Americans at the Hotel Sacher where I'm employed as a violinist. And as I indicated on my papers, I recently took a job as a bookkeeper at Erste Österreichische in one of their branches. And when I lived in Shanghai I graduated from Deaman

Gregg School of Business and worked part-time for Schmidt Engineering. But that was only for a short while. As soon as Herr Schmidt could, he closed down his operation and moved to Canada. But I learned a lot working there, and so I can always fall back on my bookkeeping skills if I need to, for a little while at least, until I'm employed by an orchestra or chamber music group."

Miss Jenkins nodded. "A double threat, as we Americans say, meaning you have two skills."

Walter laughed, although he thought the expression sounded derogatory and condescending. "I hadn't thought of playing the violin as a skill, Miss Jenkins. It's more a gift from God, and there are very few people who have been so endowed."

"I wouldn't know about that, Herr Kolber. I don't get to concerts very often. I have too much to do right here, taking care of all you refugees."

"May I say how grateful I am that you are taking a special interest in my situation?"

"I didn't say that, Herr Kolber, but I will. I can only surmise that you and your Chinese wife must be having a tough time here in Vienna. The community is not the most welcoming of foreigners."

"How right you are, Miss Jenkins. And it's been very hard on my three boys too." He looked at his watch. "Oh my, I'm already a half hour late for work. Herr Richter expects me at my desk by nine and here it is already nine thirty."

"Here, I'll process this document for you quickly. I certainly don't want you to lose your job. It's the least I can do, after all you have been through."

"That's most kind of you." How many times would he play the sympathy card? As long as it worked. He then hailed a cab and slipped into his seat before Herr Richter even noticed that he was late.

When he returned to his apartment at one o'clock in the morning, Chao Chen and the children were fast asleep. Two envelopes addressed to him lay on the table: one from his sister, Lilly, and the other from the music director in Salzburg. Lilly's letter could wait. His heart was pounding in his chest. What could the director possibly want after he had told Walter that there were no openings for him for the summer music festival?

He could barely contain his excitement. The director had written that one of the violinists had suffered a fatal heart attack, and auditions were held but no one turned up who met the director's standards. Walter read on excitedly:

> We will need you here in Salzburg immediately. You will be performing in the Landestheater for a new production of *The Rape of Lucretia* conducted by Josef Krips. Of course, he will have the final say, but I have recommended you. Please telephone me the minute this letter reaches you with your answer. Rehearsals are already in progress for a July 27 debut.
>
> Cordially,
> Heinz Steiner

Walter poured himself a glass of whiskey and drank a toast to himself and to this extraordinary turn of events. Then he read Lilly's letter:

> 5 July, 1950
> Tel Aviv
>
> Dear Walter:
>
> I'm writing to give you some bad news. Mutti passed away on April 1 of last year. I would have written sooner, but I only just now received your letter with your address in Vienna. What took you so long to write to us?
>
> You probably don't want to hear this, but Papa claims that Mutti never recovered from the blow of your marriage to Chao Chen. I'm not sure I agree with him, but the last few years have been very difficult ones for her. She was always a fighter, but between her health, the demise of the business, and you, it was all just too much for her. She is buried here in Israel. Papa visits her grave every day. I go with him sometimes, but honestly, I'd rather look at our photo album

and enjoy pictures of all of us surrounded by her love than at a scrubby plot in the middle of a dismal cemetery.

Also, we've heard from Dolfie and Margot. They are making plans to go to the United States under the quota system put in place by the Displaced Persons Act. Have you heard about it? It's in effect until May 1952, and so I imagine they'll be moving very soon to take advantage of that. According to our brother, they've had enough of Bolivia.

So promise to send me a photo of you, Chao Chen, and the boys. Maybe someday we'll meet them.

Take care of yourself, Walter.

Your sister forever,
Lilly

Walter was indifferent to his sister's news about his mother. He had stopped caring about her because she had proved herself to be of no use to him. But learning that Dolfie was going to the United States felt like someone had poured salt into an open wound. What had Dolfie ever done to deserve that blessing? Nothing, except lick his father's boots and then marry Margot.

He turned off the light and sat in the dark, sipping his whiskey and listening to the sounds of night: cars passing on the street below, the light breathing of his children, and over his head, a trumpet playing a dance tune on the radio. He recognized the melody: "Just One of Those Things." Oh, how he loved to do the fox-trot to that song. If only he could just turn back the clock for a few minutes to when Shanghai held its arms open for him and he had no care in the world.

chapter 62

The Sale

The door to the reception area of Herr Stade's office was open. Walter stood in front of Fräulein Wyler's desk.

"Ah, Herr Kolber, how nice to see you." She took off her reading glasses. "I suspect that you aren't here to look into my baby-blue eyes."

"I always enjoy seeing you, but I need to speak with Herr Stade if he has a minute."

She stood up, tugged at her skirt to make sure it covered her knees, and knocked on Herr Stade's door. After speaking with Herr Stade, she ushered Walter in.

"*Guten Tag*, Herr Stade. Thank you for seeing me on such short notice. I'm sure you must be very busy, what with business being so brisk these days."

"I'm sure you can tell that we've had an influx of representatives here to make sure that the provisions of the Marshall Plan are being adhered to. Thank God for that. Without American dollars our economy would be in the toilet. But instead, things are looking up."

Relieved that Herr Stade was in a cheerful mood, Walter said, "I have a slight favor to ask of you, and it's not about my salary. I have an opportunity to perform in Salzburg for the rest of the summer. I wouldn't want you to think that I was looking for this, and indeed, it came about rather unexpectedly. I applied for a job there more than a year ago and the director remembered me. I am to replace a musician who suffered a fatal heart attack, and they need a replacement immediately. I was hoping you would give me the time off—without pay of course."

"This is rather unusual, Herr Kolber. I don't want to stand in the way of this opportunity, of course, but I can't guarantee that we can rehire you at the end of the festival. I will need to find a violinist to take your place because we are coming into our strongest month; but if your replacement doesn't meet our tastes, why then, we'll certainly consider bringing you back. Herr Gürtler has listened to you on several occasions in the lounge, and he is very pleased with what he hears."

"I suppose that is the best that I could have hoped for, Herr Stade. I'm expected to be on the train to Salzburg by the end of the week."

Herr Stade glowered at Walter. "You haven't given me much notice, have you? Today is Monday."

"Yes, but if you'd like I'll try to help find someone to take my place."

Herr Stade opened his drawer and took out a file. "That won't be necessary. I have plenty of candidates just waiting in the wings. So, be off with you, and tell Fräulein Wyler to come in. I want her to start making calls right away."

"Thank you, Herr Stade. I hope to see you again in September. I will play through Thursday night in the lounge, and I would appreciate it if you have my pay ready for me to pick up early Friday morning. I want to give it to my wife so she isn't left short."

"What a considerate husband you are, Herr Kolber." Herr Stade sneered and then added, "You might have shown a bit more consideration to your employer as well. Now go."

The same conversation played itself out the next morning with the branch manager of Erste Österreichische, but the outcome was not what Walter wanted.

"Well, if you won't hold my job for me, Herr Richter, would you at least be willing to write a letter of recommendation so that I can find another bookkeeping position when I return? I have four mouths to feed."

Herr Richter picked up the telephone and instructed his secretary to bring in her stenography pad. He dictated a letter: "To whom it may concern, I see no reason why you should not consider Herr Kolber for a position as bookkeeper. He has worked part-time for the branch for the past four months. If you wish for a character reference, please telephone me at the number shown above. Yours sincerely, et cetera, et cetera."

Walter shoved his hands into his jacket pocket. "That wasn't exactly the rousing endorsement I had hoped for…"

"You don't deserve more than that after leaving us in the lurch like this. You should be thankful that I'm willing to confirm your employment, Herr Kolber. Honestly, you Jews have some nerve. And don't bother working for the rest of the week. We'll send you a check for what we owe you. Just pack your things, give my secretary the key to your desk, and leave."

Walter waited while the secretary typed up the letter. Handing it to Walter, she whispered, "I apologize for what Herr Richter said to you in there."

"Don't worry. I've heard a lot worse." He slipped the letter inside his breast pocket and went about tidying up his desk, taking out the few personal belongings he kept in one of the drawers, and left.

He had the rest of the day ahead of him before he had to report back to the Hotel Sacher, since he had to perform nights until the day of his departure for Salzburg. He needed to tell Chao Chen that he was leaving. But when he arrived at their apartment, she and the children were not there. He told himself, *They're probably at the park. Good. That will give me enough time to run an errand.*

He was relieved that he could forestall the confrontation that would surely ensue when he told Chao Chen he was leaving for Salzburg at the end of the week and would not be back until the end of August.

A shaft of sunlight caught his eye. Tiny flecks of dust swam through the beam, landing upon Chao Chen's nightingale music box, which sat on the dresser opposite the window. Walter stared at it. Its little cocked head seemed to mock him. He turned the key and the tinny sound of *"Für Elise"* grated on his nerves. He suddenly had an idea. He needed a new tuxedo for his appearance in Salzburg. The shabby jacket he wore every night at the Hotel Sacher would never do. He'd be ridiculed right off the stage if he showed up wearing that. He thought, *How much could I get for this thing?* He placed it in its box and tucked it into his briefcase.

The antique shop displayed a few Japanese ivory *netsuke* and Chinese carved wooden stools in its window. The owner was sitting behind the counter reading the morning newspaper, seemingly oblivious to Walter's presence. Walter cleared his throat, and the owner glanced up but then went back to reading his newspaper. Apparently he judged Walter to be someone who would have nothing of value to sell.

Walter said, "Sir, are you the person I should speak to? I may want to part with a rare Oriental treasure."

The owner gestured for Walter to come closer. "What have you got?"

Walter placed Chao Chen's jeweled brocade box on the counter and carefully lifted the mechanical nightingale out of its satin bed. The owner turned on a light and examined the object closely with a jeweler's loupe.

"Well, the gems are fakes, of course. But it looks like a rather old piece. I'd say turn of the century or earlier. Where did you get this?"

He lied. "In a shop in Shanghai. I lived there during the war. I don't have papers on it, but I assure you it is very old and was once owned by a Chinese nobleman from Baoshan Province." Walter thought this would impress the owner.

"Ah, you know quite a bit about China. Chinese history happens to be one of my hobbies, and we have a few lovely things in the shop from there. Japanese *netsuke* as well. They were very much in vogue for a while, but since the war, Viennese tastes have changed somewhat. But everything that goes out of fashion eventually comes back into vogue. Don't you find that to be the case?" He stopped. "And you are...?"

"Walter Kolber. I was born here in Vienna and lived on the Esteplatz. I haven't been back to see the old family apartment yet."

"It's still a lovely area. Why don't you stay there?"

"There's nothing for me there now. My family is all gone. I'm the only one in my family to survive the war. I got lucky, but..."

The shopkeeper interrupted. "Tsk, tsk, too bad. An all too common story, I'm afraid." He lit a cigarette, took a puff, and blew a long stream of smoke into the air. "Does it play a tune, your nightingale?"

Walter turned the key and *"Für Elise"* came out of its beak as the wings opened and closed.

"A popular tune for our sentimental Viennese customers. So, you are looking for a buyer for this, I presume?"

"Yes. Are you interested?"

"I might be. What will you take for it?"

Walter had no idea what the nightingale was worth, and so he pulled a number out of the air.

The owner disappeared for a moment. Walter could hear him turning the dial of a safe from left to right and left again. He returned. "I'll offer you two thousand Schillings."

"I couldn't possibly part with it for less than three thousand."

"Well, it's a lovely piece, and the Beethoven tune will make it a bit more saleable. But two thousand five hundred is my final offer. Business is not what it used to be before the war. I lost many of my steady customers." He looked out the window as if he expected to see someone he knew passing by. "Ah, this city holds so many memories for me, and not all of them are good."

Walter calculated that the owner's offer would cover the cost of a barely-worn tuxedo and perhaps leave something to buy Lotte a present. "If I weren't in a hurry to sell it, I'd say no. But I don't have time to find another buyer. So, the nightingale is yours." He pushed it in the shopkeeper's direction while the man counted out the money.

Walter didn't want to take a chance that some thief might try to steal from him, and so he put the money in his briefcase rather than his jacket pocket. Turning toward the door, he realized that it had starting raining.

"I see you don't have an umbrella, Herr Kolber,"

"No. It was sunny when I left my apartment earlier today, but I see that I misjudged the weather."

The owner handed him an umbrella. "Someone left this a few weeks ago. Consider it a gift."

"Why? Do you think I'm in need of a handout?"

"Most people who come here to sell something are in need of a handout, Herr Kolber. Don't take offense. I'm just trying to be friendly."

Walter left the umbrella. Turning the collar of his jacket up, he picked up his briefcase and stormed out of the shop, leaving the door wide open. He ran to catch a trolley, but he was too late. It seemed as if the skies had opened up and dropped a bucket of water on his head. His clothes were soaking wet. He sat down on a bench to catch his breath, regretting that he had not taken the umbrella. Another trolley stopped in front of him and he boarded. Puddles of water pooled at his feet. He replayed the scene in the antique store in his mind, wondering if he had been swindled.

chapter 63

Summer Heat

Wu-An Wong, Dr. Fritz Jensen's wife, routinely visited Chao Chen in her cramped apartment, bringing food and clothing for the children. They usually took a walk to the neighborhood park during the hot summer months. On this day, Wu-An held Harry's hand while Chao Chen pushed the baby carriage in which George lay on his back and Charles was settled into a portable seat in the front.

At the park, Harry ran to the seesaw and waited until one of the other children took a seat. Chao Chen watched them going up and down, somewhat nervous that Harry might fall off. How many times did she warn him to hold on? Hearing his laugh and seeing how happy he was, she told herself not to worry.

Handing Charles a biscuit to keep him occupied while George fell asleep in the fresh air, Chao Chen confided in Wu-An, who had become like a sister to her since they first met at the hospital three months earlier. "I think about leaving Walter every day, but where would I go? I can't go back to Shanghai. My brothers have troubles of their own, and Rui-De Xu has no use for me. And my poor mother, Ya-Nan... By now she's lost her mind completely. I'm not even sure that she knows I'm no longer living in the house, even though she doesn't hear me practicing the piano. That was the one thing she loved, to hear me play."

Chao Chen sighed. "I used to live for my music. But then something happened to me in the DP camp. I haven't sat in front of a piano in so long. But I still look at my music every once in a while. Do you know Beethoven's *Spring Sonata*? That used to be one of my favorite pieces, and Walter and I performed the first movement at a recital in Shanghai." Chao Chen felt like she was drifting away. "I wore such a pretty red dress." Then she stopped speaking.

Wu-An patted her hand. "Perhaps you'll get back to the piano someday, when the children are in school, Chao Chen."

"I can't see Walter ever allowing it. In fact, I cannot envision any sort of future for myself. I feel as if I'm standing at the edge of an abyss and that one day I'll just fall in. I used to be such an independent person, but now I can barely pick out my clothes in the morning." She looked down at her skirt. "Come to think of it, I wore this yesterday, and the day before too. Sometimes I don't know if I can go on."

"Don't speak that way, my dearest. Both Fritz and I are here for you. You know that. And frankly, we're very worried about you. What more can we do to help you?"

"Nothing, really. You're already doing more for me than I could have wished for. Just being able to unburden myself to you makes everything more bearable." Chao Chen took out a handkerchief and blotted the perspiration on the back of her neck. "It's so hot today. Perhaps we should go back to the apartment."

"Why don't we find ourselves a little café, and I'll treat you, Harry, and Charles to some ice cream. Would you like that?"

"Yes. I hardly think of such luxuries these days. Walter has left me with barely enough money to feed the boys. And there are some days when I simply go without eating because I don't remember to eat."

As they walked on the shady side of the street, Chao Chen told Wu-An of Walter's intentions to go to America. "I really have no idea what to expect there, and I don't know how Walter intends to support us. He assured me that Salzburg is a good place for him to make connections in the classical music world."

Wu-An nodded. Chao Chen continued. "He promised he'd write to me, but I haven't heard a word from him in over a month." Chao Chen hesitated. "I think he has a mistress."

"Have you confronted Walter?" Wu-An watched closely for her reaction.

"What would be the point? He'd deny it. And unless I'm willing to do something about it, why anger him? He has a way of turning things around and making any bad situation my fault."

"That is the mark of a true narcissistic personality. They are always blaming others for what is their fault."

"I don't know anything about psychology, but your description sounds accurate. And what is the diagnosis when this same person has a violent temper and hits you?"

Wu-An gasped. "So Walter is still hitting you?"

"It's becoming more frequent. He always makes me think that it is my fault, that I've done something terrible to provoke him. And frankly, I no longer know what's true and what isn't. Maybe I deserve it."

"The next time he takes a hand to you, I'll ask Fritz to get in touch with the Jewish Welfare Agency. They bear some responsibility for what goes on with the refugees here in Vienna. It's more common than you might imagine. I've seen it with some of Fritz's patients. When couples have endured terrible things, they take it out on each other. And it's usually the wife who suffers in silence."

"Please don't say anything. Do you think they'll have any sympathy for a Chinese woman? No! I'm the least of their concerns right now. And Walter would just find another way to punish me. He's already done what I would have thought unimaginable. He stole the one thing I valued that connected me to my father, my beautiful nightingale music box. He said he needed to sell it to buy himself a new tuxedo, and he showed no remorse when I broke down in tears. He has no compassion for me whatsoever. All he thinks about is himself and his so-called career. I used to think he had great promise, but in the music world, talent takes you only so far. You have to get along with people too. He has a habit of antagonizing everyone, unless he thinks they can do something for him. And if they do, he turns on them as if he resents their offer to help him."

Wu-An minced no words. "Fritz and I have noticed that about your husband."

Chao Chen continued, "Perhaps in Salzburg he will show a more pleasant side to his personality. He can be very charming when he wants to be, especially with the ladies."

The two women walked along without speaking further about Walter, only the birds in the trees overhead breaking the silence that fell upon them.

The Salzburg Music Festival ended on August 31, 1950, but Walter was asked to participate with a chamber music group that had been booked at several monasteries and castles in the Austrian countryside through October. In his letter to Chao Chen, he apologized for his extended absence but explained that this was all in the service of his career and their future:

> I'm asking Herr Steiner to write letters of introduction to a few orchestras in America, before we are cleared to go. I'm more convinced than ever that the United States is the "land of opportunity."
>
> Ask Dr. Jensen to take a picture or two of you and the boys. I am curious to see how big they are getting. At their ages they change every month. Does Harry ask about me? Tell him his papa will be home very soon. He probably won't understand what that means, especially at his age. I'll send one of the pictures to Lilly. She is curious to see what her nephews look like.
>
> Your devoted husband,
> Walter

Walter read his letter to Lotte before he mailed it. She rolled her eyes. "Is your wife so naïve to think that you are alone in your bed every night? You're insatiable, Walter. With three children, she's surely aware of your appetite and knows that you can't be without a woman for very long."

"Where else is she going to go, and what's the difference if I cheat on her? So long as she and I are still married, she's going to have to put up with me." He leaned over and slid his hand inside Lotte's peignoir. "That is, unless you would consider becoming my wife."

"Despite what you may think, I feel sorry for your three little boys. Whatever made you think that it was a good idea to marry that woman in the first place? It was a rash and impulsive decision on your part. But you made your bed and so there you are. Anyway, I've just met someone who might be a good match for me. He's short and fat, but when he stands on his wallet, we are eye to eye. He's a widower with three children, which could present a problem because being a stepmother is the last thing I want. But he has enough money to hire a nanny for his little brats. I've told him that

that is the only condition on which I would marry him. He knows my career comes first."

"So, he's already proposed to you?"

"I haven't yet given him an answer. If I do say yes, you and I will have to cut off our relationship. Unlike your wife's seeming lack of attention to what you are up to, he watches me like a hawk. He's extremely jealous. He wants me to come live with him in his villa at Velden am Wörthersee. It's quite lovely there, but I'm afraid I might get bored very soon. So I must keep my career moving full steam ahead, and he can help me on that account. He's a very powerful man in the music world. I can't mention his name but trust me. He'll do miracles for my career!"

"And why should I be surprised? You always do what's in your best interest."

Lotte bent over laughing at him. "Oh, Walter. You're the pot calling the kettle black. If you honestly cared about anyone but yourself, you wouldn't be in my bed. You'd be at home helping out your vulnerable, trapped wife."

Walter got red faced. When Lotte lifted her pretty face, Walter grabbed her arm and pulled her down on the bed. "You bitch, don't you ever speak to me that way." She tried pushing him off her, but he was much stronger than she was. He ripped off her peignoir and forced himself on her.

After he was finished, Lotte screamed, "You're going to be sorry for this, Walter. I'm not going to let you get away with it. I'll just let Herr Steiner know what happened here, and you will find yourself and your violin out on the street. Now get out this minute."

Walter returned to Vienna in October, fabricating a story about why he had come back earlier than expected. Picking Harry up, he swung him around the room by his arms. Harry squealed in delight, but Chao Chen chided him, "Don't do that. You can pull his arms right of their sockets if you aren't careful."

Charles was playing with a set of blocks, but at the sight of his father, he knocked them over and threw them across the room. Walter grinned. "Is that any way to greet your father?"

"I think he's confused. After all, you've been gone for almost three months. He barely knows you."

"Well, we're going to change that, aren't we, Charles? Why don't you stand up and show your papa how well you are walking?"

Charles did as he was told, stumbling toward his mother and hiding behind her skirt.

Chao Chen whispered, "George is asleep in his crib. Don't wake him. He'll be up soon enough."

Walter shrugged his shoulders and then opened the small icebox, looking for something to eat. Ice was dripping water from the upper compartment and most of the shelves, except for a bottle of milk for the children, a slab of hard Emmentaler cheese, and some sliced ham, were bare. Walter unwrapped the ham. It was covered in mold. A loaf of bread sat on the counter. He cut himself two slices, slathered them with mustard, and put some cheese between the slices. "I don't suppose you have a bottle of beer?"

"I'm afraid it's not in my budget." After making her point, Chao Chen poured him a glass of water and placed it on the table.

"Tomorrow I'll go straight back to the Hotel Sacher. Hopefully Herr Stade will be glad to see me. I can't say the same for you, Chao Chen. I find your sour expression most unappealing, and you look as if you've lost a lot of weight. I'm used to seeing women with more flesh on them."

Chao Chen thought, *Just like your mistress*. But she said instead, "I've been so sad and lost without you, Walter. Perhaps now that you are home I'll have more of an appetite."

Walter smiled and patted her cheek. "That's more like my Chao Chen."

chapter 64

Overwhelmed

Chao Chen turned the radiator up to its highest setting. The pipes clanked and wheezed. It was January of 1951, and so cold in the apartment that some days she wore a pair of gloves indoors. Harry and Charles were bundled up in puffy snowsuits that Wu-An had found at a thrift store. When Chao Chen had to go to the grocery store for some last-minute item, she tied wool scarves around their little faces to keep their noses from getting frostbitten. Trying to push the carriage along the snow-covered sidewalks, George under several blankets and Charles in the front seat, was almost impossible; but she did her best to maneuver the children along the street. Harry pulled away from her whenever he could to jump into snowdrifts, which would tempt any little boy. He was strong for a three-year-old, and she had trouble keeping him close to her side, constantly worrying that he might run in front of a passing car.

Once back in the apartment, she put Charles in the empty bathtub to play with his toys. This was a way to contain him because they had no playpen. While he amused himself, she spent a few minutes reading a book with Harry. George stood up in his crib, looking out at his mother and brother. Chao Chen wanted Harry to learn English to prepare him for America.

Chao Chen, holding a book, sat in the middle of the room with Harry on her lap. "And so the big bad wolf said, 'I'll huff and I'll puff until I blow your house down.' Do you know what 'huff and puff' means, my treasure?"

Harry shook his head. Chao Chen demonstrated the sound and then instructed Harry to do the same. She nodded to Harry, indicating that he should turn a page, and in that manner, they reached the end of the story: "The third little pig, who had built his house of bricks, took off the lid from the pot of boiling water. Into the pot fell the wolf with a big splash. And that was the end of the wolf. The third little pig was too clever for him."

Harry grabbed the book from Chao Chen and turned to the beginning of the story. "Again, Mama."

Chao Chen shook her head. "That's enough of *The Three Little Pigs* for today. We can read it again tomorrow if you'd like. Now I must wash your brother's diapers, or they won't be dry and he'll have nothing to wear, and we can't have that, can we?"

Harry nodded and pulled out a wooden toy car, which he tried to push on the floor. But one of its wheels had come off, and so he gave up and wandered into the bathroom to play with Charles.

Chao Chen lay down on the bed for a few minutes and fell into a deep sleep. When she woke up, Harry and Charles were standing by her bed banging on a pot with a wooden spoon. She looked out the window. It was pitch black. She groaned and buried her head in the pillow. Harry pulled at her hair, trying to rouse her. She finally stood up. The room seemed to spin around. She realized that she had not eaten since breakfast yesterday. She said in a stern voice that frightened the babies, "Have you no patience? I'll get your dinner, but you must promise you'll stop whining. I can't stand it."

Harry looked at his mother, and with tears streaming down his cheeks, he said, "Huff and puff. Mama, huff and puff."

Chao Chen blinked as if awakened from a bad dream. She pulled both her children close to her breast and begged for their forgiveness. "Oh my little angels, you don't deserve such a naughty mother." She felt like the first little pig who had built his house of straw, and it was falling down around her. And who was the big bad wolf in her personal story? Walter, of course.

Chao Chen flinched when she thought of him. Other than insisting on having sex with her, he avoided her and the children, using his work schedule as an excuse for his absence. Fortunately, when he returned from his tour in October, he had been rehired by Herr Stade to play violin at the Hotel Sacher. That was three months ago. He had also found a day job working in the men's clothing department of M. Neumann, the fancy department store on Kärntner Straße. Chao Chen sometimes glanced at their newspaper display ads for women's dresses. She couldn't imagine ever being able to afford the merchandise in the store, even with the employee discount. But where would she wear such lovely clothes, anyway? She and Walter never went anywhere together.

One day, without an explanation, Walter surprised Chao Chen with a pretty silk scarf from Neumann's. She tied it around her neck and admired herself in her hand mirror. She rarely looked at herself, but she had to admit that despite the stress of the past three years, there was still a hint of beauty in her tired face. She put down the silver hand mirror and sighed.

Walter remarked, "Is that all the enthusiasm you can show for my gift? It cost me a pretty penny, but I thought you'd like it. A very nice salesgirl helped me to pick it out. She said that this one would surely please you because of its pretty floral pattern, but she seems not to have known what she was talking about. I can always take it back."

"No, don't do that. I was imagining just the two of us going to a concert or spending a day in the mountains without the children. I'd be wearing this scarf, and you'd tell me how lovely I looked. That's why I sighed. The gift is bittersweet to me."

Walter smiled. "Maybe when we're living in America we'll do just that, Chao Chen."

"Have you heard anything from the embassy about our immigration papers?"

"Not yet. It's already been six months, but they warned me that it could take up to a year before we know of our status. These things can't be rushed. And our case is out of the ordinary, what with you being a Chinese citizen and all."

"Are you blaming me for the delay, Walter?"

"No. It's just a fact. Communist China is an enemy of the United States. The only reason they will grant you entry is that you are my wife. Otherwise, you'd be stranded in Austria indefinitely. And you wouldn't want to go back to Shanghai, would you? I suspect that your brothers and your mothers, if they are even still alive, are being targeted for being members of the bourgeoisie. I've overheard some of our customers at the hotel talking about the way the Communists are treating their people, sending them away to farms for retraining and shaming them in the streets by making them wear dunce caps. I don't know what to believe, but if only ten percent of it is true, you're lucky to be Frau Chao Chen Kolber, I can tell you!"

Chao Chen muttered, "I don't care what's happening to Rui-De Xu and Ya-Nan after the way they treated me. But my brothers… I miss and love them dearly."

"Really? Fu-Chan and Fu-Ti, other than pay for a few meals at our wedding reception at the Promenaden, did nothing to help you. And what a dump that was. Honestly, Chao Chen, you're much too forgiving."

"You're lucky that I am. A less forgiving woman would have left you a long time ago. I'm staying with you only because of the children. Otherwise, I'd pack my bags and leave you tomorrow."

Raising his voice, he snapped, "Really? Well, don't forget to shut the door behind you, Chao Chen."

She matched his anger. "Don't you dare raise your voice. You'll upset the children." Then she picked Harry up from underneath the table, and as she held him in her arms, all the fight went out of her. "Oh, Walter, I don't know what I was saying. I would never leave you or the children. We're a family and we belong together, don't we?"

Walter grabbed the scarf he had given to Chao Chen. "I'm taking this back to Neumann's Department Store. You don't deserve it." He then put his coat on and pulled a cap down over his head.

"Where are you going?"

"Out. I need a drink. Don't wait up for me."

The following evening, after the children had been put to bed, Chao Chen pulled a chair next to the window. She traced the ice crystal formations on the window panes that were illuminated by the headlights of an automobile making its way down the snow-covered street. The church bells rang out, marking the midnight hour. It felt to Chao Chen that all of Vienna was wrapped in slumber. She opened the score to Chopin's *Nocturne in C Minor*, laid it in her lap, and stared at the music. She could hear the notes in her head, and she started "practicing" the piece, her fingers moving through the air like they would over the keys. How she missed playing the piano. But the last time she sat in front of the keyboard, she froze, the very thought of performing for an audience at the DP camp more than she could cope with. In the loneliness of this room, however, she found comfort in reconnecting with Chopin's haunting melody.

The trees burst into leafy profusion and spring wrapped its arms around Vienna. Wu-An Jensen climbed the stairs to Chao Chen's apartment. She knocked on the door several times, but no one answered. She tried the knob and the door opened. Chao Chen was sitting by the window, oblivious to the chaos around her. Harry was pulling Charles's hair, and George, now ten months old, was sitting on the floor; he smelled of a dirty diaper. Wu-An gently touched Chao Chen, trying not to surprise her.

Chao Chen looked up at Wu-An and smiled, "How sweet of you to visit us today. I was just thinking how lovely it would be to take a stroll in the park. Spring is finally here. I thought that winter would never leave us."

Wu-An tied an apron around her waist. "Not before I've done the dishes piled in the sink and changed George's diaper and dressed him in something fresh. His pajamas look as if they have not been laundered in weeks."

"You're probably right. I haven't been feeling up to doing very much these days."

Wu-An set to work, and in less than an hour, everything was in order. Then she opened the ice box. There was a half-empty bottle of milk inside. She unscrewed the cap and smelled it. It was turning sour, and if the boys drank it, they would certainly contract a case of diarrhea. In the cupboard were a few boxes of cereal and an assortment of canned goods.

"Chao Chen, is this all you have to eat?"

Chao Chen nodded. "I suppose so. Walter promised he'd do the shopping, but he hasn't gotten around to it." As if trying to make an excuse for him, she added, "He's been so busy lately, with his job at the department store and playing every night but Mondays at the hotel. Oh, he's looking so tired these days. I do worry about him."

"I'm more concerned about you, my dearest. I think that Fritz needs to come and see you and the children."

"Whatever you think, Wu-An. I really can't seem to make any decisions for myself."

"And do I have your permission for Fritz to speak with Walter once he has had a chance to examine you?"

"Yes, of course. Walter is growing more impatient with me as each day passes."

"He should be ashamed of himself. He's neither a husband to you nor a father to his sons. I simply cannot understand his total disregard for your well-being."

"If he wasn't afraid of going to prison, he'd probably push me off a bridge into the Danube River just to be rid of me. But then he'd have no one to look after the children." Before the last words were out of her mouth, Chao Chen burst into tears.

Wu-An embraced Chao Chen. "Oh, my dear friend. I have an idea that might bring you some relief. Fritz and I would like to take Harry to live with us for a few weeks. Your son might enjoy a change of scenery, and it will give you a bit of a respite."

"I cannot bear the thought of relinquishing Harry for even an instant, even to you and Dr. Jensen, as much as I trust you. I would feel that I am shirking my duty as a mother."

"I understand. Let's wait and see what Fritz advises, but you must consider your own health. If you don't take better care of yourself, you'll be of no use to yourself or your darling children."

Chao Chen looked at Harry and gestured for him to come to her. She picked him up and hugged him with a force that Wu-An had never witnessed before, especially in a Chinese woman.

After several lengthy arguments, Walter capitulated. He couldn't deny that there was something wrong with his wife.

Walter reluctantly admitted to Dr. Jensen that it might be in everyone's best interest if he and Wu-An took care of Harry for a few weeks to give Chao Chen some relief. Walter showed no appreciation for their offer, however. "I expect that you will bring Harry back the minute we see that Chao Chen is doing better. For all I know, as you have no children of your own and Harry could easily pass for your own son, you want to take him from us permanently."

Dr. Jensen was insulted by Walter's accusations, but he saw no benefit in arguing with him. Instead, he diplomatically assured Walter that fostering Harry was the furthest thing from his wife's and his mind. He told him that he was just trying to be helpful and pretended to express his sympathies for Walter. "Look, when I was twenty-eight years old I was still in medical school, building my career as you are doing now. I could not imagine having three children at that age and dealing with a wife's malaise to boot."

"Is that what you're calling it, malaise? I'd call it selfishness."

Fritz Jensen carefully chose his words. "I hesitate to make a diagnosis of Chao Chen's mental and physical condition. Let me just say that we see many refugees suffering from all sorts of mental anguish. That combined with having three needy young children to care for is incredibly stressful. We in the medical profession are just learning about postpartum psychosis. Sometimes, after a woman has given birth, her hormones do terrible things to her mental state and she may need specialized care and treatment. We just need to watch Chao Chen carefully. Hopefully, with the summer months approaching, she will feel better. At the risk of getting too personal, Walter, may I suggest that you take extra precautions when having relations with your wife? I don't think she could withstand another pregnancy."

"Keep your nose out of our business, Dr. Jensen. I will do exactly as I wish with my wife. I have my conjugal rights and I intend to exercise them. Besides, Chao Chen enjoys having sex just as much as I do. She often begs me to initiate it. Frankly, she tells me that making love to me brings her the greatest joy. Would you want me to deprive her of this pleasure or have me take a mistress and be unfaithful to my wife? I don't think she could survive an infidelity on my part, and I couldn't do that to her."

Wu-An had already shared with Fritz what Chao Chen suspected of her husband, but this was no time to call him out in a bold-faced lie. "Of course, you're right. I must point out the risks. Your wife is in a very delicate state."

"I appreciate your observations, Dr. Jensen. Thank you for coming to the apartment. Now, if you will excuse me. I must report to work at the Hotel Sacher. Perhaps you and your wife will have a drink in the lounge some evening. I'd be more than delighted to dedicate something to you. You just have to make a request and *voilà*! Your wish is my command."

"Thank you, Walter. I appreciate the invitation, but I have my hands full at the hospital, and when I'm not there, I'm busy writing. I want to inform our Austrian brethren of what great strides China has made under the leadership of Mao Tse-Tung. We here in Vienna suffer from xenophobia and are ignorant of what is going on in the rest of the world. I intend to cure that illness with a pen."

Walter observed, "Which is mightier than the sword—the pen that is. Am I right, my good doctor?"

Dr. Jensen picked up his black medical bag and shook Walter's hand. "We'll be by in a few days to pick Harry up. Once he's staying with us, feel free to call upon him anytime."

Walter smirked. "How kind of you to offer. I'll be sure to take you up on that. And I'll bring Chao Chen. I'm sure it'll speed up her recovery to see Harry in your arms."

As difficult as it was for Chao Chen to be separated from her eldest son, she had to admit that having only Charles and George to care for lessened her daily burden. She began to eat regularly and made more of an effort to keep the apartment clean. She even paid attention to her appearance. Digging into her pocketbook, she found a tube of pink lipstick and small pots of rouge and powder, which she applied sparingly to bring some color to her face. And she slipped a headband on to keep her hair from falling into her eyes. When she went out on the street with the two boys in their carriage, she wore one of her beautiful silk cheongsams—no matter that it was inappropriate for a hot and humid summer's afternoon. She noticed that some of the gentlemen passing by gave her admiring glances.

Walter didn't know how long this marked improvement would last, but by the middle of August he would no longer tolerate Harry living with the Jensens. He declared that Chao Chen was well enough to take care of all three boys again.

Dr. Jensen observed, "I have to admit that Chao Chen seems somewhat better. Hopefully her return to health is not temporary."

Walter took a trolley to the Jensens the following Sunday. Harry was sitting on their floor putting the pieces of a puzzle together. When he heard his father's voice, instead of running to him he froze, and his lower lip quivered. Walter scooped him up in his arms. "My, you're getting heavy." He put his son down.

Wu-An handed him a small valise. "Everything he came with is in there, and I added a few shirts and pants. He's growing a lot now. He loves my cooking." Dr. Jensen and Wu-An hugged Harry and assured him that they would see him again.

As he and his father rode on the trolley, Harry looked worried. "Where are we going, Papa?"

"Home. Your mother will be waiting for you."

"Will she be happy or sad?"

"I don't really know. Now, I don't want you upsetting your mother. She has been ever so much better without you."

Walter didn't know why he said something so heartless to his innocent child, but the words flew out of his mouth before he knew what he was saying. He looked into his son's eyes, which were filled with tears. His son was afraid to say a word.

At the sound of their footsteps, Chao Chen rushed to the door and screamed Harry's name. He reached up for her to pick him up and cooed, "Mama! Mama!"

She kissed his chubby cheeks and danced around the room with him in her arms. "I have missed you so much, my treasure, and so have your brothers."

Nearly one year old, George tried to take a few steps toward Harry, but he fell, bumping his head against the table. He wailed and Chao Chen had to put Harry down in order to comfort her youngest child. Charles stood over in a corner, rocking back and forth, trying to stay out of the confusion.

Walter ran his hands through his hair. Then, grabbing his hat, he told Chao Chen, "You deal with this. I can't stand the noise. I'm going out for a walk. I'll be back in an hour to change into my tuxedo. Saturday evenings are usually very busy at the Sacher, and so I certainly won't be home before one o'clock at the earliest. But if it's any consolation, I should make a lot of tip money tonight." He kissed Chao Chen on the forehead, grabbed his violin, and dashed out the door, leaving Chao Chen with her hands full.

chapter 65

The Breakdown

Chao Chen's three sons were her only anchor to reality, but even in spite of her love for them, many days she felt as if she were in a rowboat being carried by a strong current out to a sea of despair. She experienced severe mood swings. One day she'd be laughing and playing with Harry, Charles, and George, singing to them and pretending to play the piano for their amusement, and the next day she'd stare out the window until one of her children cried for attention.

In mid-November of 1951 a heavy chill descended upon Vienna, forcing Chao Chen to keep the children indoors. Harry had outgrown his snowsuit. She wrote a note to herself to ask Wu-An if she might buy one for him, and Charles could then wear his brother's hand-me-down. She thought she might go mad if she had to spend another day inside the apartment.

A letter arrived from the American Embassy addressed to Walter and Chao Chen Kolber. She suspected that it contained their visa, allowing the family to emigrate to the United States. She was afraid to rip open the envelope, anticipating that Walter would want to read it first and give her the news that they had been cleared for passage. She wondered if the visa would have to be amended now that she was pregnant with their fourth child. Dr. Jensen examined her with Wu-An present and predicted that the baby would be born in July. She hadn't yet told Walter that she was pregnant, although it would not have surprised him because he forced himself on her several times a week. Had she the strength or mental fortitude, she would have pushed him off her, but she feared his rages and did not want to expose the children to his outbursts that would have followed if she rebuffed him.

Walter's eyes lit up when he saw the envelope lying on the table. Chao Chen watched as he eagerly read every word. He announced that they would have to leave Vienna no later than the middle of May because the visa was valid for only six months. To complicate matters, the Displaced Persons Act expired in August 1952 and there was no guarantee that it would be extended. Once the Act expired, normal quotas for all countries would be reinstated.

Chao Chen took a deep breath. "Walter, I'm expecting another baby. Dr. Jensen said it is due in July, which means, if we leave in May, I'll be seven months pregnant. I don't know if I'll feel well enough to travel."

"Would you like me to leave you behind? Because I can do that, you know."

"How could you even suggest such a plan, Walter? That would mean that the baby and I couldn't join you in the United States for a very long time."

Walter sawed at a piece of meat with his knife, dipped it into a puddle of mustard on his plate, and popped it into his mouth. He chewed slowly. "So, I guess you'll just have to waddle onto the boat dragging George and Charles by their hands. Harry will follow behind and I'll handle the luggage. We'll be the talk of the ship, I can assure you."

Chao Chen marshaled the energy to leave the apartment several days later. She struggled to zip up Harry's snowsuit, which Wu-An had found in the bins at the secondhand shop. Harry tugged at it, trying to help his mother, but it was no use. Chao Chen used a few safety pins, which would have to suffice to keep it closed. "Just sit there quietly, Harry, while I change George's diaper and then we can go outside. If we walk down to the end of our street, we can see the Christmas lights. Won't that be fun?"

"Santa Claus, Mama?"

Chao Chen ignored Harry's innocent question. She realized that there were no clean diapers and that George would have to wear his dirty diaper. She pulled several soiled diapers from the hamper, threw them into the sink and scrubbed them. She hung some on a rack in the bathroom but put one in the oven and turned on the temperature so it would be dry when they returned.

The snow was coming down hard by the time they reached the end of the street. Harry stuck his tongue out to catch the flakes, and Charles skidded across a patch of ice, laughing even when he lost his balance. George was afraid to leave his mother's side and held her hand as the lights on the Christmas tree twinkled through the falling snow. They stood at the corner for several minutes, watching shoppers carrying packages, their heads bent in the falling snow and their breath hanging in the air. Chao Chen had no money in her pocket, but if she did she might have tried navigating her brood across the street to a nearby café for some hot chocolate and a sweet biscuit.

As they turned back Chao Chen noticed a crowd had gathered in front of their apartment building. A plume of black smoke came out of the second-floor window. She was surprised to see Wu-An running toward her. "Chao Chen, there's an emergency. The custodian smelled smoke coming from your apartment. He opened the door with his key and flames were coming out of the oven. He was able to douse the fire. When he opened the oven door he discovered the remains of a charred diaper. What was it doing in there?"

In a deadpan voice Chao Chen admitted, "I thought that it was the best way to dry it. I guess I was wrong, wasn't I? But I had run out of clean diapers for George."

Wu-An's tone became calm. "Of course, accidents happen, but I wish you had told me you needed more diapers. I would have bought them for you when I picked up the snowsuit, Chao Chen."

"It slipped my mind."

The crowd was dispersing as the women led the children upstairs. The apartment smelled of smoke and was covered in a fine layer of ash. Grabbing several rags, Wu-An and Chao Chen set about cleaning the apartment. But they could do nothing about the oven.

"What shall I tell Walter? He'll probably beat me if he finds out that I've destroyed the oven." Chao Chen was overwhelmed. "I'm worried we're going to have to replace it, and we don't have the money."

Wu-An said in a comforting voice, "I'll take care of that. I've already spoken to the custodian, and he says he'll fix and clean it tomorrow. Hopefully it will still work. If not he'll have to order another one for you, and that could take weeks because of the Christmas holiday."

Chao Chen looked puzzled. "Is it Christmas? And then New Year's must be coming soon after. What year will it be, Wu-An? I've lost track of time."

"It will be 1952. You and Walter have been in Austria since 1947—for five years."

"Is that so? And now we'll be going to America. It will be much better for me there. I speak good English. I'm teaching the boys to speak the language too so that they'll make lots of friends." In a manic state, she smiled and clapped her hands. "Oh, it will be wonderful, and it will make Walter so happy." She picked George up and twirled him around the room.

"Chao Chen, why don't you sit down? Let me prepare lunch for you and the children, and then I think Fritz should come by to see you."

Although her hands were shaking, Chao Chen managed to unbutton her coat and hang it in the wardrobe, ignoring her children, who were still in their wet snowsuits. She lay down on the bed mumbling to herself. Suddenly her voice became very loud and she yelled out to herself, "Oh, you stupid girl. Look what you have done! I'm going to poison your little birds, you devil-child."

Wu-An wanted to keep the boys from becoming frightened and so she turned on the radio to drown out Chao Chen's gibberish. After she prepared lunch for them, she gathered the boys around her and read a story. She had to keep the window open to clear the air of the lingering smell of smoke and ash. Every few minutes she wiped the drifting snow from the sill.

Chao Chen barely recognized Dr. Jensen when he arrived. Speaking to her in a soothing voice, he asked her a series of probing questions and then took out his stethoscope to listen to her heart and lungs. "Chao Chen, why don't you lie down again? Wu-An will watch the children until the ambulance arrives."

Chao Chen's eyes widened. "Is one of the children sick?"

"No. I want you to go to the hospital for a few weeks. You need complete bed rest or you'll risk losing your baby. You don't want that to happen, do you?"

"No." She did as she was told and lay back down.

Dr. Jensen whispered to his wife, "I'm afraid that I had to lie to Chao Chen. She is in no danger of miscarrying, but I believe that she would not be cooperative unless she thought her admittance to the hospital had everything to do with the baby and nothing to do with her mental state."

Wu-An also whispered, "I shudder to think how they'll get along without Chao Chen, but she is in no condition to take care of the children now. That's obvious. I hesitate to suggest to Walter that we take care of the boys. I think he'd rather put them in an orphanage than voluntarily turn them over to us, but I'll offer to help so he can go to work." Wu-An broke down. "Oh, Fritz, I love Chao Chen. I can't bear to see her in so much pain. Do you think she's ever going to get better?"

"The professors at the University of Vienna who practice at the hospital are the best in the city, and from what I can tell, Chao Chen will need their expert care if she's to pull out of this."

The sound of an ambulance's siren cut their conversation short. Wu-An stayed with the children while Dr. Jensen accompanied Chao Chen to the hospital. He held her hand as the ambulance skidded through the wet streets. He rehearsed in his head what he would say to Walter. He dreaded the confrontation that was sure to ensue, but he felt he was doing what was in Chao Chen's best interest by having her admitted for an evaluation.

chapter 66

The Promise

Walter quit his bookkeeping job at Neumann's Department Store to watch over the children during the day, but he continued playing the violin at the Hotel Sacher, as much for the gay atmosphere as for the salary and tips. He made sure to chat with American guests whenever they showed an interest in him, certain that every contact he made might lead to an opportunity once he was in America. And he had little trouble making contacts. Dressed in his tuxedo jacket, with his wavy brown hair and mischievous dark eyes, he attracted the attention of more than one or two guests every night.

Walter paid Frau Waldheim, the building custodian's wife, to look in on the children until he got home at night. He thought that this arrangement would be a temporary one, but by February 1952, Dr. Jensen concluded that Chao Chen was worse than he had initially thought. So he had her transferred to the Steinhoff Psychiatric Hospital in Vienna's Fourteenth District.

Walter looked at Dr. Jensen. "What's the likelihood that Chao Chen will be over whatever is attacking her mind by May? We are scheduled to leave for the United States by then."

"It is impossible to say. The doctors are optimistic that, once she has her baby, she'll be on the road to recovery. To be quite honest, Walter, the doctors are rather perplexed by Chao Chen's condition. They believe that many factors, both physical and psychological, are at play here, and it is difficult to separate one from the other."

"You've just answered my question. The baby isn't due until July, but we cannot wait until July. We have to leave by the end of May or else we'll be trapped here for who knows how long—maybe forever. I expect to have a hearing any day now with the JDC. Let's hope they come up with a solution. When they consider the factors of our case, they may be able to bend the rules so that Chao Chen, the children, and I won't be separated. That would be a fate worse than death, I can assure you." Then Walter threw his hands up in the air and looked at the ceiling as if calling upon divine intervention.

On March 24, 1952, after a routine investigation of the medical records and personal observations by Dr. Jensen and staff members of the Steinhoff Psychiatric Hospital, the U.S. Public Health Service (USPHS) notified the HIAS-AJDC Coordinating Committee that, due to Mrs. Chao Chen Kolber's mental condition, the woman was "mandatorily excluded" from entering the United States.

Walter initially thought this welcome news: *I can leave with the boys and start a brand-new life in America.* Chao Chen would no longer be his burden to carry, and he would never have to think about her again. Once in America he would tell anyone who asked that his wife and the mother of his three children had died tragically, leaving him a widower and the sole custodian of his three boys. It made for a good story, and Walter was convinced that the Jewish agencies in the United States would give him preferential treatment, doing their best to find him a job and housing for the four of them, the widower and his three motherless Jewish boys. As for his fourth child, who would be delivered sometime in July, he'd just forget about the infant altogether, leaving it up to the government of Austria to sort out that mess.

Lillian Cohen was assigned to Walter and Chao Chen Kolber's case. She had been the first JDC representative to greet the couple and their little boy, Harry, when they arrived in Linz. She had immediately taken a special interest in them then, and now her mandate from HIAS was to expedite the transfer of as many Jewish refugees as possible out of Austria and into the United States before the Displaced Persons Act expired.

The office was swamped with requests for emigration to meet the deadline. Lillian Cohen was always assigned the most difficult cases because she was persistent by nature and could usually figure out a solution to almost any technical problem presented by an applicant. But the Kolbers' case was daunting even for her, and she wasn't convinced that sending the father and three boys to the United States was in the best interest of the family or the Agency.

And then there was the practical problem of where to relocate Walter Kolber and his three sons. Several cities had already turned them down, and now their last hope, Los Angeles, had sent bad news. The Jewish Welfare Agency in Los Angeles had just informed the Committee that they were not willing to accept the Kolber family. They questioned who, without the mother accompanying them, would take care of the children? Their situation would just be too costly and too complicated. California officials also raised the question of the boys' religion. Were they even technically Jewish? Perhaps the Agency had no legal or binding responsibility for these half-Chinese children? After some deliberation, the Los Angeles JDC concluded that there were other families on their lengthy waitlist better suited to relocation than the Kolbers.

Lillian took her glasses off and rubbed her eyes. There were so many forms in the Kolber file, but the most important one still wasn't among them. She had instructed Mr. Kolber that he needed permission from his wife to take their sons out of the country without her. Talking to herself, Lillian considered, "Maybe I should just recommend to the Committee that they disqualify the entire family." She thought back to the day she had first met Chao Chen Kolber and her husband and assigned them to the Asten Displaced Persons Camp. It had struck her how uncomfortable Chao Chen looked standing next to all the Jewish refugees. Lillian remembered how pretty she was, and how the Jewish refugees, especially the women, stared at her. Life had not been kind to this woman. And now Chao Chen's fate was in Lillian's hands once again. It was a heavy burden to bear because her decision would affect the lives of three innocent little boys, their parents, and an unborn child. She felt in her heart that she would regret whatever decision she made.

The medical and nursing staff at the Steinhoff Psychiatric Hospital had difficulty communicating with Chao Chen. No one spoke Chinese, and very few had more than a rudimentary knowledge of English. From everything that Dr. Jensen told them, the doctors determined that Chao Chen suffered from severe depression and perhaps schizophrenia. While there were days when Chao Chen appeared happy and animated, singing songs to herself and smiling at the other patients, other days she lay in bed seemingly comatose and barely aware of her surroundings. The doctors were reluctant to prescribe mood enhancers such as glutethimide or lithium, fearing its effect on her unborn child. They eventually resorted to electroshock therapy, which they determined would level out her mood and be of no great risk to her or her baby. Three treatments per week for four weeks was the prescribed course of treatment.

Although she often pressed her hands against her head as if to communicate that she suffered from headaches, one of the side effects of the treatment, Chao Chen was unaware of these treatments. She confessed to Dr. Jensen that there were days she could barely remember the names of her children. She asked repeatedly, "Where is Walter? And why can't I see my babies?"

Dr. Jensen did his best to comfort her. "They are fine. They are playing in the park every day, now that the days are sunny and bright. Wu-An will bring them by any day now." He silently cursed Walter.

Walking through the corridors for the first time since Chao Chen had been admitted, Walter shuddered at the gloomy atmosphere of the Steinhoff Psychiatric Hospital. Was it his imagination or were there children crying in some of the rooms? He knew that, during the Second World War, more than seven hundred children had been tortured and murdered by the Nazis here, in the shadow of the Church of St. Leopold, a Roman Catholic Church situated on the hospital grounds.

Walter knocked on Chao Chen's door and then entered. Dressed in a rumpled hospital gown, she held an open book in her hands, but she seemed to have lost interest in whatever she was reading and was staring out the window instead. She turned when Walter lightly touched her shoulder. Looking down at the book in her hands and feigning interest, he said, "Ah, I see that you are looking at Chopin's *Nocturne in C Minor*. One of your favorite pieces."

Chao Chen looked puzzled. "Is it?"

"Yes, my dearest. Don't you remember? You and Miss Liang struggled through that piece over and over again until you finally managed to master it."

Chao Chen smiled as if seeing herself at the piano with her teacher. "So I did, but that was a long time ago. Where was I?"

"Don't you remember? You were in Shanghai. That's where we met and fell in love—over Beethoven's *Spring Sonata*."

Chao Chen rubbed her head. "And now I'm in Vienna. Is that right?"

Walter, unmoved by her deteriorating condition, sat down next to her and got right to the purpose of his visit. "I need you to sign a form that will allow me and the boys to go to America. You are in no condition to travel, and so you'll have to join us later." He touched her belly. "You wouldn't want to risk losing our baby, would you?"

"How do I know you won't leave me here forever, Walter?"

"It will only be for a short while, Chao Chen. I promise. I'll come back for you once we are settled in America, and once you've had the baby. The doctors here will take good care of you, and Wu-An and Dr. Fritz Jensen are on hand to help you at a moment's notice."

"So why are you here?"

He took the form out of his briefcase and handed her a pen. He stated emphatically, "I already told you. Now sign this document and put today's date next to your name. It's May 7, 1952."

Chao Chen screamed, "No! I won't give you permission to take my children away from me. Not now, not ever." She stood up and threw the music she was holding across the room; the pages came unglued and fluttered to the floor. Then she tried to yank the paper out of Walter's hand.

He pushed her down into the chair and growled, "Stop behaving like a madwoman. Listen to me. If the boys and I aren't out of the country in the next few days we all will be stuck here forever. You too." Realizing his harsh tone, Walter said softly, "Chao Chen, I love you and I need you. I promise I'll come back for you. After all, Harry, Charles, and George will need their mother. And I can't take care of them by myself." He hesitated for a moment because he noticed that a veil seemed to have dropped over Chao Chen's eyes; she was calming down. Handing her the pen a second time, he whispered, "Now just sign here, and don't forget the date."

Chao Chen gave in. Walter looked at her signature. "It's very shaky, but I guess the authorities will be able to read it. If not, I'll have to come back again, which will inconvenience me to no end because I have a lot to take care of before we leave."

Chao Chen begged, "Tell me again that you still love me, Walter, and promise you'll come back for me."

"Of course I will. I do love you, now more than ever." Walter put the signed document in his briefcase, and without kissing his wife goodbye, he quickly started toward the door. Chao Chen grabbed his coat sleeve, trying to keep him from leaving. He shouted, "Let go of me! I must hurry." He pried her hand away, slamming the door behind him.

The staff heard Chao Chen's screams and the nurse on duty telephoned Wu-An, hoping that she might speak with their patient and find out what had transpired between her and her husband; but by the time Wu-An arrived, Chao Chen had cried herself to sleep.

The nurse apologized to Wu-An for disturbing her. Speaking in German, she said, *"Entschuldingen Sie, bitte.* You are always so kind to your sister."

Wu-An did not bother to correct the nurse. "My husband, Dr. Jensen, and I are more than happy to do whatever we can to help our dear Chao Chen. I pray that when the baby comes in July, her condition will improve, and she can be released from the hospital. Then we'll have to figure out a way for her to emigrate to the United States with her baby, if that is her wish."

The nurse apologized. "I'm sorry, but I couldn't understand what Chao Chen's husband was telling his wife. You should know that she was extremely upset by his visit."

"We knew that the Kolbers had planned to go to America together with their children. But the caseworker informed my husband that the United States will not allow Chao Chen Kolber entry due to her illness."

"Who could imagine that a husband would abandon his wife in her present condition?"

Wu-An was candid. "Nothing about Walter Kolber surprises me. There is an American saying. Let me see if I can translate it for you: 'A man murders his parents and then pleads for mercy from the judge because he is an orphan.' That is Walter Kolber. He has no conscience, and as far as Dr. Jensen and I can tell, he has no heart. That poor woman is a victim of, among other things, his cruelty."

The nurse replied, "I'm going to say a prayer this evening for Frau Kolber at the Church of St. Leopold."

Wu-An pressed the nurse's hand. "She needs your prayers, and mine as well."

Walter and his sons appeared in Salzburg before Lillian Cohen and the chairman of the Bureau of Special Investigation, Carl Lear. on May 8. Lillian was still uncertain about what she intended to recommend. Just that morning she had received a follow-up report from Clara Friedman, the field consultant in Vienna, saying that, when Mrs. Kolber learned that her husband and children were planning to leave without her, "she was frightened that she would be abandoned." The report also contained the official psychiatric diagnosis that HIAS-JDC had been waiting for: "Mrs. Kolber suffers from schizophrenia." Lillian wondered, *If Chao Chen gave her written permission for the father to take their children, is it even valid? In her condition, did she even understand what she signed?*

The heavy double doors swung open and a secretary led Walter Kolber and his three sons into a small hearing room. Lillian hid her concerns from the chairman.

Lillian started. "Good afternoon, Mr. Kolber. I remember meeting you and your wife the very day you arrived in Linz. Your eldest son was a mere baby and resting in your wife's arms. My, how he's grown. And what a handsome boy he is!" She smiled at Harry. "And now you have two additions to your family, Charles and George. Oh, you must be so proud, but I'm sure they are a handful. I have three children of my own, and it's a lot of work raising three active boys. They are active, are they not? I'm sure you and your wife take them to the park and out on little excursions whenever you can. Children need to be out in the fresh air, isn't that true?"

"Absolutely. I tell my wife that all the time, although unfortunately I've had to work around the clock, what with HIAS's aid shrinking. But you know about all of that, I'm sure, Mrs. Cohen, which of course is why I'm so anxious to leave Austria and start afresh in America. I'm counting on you to make that possible. You have been so kind to us. I remember when you arranged for a baby carriage when we first arrived in Asten. Oh, I'll never forget your thoughtfulness."

"I don't mean to be abrupt, Mr. Kolber, but we have a lot of other people in the waiting room. So let me get down to business, please. Do you have the form I instructed you to have your wife sign?"

With a flourish, Walter placed the form on the table. "I certainly do. My wife understands that it's now or never, and therefore she willingly gave her permission so that my sons and I can leave. I promised her that, as soon as she gives birth and if the doctors will allow it, I will return to Vienna to get her and our newborn and bring them to the United States."

As much for the chairman's benefit as for Walter's, Lillian pointed out, "Obviously, there's nothing we can do about your wife's present condition, either the pregnancy or her mental state. So, our best course of action is to focus on what is within our power, and that is to get you and your three boys to the United States before the door swings shut." Lillian didn't break the news to Walter that he and his sons were not welcome in Los Angeles, but she was confident that she would find another Jewish community willing to take the Kolbers in by the time their ship reached the New York harbor.

Lillian continued her questioning. "The Agency will assist you in getting settled once you reach the United States, but you will have to find employment right away. I see you list your occupation as a violinist, but being practical, it may be some time before you earn a living in that capacity—unless you intend to teach. Have you thought about this, Mr. Kolber?"

"I'll do whatever is necessary. As you can see from my file, I have always worked a number of jobs at the same time, as a bookkeeper, salesman… And I have some knowledge of auto mechanics as well. I worked for a garage in Shanghai, although to tell you the truth, I didn't do so well at that. I was afraid I might injure my hands, which would have put an end to my musical career."

Lillian made a few notes on a piece of paper. "Since you don't have a definite job waiting for you, the U.S. government requires that an immigration bond in the amount of one thousand dollars be posted in your case. It will be your responsibility to make the monthly interest payments. I trust that you will honor this obligation."

"Do I look like a man who would not be accountable? Once I have a job I will make sure that I pay the premium each and every month. My father was a businessman, and he always taught me the importance of paying on time. So you can count on me."

"Very good, Mr. Kolber. That's what I like to hear. Then we can proceed with confidence. Is that not the case, Carl?"

The chairman nodded. He then placed the visa and attached photograph of Chao Chen on the table for Walter to identify. Five-year-old Harry jumped off his chair, ran toward the table, and placed his little hand on Chao Chen's picture, screaming, "Mama! Mama!" Charles and George took up Harry's plaintive cries for their mother.

Witnessing the three little boys crying for their mother was heartbreaking. Lillian was in a quandary. She agonized. *What is in the best interest of the children? Do I have the right to separate them from their mother, even in her condition?* It was a painful decision, but she made up her mind, knowing that if they didn't go now the entire family could be stranded in Austria indefinitely, which was against the Agency's directive to get as many displaced persons out of Austria as quickly as possible. She reasoned, *With any luck, the mother can join them after the child is born. I can only worry about what is right in front of me, and what is right in front of me are three darling boys and a father who promises to take care of them in any way that he can.*

She whispered her recommendation to the chairman, and he picked up the pen and signed the document. "All right, Mr. Kolber. I think that everything is in order. Here are your train tickets to Bremerhaven and the passenger tickets for the USNS *General Harry Taylor*, all of which have been paid for by the JDC. There are also a few American dollars in the envelope. The ship leaves on May 12, and so you have just four days to get your affairs in order and say goodbye to your wife."

"Thank you so much. You are both such wonderful and caring people." Walter pulled out a handkerchief from his pocket and wiped an imaginary tear from his eye. "Someday, when they can understand what you have done for us, I will tell my boys of your kindness." He then lifted George into his arms and instructed Harry and Charles to follow closely behind him. "Hold hands, please. I don't want you getting lost." As they left the hearing room, fearing that Lillian Cohen might find something in his file that would change her mind, he didn't dare look back.

The chairman spoke up. "Lillian, how are you going to find a sponsor? We've already been turned down by Los Angeles. How will you get them bonded? And how can you be sure that a signature from a woman institutionalized in a mental hospital is legal?"

"According to whose law? Austria's? The United States'? God's?"

"I don't know. And what's going to happen to this Chao Chen whether or not her husband leaves? Anyway, I'm not sure Mr. Kolber has any intention of ever coming back to Vienna to get her. I can't quite put my finger on it, but there is something disingenuous about that young man."

Lillian patted him on the shoulder as if he were a little boy. "Don't worry, Carl. I'll figure this out."

"You know who you remind me of? Laura Margolis. She never met a problem she couldn't solve."

"I'm very flattered by the comparison. Let's see how this turns out. What concerns me most at this point is finding a safe harbor for this family. They have an awful lot of strikes against them. Now let's see who's next on the docket."

Walter left a letter for Chao Chen at the front desk of the Steinhoff Psychiatric Hospital. He thought, *What's the point of saying goodbye? She'll only find something to complain about, and I can't stand her caterwauling. Doesn't she understand that I'm doing what's in the best interest of all our children?* And with that final gesture, he closed the chapter of his life with Chao Chen.

A few days later, Wu-An and Fritz Jensen visited the Kolbers' abandoned apartment, searching for whatever might be of value to Chao Chen. A bucket, rags, and a mop leaned against the door. The apartment smelled of rotting food and everything was covered in a thin layer of dust. Dirty dishes were piled up in the sink, and an overflowing bag of garbage spilled onto the floor. Wu-An opened a dresser drawer and discovered an infant-sized knitted blue sweater, two pairs of lederhosen, and a silver hand mirror. On a nightstand was a photograph of Chao Chen in a cheap frame; George was in her lap and Harry and Charles were standing next to her. Wu-An put these items in a bag, and then the couple took a taxicab to the Steinhoff Psychiatric Hospital.

Dr. Jensen stopped at the front desk. "We're here to see Chao Chen Kolber. Where might we find her?"

The nurse on duty answered, "Ah, Dr. Jensen, she hasn't left her room since her husband was here to see her last week. She refuses to eat. We've brought all her meals to her on a tray, but she just picks at the food and leaves most of it on the plate. Frankly, we're very worried about her. Once her baby is born we're going to try to give her medication and another series of electroshock treatments. For now, let's hope that seeing the two of you will lift her spirits."

Although it was an unseasonably warm day for the middle of May, Chao Chen lay under several blankets. The curtains were drawn, the room so dark that it was hard to see that anyone was there.

Wu-An spoke softly in Mandarin. "Chao Chen, my dearest, Fritz and I are here."

Chao Chen whispered, "Come in."

After opening the curtain to let in some light, Wu-An sat down on the bed. "Fritz and I were just at your apartment. We found a few things that you may want to keep." Rousing herself, Chao Chen sat up in bed and leaned her head against her pillow.

"Show me."

Wu-An took the sweater out of the bag. Chao Chen let out a startled cry. "Oh, I love that little sweater. Each of the boys wore it in turn. Lilly Ozer made it for me when Harry was born." And then, as if uttering these few words had taken every ounce of strength she had, she slumped back beneath the covers cradling the sweater in her arms.

chapter 67

The Arrival

The HIAS office in Salzburg was bustling with activity. Telephones were constantly ringing, and a steady stream of messengers carried documents for processing throughout the morning. Lillian Cohen lit a cigarette, took a few puffs, and then let it rest in an ashtray on her desk. Inserting a piece of paper into her typewriter, she dashed off a letter[9*] to Anne Darling, the director of the Newark, New Jersey chapter of the National Council of Jewish Women:

> May 10, 1952
> Salzburg, Austria
>
> Anne,
>
> I'm in a bind. I have a father with three young boys under the age of five leaving for the United States on May 12, and I have nowhere to place them. I was counting on Los Angeles, but they've just notified me that they are no longer willing to take this family because Mr. Walter Kolber's wife, a Chinese national by the name of Chao Chen, was rejected for health reasons. Now that the husband is taking their three children without the mother, LA feels this family would be too much of a burden. To top it off, Detroit and Philadelphia have refused to consider them for the same reasons.

---

[9] * The contents of these letters were compiled based upon agency documents.

The father's twin brother, Adolf Kolber, and his wife Margot emigrated to the U.S.A. from Bolivia some time ago, and I have learned that they are now living in Brooklyn but will have nothing to do with Walter or his children. There is bad blood there. I don't know the details, nor do I care to, but the brother is of no help.

I know that there is an opening as of May 15 for a refugee family in Newark, and so I'm sending Mr. Kolber and his three young boys to you. I'm sure that you'll find a way to get that spot assigned to the Kolbers. They are due to arrive on the USNS General Harry Taylor on May 24 in New York City.

I can't take a "no" here. You are the last and final hope.

Your friend,
Lillian

Lillian felt personally invested in the future well-being of Walter Kolber's three young sons. Looking at the sweet faces of those boys at the hearing, she felt as if her heart would break. She was ashamed of the attitude of certain Jewish communities in the United States that simply turned their backs on the Kolbers. Yes, those communities' resources were strained, and yes, the children were not technically "Jewish" according to *Halakha*, but had the lessons of World War II and the Holocaust fallen on deaf ears? Didn't the Kolbers deserve compassion after all they'd been through?

Lillian signed the letter, then sealed the envelope and put it in a special airmail delivery pouch so that it would reach her friend, Anne Darling, well before the Kolbers' arrival in New York City. She refused to consider the consequences if the Newark opening wasn't allocated to them.

Anne Darling waited at the Ellis Island reception desk as the passengers on the USNS *General Harry Taylor* disembarked and were processed by officials through immigration. She had been sent a photograph of Walter

Kolber, but she could easily have recognized him without a picture. He was the only male passenger carrying a toddler in one arm while clutching a violin case in the other. Two young boys followed behind him, dutifully holding hands. They all seemed a bit dazed and unsure of where to go. When Anne Darling stepped forward, waving and calling out, "Walter Kolber," he seemed relieved.

Anne Darling introduced herself. "I'm Anne Darling with the Newark office of the National Council of Jewish Women. Lillian Cohen wrote to me while you were en route with your boys. I'll be taking care of you for the next few days."

Walter was all smiles. "Thank you for meeting us here. It was a long journey and we're quite tired. And we have yet another long trip immediately ahead of us. I'm assuming that you have our tickets for the train to Los Angeles?"

"Actually, no. There has been a change of plans. You'll be staying right here in New York City until we have sorted things out. We ran into a little problem in Los Angeles. We are seeking a placement for you in Newark, New Jersey. It's just thirty minutes from here, right across the river."

"Really? One minute I have it in my head that I'm going to Los Angeles and the next I'm to be living in… Where? Newark? I've never even heard of it, but if you live and work there, I can only assume that it's a lovely place indeed." Then he added, "I had my heart set on Los Angeles, but I guess beggars can't be choosers, can we?"

Anne was irked by Walter's comment, but she soldiered on. "I know it must be a bit disorienting to be greeted by this news, but every major city's resources are stretched almost to the breaking point. And we want to be sure that we situate you and your boys in a community that is only too happy to have you." Anne had stuck her neck out for the Kolbers, pleading with the Agency to accommodate them as a favor to her friend, Lillian Cohen. She hoped she wouldn't regret her decision. "Please, follow me, Mr. Kolber. I'm going to put you in a taxicab and give you enough money to tide you over for a few days. Keep your receipts as we will need to account for every nickel you spend. Here is the address of the Hotel Arlington where you and the boys will be staying. It's on 25th Street, just a short ride from the ferry terminal in Manhattan. There are a few other German Jewish refugees awaiting placement staying there, and so you should feel right at home. I'll be in touch with you tomorrow morning. Hopefully I'll have good news."

As the taxicab headed up Manhattan's West Side, Walter glanced at the passing scene: tall skyscrapers that seemed to reach to the clouds, neon lights advertising the Horn and Hardart Automat and Schrafft's Restaurant, and newsstands loaded with rack upon rack of magazines. His eyes were assaulted by the size and newness of this frenetic metropolis. Even the boys seemed intrigued, but by the time they reached the hotel they were already asking for their mother.

The Arlington Hotel was located across the street from the Serbian Orthodox Cathedral of St. Sava, which was known for reaching out to the huge waves of Christian refugees and immigrants from Yugoslavia after the Second World War. The church ran a food pantry and helped place newly arrived worshippers in temporary living quarters.

The Arlington Hotel, however, under contract with HIAS and other welfare agencies administering to the Jewish immigrant community, served predominantly Jewish refugees. An eleven-story beaux arts redbrick and limestone building, its facade was decorated with cartouches of stylized pineapples and scrolled brackets, harkening back to the building's history of luxury and refinement. Now it was a bustling refugee way station.

Once they were settled in their tiny hotel room, Charles looked under the bed and Harry opened the closet door. Seeing it was empty, Harry started to cry. Walter barked, "What are you two doing?"

"We're looking for Mama. Didn't you say she would be here?" asked Harry.

"No. You made that up. It is just the four of us. Now get used to it."

Walter opened one of his valises and took out a wooden puzzle. Handing it to Harry, he was curt. "Why don't you and Charles amuse yourselves and keep an eye on George. I have an important telephone call to make. And you are to keep quiet. Do you understand me?"

Harry and Charles nodded.

Walter took an engraved card out of his wallet and had the hotel operator dial the Manhattan telephone number. After several rings, someone answered. Walter spoke into the telephone. "Is this the Annenberg residence?"

"Yes. May I ask who is calling and the purpose of your call, please?" a male voice at the other end of the line replied.

"My name is Walter Kolber. I have just arrived from Vienna. I met Miss Cornelia Annenberg in Vienna, and she instructed me to telephone her. I'm here to start rehearsals for a concert shortly. I'm a violinist."

"Mr. Kolber, the Annenbergs are in Palm Springs, California. Perhaps you can telephone again next fall if you are still in the United States."

"I am here permanently. Perhaps you could give me her number there."

"No, that won't be possible, but if you give me your telephone number, I'll let her know you'd like her to call you."

Walter hung up the telephone, then picked it up again. When the hotel operator came on, he asked, "Is the bar open?"

chapter 68

The Fourth Son

Chao Chen was rushed to the Semmelweis Obstetrics Clinic on July 16, 1952. Throughout her labor, to the consternation of the hospital staff, who were trying to care for her in the hours leading to the delivery, she cried out Walter's name and rambled in Mandarin. When Dr. Jensen finally arrived, he tried to calm Chao Chen by speaking to her soothingly in Mandarin.

The obstetrician asked, "Do you want to assist me in delivering your baby?"

Dr. Jensen looked up. Then realizing that the obstetrician mistakenly assumed he was Chao Chen's husband because he spoke her language, he replied, "If you don't mind, I'll just watch. That way my record of not delivering babies will remain intact. I'm not licensed to practice obstetrics. My specialty is internal medicine. And just to be clear, Chao Chen is not my wife but a close friend I have taken care of from time to time. That's why my name is on her records in case of an emergency. The father of this baby has gone to the United States with their three other children."

"Well, in that case, why don't you scrub up because our patient is about to give birth."

An hour later Chao Chen's newborn son entered the world. Despite the extreme adversity that she had undergone throughout her pregnancy, none of it had affected the baby, and to Fritz's relief, the infant appeared normal. The baby let out a healthy wail and was gently handed over to Dr. Jensen in the delivery room. Cradling him in his arms, he looked lovingly at the infant, "Welcome to the world, little one. Now, what are we going to do about you?"

Chao Chen was moved from the delivery area into a four-bed room. Her baby was placed in a bassinet next to her. She leaned over and lifted him to her breast. She kissed his tiny nose and stared into his large dark brown eyes, cooing words of comfort.

Dr. Jensen and Wu-An stood at her bedside. "Chao Chen, you have done very well. What do you want to call your little cherub?" asked Wu-An.

"Mischa. That's Lilly's son's name. Such a lovely boy and so well behaved. I forget what it means in Jewish, but I think it will suit my son just fine." She smiled as tears trickled down her cheeks. "You know Lilly, don't you? She's Walter's sister, Walter Kolber, the baby's father. I'm sure he'll be very pleased that I have chosen Mischa as our baby's name." She was obviously confused. "You do know Mischa, don't you?"

Dr. Jensen answered, "I'm afraid we don't, Chao Chen."

Chao Chen shrugged. "No matter. Mischa will be his name, or maybe Michael. That is a better name for a little American boy, isn't it?"

Wu-An forced a smile. "Yes, it is. And how are you feeling?"

"I don't know. I just want to see Walter. I want to show him our baby. Where is he?"

"Don't you remember? He's in the United States with Harry, Charles, and George. They left two months ago."

"You must be lying. Walter couldn't do such a thing. I would never let him take my babies away from me. They belong with me."

"I'm telling you the truth, my dearest. But we're here to look after you and your precious baby Michael. You have nothing to worry about. Why don't you try to rest? You must be very tired after your ordeal."

"I am. Please hold Michael for me. Will you do that?"

"Of course." Wu-An held the baby close, and in Mandarin she whispered, "I know two people who can take care of you and who will love you oh so very much." And then she leaned over and kissed Michael on his forehead before handing him back to the nurse, who wheeled him into the nursery.

Fritz and Wu-An hovered by Chao Chen's bedside. She suddenly sat up, and as if in a trance, babbled, "Oh, my little birds. Whatever happened to them? Yes, yes, I fed them poisoned seeds from the street vendor. How evil of him to have sold me that bag. I'll dig a hole and bury them, and in the spring when the roses bloom, it will be so pretty, won't it?" And then, just as suddenly, she sank back into her pillow, closed her eyes, and fell fast asleep.

It was obvious to the medical staff and to the Jensens that Chao Chen could not care for Michael. While staying at the Obstetrics Clinic, her moods swung wildly from smothering him with affection to utter indifference. After a week at the Clinic, she was readmitted to the Steinhoff Psychiatric Hospital.

The Jensens had acted quickly so that Michael would not be turned over to the state and placed in an orphanage. They had already petitioned the court to allow them to adopt Michael Kolber. This should have been a simple matter for the court to adjudicate, since the child's racial background mirrored that of the adoptive parents. However, after a brief hearing on July 18, 1952, a court order was issued that presented a major problem:

> WHEREAS, Chao Chen Kolber is not capable of providing care of the infant Mischa Kolber, also known as Michael Kolber; and
>
> WHEREAS, Dr. Fritz Jensen and Wu-An Jensen desire to adopt the infant; and
>
> WHEREAS, the infant's father, Walter Kolber, cannot be located and therefore has not been provided notice of his parental rights and therefore has not provided consent to this adoption; and
>
> WHEREAS, social services has concluded that in the best interests of the infant he be immediately placed with the Jensens:
>
> It is hereby ordered that every effort be made to contact and advise the father of his parental rights and to inform him of this pending petition for adoption.

It is further ordered that the infant be placed in the temporary care and custody of the Jensens until the father agrees to the adoption.

The court will reconsider this petition if the father cannot be contacted within six months.

This decision to delay any action placed the Jensens in a double bind. Fritz had accepted a job as a news correspondent for *The People's Voice*, a Communist publication in Peking. He was expected to report for his first assignment within weeks. According to both Chinese and Austrian law, unless legally adopted, Michael could not be taken out of Austria. Furthermore, the Jensens had no idea where Walter was, and they were not sure that he would ever give his permission if he were found.

Wu-An was in a panic. "If Michael becomes a ward of the state, his prospects for adoption are grim. I don't mean to cast aspersions on your fellow Austrians, Fritz, but I can't see any Christian Austrian willing to take in a mixed-race Jewish child, can you? And those Austrian Jews who are living in Vienna would probably have no interest in him either."

"You're right. We're his only hope."

Through his contacts with HIAS and the JDC, Fritz tracked down Lillian Cohen, who had been assigned to the Kolber case. He quickly told her of Michael's birth, Chao Chen's current mental condition, and the court's order requiring them to obtain Walter Kolber's permission to allow them to adopt Michael.

Lillian immediately understood. "I am so relieved to hear from you, Dr. Jensen. I have been worried about Mrs. Kolber and the fate of her baby. I was responsible for getting her husband and three children to America, and every day I ask myself if I made the right decision."

"Mrs. Cohen, you can see this is quite urgent. Do you know, by any chance, how we can reach him?"

"Yes. I understand he's living in Newark, New Jersey, and his sons have just been placed temporarily in the Jewish Child Care Orphanage there. My colleague and friend is handling their case. She is hoping to place the children in homes very soon." She continued, "Please send me the official documents that Mr. Kolber has to sign and I'll make sure they reach him immediately."

"My wife and I are very grateful for your assistance, as time is of the essence."

The July 23, 1952 letter from Fritz, which was written in German, read:

> Walter,
>
> Your healthy newborn son, Michael, was born on July 16, 1952. Wu-An and I have taken care of him since then. Chao Chen still remains hospitalized and her prognosis for the moment is not that good. I believe it is in the best interest of everyone if you allow us to adopt Michael. You know we will take excellent care of him. Enclosed is the court order and a document that you must sign. Please sign it and return it to me immediately.

Lillian airmailed the sealed letter to Anne Darling in Newark, New Jersey, and waited.

Wu-An devotedly visited Chao Chen almost daily at the Steinhoff Psychiatric Hospital. She could not bring Michael with her because it was against hospital policy. When she shared bits of good news about the baby, Chao Chen was only mildly interested, nodding at the reports: "Michael is getting big so fast. He eats well, sleeps well, and always smiles when he sees Fritz." The most that Chao Chen could muster was a weak smile.

Wu-An dreaded the day she would have to tell Chao Chen that she and Fritz were returning to China and taking Michael with them.

Wu-An sat on a bench on the grounds of the hospital, watching the nuns hurrying by as the clock in St. Leopold's Church rang in the hour. She burst into tears of pain and regret for her sisterly friend. When she and her husband left the country, Chao Chen would be all alone in the world, with no one to care about her, no one to comfort her, and no one to give her words of encouragement that one day she would recover from this seemingly endless darkness and despair.

Two weeks later Fritz Jensen received a special delivery letter from Walter Kolber:

Fritz,

How are you and Wu-An? Life in America is not as good as I hoped. The boys are being placed into Jewish foster homes as my job doesn't pay much. I want to bring the boys to be with me, but I can't afford an apartment big enough or pay anyone to care for them while I am at work. If you can send me $1,000 to help me I will gladly sign the paper giving you permission to adopt my son. Otherwise, I will see what I can do to get Michael here. After all, I am his father.

Walter

Fritz was enraged. He shouted to the empty room, "This is extortion! Until he received my letter he didn't give a damn about the baby!" Then banging on the table, he yelled, "He didn't even know his name! Now I know why Chao Chen went insane, just living with that monster."

It took hours for Fritz to calm down. He decided not to tell Wu-An about Walter's letter. It would be impossible for him to suppress his anger, and there was no reason to upset her—at least not yet. Wu-An had already begun to think of herself as Michael's mother. After so many years of being childless, she finally had a child to love and care for, and Fritz was determined to find a way to give Wu-An what both of them fervently desired.

Now that Fritz had Walter's return address, he sent him a special delivery letter containing a ploy to force Walter into cooperating:

Walter,

I received your letter and I let the court and the Austrian government know your position. They have advised us that they intend to hold you financially responsible for the daily care of your wife and the obstetric costs for the baby's birth. They say you must also reimburse me for taking care of Michael since he was born. So far you owe almost 3,000 U.S. dollars, and you will have to continue to pay for your wife's monthly care at the Steinhoff Psychiatric Hospital. I believe

I can convince everyone to waive these costs, but only if you sign the adoption papers.

Ten days later, Fritz received an envelope from Walter Kolber containing the signed and notarized documents. No note accompanied it.

chapter 69

Special Deliveries

On a warm September afternoon, two months after she had greeted them at Ellis Island, Anne Darling drove Walter and two-year-old George to the home of Joseph and Frieda Hirschfeld, Hungarian Jews with a history with Newark's Jewish Family Services. Since 1949 their small, second-floor walk-up on Columbia Avenue in Newark had served as a temporary shelter for several Jewish refugee children needing assistance.

After they turned onto Columbia Avenue, Anne saw Frieda and her daughter Adele waiting on the front stoop of their walk-up. When the car pulled up to the curb, the Hirschfeld women ran to open the door and then led Anne and Walter, who was holding George, up the dimly lit stairs to their second-floor apartment.

Anne Darling spoke first. "Mrs. Hirschfeld, let me introduce Walter Kolber and his baby son George, whom you already met at the orphanage."

Frieda replied with a distinctive Mittel-European accent. "Welcome. This is my daughter, Adele. She was so anxious to be here to greet you that she took off from work. I'm sorry that you won't get to meet my husband, Joseph. He's at work, and so is my son Danny and Adele's husband, Ray. Our youngest son Bobby is practicing football. They won't be home until this evening. But at least Adele and I are here to welcome you, Mr. Kolber."

Adele interrupted, "Mr. Kolber, I'm glad to meet you, but it's obvious that little Georgie's diaper needs changing. Please give me his sack. There is a diaper inside, isn't there?"

Anne knew that Walter had no idea. He had not seen George in several weeks, and the workers at the orphanage had taken care of his few belongings. Anne came to the rescue. "I'm sure we have given you an ample supply."

Walter eagerly handed George over to Adele and turned his attention to Frieda. "I'm very sorry that you have to take care of George. Don't get me wrong. I can see that you're a lovely woman, and so is your charming daughter, but I feel so guilty that I personally cannot provide George and my other two sons, Harry and Charles, with a proper home. I'm living in a boardinghouse right now. The only thing good about it is that it's cheap."

Patting Walter's arm, Frieda forged ahead. "We understand your unfortunate circumstances, Mr. Kolber. We do what we can to help our Jewish refugees. You have all gone through so much, and we here in America are glad to be of some help. It is written that 'He who saves one life, saves all of mankind.' So, taking care of little Georgie is a blessing to us."

Walter sat down as if he were carrying a heavy burden. "I've had more than my fair share of bad luck. My wife died recently, back in Vienna. As you can imagine, that has been very hard on me and the boys, even though they don't fully understand what's happened to their mother. My wife was very sick for a long time, and, well, I'd rather not speak about it. In any case, right now I have no job. I'm a concert violinist, but I expect that I'll have to do something else to earn a living. Perhaps the next time I come to visit George I'll bring my violin and play for your family. Would you like that, Mrs. Hirschfeld?"

"I always love to hear a well-played violin. Perhaps you'll give us a bit of Chopin."

"With pleasure, Mrs. Hirschfeld. And I plan on visiting regularly, with your permission. I can easily take the bus from where I'm staying in Newark."

"Of course. You are always welcome in our home. And perhaps next time my husband and son will be here so they can meet you as well. I'm sure they'll want to meet little Georgie's father. For the time being they'll just have to be satisfied with my report: that you are a charming young man, and handsome too."

Walter smiled.

Adele, with George in tow, added, "It will be quite interesting to see how Daddy, Bobby, Danny, and my husband Ray, react to hearing a genuine violinist. We can't really afford to go to concerts."

Anne interjected, "Mrs. Hirschfeld, once again, the Agency thanks you and your husband so very much. I myself have been here before, but of course Mr. Kolber has not. I'm quite sure that, after seeing your warm and loving home, he feels much better about leaving his son in your care. Now, I think Mr. Kolber and I should leave so that you and George can get acquainted."

George was sitting quietly on a worn-out love seat, swinging his legs back and forth. When his father leaned over to kiss him goodbye, he turned his away.

Walter patted George on the head instead. "Don't give these nice ladies any trouble, you hear me?"

Adele swooped down to pick Georgie up, but he ran behind the sofa to play peek-a-boo instead. He didn't notice that his father left.

Walter stared out the window of Anne Darling's car while Harry and Charles sat quietly in the back seat. Walter noticed a sign that read: WHAT HELPS YOUTH HELPS UNION. It was as if the sign had been posted just for him. *Yes, indeed, what helps my sons will help me.*

It had been only a few weeks since George was placed with the Hirschfelds. As he passed through the tree-lined streets of Union Township toward Caldwell Avenue, Walter admired the quiet and predominantly German suburban community and thought, *Maybe I can find a way to live in this neighborhood too? It's certainly many steps above where I'm living in that boardinghouse in Newark.*

Anne hummed to herself as she navigated the streets toward the Rothblooms' home. What luck that she had been able to find a placement for both boys together. Harry Rothbloom, a Russian Jew from Kiev, had fought in the Bolshevik Revolution, and Rose, his wife, was an American Jew of Romanian descent. Only last week, Rose, Harry, and their daughter, Cindy, had gone to the orphanage seeking a little blond-haired girl they had seen on a previous visit. When they arrived a staff member mentioned that there were two young brothers from Vienna who were hard to place because of their mixed race and older ages. Watching the two boys holding on to each other as if their little world would fall apart if they were separated, the Rothblooms started playing with them and quickly fell in love. They didn't have the heart to let the boys be separated, and so they agreed to foster both Harry and Charles.

Rose Rothbloom greeted everyone with a warm smile. Her husband and daughter had brought out drinks and cookies in anticipation of their arrival. The Rothblooms' sons, Edwin and Jerome, were away, serving in the army in the Korean War.

Anne Darling spoke first. "Mr. and Mrs. Rothbloom, I cannot tell you how pleased we all are at the Agency that you've agreed to provide a home for both boys. It's all that anyone at my office has been talking about." Before Walter could begin his prepared speech of "trouble and woe," she hurried on, addressing the two boys. "Harry and Charles, these nice people are going to take good care of you."

Rose bent down and pressed the boys' expectant faces to her chest, then handed each boy a gift. They eagerly tore the paper off and opened the boxes; inside were two miniature racing cars with metal wheels that turned when the boys brushed them hard against the carpeted floor.

As Anne expected, Walter launched into an embellished story that she knew had been crafted to elicit the Rothblooms' sympathy. After rambling on for a bit, he finished with: "I'm sorry, but I have only two paper bags containing all the boys' belongings."

Mrs. Rothbloom interrupted the rhythm of his speech. "You have nothing to worry about. We'll get the boys some clothing and more toys. I can see that they enjoy playing with the cars. Cars are always a big hit with boys and take their minds off the pain of separation from their parents in the beginning."

"How kind of you. Now, where was I? Oh yes, the Nazis forced my family to flee from Vienna to Shanghai, where life was horrible. There was no food and it was dirty, but it's where I met their mother, Chao Chen, whom I lovingly cared for along with our three young children. You know I have another son, don't you?"

Mr. Rothbloom nodded. "Yes. I was told he is staying with the Hirschfelds over in Newark."

"Yes, thanks to Anne Darling. *Gott sei Dank*. Well, now I am a widower."

Mr. Rothbloom interrupted, "I thought, Mr. Kolber, that your wife is living in Vienna, although the reasons for her remaining there were not explained to us."

"Unfortunately, your information is incorrect. She passed away. It's very hard to talk about." Walter's face reddened as he changed the subject. "You're all wonderful, fortunate people. You are so lucky to be Americans. I hope someday to earn my U.S. citizenship, but first I have to find work."

"What is it you do? Perhaps we can help you," Mr. Rothbloom offered.

Rose added, "Mr. Kolber, I recall reading that you are a trained concert violinist."

"You are correct, but I don't seem to be having much luck with that just yet." Walter paused for a moment and looked around their house. "I can see that you live in a lovely neighborhood, a neighborhood not unlike the one where I lived in Vienna when I was a young boy so many years ago. That is, before Hitler ruined everything. But I ought not to dwell on the past. I promise that, after I find a job, I intend to work day and night so that I'll have enough money to one day bring my sons back to me. It pains me to no end to have to give them up, but at least I know that they'll be well cared for in your beautiful house."

Mrs. Rothbloom was feeling uneasy. "Mr. Kolber, our circumstances mean nothing. What is important is the love we have for your two enchanting boys."

"How right you are. That goes without saying. Thank you for agreeing to care for them until I can do so on my own. And I promise that I'll repay you in whatever way I can. If you don't mind, I will visit often—and the next time I'll bring my violin."

Cindy was delighted. "As you can see, we have a piano here. Our family loves music."

Rose continued, "We're a large family, and the boys will fit in perfectly. The school is close by and there are many children in the neighborhood I'm sure will be eager to be friends with them."

Harry Rothbloom said proudly, "You should know, Walter, that in this home we keep kosher, and we are active members of Temple Beth Shalom."

Walter turned to Mrs. Rothbloom. "I'm delighted to hear that you think my sons will be accepted by the other children. I hope you're right. After all, they are half-Chinese, and there are mean-spirited people who aren't as open-minded as you are. In fact, there are Jews who don't consider my children Jewish. Their mother never converted, although we talked about it—but we couldn't find a rabbi willing to tutor her."

Anne Darling rolled her eyes as Rose replied, "You have nothing to worry about, Mr. Kolber. As you yourself pointed out, this is a beautiful and safe neighborhood."

Cindy had already taken the boys out to the backyard. When Walter made an attempt to say goodbye, they hardly noticed.

Leaving the Rothblooms' home, Anne Darling gripped the wheel of the car to keep herself from pointing out the lies that Walter had told about his wife's death. But what was the point of bringing this up to Walter? All she cared about was that the three boys were appropriately placed with the Hirschfelds and Rothblooms and both families could be counted on to take good care of the motherless children.

Pulling out a pack of cigarettes, Walter asked Anne Darling, "Mind if I smoke?"

"Roll the window down if you must. It's really a filthy habit."

"You women, you're all the same."

Anne bristled. "Why don't you try to break yourself of the habit? Cigarettes are expensive."

"Maybe you should mind your own business, Miss Darling."

In her report to the Agency, Anne gave her portrayal of Walter Kolber:

> He is proving himself to be a fabricator who spins a good yarn. But eventually he will be caught in the web of his own lies. In my opinion, it is in the best interest of Harry, Charles, and George that they be kept in foster care for the foreseeable future.

chapter 70

Journey's End

Chao Chen stripped her bed at the Steinhoff Psychiatric Hospital and folded the linens. Taking a rag from the bedside table, she dusted the bed frame, the top of the table, and the mirror frame, making sure that the room was spotless. Just to be sure that she had packed everything that belonged to her, she looked inside each drawer and then closed them. She left the bar of soap lying in the dish for the next patient or for the custodians who would be cleaning her room after she left.

She had saved a piece of paper and an envelope for this day. Taking them out of the desk drawer, she turned on the lamp and sat quietly for a few minutes to gather her thoughts. The ticking of the clock brought back memories of periods when she thought the clock was giving her messages or the ticking was so loud she felt as if her head would split open. But all that was over for now. She picked up her pen and began to write:

14 June 1962
Dear Dr., Leder:

I am finally resolved to leave the hospital. I have not heard from Walter since he abandoned me ten years ago, taking my sons with him. I so believed him when he promised he'd come back for me, but I have given up hope of ever seeing him or my children again. I wish I knew where they were, but my husband has never written and I have no way of finding them.

As you know, I tried leaving the hospital five years ago, but after I got on the train for Shanghai, my mind could only see my boys searching these halls calling for me. I thought, how can they ever find me if I'm not here? And if I'm not here, they will think I don't love them anymore. So, my heart made me get off the train in Prague to return here and wait for them. Thank you for understanding that I needed to do this.

Today I feel like a reluctant little bird finally pushed out of its nest to fly on its own. I have been away from home for so many years that I do not know what awaits me in Shanghai. But with the love and help of my brothers, perhaps I'll make a new life. No matter where I am, I will always dream of the day when I see my children at last.

Gratefully,
Chao Chen Kolber

Chao Chen pressed the blue hand-knitted sweater and lederhosen that Harry and Charles had once worn to her cheek, then lovingly placed them on top of her few belongings. So that it would not crack, she tucked her silver hand mirror between the folds of her clothes. As the latches of her suitcase clicked loudly shut, she heard the ringing of the St. Leopold Church bell across the courtyard on the grounds of the hospital. As she parted the curtains one last time, she saw the taxicab turning into the driveway, its wheels splashing through the rain puddles and the nuns hurrying past so as not to get wet.

Before leaving her room, she gathered together the white handkerchiefs she had painstakingly embroidered with flowers, butterflies, and birds. Her early attempts had been rather crude, but the handkerchiefs she decorated in the last year showed a certain skill and artistry. She hoped that the staff would understand that they were meant as simple tokens of her deep appreciation for all that they had done for her. She put the handkerchiefs in a paper bag and tied it with a red satin ribbon that she had hidden under a chair cushion so that no one would take it. Things had a way of disappearing in the hospital.

Taking a vial out of her pocketbook, she filled a glass with water and counted out two tablets, which she hastily swallowed to calm her nerves. She breathed deeply, waiting for the medication to take effect. Leaning over the sink, she stared at herself in the mirror. She barely recognized the face reflected back at her, that of a forty-four-year-old woman with streaks of gray in her black hair and eyes that had once sparkled at the possibilities of life but now wounded by sadness. Sighing, she picked up her suitcase and paper bag. Passing by rooms with locked doors, she looked ahead at the arched doorway at the end of the corridor, and beyond it, at the gates of the hospital that were swung wide open.

Chao Chen stood under the portico with Dr. Leder, who held an umbrella for her. Members of the staff gathered around her to say their goodbyes. Chao Chen was embarrassed by all this attention, but she forced herself to hand Dr. Leder the letter and paper bag. She spoke so quietly that everyone had to lean in to hear her. "You have all been my family, and this has been my home, a place I have felt safe and protected from the outside world. But now I am ready to leave. I do not know what awaits me, but does anyone? I have both prayed for and feared this day. I hope I have enough courage left in me to carry me home."

Dr. Leder placed a reassuring hand on Chao Chen's shoulder. "All of us will miss you, and we wish you the best of luck. *Auf Wiedersehen*, dear Frau Kolber."

Before stepping into the waiting taxicab, Chao Chen looked into Dr. Leder's eyes and asked, "Will you do me a favor, Dr. Leder?"

"What is it?"

"If Walter and my sons write to me or come looking for me, will you tell them where I am?"

Dr. Leder nodded, then opened the door of the taxicab. Chao Chen hesitated for a moment, and then she stepped into the darkness. As the taxicab passed through the gates of the hospital, Chao Chen turned around and waved goodbye through the rear window.

The staff stood in the rain, holding on to a final glimpse of Chao Chen Kolber.

Epilogue

1972

Dr. Leder took a gulp of hot coffee to jolt himself awake. His desk was covered with paperwork. Besides reviewing the monthly patient reports, he needed to prepare a list of duties that the associate director of the hospital would need to fulfill during his absence. He and his wife were leaving the next day for a much-needed two-week vacation in Italy. He was feeling the effects of his age. Other physicians were already retired at sixty-six, but he was dedicated to the Steinhoff Psychiatric Hospital and kept up a hectic pace, taking care of his patients, many of whom had been under his care for years. The hospital was his baby, and in his mind, no one else could or should be at its helm, at least not while he still had his wits about him.

Talking to himself, he said aloud, "All right. Next Tuesday at the staff meeting we will discuss revising our intake procedure."

Hilde, the hospital's receptionist, stuck her head into his office. "Dr. Leder, I hate to interrupt you, but perhaps you should come out here. I have some people with the last name Kolber asking questions about a patient who, it seems, was here a long time ago. By any chance do you remember a woman from China named Chao Chen Kolber?"

A sad smile came over his face as the doctor instantly replied, "Please tell them to wait right there. I'll be out in just a minute. In the meantime, ask them for some identification. We can't have strangers investigating patient histories, can we?"

Hilde blushed. "I hadn't thought of that, Dr. Leder. They seemed so genuinely concerned and honest."

"Well, in our business, you can't be too careful."

Dr. Leder opened a drawer of a large mahogany cabinet brimming full of patient files. He thumbed through the Ks, and with little difficulty he found a five-inch-thick folder marked: KOLBER, CHAO CHEN February 10, 1952 – June 14, 1962. *Of course I remember her! Hers was one of the most complex cases I ever treated: a combination of postpartum depression, bipolar disorder, and schizophrenia.* He recalled the first day she arrived at the hospital. She was four months pregnant. *And that miserable bastard husband of hers...* The doctor's memories of Chao Chen Kolber were still vivid in his mind after all these years.

Carrying the file under his arm, he took Hilde aside before greeting the young couple who sat in the reception room. "Well?"

Hilde whispered, "Charles Kolber—that's the gentleman's name—showed me his U.S. passport. It indicates that he was born here in Vienna. Does that make sense?"

"Yes. And who is the attractive blond woman with him?"

"His bride, Christa. They are here on their honeymoon. She's originally from Germany."

"Thank you." Dr. Leder put the file down on Hilde's desk. "Hold on to this."

He then walked over to the couple. "So, Hilde tells me that you are inquiring about Chao Chen Kolber."

Charles was quick to respond, "Yes, Dr. Leder. She is my mother. We were telling your receptionist that we are here on our honeymoon. After doing some research, thanks to Christa being able to speak German, we heard that my mother was treated at this hospital. Can you help us? Can you give us any information? As you can surmise from my questions, neither I nor my brothers, Harry and George, ever had any information."

"I can confirm that Chao Chen was indeed treated at this very hospital."

Charles's eyes widened. "What else can you tell us?"

The doctor hesitated. "Mr. Kolber, I remember her very well. I certainly recall that she gave birth to a boy shortly after she arrived." He opened Chao Chen's file and turned over one page after another. "Ah, here it is. My records show that Michael was born to her on July 16, 1952 and was adopted immediately thereafter."

"So we have a brother?" Charles was surprised and confused.

"It seems that you do. But I have no other information because he was adopted." Then the doctor looked up. "I am sorry to tell you that you missed your mother by about ten years. She was released from the hospital in June of 1962. I can tell you that, in the ten years she was under my care, she never stopped hoping and praying that she would see her children again. I remember coming into her room to find her sitting by the window, holding your baby clothes. It was so sad."

Charles was stunned. "But we were told she died right after George was born. This is a miracle, just hearing about her!"

Adjusting his glasses, Dr. Leder said, "I may have something for you and your brothers." Continuing to thumb the file, he said, "Ah, here it is. It's a letter to the hospital staff from her brother, Fu-Ti, thanking us for taking care of her and informing us that she arrived safely. She traveled all the way back to China by train. You can see the envelope has a Shanghai return address, and it's in English, no less." Handing over the letter he said, "I certainly hope you find your mother—and perhaps your brother Michael too."

1981

The annoying ringing coming from the fax machine at the *Jewish News* wouldn't stop. Charlie Baumohl, the paper's editor, was irritated that Marion had once again forgotten to put paper in the fax machine, and as usual she had left for lunch promptly at noon. She was a hopeless case. He wasn't sure why he didn't just fire her; but, he reasoned, she had been around for so long that, despite her failings, he had to admit he relied on her. What did they call it that she so expertly displayed? Institutional memory? She could remember the smallest detail of what happened ten years ago, but she couldn't remember to refill the paper in the fax machine. Maybe it was time for him to retire, but life at the *Jewish News* was always full of surprises, and that's what kept him going.

Worrying that the fax transmission would be lost, he rushed to the machine behind the clerk's desk and quickly loaded the roll of thermal paper. Last week had been a short week because of the Thanksgiving holiday, and so he had only three business days to get this Thursday's edition out and was feeling the pressure. He replenished the supply of paper but not in time to receive the fax. He just hoped that whoever was sending the message would see the *"Error in Delivery"* message and try again. He still needed one more story to fill the pages, and he always needed more ads.

Rushing back to his desk, he suddenly saw a stranger standing in the doorway staring at him. Clearly the man must have been lost, since few outsiders ever needed to step into the paper's office in East Orange, New Jersey. Now acting as a clerk, he asked, "Sir, what can I do for you?"

The young man looked disheveled and wore ill-fitting clothes but seemed friendly enough. In broken English, he asked, "Maybe you can help me?"

"I'll try. What is it you need?"

"I'd like to put – how do you call it? – an ad…advice, or maybe notice in your newspaper."

The editor-in-chief grabbed a piece of paper and a pencil. Normally this would have been someone else's job, but the copy room was empty because everyone had left for lunch. "We haven't put the paper to bed yet. It comes out on November 26 and so I should just be able to get your ad in."

The man replied, "Thank you. I wait a long time to do this."

"Okay. What would you like it to say, sir?"

Taking a note out of his pocket, the man read his message aloud: "Looking for my brothers, Harry, Charles, and George Kolber, born in Shanghai and Vienna, now living somewhere in New York or New Jersey, maybe. Your brother, Michael, the fourth son of Chao Chen and Walter Kolber, is here in New York." He included his phone number in the Bronx.

Afterword

Chao Chen returned to Shanghai in 1962, where she lived under her brother Fu-Ti's care. While she improved emotionally, she never overcame her depression and constantly thought of her children. Nephritis took her life on September 29, 1983. The news of her death came to her sons just as their travel plans were being finalized to visit her later that same year. Chao Chen always retained her babies' clothes that Walter had left behind in Austria. They were placed with her when she was cremated.

As soon as he got to America, Walter Kolber began the legal process of divorcing Chao Chen. The Austrian court refused to grant a divorce, concluding his wife was under duress and therefore was not competent to make that decision. Walter nevertheless continued with his life in America and lied about his marital status, telling anyone who would listen that his wife had died.

In fact, Walter married and divorced other women, and he fathered a daughter, Regina. He had numerous relationships, and each involved some physical and/or mental abuse. He died a painful death from lymphoma on September 13, 2001. He only attempted to contact his sons once asking them for money in his later years. He died penniless and was buried by the state of Florida. No one knows what happened to the Lowendall violin.

In April 1955, journalist Fritz Jensen was covering the first Premier of the People's Republic of China, his personal friend, Zhou Enlai. Jensen, along with eight other Chinese dignitaries, was killed in an assassination attempt on the Premier when the wrong plane was blown up by the assassins.

Dr. Fritz Jensen and his wife, Wu-An, always treated Michael as their own child, leading him to believe they were his biological parents. In 1980 Michael got a student visa to come to America. Just before he left, Wu-An explained the story of his adoption and tearfully told him to look for his Kolber family in the U.S.A. Wu-An, whom Michael always considered his mother, died in Beijing in 2012.

After posting a notice in the *Jewish News*, Michael located his brothers and met them for the first time in December 1981. Tech-savvy, Michael found a home in America, got married, and fathered a daughter, Maria. He currently lives in Texas.

In 1993, Josef Kolber met his grandsons Charles, George, and their families for the first time in Israel. He was ninety-nine years old. He died just months later.

Lilly Kolber and her husband Joseph (David) Ozer left for Israel in 1949 with their children Mischa (8) and Judy (5). In 1955 they started a life in Chile only to return to Israel ten years later. Joseph died in 1987. Lilly died in 2008.

Harry Kolber, who grew up in Union, New Jersey, served in the U.S. Navy and later worked for the postal service. He was also a ballroom dance instructor. He died in 2012.

Charles Kolber grew up in Union, New Jersey and was an engineer for Fortune 500 companies and later operated a family-owned business with his wife, Christa. He and his wife have three children and eight grandchildren.

George Kolber grew up in Newark, New Jersey and found successes in retail, real estate and finance. He and his wife, Vita, have two children and one grandchild, and they are involved in numerous philanthropies, including Holocaust awareness.

Family Photos

Kolber Family Circa 1936 (left to right) Eva, Dolfie, Lilly, Walter, Josef

Chen Family Circa 1933 (left to right) Fu-Ti, Fu-She, Chao Chen

Notes and References

Endnotes

1 "German Mobs' Vengeance on Jews," *The Telegraph*, November 11, 1938. http://www.telegraph.co.uk/history/britain-at-war/3418286/German-mobs-vengeance-on-Jews-Nov-11-1938.html
2 David Kranzler, *Japanese, Nazis and Jews: The Jewish Refugee Community of Shanghai, 1938-1945* (Hoboken: KTAV Publishing House, Inc., 1988), 454.
3 Ernest Heppner, *Shanghai Refuge: A Memoir of World War II Jewish Ghetto*, 96 ff. University of Nebraska Press; Reprint edition (August 1, 1995).
4 Audrey Friedman Marcus and Rena Krasno, *Survival in Shanghai*, 78-79.
5 Ibid, 113.
6 Berl Falbaum, ed., *Shanghai Remembered*, 134.
7 Clifton Daniel ed., *20th Century: Day by Day* (Dorling Kindersley, 2000), 627.

Nonfiction

Bacon, Ursula. *Shanghai Diary: A Young Girl's Journey from Hitler's Hate to War-Torn China*. Milwaukie: M Press, 2004.

Barilich, Eva. *Fritz Jensen, Arzt an vielen Fronten: Biografische Texte zur Geschichte der österreichischen Arbeiterbewegung* [Fritz Jensen: Doctor on Many Fronts]. Globus-Verlag, Vienna, 1991.

Berenbaum, Michael, ed. *A Promise to Remember: The Holocaust in the Words and Voices of Its Survivors*. Boston: Bulfinch Press, 2003.

Bonyhady, Tim. *Good Living Street: Portrait of a Patron Family, Vienna 1900.* New York: Pantheon, 2011.

Bostridge, Ian. *Schubert's Winter Journey: Anatomy of an Obsession.* New York: Alfred A. Knopf, 2015.

Boyle, Nicholas. *German Literature: A Very Short Introduction.* Oxford: Oxford University Press, 2008.

Bullock, Alan. *Hitler: A Study in Tyranny.* New York: Harper Torchbooks, 1964.

Chapman, Patricia Luce. *Tea on the Great Wall: An American Girl in War-Torn China.* Hong Kong: Earnshaw Books, Ltd., 2015.

Chen, Jian (curator). *Jewish Refugees and Shanghai.* Shanghai: Shanghai Jewish Refugees Museum, 2013.

Chen, Yi Ming. *The World of Mortals/Dreamland.* Hong Kong: Sotheby's Gallery, 2015.

Clare, George. *Last Waltze in Vienna*, 2nd revised edition. Pan Macmillan, May 4, 2007.

Coble, Parks M. *Chinese Capitalists in Japan's New Order: The Occupied Lower Yangzi, 1937-1945.* Berkeley: University of California Press, 2003.

Cornebise, Alfred Emile. *The Shanghai "Stars and Stripes": Witness to the Transition to Peace, 1945-1946.* London: McFarland & Company, Inc., 2010.

Cowen, Ida. *Jews in Remote Corners of the World.* Englewood Cliffs: Prentice-Hall, Inc., 1971.

Daniel, Clifton, ed. *20th Century Day by Day: The Ultimate Record of Our Times.* London: Dorling Kindersley Limited, 2000.

De Sousa, Ronald. *Love: A Very Short Introduction.* Oxford: Oxford University Press, 2015.

De Waal, Edmund. *The Hare with Amber Eyes: A Hidden Inheritance.* New York: Picador, 2010.

Earnshaw, Graham. *Tales of Old Shanghai.* Hong Kong: Earnshaw Books, Ltd., 2012.

Eber, Irene, ed., trans. *Voices from Shanghai: Jewish Exiles in Wartime China.* Chicago: The University of Chicago Press, 2008.

Eisfelder, Horst. *Chinese Exile: My Years in Shanghai and Nanking, 1938-1947.* Melbourne, Australia: Self-published, 1992.

Falbaum, Berl, ed. *Shanghai Remembered: Stories of Jews Who Escaped to Shanghai from Nazi Europe.* Royal Oak: Momentum Books, L.L.C., 2005.

Felton, Mark. *Japan's Gestapo: Murder, Mayhem and Torture in Wartime Asia.* South Yorkshire: Pen & Sword Military, 2009.

Field, Andrew David. *Shanghai's Dancing World: Cabaret Culture and Urban Politics, 1919-1954.* The Chinese University Press, 2011.

Fritzsche, Peter. *An Iron Wind.* New York: Basic Books, 2016.

Goldstein, Phyllis. *A Convenient Hatred: The History of Antisemitism.* Brookline: Facing History and Ourselves, 2012.

Hahn, Emily. *China to Me.* New York: Open Road Integrated Media, Inc. 2014.

Harmsen, Peter. *Shanghai 1937: Stalingrad on the Yangtze.* Philadelphia: Casemate Publishers, 2013.

Harrison, Henrietta. *The Man Awakened from Dreams: One Man's Life in a North China Village, 1857-1942.* Stanford: Stanford University Press, 2005.

Heppner, Ernest. *Shanghai Refuge: A Memoir of World War II Jewish Ghetto.* University of Nebraska Press; Reprint edition (August 1, 1995).

Hibbard, Peter. *All About Shanghai and Environs: The 1934-35 Standard Guide Book.* Hong Kong: Earnshaw Books, 2008.

Jackson, Beverley. *Shanghai Girl Gets All Dressed Up.* Berkeley: Ten Speed Press, 2005.

Kaplan, Vivian Jeanette. *Ten Green Bottles: The True Story of One Family's Journey from War-torn Austria to the Ghettos of Shanghai.* New York: St. Martin's Press, 2002.

Kranzler, David. *Japanese Nazis & Jews: The Jewish Refugee Community of Shanghai, 1938-1945.* Hoboken: KTAV Publishing House, Inc., 1988.

Leck, Greg. *Captives of Empire: The Japanese Internment of Allied Civilians in China and Hong Kong, 1941-1945.* Shady Press, 2006.

Lee, Leo Ou-Fan. *Shanghai Modern: The Flowering of a New Urban Culture in China, 1930-1945.* Cambridge: Harvard University Press, 1999.

Marcus, Audrey Friedman and Rena Krasno. *Survival in Shanghai: The Journals of Fred Marcus, 1939-1949.* Berkeley: Pacific View Press, 2002.

Martineau, Lisa. *Caught in a Mirror: Reflections of Japan.* London: Macmillan, 1993.

Mayer, Hanns Chaim, a Holocaust survivor and essayist now known as Jean Améry.

Miyazaki, Ichisada. *China's Examination Hell: The Civil Service Examinations of Imperial China.* Translated by Conrad Schirokauer. New Haven; Yale University Press, 1981.

Neville-Hadley, Peter. *China: The Silk Routes*. London: Cadogan Books, Plc., 1997.

O'Connor, Anne-Marie. *The Lady in Gold: The Extraordinary Tale of Gustav Klimt's Masterpiece, Portrait of Adele Bloch-Bauer*. New York: Alfred A. Knopf, 2013.

Peng, Xiancheng and Wei Peng. *Two Generations: Ink Art*. Hong Kong: Sotheby's Gallery, 2015.

Pyrah, Carolyn, ed. *Eyewitness Travel: Vienna*. London: Dorling Kindersley Limited, 2014.

Ram, Uri, ed. *The Jews of Kaifeng: Chinese Jews on the Banks of the Yellow River*. Tel Aviv: Beth Hatefutsoth, the Nahum Goldmann Museum of the Jewish Diaspora, 1984.

Rilke, Rainer Maria. *Letters on Life*. Translated by Ulrich Baer. New York: The Modern Library, 2005

Ristaino, Marcia Reynders. *Port of Last Resort: The Diaspora Communities of Shanghai*. Stanford: Stanford University Press, 2001.

Robbins, Michael W., ed. *MHQ: The Quarterly Journal of Military History* (Autumn 2015).

Sebald, W. G. *On the Modern History of Destruction*, reprint ed. Translated by Anthea Bell. Modern Library, February 17, 2004.

Severy, Merle, ed. *Great Religions of the World*. Washington D.C.: National Geographic Society, 1971.

Solomon, Burt, ed. "World War I: How the Great War Made the Modern World." Special commemorative issue, *The Atlantic* (Summer 2014).

Speer, Albert. *Inside the Third Reich*. Translated by Clara Winston and Richard Winston. New York: Macmillan, 1970.

Thompson, Hugh and Kathryn Lane, eds. *Eyewitness Travel: China*. London: Dorling Kindersley Limited, 2014.

Tobias, Sigmund. *Strange Haven: A Jewish Childhood in Wartime Shanghai*. Urbana: University of Illinois Press, 2009.

Tsao, Christine Ching. *Shanghai Bride: Her Tumultuous Life's Journey to the West*. Hong Kong: Hong Kong University Press, 2005.

Xu, Meihong and Larry Engelmann. *Daughter of China: A True Story of Love and Betrayal*. New York: John Wiley & Sons, Inc., 1999.

Wiernick, Jankiel. *A Year in Treblinka: An Inmate Who Escaped Tells the Day-to-Day Facts on One Year of His Torturous Experiences*. New York, New York: General Jewish Workers' Union of Poland, 1945. www.zchor.org/treblink/wiernik.

Yeh, Wen-Hsin. *Shanghai Splendor: A Cultural History, 1843-1845*. Berkeley: University of California Press, 2007.

Yeh, Wen-Hsin. *Shanghai Splendor: Economic Sentiments and the Making of Modern China, 1843-1949*. Berkeley: University of California Press, 2008.

Zweig, Stefan. *The World of Yesterday*. Translated by Anthea Bell. Lincoln: University of Nebraska Press, 2013.

FICTION

Baryakina, Elvira. *White Shanghai: A Novel of the Roaring Twenties in China*. Translated by Benjamin Kuttner and Anna Muzychka. London: Glagoslav Publications, 2013.

Baum, Vicki. *Shanghai '37*. Translated by Basil Creighton. Oxford: Oxford University Press, 1986.

Bomann, Corina. *The Moonlit Garden*. Translated by Alison Layland. Seattle: AmazonCrossing, 2016.

Chin, Pa. *Family*. Translated by Sidney Shapiro. Long Grove: Waveland Press, Inc., 1989.

Cummings, Alan, ed. *Haiku Love*. New York: The Overlook Press, 2013.

Döblin, Alfred. *The Three Leaps of Wang Lun*. Translated by C. D. Godwin. Hong Kong: The Chinese University Press, 1991.

Kalla, Daniel. *Rising Sun, Falling Shadow*. New York: Forge, 2013.

Kwan, Kevin. *China Rich Girlfriend*. New York: Doubleday, 2015.

Landau, Alexis. *The Empire of the Senses*. New York: Pantheon Books, 2014.

Mones, Nicole. *Night in Shanghai*. Boston: Mariner Books, 2014.

Mo, Yan. *Red Sorghum*. Translated by Howard Goldblatt. New York: Penguin Books, 1993.

Reeve, F. D., ed., trans. *An Anthology of Russian Plays*. New York: Vintage Books, 1961.

See, Lisa. *Shanghai Girls*. New York: Random House, 2009.

Shepard, Aaron. *Lady White Snake: A Tale from Chinese Opera*. USA: Pan Asian Publications, April 1, 2001. http://www.aaronshep.com/stories/062.html

Tallis, Frank. *A Death in Vienna*. New York: Grove Press, 2005.

Tong, Su. *Raise the Red Lantern*. Translated by Michael S. Duke. New York: Harper Perennial, 2004.

Xiao, Bai. *French Concession*. Translated by Jiang Chenxin. New York: HarperCollins, 2015.

Ying, Hong. *The Concubine of Shanghai*. Translated by Hong Liu. London: Marion Boyars, 2008.

Yuan, Haiwang, text and translation. "Lady Meng Jiang Wailed at the Great Wall." People.wku.edu, 2003. http://people.wku.edu/haiwang.yuan/China/tales/mengjiangnv.htm

Zhang, Henshui. *Shanghai Express*. Translated by William A. Lyell. Honolulu: University of Hawai'i Press, 1997.

ARTICLES

"1937 Battle of Shanghai, Japan's Brutal Attack on China." *War History Online,* December 15, 2013. http://www.warhistoryonline.com/war-articles/1937-battle-shanghai-japans-brutal-attack-china.html

Altman, Avraham and Irene Eber. "Flight to Shanghai, 1938-1940: The Larger Setting." *SHOAH Resource Center, The International School for Holocaust Studies,* Yad-Vashem Studies, Vol. 28, Jerusalem (2000): 51- 86. http://www.yadvashem.org/odot_pdf/Microsoft%20Word%20-%203234.pdf

"Antique Asian Furniture: Rare Carved Canopy Bed with Alcove from Zhejiang Province, China." http://www.silkroadcollection.com/rb1007x-antique-chinese-canopy-wedding-bed.html

"Architectural Wonders of Old Shanghai." http://toothpicnations.co.uk/my-blog/?p=14901

Bar-Elli, Gilead. "Beethoven: Piano and Violin Sonata in F op. 24 ('Spring')." *The Hebrew University of Jerusalem.* http://bar-elli.co.il/violinsonata5.pdf

"Battle of the Bulge: Facts, information and articles about Battle of the Bulge, a battle of World War II." HistoryNet.com. http://www.historynet.com/battle-of-the-bulge

Berenbaum, Michael. "Franklin Delano Roosevelt Was the Best." *Journal for the Study of Antisemitism,* Vol. 5, Issue 1, London: 2013: 313-322.

Berliner, Nancy. "Shanghai's Jews: Art, Architecture and Survival." March 4, 2010. Contemporary Jewish Museum video, 55:04. Posted March 26, 2010. https://www.youtube.com/watch?v=vY8PLsthnfs

Bernstein, Ignatz. *Jüdische Sprichwörter und Redensarten.* Warsaw: Im Kommission bei J. Kauffman in Frankfurt a.M., 1908. http://www.yiddish-wit.com/gallery/change.html

Bleifuss, Joel. "Shanghai in 1942." *News & Views,* September 25, 2007. http://www.focusfeatures.com/article/shanghai_in_1942

Bouchet, Ceil Miller. "In Transit: Q&A with Wm Cranley." *New York Times,* November 1, 2015.

Branton, Harry. "Speech by Harry Branton, Director, World ORT Union Austria Mission, on September 29th 1948 at the convention of the Austrian ORT Association in Vienna." *ORT and the Displaced Persons Camps.* http://dpcamps.ort.org/camps/austria/linz/

Boyd, John. "Displaced Persons Act of 1948." ImmigrationToTheUnitedStates.org. http://immigrationtounitedstates.org/464-displaced-persons-act-of-1948.html

"Butterfly Lovers." *Wikipedia,* last modified November 19, 2017. https://en.wikipedia.org/wiki/Butterfly_Lovers.

Chang, Wayne. "Ho Feng Shan: The 'Chinese Schindler' Who Saved Thousands of Jews." *CNN Edition,* July 24, 2015. http://www.cnn.com/2015/07/19/asia/china-jews-schindler-ho-feng-shan/

"Chinese Bamboo Culture." ChinaTravel.com. http://www.chinatravel.com/facts/chinese-bamboo-culture.htm

"The Chronology of the Jews of Shanghai from 1832 to the Present Day." *Jewish Communities of China.* http://www.jewsofchina.org/jewsofchina/Templates/showpage.asp?DBID=1&LNGID=1&TMID=84&FID=890

Clurman, Irene and Dan Ben-Canaan. "A Brief History of the Jews of Harbin: How a Manchurian Fishing Village Became a Railroad Town and a Haven for Jews." *JewishGen KehilaLinks,* 2007. http://kehilalinks.jewishgen.org/harbin/Brief_History.htm

Cochran, Sam. "Breguet Watches on Display in a New Exhibition." *Architectural Digest,* December 31, 2014: 44. http://www.architecturaldigest.com/story/breguet-watch-exhibit-san-francisco-article

Dangoor, Renée. "The Jews of Shanghai, speech given at TaÂ'ali, London, in October 1990." *The Scribe: Journal of Babylonian Jewry.* http://www.dangoor.com/Renee/memoirs.html

De Carle Sowerby, Arthur. "The Disposal of Shanghai's Waste Products." *Tales of Old China.* http://www.talesofoldchina.com/china-journal-august-1938/disposal-shanghais-waste-products

"December 13, 1916: Soldiers Perish in Avalanche as World War I Rages." *This Day in History.* http://www.history.com/this-day-in-history/soldiers-perish-in-avalanche-as-world-war-i-rages

"Displaced Persons Camp: Linz Area." *World ORT Austria,* Vienna: 1948: 13-14. http://dpcamps.ort.org/camps/austria/linz/

Djokan, Very Rev. Fr. "History of the Cathedral of St. Sava in New York." http://stsavanyc.org/history/

Ebeling, Richard. "The Great Chinese Inflation: Inflation Undermined Popular Support Against Communism." *Foundation for Economic Foundation,* July 5, 2010. https://fee.org/articles/the-great-chinese-inflation/

"Eric Moller: Rider's Empire; Miller's Fortune." *Racing Memories.* http://racingmemories.hk/hottopics/moller/

"Ernst vom Rath." *Wikipedia,* last modified August 26, 2014. https://en.wikipedia.org/wiki/Ernst_vom_Rath

Fein, Judie. "Jews in the Land of the Waltz: Jewish Vienna." *Chabad,* January 12, 2011. http://www.chabad.org/library/article_cdo/aid/1388659/jewish/Jews-in-the-Land-of-the-Waltz.htm

Field, Andrew David. "Dancing at the Majestic Hotel to 'Nighttime in Old Shanghai.'" *Shanghai Sojourns* (blog), February 10, 2011. http://shanghaisojourns.net/blog/2011/2/11/dancing-at-the-majestic-hotel-to-nightime-in-old-shanghai-by.html?rq=Whitey%20Smith

Friedman, Gabe. "How Jews Built New Life in 'Shanghai Ghetto.'" *Forward Thinking,* February 8, 2015. http://forward.com/opinion/214437/how-jews-built-new-life-in-shanghai-ghetto/

Gavin, Philip. "The Triumph of Hitler: Nazis Take Austria." *The History Place,* 2001. http://www.historyplace.com/worldwar2/triumph/tr-austria.htm

"German Mobs' Vengeance on Jews." *The Telegraph,* November 11, 1938. http://www.telegraph.co.uk/history/britain-at-war/3418286/German-mobs-vengeance-on-Jews-Nov-11-1938.html

Gewirtz, Julian and James McAuley. "Shanghai is One of the Greatest Jewish Cities Ever Constructed." *New Republic,* June 30, 2014. https://newrepublic.com/article/118477/shanghai-one-greatest-jewish-cities-ever-constructed

Gluckman, Ron. "The Ghosts of Shanghai." June 1997. http://www.gluckman.com/ShanghaiJewsChina.html

Goldstein, Jonathan. "Shanghai as a Mosaic and Microcosm of Eurasian Jewish Identities, 1850-1950." *Religions & Christianity in Today's China,* Vol. III, 2013, No. 2: 18-45. http://www.china-zentrum.de/fileadmin/downloads/rctc/2013-2/RCTC_2013-2.18-45_Goldstein_Shanghai_as_a_Mosaic_and_Microcosm_of_Eurasian_Jewish_Identities_1850%E2%80%931950.pdf

Gourgey, Percy, ed. "40 Years Ago: The Jews of Shanghai." *The Scribe: Journal of Babylonian Jewry,* October 1986, No. 20: 4. http://www.dangoor.com/TheScribe20.pdf

"Grace Nicholson: How It All Began." *USC Pacific Asia Museum.* https://uscpacificasiamuseum.wordpress.com/2013/03/08/grace-nicholson-how-it-all-began/

"Guangxu Emperor." *Wikipedia,* last modified December 11, 2016. https://en.wikipedia.org/wiki/Guangxu_Emperor

Ha-Levi, Elimelech David. "Ashkenazi Passover Customs and Traditions for Pesach." http://www.angelfire.com/pa2/passover/ashkenazicpassovercustoms.html

Harmon, Joanie. "Julie Kalmar: IS Student Curates Exhibit on Jewish Refugees in Shanghai." *& Ampersand UCLA,* November 25, 2013. https://ampersand.gseis.ucla.edu/julie-kalmar-is-student-curates-exhibit-on-jewish-refugees-in-shanghai/

Harmsen, Peter. "German Spies in China." *China in WW2,* October 9, 2016. http://www.chinaww2.com/2016/10/09/german-spies-in-china-1/

Henken, John. "About the Program: Ludwig van Beethoven." *Performances Magazine,* Los Angeles Philharmonic, Perlman in Recital, January 24, 2017: 2.

Heyman, Stephen. "Freud's City, From Couch to Cafés." *New York Times,* Travel, August 31, 2014.

"The Holocaust: Timeline of Jewish Persecution, 1932-1945." *Jewish Virtual Library.* http://www.jewishvirtuallibrary.org/jsource/Holocaust/chron.html

"Horst-Wessel-Lied." *Wikipedia,* last modified March 7, 2017. https://en.wikipedia.org/wiki/Horst-Wessel-Lied

"Israel's Messenger." *Wikipedia,* last modified October 27, 2016. https://en.wikipedia.org/wiki/Israel's_Messenger

"Italian Front (World War I)." *Wikipedia,* last modified December 13, 2016. https://en.wikipedia.org/wiki/Italian_Front_(World_War_I)

"Jacob Schiff: National Loans." *Wikipedia,* last modified February 9, 2017. https://en.wikipedia.org/wiki/Jacob_Schiff#National_loans

Jamieson, Amber. "Song Plays On: Holocaust Survivor's Violin a Gift to Bronx Girl." *New York Post,* Metro, June 7, 2015. http://nypost.com/2015/06/07/holocaust-survivors-violin-plays-on-in-hands-of-13-year-old-girl/

The Jewish News, November 26, 1981 (East Orange, New Jersey, now Whippany, New Jersey).

"Jiangsu." *Wikipedia,* last modified December 23, 2016. https://en.wikipedia.org/wiki/Jiangsu

Kadosh, Sara. "Encyclopedia: Laura Margolis Jarblum." *Jewish Women's Archive,* March 1, 2009. https://jwa.org/encyclopedia/article/jarblum-laura-margolis

Kanagaratnam, Tina. "Columbia Country Club." *Historic Shanghai,* February 22, 2015. http://www.historic-shanghai.com/columbia-country-club/

Kranzler, David and James R. Ross. "Tribute to the Artists: Their Talent and Devotion Helped Us to Survive." Archives of Gerhard Gottschalk. https://archive.is/SURe6

"Kristallnacht: A Nationwide Pogrom." *United States Holocaust Memorial Museum,* encyclopedia last updated June 20, 2014. https://www.ushmm.org/wlc/en/article.php?ModuleId=10005201

"Kristallnacht." *Wikipedia,* last modified January 3, 2017. https://en.wikipedia.org/wiki/Kristallnacht

"Label Resource: Bernhard Altmann." *Vintage Fashion Guild* (July 5, 2010). http://vintagefashionguild.org/label-resource/bernhard-altmann/

Laqueur, Walter. "The Riegner Cable, and the Knowing Failure of the West to Act During the Shoah." *Tablet Magazine* (August 10, 2015). http://www.tabletmag.com/jewish-arts-and-culture/books/192421/riegner-cable-shoah

Larson, Parker Bowie. "Most Wanted." *Architectural Digest,* Shopping, December 31, 2014: 50.

Levy, Raphael. "12,000 Refugees in Shanghai Depend on JDC, UNRRA Aid, Jewish Army Chaplain Reports." *Joint Distribution Committee* (June 21, 1946). http://archives.jdc.org/assets/documents/shanghai_twelve-thousand-refugees-in-shanghai.pdf

Lowenstein, Jonathan. "The Journey of a Lifetime: My Grandmother's Escape on the Trans-Siberian Railway." *Telaviv1* (April, 26, 2010). http://www.telaviv1.org.il/2010/04/journey-of-lifetime-my-grandmother.html

"Lwow Pogrom (1918)." *Wikipedia,* last modified November 24, 2016. https://en.wikipedia.org/wiki/Lw%C3%B3w_pogrom_(1918)

Lustig, Mordechai. "Ghetto of Nowy Sacz under German Occupation." Translated by William Leibner. *Jewish Gen* (June 2006). http://kehilalinks.jewishgen.org/Nowy_Sacz/ghetto.htm

Lyons, Erica. "Laura Margolis in the Spotlight: Portrait of a Heroine in Shanghai." *Asian Jewish Life,* Issue 8 (January 2012). https://issuu.com/asianjewishlife/docs/ajl-issue8-whole-bis-1

Margolis, Laura L. "Race Against Time in Shanghai." *Survey Graphic: The Magazine of Social Interpretation* (March 1944).

Meacham, Jon. "Opinion: Which Date Should Live in Infamy?" *New York Times*, November 1, 2015.

Meyer, Maisie J. "Baghdadi Jews in Early Shanghai." *The Sino-Judaic Institute*. http://www.sino-judaic.org/index.php?page=shanghai_history

Miller, Tom. "The 1902 Arlington Hotel, Nos. 18-20 West 25th Street." *Daytonian in Manhattan* (August 14, 2015). http://daytoninmanhattan.blogspot.com/2015/08/the-1902-arlington-hotel-nos-18-20-west.html

"The Nanking Massacre." B-29s-over-korea.com, 3. http://b-29s-over-korea.com/Nanking-Massacre/index3.html

"Nanking Massacre." *Wikipedia,* last modified December 21, 2016. https://en.wikipedia.org/wiki/Nanking_Massacre

"Nazi Shanghai." *The Allies & the Neutral States: China at War 1895-1949* (December 17, 2008). http://forum.axishistory.com/viewtopic.php?t=147093

"Nazis Smash, Loot and Burn Jewish Shops and Temples until Goebbels Calls a Halt." *New York Times,* November 11, 1938.

Oestreich, James R. "On the Sinuous Course of a Classic Immortal Love." *New York Times,* Arts, September 5, 2015: 6. https://www.nytimes.com/2015/09/05/arts/music/review-zhang-huoding-makes-american-debut-in-two-operas.html?_r=0

Pan, Guang. "Shanghai: A Haven for Holocaust Victims." *The Holocaust and the United Nations Outreach Programme*. http://www.un.org/en/holocaustremembrance/docs/pdf/chapter6.pdf

Pine, Dan. "China's Jewish Dynasty: Local Jews Recall a Childhood in the Far East." *JWeekly.com* (February 25, 2010). http://www.jweekly.com/article/full/41505/chinas-jewish-dynasty-local-jews-recall-a-childhood-in-the-far-east/

"Proclamation of Restricted Zone in Shanghai for Refugees." Courtesy of Eric Goldstaub, United States Holocaust Memorial Museum. https://www.ushmm.org/wlc/en/media_da.php?ModuleId=0&MediaId=5282

"Profiles: Laura Margolis Jarblum." *Jewish Women's Archive.* https://jwa.org/people/jarblum-laura

Qiao, Michelle. "Demolished Synagogue Reflects Strong Ties to Jewish Community." *Ideal Shanghai* (April 25, 2014). http://www.idealshanghai.com/focus/2532/

Ray, Milton S. "Winter Birds of Shanghai." *Bulletin of the Cooper Ornithological Club*, published by the American Ornithological Society (1899).

Sessions, Debbie. "What Did Women Wear in the 1930s?" *Vintage Dancer* (April 10, 2014). http://vintagedancer.com/1930s/women-1930s-fashion/

Shabi, Aviva. "Baghdadi Jews in Shanghai." *The Scribe: Journal of Babylonian Jewry* (1992). http://www.dangoor.com/72page34.html

"Shanghai, A City for Jews in China." *Haruth Communications.* http://haruth.com/jw/China/Kosher%20in%20land%20of%20Peking%20Duck_files/JewishHistoryChina.htm

"Shanghai Ghetto." *Wikipedia,* last modified December 29, 2016. https://en.wikipedia.org/wiki/Shanghai_Ghetto

"Shanghai Municipal Council 1936-37, in front of war memorial." *Visualising China: 1850-1950.* http://visualisingchina.net/#hpc-bi-s0815

Shillony, Ben-Ami. "Shanghai Sanctuary: Chinese and Japanese Policy toward European Jewish Refugees During World War II by Gao Bei." *The Journal of Japanese Studies* (January 2014).

Stanton, Craig (archivist). "Famous Shanghai World War II Personalities, 1937-1949." *Miskatonic Debating Club & Literary Society* (August 5, 2013). http://mdcls.blogspot.com/

Sulcas, Roslyn. "'The Red Shoes' Takes the Stage." *New York Times*, December 11, 2016.

Szajkowski, Zosa and Sarah Ponichtera, trans., electronic indexer. "Guide to the Records of the Displaced Persons Camps and Centers in Austria 1938-1960 (bulk 1945-1950)." *Center for Jewish History* (November 2014). http://digifindingaids.cjh.org/?pID=2449175

Trachtenberg, Barry. "Did U.S. Anti-immigrant Hysteria Doom the Passengers on the 'St. Louis'?" *Tablet* (February 27, 2017). http://www.tabletmag.com/jewish-news-and-politics/225648/immigrant-hysteria-st-louis

Truman, Harry S. "Special Message to the Congress on Aid for Refugees and Displaced Persons, speech given on March 24, 1952." *The American Presidency Project*. http://www.presidency.ucsb.edu/ws/?pid=14435

"Turning an Eye on Jews of Shanghai." *Haaretz*, Shanghai Jewish Refugees Museum, August 25, 2012. http://forward.com/news/161716/turning-an-eye-on-jews-of-shanghai/

Walden, Geoff. "Adolf Hitler Visits Vienna." *Third Reich in Ruins* (July 20, 2000). http://thirdreichruins.com/vienna.htm

"White Friday (1916)." *Wikipedia*, last modified December 20, 2016. https://en.wikipedia.org/wiki/White_Friday_(1916)

Wu, Annie. "Ancient Chinese Furniture." *China Highlights* (September 8, 2015). http://www.chinahighlights.com/travelguide/culture/ancient-chinese-furniture.htm

Žakelj, Anton. "Anton Žakelj's Refugee Camp Diary – Commentary and Summary." *Anton Žakelj – Diaries and Memoirs* (November 14, 2007).

Zhou, Su. "The World's Toughest Exam." *China Daily*, November 23, 2012. http://europe.chinadaily.com.cn/epaper/2012-11/23/content_15952562.htm

Theses

Chen, Lipeng. "Transitional Style Traits in Beethoven's Sonata no. 5 in F Major." Master of Music Thesis, Ball State University School of Music, 2010.

Hyman, Elizabeth Rebecca. "An Uncertain Life in Another World: German and Austrian Jewish Refugee Life in Shanghai, 1938-1950." Master of Arts Thesis, University of Maryland, College Park, 2014.

Kerssen, Julie L. "Life's Work: The Accidental Career of Laura Margolis Jarblum." Theses and Dissertations, University of Wisconsin, Milwaukee, 2000, UWM Digital Commons (Paper 548).

Lipp, Carolyn Meredith. "A Fragile Home in the Waiting Room: The Ambivalent Postwar Relationship between Americans and Jewish Displaced Persons in U.S.-Occupied Bavaria." Theses and Dissertations, Wesleyan University, Middletown, 2014.

Reichman, Alice. "Community in Exile: German Jewish Identity Development in Wartime Shanghai, 1938-1945." CMC Senior Theses, Claremont McKenna College, Claremont, 2011 (Paper 96).

Film

Shanghai Ghetto. Directed by Dana Janklowicz-Mann and Amir Mann. Rebel Child Productions, 2002.

Zuflucht in Shanghai: The Port of Last Resort. Directed by Joan Grossman and Paul Rosdy. Munich: Winter & Winter, 2005.

Unit 731: Nightmare in Manchuria. Directed by Chris D. Nebe. Los Angeles: Termite Art Productions, *History Channel.* August 1, 1998. https://www.youtube.com/watch?v=rsCUxfZswhw

Archived Interviews

Adler, Frederick. Videotaped testimony, USC Shoah Foundation.

Au, Mary (Chinese musicologist), e-mail correspondence with author, September 7, 2015, January 12, 2016.

Emihovich, Erica. Videotaped testimony, USC Shoah Foundation.

Hoschstadt, Steve, director. "Shanghai Jewish Oral History Collection" (Muskie Archives, Bates College). http://scarab.bates.edu/shanghai_oh/

Jedeikin, Joseph. Interviews September 2, and September 18, 2015.

Kolber, Dolfie, Margot Rosengart Kolber, and Lilly Kolber Ozer. Interviews, 1994.

Kutner, Trude. Videotaped testimony, USC Shoah Foundation.

Ozer, Lilly Kolber. Handwritten recollections (pp. 1-9).

Rosengarten, Malvena. Interview by Benjamin Ruxin. *U.S. Holocaust Memorial Museum*, 2005, audio recording RG-50 824*0001. Accession Number: 2006.85 https://collections.ushmm.org/search/catalog/irn518054 (sound recording)

Wendel, Charlotte. Interview by William B. Helmreich. *U.S. Holocaust Memorial Museum,* donated October 30, 1992, audio recording RG-50.165*0131 Accession Number: 1992.A.0128.131 https://collections.ushmm.org/search/catalog/irn511348 (sound recording) RG-50.165.0131_trs_en.pdf (English)

Wendel, Charlotte. Telephone interview by Loren Stephens, May 26, 2015.

George Kolber grew up in Newark, New Jersey, and found successes in retail, real estate, and finance. He and his wife, Vita, have two children and one grandchild, and are involved in numerous philanthropies that include Holocaust awareness.

Charles Kolber grew up in Union, New Jersey. He was an engineer for Fortune 500 companies and later operated a family-owned business with his wife, Christa. He and his wife have three children and eight grandchildren.

CPSIA information can be obtained
at www.ICGtesting.com
Printed in the USA
FSHW010637201218
54593FS